AMERICAN GROTESQUE

BY JAMES KIRKWOOD

There Must Be a Pony!

UTBU *(Unhealthy To Be Unpleasant—
a play produced on Broadway
and published by Samuel French)*

Good Times/Bad Times

American Grotesque

Some Kind of Hero

JAMES KIRKWOOD

AMERICAN GROTESQUE

An Account of the
Clay Shaw–Jim Garrison
Kennedy Assassination Trial
in the City of New Orleans

HarperPerennial
A Division of HarperCollins*Publishers*

First HarperPerennial edition published 1992.

Library of Congress Cataloging-in-Publication Data

Kirkwood, James, 1930–
American grotesque : an account of the Clay Shaw–Jim Garrison Kennedy assassination trial in the city of New Orleans / James Kirkwood. — 1st Harper-Perennial ed.
    p.   cm.
Originally published: New York : Simon and Schuster, 1970.
Includes index.
ISBN 0-06-097523-7
1. Shaw, Clay, 1912?—Trials, litigation, etc. 2. Trials (Conspiracy)—Louisiana—New Orleans. 3. Trials (Assassination)—Louisiana—New Orleans. 4. Garrison, Jim, 1921–   . 5. Kennedy, John F. (John Fitzgerald), 1917–1963—Assassination. I. Title.
KF224.S45K54   1992
345.763'3502524—dc20
[347.6335052524]   92-53408

92 93 94 95 96 CW 10 9 8 7 6 5 4 3 2 1

Contents

Part Three   Encores

A Dedication and a Preface

For James Leo Herlihy

If it had not been for you, Jim, I would not have become involved in this bizarre matter in the first place. We have barely seen each other since it all started, so there is every reason to fill you in on what the inside of the haunted house looked like after you opened the door and unknowingly nudged me in, so to speak.

To begin with, there is a strong inducement to tell this story to an individual. Mainly because this involvement—and involvement is the word, for I do feel and have felt more strongly about this than anything outside of an extremely personal nature—because this involvement has set off unimagined mushroom clouds of wonder at human behavior, along with strong crosscurrents of conflicting emotions and one other item, namely this: it has handed me one of the memorable scares of my life. I feel more the quiet shakes down deep in the intestines, the way I would stomach-react chancing by a darkened cabin in the woods and peeking in, as would be my wont, only to hear a pride of ghostly Klansmen discussing, over their trussed-up, bug-eyed victim, which tree would be best for the lynching. The impulse is strong to nab a friend, preferably a close one, and say, clinging to him all the while, "Jesus, you won't believe this but— Have you a slug of scotch? . . . What? . . . Yes, I know I'm shaking— Now listen, because I have got to tell you . . ."

Since we react similarly to many situations and I would as soon spend an evening speaking with you as anyone I know, I am keeping you very much in mind as I start this off. Then, too, I have the utmost respect for your sense of right and wrong. I have seen this great wrong done and perhaps in telling of it I can, in some fractional way, if not exactly right the offense, at least shine a light on the damage done and help make people aware, so that it might not happen again.

So there is a certain direct plugged-in connection that compels me to set this down as if I were telling my story to you, in the hope I can funnel it through without an excess of attempted literary flimflammery. It is, also, harder to dissemble to a friend, and I would like to tell it as it happened, to strip it down to the level of an adventure, not pump it up into a treatise. You have been picked as the target area.

Now to dispose of a controversy that has been raging within for months, set off by a score of friends, a few agents, and an editor or two, to the effect: "You know, when you get into nonfiction, which is something new to you, and why you even want to get involved in the first place is beyond—but if you insist, you must be *objective*. Objectiveness, objectivity, that is what is called for." This reminds me of my initial reaction to the statement "The Show Must Go On": Why?

The reason everybody has been clubbing me over the head with objectivity is not, to be honest, beyond comprehension. It is undoubtedly because subjectivity sticks out all over me like so many porcupine quills. All along, this has been a tussle, though; ever since I stumbled into the Shaw-Garrison matter, objectivity and subjectivity have been slugging it out in my head. The sneaky hunch that subjectivity would win out must be acknowledged. Acknowledgment must also be aired that for ages I planned rigging the game so that objectivity would be the victor. But I knew the results would not be pleasing. To be candid, in that case I would be faking; and if *I* knew I was faking, I could not help conveying that to others. I would as soon level at the start and have someone see my subjectivity head on, rather than see *through* my feigned objectivity.

At any rate, "objective" brings to mind a stalking automaton who strides through the wall of a house, demolishes the living room, steps on the kid, crushes the dog and crashes out through the far wall, all precisely because it (he) is so bloody objective all he knows is he has to get from point A to point B and bugger the consequences.

My bag is so full of human frailties, how can I be objective? I've been through a war, stolen when I was hungry (and a few times when I was just cranky), watched a sheepherder couple with one of his flock, at the age of fourteen viewed a lady doing it with a donkey in Tijuana (all right, maybe she wasn't a "lady"), been arrested for growing seven pet marijuana plants in a spare bedroom, deserted the Catholic Church until they stop aiding and abetting the population explosion, pulled a holdup with a squirt gun, discovered five dead bodies while in my teens (not all stacked together in a clump, mind, separately, three of them suicides), been an actor and nightclub performer, and made love in the safe in the basement of the old Tiffany Building on Fifth Avenue during business hours. Not that I feel mauled by life—but it has certainly had its fingers on me and I don't really feel objective about stepping from the living room into the kitchen.

How, really, can any of us not be subjective? That's what we're all about, isn't it? What we experience, what we feel emotionally and mentally, how we react, how we are set into motion by stimuli and environment, what we do, what makes us do it—not only what we do to ourselves, but Heaven Help Us, what we do to one another.

PART I

PRETRIAL

1

Hang On, Mister!

My initial interest in the Shaw-Garrison affair might best be explained by the following profile which was published in the December 1968 issue of *Esquire* magazine. The only piece of nonfiction I have ever attempted, it was submitted with the succinct title "Hang On, Mister!" I was surprised, but not necessarily miffed, to find the article in print under this bold-print heading:

SO HERE YOU ARE, CLAY SHAW, TWENTY MONTHS AND THOUSANDS OF DOLLARS AFTER BEING CHARGED WITH CONSPIRACY IN THE WORST CRIME OF THE CENTURY. WHAT ARE YOU DOING ABOUT IT?

Surviving
BY JAMES KIRKWOOD

Now I sit in my hotel room in the French Quarter of New Orleans, trying, and nowhere near succeeding, to ignore the insistent laser-beam razzmatazz of an army of Dixieland combos blasting out from Bourbon Street. I sit practically on top of the wheezing, gently vibrating air conditioner because it's hot and muggy and my eyes are giving me hell for making them read, in one day, all 491 pages of the Preliminary Hearing of the State of Louisiana against Clay L. Shaw. Shaw had been charged with criminal conspiracy to assassinate President John F. Kennedy, a felony under Louisiana law carrying a penalty of one to twenty years in prison.

Without too much of a stretch, the transcript brings to mind the Spanish Inquisition. Hearsay was freely allowed, dead men spoke, objections by the defense were mostly overruled, those of the prosecution were mostly sustained, and even the state's star witness, Perry Russo, it turned out, had been placed under hypnosis three times at District Attorney Jim Garrison's bidding to "refresh his mind" and was, in fact, testifying in court under posthypnotic suggestion.

It's a scarifying document in itself, regardless of one's opinion of the guilt or innocence of the accused. I'm probably feeling the heat and eyestrain all the more because, from the smell of things in this charming, colorful, quaint, maddening funny-farm of a city, I'm afraid I've come to the conclusion that, yes, it could happen to me. Or to you.

So, to get to why I'm sitting here in New Orleans in this far from peaceful state, both of mind and of the Union. Last November I was holed up in my East Hampton cottage, having made a resolution to myself and friends that I now had a stranglehold on the final chapter of a new novel and that nothing, repeat nothing, was going to lure me away from my writing machine and into New York City. Not *Bonnie and Clyde,* nor *Rosencrantz and Guildenstern.* I'd even said to a weekend guest and old friend, author James Leo Herlihy, that I wouldn't come into town if Marlene Dietrich asked me to an intimate supper for G. Garbo—with De Gaulle serving. That was on a Sunday evening as I drove Jim to the train.

Monday noon the phone rang and it was Jim Herlihy saying in a loud voice, "Guess who's coming to dinner?" I could hear the smile on his face and I knew he had more than fair bait. I swore generously at him before asking.

"Clay Shaw," says Jim, knowing I'm an archfiend when it comes to real-life trials of any kind and their participants. Celebrities to me are not necessarily Liz and Dick, they are just as likely to be Perry and Dick or Dr. Sam Sheppard or Candy and Mel. Jim went on to say that a friend of his was a friend of Clay Shaw's and had suggested Shaw call Jim when he was in New York. Jim had invited him to dinner. I swore a bit more and said I'd be there.

I'd seen pictures of Clay Shaw in the newspapers, briefly glimpsed him on television, but I had no idea what kind of a man to expect. Mostly I'd seen New Orleans D.A. Jim Garrison who for a while had turned up almost nightly on the six o'clock news. I'd read slews of articles about the case and heard all sorts of people sound off about it. The only person who hadn't really sounded off in detail was the accused himself, outside of a quiet but firm "not guilty."

So, in meeting Clay Shaw, accused of participation in the "Case of the Century," as Garrison has called it, you kind of had the feeling you were being introduced in person to a brand-new movie star who'd had a blockbuster publicity campaign but whose first big film hadn't been released yet.

What do you do? You shake hands—mine got lost in his, he's a barrel-chested six-foot-four, two-hundred-twelve-pound giant of a man with close-cropped white hair, striking blue eyes and, at first sighting, almost handsomely fierce of face—and sit down opposite him while you're served your first drink, all the time trying hard not to stare through him, inside him, to see if you can possibly detect the answer to the bald question that can't help rattle around in your head: Say, listen, you didn't really conspire to assassinate the *President* of the United States, did you? I mean, did you really hang out with Lee Harvey and all that bunch?

But you don't. You get your drink, hoist it, and say something bland like, "Here's to your stay in New York." Then there's more light talk: Yes, I've been to New Orleans once, fascinating city. No, I've never been to Mardi Gras but I hear it's wild, etc.

And finally, because I sensed a leveling *something* in the man, I couldn't help putting my glass down and asking, "Would you mind, or does it bore you, to talk about your [oh-oh, watch the word] predicament?"

"No," he said with a smile, adding he'd be a liar if he said his "predicament" wasn't the most ever-present thought-consuming experience of his lifetime.

He spoke with a combination of wisdom and wonderment and a sort of Somerset Maugham knack for storytelling and also humor —but certainly not flippancy—of this most traumatic event from beginning to middle, which is smack where he is, between the indictment of a preliminary hearing and jury trial. By three in the morning we were still listening to his account. You spend eight hours with a man and, though it's only eight hours, you get a definite feeling about whether you'd trust him with *his* word, *your* money, wife, life, or even whether he'd be on time for a luncheon appointment. Call it the scratch test, the intuition test, whatever it is, Clay Shaw passed it, at least for me.

Back to work in East Hampton, where I finally finished the novel. In the meantime there were news flashes from New Orleans, dates set for the trial, appeals by the defendant's lawyers, appeals denied, the trial rescheduled, and all the time I was thinking about this man down in Louisiana and wondering what his life was like during all this, wondering if my hunch about him had been 100 per cent on the nose. Articles were appearing in almost every national magazine and all those authors who have stumbled upon a second livelihood challenging the Warren Commission were courting hemorrhoids, applying seat of pants to seat of chair, pounding out their theories in staggering quantity that, if nothing else does, should certainly bring on a paper shortage.

I finally wrote Clay Shaw a brief note, months later, telling him I had enjoyed meeting him and wishing him luck. He replied soon, thanking me and saying the evening in New York had been a welcome respite from the situation in New Orleans and that his trial was tentatively set for April.

There was no further correspondence and I started, haltingly on little cat feet, into another novel. One morning I suddenly found myself reaching for the phone and dialing my agent: "Say, do you suppose you could get me a magazine assignment to cover the Clay Shaw–Garrison trial?" She was surprised. First, I'd never written a magazine article; second, as far as a trial was concerned, a magazine would be scooped by the daily papers; and third, how had it even occurred to me? I told her of meeting Clay Shaw and of my impressions, which time had strengthened. She said to jot them down, send them to her, and she'd get them off to a magazine. But not to hold my breath.

I didn't, but oddly enough in about ten days I found myself on the Terrifying Silver Bird for New Orleans with a strong suggestion to stick to Clay Shaw's impressions and go light on the actual evidence in the case which had been presented at length all the way from *Playboy* to *The New Yorker*.

Having forewarned Clay Shaw of my arrival, I rang from my hotel and was invited for drinks and dinner. Toward the end of the conversation, it was dropped that his lawyer, one of four, would also be stopping by for a drink.

After cleaning up, I strolled the twelve blocks through the Vieux Carré, gawking at the undisturbed architecture of those hardy yet delicate buildings with their shutters and balconies and iron grillwork, until I came to a white brick wall on Dauphine Street with a red door splashed in the middle.

Clay Shaw greeted me and again I realized what an impressive figure of a man he is as he showed me into the high-walled patio bordered on two sides by ferns, with an oblong glass table at the far end for outdoor dining. Then inside for a look at the immaculate kitchen and good-sized living room which compose the ground floor of the small, charming carriage house he had restored with loving care. The furnishings are French, grouped comfortably around a low coffee table, the floors are polished cork topped by several fine Oriental rugs, there is a small desk and a splendid large gold-leaf mirror. At the top of an angled red-carpeted flight of stairs are a large sparsely furnished bedroom and a bathroom. To city dwellers, the house would be comparable to a duplex apartment. Though it might be described as elegant, good taste and simplicity of choice are manifest.

His lawyer of twenty years, Edward F. Wegmann, soon arrived and it is difficult to describe him physically. His height, weight, age, face and eyes melt into one word—concern. As he sat opposite me I felt I was being looked into the same way I had looked into Clay Shaw that evening in New York. I was being X-rayed, enough to induce a twinge or two of stage fright. He was curious to know how my interest in Mr. Shaw had come about and what my angle would be. I did what I could to allay his concern. Later, when we'd relaxed somewhat, I could still read the tacit message printed across his face and imbedded in his eyes: *Don't hurt this man; I'm not only his lawyer, I'm his friend; he's been made a target and I'm intercepting all possible potshots.* If you've ever seen a lioness guarding her cubs, you'll know the look.

After Mr. Wegmann had gone, dinner was served in the patio by Willie Mae, who keeps a quieter but nonetheless carefully concerned eye upon her employer. During dinner the talk was easy and I asked Clay Shaw about his political background. "I suppose I'd describe myself as a Wilsonian-F.D.R.-Kennedy liberal. By that I mean I agree with those men who have seen that the capitalist system had to be adapted to give a better life to more people. These days a man has some kind of income when he's finished working, what with Social Security, and now there's even Medicare, so that the fundamental needs for a basis of decent living have been assured. I thought John Kennedy was in the same tradition, a man who looked hard at the foundations of things and would move to further adapt the system to provide a better life for the most people, which is what any political system should be about. Most of my friends consider me very liberal indeed. I remember when Kennedy was running against Nixon. I went to visit friends of mine at their farm and when the hostess asked me who I was going to vote for and I told her Kennedy, she was extremely chagrined. If she hadn't been a well-brought-up Southern girl I don't think she'd have given me any lunch." ·

After dinner, on the way back to the hotel, I stopped by a Bourbon Street bar for a nightcap. The shapely barmaid, who'd blown at least one full can of hair spray to concretize her teased soufflé of blond hair, turned out to be Shirley. When Shirley asked me with misty eyes and a baby-whisper voice if I'd care to feed the jukebox, I figured I could ask Shirley a favor in return. "What do you think of this whole Clay Shaw thing?"

"Clay Shaw?" she mused. "Oh, yes, Clay *Shaw* . . . Oh, well, I wouldn't know anything about him. You mean the whole thing?" she purred.

"Yes—well, then, what do you think of the District Attorney?"

The eyes sharpened into baby-blue bullets, the voice unfurred and she boomed, "Garrison! *Garrison!*" She leaned close in over the bar, threatening my vodka and tonic and, giving each word equal time, drummed out the following message: "Baby, Jim Garrison is on a bad trip." This brought Louisiana State University drama student Buddy Campbell up out of his glass of beer and into it. "Man, I'll tell you something else. Shaw's on a bum rap."

The following morning I arrived at the red door on Dauphine Street with yellow legal pad and pencils, anxious to start at the beginning. One day Clay Shaw was all of this: a respected business and social leader of New Orleans, possessed of a fine war record ending with an honorable discharge as a major in 1946, having served as a secretary to the General Staff and having been decorated by the United States with the Legion of Merit and Bronze Star and by France with the Croix de Guerre; a man who, besides being Managing Director of the International Trade Mart from its inception in 1946 until his retirement in 1965, is widely known as one of the pioneers who began the rehabilitation and restoration of New Orleans' famous French Quarter; a man who believes firmly that hopes for world peace and understanding might well be enhanced by increased and closer trade between nations and who worked to bring this about, at the same time drawing added revenues into the Port of New Orleans; a man who was present at and supported most of the artistic and cultural events in the city from theater to symphony to opera; the author of several published plays, one of which, a one-acter called *Submerged,* has had thousands of performances and is still widely played by amateur groups around the country.

One day he was all of this, the next day his credentials were irrevocably smeared, squirted upon by inky stains charging him with conspiracy to assassinate the President. How did this happen? How does a nightmare begin? Very easily.

First off, why the retirement at such a comparatively early age? Clay Shaw smiles. "Well, I'd worked hard from the age of fifteen and upon the realization of the new ITM building, designed by Edward Durell Stone, I felt I'd achieved what I'd set out to accomplish in that area of my life. Although I wasn't a millionaire, I had enough put aside to carry me along until the time at which I reasonably expect to shuffle off. I wanted, from here on in, to devote my life to writing. I also wanted to travel and I thought it might be more pleasant to do this while I could still get up a gangplank unaided. So, in 1965, I retired and on October 1 there was a testimonial luncheon, all of that, and the Mayor presented me with the International Order of Merit medal." Shaw smiled, took a deep breath and smacked his hands together. "And I was free. Right away I took a couple of months off and went to Mexico. Then in the summer of 1966 I boarded a freighter, spent a month in Barcelona and a month in London, getting back here in the early fall. I probably would have continued traveling if it hadn't been for my father's death in November of 1966. This held me here, keeping an eye on my mother who lives in Hammond, a small town very near New Orleans. Then, when this period of transition for her was over, I had every intention of—" Clay Shaw broke off, smiled and held his hands out, palms up. "But the best-laid plans of mice and men . . ."

"When did you first have an inkling there was a diversion being planned for you in New Orleans?"

"On December 23, 1966, I had a call early in the morning from a Detective Otillio in the District Attorney's office; would I be good enough to come down and answer some questions? I was curious and asked what about. 'Well,' he said, 'we'll talk about that when we see you.' I said all right and he came by and drove me to the D.A.'s office, where I was questioned by an assistant D.A. named Sciambra, who told me they'd come across the fact that Lee Harvey Oswald had known someone named Clay Bertrand when he was in New Orleans. They'd gone over a list of Clays, thought about me, and wanted to know if I'd known Oswald. I said no,

that I'd almost met him when he'd come to distribute Fair Play for
Cuba leaflets in front of the Trade Mart, but that my assistant had
dealt with him. I added, with what in retrospect seems irony, that
I guess I missed my tiny footnote in history by not meeting the
bird. They wanted to know more about the Cuban consulate—it
was the presence of the consulate in the building that drew
Oswald to that point to distribute the leaflets—and most of their
questions concerned that. I was asked if I knew a man by the name
of Dave Ferrie. No, I hadn't. Then Jim Garrison came in and we
rehashed what I'd already told Sciambra. It was all very friendly
and then they thanked me profusely for being a good citizen, for
being cooperative and coming in and talking to them, and I left.
Went on to a Christmas party at City Hall."

I asked Clay Shaw how he felt about this and he smiled and
waved a hand in the air. "I felt it was interesting dinner conversation. You know, being called down to the D.A.'s office and grilled.
I thought it was kind of entertaining. I didn't take it seriously at
all. After that I read in the papers about Garrison's probe, read
about Dave Ferrie's death and about someone named Russo
writing a letter to the District Attorney saying he'd known Ferrie.
But I had no more than a cursory interest in what was going on.

"Then on Sunday evening, February 26, a Walter Sheridan
from the NBC Washington Bureau got in touch with me, wanted
to know if he could come over and talk with me. I said yes, and he
arrived soon after." Clay Shaw hesitated and lifted a hand in the
air, one finger pointed up. "You know, it's funny but a faint alarm
sounded when I asked him if he'd like a drink and he hesitated
perceptibly. I thought this was strange, but he recovered and said
he'd have one. I wondered why this man wouldn't want to take a
drink with me, but then I thought, Oh, well, I'm imagining
things. I fixed our drinks and he said there were rumors in town
I was the mysterious Clay Bertrand that a man named Dean A.
Andrews, Jr., had talked about in connection with Oswald. I
pointed out to him that it would be ridiculous for me to try to use
an alias of any kind, that I was well known in the city, I'd been on
television, given speeches, my picture had been in the papers over
a period of years and, because of my size alone, I couldn't very
well get away with running around using a fictitious name. I told
him I had no idea what was going on, but I did know that I was
not now nor have I ever been Clay Bertrand. We talked in general
about Garrison's probe, then he thanked me and left. I still

thought the whole thing was silly," Clay Shaw added, sloughing it off with a shrug that belongs back in time more than a year.

"Two days after Mr. Sheridan's visit, on Tuesday, February 28, a friend of mine came over to see me and mentioned that there were two men sitting outside in a car and that they looked like detectives. I glanced out of an upstairs window and there *were* two men in a car, but I thought if they were detectives they must be watching someone else. Later on, after an hour or so, I answered the doorbell and found two youngish men standing there, one dark, one fair. The dark one presented me with a card, saying he was from, I believe, Mutual of Omaha, that they were making a survey of people's insurance needs and would I talk to them. I said it was a bad time, I had company, and I also told him that I was, if anything, overinsured and was not a good prospect. The dark man—I'd never seen him before, but he turned out to be Perry Russo at the preliminary hearing—anyway, he asked if he might phone and speak with me further sometime. I said yes, but again reiterated that my insurance needs were well taken care of, and they left.

"The following morning, March 1, I went to the office of a friend of mine and a woman, a mutual friend, phoned about ten-thirty to say that she'd heard on local television that the District Attorney had issued a subpoena for me. I said, 'Well, that's nutty, I'll find out about it.' I called the D.A.'s office, asked to speak to Mr. Garrison and was told he wasn't there. I got a Mr. Ivon and said, 'Do you people want to talk to me?' Well, yes, they did. 'You don't have to issue a subpoena, just call me up,' I told him. 'What time would you like to see me?' Ivon said about one o'clock and I said fine, a friend of mine would drive me out. I stopped by my house to pick up my mail and there were two or three sheriff's deputies in the patio—I don't know how they got in—and Detective Otillio, my old friend of December 23. They had the subpoena and asked me to sign it. I thought it was ridiculous and told them I'd just talked to Ivon and had arranged to go out there at one, to check with him. They did and then Otillio said, well, it was getting on toward noon and that I could either come out at one or drive out with him then."

I interrupted Clay Shaw. "Did you call your lawyer or—" He waved a hand in the air. "No, I didn't even think about it. Who needs a lawyer?" he asked rhetorically. "I rode out to the D.A.'s and was kept waiting until about two-thirty in various offices

talking to Otillio, who incidentally told me the story of his life."
Shaw grins but the grin soon disappears. "I began to get a little
annoyed. I was being cooperative but by this time I'd been there
two and a half hours. I hadn't had any lunch and I was hungry
and I began to be a little sharp about the whole thing. Finally I
was told that Sciambra and Ivon wanted to talk to me, so I was
taken into a room where they were. They got me a sandwich and a
Coke—on the state, I didn't have to pay for it; however, the price
turned out to be rather severe. I asked them what they wanted and
they began to question me. Did I know David Ferrie, had I ever
been to David Ferrie's apartment? The answer was no. And on
and on. They showed me pictures of Ferrie and others. Did I know
Lee Harvey Oswald? No. 'You've never been to David Ferrie's
apartment?' No. Then finally: 'What would you say if we said we
have three witnesses who would testify that you'd been to David
Ferrie's apartment?' I told them I'd say that either the three
witnesses were mistaken or lying—that I'd never been there,
period. This went on for the better part of an hour or so. Finally I
was asked if I'd take a lie-detector test. 'No,' I said. 'I've come
down here, I've been cooperative, I've told you the truth.' They
told me that if I wouldn't take a lie-detector test they were going
to arrest me and charge me with conspiracy in the murder of
President Kennedy."

Clay Shaw's eyes, even now, widen in disbelief and he flings his
arms out to the side of his chair. " 'You've got to be kidding,' I
said, 'you've *got* to be kidding!' No, they said, that's the way it is.
'In that case I want a lawyer and I want one now.' "

He called his lawyer, Eddie Wegmann, who was out of town;
called his brother, William J. Wegmann, who was also unavail-
able; finally contacted an associate of the latter, Salvatore Panzeca,
who said, "Sit tight, don't say anthing, I'll be right down." Shaw
was left alone, locked in a room, until Panzeca arrived and took
out a pad on which he wrote that the room was bugged, the mirror
was two-way, and they'd best communicate in writing. He asked
Shaw what this was all about and Clay, now completely stunned,
could only scrawl, "I don't know." Panzeca then left to speak to
the D.A., telling Garrison that his client would not object to
taking a lie-detector test but that he, Panzeca, would like him to
have a good night's sleep first and they wanted the right to look at
the questions; anything pertaining to the President's assassination
was fine, but the questions should be limited to that.

Garrison, however, smarting from a baying press, from the world, in fact, shouting for him to come up with something or someone solid after days of dropping tantalizing hints that he had solved the riddle of the assassination, swung into high gear and said, "No deals, he's got to do it right now or we'll arrest him."

Panzeca immediately set about arranging bail and, with the Wegmann brothers now contacted and on their way and approximately 150 members of the press and TV swarming all over the building, Shaw was formally arrested. The statement was read by William Gurvich, a chief investigator on Garrison's staff who later defected, even going so far as to appeal to Robert Kennedy to aid in calling a halt, and later appearing before the grand jury under oath. After that grand jury hearing, he repeated publicly that Garrison's probe had no basis in fact and that there were absolutely no legitimate grounds for the charges against Shaw. At the time of the arrest, however, on behalf of the District Attorney, Gurvich read the formal statement which avoided any specific link of evidence, bluntly saying, "Mr. Shaw is under arrest and will be charged with participation in a conspiracy to murder President Kennedy."

The nightmare was entered into. On the part of Clay Shaw, what was it like? "I could feel the ferment building around me." Kaleidoscopic memories of detectives and flashbulbs, of handcuffs clamped on, of being led through mobs of shouting reporters, buttressed by his equally stunned attorneys, taken to Central Lockup, mugged, fingerprinted, told a search warrant had been issued for his house and he might as well give them his keys, they'd only break in if he didn't, and finally, by about nine-thirty in the evening, released on $10,000 bail.

There is still disbelief in Clay Shaw's eyes as he says, "I drove with Eddie Wegmann, neither of us knew what to say, until we parked near his office. There was a bar, we went in and I had two tremendous bourbons," Clay Shaw adds, nodding his head, and a flicker of an appreciative smile crosses his face. "You know, I had my first small bit of encouragement then. The barmaid told us she'd heard it on television, said she'd known me for years, knew I never could have been involved in anything like that and absolutely refused to take payment for the drinks."

Shaw and Edward Wegmann repaired to the latter's office, where they talked for a while in tones of pure incredulity, phoned a few close friends from whom they learned the astonishing news that Shaw's house was a fortress besieged by policemen lugging off cartons of his belongings with a battery of newsmen and cameras set up to record the indignity of the proceedings.

It was difficult for Shaw to accept this. He did not go home that night, nor did he enter his house for the following six weeks. He went to stay instead at the home of an old friend, a woman he'd been associated with in business and socially, who insisted he accept her hospitality at this time. At this point in our interview we broke off and went to pick up this very same lady for lunch. Although there's no doubt that the District Attorney's office knew of his whereabouts every second, he asked me not to use her name, for fear of harassment, and I will respect his wishes.

What's it like to step out in public with Clay Shaw, who twenty months later is still out on $10,000 bail, still accused of this heinous crime? It's about like standing at Hollywood and Vine with Paul Newman. It does not cover one in a cloak of anonymity. A teeny-bopper in faded blue denim jeans and work shirt topped by a contradictory floppy yellow wide-brimmed hat of the thirties gyrated gently in a sunny noonday frug on the porch of an old unrestored cottage across the street. "A nest of hippies," Clay Shaw whispered to me. Still frugging, she waved and called out a happy "Hiya, Mr. Shaw!" The walk covered five or six blocks; no one failed to react; people either looked, waved a hand, or shot a friendly "Hi, there, Mr. Shaw, how are you?" to which he invariably replied with a brief, smiling "Fine, what have I got to be worried about?"

Clay Shaw's friend, a charming widow, when questioned about the time he spent at her house, laughs and waves a fanless hand in front of her face. "Yes," she says, "dear Clay 'shacked up'—I guess that's what they call it nowadays—with me, but then I'm an aging matron type, so I suppose that's all right." (Aging matron type is an attractive blonde with striking, thin rich-lady legs.) Over lunch there was talk of his arrest, his life, and later on I had a private chat with her.

"Here I was," she says, perched in her comfortably furnished living room, "sitting right here watching Huntley-Brinkley and—my God, there's Clay in handcuffs and they're announcing that Jim Garrison's arrested him for conspiracy to assassinate the President. To assassinate the *President!*" she repeats, still unable to comprehend it. "I was stunned, shocked. This man has never done an unkind thing to anyone in his life. Well, of course, all of

Clay's friends, and he has many, were on the phone and we were all trying to find out what the almighty devil was going on. It was a madhouse. Later on that evening, when he was out on bail, I told his lawyer to bring him right on down here. That poor man, he was in a complete daze." I asked her what he did upon arriving. "He didn't do a thing," she says, slamming a hand to her chest. "*I* did. I fixed him a Beefeater martini that was the strongest thing you ever *saw*." She laughs. "We call that the thousand-dollar martini. You know, out on $10,000 bail and the bondsman gets ten per cent. Then I fixed him some eggs and bacon and put him to bed. The worst day of my life, absolutely the worst.

"Clay was in a state of shock for a week or so, everyone was in New Orleans, nobody could believe it. But Garrison wouldn't let go and then along came the preliminary hearing and, of course, what can you do? Then, after the hearing, Clay hadn't been out in public since his arrest and one night he said, 'All right, I'm taking you out to dinner tonight.' I got all dolled up and we went to the Royal Orleans, and don't you know we're sitting at our table and who comes walking right by?" Her voice rises several decibels and once again her hand flies to her chest. "*Of all people,* the Jolly Green Giant, Garrison himself, and his guru, Mark Lane. Ohhh!" she expels. "But we just sat there staring straight ahead until they'd gone by, then we finished our dinner and left. You know"— she leans in toward me—"I think Garrison's always been jealous of Clay. People in this town adore Clay, wherever he goes people are always swarming all over him, pumping his hand, you can feel the warmth go out to him. I don't know about any conspiracy but I know Clay Shaw didn't have any part of it. Why, he *voted* for Kennedy, he adored him. Kennedy was a builder, just like Clay was, why would he want to harm him?"

Later that afternoon, a reporter on the *Times-Picayune* said, "The whole case has taken a turn hinging on the personalities instead of the facts. Look at Garrison and Shaw, both tall, both middle-aged, both handsome imposing figures, both extremely bright and both possessed of charm. The similarity between the two of them is so apparent it would take a blind person not to see it."

William Gurvich, whose defection from the D.A.'s staff has been mentioned, sat in the inside office of his private detective agency. He explained that he could no longer go along with Garrison and his methods. Like Clay Shaw, Gurvich speaks not emotionally, no ranting about Garrison, but he speaks with firm conviction and concern of the office of District Attorney, of the pitiful state of politics in New Orleans, of the fact that Garrison is convinced of a conspiracy, although he should know that Clay Shaw had nothing to do with it, but that he is hanging on to anyone and anything to keep the case open, believing, as many reckless men in history have, that his means, no matter the cost to others, will most certainly be justified by the end. When asked if he would testify for Shaw if and when his case comes to trial, Gurvich said, "Only one thing would keep me from it—death." His parting sentence to me was a quiet and, in a way, sad one: "I feel sorry for Jim Garrison, but I believe he's an extremely dangerous man."

If this is a viable opinion, and it seems to be among many good citizens of New Orleans, why hasn't there been more of an outcry? Maybe they take their lead from the Governor of the State of Louisiana, John McKeithen, who, when asked if he had any criticism of Garrison and his probe, stated publicly to the press that he did not but added, just as publicly, "And even if I did I wouldn't voice it. I have learned that most of Garrison's enemies are buried—politically speaking—and I don't want to join the list of the deceased."

(Interesting note: Although major newspapers all over the United States have featured editorials highly critical of the methods of Jim Garrison, neither one of the New Orleans papers, the *States-Item* and the *Times-Picayune,* has so much as uttered an editorial peep.)

So here is Clay Shaw, twenty months, a battery of lawyers, and many thousands of retirement dollars later, still in the talons of the persistent District Attorney with the nasty shadow of conspiracy to murder the President hanging over him. One has to ask, even if these charges eventually dwindle and die, if the accused will ever be completely free of the original smear.

The press, for instance, has frequently hinted at a duality in Clay Shaw's personal life and when his house was searched and his personal possessions were seized not so much was made of "One Underwood typewriter and case" or "One calorie counter" or "Three manuscripts" but there was a flurry of chop-licking over "One chain . . . One black hood and cape . . . Two pieces of leather . . . Three pieces of rope . . ." etc. It is also fascinating to note that while the dossier contained "Four paperback books and twelve hardcover books" it listed separately "One book entitled *A Holiday for Murder.*"

I interviewed a long-time friend of Clay Shaw's, Mrs. Lawrence Fischer, who designs many of the floats and costumes for Mardi Gras, or as she puts it, "New Orleans Annual Climactic of Civil Lunacy!" and a snappier woman I've never talked to. A day or so after Shaw's arrest her doorbell rang and an investigator for the D.A. identified himself. "Oh," she said, curled up in her armchair and re-enacting the scene with relish, "you come right on in, you're *exactly* the man I want to talk to." She winked at me. "I think I took him by surprise. Anyhow, this joker wants to spread a mulch of sinister deeds over Clay. Wanted to know how long I'd known him. Since he was seventeen. Wanted to know if we'd ever discussed sex." Mrs. Fischer slapped her leg. "Well, it would be pretty unusual to go for over thirty-five years with a good friend and never bring the subject up, now, wouldn't it? Of course we had. Then this young man asked, 'Has Mr. Shaw ever told you the intimate details of his sex life?' 'No,' I shot back at him, 'and furthermore I haven't told him the intimate details of *my* sex life either. Are you here to discuss his political leanings with reference to the Garrison farce, or are you conducting a sort of Kinsey report?' Then he wanted to get into the black robe and the hood and the black hat and finally I just couldn't take it any longer and I said, 'Listen, my good young man, I don't know whether you've ever heard of it, but we have something here in New Orleans every year and it's called *Mardi Gras!* Everybody in town gets dressed up in costumes. My God, you could raid any apartment or house in New Orleans and come up with some pretty far-out ensembles—I can assure you. While you were at it, why didn't you take his Chinese costume or the Western one or the Dutch one?'" Mrs. Fischer chuckled with pleasure. "I think that investigator was damned glad to get out of here." She raised a hand to her forehead and sighed. "Good Lord, since this case began, New Orleans—never what you'd call a sane place anyhow, I mean think of Huey Long and all that—has turned into one vast walking lunatic asylum."

Later that afternoon, I spoke with a former business associate of Clay Shaw's. "Clay was so completely stunned and mystified by the charges leveled against him that we were all worried, especially when it dragged on and on, whether he could withstand the strain.

After months of trial of preliminary motions by his lawyers, all of them turned down, change of venue, turned down, it was one remark that let us know he was going to come through all right. At a dinner party we were discussing the morass of legal procedure, the endless entanglements of the law, and Clay finally shook his head and said, 'Can you see me for the rest of my life running around with stacks of documents and sheafs of papers tucked under my arm, knocking on every judge's chamber in the land, crying out, "I didn't kill Cock Robin, I didn't!" ' "

Further sessions with Clay Shaw gave sound indications of his rationale and the philosophy which has enabled him to keep his balance and remain on course.

On the theory of conspiracy: "I'm no authority to judge and it's difficult to sift through all that's been written about the Warren Commission, the CIA, the FBI, the Attorney General, the Right and the Left, the Cuban situation and so forth. I only know I had no part in any plot. But I do feel many people believe in a conspiracy, because when death comes to the figure of a prince, as it did to Kennedy, struck down in his prime, it should come under a panoply of great tragedy with all the resulting high court intrigue—almost something out of Shakespeare—not from some poor little psychotic loser crouched with a mail-order rifle behind a stack of cardboard boxes in a warehouse."

On the question of what has sustained him most during this troublesome year and a third, Clay Shaw leans back in his chair, rests his head against the high back for a long time before sighing and leaning forward, hands clasped in front of him. "It's difficult to isolate any one factor in your psychic makeup. To be perfectly pragmatic, I suppose the knowledge of my innocence has been the great sustaining factor and against that, I believe, nothing in the long run can fail me. I have found religion helpful. Although I'm not a member of any church formally, I think of myself as a religious person. I've found several works supportive, *Confessions of a Guilty Bystander,* a book of meditations by Thomas Merton and"—he picks up a volume from the coffee table—"this, of course, the Bible." He puts the book down and adds with a smile, "I might say that I've particularly been reading the Book of Job."

At this point I mention that I would have thought Kafka might have come to mind and he reacts with a hearty burst of laughter and smacks his hands together. "Oh, yes, by all means. Yes, I've often had the feeling that I might just be living in a Kafka novel.

Ironically enough, I was always the one who thought that Kafka rather overstated things: Now, come on, all right, so K. can't communicate with the Castle and man and God are incommensurate, but do you have to go on at such tiresome lengths? Boy, have I changed, what a fellow feeling I have for K. now!

"Then, too, this entire experience has rather convinced me of the validity of Christian existentialism as far as philosophy is concerned. In other words, whatever plans you make, you must be prepared, in one moment, that they can be demolished. Of course, man being what he is, he must make some plans for the future." He hoists a warning hand in the air. "Bear in mind, however, that they might all collapse! Another book I've found interesting, *Religion and Personality*. There's a marvelous line in it: 'Life is not a puzzle to be solved, it's a mystery to be lived minute by minute, hour by hour, day by day.' Oh, and a fine piece of advice given me by a Jesuit friend of mine, a quote from Ignatius Loyola: 'Work as though everything depends upon you and pray as though everything depends upon God.' You see, many people say, 'Oh, well, let us do God's will,' and then they relax. It's not quite that simple, it's a matter of *finding* what God's will is—not easy, granted—and to find it moment to moment and live accordingly."

How does this apply to his daily life? A large smile from Clay Shaw, a long drag on his cigarette followed by a deep cough. "I must give this habit up," he says, holding the offending weed in front of him, "but at this point in my life circumstances are not all that conducive to it." He sighs and then continues. "Well, I'll tell you, soon after this bombshell was dropped on me I had a long talk with myself, told myself I was going to attempt to lead my life, as far as possible, as I did before. This is not one hundred per cent possible, but within the limitations placed upon me I decided I was going to do the best I could. I've pretty well carried this out. I have to admit that there has never been a twenty-four-hour period when this current situation hasn't occupied some of my mental concentration. Because of this, writing is not as easy as it was before. Incidentally, I'm keeping a journal"—he chuckles and adds a wink—"in the hopes that one day it might help keep me. I find that when I wake up in the morning, I'm at my lowest— heavy, heavy still hangs over my head—but then as I begin to distract myself with the activities of the day I work out of it. I then try to enjoy each and every minute to the fullest, whatever it is, a book I'm reading, the birds in the patio out there, a sunset, an enjoyable meal, the companionship of friends, a game of bridge. Perhaps, with the Sword of Damocles hanging over me, I'm even made more aware of the simpler pleasures of life."

What about the future? "Hard to say," Shaw says, shaking his formidable head. "There's no way of knowing how long this will drag on. My most cherished dream would be to continue what I originally planned, my writing, to combine it with travel. Of course, I might not have any money left to do that, I might have to—as they say—open up the shop again." A rueful smile. "Justice may or may not be blind, but she's the most expensive gal I've ever walked around with! But I'll go on writing, I'll work it out. I'm working now on a play which deals with the age-old problem of the human race. Namely, if we're going to be a society at all, we have to give power to administer things to somebody. But we've never worked out any satisfactory solution as to what happens when this power is abused, when it hardens into a privileged cast of nobles. The dynastic principle doesn't work, because a good king is followed by a weak king. Democracy has tried to put institutions in the place of the dynasty, but then the institutions must be headed by individuals, either elected or appointed. So we still have the problem of what to do when somebody in high office totally abuses this power, or even becomes mad. Witness Hitler, Mussolini, Joe McCarthy. This is implicit in the theme of the play. If my reach is equal to my grasp, if I have the technical ability to do it as I see it, I think it will be a good play."

Obviously, I ask, the germ of this idea came from his recent experiences with a certain someone in power. He grins. "Let's just say this has been a watershed in my life; anything I write hereafter will have to be influenced directly or indirectly by it."

What about friends, have any of them dropped out of sight during this period? "Not friends. Perhaps a few acquaintances have shied away, but not friends, they've been closer than ever. You know"—he smiles—"immediately after my arrest, there was something almost every night on the evening news. It was extremely painful to have to sit and hear of the charges against me, but one had to keep in touch with all the developments, it was something that couldn't be ignored. I was speaking about this unpleasant task to a friend, who immediately volunteered to come over every evening when I turned the set on—and *wince* for me!"

Has he made any new friends as a result of his trouble? Clay Shaw's face lights up now. "About ten days after my arrest I called a cab to take me to my lawyer's, almost a daily pilgrimage. The cab arrives, I get in, the driver flips the flag and off we go. He could really have been sent by Central Casting—dark, stocky, Italian. I see him looking back at me in the mirror and finally he says, 'Haven't I driven you before?' 'No, I don't think so.' He kept an eye on me. 'You look so familiar, I could swear I know you.' I finally thought, What the heck, and I said, 'Well, you probably recognize me from the papers, I'm Clay Shaw.' 'Oh, Mr. Shaw, of course,' and he flips the flag off. 'No charge for you, everybody knows it's a bum rap.' I insisted on paying when we arrived at my lawyer's but he wouldn't hear of it, wanted to know how I was going to get home. I told him I'd call a cab. 'No,' he said, pointing to the opposite curb, 'you take your time, I'll be parked right over there.' I told him I couldn't impose upon his time, I wasn't even sure when I'd be leaving, it might be an hour or so. 'Are you kiddin'? I got the whole *Daily Racing Form* to figure out.' Sure enough, when I came out, there he was. Again he refused to flip the flag. Now I really had to protest, but he wouldn't give in. 'No charge, Mr. Shaw. Listen, your lawyers are gonna cost you enough. Now, you know, Mr. Shaw, it's going to be tough for you to get around, everyone knows you. I want you to use my services. I'm either in my cab or at home and my wife knows how to reach me all the time. I want you to take my number and call me anytime. I don't give a damn, three in the morning and you want a carton of cigarettes, a bottle of booze, a magazine—you call me.' "

Clay Shaw shrugs. "That's the way it's been for almost a year and a half. He's never charged me. Oh, I've given presents, to him, to his wife and kids, sent them to my doctor, no bills, things like that. I go out there for Sunday dinner, they're part of my family. You can't realize what this has meant to me. Here's a man who saw injustice being done and had nothing to offer against it but himself and his cab. It reminds me of the tale of the Juggler of Notre Dame. He had no money to offer, only his talent, but that he gave freely. He juggled in front of the statue of Our Lady and surely enough—the statue smiled." And Clay Shaw does more than smile when he speaks of his cab-driver friend—he beams.

This cab-driver friend, whom Clay Shaw requests I refrain from naming—"After all, he's in business here, he could be caused trouble"—I'll call "Tony." It was Tony who drove me on the next to last day of my visit to the Criminal Court Building which houses the District Attorney's office. I had been warned, by almost everyone with whom I'd spoken, to make it easy for myself and stay away from Garrison. I might be subpoenaed, harassed, and a few other things. I was also warned that he can charm the birds when he wants to. But curiosity had me by the throat and I wanted to get a close look at this controversial man. A newspaper reporter asked me what I had in mind to say to him. "I'm just going to say I think Clay Shaw is completely innocent and see what *he* says."

"You're going to—Jesus—" He shook his head and walked away from me.

Lest the reader's hopes rise, I didn't see Jim Garrison. I walked into his most impressive office and found the switchboard operator and several secretaries at the tail end of a *Kaffeeklatsch*. When they'd scattered, I straightened my tie and approached the least formidable-looking one. "I'd like to see the District Attorney," I said, unable to come up with anything more original and sounding like a bad actor in a 1940's B picture. She asked what my business was; I told her I was writing an article and wondered if I could just speak with him for a few minutes. She asked me what publication I represented.

"*Esquire*," I said.

"*Esquire!*" the secretary trilled. "*Esquire!* Oh, honey, it's a good thing the District Attorney's in California. Don't you know *Esquire* named him Bigmouth of the Year last year?"

"No," I replied. (And I hadn't recalled that fact.)

"Well, if you really want to see him, leave your name and number and I'm sure he'll be in touch with you when he gets back next week."

"I'm going to New York tomorrow."

"That's good," she said, pointing toward the door. "Have a nice trip."

It was Tony who drove Clay Shaw and me for a last lunch at Antoine's in New Orleans. Megatons of warmth exploded from the employees of this famed eatery as we entered. "Ah, Mr. Shaw, good to see you," the maitre d' said, reaching for his hand. "How are you, Mr. Shaw?"

And the familiar, smiling reply: "Fine, what have I got to be worried about?"

Over our meal a few last questions to him. "Has anything particularly humorous happened as a result of all this?"

"Nothing really hysterical." He grins. "Except when I was in

New York, I was waiting for a stoplight on Lexington and I noticed a woman eying me closely. She finally sidled up to me and said, 'Aren't you the man who's being bothered by that lawyer down in New Orleans?' I had to smile; that's one way of putting it—Department of Understatement. 'Well,' the woman added, 'my family and I saw you on television, we think it's terrible and we're all praying for you.' "

"Has anyone ever done or said anything vicious to you since your arrest?"

"No, I must say they have not," he says without hesitation, then quickly adds, "I must also express my cynicism by saying I'm surprised. Oh, there have been a couple of unpleasant predictions. In the early days of my arrest, Mr. Garrison said to a journalist that I'd never come to trial, I'd commit suicide first. That gave me very little worry—not the type. And I've heard it said by those who are aware of such things that I wouldn't come to trial because I'd be assassinated." Clay Shaw shrugs and waves it away. "What can you do? If somebody really wants to kill you, seems they have a good chance, witness Lee Harvey Oswald being killed on television with an entire phalanx of Dallas policemen standing by.

"So, while it's not pleasant to contemplate, since there's nothing one can do outside of taking the reasonable precautions, I just try to put it out of my mind."

"Have you received any mail and, if so, what kind of mail?"

"To date, about three hundred letters have arrived from all over the world. All of them were sympathetic, except for three, which were hostile."

"Did you answer any of them?"

"Yes, I hired a secretary and answered all of them. I figured if people could take the time and effort, the least they deserved was a reply from me."

"Did you answer the hostile ones, too?"

"No, none of the three were signed, as is the way with crank letters, I suppose. Oh, I must tell you about one letter from a retired minister in New Jersey and with it a large photograph of me. He'd gone to the bother of contacting one of the wire services and he'd bought this photograph for five dollars. At the end of the letter he asked if I'd please autograph it and send it back to him. He said he was going to hang it in his study next to a picture of Captain Dreyfus."

When we said our goodbyes, I wished Clay Shaw well, and then

Tony, refusing to flip the flag, drove off toward the airport. "I sure hope this thing is over for Mr. Shaw soon," Tony said. "I worry about him. I wish he'd be more careful, like maybe even hide out for a while until his trial comes up. But he goes right on living the way he always lived. See, if you never done anybody harm, you don't expect anyone to do you harm. But they're out to convict Mr. Shaw. I tell you, he's dealing with a dangerous man." Tony glanced over at me. "You know what kills me about Mr. Shaw? He doesn't even run down the guys that are running *him* down. He's got this great outlook on life." Tony grinned and began to thump the steering wheel. "He's really hanging on good!"

As the plane circled New Orleans, gaining altitude, I looked back down at the city with the Mississippi curling around it like a giant python and realized that Clay Shaw *is* hanging on down there in his own quietly tenacious way. There's no doubt that the District Attorney has dedicated himself to getting a conviction but the scapegoat is being stubbornly resistant about playing the villainous part assigned him. And trying to assemble the tenuous evidence and make it stick is about like trying to stuff twelve pounds of Jell-O into a ten-pound bag. But watch out—Mr. Garrison is determined to pull off this stunt. Hang on, Mr. Shaw!

2

Commitment

The December issue of *Esquire* hit the stands around November 15, coinciding exactly with the appearance of my second novel, *Good Times/Bad Times,* with the consequence that I was not giving the Shaw affair my first attention. Publication time is a tricky period when the artist, the ego, the id, the show-off, the invert, patience, temperament and paranoia all jump in the ring for a tag bout, and the best you can hope for is partial recovery by spring.

At this point, however, my spirits had been buoyed by an amalgam of prepublication good fortune: a healthy movie sale to Warner Brothers-Seven Arts, a good paperback deal, English rights sold, both hard and paperback, and finally a happy phone call from my dear lady novel-agent, Phyllis Jackson, with the news of a Book-of-the-Month Club alternate selection.

Hot damn, I was thinking, not bad for a poor kid from the other side of the tracks who never went to college—even though his parents were movie stars amongst that caravan of wild and woolly film pioneers who were chopping down orange trees and slapping up great fakey one-sided movie sets in their place. Still, I grew up as my parents' careers were on the slide; I never caught their act on top. The adoring public, they learned, could pull a disappearing act that would have had Houdini down on all fours looking under the rug. The real memories began there and most of those gruesomely impressionable childhood years were spent, eyes glommed to my parents, both disastrous with a buck, and their friends, who were trying to step out of their personal career depressions, to say nothing of *the* Depression, with all the success of a troupe of trained fleas attempting to perform a peppy Charleston on a dance floor made of flypaper. So my personal memories of all that glitter-glam-Malibu-Hispano-Suisse-tennis-anyone-Pickfair-San Simeon who-hah are nil and I have never gotten over an itchy suspicion of success.

Still, every so often, Clay Shaw would pop up in my toasterlike brain. I would wonder, How goes it down there, sometimes even place a long distance call. How goes it, I would ask. Oh, chugging along, a new brief had been filed by his lawyers; a judge had ordered temporary injunctive relief for the patient from Garrison's attempt to bring him to trial, until a three-judge panel could sit on it and rule; the three-judge panel would throw him back into the lion's cage; his lawyers had exhausted the higher state and lower Federal courts and were now preparing an appeal to the United States Supreme Court, etc. There was always a petition in the hopper and there was always a trace of optimism in his voice, if not in his heart. He spoke never in a downdraft, although as petition after petition was eventually denied, he must often have felt like hopping the nearest freighter. Still, he never allowed the tone of his voice to burden the party on the receiving end of the news, no matter how bad. If he had recently suffered a setback he would nevertheless speak like a man who had just rolled up his sleeves and smacked his hands together: All right, now we'll get on to the next step, which, because it is to a higher court, might also result in a loftier meting out of justice, or perhaps even in sensing injustice.

On the contrary, he was always quick to ask, How goes it with you? What word on the book? What are the signs? How's the work coming on your house?

After the few times we spoke on the phone I would hang up in wonder at his complete lack of self-pity. Not the hint of a whimper in a carload. He was getting on with what had to be gotten on with, his fix, as best he could. And because of that, of course, he was much more unforgettable than if he were sitting around crooning his fate. The better-spirited he was, the more he lingered in my mind.

On my publication day I received a telegram from him:

> Dear Mr. K.
>   What a fabulous day
>   May your book be found without flaw
>   May it sell both widely and well
>   Is the wish of yours truly   Clay Shaw.

This got to me. Had I been immersed in his dilemma for the

past two years, I doubt if I'd remember to change my socks, let alone the publication date of someone's book.

A few days later, I opened the *Times* and found a small squib saying the Supreme Court had turned down Clay Shaw's appeal, that he had no further recourse and would most likely be brought to trial.

Although I was now in the midst of plugging the novel, and was some two hundred pages into the next book, I phoned Roberta Pryor at my agency and asked her to please see if she could secure an assignment for me to cover the trial from one of the national magazines. Both she and Phyllis Jackson were pessimistic, reminding me any magazine would be well scooped by the national newspaper coverage. Still, I insisted they give it a good try.

Then I phoned Clay Shaw, a consolation call. On the surface he was bearing up as well as usual, but I could tell that behind the façade of "Well, so be it—maybe now we'll just go ahead and get the whole thing over with" there was enormous disappointment. What gave me a further clue was the pickup of enthusiasm in his voice when I said I was trying to get an assignment to cover the trial. I gathered he actually wanted me to be there as a friend and a supporter as much as he cared whether I were to write about the trial. I could not help being affected by the hope he expressed that I would somehow manage to be on hand. I asked him to let me know when a definite trial date was set.

A few days later, Clay called and said it looked as if January 21 was a firm date. He seemed anxious to know if I was meeting with any success in securing an assignment. Within a week or so I decided to phone Jim Goode, articles editor of *Playboy* in Chicago, and an acquaintance. We'd had drinks together in New York a year or so before and he'd said if I was ever struck by an idea for a humorous article to let him know, he'd be interested. Although this could not *really* be classified as hilarious source material, it was an idea, so I phoned him. He listened attentively and then asked me to write him, outlining my idea, my angle. I got a letter off the following day, concentrating on my enthusiasm for the task, with a feeble concluding sentence indicating—what with New Orleans and all the characters involved—there just might be some humor to be siphoned from the trial. The next day I took off for a Christmas visit to my mother in Key West.

On December 26 Jim Goode phoned me there. He'd received my

letter and was intrigued with the idea, but he was not actually jumping up and down. He knew I was sympathetic to the defendant and he let drop there were some employees of *Playboy* who were equally sympathetic to Jim Garrison. (*Playboy* had printed a lengthy interview with the District Attorney in October 1967 entitled "A Candid Conversation with the Embattled District Attorney of New Orleans." If Garrison was embattled, what was Clay Shaw?) He kept ferreting out my reasons for wanting to cover the trial, what my angle would be, would I be able to be objective? Objective? Hmn . . . well, all I could say was I had heard the defendant's version and now, in all honesty, it would well behoove me to listen to the prosecution's case, which would certainly be aired in its entirety. Yes, but how was I going to treat the trial? Well, it was hard to say, because the trial had not *occurred;* that's a little like asking Clive Barnes how he's going to review next Thursday's opening night; he hasn't *seen* it yet. Then he hit the word "enlightening." He wanted to know what would be enlightening about my coverage. *Playboy* was not at all interested in simply chronicling some morbid trial proceedings unless they could be made somehow enlightening to the reader. Would they display qualities that might prove uplifting to the human condition?

Playboy?

After we'd been talking an hour—yes, an hour—I began to hanker for a broken connection. The long distance is never a satisfying medium over which to conclude important business. I have never gotten over the wonder of its being long distance, still tend to raise the voice several decibels and can never quite tear my mind away from the profit the phone company is racking up. It does not breed relaxation. So lest I blow the deal by faulty ad libbing, I requested Jim Goode to let me phone him in a few days with a firm prospectus outlined. He suggested the next day, instead of a few, and I agreed.

That evening was spent rehearsing. I wanted the assignment so badly I did not want to leave my argument to chance. I even scribbled out a few cue sheets with my ideas, knowing that if I ever stopped talking, or lost my point, I would have to yield the phone. I could hardly wait for business hours so I could place the call, which went, roughly:

KIRKWOOD: Hi, Jim, how are you? [No time left for reply, don't let him get in a word.] I got to thinking about what we were talking about yesterday. About the importance of this trial and what would be enlightening? Here we have the first man accused—outside of Lee Harvey Oswald who was put away before he could shed any light on the tragedy—the first man accused and now actually brought to trial for the murder of probably the most popular man on earth at the time of his death.

GOODE: I know, but—

KIRKWOOD: So here you have someone, a writer of sorts, who has a direct line to the mind and heart and visceral reactions of the defendant and also someone who has the trust of his lawyers—

GOODE: That may be true—

KIRKWOOD: And, remember, this defendant is not just some vagrant they've picked up. He's been a respected man in the community, a man with a fine war record, a self-taught man, a man known as a builder, a booster, even a philanthropist.

GOODE: Nobody said he—

KIRKWOOD: So if it isn't enlightening to chronicle this man's day by day reactions to his trial, when he claims total innocence, to have access to his thoughts as he's dragged into the ultimate confrontation with the government, with the law of the land, as few citizens ever are, a most personal and terrifying confrontation at the most dangerous level—

GOODE: It's obvious from your—

KIRKWOOD: I know, you think I'm prejudiced and that will color the microscope I look through. All right, suppose—and I would be surprised—suppose the state comes up with incontrovertible evidence linking Clay Shaw up to this crime. If he should be proven guilty, then you have the inside track on the man found guilty of one of the most heinous crimes in history. Who would not want to know how Hitler felt, how he would have reacted had he been brought to trial? The observance and study of mankind in itself is illuminating, isn't it?

GOODE: Yes, but—

KIRKWOOD: As I see it, the magazine can't lose. No matter how the trial comes out, it can't be a dud, it has got to be fascinating. If Shaw wins, then you've got a line to the inner spirit that allowed an innocent man to endure two years of persecution and financial ruin. If it should turn out that Garrison wins, there are two alternatives.

GOODE: But if Garrison—

KIRKWOOD: If Garrison wins, either Shaw is guilty or the alternative is that Garrison's dragged his victim through the mud this far, then there's some reason to believe he might just put one over on a jury. Then we would have an innocent man unjustly convicted, now facing years of appeals in the higher courts.

GOODE: You sound as if—

KIRKWOOD: The way I see it, it's not necessarily the Shaw trial, it's the Shaw-Garrison trial. These two giants slugging it out and if Garrison should lose, if it turns out he has persecuted an innocent man, whatever his motives, then we might just see the disintegration of a man and his public career, much the same as we saw the undoing of McCarthy during the Congressional hearings.

GOODE: You certainly—

KIRKWOOD (chugging into the home stretch): In the end, you have to go with my enthusiasm, my strong impulse to cover this event, to be there and soak it up. You have to sniff my taste for it. I know you still want to know what my angle would be for covering the trial itself, but that's the third side of a missing triangle. It hasn't unfolded, it's a mystery as yet, but a mystery I want to observe every second it's unraveling. Also, don't forget the pur drama of a trial—the unexpected moment-to-moment—

GOODE: All right, okay, you've got the assignment.

KIRKWOOD: I'm not finished yet.

GOODE (laughing): Yes, you are.

KIRKWOOD (also laughing): Sure, because *you* want to talk now.

And he did, reaffirming the assignment and adding he would write a letter to the Criminal Sheriff requesting a courtroom seat for me.

The fee was to be $2,000 for the article, plus $1,500 total expenses, even if the trial should last five months. Should *Playboy* decline, in the end, to print the article, I would get no part of the aforementioned $2,000. I would only have received expense money. In that event, should my agent manage to place the article with another magazine, I would then have to return even the expense money to Hugh Hefner.

Not a get-rich-quick deal by any means. Still, I was awash with high spirits for the rest of the holidays and I had to admit to myself that, assignment or no, I would somehow have ended up at the Criminal Court Building in the Parish of Orleans in the State of Louisiana when court was called to order.

Why? Outside of being catnipped by trials and possessing an overdose of curiosity—I cared. Not usually attracted to causes, at least those which do not affect me personally, here I was caring strongly. It was a good feeling.

3

A Doubleheader

When I phoned Clay Shaw to tell him of my assignment, his voice projected the good news my arrival meant to him. It was warming to hear. "Come on down, I think we'll show you a high old time."

Flying is not my favorite form of relaxation, especially the getting up there and the coming back down. Still, as the act of flight hurtles the body through space, so does the mind, once the initial fright has passed and one gives up to the fates, tend to soar.

Therefore, on the trip to New Orleans, my mind conjectured a few of the possibilities.

Among the fringe benefits, there was a world of gumdrops promised by the colorful District Attorney, who had legally and in the manner of many movie stars changed his unwieldy name of Earling Carothers Garrison to—just plain Jim. In frequent head-on statements he had pointed a many-fingered hand in accusation of sins of commission and omission at the CIA, the Secret Service, the paramilitary, the regular military, war lovers, the neo-fascists, the FBI and J. Edgar Hoover, the Attorney General and the Justice Department, Earl Warren and the entire Warren Commission, the homosexual underground, the Eastern Establishment, the doctors at Parkland Hospital, those at Bethesda, the right wing, the Dallas police, the anti-Castro Cubans, L.B.J. and NBC—to name a few.

As a New Orleanian had cracked on my previous visit: "Holy Smoley, the only group not charged is the Girl Scouts—and they'd better stop pushing cookies!"

Jim Garrison had not been beating around the bush when he made these accusations; they were not glancing blows or love taps. They were broadsides. For instance, in his many blasts aimed at the then Attorney General, Ramsey Clark, accused by Garrison of hiding the truth of the assassination from the American people, the District Attorney called Clark "a political appointee who, if his father Tom Clark had not been on the Supreme Court, would probably be cleaning the streets with a broom."

Of the then President of the United States, Garrison had the temerity to ask and answer this question in an interview for *Ramparts* magazine in January of 1968:

Who appointed Ramsey Clark, who has done his best to torpedo the [my] investigation of the case? Who controls the CIA? Who controls the FBI? Who controls the Archives where this evidence [the autopsy photographs and X rays, etc.] is locked up for so long that it is unlikely that there is anybody in this room who will be alive when it is released? This is really your property and the property of the people of this country. Who has the arrogance and the brass to prevent the people from seeing that evidence? Who indeed? The one man who has profited most from the assassination—your friendly President, Lyndon Johnson.

Who, one couldn't help think, has the balls to drop that far from subtle implication? Jim Garrison. Yes, he does that. He might well have surprises up his sleeves and magic in his pockets; one thing is certain—he has chutzpah running in his veins.

What if he had, indeed, hooked a couple of big ones? I mean really hooked them, with evidence to back him up. Yes, there might well be surprises. In fact, the very essence of Jim Garrison is not only his craving to surprise, but his ability to satisfy this urge.

By the time the plane landed I was salivating; all right, let's get this much-heralded show on the road.

My first big surprise was being met at the airport by a reporter friend from the *Times-Picayune* with a sly, grinning "Guess what?"

"What?" I asked as we walked toward the baggage pickup.

"Looks like the trial is off!"

"*What?*"

"This afternoon the D.A.'s office flatly said if they don't get the autopsy X rays and photos from Washington they cannot—underline cannot—come to trial." He waved the afternoon paper in my face in bold-headline proof.

"But I've rented an apartment for two months," I said.

"So—you'll sublet."

I hadn't even picked up my baggage and it looked as if the game had been called. According to the article in the paper, the District Attorney's office had taken a firm stand. Washington had been equally adamant about releasing this material and there was no reason now to think there would be a change of policy. So, if one went by the papers, there seemed to be a distinct possibility of a stand-off.

Riding into town to see an apartment I wasn't so sure I'd be needing, my emotions were on dual control, marked dichotomous. There was relief that Clay Shaw might well be spared the trial of a trial. There was also a certain depression at being all geared up for a high old time only to have the party canceled. Put away your paper hats and noisemakers, the fun's off. Still, when I thought about it, the fun was at the expense of Clay Shaw, he was the one in the barrel, so why should I feel disgruntled by a move that could only be described as beneficial to him?

Perhaps it was that small morbid subdivision of the brain that, sometimes against our conscious wishes, makes us press forward on tiptoe, necks craning, to look over the crowd at the victim of an accident—an eyeful we know will be repellent to the sight. Although we don't *want* to look, we can't *not* look, rationalizing, It's a shame but it's happened and I might as well see just how badly injured a person riding a bike can *get* when struck by an express train.

The apartment turned out to be perfectly suitable, if uninspired, right on the corner of St. Philip and Royal and across the street from a school playground. There was even a small elevator in the four-story building, so small that if three people happened to get in at one time they could all have been arrested for indecent mauling.

The door to the apartment itself, on the third floor, led into the oblong living room, which, unless the louvered doors separating it from the bedroom straight ahead were pulled, really made one long room with the bed facing the front door at the far end. A small bathroom led off left from the bedroom part of the room and a small kitchen led off left from the living-room portion. Two large windows sided the bed, looking down into St. Philip Street and across into the playground. Not a picture, painting, print or anything on any of the off-white walls, nor the sign of anything ever having been there.

There was nothing at all unusual about the apartment, except the three lamps in the living room. These wood-based shiny-white-shaded lamps were giants; if huge banquet halls in feudal castles had been wired for electricity, these lamps would not have been dwarfed. As it was they were definitely out of scale. I remember one night later on, coming home with a buzz on and thinking three of Jim Garrison's spies were standing on my tables disguised as lamps. That's how tall they were. Another item of more than routine interest was an electric heater in the ceiling of the bathroom with a heating capacity not only to instant-dry your hair after a shower but to grill a steak, if you happened to be drying your hair with a sirloin instead of a towel.

The apartment was air conditioned and the bed was large and comfortable, so if you didn't linger too long under the ceiling heater and if you could condition yourself not to imagine the lamps were closing in on you, the setup was not bad at all.

The evening was spent in conjecture, as was the entire weekend, for that matter. Despite Garrison's earlier statement that only death could keep him from bringing the case to trial, the newspapers, radio and TV were hawking this latest no-trial flash, causing arriving pressmen from all over the nation to scratch their heads and look up return flights.

There were rumors in every corner and hanging from the walls: Garrison had not been seen around lately and he was "away someplace" taking "a rest." His subordinates, most particularly those who would be in charge of actually trying the case, were out to dodge the trial because they would be doing all the work and getting none of the credit, if credit there should be. Garrison himself was using the autopsy photos and X rays as an out, knowing he hadn't a hope in hell of winning the case; this way he could claim forever that the Feds had prevented him from going to trial, fitting in with his persistent accusations that everyone from the President and Earl Warren on down was burning the midnight oil to sabotage his investigation. New Orleans was a grab bag of rumors and you could take your pick.

Clay Shaw received me the next afternoon, Saturday, at the now infamous red door on Dauphine Street. I had not seen him, except for brief glimpses on the television news and in newspaper photographs, since coming to New Orleans to do the profile the previous May, and I was startled again at the size of the man. I'd forgotten how truly large and barrel-chested he is. He greeted me warmly, actually as more of an old friend than a new one. When I'd sat down opposite him, drink in his hand—a drink and a cigarette were almost necessary security blankets at this time and one could not have blamed him had he kept a teddy bear at the ready—I realized I'd also forgotten how striking and unusual his light agate blue eyes were. Eyes, the size, shape, especially the way they either look at or avoid the subject—their personality—are most important and memorable characteristics. Despite this, I am always hard put to remember the color.

These eyes look directly at you. The simpler questions first: How was he feeling? The answer came back high-spirited and energized. "Feel like a spring lamb!" He smiled. The face smiles easily, pushing everything up until the high broad cheekbones prohibit further movement except for the spread of the eyes. Was this because of the sudden no-trial gambit? "Hell, no, I'm ready to go," he said, smacking his hands together. "I'm all revved up— let's have the trial."

Clay shot a quick glance over his shoulder toward the corner bookshelves and asked, "What about you, Garrison?" He paused a moment, then delivered a brisk "Fuck you, Big Jim." He laughed, telling me to say hello to the District Attorney. I greeted him similarly. Explanation: Because of the preponderance of cloak and dagger work in the case, everyone connected with it, including Jim Garrison, who claimed the FBI had his phones tapped, was aware of the possibility that the privacy of their homes was being electronically raped.

I thought this brio on the part of the defendant might be affected, but as we spoke further, his attitude remained constant. Why? Who could possibly want to endure the ordeal of such a trial? "Nobody, surely, but I can no longer endure the time out of my life *waiting* for the trial. It's gone on too long, the pressures are as great in this limbo I've been in, going on two years now. I want it over with. If I weren't innocent perhaps . . . but I am. I'm ready to prove it. I'm ready for the trial." There was not only his readiness to stand trial, but there was an added fight, a definite hint of a future offensive in the defendant. "I don't want to let Garrison off the hook. All right, Mac, you started it, now let's see exactly *what* you've started." (Clay Shaw uses "Mac" occasionally in a certain half kidding, half don't-fool-around-with-me-any-more tone.) "There's a Federal law giving redress if a man is falsely arrested with malicious intent. Of course, I don't know how you prove malicious intent, but I intend to do my damnedest." He went on to indicate he would do everything possible to sue Garrison, not only because of the wrong done him, but because he felt a stand should be made to prohibit other public officials from persecuting innocent persons whose private lives might be questionable on the grounds that they are fair game. There was a kick in seeing him in such a good mood, and the scent of the extra added fight was refreshing to whiff.

That evening, at what was supposed to be his pretrial "last supper" at the New Orleans equivalent of Tara, the home of spunky, gravel-throated Mrs. Edith Stern—Sears-Roebuck heiress and benefactress of the arts, Negroes, and almost anyone in need who might be brought to her attention—Clay Shaw was greeted affectionately by a few close friends who were switching the status of the dinner from last supper to victory celebration. "No," he reiterated while we were being served cocktails, "as much as I'd like to avoid a long-drawn-out messy trial, after all this time I don't want the charges to linger on by innuendo. I want to be vindicated."

But the guests—painter Leonard Flettrich; a prominent civil lawyer and his wife, Mr. and Mrs. Moise Dennery; and Muriel Bultman Frances Bogner, another slim, energetic philanthropist, a one-woman committee of twelve—were decked out in high spirits, obviously concentrating upon the possibility that the ordeal of a trial might be spared their friend. Mrs. Stern is the perfect hostess; she showers the visitor with warmth and her delight that you could be with her. One got the idea that if she and Mrs. Bogner put their minds and energy working together they could undoubtedly have the pyramids shifted to New Orleans. As it is, they are up to their bankbooks and vitamin B-12 in the symphony, the museum, the civic theater, civil rights and you-name-it.

Leonard Flettrich's wife, Terry, who hosts a noontime television hour, a sort of New Orleans *Today,* could not be with them that evening; she was in Washington covering the inauguration. There was some talk of Nixon and at that time most of us could not believe, or take seriously, the idea that Richard Milhous Nixon was alive and well and about to start living in the White House. Mrs. Flettrich's presence in Washington, however, confirmed that, yes, he actually was being installed as our President.

Still, optimism was in the air over Clay Shaw's current no-trial status—enough, along with a few cocktails, to permit Leonard Flettrich to call across the room, in what is currently referred to as black or sick humor, "Hey, Clay, when you're clear of this one, what are we gonna do about Nixon?" Because these people, if anything, signify the antithesis of ill will, there was only laughter as Mrs. Dennery cried out, "God, don't say that, not in this town. We'll *all* be arrested!"

So the evening progressed in testimony of the friendship and concern this small sophisticated cabal of Shaw-ites felt for their guest of honor. The talk could never stretch more than a twenty-minute span without snapping back to Topic A, no doubt because the culmination, one way or the other, was only a day off. Judge Edward A. Haggerty, Jr., had set Monday morning to hear the state's official motion that would supposedly ask for indefinite continuance or perhaps even drop the charges on the basis of lack of cooperation, harassment and severe blockade by various agencies of the Federal government.

They were sensitive enough to Clay Shaw to change the subject away from Topic A whenever a certain faraway look clouded his eyes, as if he'd forgotten to bring something terribly important with him—a look that must have mirrored the sudden reminder that My God, this is real, yes, here I am laughing on the inside with my friends, but on the outside I still stand seriously accused of conspiracy to—I can't believe it! This could be triggered by any overly long serious discussion of the case.

There was another look, an almost tacit sigh of boredom that would seem to generate from his eyeballs and could be interpreted as saying, Time out! Enough! I'm tired of having my nose rubbed in it. I need to come up for air.

Change of subject, sigh, smile, there, that's better.

The way to treat *it* that evening was with humor, riddled with brief and widely spaced machine-gun bursts of solid caring.

Clay Shaw had mentioned that his mother was coming in from Hammond, the small Louisiana town that is her home, the next afternoon, Sunday. This was to be their last visit before the trial, and they were sticking to the schedule despite the recent developments, perhaps because if they counted too much on the charges being dropped they might nix old devil luck. I had never met her and was curious, so although I felt pushy, especially intruding upon a relationship that seemed both close and extremely private, I asked if I could drop by for a few minutes in the afternoon, simply to meet her. Permission was granted.

A small family group was present by the time I knocked on the red door that Sunday afternoon: Mrs. Alice Shaw, Clay's mother; Mrs. Tulip Atkins, a cousin, also from Hammond; a nephew, Jim Wall; his wife and baby; and Father Sheridan, a Jesuit friend who had remained close to Clay Shaw since his arrest.

Someone asked Clay how well he'd known Jim Garrison before this all started. "Oh," Clay said, "we only had a nodding acquaintance, no more than a brief hello when we'd served on committees or seen each other at social or civic events. I'd never had a drink or a talk alone with the man. I was seated at the next table one night at Brennan's, the night Garrison flipped a glass of wine in his wife's face. Some people have hinted my presence at the scene of his embarrassment might have something to do with his attitude toward me. But I think not, that would be highly overreacting on his part."

Mrs. Shaw, thin, frizzy-haired, wearing a longish maroon dress, and smack out of Grandma Moses, sat smoking a cigarette in that gingerly manner older people sometimes employ—almost as if, were they to take too firm a grip on it or too deep a puff, it just might explode. She sat there, saying little, only nodding in agreement at the many indignities foisted upon her son. Again there was talk of the whips, the chain and the black hood and cape and of the dark hints of a den of sado-masochist activity dropped by the D.A.'s office, even though this paraphernalia was part of a Mardi Gras costume Shaw had worn and been seen in by numerous Quarterites over a period of years during the carnival season.

Father Sheridan asked Clay Shaw if any of his possessions, including less sinister items such as a calorie counter, typewriter, various manuscripts and books, had ever been returned to him. No, Clay said, they hadn't. The room was filled with clucking over this minor inconvenience when Mrs. Shaw suddenly turned to her son and said with a mixture of annoyance and motherly concern, "That's right, Clay. They never did give you back your *whips*, did they?"

The incongruity of choice from this gentle, quiet elderly woman filled the room with laughter.

"That's my mom," Clay Shaw said, on the edge of his own laughter, reaching over and patting her knee with affection. Nothing could top that and I soon left, wishing Clay Shaw luck and saying I would see him in the courtroom the next day.

Elsewhere in "The City That Care Forgot"—the motto New Orleanians have fondly pegged onto their home town—I nosed around, taking the pulse of what citizenry I came up against and by late Sunday night there was no doubt that a dyspeptic nimbus, a certain disgruntlement, hung over many local folk that weekend. By mid-January Mardi Gras activities are well under way and the nervous sensual aroma of that legalized time of civic madness shimmered in the air even more than usual this year, for a highly publicized extra-special sideshow, the Shaw trial, had been firmly promised.

A doubleheader had been scheduled for the winter of 1969 but now, with everyone gathered around the pre-Lenten groaning board, it looked as if dessert might not be served and the guests would be cut off, still salivating. Yes, the average citizen of New Orleans was cranked up with displeasure at the prospect of a no-trial.

Monday would tell the tale.

4

All Systems Go

Monday morning I met with Clay Shaw's lawyers—Irvin Dymond, the Wegmann brothers, Eddie and Billy, and Sal Panzeca—in the coffee shop of the National Bank of Commerce Building. They were all in fine high spirits, mostly speculating on the prosecution's about-face regarding not coming to trial. They laughed, kidded one another, cracked jokes about themselves and Garrison, and their jocularity was completely surprising. I wondered at their ease in this deadly matter, at the same time I noticed that Eddie Wegmann's participation in the fun and games was measured.

Eddie and Billy Wegmann actually share the same solid, up-turned, even-featured face, with one exception: Billy's ease allowed his features to assume the mask of comedy, while Eddie's expression, because of his intense personal concern for Clay Shaw, was more often than not frozen into the mold of tragedy.

Irvin Dymond, ex-boxer, Navy man and self-made lawyer, now wildly devoted to his pretty third wife—between them they share ten children—gives the first impression of being tough and unyielding. As a lawyer, he is. But when he laughs, he throws his head back, his cheeks convert to two enormous dimples, and one can see the delight, the zest for living and comradeship that make up the whole man.

All three are mellow men in their fifties, men of conservative dress, medium height and stocky builds. Sal Panzeca, the junior member of the defense team, is short, dark, compact and energetic, with a face that grins more easily than it frowns.

The District Attorney had been lying dormant for a spell; there had been no personal proclamations issued in the last week and he had not been seen locally, at least by the opposition or friends of the opposition, so Clay's lawyers sifted through the full winter line of rumors: Jim Garrison had been hiding out in the New Orleans

Athletic Club, sleeping the days away in the slumber room or he'd been undergoing psychiatric treatment (there was frequent talk of a family history of mental disturbance) or he was perhaps in California in a last-ditch effort to round up additional witnesses or he really wanted out of the investigation.

The defense team was sure there would be a motion on the part of the state for continuance, most likely indefinite continuance. The general air of response was not to let Garrison get away with this latest ploy. At least that was the opinion of these lawyers in consort, but privately there were ambivalent trickles: No, we're not going to let the Jolly Green Giant slip out of this valley with anything approaching ease, yet, on the other hand, it would be fine for the other giant, the defending one, if a long, messy trial could be spared him.

Riding out in the car to the sinister-looking Criminal Court Building, they were even more jovial, now concentrating upon Eddie Wegmann's driving prowess, their golf games, a drinking bout or two, and the presiding judge, Edward A. Haggerty, Jr., whom they delighted in twitting. The car was parked across the street from the building, kitty-corner, in one of the trio of gas stations occupying the three remaining corners at the intersection of Tulane and Broad. As the lawyers crossed the street and made for the garage entrance of the building a battery of television and news photographers swarmed around the corner toward them, shouting and sending them into a quick-paced escape down into the garage.

Now hilarity took a powder and a no-nonsense military bearing starched up the men as they strode across the concrete floor of the garage, past the many parking places with the Criminal District judges' cars parked at rakish angles in no seeming order. I noticed a large center empty parking space with the sign JIM GARRISON DISTRICT ATTORNEY posted in front of it. Someone was missing.

Up in the elevators to the top floor, what seems to be the second floor but is counted as the third because of the basement, to be met by an eye-confusing hubbub of activity in the large vaulted-ceilinged marble corridor leading to the courtroom of Criminal District Judge Haggerty at the far end of the building. More newsmen, spectators, the curious who are drawn to trials and courthouses when big doings are afoot. Lawyers are used to this and their pace quickened once more, giving them momentum to plow on through the crowd as if court had been called to order already and they were late arriving.

This was not considered a day of the trial itself, and there was not much order to it, undoubtedly because almost everyone presumed the morning would contain a series of motions for continuance by the state and objections and motions for a speedy trial by the defense. One got the impression the proceedings were going to be indefinite and highly arguable by both sides. Not having credentials yet, I simply tagged along with the defense and soon found myself sitting in the large courtroom, up front in the jury box to the audience left of the judge's bench, with other members of the press, all of whom were strangers to me.

Within seconds the judge was announced and from his chambers came silver-haired, black-robed Edward A. Haggerty, Jr. We all stood in deference for a few seconds and then the courtroom was filled with the clatter of people taking their seats. Right in front of me, I spotted Clay Shaw at the defense table along with the Wegmann brothers, Irvin Dymond and Sal Panzeca. The missing link for the first few minutes was not only Jim Garrison but James Alcock, the Assistant District Attorney who, it was understood, would be handling the bulk of the state's courtroom work. A deputy announced he was not yet in court, that someone would be sent to fetch him, to which the judge, looking a great deal like Jed Prouty in one of those old Jones Family movies, with a son like Jimmy Lydon, replied, "Why don't you have someone get on the phone instead of having to trek all the way down there?"

Soon James Alcock, a stocky 36-year-old attorney with the earnest appearance of someone who might be in charge of the local youth movement at the YMCA, arrived and the day began.

Judge Haggerty, who has a reputation for liking his spirits not infrequently spaced, and who was rumored to have taken a vow to go on the wagon for the duration of the trial, asked Alcock, "Does the state wish to be heard orally on the motion?"

As Alcock replied in the affirmative, Irvin Dymond rose from his seat but before he had time to make his intentions known, the judge, immediately rattled, a tremulous hand flying to adjust his glasses and then remaining to vibrate about his face, objected: "Don't do that!" Irvin Dymond attempted to explain he was merely about to hand in a written motion when the judge snapped, "Yes, I know, but you disturb me when you get up. I always think you're going to interrupt me." His fingers quivered about his face and then fluttered down.

Smiles on the faces of many members of the press and on the lawyers' faces as well. If he were, indeed, going on the wagon, his hands indicated he had not quite begun the night before.

That small disturbance out of the way, Alcock repeated that he did indeed wish to make an oral statement, after which Dymond was allowed to hand up to the judge a document in answer to Alcock's motion of three days before (Dymond's motion was for a speedy trial).

On the previous Friday a report of four medical experts appointed by Attorney General Ramsey Clark had been released. The men on this panel had examined the clothing of the late President, sixty-nine black-and-white photographs, plus color transparencies and X rays taken at the autopsy, and their report agreed with the conclusion of the Warren Commission that the President had been killed by two shots fired from behind. The Justice Department announced that the examination had been conducted February 16 and 17, 1968, almost a year before the report was made public.

James Alcock began his speech by saying the state was entitled to a fair trial, just as the defendant was, adding he would like to submit an outline of "the offense that prompted the filing of this motion at the eleventh hour." He then rapped the Attorney General, saying the original autopsy report obviously needed buttressing and therefore Clark had rounded up a panel of "so-called" experts. The idea that this panel reviewed the original autopsy reports—the same ones denied Garrison—in secret almost a year ago and that Ramsey Clark had chosen to make this latest report public only three days before he was to leave office and on the eve of picking a jury for the Clay Shaw trial he called "unconscionable" and "a blow to the administration of justice." He added it could not help influencing prospective jurors.

Alcock had already worked himself up to a good healthy degree of indignation by this time. Now he allowed for a sudden and brief pause, then dropped his surprise package: "The state will trust the good judgment, common sense and spirit of justice which the state feels prevails among the people of New Orleans and will withdraw its motion and announce at this time the state is ready to go to trial tomorrow."

People sat there, mentally knocking the palms of their hands against their foreheads. What? How's that? Play it again. The judge appeared stunned, the four defense attorneys and the defendant himself sat motionless, no one gasped, cried out or even murmured until this about-face sank solidly in: Yes, that's what the man said.

Then, within a matter of minutes, Judge Haggerty announced the trial would, indeed, commence at ten the next morning with jury selection, and having stated that, glanced over the motion Dymond had handed in and complained that the proper documents were not affixed to it. Dymond replied that the matter was now moot. "I know it's moot, Mr. Dymond," the judge once again snapped at him. "You don't have to tell me."

I noticed the trace of a grin on Dymond's face and later learned that Billy Wegmann had offered to set Dymond up to a dry martini for every time he managed to rattle the judge.

Court was adjourned for the day and reporters skidded down the marble hallway to the phones. An infectious spray of excitement flowed from Judge Haggerty's courtroom and diffused throughout the building as small clusters of spectators and courthouse employees chattered and giggled: Yes, the trial was on.

Those of us who were embarking on long-term papers and those who did not have to file stories immediately made our way down the stairway to the Sheriff's office to secure our courtroom visas, where we had earlier thought none would be necessary.

The smiling Sheriff's administrative assistant, dark-haired, attractive Nina Sulzer, sat behind her typewriter (and a full quota of sex appeal), collecting drivers' licenses from four or five reporters and typing up identification cards. It was apparent from the sudden burst of activity in the Sheriff's office that they were as surprised as the rest of the courthouse. "Will I have a regular seat?" asked one press lady. "Oh, we're long out of seats," sighed Nina Sulzer, "but we'll do our best. You'll get in, but I can't be sure about the rest." At that point the Criminal Sheriff, Louis A. Heyd, Jr., breezed past on his way to his inside office.

"Surprise!" Miss Sulzer said.

"Surprise!" he echoed.

"I'm going to quit." She shrugged.

"I already quit, five minutes ago," replied the Sheriff.

They laughed and the Sheriff went into his office as a young Parish Prison inmate arrived to help set up the picture-taking equipment for our press cards. I'd heard that Miss Sulzer was friendlily disposed to the accused, in fact Clay Shaw had phoned her about a seat for me. She knew of the *Esquire* piece, knew which team I was rooting for. We eyed each other as potential friends but we did not document the possibility with words. While she was processing me, she winked and said, "It's a madhouse. I don't know what we're going to do. I've already got a list of at least seventy-five housewives, mostly friends of the judge and a few other officials, but not really the best audience for Clay."

The use of his first name broke down the formality between us and I was grateful to her for that small sign of trust.

Once Nina Sulzer was finished with me I was ushered into the inside office to await having my picture taken. I sat down and introduced myself to Sheriff Heyd, a most amiable man both in appearance and attitude, not at all the image one would ascribe to a criminal sheriff, let alone a Southern one. The phones were ringing, employees and newsmen darted in and out, and an exceedingly attractive local TV reporter, Rosemary James, formerly part of the *States-Item* team that had first broken the story of Garrison's investigation, was being snapped by the young prisoner. The atmosphere in the Sheriff's office was suddenly quite jazzy: Yes, we're going to have the party after all.

This was a majority reaction in the city. "We gonna have Mardi Gras *and* the trial," a cab driver told me on the way back from the courthouse. "Shee-it, what a time!"

5

The Power Game

Even on a sunny day the very sight of that fortress of the administration of law and order, the ominous oblong-block-long stony-gray-beige twelve-columned Criminal Court Building at the corner of Tulane and Broad invites strong suspicions that nothing particularly good is going to happen to anyone officially summoned to enter it. The sightseer begins to wonder where the guillotine might be set up—in an inside courtyard perhaps, or maybe they've hidden it around the corner. A local reporter, Don Lee Keith of the *Times-Picayune,* put it this way: "Every time I step inside the Criminal Court Building I feel like a big black vulture has just lit on my shoulder."

Once inside you come face to face with a door marked Louis A. Heyd, Jr., Criminal Sheriff. To the left of the Sheriff's office and the lobby, a corridor runs past various offices, few of which I ever saw in use, to the end of the building and a small candy-sandwich-and-coffee counter, at the bottom of an end staircase leading up to the top floor. To the right of the lobby the corridor begins with a setup of pay phones for the reporters attending the trial and proceeds down past the local newspaper pressrooms to the coroner's office and a massive men's room at the foot of another staircase. Besides these two end staircases, to the right of the Sheriff's office the main stairway spirals up to the midpoint of a wide marble corridor stretching the entire length of the block-long building from the D.A.'s impressive office at one end, past the other Criminal District courtrooms to the courtroom of Judge Haggerty at the far end.

By the ropes of this forbiddingly official spot, cordoned off for the Clay Shaw trial, stood Nina Sulzer, who turned out to be not only administrative assistant to the Sheriff, in charge of seating and security for the trial, but also Lady Domo of the Parish Prison, for lack of funds a certified hell hole abutting the backside of the Criminal Court Building. There she was the first day of jury selection, clipboard in hand, pleasantly harassed, bright and candid, dealing with a swarm of press, spectators, and prospective jurors, making trips from the ropes to the security desk set up near the courtroom door with the pulled-in sexy walk of an assured airline hostess. As a matter of fact, from her good looks and shapeliness, she could very well have been welcoming us aboard a 500-seat supersonic flying machine instead of into a courtroom. The idea of her walking down the Parish Prison corridor, with cells of raunchy prisoners ogling her from both sides, boggled the imagination. She must be, I thought, surely the prettiest, swingingest jailer on active duty.

This was all foreign country to me, and I admit to a bit of *Front Page* excitement as she called out, "Waldron, New York *Times;* Parks, Baltimore *Sun;* Cohen, L.A. *Times*," and I felt a bit silly when she read off "Kirkwood, *Playboy*," as if I should come skidding up with a white knit crew sweater and tennis racquet in hand, shouting, "Anyone for doubles?"

Once through the ropes, checked at the desk for proper credentials, frisked by two deputies and allowed to enter, I found the courtroom to be in pleasant contrast to the cold marbleized Judgment Dayism of the building that housed it. The abrupt proceedings of the day before and the strangeness of the place had prevented me from giving it the eagle eye. It is actually an agreeable-looking courtroom: large, high-ceilinged, pale green where it isn't decorated with handsome fluted wood paneling. It has dignity and would make a perfect setting for Perry Mason, with three enormous venetian-blinded windows on each side, four large chandeliers, and rows of solid shoulder-high backed wooden pews for press and spectators leading on either side of a wide aisle up to the railing and official working area of the court: prosecution table back nearest the rail, defense table in front and slightly to the right, well beneath the massive raised judge's bench, and two ample jury boxes, one to the far left and one to the far right, facing across the room at each other. The witness chair, audience left of the judge's bench and also raised, but not quite as high as the judge's—let's keep them in their place—is comfortable in appearance, if not in actuality, which is probably the best that can be said of any witness chair.

The state seal in color, an ungainly-looking pelican, is implanted on a large wooden panel behind the judge's bench and repeated ten times in smaller plaques around the room toward the top of the walls. These birds are the only frivolous touch, adding just a smattering of Walt Disney, and they struck me as being out of place. If I were on trial I don't think I'd care for a bunch of nesting pelicans staring down at me.

Soon the room began filling up with the principals: Assistant D.A.s James Alcock, Andrew "Moo-Moo" Sciambra and Alvin Oser for the state; ample deputies for courtroom security now fringing the room; the defense team, Irvin Dymond, the Wegmann brothers and Sal Panzeca; the judge's minute clerk, George Sullivan; a court reporter; more press; and now those empaneled to serve as jurors, as many of this original panel of 169 as would fit into the right side of the courtroom and even spill over into the right front, ahead of the railing, where there were several rows of benches, and also into the right jury box.

And there was the defendant, well dressed in a conservative suit, but looking a bit gray around the gills and smiling and smoking the way one would if dragged to a cocktail party one didn't want to attend, enduring it but not necessarily enjoying. It was a warm day in New Orleans for January, and Clay Shaw looked warmer than most of us.

There was a great businesslike air of settling down to the pre-proceedings—the beginning business day of a large corporation, perhaps a stockholders' meeting. At least this was true of the working area of the court.

It was not true of the right side of the spectator section, now jammed with jury prospects who, as a group, resembled nothing more than a meeting of dock workers. Unless they specifically volunteer, Louisiana women are not empaneled in criminal cases, so half of the qualified citizenry was absent, a half that, were I the defendant, would sorely have been missed. True or not, the sight of a woman, or women, on a jury gives indication that there will be a predisposition to mercy, to special pleadings, to even, in a strange nameless way, a sort of logical outcome. Instead, this group of womenless no-nonsense vigilantes crowded the pews and looked downright ill at ease. There were few white-collar workers noticeable among them. Many had made no attempt to dress up for the occasion and most of those who had, looked as if they belonged back in the late thirties or early forties. They would have looked better, more natural certainly, in their work clothes. If those empaneled for jury service are supposed to represent a cross section of the community, then a section or two must have, indeed, been crossed out.

Now the door to Judge Haggerty's chambers opened and out he came, his craggy Irish face looking scrubbed and pink as a baby's dimpled bottom and his silver hair immaculately groomed. A local reporter said, "Check his hair, he has it 'done' before court." An out-of-towner asked, "Has it *what?*"

"Done, he has it *done.*"

The other out-of-towner and I looked at each other and shrugged. I made a note to check on it.

We were standing in deference, while court was called to session and soon after we were seated, various peripheral matters were attended to, including the judge's signature on a subpoena for Mrs. Marina Oswald Porter, who had agreed to testify for the defense, with a check attached to it for $170 to cover travel expenses for the remarried widow of the man the Warren Commission dubbed the sole assassin of the late President. So here was one feature player due, and those in court perked up at the prospect of hearing the lady who had shared the bed and board of that disaffected young loner.

Then local witnesses under subpoena for the trial were called in. And if the former Marina Oswald was a featured player, most of us got our first look at a young man who could be considered a star performer, Perry Raymond Russo, the one and only witness at the preliminary hearing who testified to overhearing dark talk of conspiracy between David Ferrie, Lee Harvey Oswald and Clay Shaw, a man he identified in court as having been introduced to him at Ferrie's under the name of Clem Bertrand. He appeared in the center aisle, along with a herd of twenty-some defense and prosecution witnesses, who just stood there like so many corralled sheep, hemmed in by prospective jurors on one side and the press on the other. Russo, easily recognizable from his photographs, placed himself in the middle of the witnesses, self-consciously aware of his importance but, it seemed to me, attempting to smuggle his identity in with this gaggle of bit players and not stand out unduly as the star. Despite the unseasonably warm weather that day, Russo wore a smart three-quarter-length gray topcoat, almost mod in style. He was well groomed and smoothly shaven, and his head, with tightly cropped dark hair, struck me as being just a bit too large for the rest of his body.

The witnesses' names were called out and when Russo's turn came, all heads in the press section pivoted to him as he replied, "Here." I immediately looked toward Clay Shaw; he had not turned around but sat completely motionless, facing the judge's bench.

After roll call was completed, the witnesses were admonished not to sit in the courtroom before their participation in the trial and were then excused until the jury was chosen and they were called to give testimony. They straggled out as they had in, Perry Russo remaining in the middle, head not down, but not up either.

A brief recess followed. In just this short time in court that morning, a half hour or so, it was obvious that serious business was under way, the machines of trial were spinning, perhaps slowly at first, but they were under way.

Recess over, the judge had a few statements to make. Attorneys for the state, for the defense, and the defendant himself would be allowed to smoke in the courtroom at all times, if they so desired. Once a juror was sworn in and took his seat in the jury box to the left, he too would be allowed to smoke. There would be, however, no smoking in the press or spectator section.

Now Judge Haggerty addressed himself to the prospective jurors. The jury would consist of twelve and two alternates. From the moment a juror was accepted by both sides and sworn in, he would be spending his time either in the courtroom or sequestered at a nearby motel for the duration of the trial. He would be allowed one phone call to his wife (or some member of his family or a friend) . After that he would not be allowed to communicate with anyone except through a deputy sheriff for the duration of the trial. He would not even be allowed to go home to pick up additional clothing or his Waterpic or the paperback he was reading. These would be brought to the motel by a member of his family or a friend.

The austerity of all this appeared to have a sobering effect upon the gathering to the right, especially since all predictions for the duration of the trial ran from six weeks to two months. Despite the large hunk of time out of a juror's life, the Parish of Orleans is the only parish in the state of Louisiana that does not provide one penny in recompense for its jurors—limiting candidates to the retired, to employees of the city, state or Federal agencies who would be kept on the payroll, or to persons working in more or less nonessential positions for large corporations willing to be altruistic in continuance of their employees' salaries. As if these negative inducements were not enough to make the task of completing a jury gargantuan, a juror to be seated must also have no fixed opinion of the case—and it was doubtful if any criminal trial in the history of Louisiana had achieved as much flamboyant pretrial publicity as this.

But the search was on. As a deputy passed around printed lists with the 169 names of the prospects to the grateful press, another courtroom deputy shook up a cage filled with slips containing the jurors' names and numbers for the drawing of the initial 14 to be questioned in the voir dire, the name given to the process of questioning candidates for the jury and defined by the Random House Dictionary as: "1. an oath administered to a proposed witness or juror by which he is sworn to speak the truth in an examination to ascertain his competence. 2. the examination itself."

Irvin Dymond had another definition of the voir dire: "Jury selection is a vicious poker game for the highest stakes you can imagine—a man's freedom."

The very first name and number called out at the beginning of this trial for conspiracy to murder President John F. Kennedy produced a gasp in the courtroom, then a ripple of nervous laughter, followed by whispers of pure incredulity.

"Number ninety-two—John W. Kennedy." True enough, loud and clear came the name and number.

"Jesus, they're kidding," one reporter mumbled and the rustle of lists filled the room as we all tore at them to find that the ninety-second name was for fair—John William Kennedy.

"Not funny," one reporter cracked.

"Bad taste," another said, giving the thumbs-down.

Necks craned to see who belonged to the name as a rugged white-haired, ruddy-faced Irishman, probably in his late fifties, wearing an open shirt and a dark jacket, rose from the assemblage and came forward.

He was sworn in and barely had time to warm the witness chair before he was asked if he had a fixed opinion. In a gruff voice he quickly replied that he had, indeed, formed a fixed opinion of the case. He was quickly and happily excused for cause by both sides. The wave of relief was audible as he made his exit from the courtroom. The idea of having a John Kennedy sitting in the jury box, a grim specter at the trial of his name-alike, was not fitting.

The next name was called out quickly, as if to erase the ghostly reminder of the tragic death responsible for this trial. "Number 107, Irvin Mason."

A distinguished-looking silver-tipped crewcut Negro stepped up to take the witness chair. The judge asked if he had a fixed opinion, and Mr. Mason replied that he had no opinion as to the guilt or the innocence of the defendant. Judge Haggerty then reminded him that the burden of proof was upon the state, not the defense, and turned Mr. Mason over to Assistant D.A. James Alcock for questioning. It soon turned out that the jury candidate was married with two children, a son, 21, in the service, and a daughter, age 5. Mr. Mason, who had obviously dressed for the occasion —black suit, white shirt, dark tie, black shoes and socks—was soft-spoken as he told of his job as a machine operator for Freeport Sulphur Company and gave indication that his company would keep him on the payroll for the duration of the trial.

Alcock then went down a list of publications and television shows, asking Mr. Mason if he had read of the case or heard talk of it in or on: *Plot or Politics, Rush to Judgment,* television specials on both NBC and CBS devoted to the Warren Report and the Garrison investigation, the Johnny Carson show, *New Orleans* magazine, the *Saturday Evening Post, Newsweek, Time, The New Yorker, Ramparts, The New Republic,* the *New York Review of Books, Playboy, Look,* the Los Angeles *Free Press,* various television appearances of Jim Garrison, the *Wall Street Journal,* the Chicago *Daily News* and *Esquire.*

No, Mr. Mason had not been exposed to the case through any of these books, magazines or television shows. He had discussed it with his wife, although not in extended conversations, and he had read news items pertaining to the case in the local papers from time to time, but neither he nor his wife had ever discussed the guilt or innocence of the defendant.

Under further questioning by Alcock, Irvin Mason warmed up a bit and indicated that although he knew nothing about the case and believed little he'd read, he thought Mr. Garrison had more evidence than he had made public or else Mr. Garrison "was going out on a very long limb." He also aired his belief that the government should have released the autopsy reports.

In his questioning, Alcock reinforced my initial impression, that he was a young man determined to do a thorough job. His voice at times was a bit high and nasal and although his accent was decidedly Southern, it was not gratingly so. He took great pains to familiarize the prospective juror with the nature of the charge and with the essence of what the state must prove.

And here, for the first time, the spectator became aware of what I came to think of as the simplistics of the prosecution's case. Although Clay Shaw was charged with conspiracy to kill John F. Kennedy, the state did not have to prove that anyone he had conspired with had actually assisted in killing or had, in fact, killed the late President. In other words, the Louisiana conspiracy law is rather loose, for, as we were to learn, the crime itself need not even have been carried out for this conspiracy trial to take place. If John Kennedy were walking around today, Clay Shaw still could have been tried for conspiracy to murder him. Here is the brief definition of criminal conspiracy as set forth by the Criminal Code of Louisiana:

> Criminal conspiracy is the agreement or combination of two or more persons for the specific purpose of committing any crime; provided that an agreement or combination to commit a crime shall not amount to a criminal conspiracy unless, in addition to such agreement or combination, one or more of such parties does an act in furtherance of the object of the agreement or combination.

Now Alcock outlined six overt acts the state would prove were connected to this conspiracy, any one of which would be enough, together with the proof of conspiracy itself, to fulfill the requisites under the Louisiana Criminal Code.

1. A meeting of Lee Harvey Oswald, David W. Ferrie and the defendant, Clay L. Shaw, in the apartment of David W. Ferrie at 3330 Louisiana Avenue Parkway in the City of New Orleans during the month of September 1963.
2. A discussion of high-powered rifles and how they could be used in the assassination, a discussion of escape routes to points outside the continental United States, and a discussion of alibis to be established.
3. A meeting among Mr. Shaw, Oswald and Jack Ruby, who

killed Oswald, at the Capitol House Hotel in Baton Rouge in October 1963, at which time Mr. Shaw gave Oswald and Ruby a sum of money.

4. A trip to the West Coast of the United States by Clay L. Shaw during the month of November 1963.

5. A trip by David W. Ferrie from New Orleans, Louisiana, to Houston, Texas, on the day of November 22, 1963.

6. Lee Harvey Oswald taking a rifle to the Texas School Book Depository in Dallas, Texas, on or before November 22, 1963.

The last three were as well known as they were simple. If, in fact, only one of these had to be proven, then we could all forget about the overt acts, three were in the bag, and all that had to be proven was agreement to conspire.

Before court recessed for lunch, Alcock made a point that the overt acts did not have to be criminal in themselves, they could be innocent, as long as they, in some way, furthered the *idea* of conspiracy. That could be the purchase of an automobile, the purchase of a gun, or the taking of a trip. It was also made clear that one conspirator could carry out an overt act without the knowledge of the other conspirators and that act would still be inculpatory and binding upon the other members, as long as he or they had not formally disavowed the conspiracy. When Alcock finished with Mr. Mason, the prospective juror remained steadfast in his assertion that he could be a fitting member of a fair jury.

Now there was a short hassle. Irvin Dymond claimed the state must either accept a juror before passing him on to the defense for further questioning, or else reject him, thereby using up a peremptory challenge, of which each side was allowed twelve. These challenges are considered most precious, permitting a lawyer from either side to dismiss a person from serving without stating a reason. The reason in fact could amount to anything from a lawyer's not liking the way a man combs his hair to a smirk on his face in response to a question—or just to plain chemistry. Or the lawyer could have psyched the man through questioning and decided he would most likely be antipathetic to the defendant by virtue of background, education, occupation or politics.

James Alcock fought Dymond on this, arguing it was proper for the state to keep judgment to itself until after the defense had questioned the prospect. Judge Haggerty cited confusion in the law and ruled the state did *not* have to accept or reject a juror before passing him on to the defense for examination. Irvin Dymond immediately filed a bill of exception, the first of many official exceptions to the court's rulings, as grounds for possible appeal.

We took our first lunch break. Reporters raced for phones, although there didn't seem to be much to break a leg about; perhaps it was just plain conditioning.

Nina Sulzer asked if I would like to visit Clay Shaw; she was worried about his health and thought he could afford to see a friendly face. I was told he would spend his lunch hours in one of two offices requisitioned for the defense team, right off the main lobby downstairs, in the group of offices belonging to the Criminal Sheriff. I found Clay in a small office, sitting behind a desk in front of a window whose view was obscured by clouds of steam rising up from the basement of the building. He was, on close inspection, looking quite gray and he was perspiring profusely. He'd been having trouble with his back and he'd taken muscle relaxants, which he felt had disagreed with his system. He was also feeling the heat. The courtroom's air conditioning had not been operating at maximum efficiency and the electric fans by the windows had been turned off to reduce courtroom noise. Outside of the heat and his back—his chair in court was a hardwood armchair that looked as if it might take a bit of settling into before comfort could be arrived at—he had no complaints.

He did mention he thought Mason was a bit too eager to serve on the jury, although he was in favor, as were his lawyers, of having at least three Negro jurors. The philosophy behind this maintained that Negroes knew what it was like to be the underdog, to be persecuted, and they would be likely to sympathize with Clay Shaw, a man who had so patently been residing in Jim Garrison's dog house for two years.

His lawyers popped in and out—they had a larger conference room adjoining his—and Nina Sulzer arrived, more concern behind the mask of her attractive face than she gave words to, and took orders for luncheon. Orders meant taking the number of sandwiches, not the variety. The sandwiches were thick baloney on French bread that had been prepared in the Parish Prison by inmates. Nina apologized for the lack of New Orleans cuisine and when she left the room, the defendant apologized, too, as if he hadn't enough on his mind. Clay Shaw is actually a gourmet, and this gourmet was to lunch on thick baloney more times than not in the next month or so.

Louis Gurvich, feisty and outspoken brother of Leonard and William Gurvich, all staunch friends of the defense and partners in their own private detective agency, showed up for lunch. (William Gurvich, who had defected from Garrison's team and had been eagerly counted upon as a defense witness to blow the whistle on some of the shadier shenanigans of Garrison's staff, was now badly out of commission in the hospital with bleeding ulcers, and the purple flag was up that he would be missing from the courtroom.) Lou Gurvich was shaking his head that this trial had even come to pass. "Of course," he said, "Garrison can charm the birds when he wants to. Oh, they fall down out of the trees, but he's not to be seen in moments of stress. People don't know what a psychological yo-yo he is." There was talk about Garrison's discharge from the National Guard in 1951 for reasons of physical disability (psychological) and there was further talk of his younger sister who had reportedly spent time in the Mississippi State Mental Hospital, suffering from schizophrenia.

At one point, and this was while Clay Shaw was bravely chewing his way through his sandwich, Lou Gurvich suddenly turned to me and said, "You know, the local FBI are betting six to five Shaw will be found guilty. One of them is giving three to one odds." He misinterpreted the look of shock upon my face; it did not pertain to the FBI or the odds, but it did have to do with dropping a cheery tidbit like that in front of the defendant on the first day of his trial—especially while he was eating.

I think Gurvich misinterpreted my expression because he went on quickly to explain, "Oh, they know Shaw's innocent, but that's not the point. The point is they also know how Garrison works. If he's gotten this far with the hoax there's no reason to believe he won't get a conviction."

I glanced over to catch Clay Shaw's reaction; he merely shrugged, gave his eyebrows a short ride up and smiled. Although I knew Lou Gurvich's intentions were on the up and up and his best wishes were for the defendant, I excused myself to go to the men's room in order to cut the conversation short, without having to say: For Christ's sake, keep the good news to yourself.

The afternoon session began with Irvin Dymond taking over the questioning of candidate Mason. He began by asking if he thought he could give the defendant a fair trial.

"I think I can," replied Mason, and just as *I* was thinking, You better be a little more definite, the man added, "In fact, I know I can."

Dymond asked him if his feelings about the release of the autopsy reports would influence his fair judgment.

MASON: No, it wouldn't. As long as they [his company] pay me, so I can take care of my wife.

Dymond went on in his low, throaty voice, a sort of friendly come-into-my-cave growl with a muffler on it. At one point he paused, looked down at the table in front of him and then back up at Mr. Mason. "Clay L. Shaw will take the witness stand in his own behalf. Will you give him the same consideration as other witnesses?"

This caused a flutter in the courtroom as notebooks were whipped open, and some reporters turned around to look at the large clock over the main entrance. I wondered what the excitement was all about, and then realized that this was the first formal indication that the defendant, who has the option of remaining silent or testifying, would speak up in his own behalf. I suppose the reason it had not struck me as news was that it had never occurred to me he would not testify. Surely no one in recent courtroom history, to my knowledge, would make a better witness for himself than Clay Shaw.

Now came something that *was* news to me. Dymond's next statement to the prospective juror: "Although it is not necessary for the prosecution to prove a motive in the State of Louisiana for the crime of criminal conspiracy, still, if no motive is shown, that should show favorably for the defendant. Would you—"

Alcock objected and there was a short skirmish. He contended that as long as motive was not an element under the Louisiana statutes, he did not want Dymond to delve into that area. For the second time that day Judge Haggerty settled the matter by ruling for the state and instructing Dymond not to ask jurors whether they would give any weight to the state's failure to prove a motive.

Dymond continued, asking Mason for reassurance about his ability to be a fair juror, such questions as whether the length of the trial, estimated at from six to eight weeks, would influence his consideration of the case. Always Mason politely replied that he would give the defendant a fair hearing. Finally Dymond leaned way back in his chair, paused, and looking squarely at Mason, said, "I take it you are anxious to be a juror in this case?"

Judge Haggerty quickly blocked an answer. Shortly afterward, Dymond, a smile in his growl, said, "The defense will accept Mr. Mason."

ALCOCK: The state will accept Mr. Mason.

Necks craned to document this moment by the clock. First juror chosen at 2:28 P.M.

By 2:30 we were all engaged in another recess, a commodity Judge Haggerty was generous in dispensing. Irvin Dymond came out into the corridor and was mobbed by the press. He was smiling when he said, "If we can get eleven more like him we'll be okay." The general consensus regarding juror Mason was that he would give the defendant a fair shake. Clay Shaw seemed pleased, too, although he was still perspiring heavily. I'd noticed during the questioning that he took time out from his chain smoking to every now and then pat his face and neck with a folded up handkerchief. He could not manage to sit in any one position comfortably for any length of time without shifting.

We soon learned to double the announced time of the recess: if it was announced as five minutes, that meant ten, ten meant twenty, and so on. As the trial wore on, the ratio was tripled and toward the end sometimes it quadrupled. When court resumed, the third prospect for the day, a Mr. Harris, was called up and asked by Judge Haggerty if he would be paid by his company. Mr. Harris did not know and the judge sent him into his chambers to make a phone call and ascertain if he would be kept on the payroll. When Mr. Harris returned, he told the Judge, "They won't pay men who work by the hour." Judge Haggerty wanted to know who told him that and the man said, "One of the bosses." Judge Haggerty: "Call the president of the company you work for, instead of a lower boss, tell him Judge Haggerty told you to call and ask him." Again the man left and soon returned with the assurance that he would be paid. Now the judge questioned him about his number of years in New Orleans, schooling, family, etc., and eventually asked if the man had formed any fixed opinion of the case. Mr. Harris said he had and was promptly excused. There was a small sigh in the courtroom, indicating perhaps that should be the first question asked, thereby saving time in peripheral questioning.

The fourth prospect, Junius Johnson, a worker for the U.S. Post Office, was sworn in and his questioning had barely begun when a few whispers to the rear of the courtroom caught my ear and I turned around to see—my very first in-person sighting—the Jolly Green Giant himself, Jim Garrison, walking down the center aisle of the courtroom in an easy yet slightly self-conscious lumbering gait. Everyone looked at the clock; I looked too: 2:57 P.M. His face appeared puffier than I'd recalled from his pictures; there was also a hang of jowl beneath his chin that was unfamiliar. He walked quietly to the rail, a deputy swung the gate open for him, whereupon he took his seat at the right end of the prosecution table, nearest the gate and perhaps two yards behind Clay Shaw.

He was immaculately groomed in a dark blue blazer that looked to be cashmere, gray slacks, white shirt and a quietly handsome small patterned tie. His dark hair was well barbered and clung close to his head.

He sat quietly listening to his assistant, James Alcock, take Junius Johnson through a list of questions:

ALCOCK: Does your wife work?
JOHNSON: No, she don't.
ALCOCK: Has anyone ever discussed the guilt or innocence of the defendant in your presence?
JOHNSON: Only in passing, employees I work with might have.
ALCOCK: Has your wife ever expressed an opinion?
JOHNSON: She have [sic] never expressed it to me.

Garrison did not utter a word during this first appearance. Maybe twice he leaned over and whispered something in Andrew Sciambra's ear, or was whispered to, nothing more. Although he was silent, his presence was felt in the courtroom. The air was charged with a few more atoms; you could feel it. A real star in attendance, who, because of his true love and talent for unfailingly hitting his mark in the klieg-light beam of whatever branch of the news media he chooses for illumination, had steadily built up his career into one of the All-Time Louisiana Hall of Famous Leading Men, right alongside Huey Long and Earl Long and a step above Singing-Swinging Governor Jimmy Davis.

I kept my eyes on him; if he was reacting at all to the setting or the proceedings he was not showing it. There was no flamboyance evident in his presence, only the presence itself, and when he suddenly stood up at 3:15—an eighteen-minute cameo appearance—all eyes followed him.

The walk seemed self-conscious again, lumbering forward and bent a little as if its owner had become indoctrinated, in public places, to stooping so people could see past his massive six-foot-six-inch frame. Usually, for men of extraordinary height, there is something out of whack in their proportions, head to shoulder, shoulder to trunk, or trunk to legs. Jim Garrison appeared to be well put together; he had been scaled up from the size of a normal man without fault. Oh, there was the matter of puffiness of cheek and jowl underneath, but those were minor and possibly—from whispers of those in the press who'd known him personally: "He's put on weight"—only temporary, but they did distract from the overall handsomeness attributed to him in many written articles and by the citizens of New Orleans. There was a slight grimace to his mouth as he walked out of the courtroom but that, too, was undoubtedly self-consciousness at the dozens of eyes tracking him. He nodded to one pressman at the rear of the room and then was gone, as quietly as he'd arrived.

When Alcock tendered the witness, Mr. Junius Johnson, to the defense for questioning, we were afforded another recess. Again we all trooped out to the huge vaulted corridor, lit our cigarettes and speculated. Everyone seemed pleased that Jim Garrison, having spent approximately 350-some days out of each of the past two years tenaciously bringing his case formally to trial in a courtroom, had at least checked in. As one petulant woman spectator had snorted earlier in the day when there was no sight of the D.A., "It's like doing *My Fair Lady* without Professor Higgins!"

Several reporters mentioned Jim Garrison's tan and speculated whether he'd picked it up in California, a state he'd taken trips to several times in search of witnesses and, also, outside financing, or Las Vegas, where he would weekend now and then to get away from it all, or under the sun lamp at the New Orleans Athletic Club, a favorite in-town haunt of his.

After recess, we were searched again on our way back into court—it was our seventh frisk of the day.

Irvin Dymond took over the questioning and soon led into the Warren Report, at which point Mr. Johnson indicated that although he hadn't read it, he was not all that sure the Warren Report was a complete report. This area of opinion interested Dymond; if the prospective juror tended to disbelieve the report, the state might have on its hands a most receptive man upon whom to lay its theories. Alcock saw what was coming, that Dymond might try to get the juror excused for cause on this basis and now they got into a round robin over the Warren Report, and which questions pertaining to it were allowable. Dymond emphasized that the man indicated it might not be a complete report, to which statement Judge Haggerty snapped, "How can he know if the Warren Report is correct or not, if he hasn't read it?"

Logically, not a bad question, but it would be interesting to know what percentage of the vast army of American Warren Report doubters had actually read the report. As Clayton Fritchey wrote in his New York *Post* column the day before the trial began:

> The charges of Garrison and other detractors of the Warren Commission report have poisoned the public mind against the official assassination findings to such an extent that the Harris Poll reports that two-thirds of Americans are now convinced that President Kennedy was the victim of a "conspiracy" and conspiracy is what Shaw is accused of.

It is a fairly sure bet two-thirds of the citizenry had not read the report. But if two-thirds of the American people thought the President's death was caused by a conspiracy, and Clay Shaw was the one and only man arrested and brought to trial for same, then it must follow that approximately two-thirds of prospective jurors would be apt to regard him with a cocked eye and suspicions of dirty work in Dealey Plaza. These statistics must not have aided Clay Shaw in getting a good night's sleep.

The Warren Report controversy and questions pertaining to it came to a stand-off that afternoon. Reviewing my handwritten notes on a long yellow legal pad, I next find a quote from Judge Haggerty.

"Although the jury will be locked up, they will be able to read the papers, except for articles about the trial, and watch television, except for news accounts of the case, and they will be able to see the Mardi Gras parades on television."

At first I was puzzled by this but I soon recalled that every now and then Judge Haggerty would up and drop a totally gratuitous, albeit well-meaning and sometimes educational, tidbit of information upon us, usually relating to the comfort of the jury or a clarification of the law or an interesting statistic. These nuggets were usually released after one phase of the courtroom proceedings was ended, and before the next segment was entered into. They were the equivalent of short subjects, commercials, or newspaper filler items. After a while the observer could sense one coming up, as if the judge sitting high on his bench refereeing this legal ball game could stand the passive act of observing only for so long without wanting to get up and pitch one himself. He would fiddle with his glasses, sit forward, give his mouth a stretch, blink, lean back, sit forward again and by then it was pretty certain the next time he found an opening he might just unload a goodie on you. This trait was not unattractive; there was a certain friendly hey-you-guys-wait-for-me-ness about Judge Haggerty.

When Dymond got the floor again he went once more into the business of motive, explaining that although it was not incumbent upon the state to prove a motive, still the lack of proof should constitute a fact favorable to the innocence of the defendant.

Dymond and Alcock locked horns on this issue now; they were both adamant, Dymond insisting he had a right to pursue this line of questioning and indoctrination of a potential juror and Alcock insisting that he be blocked in his efforts to introduce motive into any line of questioning. For the second time that day, Judge Haggerty settled the matter by ruling for the state and instructing Dymond not to ask jurors whether they would give any weight to the state's failure to prove a motive.

Shortly thereafter Dymond finished his questioning of Mr. Johnson and turned him back to the state for acceptance or rejection.

"The state will accept Mr. Johnson," said Alcock.

"The defense excuses Mr. Johnson," said Dymond, using the first peremptory challenge of the trial.

Mr. Johnson probably wondered why he was excused; I did, too. I supposed it was the airing of his belief that the Warren Report might not be all inclusive, together with a liberal smattering of wrong pronouns and problems of syntax that did not add up to the perfect juror for Clay Shaw.

Another recess. This one around 4:30. By this time the wooden benches gave a hint of the torture racks they would soon become, long day after day. The courtroom was becoming stuffy; as we all began to wilt, so did the air-conditioning system. Clay Shaw rose from his hardwood chair and walked stiffly to the jury box, where he sat in one of the more comfortable red-leather-backed jury chairs. Outside in the corridor, reporters who had late afternoon deadlines were phoning in their stories on the first day of this trial.

Interesting to note that when this recess was over and we all straggled back into the courtroom, not a hand was laid on us. No search at all. The deputies, also weary now that the proceedings had settled down and in, merely stood and gazed at us impassively. This turned into routine, in what might be called the law of diminishing security.

It was after 5 o'clock that afternoon when Oliver Marion Schultz, a balding 39-year-old employee of the New Orleans Public Service was sworn in. He wore slacks and a plaid blue-brownish sports shirt, dark shoes and white socks. There was a pleasant sleepy look about him and as Alcock took him through the preliminary questioning, he displayed an easy good humor, perhaps *nature* more than humor. He was a truck driver, native of New Orleans, one child, three stepchildren, and when asked if he'd ever served on a jury before he replied in the affirmative, smiling and adding, "You was the attorney." At which point a reporter near me said, "The state will accept him." "Why?" I asked. "On his English alone."

In further questioning, Mr. Schultz indicated he'd read no books or magazine articles about the case, but had read a few local newspaper stories. No one, he asserted, had ever discussed the innocence or guilt of the defendant. Finally Alcock asked Schultz virtually the same question Dymond had asked Mason: "Do you want to serve on this jury?"

Before the judge could block an answer Mr. Schultz grinned and replied casually, on a shrug, "Not necessarily."

He was soon passed to Dymond, who asked him early on if he had any opinion as to whether Lee Harvey Oswald killed John F. Kennedy. Mr. Schultz indicated he had no opinion whatsoever. It was incredible to think a 39-year-old citizen of the United States could have no opinion whatsoever, but that is what he maintained. Irvin Dymond wanted to know if he understood what the overt acts meant and in the course of the questioning the judge spoke up, pronouncing them "ovoit" acts, in the strange Southern accent with, to Eastern ears, a bit of Brooklyn thrown in on certain vowels. Dymond also wanted Mr. Schultz's assurance that he would require the state to prove its case beyond every reasonable doubt. Alcock disagreed with the choice of "every" and they got into a swivet over semantics. Alcock wanted the question put: "beyond *a* reasonable doubt."

Judge Haggerty finally interceded and ruled against the prosecution for the first time that day, instructing the juror that, in the event he should be chosen, the state would have to "remove from your mind *every* reasonable doubt."

Dymond questioned Mr. Schultz for perhaps ten more minutes, during which the jury prospect calmly maintained he had no beliefs one way or the other about the case, was wide open to giving a fair trial, and had not been affected by the barrage of pretrial publicity. Then, surprisingly enough, he was accepted by both the state and the defense, was sworn in and took his seat as juror number two in the second row of six jury seats next to Mr. Mason. They shook hands and smiled wanly at each other.

Oliver Schultz was perhaps not a quiz kid by any means but there was a certain ease about him, behind which there appeared to be no hidden axes to grind. He had also not been jumping up and down to get on the jury and he did not seem to be dissembling when he said he harbored no specific beliefs.

Still one woman spectator was heard to grumble, "No opinion, hasn't read anything, hasn't ever heard anybody discuss the innocence or the guilt of the—Why," she snorted, "anyone ends up on that jury's got to be a moron or a damn liar."

By this time it was 5:45 and court was adjourned for the day.

6

He Must Have Something

During a recess that first day, I had met James Phelan, a gravel-throated mick-faced journalist of the old school. Lean and spare and in his fifties, he would be at home in a revival of *The Front Page*. I could easily picture him in another era, panning for gold up in the Yukon.

Early on, soon after Clay Shaw's preliminary hearing, Phelan had written an article for the *Saturday Evening Post* that was highly critical of Garrison's investigation. Jim Phelan was the man who discovered the vast discrepancy in a copy of a detailed memorandum written by Assistant D.A. Andrew Sciambra covering his first interview with Perry Russo, between what Russo had originally told Assistant D.A. Sciambra he knew about David Ferrie, a man Garrison had been investigating before Ferrie's untimely death, and the much more dramatic and highly inflated account of the assassination plot Russo outlined a few weeks later during the preliminary hearing. Jim Phelan had confronted Garrison, Sciambra and Russo himself with this discrepancy and was now on hand as a witness for the defense. He was regarded as a key man who might well torpedo the credibility of the state's star witness.

Phelan came to the trial with an assignment to write an article for *True* magazine; because he was slated to take the witness chair he was not allowed inside the courtroom prior to his appearance. For a man who was a curious journalist and, moreover, vitally concerned with what he believed to be a gross miscarriage of justice, this was frustration in the nth degree. For many days to come, Jim Phelan could be seen cooling his heels outside the courtroom in the corridor, or warming a bench, only to get up when court recessed and corner a fellow journalist: "What's going on in there? What's happening? What did so-and-so say?" There was something immediately likable about Phelan. We made a date to meet that evening at the Press Club, and Jim promised to tell me the story of his involvement.

Before returning to my apartment to get cleaned up and pick up my tape machine, I phoned Clay Shaw to see how he was feeling. Not well. His back was bothering him. He was having his regular evening martini and had a call in to his doctor. He did not appear to be hysterical with joy over the initial choice of jurors, but he was mildly sanguine and attempting to be his usual philosophical self. He sounded dog tired. I suggested if he got to feeling really ill, he should take to his bed for a day or so. He could not be faulted for sickness. School would simply not be held that day.

The New Orleans Press Club on Chartres Street in the Quarter possessed, at that time, all the warmth and atmosphere of the waiting room in Grand Central Station. It had recently moved there from an old location and as it stood that evening it was a bare hall with a bar running along one side. There were not even any stools. I would have imagined the New Orleans Press Club, of all press clubs, might have a great funky Belle Watling whorehouse parlor *gashpritz* about it, where gentlemen could mix, mingle, down a few and shoot the bull until they got about the more serious business of the evening.

Jim Phelan, already elbowing up to the bar, introduced me to a great beefy teddy bear of a guy with a cracker accent you had to dip your ear into in order to snatch the specific words strung together in his Dixie melody twang. If there are now such clothes as perma-pressed, his were perma-rumpled. Large of body and large of head and face, large of good humor, filled with a great zest for food and drink, this turned out to be Martin "Moe" Waldron of the New York *Times,* currently working out of Houston. If I had been asked to pick out the *Times* correspondent from the eighty or so average daily press attendants, he would be one of the last I would have pointed to.

We were soon joined by Hugh Aynesworth of *Newsweek,* a man acknowledged to be an expert on Dealey Plaza, the assassination, and the many spiraling leads, investigations, mysteries, theories, rumors, quacks and frauds that have sprouted therefrom. He was known to be violently anti-Garrison to the point of battle and intensely pro-defense. His associate on *Newsweek,* Kent Biffle, was with him. Jerry Cohen from the Los Angeles *Times* soon arrived, as did Roger Williams, Atlanta-based correspondent for *Time* magazine.

Rounds of drinks were set up and the camaraderie of these men was immediately evident. Most, if not all, had covered the preliminary hearing two years earlier and they were like war correspondents. The hearing had been their Korea and now they were once more gathering at the battleground for Vietnam. They were all ,seasoned journalist-reporters and I felt like the lowliest cub in the den. What they did not make me feel was an outsider. These are men of extreme good will and they possess, despite a sort of exterior newspaper-print brusqueness, a strong sense of perception and sensitivity. They extended to me instant professional courtesy. I took to them immediately and hoped they would allow me permanent membership in the club.

This group turned out to be the hard-core out-of-town stick-together press gang. They had other cases and news coverage in common, so there was no lack of conversation as the drinks came, the glasses were emptied and refilled. There were tales of memorable binges, memorable broads—they're not an unbawdy bunch —and memorable assignments, all served up between speculations about Garrison, first impressions of the men empaneled for jury duty, anecdotes about the judge, Louisiana politics, and the usual smattering of rumors.

It was soon apparent the tape machine I'd brought would be as useful as my appendix. There would be no interview tonight, at least no sensible one. We were, as they say, well on our way. At 9:30, Broussard's Restaurant became the recipient of our favors. The waiters assigned to serve this highly mellow bunch of put-ons were to be pitied and well tipped. Moe Waldron sat at the head of the table and his position was prophetic, for he turned out to be most definitely Master of the Games for our stay in New Orleans.

The talk covered Garrison's career, back to his first election to office of District Attorney and his highly publicized clean-up of Bourbon Street, a tidying-up that supposedly swept away the lewder strippers, B-girls, pimps, prostitutes and homosexuals. The majority opinion was that they had not been swept away as much as they had been swept under the carpet for a brief vacation. This brought forth an anecdote from Jim Phelan regarding reform in Louisiana, the name of the ticket that has given birth to so many of its colorful politicians. It is attributed to a famous New Orleans madam named Norma:

"I've seen reform governors get elected and become ex-governors, I've seen reform mayors elected and become ex-mayors, and I've seen reform district attorneys come in and now they're ex-district attorneys. But isn't it funny, with all this reform business going on, Norma's never become an ex-madam!"

Someone else came up with the definition of reform, Louisiana style: "A reform candidate is someone on the outside looking at all the graft going on and trying to get in on the inside—to grab his share."

It was that evening that Jim Phelan, awash in mellow leprechaun spirits, dropped the first limerick of the trial on us:

> Cried Big Jim, the world owes me praise,
> And I'll get it, come one of these days.
> Earl Warren, the dunce,
> Solved the killing just once,
> But I solved it seventeen ways!

Later on, much was to be written and discussed about the journalistic passions stirred up by the Shaw-Garrison matter. It was unanimously acknowledged by those in attendance that never had a case surfaced such strong personal emotions in the covering journalists. Even at this stage of the proceedings, this evening was a measuring stick for escalated passions to come. Of the reporters present I believe all, even at this time, would have bet money on Clay Shaw's innocence—not his acquittal, his innocence. That is to say, the representatives of the Los Angeles *Times,* the New York *Times, Newsweek, Time, True,* and *Playboy,* a fair minor sampling of the national press. It is true that Martin Waldron and Roger Williams were, at that point, not so much personally pro-Shaw as they were highly skeptical of Garrison's tactics and of his case. There was a policy of waiting to see what Garrison might possibly come up with; there was no burning personal involvement. Which is perhaps how it should be. I envied them the ease of detachment, but it is difficult to brainwash your feelings when you have gotten to know the defendant personally, as had Phelan, Aynesworth and myself.

Despite the joking, the good humor, the overall verbal grab-ass, every now and then the gathering would pull down, a serious remark would be spoken about the case, a speculation aired. Then eyes would meet and acknowledge for a second that, Jesus, we are in on *something,* something unusual, to put it mildly, and we can't be quite *that* sure what it is. There was a catch phrase in New Orleans that dropped from the lips of almost everyone you spoke to as rain droppeth from the heavens: "Jim Garrison must have something." You got into a cab, spoke to a clerk in a store, or engaged in conversation with a bar-mate and you were bound to hear it.

We all got to talking about it that evening and even one of our group of disbelievers said, "Well, hell, of course, he might just *have* something!"

Wouldn't that be a laugh on us, was the response.

Leaving the restaurant—you could hear the sighs of employee relief—we were drenched with a humid urine-like rain, so popular in the South, the kind that has your clothes reeking, no matter if they have just come from the cleaners.

The rain added to the general buzz of the occasion as we proceeded in a sort of Gene-Kelly-Dancing-in-the-Rain lope to Bourbon Street. Well, hell, we had to get in out of the rain, didn't we? Where else to get in out of it from but a bar. There was every indication that, although this was now around midnight, the shank of the evening had not been touched. It had for me, however. I was feeling warm and fuzzily content with a bellyful of spirits, good food and even better companionship, so I decided to peel off and stagger home to bed before I was taken really drunk and made an ass out of myself. Warm goodbyes all around, the first few shouted insults from new friends and off down Bourbon Street.

Bourbon Street! That thesaurus of jazz and strippers and honk and tonk and tacky, tacky, tacky. The barkers were out in full voice and there was a lady barker, and over on the right side, another lady barker.

Every kind of stripper was on display. There was Tiny Alice, the world's weeniest stripper, and there was Big Bertha, the world's largest, and over there one worked with a cheetah and down the street another worked with a basket of snakes. Something for everyone.

The rain fell harder now and I hailed a cab. Just for the hell of it, I said to the driver, "Well, what do you think of the trial, what do you think's going to happen?"

The cabbie sighed, shook his head and delivered his line right on cue: "I don't know, but I'll tell you one thing—Jim Garrison must have something."

Beautiful.

7

A Jury of Whose Peers?

The early morning frisk was a wahoo-everybody-up! and we were passed in and took our seats in that section of pews to the left of the aisle. The first two rows were reserved for sketch artists from the television networks, newspapers and wire services. No cameras allowed inside. One deputy, a heavy molelike fellow usually stationed by the railing separating the press from the prosecution table, never conquered his fascination with the sketching. Lawyers could be having a shout-down, witnesses could be describing the bizarre, bizarre witnesses could be describing the outrageous—still he remained glued to those front-row sketch pads, as if they were limning out the absolute truth of the trial, if not the universe.

As if at a given signal, the defense and prosecution teams marched into the courtroom at precisely the same moment. James Alcock, Moo Sciambra, Alvin Oser and William Alford paraded out of the door leading from the judge's chambers to the right as Irvin Dymond, the Brothers Wegmann, Sal Panzeca and the defendant himself strode from the door to the rear left. Perhaps it was the timing of the entrance march, but it reminded me of the bullfights, each team of attorneys a cuadrilla, representing their matadors—Clay Shaw and Jim Garrison. Except Garrison had defaulted. He'd sent his cuadrilla in to fight the bull, to pic him, to sentence him, if not to death, to twenty years at hard labor.

Judge Haggerty's entrance on this second day again brought forth whispered comments about his hair; he did look spankingly well groomed on top. As I was making a scribbled note to check on this, someone, I don't remember who, asked what I was writing down. I replied I thought it would be interesting to find out if the judge was concerned enough about his personal appearance to keep in constant touch with his barber during the trial. I was to hear of my comment later.

Now came the selection of the prospective jurors for the day's voir dire. Three fixed opinions came to bat in succession and were quickly dismissed. Then Alvin Oser took over for the state, spelling James Alcock. Oser is a large man with a modified crew cut, soft-spoken and more rambling in his questioning than the ferret-like Alcock. His eyes, the set of them under his brows, give him at times a frowning look, almost a scowl, but this was not evidenced in his manner until later on, when he and William Alford swung into action against the Warren Report.

His first prospect had never expressed an opinion as to the guilt or innocence of the accused, but did comment he'd always thought the assassination had been the work of one man alone. The defense team perked up at hearing this; here was a man after their own hearts. The prosecution, Alcock and Sciambra, went into a whispered confab; here was a man to beware of. When he was tendered to the defense, Dymond did not question him at length, undoubtedly not wanting the man to highlight his opinion by elaboration. When Oser got the man back, he again probed his assassination beliefs. The man reiterated his belief that John Kennedy had been shot by one man, and the state used its first peremptory challenge to excuse him.

Now the score was one and one. Peremptory challenges were watched closely, for whichever side ran out first would most likely have an unappetizing juror or two shoved down its throat.

A few jurors bit the dust for lack of pay before a Negro mailman took the seat. For some reason a preponderance of mailmen trooped up during the voir dire; it seemed almost every fifth prospect was a mailman or else worked for the Post Office Department in one capacity or another. This mailman, however, was special, as it turned out that the National Bank of Commerce Building was on his route and he delivered mail to Eddie Wegmann and Irvin Dymond, both of whom have their offices there. Judge Haggerty immediately asked if he received Christmas presents from various offices he serviced. There was a slight pause and the mailman replied in a flat voice, "From some of them I do." This brought a few grins to the assembled; it was obvious from the reading that someone, either Wegmann or Dymond or both, was not coming through at Christmas. The man appeared to be bright, with a mind of his own and not easily led, as questioning by the state continued. He had not read much about the case, except in the newspapers. He had no fixed opinions, but he had experienced *mixed* opinions. The longer he was questioned, the more likable he became. It was obvious he would make a strong effort to be fair and his honesty about harboring mixed opinions was refreshing. Then, somehow, as he was passing the test, Judge Haggerty suddenly asked if there was any other reason he could possibly think of that might prevent him from giving his full attention to the matter at hand in the event he was picked. The mailman thought a bit, then said, not really, only that his wife didn't much like to be alone at night. At this, he was quickly excused for cause. Had the judge not pressed this point, I believe the defense would have chosen him and either the state would have agreed or been forced to use a peremptory challenge. The rest of the jurors questioned during that morning session were excused for lack of pay, illness, fixed opinion, or invincible ignorance.

In the corridor I met up with Father Sheridan, who was concerned about Clay's health and suggested we drop down to his cubicle. Near the stairway he introduced me to a local television and radio reporter, Jim Mitchie, who said about the jury prospects' professed lack of knowledge of the case, "Everyone on this panel must have been in a closet or dead for the last two years." Mitchie is a good-looking small-boned slight young man who has a reputation for dogging Jim Garrison at press conferences. The idea of his persistently questioning Garrison brought forth the mental picture of a Chihuahua snapping at a Great Dane, but snap he does. The story is told that Garrison became unusually annoyed one day when Mitchie wouldn't give up without getting an answer to a particular question. "Mitchie, you're an asshole, and a stupid asshole, at that," Garrison is supposed to have shouted. To which Jim Mitchie, still holding his mike up to Garrison's face, replied, "Nevertheless, sir, will you answer my question?"

While we were talking, Judge Haggerty came by on his way to lunch and spoke to us briefly, saying he wished the mailman had qualified as a juror. If so, I wondered why he'd taken over and pursued the man's mild comment that his only concern would be over his wife's possible nervousness at being left alone.

Downstairs we found the defendant still not feeling well; his back was bothering him and the prescribed medicine was not agreeing with him. But he would not dwell on his state of health, merely answered our questions of concern and then got off it. The talk naturally centered around the prospective jurors and Irvin Dymond said, regarding the vast disclaimers of no opinions, no knowledge of the case, no television, no magazine articles, no books, no beliefs in the guilt or innocence of the accused, "When we get a jury seated in this case it's almost impossible not to end up with twelve liars."

I learned now for the first time that Irvin Dymond had run against Garrison in his first campaign for office of District Attorney back in 1961 and that, according to those in the know politically, Dymond was considered the front runner, a certain winner, until all the candidates appeared on a television show together. Much had been spoken at that time of officials who, in addition to their elected office, were also keeping their hands in private practice. Garrison vowed to devote all of his time to the office of D.A. if elected. Dymond declared he could not possibly support his wife and children on the D.A.'s salary alone, that he would give of his prime time and energies, but that he would have to resort to some outside practice to maintain his standard of living, ending up with: "If you want a $17,000-a-year man, I'm not it." That bit of candor, again according to the majority of local pundits, cost him the election. "And now," Clay Shaw said, "here's Irvin battling it out against Garrison in a case that might well destroy him as District Attorney." Someone else cracked, "Yep, Irvin made him, now he's doing his best to break him."

When court convened after lunch, Judge Haggerty issued the second warning about respect for his guidelines; he let it be known violations would not be tolerated and that several newsmen were already high on the list when the time came for drawing up citations for contempt.

Several jurors were quickly excused for various reasons, until William Ricks, Jr., a 31-year-old Negro high school teacher, took the oath for questioning. Ricks, sporting a tidy mustache, was well dressed in a plaid sports jacket, brown slacks and pale yellow shirt. When he answered the preliminary questions about his exposure to the case, acknowledging that he had read the papers, some periodicals and had listened to reports on radio and television, I heard a reporter sigh, "Thank Christ!" When asked if he had formed any opinions one way or the other Ricks replied, "No, I'm more of an agnostic where this case is concerned." He admitted he had spoken of the case to friends, but mostly about whether or not there would be a trial. When Dymond took him over, Ricks seemed more at ease than when he had been questioned by Oser. During this questioning by the defense there was a thick huddle in progress at the prosecution table between Alcock, Sciambra, and Alford. The feeling among the reporters near me was that Ricks was too smart, too much of an individualist and the state would turn him down. Yet when Dymond was finished with him, the state announced the school teacher was acceptable and Dymond also agreed on him. William Ricks was sworn in as juror number three at 2:10 that afternoon.

The next man questioned was the director of personnel for the New Orleans Public School System. He'd been introduced to the defendant once or twice at functions but said he would not allow that to influence him. He was an intelligent man, well educated, and acknowledged having discussed the case with his family and friends, although he did not recall ever expressing an opinion and claimed that his exposure to all the publicity given Garrison's investigation had only resulted in confusion. Not only was he a literate and thinking man but his assertion that he would be a fair and impartial juror was totally believable.

When Dymond tendered him to the state we were given a 3 P.M. recess and the word outside the courtroom was: Now we've got a live one. If Clay Shaw is to be tried by a jury of his peers, this is more like it. Martin Waldron and Jerry Cohen both shook their heads. "Not a chance of him getting on," Waldron said. "The state'll bump him, too much up here." Jerry Cohen agreed, tapping his head.

They were right. The state was not really interested in pursuing the director of personnel for the Public School System; after several questions they soon used a peremptory challenge, their second, to excuse him. There was something disquieting about this man's dismissal. And the longer the jury selection continued, the more patently and uncomfortably clear became the preferences of the state. And the stronger the smell that there was indeed something rotten in New Orleans.

More prospective jurors down the drain until Charles Daniel Ordes, a 39-year-old supervisor in the assembly department of the American Can Company, currently on the 2:30-to-1 A.M. shift, married with three children and a native of New Orleans, took the stand. Mr. Ordes—coal black hair, trim little mustache, slim-faced, soft-voiced—had the look of someone who might turn up with his wife or girl friend as winner of the tango event in the Harvest Moon Ball Contest.

Mr. Ordes was dressed in a well-tailored gray suit, white shirt and dark tie. After questioning by the state and the admission that he had spoken to a few people about the case but had no fixed opinion at this time, he was tendered to Irvin Dymond, who asked, "Would you go into this case presuming Mr. Shaw is guilty—I mean *not* guilty?" That slip brought a smile to certain lips in the courtroom and a short sideways glance from Clay Shaw himself. Mr. Ordes asserted he *would* presume the innocence of the accused.

Toward the end of the questioning Dymond paused, looked down at the table in front of him, then squarely back up at Mr. Ordes and addressed him with a deadly serious voice. "Then, Mr. Ordes, you are certain you would, if chosen, presume Mr. Shaw to be guilty—" This second slip brought murmurs to the courtroom, especially in the press section, as the lawyer corrected himself, "I mean, innocent."

A reporter whispered, "Hey, Irvin, take it easy." Clay Shaw did his attorney the courtesy of not even looking over, although there was a brief lowering of his massive head and at the very least he must have squeezed back a wince.

Finally Dymond indicated he was finished questioning Mr. Ordes, at which point the state accepted him. There was a brief huddle at the defense table and then the defense also accepted him as juror number four.

Several more candidates fell by the wayside and so ended the second day of the voir dire.

8

Smashing the Guidelines

The New York office of my publisher, Simon and Schuster, had put me in touch with their New Orleans–based salesman, John Mourain, who had phoned over the weekend and asked, providing spare time was available, if I would mind stopping by a bookstore or two to scribble my name in the available copies of *Good Times/Bad Times* and perhaps squeeze in a few radio and television interviews. A date was set up for Thursday, January 23, the third day of jury selection, for an appearance on the New Orleans equivalent of the *Today* show on WDSU, the NBC affiliate. The show, an hour from noon to one, called appropriately enough *Midday,* has a wide following and is hosted by Terry Flettrich, a friend of Clay Shaw's whom I had not met but whose husband, Leonard, had been at Edith Stern's for dinner several nights before the trial began. John Mourain was to pick me up at the courthouse a little before noon.

That morning in court Clay's face was gray and showed fatigue. Nina Sulzer was most concerned about him. He was displaying his usual good front, smiling and saying hello to reporters he knew before court began or when he would come out into the corridor during recess flanked by his guards on the way to the nearby men's room. At one recess I had an opportunity to speak with him. His guards stepped back diplomatically. (The two men assigned to protect Clay during his time in the courthouse were Severio Loyacano and E. A. Ciaccio, Jr., both seasoned deputies in their fifties. Their respect and admiration for Clay seemed to grow day by day; toward the end of the trial I would not have wanted to tangle with either of them over the merits of the defendant. Although they avoided documenting their feelings in words, at first, their sentiments were made apparent by the warmth and courtesy they extended to those in the courthouse who were friends of Clay's.)

As we stood talking in the corridor, Clay told me his back was playing hob with his nerve ends. He had not been sleeping well, and the medication prescribed was not agreeing with him any better.

I remembered I'd be leaving before the lunch recess for the *Midday* show and kiddingly asked Clay to see to it that no jurors were picked in my absence. He told me arrangements had been made by Nina Sulzer for him to have a bed in the Parish Prison hospital ward during lunch. He would be able to lie down for an hour and also receive medical attention. He was sure he'd have access to a television set and he'd look in. He made his way through the scattered groups of people gathered outside, smiling, a brief wave here and there to a local reporter in the hall. Although his head was held up, he walked with obvious discomfort, moving toward his hardwood chair where he would sit in a certain amount of pain, an impotent spectator as the men were picked who would decide whether he would spend the last third of his life in prison or as a free man.

During the morning session, some of the out-of-town press were discussing the policy of the two local sister papers, the *Times-Picayune* (morning) and the *States-Item* (afternoon), neither of which had been in the habit of printing pro-Shaw phrases in the two years since his arrest, outside of referring to him as "the tall, distinguished-looking defendant." Neither paper had elected to criticize the tactics of the District Attorney or his office in all that time, nor had they editorialized against what was generally looked upon by a majority of the national news media as a highly questionable investigation, employing undisclosed private funds contributed by personal and business friends of Jim Garrison to aid him in the hot pursuit of anyone he chose to prosecute or, even worse, persecute. Their alleged excuse for such silence was that they did not wish to violate the court's guidelines by publishing anything which might prove prejudicial to either side.

Fair is fair. If the papers had stuck to their neutral position, all well and good. But, the two local sheets were quick to set up in bold print, and nowhere near the obits, any statement issued by Jim Garrison or his office, regardless of whether it smacked of an incriminating flavor. They were, in effect, willing and eager public relations outlets for the District Attorney, trumpeting each succeeding claim to issue from his vast warehouse of charges and thereby giving it a measure of public acceptance. As Garrison himself acknowledged in his lengthy *Playboy* interview (which violated guidelines on a gargantuan scale), "The very repetition of a charge lends it a certain credibility, since people have a tendency to believe that where there's smoke there's fire."

The two local newspapers were responsible to a significant degree for keeping the captive readership of New Orleans beclouded by Jim Garrison's smoke screen for two years. There is no competition; both papers are owned by the Newhouse chain and shared, at that time, the same president-publisher and executive editor. They neither questioned the veracity of the many charges made by the District Attorney nor did they bother to investigate the specifics or to separate fact from fiction. They simply printed the press releases as fast as they were turned out from the Jolly Green Giant's rumor workshop at 2700 Tulane.

I slipped out of the courtroom early and found John Mourain, who turned out to be a completely affable gent and quite the opposite of most publishers' representatives in his familiarity with the product involved and, more than that, his enthusiasm for both his job and the books he represents.

A quick stop at Doubleday's to sign fifteen or so books in my retarded scrawl, for which I apologized profusely, and then on to Station WDSU in the heart of the French Quarter. There was the usual pre-going-on-the-air bustle: commercials were being rehearsed; lights adjusted; a women's luncheon group of guest viewers was being seated on a terrace set above and to the side of the studio floor. A production aide advised me I was being given an entire five-minute segment. The look on my face must have translated well because he added, almost in rebuke, "Many of our spots only run three or *four* minutes." There is nothing as dull as a quickie interview; it is as relaxing as the simultaneous ringing of phone, doorbell and burglar alarm and allows for the same display of personality that emerges in the running of the 100-yard dash.

Soon the show was on the air and I was ushered forth and placed next to Terry Flettrich, who is an attractive, poised, professionally pulled-together cool lady. The interview was supposed to be about the book and she started off by way of mentioning why I was in New Orleans (to cover the trial). She then spoke of the *Esquire* article, saying how much she had enjoyed it and also dropping word that she had read some of it over the air. I believe she asked me something about how I happened to write the article in the first place, and the next thing I heard myself saying was: "Well, you see, I met Clay Shaw by accident in New York. He told me his story and—well, I became involved because I strongly believe—I have no way of knowing, of course, it's just my personal belief—that he's completely innocent of the charges against him." I delivered a few more words about Clay and his situation.

It is possible that Terry Flettrich got out one other sentence like "Mm-hmn, yes, well that was obvious from your—" And then from the waving of arms off-camera you would have thought you were aboard an aircraft carrier at crash-landing time. I was bade the quickest of goodbyes and they were into a commercial so fast I'm surprised the film didn't snap.

As I was hauled away from the cameras by a floor manager, the next thing I remember was the specter of two men; one's face was purple and the other's was drained completely of blood. They were both literally jumping up and down and shouting in hoarse whispers, "Jesus Christ, what was *that*! Why did you—how could you—Jesus!" Then they flew into a garble of strangled words about the station and lawsuits and contempt and fines and, I believe, jail, followed by so many self-inflicted forehead blows that concussion seemed imminent. And then Terry Flettrich was standing near us, looking stunned by their reaction, and apologizing to them and to me and also, very nicely, taking the blame for leading the questioning to Clay Shaw and not the novel. But the words were mine, the stupidity was mine, even though I was more shocked by their violent reactions than by my gaffe at that point.

There was no reasoning with them. The only thing that occurred to me was to absent myself from the studio. I'd dropped my bomb and now I was being flakked to death. Best to flee the area like any sensible bomber would. With John Mourain behind me I soon hit the streets. "I don't see what all the shouting's about," said John, looking every bit as if he meant it. "I mean, you think the guy's innocent and you said it was only your opinion so what's the big deal?"

We ducked into the Royal Orleans Hotel for lunch. By the time my Crab Louis arrived my stupidity had thoroughly sickened me. Here I was going on one of the most popular television shows in New Orleans *during* jury selection and blithely shooting off my mouth about the innocence of the accused, when undoubtedly many prospective jurors in the days and weeks to come would have seen the show. With feelings pro and con over the Shaw-Garrison match running to fever pitch in the town, it would be highly possible for someone, perhaps the wife of one of the many assistant district attorneys, or the judge's wife, sister, friend, clerk, former teacher, or just a plain pro-Garrison citizen—somebody had to register a complaint. There was no way out of it. The more I thought about it the more certain I was the wheels of reaction were in motion at that very moment. Phones were ringing someplace and they were ringing me no good. It seemed probable to me at that moment that my credentials would be revoked and I would be barred from further attending the trial.

"You don't want to eat, do you?" It was John Mourain. Gratitude for his sensitivity has still not worn off. "Do you want me to call the station and see what's happened, if they're getting calls or—"

I didn't want to know about what was going on at the station; I wanted to know about what was going on at the courthouse. We left our luncheon uneaten and drove over to the intersection of Tulane and Broad in virtual silence and when John let me out, he asked, "Do you want me to stick around?" I told him no and thanked him. I would have liked him to, actually, but it was my bag, I'd jumped in it myself, and it was time to shape up now. He said he would phone me later, and to let him know if there was anything he could do.

Lunch break was still in progress, so I quickly went to the corridor leading to the Sheriff's offices and entered the small room designated to the defense team. Clay Shaw was still in the Parish Prison sick bay; his lawyers were on hand and I quickly blurted out my stupidity, ending with a feeble joke about how I hoped they'd have time to represent another client. They were concerned but they certainly had more important matters on their minds. I had thought of asking to see the judge and simply saying, Look, you won't believe what an asinine thing I did but it's true and you're going to hear about it, please put it down to temporary insanity. But the lawyers' advice was to play it cool and see what happened, not to initiate talks.

Once checked, frisked and passed in for the afternoon session, I sat down and waited for the boom to lower. The courtroom began to fill up with the press, prospective jurors, and a few spectators; I kept my eyes on all those up front in the working area of the court to see if I could discern any undercurrent. The attorneys soon filed in and then Clay Shaw entered through the door to the left of the judge's bench.

Now the clerk of court came out of the judge's chambers followed by Judge Haggerty, all seriousness. Was that a censorious squiggle that held up his brows, or just routine court business? He took his seat high up on the judicial bench, glanced down at some papers, then up and out at the court. I would not have been surprised if he had said, All right, is there some stupid dumb-headed klunk named Koikwood (I'd already heard him pronounce Hoiboit and Oynest for Herbert and Ernest) in this courtroom?

Yes, sir, Your Honor, I'd say, my voice cracking like Henry Aldrich's.

Koikwood, are you out of your fuckin' *mind!*

Yes, sir, Your Majesty.

He would thereupon unload the incident upon the court, which would then, to a man and a woman, turn and fix me with eye sockets brimming in scorn and, after I had been properly seared, would come the laughter, derisive and hollow and then, finally, I would be officially drummed out of the corps.

Oh, come on, Judge, out with it! Instead he offered up a few statistics, how many prospects—fifty-eight—had been questioned so far to yield up the four jurors they'd acquired; fifty numbers would be drawn presently and the men representing those numbers would be summoned to appear the following morning. Also, now that it appeared jury selection was not going to be a shoo-in, court would convene at 9 A.M. instead of 10, Monday through Saturday.

My concentration upon the proceedings early that afternoon was, unattractive as it is to admit, in a deep freeze of self-involvement. My notes are slimmer than usual. Various candidates were excused for the usual: fixed opinions, lack of pay, one man whose answers were far too pat and whose intelligence was not all that apparent was excused peremptorily by the defense, and a draftsman who was obviously above average intelligence and concerned with being a fair juror, and who displayed admirable qualities of humor, concern, and civic involvement, was dismissed by the state through use of a peremptory challenge.

During an afternoon recess Eddie Wegmann sidled up to me in the corridor outside the courtroom. "Heard anything?" he asked. "No," I replied. "You?" "No." We drifted away from each other like co-conspirators, the less said the better.

I relaxed somewhat in midafternoon, delivering myself up to the fates—that is, until a deputy would stride in, or the clerk of court or some other courtroom official would approach the bench and hand the judge a slip of paper or crane a neck into him for a whispered conference. Then my stomach would tighten and I'd hang by my thumbs for a spell.

Late in the afternoon, Herbert John Kenison, a 28-year-old microfilm printer and native of New Orleans, came up to bat. Mr. Kenison has a foxlike appearance, a friendly fox. A thin man, thin-faced, rather hawk-nosed with prominent ears, he was well groomed, in a brown suit and striped tie. He was a high school graduate, had read no books or magazine articles, claimed to have seen no television reports. His only exposure to the case had been through the coverage in the local papers and he intimated he hadn't exactly been glued to them. When Mr. Kenison was tendered by the state to Dymond, the attorney asked with a distinct trace of incredulity to his voice, "You have never heard *anybody* express an opinion?" "No," replied Mr. Kenison. This brought forth such a sigh from the reporter seated behind me that I felt his breath graze my neck. Dymond did not question him at length and when Mr. Kenison was turned back to the state, Alcock quickly accepted him. The defense surprised many of the press by also accepting him. Herbert John Kenison was sworn in as juror number five.

Now a string of candidates bit the dust in rapid succession, until well after 5 P.M., when James Gary O'Quinn, a 30-year-old petroleum engineer for Chevron Oil took the witness stand. He was not dressed with great class—red cardigan sweater, plaid shirt, slacks and white socks with black shoes—but he had a pleasant roundish open face and was easy of manner and pleasant of speech as we learned that he was born in Beaumont, Texas, had lived in New Orleans for nine years, was married with one daughter, wife a schoolteacher. He had read articles in *Look* or *Life,* couldn't recall which, had seen Garrison on the *Tonight* show and had heard various discussions of the case but had not himself ever expressed an opinion. He had, he said, formed no opinion. He looked to be a friendly sort, as if he would give both sides a fair shake, then make up his mind in his own quiet way. He was sworn in as juror number six at six minutes to six on the third day, thereby filling the back row of the jury box—it was not a case of first come, best seats—and completing half the jury, not counting the two alternates.

When I arrived back at my apartment, John Mourain phoned to see if I had gotten the axe and was as surprised as I was that no counties had been heard from. That evening I had dinner with a deskman of the *Times-Picayune* and I confessed my gaffe of that noon along with my wonder that I had not been brought to heel. I was again reminded that one of Jim Garrison's most interesting traits was his fondness for surprise. There was a certain unpredictable panache about his moves. That thought did not allow me to rest easy on my pillow that night.

9

All Fifty-seven Varieties

I met John Mourain in the hall the next morning and guided him to the Sheriff's office for a courtroom pass. He became severely mesmerized by the trial and often would show up for half a day, or even an entire session and toward the end, when suspense and tension were at an all-time unleashed high, he was in constant attendance.

Clay Shaw entered the courtroom looking much better than he had the day before. There seemed to be a genuine smile upon his face as he said, "Good morning, good morning!" to members of the press and then took his seat. It was the difference, in what used to be pointed out in acting class, between *"acting* happy" and *"being* happy." Not that Clay Shaw had reason to be overjoyed, but his early morning spirits were not dampened by apparent ill health and he was walking better.

Judge Haggerty, silver hair smoothly in place, hands not nearly so smooth in movement—to see him juggle his first cup of morning coffee must be an unnerving sight—did not appear to be on the lookout for a specific member of the press and the day's voir dire began. The first prospective juror, the eighty-fourth to take the stand, was excused because of migraine headaches.

Soon the clerk called up a 24-year-old cashier for the George Hormel Company. Under questioning by James Alcock he admitted to having read articles in *Life* and other magazines pertaining to the case; he had also seen Jim Garrison on the *Tonight* show and added, "I didn't like Johnny Carson's treatment of Garrison." A sideways glance between Irvin Dymond and Billy Wegmann. Regarding the publicity surrounding the case, he had this to say: "What are they [the District Attorney's office] going to come up with next? You have no way of knowing whether what you release to the newspapers is evidence or just something to fill up the papers." No dummy, this cashier.

When Dymond took him over, the young man admitted to

having seen the movie *Rush to Judgment,* taken from the widely read book of the same name by Mark Lane, that irrepressible suspicioneer of secrecy and conspiracy in high, middle and low places, the purveyance of which had earned him a small fortune. As a result of seeing the film, the jury candidate was left with the opinion that the murder of J.F.K. was probably due to a conspiracy. After making that statement—raised eyebrows at the defense table—he hedged, saying he got the *impression,* but that it was not an absolute opinion. Dymond, however, zeroed in on this and got him to admit it would take evidence to change his impression, at which point the lawyer challenged him for cause. James Alcock immediately objected and Judge Haggerty sustained the objection, saying, "We're not trying the Warren Report. We're not trying the death of the President in Dealey Plaza, we're trying a conspiracy in New Orleans."

Dymond quickly asked, "Is the court ruling that the state cannot get into Dealey Plaza in their case?"

Knowing full well Jim Garrison planned to demolish the Warren Report to the best of his and his staff's abilities, those in the courtroom hung in wait for the court's reply. Judge Haggerty said, "We'll cross that bridge when we get to it."

If you could not hear the groan in court, you could feel it. Dymond still wanted the juror challenged for cause, arguing, "One of the necessary elements of the state's case is that it must prove conspiracy. If a prospective juror already thinks there *was* conspiracy . . . the state is halfway home."

Judge Haggerty continued to sustain the state's objection to Dymond's plea that the prospective juror be excused for cause until Dymond was forced to use his third peremptory challenge to vacate the young man from the chair.

This ruling had barely sunk in when a field engineer took the stand. He indicated he had an opinion, but not a fixed one, saying he had grave doubts as to the Federal government's position that there was *not* a conspiracy. Irvin Dymond immediately, despite the judge's previous ruling, leaped in: "This man already feels there was a conspiracy—there's no point in further questioning."

To which the judge replied, "What the prospective juror thinks makes no difference, the state has to prove conspiracy."

To those of us sitting there, this was most confusing. What a prospective juror thinks about almost *anything* had been, up to this point, most crucial. Else why the prolonged and difficult task of jury selection, why the prediction that jury selection might stretch into three weeks, if, in fact, a jury could be found at all in the Parish of Orleans?

Dymond would not give up: "But the [prospective] juror already *believes* conspiracy!" He challenged for cause. Judge Haggerty overruled the challenge, and Dymond filed a bill of exception. Now the questioning continued with Dymond concentrating on the man's already formed impression. Judge Haggerty eventually entered into the discussion and after getting the juror to say he thought he could weigh the case on the evidence presented and as Dymond was questioning him further, the judge suddenly pulled an about-face and indicated he would excuse the man for cause, on the basis of his impression. Now the confusion doubled as members of the press regarded one another with quizzical looks and James Alcock sprang to his feet and strongly objected to the judge's intent to excuse for cause. Now Alcock indicated *he* would file a bill of exception, adding that "Every juror that's been selected so far has an opinion."

More puzzled looks in court as the implication of this remark sunk in, meaning, in effect, the prosecuting attorney was casting grave doubts on the veracity of those six jurors already sitting in the box, all of whom claimed no opinion. Edward Wegmann, in a spurt of gamesmanship, held this remark up to the magnifying glass by rising in outrage and saying, "That's an insult to this jury!".

Alcock, knowing he would have to win or lose by the decision of these men he had just maligned, quickly apologized and added he was only trying to say that anyone who might be selected would be apt to have *some* kind of opinion and not a completely open mind because of the wide publicity dealing with the assassination.

At any rate, the judge excused the man for cause and Alcock filed his bill of exception.

The expressions of the six men in the jury box to all of this formed a clue to a case of phenomenal group inscrutability to come. Mason sat smoking impassively. Oliver Schultz's head was down, chin cradled in his left fist, indicating his thoughts might be centered more around nap time than the imputation of his honesty. William Ricks gave indications of mild interest, and the other three registered emotions somewhat below that.

Now a small army of candidates trooped to the stand and were excused one after the other for the usual variety of reasons, until Larry Dean Morgan, a 24-year-old aircraft mechanic, appeared. Married, with a 5-month-old son, Morgan is a good-looking dark-haired, smoothly olive complexioned young man who was not cheated when solid sets of prominent white teeth were handed out. Having listened to Alcock's theory of prospective jurors' almost certain propensity for some opinion, Morgan claimed he had no opinions whatsoever. None? No, none. He admitted to knowing a detective on the New Orleans police force but this, he said, would not influence him in weighing the testimony. He had also seen David Ferrie twice, maybe three times, at the New Orleans Lakefront Airport, where Morgan had worked, but he had never met him. (Every prospective juror was asked if he knew any of the principals involved in the case.) He maintained that he had no more than general discussions about Ferrie and the case. It turned out that Perry Russo used to play ball in a park across the street from where Larry Morgan lived but he had only seen him, had never met the preliminary hearing's star witness. Upon further questioning, young Morgan alleged he had read nothing about the case. "I never read newspapers, that may sound funny," he said. He claimed little interest in the matter. That might have been true, but at this stage of the game he seemed to have a very definite interest in being on the jury. Later, when I interviewed his pretty young wife, Kathleen, asking if she'd had any idea that when he left for court that morning he'd end up on the jury, she said, "Yes, woman's intuition, I knew they were going to take him. I knew Larry's kind—he'll try anything once. I knew that when I married him."

When Dymond questioned him, Larry Morgan was careful to answer in a way that maintained strict impartiality. He did utter one sentence that was passed over by both sides, but which struck me as worthy of further investigation: "If he's [Shaw's] not guilty he would have to show his innocence." A reminder that the defendant is presumed innocent until proven guilty would not have been out of place.

Without too much questioning, Dymond tendered Morgan back to the state, and James Alcock accepted him. Dymond indicated the defense was of a like frame of mind, and Larry Dean Morgan was sworn in as juror number seven at 1:45 that afternoon. Those of the press who were pro-defense were not all that certain they would have chosen him.

Clay Shaw, in response to the question of his health, smiled during a recess and said in a hearty voice, "Fine, feel fine today, like a spring lamb." Curious to get his impression of jury selection and assured he was feeling up to it, I asked him to dinner that evening.

An entire parade of jurors was excused after Larry Morgan was sworn in, and finally a man named Lloyd Heintz was called up. Judge Haggerty made a little pun about Heinz Foods and their seventy-seven varieties, but it got muddled when someone reminded the Judge that Heinz claimed *fifty*-seven varieties. Wan smiles all around. Mr. Heintz, a 40-year-old draftsman and geophysicist for Chevron Oil, was a dapper, well-dressed handsome man with premature silvering hair. If Mr. Ordes looked as if he might enter the Harvest Moon Ball in the tango department, then Mr. Heintz could be imagined entering the fancy ballroom division.

The prospective juror said that although he had not made a conscious effort to follow the case, he had read quite a bit about it in the newspapers; he'd also read several magazine articles and excerpts from *Rush to Judgment,* which at the time caused him to have certain misgivings about the Warren Report. He felt now, however, that he had a completely open mind regarding this specific trial. There was something forthright and honest about this man; although not overbearing in any sense of the word, he had a certain quiet strength and it would stretch credibility to imagine him being pushed around or led in any way.

Irvin Dymond felt that way, too. He barely questioned Mr. Heintz when he announced the defense would accept him as a juror. I wouldn't be surprised if he thought the state would excuse Heintz peremptorily, but, to its credit, the state accepted him and he was sworn in as juror number eight. To this I heard a reporter remark, "They got a live one there."

It suddenly occurred to me I had still not been called to the principal's office for my faux pas of the day before and I crossed myself; I did not dwell on this for fear that even my thoughts might summon forth a reprimand, if not the hook.

There was no further lengthy questioning that afternoon as prospects were excused left and right. Questioning a candidate about his family status and learning the man had eight children and "another one on the way," Judge Haggerty earned a laugh for his good humor when he excused the man with a sigh and a heartfelt "God bless you!" By 3:30 that afternoon the entire original panel of 169 jurors had been exhausted. The judge announced court would reconvene at 9 A.M. Saturday morning when forty-four prospective jurors from the panel of one of the other Criminal District judges would be tapped to appear for possible duty.

The box score accounting for the 169 read: 8 jurors accepted; 44 excused for lack of pay; 35 dismissed for fixed opinions; 22 wiped out for reasons of health; 50 excused for all other reasons: concern for family, wife pregnant, attending night school, self-owned business, friendship with one of the lawyers or a witness in the case, 3 were excused because of attachments, and 7 jurors had been dismissed by the use of peremptory challenges, 3 by the defense and 4 by the prosecution. Only four more needed, plus two alternates, and the Big Show would be under way.

That evening Clay Shaw and I went to Antoine's for dinner. It was Friday night and there were lines of people outside the restaurant. Clay was familiar with the side-alley private entrance. He phoned on an outside intercom, and the door was soon opened. He was explosively greeted by a maitre d'—"Ah! Mr. Shaw!"—and we were ushered in. As we were led through several packed dining rooms to a final room and our table, one heard the murmurs: "Clay Shaw." "Look, there he is." "It's that man on trial." "Look, honey, there's Clay Shaw!" On he strode, head up, walking tall, as several people who knew him called out, "Hiya, Clay" or "Good luck" or "We're with you!" He would smile, nod, wave a hand and proceed on. When we sat down I noticed several reporters I did not know by name and one of the television sketch artists at the next table. We all nodded.

Our waiter turned out to be Thomas Williams, nicknamed "Chico," a long-time acquaintance and admirer of Clay Shaw, as are most of the waiters, captains and bus boys in New Orleans, it seems. His greeting at any of the restaurants he patronizes is invariably the kind of welcome actors pray for when taking out-of-town visitors to Sardi's. Like you own a piece of the action.

Chico asked how it was going, how he was feeling. "Feel like"—and I could finish it for him—"a spring lamb." After two years in the public eye, he was programmed to a certain degree when it came to the social amenities. I suppose it was inevitable. And this programming sometimes extended to a few of the larger issues. Later, when the waiter had served Clay his customary martini, and a discussion of the case was inevitable, Chico asked, "Mr. Shaw, what do you suppose is in his [Garrison's] mind?" To which Clay shrugged and replied, "I have no idea, I'm afraid you'd have to ask Mr. Garrison that." It was a sentence I had heard often and would hear again and again.

Chico was also currently moonlighting as a guard at the courthouse and the adjoining Parish Prison. He smiled when he told Clay that only that day he had been assigned as guard on the roof of the courthouse, adding he was on the lookout for him against attack "by any nuts." Chico also mentioned that Judge Haggerty had been in Antoine's the night before.

"Was he drinking?" Clay asked.

"Not much—just four White Label and waters."

There were still rumors that the judge had gone on the wagon for the duration of the trial, but the wagon must have been a modified one. There was also speculation that if he did not, he would find it difficult to withstand the strain of a long and complicated trial. (The judge himself makes no bones about liking the sauce.)

During dinner I asked Clay how he *really* felt. He who had been the epitome of Mr. Cool took a long sip of his martini, flicked his eyes up and over to me and grinned. "Now that it's past, I have to admit to a severe case of nerves the first day. [Praise be to God, I thought.] Oh, my back was no help and the medicine wasn't agreeing with me, but suddenly there it was, in reality, the trial, *my* trial was under way, the wheels of justice"—a sideways glance and a shrug—"or injustice, I'll let you know later, were officially spinning and it got to me, hit me. But now my back feels better, I actually had a good night's sleep last night and—I suppose the show is under way and I'm getting used to it. Like an actor on opening night, after the curtain's up and the plot's unfolding, then you get used to the play and your role in it and relax. Mind you, I don't mean enjoy, but relax."

Was he aware when jurors or prospective jurors were scrutinizing him? "Oh, yes"—he nodded—"and there's a tendency to—you can't help it—want to show them various sides of yourself. Now smiling, now relaxed, now interested." He paused for a moment and there was a trace of wry humor when he added, "Concerned, but not overly *worried*, I suppose that would be best." I agreed with him it would be humanly impossible not to want to impress the men who are to be your judges.

We talked further of jury selection, of the trepidation he felt as a prospect was being questioned, of the dangerously ill-defined game of second-guessing when one tries to glimpse the inside of another man's psyche. Clay remarked, "The dichotomy of it strikes me—how can you watch with such apprehension the picking of these people who are going to be the arbiters of your fate and still experience the stultifying boredom of jury selection at the same time? But that's the way it is!" Clay suddenly sat up straight, shook his head and spoke with wonder. "One thing keeps me very much awake. It invariably comes as a shock, like someone splashing cold water in my face, every time someone reiterates the charge that I conspired to kill the President of the United States!"

He sat there for a moment, in silence, still in wonder; it was apparent he was even now experiencing the eerie playback of his own voice mouthing these incredible words. He went on to say his defense counsel would like to have at least two more Negroes on the jury, again voicing their theory that Negroes have been the underdog, the oppressed, and they know what it's like to be hounded and persecuted. There were many in New Orleans, though, who lumped it the other way. All Negroes, they professed, loved John Kennedy and their emotional hangover was still ripe, full-blown and full of ache.

Now we touched on some of the courtroom personalities. Of his chief prosecutor, James Alcock, he said, "I believe he's extremely bright. I think he knows the truth, or maybe he's closed his mind to it, shut it out. I believe he's prosecuting this case because the job was assigned him, he's treating it like any job. And he'll do his best to win. I think he's extremely ambitious, earnest and anxious to improve himself in the good old American tradition." This last sentence was declaimed with distinct humor.

As for Jim Garrison's seeming lack of interest and attendance in the day-to-day proceedings, Clay noted, "If Alcock handles the whole thing, the entire case, and it misfires—it wasn't Big Jim what done it, it was Alcock."

I asked Clay how he felt when Irvin Dymond rises from his chair with a big smile to walk back and confer with James Alcock, sometimes even putting an arm around his shoulder. "I was shocked the first time I saw that, really shocked. I wanted to say, Hey there, wrong team! But you realize this is their work, a way of life. They couldn't possibly contain the degree of hostility exhibited during their arguments and live."

What goes through his mind, what does he think when a man says he's formed a fixed opinion? "I try not to think about what that opinion might be! To dwell on each one would be extremely unhealthy."

We spoke of lesser matters: the reported $15,000 a month it cost to sequester the jury at the Rowntowner Motor Inn, a mile or so away from the Criminal Court Building on Tulane Avenue; the hardness of his wooden chair and of the press benches; the falling off in spectator attendance from the first day, now that jury selection was down to a daily and highly publicized grind; the growing number of excuses and rapid dismissals now that jury prospects had caught on to *How Not to Serve* through the detailed accounts in the local newspapers, which listed every jury candidate called for questioning and the reason for his excusal. So that, after the third or fourth day, anyone who did not wish to serve, for whatever reason, had an easy out. All it took were the magic words "fixed opinion." Or the lesser reasons: I would feel undue concern at being away from my family; I'm taking a night course at Tulane and would lose credits; my mother suffers from hiccups and I have to stick around to scare her. Instead of the court taking a firmer stand regarding excuses, the longer the voir dire dragged on the more lenient the court seemed to become.

There was now talk, as Chico brought us our steaks, of a costly libel suit Perry Russo had instigated against *Time* magazine. *Time,* in a pretrial piece, had listed the qualifications of a few of the state's witnesses, among them Vernon Bundy, a self-admitted petty thief and narcotics addict, and Perry Russo, who had testified he trafficked in pornographic films with David Ferrie, and who had probably had his fingers, as he was later to admit, in some pretty sticky wickets, but who had not, as far as anyone knew, been connected with narcotics. Still, in their roundup, Perry Russo was listed as a narcotics addict. This was reportedly an error made by a copy editor who mistakenly transferred the phrase from Vernon Bundy's list of credits; still it had come out in print before the error was caught and that was enough to bring suit.

Most of the remainder of our dinner at Antoine's was spent in talk of the theater, books, Louisiana politics, and the problems of the city of New Orleans. Had I been in his place, having the one-track mind with which I am stuck, I would have found it difficult to wrench myself free from the quicksand of my immediate dilemma, but Clay had the capacity to shelve entire disaster areas.

As we left the restaurant Chico Williams shook Clay's hand, saying he would like very much to come down off the roof some day and sit in on a court session. Clay said he would speak to Nina Sulzer. Chico then looked at Clay for a long mement, shook his head and said sadly, "If I was you I'd lose all faith in humanity after this."

10

The City That Care Forgot
and Vice Versa

On our first Saturday morning in court, the mood smacked of a holiday procedure. Most of the press were disgruntled at having to labor six days a week and showed their scorn by appearing in extremely casual dress—a number of far-out sports jackets with open-necked shirts—and a few reporters appeared in sports shirts or sweaters without jackets. The other courtrooms were not in session, so the corridors had been swept clean of humanity and its leavings—newspapers, paper coffee cups, and brimming cigarette receptacles. Even security precautions were on half-holiday. We were checked in and searched, but no more than a tickle—as if assassins don't work on Saturdays. By this time there was a grand gal joining in on the search, Sadie Little, an employee of the Parish Prison, usually in charge of the laundry but now switched over to courtroom security. In her sixties, and craggy of face to prove it, Sadie Little affected large dark glasses, a brownish wig with streaks of gray in it, and longish shapeless shift-type dresses. She was immensely good-natured and toward the end of the trial finally confided to me, "I'll be glad when this crock of [she skipped the word] is over." Sadie's sheriff's badge, a starred rosette pinned above her pendulous breasts, was an added touch I will always fondly remember.

Clay Shaw appeared to be in even better health than he had the day before. It was also possible Judge Haggerty might just have had a big Friday night. When a sheriff's deputy reached in front of a prospective juror's face to adjust the microphone and thereby produced a noise like a creaking door, the judge snapped, "Sheriff, leave that alone, let the jurors do that!"

Twenty-six candidates were wiped out in a relatively short period and a certain boredom set in. Newspaper reporters fell to doodling, a few attempted to doze off without being spotted by a deputy, especially auctioneer-voiced Sal Brocato who had an aversion to the press catnapping in court. I noticed Moe Waldron, at one point, sitting extremely erect, head up, hands folded in his lap, looking for all the world as if he were watching a championship fight, except for his eyes, which were closed.

As the men trooped up to the stand with their fixed opinions, no pays, and family illnesses, I ran down the names on the jury lists, marking some of my favorites. I believe the names in New Orleans are slightly more colorful than would appear on a jury panel, say, in New York: E. Gaston Ralph Alciatore, Carroll Edward Delacroix, Ashton Raymond Delahoussaye and Harold Merdic du Charm—the last three right out of the picnic scene in *Gone with the Wind*.

By the time the forty-ninth prospective juror of the day sat down on what must have been a highly warmed up seat, we were in for another contradiction. Number forty-nine was an engineer-technician for the J. Paul Getty Oil Company, who turned out to know Raymond Wegmann, a brother of the two defense lawyers and a monsignor in the Catholic Church. The engineer claimed never to have spoken of the case with the monsignor but he had occasionally discussed the matter with fellow workers. He'd read no magazine articles but he had seen the CBS special devoted to the assassination and the Warren Report and read about Garrison's investigation in the newspapers—"if it was on the front page." At the time of the assassination he felt Lee Harvey Oswald did *not* kill the President by himself. Upon further questioning by Alcock, he admitted he would require presentation of evidence to change his impression.

Surprisingly enough, it was James Alcock who challenged for cause, surprising because the man, if he did not believe Oswald was alone in killing the President, must therefore have concurred with the theory of conspiracy. Unless the challenge was inspired by his acquaintance with Monsignor Wegmann, or perhaps Alcock's reticence was ruled by the man's obvious intelligence and his job as an engineer, which would tend to draw a decision based on hard facts rather than emotional appeal. We were surprised again when the judge refused the challenge for cause. Alcock was no less surprised, and when he reminded the judge that only the previous day his honor had upheld a similar challenge after a man had admitted he would require evidence to change his impression, Judge Haggerty jerked back his head, adjusted his glasses and said, "I've had a change of heart." Alcock persisted, his nasal voice now rising to a whine, as he reiterated this was the identical situation as the day before but now the judge had switched his ruling. Said Judge Haggerty, hands buzzing about his glasses, "That may be, but I've read some law since then and I've changed my mind."

If this was confusing, the matter became doubly puzzling when Dymond also soon challenged this same man for cause and the judge changed his mind once more and excused the prospect.

Shortly before noon the entire list of jurors was exhausted, and Judge Haggerty indicated he would raid jurors from every panel of the remaining Criminal judges, if need be. Now he made a short speech regarding the eight men already selected. He was, throughout the trial, genuinely interested in their comfort, as he was vitally concerned that they do nothing to violate the laws set down for jurors in criminal cases, which violation could be cause for a mistrial. Judge Haggerty announced the jurors would be allowed to attend church on Sunday, if they so desired. He also added he'd arranged a sightseeing tour for them.

This brought smiles to the faces of the newsmen. After all, most of the jurors were natives of New Orleans and the idea of piling them into a bus and hauling them to the French Quarter, where the driver would say, "This, gentlemen, is world famous Bourbon Street!" tickled the press.

Court was adjourned early and we were happy to be let out into the brisk, clear day. Some of the press were going home for what was left of the weekend, but it never occurred to me. New Orleans, even that early on, seemed much farther away from New York than it was in actuality. As the trial progressed and my stay lengthened, this impression increased until, toward the end, I had the distinct feeling of being in another country, and the mighty Mississippi, circling the city and augmenting the illusion that New Orleans is an island, could have been the Amazon or the Nile. Perhaps the notion that this trial could not actually be taking place in the United States fostered this impression. I remember especially receiving long distance phone calls and thinking of them as coming in from overseas.

That Saturday evening I went to several cocktail parties, out to dinner, and on Sunday, to a luncheon with Clay Shaw at Edith Stern's, then in the evening to dinner with friends of friends in New York—people I'd not met before but had letters or phone calls of introduction to. Not that I was in a party mood but outside of Mrs. Stern, and one or two others, none of the people I associated with that weekend were personal friends of the defendant. It had occurred to me that since arriving for the trial I had been too isolated; I'd been consorting almost exclusively with people who knew Clay and therefore would be sympathetic to him as well as antipathetic toward Jim Garrison. I decided to nose out the reactions of others and see which way the tide of opinion ran.

These cocktail and dinner companions were all fairly intelligent, well-to-do, very much with-it folk: lawyers and their wives, insurance brokers and their wives, a lady who ran an art gallery, a young couple in public relations, a photographer and others. Now, in my social meanderings, usually with a question on my lips (and a glass not far from them; New Orleanians tend to force wine-and-dine visitors), I was hard put to find one person who believed Garrison had a trump card up his sleeve; I did not unearth one person who believed Clay Shaw guilty. One or two said, "Well, you know, he could have known this David Ferrie, but who couldn't have? New Orleans is really a small town. But Clay Shaw conspire to kill Kennedy—ridiculous!"

To some of these people I would venture to ask, "If no one believes the District Attorney has anything and if everyone believes Clay Shaw is innocent, why hasn't anyone done anything about it?"

"Listen, Clay Shaw has the best criminal lawyer in town. Irvin Dymond is—"

"No, I mean *do* something, why didn't you do anything before the trial, in the two years Garrison was, so you think, persecuting this man?"

Over and over, though, I would hear that Garrison was the most powerful man in the state. "Why, I remember when he took on the eight Criminal judges singlehanded," I would be told and then hear for the fifth time how, when the Criminal judges, including Judge Haggerty, had sought to oversee the funds Garrison was using on his Bourbon Street cleanup and vice investigation, the District Attorney turned around and took on all eight of them, charging their actions "raised interesting questions about racketeer influences," and intimating strongly that the judges would be on the losing end if his vice cleanup succeeded. The judges hauled him into court for criminal libel. He was convicted and fined $1,000. If he had forked over the money it would have gone into the fines and fees fund which the District Attorney uses to help run his office. The tag end of the story is a remark Garrison made to a friend that if he were forced to cough up the grand, he would "immediately commission a $1,000 portrait of myself to hang in my office!" The portrait did not have to be executed, however. The U.S. Supreme Court reversed his conviction, claiming the right of the individual to criticize duly elected public officials. He soon managed to unseat a judge or two who had particularly irked him, and the other judges rolled over, played good dogs and stopped jumping on the furniture. Garrison had guts and daring, everyone gave him that.

I would also ask about his popularity with the voters, with those who might be slightly less thinking—though they could scarcely be less acting—perhaps a bit lower on the social and economic scale. I would be told that Garrison had, after all, accomplished some good deeds, that he'd galloped into office as the White Knight, the reformer—the Vice Man Cometh. I would be reminded of his good looks, his appeal, his powers of persuasion, and his image as a maverick, owing nothing to "the machine," although one could not help thinking he *was* the machine.

So it was La Ronde, New Orleans style. They could see in my eyes and the slight tightening of my lips that satisfaction had not been given. "Of course," these attractive, well-heeled people would say, "it's a crime and we certainly hope Clay Shaw is acquitted, that'll fix Garrison's wagon." And there would be a great deal of sympathetic clucking about what the defendant must be going through. Then finally one of the wives would pass me a canapé and say, "Aren't you lucky we're having Mardi Gras during the trial? Have you ever seen it before or is this your first?"

And that was the end of topic Shaw and on to topic A, Mardi Gras, which would be described in the minutest detail. ("Darling, when did that man fall off the float and get killed—was that last year or the year before?" "No, honey, last year the man fell off his *horse* and got killed, the year before was the year the man fell off the float.")

Even Mardi Gras has its nasty taste, because, if you think you're running into prejudice against the Negro in this Southern city, another severe jolt arrives with the discovery that they also indulge themselves in a king-size portion of anti-Semitism. Today, in New Orleans, Jews are most definitely excluded from the official Mardi Gras functions. They cannot belong to the select Boston Club, they cannot take part in the hundreds of balls, banquets and parties spawned by this festival, they cannot attend their friends' daughters (and their children cannot attend their classmates') coming-out parties. I *know* New Orleans is not the only city that subscribes to anti-Semitism—it's just that you figure they have enough *other* problems with which to occupy themselves, so it comes as a complete surprise that they have indeed managed to find time to squeeze that one in, too. I suppose where there's ill-will there's a way.

And so, prejudice's ooze rises to the surface at carnival time to affect a vast section of New Orleanian activists for civil rights, improved housing, a more equitable real estate tax, better local government, and yes, culture: the museum, the civic theater, the libraries, the opera, ballet and other worthy institutions. Still, at this time of year they are barred from taking part in the organized festivities that are supposedly the culmination of the work year in The City That Care Forgot—which one cannot help scramble to read, The City That Forgot to Care.

At luncheon at Mrs. Stern's on Sunday there was little conversation about the trial. Clay and Mrs. Stern were vitally concerned with the upcoming elections for Mayor and, of course, District Attorney. Both felt strongly that New Orleans is slowly relegating itself to the status of a museum city, like Charleston, happy to rest on past laurels, its quaint charm, its legends, the Garden District, the French Quarter, and, of course, always Mardi Gras. Both felt the dire need for strong, concerned leadership that would boost the city economically and culturally and vitalize the port of New Orleans, now being bypassed because of rotting piers, sagging docks and obsolete loading machinery, in favor of Houston and other forward-looking cities. Mrs. Stern hit upon an idea for a mayoral campaign slogan whereby New Orleans would be pictured as the Sleeping Beauty. Was there in all of the city a

Prince Charming (Mayor) who would kiss her and bring her back
to life? I could picture her high on a ladder slapping up the
billboards herself.

The afternoon at Mrs. Stern's had been her farewell visit with
Clay—and why? "Because," Clay said, after we'd left and in a
voice that carried the shame he felt it was, "although she doesn't
say why, she takes off on a three-week trip every year around
Mardi Gras time, so she won't have to embarrass her non-Jewish
friends by being in town when she would have to be excluded
from the many activities and celebrations."

And then this septuagenarian guardian angel of much we hold
dear flutters back to town and breaks her back for another eleven
months, trying to pull New Orleans up out of the quagmire of
civic, economic and cultural indolence it is slowly sinking into.
True, she is immensely wealthy and has her own private jet with
which to escape, but I think, were I she, I might just wing back to
town someday with the bomb-bay doors open.

11

Fun Couple

The first word Monday morning was not good for the defense. Judge Haggerty announced that the last juror sworn in, Lloyd Heintz, had been taken ill over the weekend and was in the hospital. The judge dropped him from the jury over Irvin Dymond's objections. Dymond preferred holding the matter in abeyance, in the event Mr. Heintz should recover, but the judge overruled Dymond and the defense lawyer droned out another bill of exception. Heintz was the one juror so far who had given the impression he would not be easily led by the state, would not include Clay Shaw in a general denunciation of the Federal government or the Warren Report, and would keep his mind and full attention on the specifics of the case.

The first prospective replacement to take the stand was excused for cause when he said, "I'd be looking for Mr. Shaw's attorneys to prove his innocence, than for the District Attorney to prove his guilt." A cheery early morning theorem for the defendant's ears.

This turned out to be the day of peremptory challenges, with the defense using up four and the state three. Irvin Dymond spent one early on to excuse a man with a patently low IQ, aggravated by a pair of shifty, mean-looking eyes. He had the appearance of a man who might be known in his neighborhood for killing cats at random and notching his belt in memoriam. An earnest, elderly Negro prospect who, when asked by the judge if he would suffer undue concern being absent from his family for a long period of time, replied, "Yes, on account of my wife don't keep too well." For this the man was rewarded with snickering laughter from a majority of those present. He looked up in confusion. I was reminded that the simple cruelty of high school youngsters often extends beyond graduation.

The twelfth man to be interrogated replied to the question about his family status, "Married with nine kids." Judge Haggerty adjusted his glasses, smiled and asked what their ages were. The man gave him a stricken look as if to say, Why throw me a curve like that, Judge? He managed to run down the list, squeezing out the ages of seven children, but was able to go no further. Another prospective juror, when asked if he had an opinion, said, "Yes, I do. No reflection on Mr. Shaw, but—" Judge Haggerty quickly cut in, silencing and excusing him and at the same time adding, "Trials can't be held in a vacuum."

Before luncheon there was a skirmish when one of the jury candidates indicated he harbored doubts about the veracity of the Warren Report. Irvin Dymond wanted the man excused for cause but the judge refused, saying, "The Warren Report is not a legal court decision, it is not an official document and is fraught with hearsay and unsworn testimony." That gave some indication of what the judge's inclination would be when it came time for Jim Garrison's staff to begin lobbing hand grenades at the report.

The morning session yielded not one juror. That noon I lunched with Rosemary James, one of the reporters to first break the story of Garrison's investigation into the assassination of the President. She, Mike Parks, a young reporter for the Baltimore *Sun,* and I went across the street to a beer and sandwich joint. Rosemary now reports the news for WWL, a local television station, and had been closely involved with the Shaw-Garrison affair from the start. She was most knowledgeable about the cast of characters, of which she said, "There's hardly a normal person connected with the entire case." She had, in fact, written a paper-back book with another local newsman, Jack Wardlaw, in 1967, entitled *Plot or Politics?—The Garrison Case and Its Cast.* The question of politics referred to the possibility that Garrison might be pursuing his investigation for personal aggrandizement leading to higher political office. The book served as a primer-playbill for most out-of-town reporters who were not all that familiar with the scoreboard and supporting cast.

Rosemary told us Jim Garrison had presented her husband, Judson James, a writer and public relations man, with an auto-graphed photograph. In it, Rosemary explained, Garrison is pic-tured with a cigar in one hand and a drink in the other as he leans back in his chair, roaring with laughter. The District Attorney's signature reads, "To Jud—I have just read the inscription on the outside of the Criminal Court Building!" The inscription referred to reads, "This Is a Government of Law Not of Men." I later saw this picture hanging on the wall of the James apartment. It is even cuter than it sounded that day.

Rosemary attributed Jim Garrison's great appeal to the press to his quotability and his fondness for the game of "Surprise!" Although Rosemary was completely pro-Shaw, she held a certain amount of admiration for Garrison, as did many New Orleanians who nevertheless thought he'd spun way out of orbit. Oddly enough, there are even those who have been charged and indicted by the District Attorney who still have a lingering crazy little pocket of affection for the man. Perhaps this is due, no matter what, to his contribution to livening things up. Whatever can be said about the District Attorney, I don't ever recall anyone applying the word dull to him. He was also widely praised for his sense of humor.

Rosemary spoke, too, of Liz Garrison, whom I had not yet seen but who, I had heard, was most attractive. Rosemary quoted her as having said, apropos of her five children by Jim Garrison: "He keeps me pregnant in the summer and barefoot in winter."

Early on in the afternoon session one man again said he had read excerpts from the Warren Report and there were some things in it he found hard to believe. Dymond immediately challenged him for cause, once more arguing that the state had to prove conspiracy before they could connect Clay Shaw to it and if this gentleman already believed in conspiracy the state was free of that burden. The judge had ruled both ways, so no one knew what the outcome would be. This time he refused to excuse the man. Dymond filed yet another bill of exception and was forced to use a peremptory challenge. There was a repeat performance later when another man said, "I have some thoughts it [the assassination] just couldn't be one person." Again Dymond, Alcock and the judge fought it out, with Dymond being ruled against, and another peremptory challenge was squeezed out of the defense's precious quota.

The seventy-fourth man of the day to sit in the witness chair was Sidney Hebert, Jr., 55—the same age as the defendant, the judge and Irvin Dymond. Mr. Hebert, a retired fire department captain, is a short mild-looking bespectacled man, with thinning hair and thin lips. He had never served on a jury before and had no fixed opinions or impressions. He'd read excerpts from the Warren

Report, couldn't recall reading any magazine articles, and had seen Garrison on the *Tonight* show. He'd heard people express their opinions as to the guilt or innocence of the defendant but he had certainly never given voice to any because he had none. Mr. Hebert was sworn in without undue enthusiasm on either side as juror number eight at 5:10 that afternoon, replacing Mr. Heintz.

Close to adjournment time, a volunteer, Miss Nancy McDaniel, took the stand. Miss McDaniel turned out to be 27, a native of New Orleans, bright, trim and attractive, the kind of a girl to whom, when she whipped off her glasses, you could imagine someone saying, Gee, Nancy, you're really very pretty. Will you go to the prom with me? Furthermore she did not have a fixed opinion. She worked for a company as an accountant, preparing statistical calculations (I immediately saw the defense perk up; she would demand nothing but facts), and she gave every indication of being extremely intelligent and, one would imagine, most fair. She had read some magazine articles, seen accounts of the case on television, including the CBS special and part of Garrison's appearance on the *Tonight* show. As the questioning continued, the press came out of their late afternoon lethargy. I turned to Moe Waldron and Jerry Cohen and expressed my firm hope that she would get on. I received a quick negative shake of the head. "She's far too bright, the state will bounce her." I should have realized that. Perhaps because she was a female my logic had scattered. Sure enough, and with great regrets, we saw her excused by Alcock on a peremptory challenge. I believe there was a tacit "boo" ringing in the courtroom, from all hands but the state. Court was soon recessed. The day had begun with eight in the jury box and it ended with eight.

Most of the people I had run into up to this point were pro-Shaw. But this day, I'd been seated behind a couple, Dick and June Rolfe, who were stridently pro-Garrison and wanted Clay Shaw skewered in the worst way, and we had struck up a conversation. They were aware I'd written the profile on Clay and that I was a Garrison doubter.

June Rolfe conducts a short early evening news program on a local UHF station, Channel 26. Dick is a writer and also a public relations man. They are also somewhat jacks and jills of all trades, most congenial in the social amenities, bright and verbal and, of course, I had no idea at this time of the depths of their passions.

When they found where I'd taken an apartment, they kindly offered me a ride home; they also lived in the Quarter.

The Rolfes, both slightly overweight, seemed to be in their early fifties. Dick affects somewhat longish, but not necessarily thick hair, which always appeared to be slightly damp, especially the feathery part that reached down to tickle his neck. He has a pleasant, if somewhat flaccid, face, which also bespoke of the damp. June Rolfe is blondish, possessed of a face that frets easily, and she rarely bothered to "fix herself up." It was obvious she did not have a fondness for giving her hair more than a token brush in the morning nor did she take pains to keep it touched up. When she did bother to fix herself up, she too was pleasant enough in appearance. Some mornings she even arrived in court wearing a wig and that made a happy difference.

While I was riding in their station wagon, they began to wax polemical. They were high on Jim Garrison and asked if I'd ever met him. I replied that I hadn't, that I'd tried, missed, and hoped I'd be able to while I was in New Orleans this trip. "Oh, he's a great guy, you'll love him. He's really terrific, fine sense of humor, terribly bright and extremely well read." Dick went on to say the District Attorney was a great Graham Greene buff and assured me I would like him inordinately well; he also said he'd see what he could do to bring about a meeting between us. They were old friends of Jim and Liz Garrison and he was sure he could arrange it. Perhaps not during the early stages of the trial when he was so busy (though not in the courtroom) but later on, when things calmed down. I told them I would appreciate this.

Then they got on to Clay Shaw. They took it easy on the main target area, conspiracy to assassinate, because they were aware of my feelings, which I had reiterated during the ride. But they were positive he was the mysterious Clay or Clem Bertrand, that he'd used that alias to monitor the homosexual underground of the city, that he'd undoubtedly known David Ferrie and, June Rolfe said, "He did an extremely vicious thing to us." What was that, I wanted to know. Clay had bought a building a few years earlier in which the Rolfes were living; they were forced to vacate their apartment at the changeover, and June Rolfe's story had it that Clay Shaw claimed they'd skipped out on the last month's rent. She maintained they had paid the rent to the real estate agent, going on to say that a year or two later when she'd sought a store to rent for an antique shop, Clay had supposedly blocked the deal by telling the people who owned the building she was unreliable. Whatever the facts, June Rolfe was left grasping an unhealthy portion of animus for Clay. She finished by admitting he was certainly an intelligent person and could be extremely charming, but that he had come to New Orleans as a country boy and gotten in with the wrong crowd, that's why he was in all this trouble now.

Later I brought this incident up to Clay and he spoke of it dispassionately, merely saying they had in fact not paid the last month's rent, that it was over and in the past, but he felt they wanted his scalp, for which he was sorry.

When they delivered me to my apartment, I thanked them, and despite our vastly different points of view I felt there would be no open hostility, providing they had no serious intentions of converting me. I had no intention of converting them. The Rolfes nevertheless took my conversion on with missionary zeal— a project that cost them atoms of energy and me endless hours of reining in my patience and temper.

12

Not a Pretty Sight

I missed the morning session of the following day, the seventh of the voir dire. The proofs of an article I had written for *Playbill* arrived, and I was to go over some cuts and changes and either agree, disagree, or change them; whatever I did, they were going to press and the proofs were needed back in New York immediately.

I arrived at the Criminal Court Building at noon to learn that two jurors had been picked, bringing the total to ten. The defense had used up another peremptory—the score was even now, and each side had only four left. Once peremptories were exhausted, a prospective juror could only be excused by consent of both sides (no pay, ill health, etc.) or by cause (fixed opinion, friendship with one of the principals, disagreement with the conspiracy law, etc.) ; otherwise, should there be a dispute between state and defense, Judge Haggerty would be the deciding factor. With ten jurors in the box and peremptories running low, it seemed that jury selection would not drag on much longer.

Before court resumed, I spoke with Irvin Dymond, who was upset over a new ruling of the judge's which had gone into effect that morning. From now on, there were to be no questions asked of potential jurors about the Warren Report or their opinions of it, no questions about believing or not believing either Lee Harvey Oswald or David Ferrie was part of a conspiracy. Dymond was amazed at this ruling. After all, his client stood accused of conspiring to murder John Kennedy in collusion with Oswald and Ferrie, and if a man believed Lee Harvey Oswald was aided and abetted in the murder, then it would be most dangerous for the defense to have him on the jury. Dymond would now have no way of discovering a potential juror's inclinations, except by second-guessing or intuition. The lawyer explained that this ruling would, of course, be reason for appeal, should that be necessary.

And then he added, "But who wants Clay to spend the rest of his life appealing?"

When the jurors were brought down for the afternoon session, I got my first look at the two new members. Juror number nine was Harold Bainum, a 24-year-old married credit corporation unit manager. Wearing horn-rimmed glasses, Mr. Bainum was tall and heavyset and appeared older than his 24 years. Despite his solid build and filled-out cheeks, there was a prim tightness about his face. Juror number ten was Warren Humphrey, a 52-year-old married Negro employee of the Post Office, father of two. Mr. Humphrey was distinguished-looking in a quiet way; there was a touch of gray to his hair on the sides, and he had a way of sitting up at attention in his chair. Both jurors were dressed in suits.

For some reason this turned into a crazy-quilt afternoon of ding-a-ling prospects. Where they came from and how they happened to appear this one session, nobody knew. Although the state and defense continued fighting each other, we were also to see several instances of them working together, not without a certain degree of compassion.

The first candidate of the afternoon was dimly lacking in intelligence, a condition that did not necessarily make him unacceptable to the state. After Alcock had finished his questioning, Dymond, with a slim bag of peremptories left, was obviously scouting for any reason to excuse the man for cause. He went on a meticulous search-and-destroy mission in his low, easy growl, and although the man was vague and his attention span was dangerously short, he was somehow managing not to disqualify himself. Finally Dymond paused, looked down at the table, then back up and said, in a manner which strongly indicated an affirmative reply would be most correct, "Would you require the defendant to prove he's innocent?" "Yes," came the nodding reply. Dymond quickly called for him to be excused for cause. Alcock jumped up, accusing Dymond of entrapping the prospective juror. But there was nothing for Judge Haggerty to do but overrule the state's objection and dismiss the man. What was said was said, and there was no taking it back. A smile of pure satisfaction creased Dymond's face as he glanced around at Alcock.

Another fight ensued when a candidate for the jury, a mumbler and an extremely lethargic young man, mentioned he had seen Perry Russo around a neighborhood ball park and had spoken to him casually. Dymond quickly challenged for cause and Alcock objected strenuously, claiming the two men hadn't really known each other. Dymond hammered home the point that Russo, of all people, was the state's star witness and any contact with him might prove prejudicial. Judge Haggerty sided with the state and refused an excuse for cause. Dymond continued, persistently questioning the young man about when he'd spoken to Russo, what had been said, under what circumstances—and again challenged for cause. This time there was a grave warning tone in his voice that clearly indicated this would be a most serious point of contention for appeal, should the judge not dismiss this man. The defense lawyer's tone conveyed itself, and it was easy to read in Judge Haggerty's expression that he might well be venturing into dangerous territory. Dymond kept headlining the importance of Perry Russo as a witness until Judge Haggerty backed off from his original decision and excused the man.

Now, for one of the first times, we saw the state and the defense work together as two obvious homosexuals in succession came up for questioning. Wide grins and a few chuckles were being suppressed in the press section. Not that there was anything inherently hysterical about these two, but they were acting extremely supercilious and at the same time slightly put out about the whole thing. Once their proclivities had made themselves known, Irvin Dymond would swing around in his chair, glance at James Alcock, who would nod, then in consort they would manage to excuse the prospect at the next slightest opportunity, without embarrassing him.

As if to compound this run of luck, now a poor retarded chap with three separate tics, all working against one another, hopped up on the stand. A reporter near me whispered, "My God, where are they coming from today?" First off, this young man, who was painful to observe, should never have been called, but there he was, fighting to pull himself together and get through this ordeal. I believe, in all fairness to the defense and the state, they did not excuse him immediately, hoping to avoid the obvious recognition of his condition and therefore salvage his pride. He was asked a series of the usual questions, ending with "Do you know any of the defense lawyers, state's attorneys or witnesses in this case?" No, he did not. "Do you know the defendant?" His answer to that was a well-and-long-thought-out non sequitur, which he mulled over while looking down toward his lap at one pathetic twitching hand. He glanced up and out at the attorneys with a shrug and then replied, "Well, a lot of people *know* him." Irvin Dymond swung around, exchanged looks with James Alcock and they excused him gently.

Clay Shaw later remarked of this stream of candidates, "Sometimes viewing humanity en masse like this is not a pretty sight—it's not encouraging to see how many disturbed, lost people there are."

The day yielded not one more juror. Still, with only two jurors, plus two alternates lacking and with peremptory challenges dwindling fast, it was unthinkable that the voir dire would drag on for seven more agonizing days.

13

"One of History's
Most Important Individuals"

Jim Garrison had been District Attorney of New Orleans at the time of the President's assassination in 1963. It was not until November 1966, however, that his curiosity became piqued into a further investigation regarding the death of John F. Kennedy. This process was sparked by a conversation Garrison had aboard a plane bound from New Orleans to New York with fellow passengers Senator Russell Long of Louisiana and Joseph Rault, Jr., a New Orleans oilman of some wealth. They fell to speculating about the implausibility of a congenital loner-loser such as Lee Harvey Oswald pulling off the murder of the President singlehanded. Senator Long elaborated, voicing his doubts about the thoroughness of the Warren Commission's investigation.

New Orleans, the Chamber of Commerce magazine for that city, later quoted Garrison in this plane conversation as recalling in 1963 that his office had briefly investigated "a very unusual type of person who made a very curious trip at a very curious time about the date of the assassination." The District Attorney indicated he might well check back on this person.

The person he checked up on was indeed unusual. David W. Ferrie was a weird, supposedly brilliant 48-year-old jack-of-all-trades—and a pilot who had been discharged by Eastern Airlines for homosexual activities that were revealed after an arrest back in 1961 for an alleged "crime against nature" with a 16-year-old boy. Ferrie, who suffered complete loss of body hair from alopecia, made his own toupees by gluing bits and pieces of orangish-brown hair to his head, sometimes achieving the effect of a bad hairpiece and other times not even making it that far. Mostly, he looked like a totally bald man who had stuck clumps of monkey-furlike hair to his head. He also pasted on false eyebrows, the thickness of which varied from time to time. Pictures show him to have been owlish-looking, broad-faced, and slightly hawk-nosed, with dark intensely shining eyeballs oval-framed by his accentuated false eyebrows, which photographed as if they had been crudely drawn on.

David Ferrie squeezed out a living after his forced retirement as a commercial pilot by working as a free-lance pilot, a flight instructor, a leader of a unit of the Civil Air Patrol, and by employment as a private investigator for a law firm that for a while represented Carlos Marcello, alleged leader of the New Orleans chapter of the Mafia. As a sideline, he also trafficked in pornographic films. He professed to be a bishop in the Orthodox Old Catholic Church of North America, a cultish underground group quite different from the Catholic Church we know. At one time he had himself listed in the telephone book as a psychologist and he was an enthusiastic practitioner of hypnosis, using it, some claimed, for purposes of salting the tails of quarry upon whom he had sexual designs. He was a pianist of some accomplishment and possessed a certain knowledge of basic medicine, chemistry and physics. He had reportedly put in extensive research on his own private cure for cancer, at one time sharing his apartment with several thousand white mice. It was said that he usually wore sloppy clothes, that his apartment was cluttered and filthy, and that he was physically not the cleanest person.

David Ferrie was a devout anti-communist and had written, in a letter in the early 1950s to the Commanding Officer of the First Air Force, "There is nothing I would enjoy better than blowing the hell out of every damn Russian, Communist, Red or what-have-you . . . I want to train killers . . ." This, in an attempt to secure an Air Force commission, which was subsequently denied him. Later, he had supposedly turned pro-Castro but reverted to a decidedly anti-Castro posture and actually, according to many sources, got his wish by training killers in the swamps across Lake Pontchartrain from New Orleans for an invasion of Cuba. He also claimed to have taken part in the actual Bay of Pigs invasion as a pilot and in a speech in New Orleans before the local chapter of the Military Order of The World Wars he had been highly critical of President Kennedy for failing to provide air support.

Whichever of his credits were true, whatever he was, he was most certainly not the boy next door. At worst he was clutched in the hand of a certain madness, at the very least he must have been a highly neurotic person with a quick, retentive mind, a leadership complex and definite powers of persuasion.

The day the President was assassinated David Ferrie was in a New Orleans courtroom where Carlos Marcello was fighting deportation. Previously Marcello had been abducted by Justice Department agents and slapped on a plane to Guatemala; supposedly David Ferrie assisted in getting Marcello back into the country. The judge ruled that Marcello's deportation had been illegal and to celebrate this victory, Ferrie decided to drive to Texas with two young friends, Alvin Beauboeuf and Melvin Coffey. They left Friday night, driving to Houston and Galveston, and visited an ice skating rink in Houston before returning to New Orleans Sunday evening. By that time a New Orleans character named Jack Martin had tipped off the District Attorney's office that Ferrie had trained Lee Harvey Oswald in the use of guns and indicated Ferrie might well have been cast as a getaway pilot.

Soon after his return to New Orleans, Ferrie was arrested and questioned, not only by the District Attorney's office but by the FBI and the Secret Service. The following extract is from the United States Secret Service report on the incident, filed by Special Agents Anthony E. Gerrets and John W. Rice.

SYNOPSIS

Investigation disclosed that information furnished by Jack S. Martin to the effect that David William Ferrie associated with Lee Harvey Oswald at New Orleans and trained Oswald in the use of a rifle with a telescopic lens, also that Ferrie had visited Dallas several weeks prior to the assassination of President John F. Kennedy, is without foundation. Jack S. Martin, who has the appearance of being an alcoholic, has the reputation locally of furnishing incorrect information to law enforcement officers, attorneys, etc.

DETAILS OF THE INVESTIGATION

. . . At 11:10 P.M. on 11-24-63 reporting agent received a telephone call from Herman S. Kohlman. He said that he was an Assistant District Attorney for the Parish of Orleans and that he was calling from the District Attorney's office. It was apparent that Mr. Kohlman was reluctant to talk about "FARRY." He finally stated, however, that the District Attorney's office was conducting an investigation on their own with regard to "FARRY"; that "FARRY" is actually David Ferrie (W; M; 42; 195; 5-11; wears a wig, having suffered loss of hair in blotches). He said that Ferrie has a record at the New Orleans Police Dept.—Bureau of Identification; that he had been arrested several times and charged with moral offenses involving young boys. . . . Mr. Kohlman stated that at the time of his telephone conversation with me his office had ten Police Officers (investigators for the District Attorney's office) scouring the city for David Ferrie and that in the event Ferrie was picked up he would notify me. (No request was made of Mr. Kohlman that Ferrie be picked up and held for this Service.)

At 12:35 A.M. on 11-25-63 Assistant District Attorney Herman S. Kohlman telephoned the reporting agent at his residence, at which time he advised that he had received information to the effect that David William Ferrie had left for Dallas on Friday 11-22-63 during the afternoon, travelling in a light blue Comet. He also advised that Ferrie reportedly *had* a plane and may still have it. He said that at the time of his telephone conversation with me Ferrie was allegedly on his way back to New Orleans.

Mr. Kohlman stated that it was his information that Harvey Lee Oswald was in Ferrie's Civil Air Patrol group in New Orleans some years ago; that Ferrie allegedly had a fraudulent charter and that the Civil Aeronautics Board checked on it.

When pressed for the full name of the informant thus far referred to only as "Jack," Mr. Kohlman stated that he was "just a fellow who worked around the Police Headquarters building" and that "Jack" did not want to become involved in this investigation and for that reason did not want his name mentioned in any way. Mr. Kohlman was informed that "Jack" would have to be interviewed in person by representatives of this Service.

During the late afternoon of 11-25-63 SAIC Rice received a telephone call from Herman S. Kohlman, advising that David Ferrie had been picked up by representatives of the Orleans Parish District Attorney's office and that he was being questioned in the District Attorney's office at that time. . . .

At approximately 7:00 P.M. on 11-25-63 SAIC Rice and reporting agent interviewed David William Ferrie (W; M; 46—DOB 3-18-18 at Cleveland Ohio; 5-11; 190; ruddy complexion; brown eyes; wears dark brown kinky wig with a reddish tint; false upper teeth; resides at 3330 Louisiana Avenue Parkway, New Orleans . . .).

Ferrie insisted that he was in New Orleans on Thursday, November 21, 1963, and on Friday, November 22, 1963, until about 9:00 P.M. He said that he is positive that he was in New Orleans on the dates mentioned because he had been in Court in connection with a trial involving Carlos Marcello. He said that he departed New Orleans about 9:00 P.M. on 11-22-63 and drove to Houston and Galveston, Texas, with two companions, Alvin Beauboeuf, about 19 or 20 years old, of 2427 Alvar St., New Orleans, and Melvin Coffey, about 26 to 28 years old, 618 N. Pierce St., New Orleans; that he was driving a 1961 blue Comet 4-door Station Wagon with 1963 Louisiana license . . .

Ferrie stated that he and his two companions mentioned above returned to New Orleans about 9:30 P.M. on 11-24-63; that he telephoned Attorney G. Wray Gill (by whom he is employed as an investigator) several times; that at Gill's suggestion he left New Orleans about midnight that same date and drove to Hammond, La., alone, where he stayed at the Holloway Smith Hall on Sycamore Street, at the Southeastern Louisiana College, where he has a friend, Thomas Compton, who does research in narcotics addiction under a Doctor Nichols, under a Federal grant. He said he left Hammond about 1:00 P.M. on 11-25-63 and arrived New Orleans about 3:00 P.M.; that immediately upon arriving at New Orleans he contacted Attorney Gill, who accompanied him to the Orleans Parish District Attorney's office, where he was wanted for questioning in connection with the Oswald case. . . .

David William Ferrie emphatically denied that he had been in Dallas for about the last *eight to ten years*.

As the interview with David William Ferrie was about to end he stated that he had a very good idea who had reported him as having associated with Oswald, training him in the use of rifles with telescopic lenses, etc.; that he was firmly convinced that one Jack S. Martin, who resides at the corner of Esplanade Avenue and N. Prieur Street, had made this false report concerning him. He stated that Martin makes a practice of hanging around the offices of various attorneys, courtrooms, etc., and is well known locally for furnishing false leads to law enforcement officers, attorneys, etc.

Subsequent to our interview with Ferrie on the night of 11-25-63 he was interviewed by FBI Agents at the First District Police Station.

On 11-26-63 it was learned the FBI Agents had talked with Jack S. Martin, who admitted that he had been the informant with regard to David William Ferrie; that Martin had admitted to FBI Agents that the information which he had furnished Assistant District Attorney Kohlman was a figment of his imagination and that he had made up the story after reading the newspapers and watching television; that he remembered that Kohlman, a former newspaper reporter, had written an article or story about Ferrie a couple of years ago and that he pieced the whole thing together in his mind and had given it to Kohlman as facts.

On the night of 11-29-63 SAIC Rice and reporting agent interviewed Jack S. Martin at length in his small run-down apartment located at 1311 N. Prieur Street, New Orleans, which he shares with his wife and 6-year-old son. Martin, who has every appearance of being an alcoholic, admitted during the interview that he suffers from "telephonitis" when drinking and that it was during one of his drinking sprees that he telephoned Assistant District Attorney Herman S. Kohlman and told him this fantastic story about William David Ferrie being involved with Lee Harvey Oswald. He said he had heard on television that Oswald had at one time been active in the Civil Air Patrol and had later heard that Ferrie had been his Squadron Commander. Martin stated that Ferrie was well known to him; that he recalled having seen rifles in Ferrie's home and also recalled that Kohlman had written an article on Ferrie and that Ferrie had been a Marine and had been with the Civil Air Patrol. Martin stated that after turning all those thoughts over in his mind, he had telephoned Herman S. Kohlman and told his story as though it was based on facts rather than on his imagination.

In view of the above, this phase of the investigation involving William David Ferrie will be considered closed.

Ferrie was released and that was the end of the matter—in 1963. Although the D.A.'s own office, the FBI, the Secret Service and, later on, the Warren Commission, who had access to these previous reports, all discounted Jack Martin's story as completely apocryphal, and even Martin admitted it was a figment of his imagination, it was still this tip to which Garrison returned for the beginning of his investigation—and it was David Ferrie who was his first suspect.

The investigation got under way in December and soon a small staff of assistant D.A.s, policemen, and friends was recruited, along with private detective William Gurvich and Thomas Bethell, a young British jazz enthusiast turned assassination buff. David Ferrie was checked on right and left, cameras were hidden across from his apartment, he was followed day and night, and his friends and acquaintances were grilled. The heat was on. The heat produced very little, however, and Garrison even returned to Jack Martin, who apparently was only too eager to reactivate his imagination and from it supplied further tidbits that titillated the District Attorney—among them, that Ferrie had hypnotized Oswald and the assassination was the result of a posthypnotic suggestion.

At this stage Garrison theorized that the entire plot against Kennedy had been carried out by rabid anti-Castroites who had turned their wrath from Castro to the President as a result of the Bay of Pigs disaster. While Oswald's 1963 activities in New Orleans had shown him to be passionately pro-Castro, the District Attorney did not let that disturb a supposed relationship between Ferrie and Oswald. It was postulated that Oswald's pro-Castro sympathies were merely a front to conceal his true feelings. At this point the District Attorney's office was eying all Cubans in exile and others who were known to be rabidly anti-Castro. Included in this group was a private detective by the name of W. Guy Bannister, who was well known to have been antipathetic toward Castro. Guy Bannister, who died in 1964 of a heart attack, is a man worth remembering. According to many New Orleanians, he bore a strong resemblance to Clay Shaw, even to the white hair, and there are those who say any possible testimony placing Clay Shaw in the company of David Ferrie, who was also employed by Bannister for a time, might well be a case of mistaken identity.

If the entire Ferrie episode—lead, milieu and suspect—was strange, the origin of the mysterious name Clay Bertrand, by which Jim Garrison eventually touched on Clay Shaw, was at least as outlandish. Undoubtedly one of the most unusual characters practicing law in the United States today—and yesterday and the day before—is a small-time New Orleans lawyer smack out of Damon Runyon by way of Our Gang comedies, one Dean Adams Andrews, Jr. Andrews, short and rotund, is rarely seen without a pair of large sunglasses, and so colorful is his swinging hip-talking gift of gab that there should always be a tape recorder at the ready when he warms up to speak.

It was widely known that Dean Andrews, while recuperating from an attack of pneumonia in New Orleans Hotel Dieu hospital at the time of the assassination, had spread word that a man had phoned him shortly after the death of the President, asking if he would be interested in going to Dallas to defend Lee Harvey Oswald. Andrews phoned fellow lawyer Sam "Monk" Zelden, also smack out of Damon Runyon, asking him if he'd be interested. The question was made moot the following day when Oswald was shot by Jack Ruby. Andrews, however, had also phoned the FBI and was soon interviewed in his hospital room by Agent Regis Kennedy. He was also later interviewed by the Secret Service. When asked to give a name to the voice on the other end of the telephone, he said it belonged to a "Clay Bertrand." His description of the man, whom he claimed at various times never to have seen, or to have seen once or twice, changed like a cloud formation. If he had the FBI and the Secret Service confused, he did nothing to make life easier for Wesley J. Liebeler, who interviewed him as assistant counselor for the Warren Commission.

According to Andrews' testimony, given to the Commission on July 21, 1964, Lee Harvey Oswald had visited his office as many as five times during the summer of 1963, usually accompanied by a man whom Andrews described as "a Mexicano" and also, the first time, by a group of young Mexicans whom he called "gay kids"— apparent homosexuals who had been arrested by police for wearing women's clothing and whom Andrews had represented from time to time in other scrapes with the law. Oswald was interested, Andrews claimed, in rectifying "a yellow paper discharge" from the Marines and also straightening out his status as a citizen as well as investigating his Russian wife's prospects for citizenship.

The excerpted transcript reads:

MR. LIEBELER: And did you talk about different subjects at different times? As I understand it, the first time he [Oswald] came there, he was primarily concerned about his discharge, is that correct?

MR. ANDREWS: Well, I may have the subject matter of the visits reversed because with the company he kept and the conversation— he could talk fairly well—I figured that this was another one of what we call in my office free alley clients, so we didn't maintain the normalcy with the file that—might have scratched a few notes on a piece of pad, and 2 days later threw the whole thing away. Didn't pay too much attention to him. Only time I really paid attention to this boy, he was in the front of the Maison Blanche Building giving out these kooky Castro things.

MR. LIEBELER: When was this, approximately?

MR. ANDREWS: I don't remember. . . .

MR. LIEBELER: He was handing out these leaflets?

MR. ANDREWS: They were black-and-white pamphlets extolling the virtues of Castro, which around here doesn't do too good.

They have a lot of guys, Mexicanos and Cubans, that will tear your head off if they see you fooling with these things. . . .

MR. LIEBELER: Did you ever talk to this other fellow [the "Mexicano" that allegedly accompanied Oswald on his first visit to Andrews' office]?

MR. ANDREWS: Well, he talked Spanish, and all I told him was poco poco. That was it.

MR. LIEBELER: Do you speak Spanish?

MR. ANDREWS: I can understand a little. I can if you speak it. I can read it. That's about all.

MR. LIEBELER (showing picture to witness): I show you a picture which has been marked "From Pizzo Exhibit No. 453-C," and ask you if that was the same man that was in your office and the same man you say was passing out literature in the street.

MR. ANDREWS: It appears to be.

MR. LIEBELER: Would you recognize this Mexican again if you saw him?

MR. ANDREWS: Yes.

MR. LIEBELER: Do you remember telling the FBI that you wouldn't be able to recognize him again if you saw him?

MR. ANDREWS: Probably did. Been a long time. There's three people I am going to find: One of them is the real guy that killed the President; the Mexican; and Clay Bertrand.

MR. LIEBELER: Do you mean to suggest by that statement that you have considerable doubt in your mind that Oswald killed the President?

MR. ANDREWS: I know good and well he did not. With that weapon, he couldn't have been capable of making three controlled shots in that short time.

MR. LIEBELER: You are basing your opinion on reports that you have received over news media as to how many shots were fired in what period of time; is that correct?

MR. ANDREWS: I am basing my opinion on five years as an ordnanceman in the Navy. You can lean into those things, and with throwing the bolts—if I couldn't do it myself, 8 hours a day, doing this thing for a living, constantly on the range, I know this civilian couldn't do it. He might have been a sharp marksman at one time, but if you don't lean into that rifle and don't squeeze and control consistently, your brain can tell you how to do it, but you don't have the capability. . . .

MR. LIEBELER: Did there come a time after the assassination when you had some further involvement with Oswald, or at least an apparent involvement with Oswald; as I understand it?

MR. ANDREWS: No; nothing at all with Oswald. I was in Hotel Dieu, and the phone rang and a voice I recognized as Clay Bertrand asked me if I would go over to Dallas and Houston—I think—Dallas, I guess, wherever it was that this boy was being held—and defend him. I told him I was sick in the hospital. If I couldn't go, I would find somebody that could go.

MR. LIEBELER: You told him you were sick in the hospital and what?

MR. ANDREWS: That's where I was when the call came through. It came through the hospital switchboard. I said that I wasn't in shape enough to go to Dallas and defend him and I would see what I could do.

MR. LIEBELER: Now what can you tell us about this Clay Bertrand? You met him prior to that time?

MR. ANDREWS: I had seen Clay Bertrand once some time ago, probably a couple of years. He's the one who calls in behalf of gay kids normally, either to obtain bond or parole for them. I would assume that he was the one that originally sent Oswald and the gay kids, these Mexicanos, to the office because I had never seen those people before at all. They were just walk-ins.

MR. LIEBELER: You say that you think you saw Clay Bertrand some time about 2 years prior to the time you received this telephone call that you have just told us about?

MR. ANDREWS: Yes; he is mostly a voice on the phone.

MR. LIEBELER: What day did you receive the telephone call from Clay Bertrand asking you to defend Oswald?

MR. ANDREWS: I don't remember. It was a Friday or a Saturday.

MR. LIEBELER: Immediately following the assassination?

MR. ANDREWS: I don't know about that. I didn't know. Yes; I did. I guess I did because I was—they told me I was squirrelly in the hospital. . . .

MR. LIEBELER: Do you remember what time approximately that Clay Bertrand did call you?

MR. ANDREWS: I will tell you: They feed around 4:30. By the time I got fed, it was about 5 o'clock. They picked the tray up. So that's about the right time. It's around that time.

MR. LIEBELER: Now you said that after Clay Bertrand called you, you called your secretary and asked her if she remembered the Oswald file; is that correct?

MR. ANDREWS: Yes; she didn't remember Oswald at all. . . .

MR. LIEBELER: And do you recall that she said that she remembered that you called her at approximately 4 o'clock on the afternoon of November 23, 1963?

MR. ANDREWS: Yes.

MR. LIEBELER: Now have you—let's take it one step further: Do you also recall the fact that your private investigator spent most of that afternoon with you in your hospital room?

MR. ANDREWS: Yes; he was there.

MR. LIEBELER: He was there with you?

MR. ANDREWS: Yes; Preston M. Davis.

MR. LIEBELER: Do you remember approximately what time he left?

MR. ANDREWS: No.

MR. LIEBELER: Would it have been before you called your secretary or afterwards?

MR. ANDREWS: Yes.

MR. LIEBELER: Before you called?

MR. ANDREWS: No; after.

MR. LIEBELER: After you called your secretary?

MR. ANDREWS: Let's see. He wasn't there when I made the phone call. He wasn't there when Clay Bertrand called me, I am pretty sure, because he would have remembered it if I didn't.

MR. LIEBELER: You discussed it and he doesn't, in fact, remember that you received the telephone call from Clay Bertrand?

MR. ANDREWS: He wasn't there. While he was there, we received no call from Clay Bertrand or no call concerning the office or business because I would have talked to him about it.

MR. LIEBELER: You say that he left before you called your secretary?

MR. ANDREWS: I think he left around chow time, which, I think, is around 4 o'clock. I could be wrong.

MR. LIEBELER: Now after giving this time sequence that we have talked about here the consideration that I am sure you have after discussing it with the FBI, have you come up with any solution in your own mind to the apparent problems that exist here? That is to say, that your recollection is that you called your secretary after you received the call from Clay Bertrand and you called your secretary at 4 o'clock, which would indicate that you must have received the call from Clay Bertrand prior to 4 o'clock, but you did not receive the call from Mr. Bertrand while Mr. Davis was there, and he left at approximately 4 o'clock or shortly before you called your secretary, in addition to which, you first recall receiving the call from Clay Bertrand some time between 6 o'clock and 9 o'clock in the evening.

MR. ANDREWS: Well, the time factor I can't help you with. It is impossible. But I feel this: I wouldn't have called my secretary—if I couldn't get her to verify it, I would tell you that I was smoking weed. You know, sailing out on cloud 9.

MR. LIEBELER: But, in fact, she did verify the fact that you did call her?

MR. ANDREWS: Yes; I often thought it was a nightmare or a dream, but it isn't. It's just that I can't place—other than what I told Regis Kennedy and John Rice, the exact time I can't help you on. But if it hadn't been for calling her and asking her— . . .

MR. LIEBELER: Well, in any event, you are not able to clarify for us the sequence of what happened?

MR. ANDREWS: Well, the sequence of events had to be this: Davis spent the Saturday afternoon with me. He probably left just before chow, and then I ate, and the phone call came in some time after chow. I am positive it wasn't as late as 9 o'clock. I think the latest it could have been is 6, but Miss Springer says I called her some time around 4, 4:30—I don't know which. . . .

MR. LIEBELER: Now do you recall talking to an FBI agent, Regis Kennedy, and Carl L. Schlaeger on November 25?

MR. ANDREWS: I don't remember—Kennedy, yes; Schlaeger, no. I don't even know if he was in the same room. I don't think I have even seen him, much less talk to him.

MR. LIEBELER: Kennedy was; yes?

MR. ANDREWS: Yes. . . .

MR. LIEBELER: Do you remember telling him at that time that you thought that Clay Bertrand had come into the office with Oswald when Oswald had been in the office earlier last spring?

MR. ANDREWS: No; I don't remember.

MR. LIEBELER: Was Bertrand ever in the office with Oswald?

MR. ANDREWS: Not that I remember.

MR. LIEBELER: Do you have a picture in your mind of this Clay Bertrand?

MR. ANDREWS: Oh, I ran up on that rat about 6 weeks ago and he spooked, ran in the street. I would have beat him with a chain if I had caught him.

MR. LIEBELER: Let me ask you this: When I was down here in April, before I talked to you about this thing, and I was going to take your deposition at that time, but we didn't make arrangements, in your continuing discussions with the FBI, you finally came to the conclusion that Clay Bertrand was a figment of your imagination?

MR. ANDREWS: That's what the Feebees [FBI agents] put on. I know that the two Feebees are going to put these people on the street looking, and I can't find the guy, and I am not going to tie up all the agents on something that isn't that solid. I told them, "Write what you want, that I am nuts. I don't care." They were running on the time factor, and the hills were shook up plenty to get it, get it, get it. I couldn't give it to them. I have been playing cops and robbers with them. You can tell when the steam is on. They are on you like the plague. They never leave. They are like cancer. Eternal. . . .

MR. LIEBELER: Now subsequent to that time, however, you actually ran into Clay Bertrand in the street?

MR. ANDREWS: About 6 weeks ago. I am trying to think of the name of this bar. That's where this rascal bums out. I was trying to get past him so I could get a nickel in the phone and call the Feebees or John Rice, but he saw me and spooked and ran. I haven't seen him since.

MR. LIEBELER: Did you talk to him that day?

MR. ANDREWS: No; if I would have got close enough to talk to him, I would have grabbed him.

MR. LIEBELER: What does this guy look like?

MR. ANDREWS: He is about 5 feet 8 inches. Got sandy hair, blue eyes, ruddy complexion. Must weigh about 165, 170, 175. He really took off, that rascal.

MR. LIEBELER: He recognized you?

MR. ANDREWS: He had to because if he would have let me get to that phone and make the call, he would be in custody.

MR. LIEBELER: You wanted to get hold of this guy and make him available to the FBI for interview, or Mr. Rice of the Secret Service?

MR. ANDREWS: What I wanted to do and should have done is crack him in the head with a bottle, but I figured I would be a good, law-abiding citizen and call them and let them grab him, but I made the biggest mistake of the century. I should have grabbed him right there. I probably will never find him again. He has been bugging me ever since this happened.

MR. LIEBELER: Now before you ran into Clay Bertrand in the street on this day, did you have a notion in your mind what he looked like?

MR. ANDREWS: I had seen him before one time to recognize him.

MR. LIEBELER: When you saw him that day, he appeared to you as he had before when you recognized him?

MR. ANDREWS: He hasn't changed any appearance, I don't think. Maybe a little fatter, maybe a little skinnier.

MR. LIEBELER: Now I have a rather lengthy report of an interview that Mr. Kennedy had with you on December 5, 1963, in which he reports you as stating that you had a mental picture of Clay Bertrand as being approximately 6 feet 1 inch to 6 feet 2 inches in height, brown hair, well dressed.

MR. ANDREWS: Yes.

MR. LIEBELER: Now this description is different, at least in terms of height of the man, than the one you have just given us of Clay Bertrand.

MR. ANDREWS: But, you know, I don't play Boy Scouts and measure them. I have only seen this fellow twice in my life. I don't think there is that much in the description. There may be some to some artist, but to me, there isn't that much difference. Might be for you all.

MR. LIEBELER: I think you said he was 5 feet 8 inches before.

MR. ANDREWS: Well, I can't give you any better because this time I was looking for the fellow, he was sitting down. I am just estimating. You meet a guy 2 years later, you meet him, period. . . .

MR. LIEBELER: I am at a loss to understand why you told Agent Kennedy on December 5 that he was 6 feet 1 to 6 feet 2 and now you have told us that he was 5 feet 8 when at no time did you see the man standing up.

MR. ANDREWS: Because, I guess, the first time—and I am guessing now—

MR. LIEBELER: Is this fellow a homosexual, do you say?

MR. ANDREWS: Bisexual. What they call a swinging cat.

MR. LIEBELER: And you haven't seen him at any time since that day?

MR. ANDREWS: I haven't seen him since.

MR. LIEBELER: Now have you had your office searched for any records relating to Clay Bertrand?

MR. ANDREWS: Yes.

MR. LIEBELER: Have you found anything?

MR. ANDREWS: No; nothing.

MR. LIEBELER: Has this fellow Bertrand sent you business in the past?

MR. ANDREWS: Prior to—I guess the last time would be February of 1963.

MR. LIEBELER: And mostly he refers, I think you said, these gay kids, is that right?

MR. ANDREWS: Right. . . .

MR. LIEBELER: Do you have anything else that you would like to add?

MR. ANDREWS: I wish I could be more specific, that's all. This is my impression, for whatever it is worth, of Clay Bertrand: His connections with Oswald I don't know at all. I think he is a lawyer without a brief case. That's my opinion. He sends the kids different places. Whether this boy is associated with Lee Oswald or not, I don't know, but I would say, when I met him about 6 weeks ago when I ran up on him and he ran away from me, he could be running because he owes me money, or he could be running because they have been squeezing the quarter pretty good looking for him while I was in the hospital, and somebody might have passed the word he was hot and I was looking for him, but I have never been able to figure out the reason why he would call me, and the only other part of this thing that I understand, but apparently I haven't been able to communicate, is I called Monk Zelden on a Sunday at the N.O.A.C. and asked Monk if he would go over—be interested in a retainer and go over to Dallas and see about that boy. I thought I called Monk once. Monk says we talked twice. I don't remember the second. It's all one conversation with me. Only thing I do remember about it, while I was talking with Monk, he said, "Don't worry about it. Your client just got shot." That was the end of the case. Even if he was a bona fide client I never did get to him; somebody else got to him before I did. Other than that, that's the whole thing, but this boy Bertrand has been bugging me ever since. I will find him sooner or later.

MR. LIEBELER: Does Bertrand owe you money?

MR. ANDREWS: Yes; I ain't looking for him for that, I want to find out why he called me on behalf of this boy after the President was assassinated.

MR. LIEBELER: How come Bertrand owes you money?

MR. ANDREWS: I have done him some legal work that he has failed to pay the office for.

MR. LIEBELER: When was that?

MR. ANDREWS: That's in a period of years that I have—like you are Bertrand. You call up and ask me to go down and get Mr. X out. If Mr. X doesn't pay on those kinds of calls, Bertrand has a guarantee for the payment of appearance. One or two of these kids had skipped. I had to go pay the penalty, which was a lot of trouble.

MR. LIEBELER: You were going to hold Bertrand for that?

MR. ANDREWS: Yes.

MR. LIEBELER: Did Oswald appear to you to be gay?

MR. ANDREWS: You can't tell. I couldn't say. He swang with the kids. He didn't swish, but birds of a feather flock together. I don't know any squares that run with them. They may go down to look. . . .

MR. LIEBELER: I don't think I have any more questions, Mr. Andrews. I want to thank you very much for coming in and I appreciate the cooperation you have given us.

MR. ANDREWS: I only wish I could do better.

To which Clay Shaw might easily have replied, You have done quite enough.

Considering the complete lack of corroborating evidence, testimony, hearsay, or even rumors that would inject reality into Dean Andrews' accounts of his dealings with Lee Harvey Oswald and the mysterious Clay Bertrand, it is not difficult to understand that the FBI, the Secret Service and the Warren Commission all finally reached the conclusion, after attempting to locate a Clay Bertrand, that there was no such person to be found in New Orleans. There was not one supportive piece of evidence, not a record, note, check, address, phone number, not one other person, secretary, assistant, or other witness of any sort to specifically connect Lee Harvey Oswald or Clay Bertrand with Dean Andrews. Or to give flesh and blood to Clay Bertrand. Despite Andrews' alleged representation of the "gay kids," there is no record, name, address, or phone number of one of them who supposedly came in with Oswald. Although Andrews says names are an improbable method of identification, they are not to the police, who have even been known to photograph and fingerprint suspects.

The conflicting identification of Clay Bertrand—5 feet 8, 6 feet 1—is also suspect, to say the least. When Dean Andrews accounts for it by saying he did not see Clay Bertrand standing up, whereas he had stated minutes before the man had "spooked and ran in the street" and "he really took off, that rascal," it has an even tinnier ring. How does a man run without standing up?

However incredible it may have been to launch into a deadly serious manhunt for Clay Bertrand after investigating Dean Andrews as the source, Jim Garrison, who was well acquainted with Dean Adams Andrews, Jr., and the character he is, did just that.

Two members of *Life* magazine, David Chandler, a reporter based in New Orleans, and Richard Billings, were in on the early stages of Garrison's investigation when he started dragnetting the city for someone named Clay Bertrand. Assistant D.A. Andrew Sciambra was assigned to scrape the Quarter and could find no such person. Nobody could come up with Clay Bertrand. Finally the question was asked: "Do we know of anyone named *Clay?*" Someone about that time dropped the name Clay Shaw.

At least here was a person with the suspect first name, a man who was important, educated, well off, who was not married and had friends in all strata of New Orleans society, including the homosexual world. David Chandler attests to this early theory of Garrison's that Clay Shaw might just be involved, this despite the overwhelming likelihood that if someone were going to use an alias in an activity as sinister as murdering the President of the United States, he would hardly use his own first name, especially if that name were as unusual as Clay. The purpose of an alias, after all, is to avoid detection. Greta Garbo never registered as Greta Brown. She went whole hog—Harriet Brown.

Because Dean Andrews had dropped the hint of homosexuality, Garrison added that to the dossier of implication. And finally, the

District Attorney, who was wholeheartedly espousing the Cuban theory, found it additionally incriminating that Clay Shaw spoke Spanish.

While Garrison embraced those scraps of reasoning leading to Clay Shaw, he shoved aside and out of sight the notion that Clay Shaw did not come close to fitting either one of Dean Andrews' descriptions of the mysterious Clay Bertrand. He also did not choose to complicate his hypothesis with possible motive on the part of Clay Shaw. Nor did he entertain the idea that if Dean Andrews, as Andrews later claimed, were attempting to protect a client, he would hardly be careless enough to give the client's true first name.

So in December of 1966 Clay Shaw was brought in for questioning and asked if he'd known Lee Harvey Oswald or David Ferrie or if he might ever have used the name of Clay Bertrand. When Shaw responded in the negative and apparently was not unnerved at being questioned, Garrison, according to Chandler, told his staff to forget about Shaw. A few weeks later, when Richard Billings inquired of Garrison as to the identity of Clay Bertrand, the District Attorney supposedly replied that he was really Clay Shaw but added he didn't think it was important.

David Ferrie was still the prime suspect. If Garrison truly suspected Ferrie and really believed Shaw was Bertrand and that both of them had known Oswald—although no one else at this time attested to it—one wonders why he never had the two men confront each other. It seems to have been his *modus operandi* that suspects were never linked until one was dead. Thus Ferrie was accused by the D.A. of having trained Oswald in the use of the rifle and in assassination techniques but Oswald was dead, so there was no danger of a confrontation there. And Clay Shaw (as Bertrand) was accused of having known Oswald and of helping him secure legal advice but again Oswald was dead—no problem. But, at the time, both Ferrie and Shaw were alive and well and living in New Orleans, and they were never brought together. Ferrie was not to live for long, though.

Despite the District Attorney's persistent efforts, all corroborative side roads were either petering out or coming to abrupt dead ends by February of 1967. Many people believe the investigation, which had been conducted in secret without notation in the press, would have expired if it had not been discovered at that time and seen the light of newsprint.

A band of reporters from the *States-Item*—Rosemary James, Jack Dempsey, Dave Snyder and Jack Wardlaw—began tracking down what project might possibly be occupying Jim Garrison's attention at that time. When Rosemary James, who had maintained good working relations with Garrison, asked him straight out, "Are you conducting an investigation of the Kennedy assassination?" she claims Garrison replied, "I will neither confirm nor deny that." To a reporter that is tantamount to saying, Yes, but you'll have to scrounge around for your own details. If he had not been conducting an investigation, he would have said no. If he had been seriously immersed in an investigation and wanted to avoid publicity at the time, he would likewise have said no, it may reasonably be argued.

Garrison's answer only spurred the reporters to a deeper dig. In Orleans Parish, the D.A.'s expense vouchers are a matter of public record and these showed up $8,000 which had recently been spent on trips to Dallas and Miami, Miami being important anti-Castro territory to be raked over by the District Attorney. These expenses, together with several leaks from the District Attorney's staff, enabled the local reporters to put together enough information to break the news in the press. Rosemary James wrote up the story and went to Garrison's office, where she handed him the copy on February 16, 1967. She claims he looked at the first page, saw what it was about and handed it back to her, repeating what he'd told her before: "I will neither confirm nor deny it." At no time, she says, was she or anyone else on the paper asked to withhold the story.

The next day, Friday, February 17, the story broke in the papers and within twenty-four hours New Orleans was besieged by the national and world press. Garrison did not call the paper or exhibit signs of anger as the hurricane eye of public and press interest swept in on the city that weekend. But the following Monday he not only excluded reporters from the local papers from a press conference he held at a nearby motel, but asserted that irresponsible and premature newspaper publicity had deeply hampered his investigation and might even endanger the lives of some of the principals involved. He maintained that arrests had been only weeks away but now, because of this most unfortunate leak, they would be months away. He claimed to be outraged by the local newspapers' recklessness, and said he would grant no more interviews but continue the rest of his probe in utmost secrecy, even if he had to resort to using borrowed or contributed funds in order to bypass checking of the public vouchers.

David Ferrie was supposedly kept under protective custody at a hotel in New Orleans for two days after the story appeared. He had contacted newsman Dave Snyder on his own the night the story broke, telling him he'd been harassed and followed. He called the investigation a big joke and added that because of the trip he'd made to Texas the evening of the assassination he'd been tagged as a getaway pilot. Ferrie indicated he might just launch his own investigation into the assassination. When the D.A.'s office was questioned about David Ferrie, the word was given out that he was not important. This was not the word for long.

On February 21, David Ferrie returned to his apartment. Late that night, a reporter from the Washington *Post,* George Lardner, interviewed him and left at 4 A.M. About eight hours later, David Ferrie's nude and lifeless body was found under a sheet in his bed. By this time, many of the national and foreign press had taken their lead from Jim Garrison, folded up their typewriters, and skipped out of town. The tragic and most untimely death of David Ferrie brought most of them flying back to the scene.

Coroner Dr. Nicholas Chetta first placed the time of death at before midnight, but after George Lardner came forth with the time sequence of his interview, it was changed to shortly after 4 A.M. Dr. Chetta said death resulted from a berry aneurysm, a weak spot in a blood vessel that suddenly blows out, causing a cerebral hemorrhage. He attributed David Ferrie's death to natural causes, ruling out murder: if the aneurysm had been caused by an external blow, there would have to be tissue damage and none was present. He also intimated it would be an unlikely way in which to commit suicide (i.e., by causing the blood pressure to rise sufficiently to effect a blowout). An autopsy also revealed no evidence of drugs which might have been used to induce such a condition; added to this was Ferrie's own doctor's report that he already had a history of high blood pressure.

None of this discouraged Jim Garrison. He heralded David Ferrie's death as suicide, interpreting a somewhat murky and bitter letter he'd written to a friend shortly before his death as a suicide note. This version of Ferrie's death naturally insinuated that he had taken his life because of some harbored guilt.

Once dead, the man was no longer insignificant. The very day of Ferrie's death, Garrison suddenly bestowed upon this unfortunate person the title of "one of history's most important individuals." He went on to claim that his office knew without a doubt that Ferrie was involved in events culminating in the murder of the President, and despite the fact that Ferrie had been under consideration for two months and had been returned to his apartment from custodial guarding only the day before, Garrison maintained that at a staff meeting that very morning, the morning David Ferrie's body was discovered, the man's arrest had been decided upon. "Apparently we waited too long," Jim Garrison said.

14

A Star Is Born

The demise of David Ferrie in New Orleans heralded the arrival of another man headed for instant notoriety. A 25-year-old insurance salesman named Perry Raymond Russo quickly surfaced in Baton Rouge and claimed to have information about David Ferrie that might or might not be of importance.

Russo contacted the Baton Rouge news media on his own, saying he had written to Jim Garrison in New Orleans, offering to divulge whatever knowledge he had of David Ferrie, whom he had known in New Orleans. Russo also taped a television interview with James Kemp of WDSU-TV (New Orleans) and claimed that David Ferrie had talked in general terms about how easy it would be to assassinate a President of the United States, but did not specify Kennedy. Ferrie used to joke about how it could be accomplished, Russo said, because the President was in public view and more or less unprotected so much of the time. He ended with "And that was all of the conversation during the summer [of 1963]." Russo also said on the taped interview that he had never heard of Oswald until the television accounts of the assassination.

The next day Andrew Sciambra was sent to Baton Rouge to talk with Russo. The Assistant D.A. spent several hours with the young man and, according to a 3,500-word memo dated February 27 that Sciambra later wrote, he showed Russo various pictures that the young insurance salesman identified as likenesses of David Ferrie; Sergio Arcacha Smith, an anti-Castro Cuban-in-exile leader; and Clay Shaw, whom Russo said he thought he had seen twice in New Orleans but gave no indication of ever meeting. According to the Sciambra memo, Russo did not give Clay Shaw a name. The young man also stopped at a photograph of Lee Harvey Oswald. He thought the picture might be of the man he knew as a room-mate of David Ferrie's, except the person he was thinking of had a beard and was usually messy-looking. He toyed with the photo-

graph by sketching a beard on the face, and this led him to entertain the possibility that he might have met the man at Ferrie's. He
added that the more he thought about it, "The more the name
Leon really rings a bell."

The next day, February 26, in the presence of Richard Billings
of *Life*, Sciambra gave Garrison an oral report of his interview
with Russo. Garrison ordered a truth test for Russo using sodium
pentothal. The following morning—the same date that appeared
on Sciambra's memo—Perry Russo was given sodium pentothal at
Mercy Hospital by Dr. Nicholas Chetta, the coroner who ruled
David Ferrie had died of natural causes. Russo, under the influence of the drug, was questioned at length by Sciambra. No
transcript of this interview is known to exist, unfortunately, but
Sciambra wrote a memorandum on it as well as on his interview
with Russo at Baton Rouge. Those familiar with the report have
stated the name Bertrand was first mentioned by Sciambra. That
evening, Richard Billings had dinner with Russo, Sciambra, and
Garrison while Sciambra went over the sodium pentothal session,
telling Russo he had identified a tall man with white hair as
"Bertrand," a man he'd been introduced to at David Ferrie's
apartment. Richard Billings has reported that this was news to
Russo, who did not recall ever meeting anyone named Bertrand.
Garrison made an attempt to smooth over this discrepancy by
explaining that the taking of truth serum undoubtedly was a
mind-rattling experience and, besides aiding Russo, it undoubtedly confused him somewhat, too.

The following day, Russo was taken to Clay Shaw's house at
1313 Dauphine Street, where, posing as a Mutual of Omaha
insurance salesman, he got a good look at Shaw.

The next day, March 1, 1967, a day of what Garrison referred to
as "a command decision," Clay Shaw was summoned to the District Attorney's office and, after being questioned for hours, after
reporters and Perry Russo had been permitted to watch him
through a one-way mirror, was finally arrested and charged with
this monumental crime. Garrison also sought a warrant before one
of the Criminal Court judges to search Clay Shaw's home, stating
he had a confidential informant who attested to a meeting between David W. Ferrie, Lee Harvey Oswald and Clay Shaw (alias
Clay Bertrand) in which they discussed the murder of President
Kennedy—the same confidential informant who, the day before,

had indicated he had never met anyone named Clay Bertrand. Even Perry Russo was later given to muse over this turn of events in the D.A.'s office when he said, "They asked me a lot of questions. I could figure out what they wanted to know."

March 1 was also the first day of a series of hypnotic sessions Russo underwent with Dr. Esmond Fatter, at the request of the District Attorney. This is how the transcript reads in part:

DR. FATTER: Perry, I am going to ask you a date, as you see that date on the television screen, lift your right index finger—all right, I wonder what date you see?

PERRY RUSSO: September 16.

DR. FATTER: I wonder what year, Perry?

PERRY RUSSO: No year.

DR. FATTER: Look at the television screen, and a picture will come on and when the picture becomes very vivid to you and the program begins, lift your right index finger and if you care to, you can tell me about that picture.

PERRY RUSSO: I see Dave Ferrie just sitting around, just talking and he asked me if I wanted a cup of coffee or a glass of water or a Coke. I wanted water from the kitchen and ice box.

DR. FATTER: Continue looking at that television program and tell me more about it.

PERRY RUSSO: Dave and I were sitting and he was on the big sofa and I was on the small sofa and he has on a white shirt and baggy pants. He asked me if I had registered in school.

DR. FATTER: Perry, look around that room. I wonder, is there a calendar on the wall?

PERRY RUSSO: Yes.

DR. FATTER: And what month is on the calendar?

PERRY RUSSO: September.

DR. FATTER: And what year, Perry?

PERRY RUSSO: 1963. . . .

DR. FATTER: Continue looking at that television picture and notice the news cast— The president, President Kennedy, is coming to New Orleans and as you look describe it to us.

PERRY RUSSO: I am at school and it is late. I was going to see President Kennedy and I remember I ran up a long ramp, an elevated incline, and I am with AL SAIZON, and we are just waiting and Kennedy hasn't arrived. I figure we were late and we just stood and waited, and he drove up on the ramp with sirens and started his speech.

DR. FATTER: Who is that white haired gentleman that is over there looking at President Kennedy?

PERRY RUSSO: He is either with the New Orleans Police Department or government because my friend remarked about it. He said that he was the only one not looking at the president—he was looking at us. Then Al went over to the exit. Kennedy was getting ready to finish. Al went to the exit which is like an airplane hangar and I stayed because I was interested in Kennedy. He talked a while to the boy and this boy left and the Secret Service men went and talked to these other two men. All the Secret Service men had on loud coats.

DR. FATTER: How about this white haired gentleman?

PERRY RUSSO: That was him.

DR. FATTER: Do you know his name?

PERRY RUSSO: No.

DR. FATTER: We are looking at the television screen again and when it is clear again your finger will lift up. Study the picture and you are in an automobile driving into a service station. Tell me about that program on the television.

PERRY RUSSO: I had trouble with my car because it wouldn't start at a red light and I didn't have any money except $4 or $5 and I just drove in and an old friend of mine came up and he said, "You remember me?" and I said yes. These boys fixed the tire, took the battery out, charged the battery, and I had to pay $2.50 and I left.

DR. FATTER: Tell me about the white haired man sitting in that automobile over there.

PERRY RUSSO: He is sitting with Dave and they are just talking and I interrupted their conversation and he thought it was rude and he left. He was sitting next to Dave and I yelled to Dave about getting the boys to hustle, I had to go because he was very ill at ease because Dave and I were suspicious of each other.

DR. FATTER: About what, Perry?

PERRY RUSSO: He told me he was going to kill me.

DR. FATTER: Why, Perry?

PERRY RUSSO: Because I broke up he and Al. . . .

DR. FATTER: Take a look at the white haired man again in the automobile and when you see him, lift your finger up— Did you ever see that man before?

PERRY RUSSO: Yes—he was a friend of Dave's.

DR. FATTER: Where did you see him before?

PERRY RUSSO: At the Nashville Wharf. . . .

DR. FATTER: Continue to go deeper and deeper to sleep. You are comfortable and blank— Look at the television screen again, picture and visualize and your finger will lift again when it is clear. That is right. A picture is going to come on and you are in Ferrie's apartment on Louisiana Avenue Parkway. Would you look at that picture and tell us the story that you see?

PERRY RUSSO: He introduced me to his roommate who was a kook!

DR. FATTER: And, Perry, I wonder what his roommate looked like. Describe him for me.

PERRY RUSSO: Looked like he would be about as tall as I and he had sandy brown hair, dirty white shirt and dirty, dirty, dirty, dirty—

DR. FATTER: And Perry, his name was—

PERRY RUSSO: Leon.

DR. FATTER: His last name?

PERRY RUSSO: Oswald.

DR. FATTER: That is right, continue looking at the picture. Who else is in the apartment?

PERRY RUSSO: Nobody, just me and him.

DR. FATTER: Just you and—Ferrie?

PERRY RUSSO: And Oswald.

DR. FATTER: That's right, Perry, keep looking at the picture and tell me what happens.

PERRY RUSSO: He introduced me and we talked and Ferrie came in and served coffee and I didn't take any, and the roommate was sitting on the piano. It was closed and he just sat and Ferrie and Leon didn't seem to get along that night.

DR. FATTER: They had differences of opinion?

PERRY RUSSO: Yes.

DR. FATTER: What about, Perry?

PERRY RUSSO: Dave never stated but I got the idea it was about a boy Dave was sleeping with and Leon made some remarks about it and Leon objected to the boy being there.

DR. FATTER: That's right, continue to go deeper and deeper—Now, picture that television screen again, Perry, and it is a picture of Ferrie's apartment and there are several people in there and there is a white haired man. Tell me about it.

PERRY RUSSO: We are having a party and I came in and everybody is drinking beer. There are about ten of us and I am there, the roommate, Dave, some young boys and some other friends of Dave's and I was with Sandra. . . .

DR. FATTER: Tell me more about that picture.

PERRY RUSSO: Well, there is a record player in the middle of the room and it is playing sounds, not music—Spanish and a guy is making a speech and everybody laughed.

DR. FATTER: And what did he say?

PERRY RUSSO: He was speaking Spanish, sorta like Hitler. He got real excited.

DR. FATTER: And how about the white haired man—

PERRY RUSSO: That is a friend of Dave's.

DR. FATTER: His name?

PERRY RUSSO: CLEM BERTRAND.

DR. FATTER: Had you seen him before?

PERRY RUSSO: Yes, I saw him at the Nashville Street Wharf.

DR. FATTER: I wonder where else—

PERRY RUSSO: Nowhere.

DR. FATTER: Is that the same white haired gentleman in the service station?

PERRY RUSSO: I don't remember the service station.

DR. FATTER: I wonder who that is sitting on the sofa with the rifle?

PERRY RUSSO: Leon.

DR. FATTER: What is he doing with the rifle, Perry?

PERRY RUSSO: He always had a rifle, he liked guns and many times he would have a rifle. . . .

DR. FATTER: Continue looking at the television program and Clay, the white haired man is going to come into the room. You are at Ferrie's apartment and there are many people. Who did he introduce Clay to?

PERRY RUSSO: He introduced me—me to everybody.

DR. FATTER: How did he introduce you and exactly what did he say?

PERRY RUSSO: Well, when I walked in everybody was sitting

around. Just voices. Everybody in the house was laughing and Dave said this is my friend Perry who lives on Elysian Fields, and he introduced me to everybody.

DR. FATTER: Make believe you are Ferrie introducing Perry around.

PERRY RUSSO: I am Perry Russo— I am Perry Russo— I am Perry Russo— I am Perry Russo— . . .

DR. FATTER: Tell me where was Bertrand?

PERRY RUSSO: Sitting on the semi-sofa.

DR. FATTER: I wonder, is this the white haired man?

PERRY RUSSO: Yes.

DR. FATTER: Could you count the Cubans that are in the room for me, Perry.

PERRY RUSSO: Four.

DR. FATTER: I wonder—are they pro-Castro?

PERRY RUSSO: I don't know, I didn't talk to them.

DR. FATTER: Anti-Castro?

PERRY RUSSO: I didn't talk to them . . . they are in green fatigues, one in khaki pants and he is short and strong and hefty and has on a T-shirt—one maybe 22 or 25 and he is dressed in dungarees and checked yellow and red and blue lots of colors in his shirt and there are two other men. . . .

DR. FATTER: Look over there, Perry, tell me what Leon is doing.

PERRY RUSSO: He is sitting beside the piano—just sitting. He does the same thing. I don't like him because he doesn't like me. He told Dave the first time I saw him in front of me—why did he have to bring every little prick off the street in the house and I told Dave I wanted to go home.

DR. FATTER: Let your mind go completely blank, Perry—see that television screen again, it is very vivid—now notice the picture on the screen—there will be Bertrand, Ferrie and Oswald and they are going to discuss a very important matter and there is another man and girl there and they are talking about assassinating somebody. Look at it and describe it to me.

PERRY RUSSO: We are sitting around on the sofas and I came in late. Dave offered me a drink and I said no I didn't want anything, and I sat down and played like I belonged. I didn't know what was going on. Dave went and got drinks for everybody—all the drinks were coffee and they resumed the conversation and I was just sitting. They planned to assassinate President Kennedy.

DR. FATTER: Tell us exactly what everybody said, Perry.

PERRY RUSSO: Dave paced the floor back and forth and he talked and talked and told them if they were going to get the President they would fly to Mexico or Cuba or to Brazil and Clem said they would not go to Mexico and Brazil—it involved too much gas expense and the cooperation of Mexican authorities and that wouldn't be possible. Leon snapped at Bertrand and said leave him alone. I guess Ferrie and Leon had made up and Leon said leave him alone because he is right because if he said we go, we can do it. It doesn't make any difference, Japan or Mexico.

DR. FATTER: I wonder what they said about Dallas, Perry?

PERRY RUSSO: Nothing about Dallas. Ferrie had a bunch of newspaper clippings about one inch thick all of them about Kennedy—Kennedy's picture or Kennedy's name in the headline. Had rubber bands and clips on them and carried them around with him.

DR. FATTER: I wonder if Ferrie ever told you that he was going to assassinate the president in Dallas?

PERRY RUSSO: He never told me that, he told me he was going to assassinate the president and I laughed at him, but I never laughed in front of his friends.

DR. FATTER: Is Clay Bertrand the same person that you saw in the District Attorney's Office and the same person you went to sell insurance to yesterday, Perry?

PERRY RUSSO: Dave never took me to his house.

DR. FATTER: You went to his house yesterday to sell insurance with somebody from the District Attorney's Office, Perry. Is that the same man that was in with Ferrie and Oswald and the same man that was at the wharf?

PERRY RUSSO: I don't understand—Dave never showed me any places like that.

DR. FATTER: Now go to sleep, Perry . . . And, now, Perry, I want you to see that television screen again and when you visualize it and it is clear you will see the face of a white haired man. You met him yesterday when you went to his apartment. This is yesterday, the last day of February. You picture him in your mind. Have you seen him before? Have you seen him on several occasions and what were these occasions, Perry?

PERRY RUSSO: He was Dave's friend and I saw him at Dave's house.

DR. FATTER: Where else did you see him, Perry?

PERRY RUSSO: I saw him later at Dave's and Al's service station.

DR. FATTER: Where else, Perry?

PERRY RUSSO: I saw him at the Nashville Street Wharf.

DR. FATTER: What is his name, Perry?

PERRY RUSSO: CLAY BERTRAND.

In connection with such a transcript, it is interesting to note the comments of Dr. Herbert Spiegel, Assistant Clinical Professor of Psychiatry and Director of courses in Hypnosis at the College of Physicians and Surgeons, Columbia University, and Assistant Attending Psychiatrist, Presbyterian Hospital, New York. These comments are backed up by Dr. Jay Katz, Professor (Adjunct) of Law and Psychiatry at Yale University and Attending Psychiatrist at the Yale New Haven Medical Center. These are taken from a sworn affidavit Dymond planned to use in the trial:

In recent years, I have become especially interested in the study of the relationship of hypnosis and hypnotizability to credibility. I recently conducted an experiment demonstrating how a fiction can be implanted into a normal person via hypnosis. Even out of the trance state, he believed it with the conviction of a true fact. . . . Upon the basis of my training, study and experience I conclude the following: Hypnosis is a state of intense and sensitive interpersonal relatedness characterized by nonrational submission and by relative abandonment of executive (ego) control. Heightened suggestibility (i.e., inclination to believe what others desire him to believe) is perhaps the most salient characteristic of the state of hypnosis. . . . There is a close correlation between a subject's suggestibility in a normal, non-hypnotic state and his hypnotizability. Persons who are not hypnotizable tend to be the least suggestible element of the population. Persons who may be induced into a deep trance tend to be among the most suggestible. . . . False ideas and beliefs can be implanted upon the mind of a subject who is in a trance without any intent on the part of the questioner to implant such beliefs, if the subject *thinks* that the examiner or hypnotizer desires him to entertain such beliefs or if such beliefs seem to him to be necessary to support other beliefs or to please the hypnotizer or whomever he represents. The ease with which such implantation can occur varies with the hypnotizability of the subject. . . . Induction of a trance may alter the relationship between the subject and the hypnotizer so that the subject is more open to suggestion by the hypnotizer (or one whom the subject identifies with him) in subsequent interrogations outside the trance state. . . . Once a subject is hypnotized he may continue to be in a trance for months thereafter, although he may not appear to an untrained observer to be in a trance. The subject may also have a previous trance reactivated months after he has, according to all normal criteria, come completely out of the previous trance. Compliance with a so-called "post-hypnotic suggestion" is an example of such trance reactivation. It may occur long after the initial trance and will often not be apparent to the observer.

The preceding made me go back over Russo's transcript and zero in on some of the leading questions: "Who is that white haired gentleman that is over there looking at President Kennedy?" "How about this white haired gentleman?" "Do you know his name?" (To which the first answer, oddly enough on the very day Clay Shaw was arrested, was "No.") "Tell me about the white haired man sitting in that automobile over there." "Take a look at the white haired man again in the automobile and when you see him, lift your finger up— Did you ever see that man before?" "Now, picture that television screen again, Perry, and it is a picture of Ferrie's apartment and there are several people in there and there is a white haired man. Tell me about it." "And how about the white haired man—" To say nothing of this most leading remark by Dr. Fatter: "Let your mind go completely blank, Perry—see that television screen again, it is very vivid . . . there will be Bertrand, Ferrie and Oswald and they are going to discuss a very important matter and there is another man and girl there and they are talking about assassinating somebody. Look at it and describe it to me."

It is unnerving to realize the name Clay is first used by the doctor, not Russo, who spoke of "Clem." The first mention of talk of the assassination also came from the doctor, not Perry Russo.

The District Attorney in Louisiana can bring a case to trial merely by filing a bill of information against the accused or else by presenting his evidence to the grand jury in secret and securing an indictment. Jim Garrison chose another and most unusual manner in which to present his case and obtain the official go-ahead for a full-scale trial. Garrison requested a preliminary hearing. Such a hearing is usually requested by the defense and is held for the purpose of determining whether or not the state has sufficient evidence to hold a defendant over for trial; it is sometimes helpful to the defense in giving that team an insight into exactly what the state's case consists of in the way of important witnesses and incriminating evidence. Rarely is this course of action requested by the state.

But there were few in New Orleans who doubted the District Attorney's reasons for desiring a preliminary hearing. It is, in effect, a trial, with only the state presenting its side of the case. Although the defense is permitted to cross-examine, they are not allowed to put their own witnesses on the stand. It is not only open to the public but, obviously, to the press. For pure drama, such a forum could hardly be surpassed. It provided Garrison with the means of reaching the widest possible audience and of having the press and public hear only his side of things; it would make his name a household word throughout the country, if not the world; it would stimulate phenomenal interest in the case, enough to flush out other witnesses, either those who might have real knowledge of a plot or that sad peripheral fringe of humanity who want so badly to get in on the act, to somehow, some way, achieve importance and whose need to do this enables them to perform lobotomies on their conscience.

The preliminary hearing was scheduled for March 14, 1967. Judge Bernard J. Bagert, presiding judge of the Criminal District Court, did not want the sole responsibility of judgment in this highly inflammable matter, so he appointed two other judges to sit with him and share the burden of ruling. He chose a mixed bag in the form of Judge Matthew S. Braniff, a political ally of Garrison, and Judge Malcolm O'Hara, who had tried to bump Garrison from office by running (unsuccessfully) against him in the previous election.

The preliminary hearing was as dramatic as any trial could hope to be. The press, both national and foreign, had converged upon New Orleans; the courtroom was standing room only. The cat was not yet out of the bag and everyone wondered who it was going to be. Although Perry Raymond Russo had made his presence known in his press interviews, he had disavowed knowing Oswald and given no indication he had knowledge of anyone besides David Ferrie, so it was not until he was called up in open court that he was unmasked as the surprise witness for the state against Clay Shaw.

Russo was asked to identify the man he had been introduced to as Clem Bertrand, the man he said he'd heard conspire with Ferrie and Oswald to kill the President at a party at Ferrie's apartment sometime in September of 1963. In a dramatic bit of courtroom play, Perry Raymond Russo left the witness stand, walked to Clay Shaw and held his hand over Shaw's head.

Now an entire story of conspiracy was spun out as Russo claimed that an assorted group of Spanish-speaking types were in attendance and that he, Russo, had arrived at the party with a girl named Sandra Moffitt and a friend, Niles "Lefty" Peterson. Although Russo was vague about the exact date, how they got to the party, how and when his friends left, he was certain of one thing: After a while everyone had gone but Ferrie, Oswald, Bertrand (Shaw) and Perry Russo, who had stuck around for no other reason than to wait for a ride home. It was not clear why he had not left with his friends, especially Sandra Moffitt, who was a girl friend of his. When this select group was left alone in Ferrie's apartment—two now dead, two alive—the conversation soon got around to talk of assassinating the President, triangulation of gunfire, means of escape for the assassin and alibis for the others involved.

When cross-examined by Irvin Dymond, Russo was asked how it was possible that three men would permit a discussion such as the one he testified to, to be overheard by a perfect stranger, as far as two of them, Oswald and Bertrand, were concerned. Perry Russo replied that Oswald had voiced a brief objection but David Ferrie took care of that by saying, "Forget him, he is all right." That weighty amount of reassurance apparently assuaged the fears of the co-conspirators and they jumped back into the assassination talk. Questioned further about the unsuspicious nature of these alleged assassins, Russo testified that none of the three ever warned or even suggested that he keep quiet about this dark meeting. Asked why he had not reported this sinister conversation to the FBI or anyone else, Russo said that at the time "I was involved with school, which was more pressing to me." He also made a statement of personal policy, which he had apparently by this time altered drastically. To wit: "I never push myself off on anybody." Later on, after the assassination, he claimed he did not give his information to the Warren Commission or any other agency because they decreed Oswald had been the lone assassin. Then he added, "I had no reason to disagree with these people. They are professionals."

Irvin Dymond also brought up Russo's taped television interview of February 24, before he'd spoken to anyone from the District Attorney's office, in which he had stated he'd never heard of Oswald until the television reports of the assassination. Asked about this discrepancy, Russo explained that he had known a *Leon* Oswald, who had sported a light growth of whiskers, and added, "I did not, myself, honestly know a Lee Harvey Oswald." When Dymond displayed shock that Russo had known a Leon Oswald, that he'd identified a photograph of Lee Harvey Oswald as Ferrie's roommate and even then he had not realized it was the same Oswald, Russo stuck to his story that he had not positively identified the picture until after a six-hour beard-sketching session in the District Attorney's office and added that the picture he'd had in mind of Lee Harvey Oswald was not positively identical with that of the Leon Oswald he'd known. This, despite the wide publicity given Lee Harvey Oswald's New Orleans upbringing and his 1963 pre-assassination stay there.

Russo remained a stickler for detail to the very end. When Dymond got him to admit he'd read of the District Attorney's investigation, which included David W. Ferrie, and suggested that Russo had waited to come forward until after Ferrie's death so there would be no one to contradict his story, Russo actually said that for all he knew, the David Ferrie he'd known in New Orleans might have been one other than the David W. Ferrie the D.A.'s office was investigating in *their* efforts to solve an allegedly New Orleans–based conspiracy. Russo capped this off with "I never knew his middle initial was W."

During the hearing Russo testified that the last time he'd seen Oswald in New Orleans had been in October in Ferrie's apartment. To this Dymond inquired, "Are you aware that Oswald left New Orleans on September 25, 1963, on his way to Houston and Mexico, and that he never returned?"

The prosecution objected to this line of questioning and when Dymond indicated he would present in evidence the Warren Report, which so stated, Judge Bagert asked, "You're going to introduce the Warren Report?" Yes, that was Dymond's idea. "You must be kidding," Judge Bagert cracked, reportedly earning a laugh from the audience and smiles from his co-judges. Dymond was quickly set straight that the judges wanted none of the Warren Report introduced in any way, shape or form. The New York *Post* commented in its coverage of the hearing that this "marked the first time that a court in this country has held the Warren Report to be without legal foundation and unacceptable as a matter of fact." And so it was.

Despite the illogicality of much of his testimony, it should be noted that Perry Raymond Russo proved to be an unshakable witness. From those who observed his performance on the stand he might not have been an intellectual but he exhibited a bright, quick mind and a sturdy talent for slipping out of a direct yes or no answer into a more general and highly verbalized response.

There was only one other witness placed on the stand to testify to Shaw's association with any of the conspirators. This was Vernon Bundy, a 29-year-old Negro narcotics addict, who was currently languishing in the Parish Prison for parole violation. There was apparently great dissension in the ranks of the D.A.'s office about putting him on the stand. From all reports, Charles Ward, Garrison's right-hand Assistant District Attorney at that time, objected strongly to using him as a witness, as did others. Garrison, however, trotted him out anyway. Bundy's story amounted to this: In the summer of 1963 he had gone out to the seawall on Lake Pontchartrain to give himself a heroin fix. Although the beach was virtually deserted he soon saw two men meet extremely near him and begin a conversation. Bundy identified one man as Clay Shaw and the other, after looking at a photograph, as Lee Harvey Oswald. Shaw, it appeared, gave Oswald a bundle of money, they exchanged a few words and left, each going his separate way. Bundy walked to where the two men had been standing and picked up a "Fair Play for Cuba" leaflet, which he said had fallen out of Oswald's pocket, and wrapped his dope kit up in it. (It had been established that Oswald had handed out similar leaflets during the summer of 1963 in New Orleans.)

Perry Russo and Vernon Bundy shared one thing in common in regard to their testimony: Neither one had ever told his story to anyone before this time.

When the four-day hearing ended, the three judges required very little time to announce their ruling that Jim Garrison had presented sufficient evidence to bring Clay Shaw to trial.

Although a preliminary hearing should have no real probative value in determining the guilt or innocence of the accused, this one, because of its widely sensational press coverage and the sea of interest it engendered, shaped up as a Garrison victory and cast an even darker shadow upon the figure of the accused. The District Attorney took the added step of going before the grand jury, presenting essentially the same evidence, and receiving from them a formal indictment on March 22. Now, in the event the case against Clay Shaw eventually fell on its face, Jim Garrison was less likely to be sued for false arrest since his actions were backed up by the ruling of the three judges and a grand jury indictment.

A local television reporter told me a story illustrating the carnival atmosphere spawned by the sensational preliminary hearing. A middle-aged woman with her young daughter, aged seven or eight, and dressed in the Little Bopeep style of early Shirley Temple, complete with long curls, pinafore and patent leather shoes, kept pushing her way through the crowds outside the courthouse, trying to engineer an appearance for her daughter in front of a television camera, any television camera. This anxious mother was warded off until she finally could stand it no longer. Marching up to a reporter, she said, "I have something of great interest for the television viewing public." She was quickly reminded that the camera crews were engaged in covering an event of great national importance, having to do with the assassination of President Kennedy. "That's exactly why my child and I are here," snapped the woman. "My little daughter has prepared a Child's Version of the Warren Report and she would like to recite it for all the people out in television land!"

And a little child shall lead them.

PHOTOGRAPHS

Stars and Featured Players

Grateful acknowledgment is hereby
made to the following studios and
photographers for permission to use
the pictures numbered as shown:
Black Star, 18 (Flip Schulke) ; Mickey
Demoruelle, 37; Greystone
Photographers, 12, 13; John Messina,
5, 11, 15, 17, 25, 27, 28, 29, 31, 32; The
Times-Picayune Pub. Co., 9, 16 (P. A.
Hughes) , 19, 20 (Ralph Uribe) , 21
(P. H. Guarisco) , 22, 23 (C. F.
Bennett) , 24 (J. W. Guillot) , 30
(Ralph Uribe) , 34 (P. H. Guarisco) ,
35; Leo Touchet, 1; UPI Telephoto,
33; Wide World Photos, 2, 3, 4, 6, 7,
8, 10, 14, 26, 36, 38.

1 ▷

The Defendant: Clay L. Shaw

"I was always the one who thought
Kafka rather overstated things. . . .
Boy, have I changed, what a fellow
feeling I have for K. now!"

2

◁ The Prosecutor: Jim Garrison, District Attorney of New Orleans

"The government's handling of the investigation of John Kennedy's murder was a fraud. It was the greatest fraud in the history of our country. It probably was the greatest fraud ever perpetrated in the history of humankind."

3

Left to right: District Attorney Jim Garrison, Assistant District Attorney Andrew Sciambra, Assistant District Attorney James Alcock

JIM GARRISON: "Who has the arrogance and the brass to prevent the people from seeing that evidence? Who indeed? The one man who has profited most from the assassination—your friendly President, Lyndon Johnson."

4, 5
Jim Garrison

"I really dislike public life. I don't enjoy backslapping, pumping hands, making public appearances or making speeches. . . . In fact, I've avoided it almost completely for two years now."

6

Jim Garrison
"Darnit, we lose one case and the next morning I'm called on to resign."

7

"I am opposed in the race [for re-election] by Harry Connick, Ross Scaccia, Charles Ward and the New Orleans *Times-Picayune,* the *States-Item,* the New York *Times,* the federal government, the CIA, the FBI . . ."

8

"To have wisdom, you must suffer. You must be a victim of the system."

9
The Prosecution Team: (left to right) Assistant D.A.s Andrew "Moo-Moo" Sciambra, James Alcock, Alvin Oser

10
Assistant D.A. James Alcock
"I wanted to win, naturally, and I thought that we'd put on—I thought we'd done everything we could. Let's put it that way."

11
Assistant D.A. Andrew "Moo-Moo" Sciambra
"There have always been leaks in the D.A.'s office—at least ever since I've been there."

The Defense Team: (top to bottom) Edward Wegmann, William Wegmann, Salvatore Panzeca

12
Edward Wegmann

"We kept the conversation to a minimum because I had been warned the room might be bugged."

13
William Wegmann

"It [sodium pentathol] allows a person to talk freely but there are indications that the person does not always tell the truth."

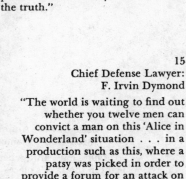

15 ▷
Chief Defense Lawyer:
F. Irvin Dymond

"The world is waiting to find out whether you twelve men can convict a man on this 'Alice in Wonderland' situation . . . in a production such as this, where a patsy was picked in order to provide a forum for an attack on the Warren Commission and the Warren Report."

14
Salvatore Panzeca

"I told him [Clay Shaw] not even to say hello or goodbye to anyone."

16

The Jury: (front row, left to right) Bob Burlet (second alternate), John J. Beilman, Jr. (first alternate), Larry Morgan, Sidney Hebert, Jr., Harold Bainum, Jr., Warren Humphrey, David Powe, Peter Tatum; (back row, left to right) Irvin Mason, Oliver Schultz, William Ricks, Jr., Charles Ordes, Herbert Kenison, James O'Quinn

Judge Edward A. Haggerty, Jr.

"The Warren Commission were told to go out and produce this and get this. And anything that didn't correspond to what they were told—if they got it, it was disregarded. Now, that's not the way you investigate the death of the President. That's not the proper way to handle something. You say—go get it, whether it's good or it's bad. This Commission Report—I've never read it."

18
Lee Harvey Oswald

The
Deceased

JIM GARRISON: "Oswald was a bright person, not stupid or a loner as so many people have claimed."

19
David W. Ferrie

JIM GARRISON: "David Ferrie was one of history's most important individuals."

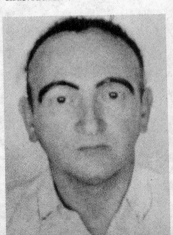 

20
Witness: Perry Raymond Russo

"If I had a message for Clay Shaw? . . . I don't just know what I could tell him. . . . You know, what would Judas Iscariot tell Jesus Christ?"

21
Witness: Lawyer Dean Adams Andrews, Jr. (left), and his former attorney, Sam "Monk" Zelden

DEAN ANDREWS: "I would like to be famous, too—other than as a perjurer."

22
Witness: Vernon Bundy

"The twisting of his foot had frightened me that day on the seawall when I was about to cook my drugs."

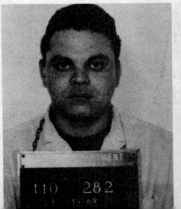

23

Witness: James Hardiman

"Names I'm not allowed to give out, but if you phrase your question so I can answer direct, I can say I delivered mail to Clem Bertrand at that address."

24

Witness: Mrs. Jessie Parker

"When the District Attorney sent for me I was frightened. I didn't know what he wanted."

25

Witness: Colonel Pierre Finck

"My particular field as an expert is forensic medicine. That's f-o-r-e-n-s-i-c. The word *forensic* comes from the Latin *forum*, which means the public place, the marketplace."

26
Witness: Charles I. Spiesel

Q.: "How many different
people have hypnotized you?"
SPIESEL: "It's hard to say—
possibly fifty or sixty."

27
Witnesses:
Mr. and Mrs. Nicholas Tadin

MR. TADIN: "They [my
friends] got on me, said I
better get down there."
MRS. TADIN: "I wouldn't be
here today if my husband
hadn't made me come."

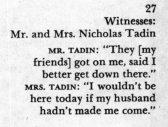

28

Witness: Marina Oswald Porter

Q.: "Did he [Lee Harvey Oswald] ever admit to you that he shot President Kennedy?"

MARINA: "No, he didn't. I didn't ask him about that."

29

Witness: James Phelan

"I realized his house was bugged . . . he had the 'on' switch rigged up in the record player. So we'd sit around and I'd talk about baseball and patriotism and mother and the flag and apple pie and so on."

30
Witness:
Elizabeth McCarthy Bailey

"It's my opinion that it's highly probable that Clay Shaw signed the name 'Clay Bertrand.' "

31
Witness: Charles A. Appel, Jr.

"The defendant Shaw did not write the entry in the book."

32
At a press conference Saturday, March 1, 1969: (left to right) William Wegmann, Edward Wegmann, Clay Shaw, Irvin Dymond

Q.: "Why did he [Garrison] pick you to prosecute?
CLAY SHAW: "I wouldn't undertake the mental processes of many people, and Mr. Garrison is one I absolutely refuse to understand. I don't know."

33
Clay Shaw, charged with two counts of perjury, arrives with his lawyer, Irvin Dymond, to post bond three days after the conclusion of Shaw's conspiracy trial.

CLAY SHAW: "You stew an old bird in a pot for two years and that old bird gets tough."

34
William Gurvich

"What I told him [Robert Kennedy] was . . . the exact words were, 'Senator, Mr. Garrison will never shed any light on your brother's death.' "

35
Aaron Kohn, Managing Director of the Metropolitan Crime Commission, given a night's lodging courtesy of Jim Garrison after appearing before the Orleans Parish Grand Jury.

"You probably see it in my face as I talk . . . I have long had the feeling I have been sitting at the ringside of the evolution of Mussolini, Adolf Hitler, any tyrant who has successfully taken over control of a massive part of society."

36
The Mayor of New Orleans:
Victor H. Schiro

"I'm tired of hearing people
tell what's wrong with this
city. This city is great! . . .
So I coined this—*Look Up,
New Orleans!*"

37
Mardi Gras

38

Judge Edward A. Haggerty, Jr. (and companions) at the time of his arrest in a police raid on a New Orleans motel stag party.

JUDGE HAGGERTY: "Oh, well, the world's not coming to an end."

15

The Sciambra Memo

In order to bypass the press checking on the expenditures in his investigation, Jim Garrison did not hesitate to be championed by a group of New Orleans businessmen who banded together and founded what they called "Truth or Consequences, Inc." Its purpose was to supply Garrison with private funds with which to conduct his inquiry into the death of the late President.

That such a *modus operandi* was antithetical to traditional American notions of democracy and could spawn an epidemic of witch hunts throughout the country, if practiced on a national scale, did not seem to daunt the good citizens of New Orleans—or at least not very many of them. Many of the fifty-some men in this group were not only wealthy businessmen but they were also up to their knees in political connections, serving on rail terminal boards, aviation boards, housing authorities and the like. But then political logrolling is as endemic to the State of Louisiana as gumbo. It is still shuddering, though, to contemplate this enclave of secret power and wealth, to realize it was allowed to flourish and, at last report, still is.

Fueled by such private funds, Jim Garrison steamed ahead. Dean Andrews, who had not been called during the preliminary hearing, was soon subpoenaed to appear before the Orleans Parish grand jury and asked whether he could identify Clay Shaw as Clay Bertrand. Andrews replied, "I could not do it. . . . I can't connect the two. I can't say he is and I can't say he ain't." And then: "I see him [Shaw] on TV—he is a tall cat—I don't believe the person I know as Clay Bertrand is as tall as him. I don't know. I can't say yes, and I can't say no. As God is my judge. I have to go back to the same thing I am telling you—I go to a fag wedding reception, and he is standing up and he is well dressed—I don't measure the guy then, I don't measure him now. I don't even think about the guy. Just like you go to any wedding reception, you mingle, you drink, you talk. I had no occasion to—to have this guy impress me." He finally said to the grand jury, "I get the impression you all want me to identify Clay Shaw as Clay Bertrand. I'll be honest with you, that is the impression I get—"

"Well?" said a grand juror.

"And I can't. I can't say he is and I can't say he ain't. . . . I cannot say positively, under oath, that he is Clay Bertrand or he is not. Even with me listening to the guy's voice on the phone, the voice I recall is somewhat similar to this cat's voice. . . . The voice I recall on the phone as Clay Bertrand's is a deep, cultured, well-educated voice—he don't talk like me, he used the King's English. Everybody thinks I am holding something back. They think I have the key to who killed Kennedy—I wish I did. I'd sell it and make a million dollars."

And on Dean Andrews went, in a merry hip game of verbal hide and seek, not saying yes and tantalizingly enough, not really saying no. For this, he was soon indicted on several counts of perjury.

His lawyer at the time, Monk Zelden, who almost matches Andrews in colorfulness of character, claimed that the indictment was faulty and that it was not specific about which statements of Andrews were considered perjurious. The grand jury then cited particular portions of his testimony and gladly reindicted him.

Despite an earlier statement that if he didn't play ball with the District Attorney about the identity of Clay Bertrand, "the Jolly Green Giant would pounce on me like a thousand-pound canary," Andrews changed his mind and volunteered to go before the grand jury again on June 28. This time he informed the grand jury he'd known all along Clay Shaw was *not* Clay Bertrand, that it was impossible, because Clay Bertrand was a name he'd made up to protect a bartender friend who *had* spoken to him on the phone in Hotel Dieu hospital but who had nothing to do with Oswald or the assassination. Dean Andrews went even further and admitted that Jim Garrison had made a deal with him by which Andrews would at least refrain from saying Clay Shaw was *not* Clay Bertrand. That he claimed, was the reason for his previous testimony. For confessing this, Dean Andrews was finally convicted on three of five counts of perjury.

The thousand-pound canary had indeed pounced.

The first in a series of public slams against Jim Garrison, questioning his tactics and the credibility of his main witness in the preliminary hearing, came in the form of an article, written by James Phelan, in the *Saturday Evening Post*, May 6, 1967, entitled "A Plot to Kill Kennedy?—Rush to Judgment in New Orleans." Through pure serendipity and the bravado of the District Attorney, Phelan had come upon a contradiction in the state's case that might well have resulted in the collapse of the prosecution.

In the middle of jury selection I asked Jim Phelan to come to my apartment and tell me his story. One evening after court, comfortably seated with our scotches and water and a bowl of peanuts, I taped his voice, full of outrage at what had been allowed to take place in New Orleans. Phelan had written a laudatory article years before on Garrison when the District Attorney was mopping up Bourbon Street and thus had entree to him. Here are excerpts from his taped account to me that evening:

When I got down here [New Orleans in March 1967] it took me about three or four days to get to Garrison, what with all the other press here. I left a message for him and he finally called me, we met and had a couple of short sessions. And he said, "Oh, hell, let's get out of here. I need a rest, meet me in Las Vegas." So I flew out there and a day or so later I met him at the airport, drove him into town, and checked him in at the Sands, where he registered under the name of W. O. Robertson, which is Willard Robertson, the Truth and Consequences guy.

So we talked, had a long session and I simply—the more he talked, the more I began to lose faith—he simply couldn't make any sense. He just rambled in every direction. He found it enormously significant that Dave Ferrie didn't put on his ice skates at the skating rink in Houston on Ferrie's trip the weekend of the assassination. This was one of the big pieces of evidence he'd picked up that the FBI *missed*. In fact in my notes I underlined that, because he made such a big point of it. I said, "All right, so he didn't put on his ice skates, so what?" He says, "Well, this is like—you know how you take a thread on a coat and pull it and unravel the whole coat?" He said, "This is the thread that I got hold of and helped me solve the whole case"—that Dave Ferrie didn't put on his ice skates! "He hung around the phone there," Garrison said, "and so that had to be the message center." I said, "What message center, did somebody call him?" "Well," he said, "no, we haven't tracked that down, but this was obviously the message center." And he rambled on like this and then jumps over to something else and I make all these notes and when I get through I begin to think this guy is off his rocker. He cannot tell a coherent story. He apparently has no evidence. I think he sensed this because I'd say, "Well, then, that means you've got proof that so-and-so did this or that?" "Well, no, it didn't work that way." I kept pushing him for some kind of evidence. I think this is why he gave me the two documents. We went up to his room and he said, "All right, I've got two documents for you. You take 'em home, read 'em tonight, because this is the heart of my case." The two things he gave me were the memorandum of Sciambra's when he first interviewed Russo in Baton Rouge and the second one was a transcript of Russo's answers when he was hypnotized by Dr. Fatter.

Russo tells two different stories. Up in Baton Rouge he, one, doesn't say anything about knowing Clay Shaw as Clem Bertrand, two, he says nothing about Shaw knowing Oswald and, three, he says nothing about Shaw and the party at which the assassination talk supposedly—he doesn't *mention* the assassination! So I took them back and I read them and I read them and read them and read them. I kept reading them, thinking I've missed something here. I read each one of them very carefully about three or four times and I then realized how they had procured Perry Russo. Either he was a born liar or a suggestible witness. One or the other. Most important, he hadn't had anything at all of any incriminating nature when he appeared and then he was processed into this other thing. Of course, at this time we're ten days before the preliminary hearing and I don't know what he's going to say when he gets on the stand. I was to meet Garrison at ten the next morning and return the documents. When he gave them to me he did not put any restrictions on them. He knew I was writing a piece. He said, "You'll now understand my case when you read them." So I got up early and made a call to Bob Mayhew at the Desert Inn and told him I needed a Xerox and needed it fast. I had to have two documents Xeroxed and I did not want anyone else reading them or knowing they were being copied. They Xeroxed the copies for me and I returned the originals to Garrison and made no comment about the thing. I wanted to wait for the trial.

I immediately called the *Post*, talked to the chief editor, Don McKinney, and told him I had a bomb in the case and it would blow Garrison's key witness right out of the water, that I had a problem with my conscience because I knew they were taking Shaw to the preliminary hearing and if his lawyers had this they could knock Russo right off the stand. But I was employed by the

Post and what should I do? He said he'd call me back and he went and talked to Otto Friedrich, the managing editor of the *Post,* who was an assassination buff, and he called me back and said, "I have a message from Friedrich, he says tell Phelan to try to refrain himself from telling Garrison how to run his investigation." So I was thereby put under wraps with what I had, insofar as the defense was concerned.

Then I attend the preliminary hearing and I sit there and listen to Russo tell this marvelously detailed story about the party that he'd not mentioned when he first appeared as a witness. The following day I called Garrison at his home and told him there was something deeply troubling me and he said, "Come out here and tell me about it." I went out to his house and he was there with his wife and children and shortly after I got out there Bill Gurvich and his wife came out and I told Garrison that—I said, "How come Perry Russo told two different stories? How come when he first appeared he did not identify Shaw as Bertrand, he did not say Shaw knew Oswald, and he said nothing at all about an assassination plot at any party." His mouth kind of dropped open and he said, "He didn't?" At that point I realized Garrison had not read the memos he'd given me. He said, "Well, I'll have to get Moo-Moo [Sciambra] out here and explain it."

Sciambra comes out there—they shoo the women out of the room—and sat down and Garrison said, "Okay, tell him your problem." I did, and Sciambra came back at me real hard and said, "Mister, you don't know what the shit you're talking about!" I said, "Look, I've got some bad news for you, Moo." I said, "I've read your memo, I've got a copy of your memorandum, and I've read it six, seven, eight times. I can almost recite it from memory and there ain't nothing in there about the assassination plot. I'll tell you how sure I am." I said, "I'll make a deal with you. If that memo isn't the way I've described it, I'll resign from the *Saturday Evening Post* tomorrow—if it is the way I described it, you resign from the D.A.'s office tomorrow. We'll shake hands and then read the memo and tomorrow one of us is going to be out of work." At that point he immediately backed off, like that [Phelan snapped his fingers]. I said, "Jim, get a copy of the memo"—because I'd left mine in the safe down at the hotel—so Garrison is rummaging around in the drawer alongside his desk trying to find the memo.

Then Sciambra changed his story. Now he says, Well, he wrote the memo in a big hurry and he said maybe he forgot to put in about the assassination plot. And I told him to come down off the wall! I said, "Come on, now, you found a witness to the crime of the century and you come down and write a 3,500-word memo and leave the crime out of it—put in all this other chicken-shit stuff—but you leave the crime *out!*" I said, "Nobody can be that stupid. . . . Besides, this hypnosis transcript shows how the thing was pulled out of him." So we ding-donged it back and forth and Gurvich sat there and never said a word, over in the corner. I said, "You know the thing that really hangs me up is that you said Russo said he saw the man twice and named the two times, once on the Nashville Wharf and once in a car with David Ferrie. So if he told you about the party you not only had to forget to leave *out* about the party but you also had to change the number of times to conform with what you told here, and that won't work." Sciambra was pretty hostile. We broke up and nobody was very friendly with anybody else. I said, "I'll call a cab and go back." And Gurvich says, "No, I'm going back to town, I'll drive you back."

I get in the car with Gurvich, who was his chief investigator, and this thing made a terrible impact on him. He said, "Man, you have just blown up the only witness we've got." He said, "I'll never forget Sciambra sitting there lying to you." He said, "This little son of a bitch, this was his little magnum opus and he sits there telling you he had a half-dozen other things to do. This was the one big thing that this little S.O.B. did and he sat there saying, 'Maybe I forgot!' " Gurvich said, "Man, he worked that memo over and polished it and repolished it." Gurvich was terribly upset.

The day after the meeting out at his house Garrison called me and had me go to lunch with him at Broussard's. He was upset by my reaction and we talked about it. Again I told him I thought he had a suggestible witness on his hands. He said, "Well, that's no problem, because we never make suggestions to anyone."

I went over to the office in the afternoon, I looked up Sciambra and said, "Look, we can resolve this thing very simply. If he told you about the three missing points, particularly about the assassination plot," I said, "you made notes up there, just show me your original notes and if you can show me where it is in your notes—then I'll agree you forgot it and didn't put it down in your memo." He told me he'd burned his notes, didn't have them. I said I wanted to talk to Russo. Sciambra said Russo wouldn't talk to anybody without their permission. I said, "Well, call him up and tell him I'm coming to talk to him." He made a call in my presence but was unable to get Russo. I called Sciambra later on in the day and he said he'd then been able to reach Russo and he'd see me if I came up there. I said, "Did you tell him what the problem was?" And he said, "Yes, I told him." I said, "Well, that's a dumb thing to do—you tip off a guy who's screwed up his testimony *how* he screwed up and he's got a lot of time to think up an answer." I raised this point with Garrison. I said, "For Christ's sake, Sciambra told him what's wrong!" Garrison said, "Well, why bother to go up?" But I decided to go. I thought it was a futile trip and in all probability Moo—well, Moo probably didn't really understand *how* he screwed up so he probably couldn't explain it to Perry—and I went up with Matt Herron, who was a photographer with the *Post*.

I told Russo, "Look, I got a copy of the memo Sciambra wrote about the interview with you and I'm going to use it for the article in the *Saturday Evening Post*. I want you to read it and tell me whether it's an accurate account of your interview with Sciambra."

So Russo sat down there and read that thing [Sciambra's memo] line by line and made two or three corrections on it. And none of them had to do with Shaw. They were just peripheral matters. I had underlined the statement where Sciambra had written, "I then showed him a picture of Clay Shaw and Russo said he'd seen this man twice." I had a ball-point pen and when I'd read it I'd underlined that because that to me was the key to the whole thing. So it was the only thing underlined in the whole memo. When Russo got down to it, he said, "Well, I should have said three times, counting the party. I'm usually pretty careful about what I say, but maybe I only said two times." Then he shrugged and went on and finished the memo. I said, "Other than the corrections you've made, is this an accurate account of what you told Sciambra?" He said, "Well, we talked for a long time, talked about a lot of different things." And I said, "No, I mean in terms of this case and what you knew about it." He said, "Yes." I said, "Then you first mentioned the assassination plot and the party *when?*" He said, "Down in New Orleans."

At that point, I'd verified the whole thing. I was astonished actually that he'd say this, especially after Sciambra had *called* him. I couldn't believe it. As soon as we got out in the car I said to Matt Herron, "Did you hear that?" He said, "Yeah." I said, "Burn it in your head, kid. I mean, right now, burn it in your head because someday you're going to be in court on this and I'm going to have to tell this story and you're my witness."

The next morning I flew out, went to New York and wrote the article. I mean I was satisfied. So about a week or so after the article came out, in May, I called Matt Herron and asked him what the reaction was. He told me at that time he'd had a couple of calls from Perry Russo and I said, "How's Perry taking the article?" He said, "Oh, he's very friendly. He doesn't understand what all the shouting's about and he said he'd like to talk to you, told me if you're ever down in New Orleans, come and see him, give him a call."

Herron gave me Russo's number and I called him. By this time he'd moved from Baton Rouge and was down here in New Orleans. He was very friendly to me, told me he didn't see what all the hullabaloo is about and he said, "People tell me I ought to get a lawyer. What do you think, what do you advise me?" I said, "Perry, there's only one thing I'm ever going to tell you and that's—tell the truth about this thing. You're going to hurt yourself if you don't." He said, "Well, if you ever come down here, give me a ring." Shortly after this I was approached by the NBC people and I told them about this conversation and this is what intrigued them—that after having written this article, the guy still wanted to talk to me and that was it. They hired me and I came down here.

By this time, they'd indicted Dean Andrews. Garrison had told me in Las Vegas—he didn't tell me Andrews' name—he said, "There's a lawyer, friend of mine, I'm going to knock him on his ass because of what he's doing to my investigation." And then they indicted him for perjury. Garrison had a rep for clobbering people and I talked to my lawyer on the West Coast. He advised me not to come here, said, "Stay out of the jurisdiction." I talked to the attorney for the *Saturday Evening Post*. He said, "Stay out of the jurisdiction." He said, "I know you're not going to do it, I know you too well."

When the *Post* article appeared, Moo Sciambra went on TV and challenged me to come down here and appear with him before the grand jury, but I was never asked by the grand jury to come down. Garrison had my home phone number, he knew the address and phone number of the *Post,* and nobody ever asked me to come before the grand jury. Sciambra just got up and shouted it out. So I figured when I came down, they'd just yank me before the grand jury and I'd tell what happened and Sciambra and Garrison would lie about what happened and they'd indict me for perjury. I expected it. So I told Pershing Gervais [Garrison's former chief investigator], said I wanted to get this monkey off my back right away, said, "Tell Big Jim I'm in town and if he's going to take me before the grand jury, here I am." I found out later they had a meeting the next day and they decided—I got word back—that they wouldn't take me before the grand jury unless I provoked them. I asked my informant what would provocation consist of?

He said, "If you hold a press conference and say you are publicly in town and defy them to take you to the grand jury, then they'll do it." And I wasn't about to—I'm not crazy!

So I started talking to Perry and, right off—the first time I talked to him—first off, I realized his house was bugged. I spotted the thing almost immediately. He reached over to the record player. Whenever I'd come into the room he'd jump up and say, "*Oh, let us play some music!*" And he'd go over and fiddle with the phonograph and he'd start a record up and he'd only let it run like fifteen seconds and he'd say, "Oh, the hell with that!" He'd go and turn it off. So I realized he had the "on" switch for the bug rigged up in the record player. So we'd sit around and I'd talk about baseball and patriotism and mother and the flag and apple pie and so on. Then whenever we'd really want to talk we'd walk out of the house.

I took him down to the poolroom the first night, about a block and a half from his house, and we shot a couple of sticks of pool. Then we started walking back to the house, got about halfway back and he stopped, all of a sudden, and just blurted it out. He said, "Boy, if Jim Garrison knew what I told my priest up in Baton Rouge after the preliminary hearing!" I said, "You want to tell me about it?" He said, "Yes, I told him I want to see Clay Shaw." I said, "You want to see Clay Shaw, Perry—why?" He said, "So I'd be sure." I said, "Man, what are you talking about? You got up in that preliminary hearing in the courtroom and put your hand over his head and positively identified him under oath and *now* you want to know if this is the right guy!" He said, "Well, I'd like to just sit in a room with him. I don't want to talk about the case. And no fucking lawyers. No *fucking* lawyers! I just want to listen to him. This is the flesh, man," he said. "I want to hear him breathe, listen to him talk and then I'd know." I said, "You want to see Shaw, I think I can arrange it." He said, "Yeah, I'd like to talk to him." I said, "Let me work on it."

So the next day I called Shaw's lawyers and we met down in Wegmann's office and Shaw was there and I told them what Perry Russo said. Shaw immediately agreed, right like that. He said, "As a matter of fact, I'd like to talk to this kid myself." He said, "I don't know what he's up to myself, he baffles me." At first his lawyers were dead set against it, thought it was some kind of entrapment. I said, "Look, I told Perry I'd set up the meeting with the provision that I'd be there. I'll set it up and we'll have Shaw in a room and I will bring Perry Russo in and when I bring him in I will say, 'Perry, you wanted to talk to Clay Shaw, here he is.' " I said, "We'll lock it down so it was Russo who sought the meeting and not Shaw." And the lawyers agreed to this. We discussed the ways and means and the technical problems and Shaw said he'd hold himself in readiness.

I went back to Russo that evening and as soon as I told him I'd set it up, he backed off. Russo said, "Oh, the hell with it. If we do it, it'll get back to Garrison and Garrison'll clobber me." He said, "The hell with it." The last time I saw him, about five nights later, the last thing he said to me as I was getting ready to leave, he said, "I lied to you about why I didn't want to see Clay Shaw." I said, "I know, I figured." He said, "The real reason I didn't want to see Shaw was that I knew if I sat down in a room with him, talked to him, listened to him, that I'd know he's not the guy and then all I could do is go on the run, go to Mexico or go out to California and become a beatnik—but I couldn't run from myself."

In the interim he told me a lot of things. He talked very obliquely. You could never get him to face up to things squarely. He talks all around the edge. But he told me that when he came down from Baton Rouge and before the hypnotic session, he said, "They asked me a lot of questions and I'm a pretty perceptive guy. I was able to figure what they wanted to know from the questions they asked. And when they got through asking me questions, I asked them a lot of questions, like Who is this guy? Who is that guy? Why is this so important?" He said, "In addition, I read every scrap of stuff that was in the papers about the case." I said, "You know, in your second hypnotic interrogation, that was the first time you mentioned Shaw setting up the alibi about going to San Francisco and you didn't come up with that until after Garrison had discovered the fact [that Shaw had made a business trip to the coast] and it had been printed in the paper." I said, "Perry, that one really rattled my tin ear. You know, come off it."

He told me that he was caught in the middle on this thing, that if he stuck to his story, Shaw and his friends and lawyers would clobber him. If he changed his story, then Garrison would charge him with perjury and chuck!—there would go his job with Equitable Life. He told me all he was concerned about was his own position, that he wished he'd never opened his mouth about it, wished he could go back to the day before he shot off his mouth up in Baton Rouge. He'd keep still and never say a thing about it. He never got in such a mess in his life. I said, "Look, boy, I told you on the phone, I've told you over and over, there's only one way to do this and just tell the truth. Just tell the truth about what happened, that's all you got to do. You do anything else and you're in trouble. Tell the truth about it!" He told me, "I no longer know what the truth is. I don't know the difference between reality and fantasy."

The last evening I talked to him I took him and Steve Derby [a friend of Russo's] out to the lake. I think it's called Fitzgerald's, a seafood place. I told Steve to try to get a table for us. I figured it would take fifteen or twenty minutes. I walked Perry over by the lake and I went over the whole thing with him. All the things that were wrong with the story. When I got through he said, "You know, all the things you've told me have been rumbling around in my head for weeks now. I'm much more critical of myself than you've been of me in discussing this. I wish I'd never got into the goddamn thing!" But he never actually said, "Yes, I lied." And *more* important, he never said, "Look, it happened the way I told it." Never once! He could have gotten rid of me just like that if he'd only said that. I'd put it to him over and over again and he'd never respond to it directly.

[At this point I asked Phelan if he felt sorry for Russo.] Oh, I felt sorry for him at the outset, but—that thing he said about not being able to run from himself, that was the only instance in all the times I spoke with him that he expressed any kind of concern for what he'd done. The rest of the time it was What's going to happen to me? What's going to happen to me? I talked to him about justice, the truth, the objective truth, and what he was doing, and what he was doing to Shaw, if his story was phony.

He asked me once if I'd heard about the Dreyfus case. He said, "What was it? I hear people talking about it." I said, "Well, it's a famous case, an instance of an innocent man getting railroaded into prison, Devil's Island, down in the Caribbean, a French guy accused of selling out his country. It was a famous case." I said, "He was finally sprung by a writer by the name of Emile Zola, who wrote a pamphlet called *J'accuse.*" I said, "It's interesting that you raise this, because if your story is false and if Clay Shaw is innocent—you're going to go down as a little footnote in history as a piece of shit that turned Clay Shaw into another Dreyfus." He said, "Oh [Phelan laughed]! *Oh!*" But after a while I lost any sympathy I had. I really did. I think what he's done is too enormous. I'm sorry for him—that he's capable of doing such a thing—but I think he ought to be in jail. I think it's a monstrous thing.

[I asked Jim Phelan if he had ever seen Garrison after this.]

Two or three days before the NBC documentary [on Garrison's investigation] was shown, I read in the paper that Garrison would be up at the Laurel Country Club in the Catskills addressing a state convention of New York district attorneys. So I thought I'd call him. Hell, I hadn't seen him since I'd talked to Perry. I thought I should tell him what Perry was saying. At any rate, I went up to the Laurel in the borscht belt. They had a large press table set up there and they had all these D.A.s and their wives and Jim was the featured speaker. I sat at the press table, which is right on the aisle, and I kept watching the door and here came Big Jim. Oh, I had talked to a CBS producer the previous week—Garrison was in New York taping his part of that CBS thing on the assassination—and I said, "Did he ever mention me?" And he [the CBS producer] said, "Yes, I asked him about you, what does he think, and he said, Well, he thinks you're wrong but he thinks you're an honest man and that of all his critics you'd still be welcome in his house." So when Garrison came in I got up and walked over to him and said, "Hiya, Jim. I haven't seen you in a long time!" He turned to the guy with him and said, "This is my most severe critic." I said, "The guys at CBS told me you thought I might be wrong but you thought I was an honest man." "Yes," he said, "I think you're an honest man." "Well," I replied, "if you think that, you better listen to what I have to tell you, because I've got some information you ought to have." He said, "Meet me after the convention and we'll talk."

It broke up about eleven-thirty, so I picked him up and we walked over to another part of the Laurel, a little bar, and sat down. I talked to him for maybe about an hour and a half, told him everything I told you here about Perry. First off, before we got into that, he said, "You know, that question you asked me out in Las Vegas. I been thinking about that and thinking about that." Well, the question was—now we're talking about ten days before the preliminary hearing—I said, "Jim, you know you described Shaw and Ferrie as kind of super criminals. You told me they were incredibly cunning. Why did these super masterminds, why, when they discussed the assassination, did they do it in front of a square like Perry Russo, who's hanging around waiting for a ride home, a guy who could be expected to run gibbering to the FBI or, as he subsequently did, come to you and incriminate them?" I said, "These are *super criminals!* Clay Shaw is a man of means. Why didn't he reach down in his pockets and give Russo two bucks and say, 'Hey, take a cab home, we got some business to talk over.' I don't dig it." Garrison said, "Hey, that's a good question." He'd never thought of it. He said, now at the Laurel, "That's the first thing we talked about and I've got the answer to the question you raised in Las Vegas." He said, "Perry Russo had to be a *part* of the conspiracy, that's why they talked about it in front of him. He's not telling the whole story. He's in the plot, too." I said, "For Christ's sake, come down off the wall! You mean you're going to take your star prosecution witness and make a co-defendant out of him!" I said, "What kind of motive would Perry Russo have if he were a part of a conspiracy? Ferrie's dead and the only two co-conspirators left are him and Clay Shaw. What kind of motives would he have for fingering his co-conspirators and coming forward? He's home free. The conspiracy has succeeded and *now* he's going to finger his co-conspirator?" I said, "If he does that, how does he know that Shaw isn't going to turn around and finger him back? And they *both* go down the tube." I said, "Come on, man, you know you're overheated." And he dropped it.

Then we go on and I told him all the stuff I told you. When I got through Garrison said, "Well, I'll tell you, I'm going to have to take a harder look at Moo Sciambra when I get back down there. It's obvious to me that Russo's got two stories. He's talking out of both sides of his mouth. He tells you one story, he tells me another. Look, I got nothing against Clay Shaw. I'm after bigger game. I'm after the Warren Report. What on earth good would it do me to go into the ditch against the wrong man?" He said, "That's crazy. I got a small staff, I don't have any critics. You know, the best way to make an investigation is to have somebody shooting holes in it and playing devil's advocate. I welcome a critical press. I don't have enough money to have a big enough staff to *have* a devil's advocate," he said, "but it occurs to me that I have a very good one in you. I value what you're doing. I welcome it."

He said, "Now here's what I want to do. I have to go back to New York for a day or two, from there back to New Orleans. Within ten days I'll call you in California and I want you to come down to New Orleans and we'll have a conference and a confrontation with Perry Russo." He said, "I'm not going to tell my staff about it, Perry won't know you're going to be there. I'm just going to set it up in a hotel room and he can come in expecting to talk to me and when he walks in the room—you be there. You confront him with the things you told me and if he cops out to half of it, I'll drop the case against Clay Shaw."

I said, "Great." I said, "Jim, you know I feel better about you now. Jim, this needs to be done. We're in a unique position to evaluate this case. Whenever you're ready, Jim, I'm ready. All I need is about twenty-four hours. It only takes about four or five hours to fly down there. Call me and I'll come. I'll keep myself loose so I can come." And I said, "I'm happy, I really am. Come on, I'll buy you a drink, I feel better about you."

He conned me, he really did. So I go back and I wait like about three weeks and I try to call him but can't get through. I wrote him a letter and reminded him of this, no answer. Then I wrote and quoted from his passage in the foreword to *Crime and Law Corrections,* in which he referred to the Kitty Genovese case about the thirty-eight gray mice who peered down from their windows while Kitty Genovese was killed and these thirty-eight gray mice might have been peering down in safety upon the destiny of their race. In other words, people have to come forward and be involved. So I quoted that quote and I said, "There are many Kitty Genoveses in this world and there are many ways to close your windows on their screams for help. If Perry Russo is a liar, you are making a Genovese out of Clay Shaw. You've suggested the confrontation and here a month has gone by. Maybe you thought I didn't have the guts to come down there and confront this kid. You couldn't be more wrong. I told you I'm ready whenever you are and," I said, "I guess you aren't going to be ready." I said, "Jim, if you want to play the thirty-ninth gray mouse, stop demeaning the other thirty-eight." That's when I got the five-page letter saying, Of course, there would be a confrontation, because he had given me his word. "Meanwhile, though," Garrison writes, "I've discussed this at length with Perry Russo and I now know he's telling the truth."

So I wrote him a final letter. And I said, "You've destroyed the basis for a confrontation. What's more, you have prejudged the confrontation before it occurred."

Jim Garrison will believe anything if it fits in with his preconceptions. He's totally uncritical, he has the sloppiest mind. This is the last guy in the United States who should be district attorney of anything, let alone a major city. This is a man that decided something happened and then sets out to prove himself right. He has a tremendous ego. Pershing Gervais told me, "Jesus, he never would have got on this if I'd been in that office. I'd have stomped the thing down so fast." But Pershing was out of there by then.

But I think Perry felt that I had actually figured the whole thing out, really the way it happened. People were saying, Why is this kid lying? Well, a part of it is true and he thinks another part of it is true. I think he thinks he saw Shaw in a car with Ferrie. I think he thinks that some little prick that was hanging around Dave Ferrie's probably did kinda look like Oswald. I mean, I think this much of it is true. Because this is what he came forward with. So all he has to do is move over and throw in that party. And with the party he throws in things that Dave Ferrie had told him earlier, independently, about being obsessed with Kennedy and about carrying the newspaper clippings around and how it would be easy to kill the President. So all he has to do is populate the party with the roommate and Shaw and let Ferrie say these things and he threw in a few things from the Mark Lane book.

And I *know* the way Garrison would put it. He'd say, Man, you're the one missing piece. We've been working this jigsaw puzzle and we knew that Shaw was the mastermind, we know that he and Ferrie plotted together. And here you dropped the piece right in there. And, Oh, boy, Russo thinks, I'm a big man and I'll help. And he thinks there's a whole lot else. He told me he was bothered about how much corroborative evidence there was. So he probably thought he's just going to invent a little something that's going to help them along, not much—there's going to be eighteen other witnesses and all kinds of other stuff to back him up. He got stuck with the thing. He got stuck with himself. He told his dirty little lie, thinking, Well, I'm helping a great big case that was built like a brick shithouse, solid as can be. I'm just one little old brick and there's all this other stuff. He got suckered into it. And, in turn, he suckered Garrison into it. Because the story he told in Baton Rouge, *without* the party, was a pretty damn good story, because Perry Russo is the only man on this planet who puts Dave Ferrie and Oswald together, the only one. Now we have some people later who come along that put *Shaw* and Oswald together, but Perry is the only one that ties Ferrie and Oswald. I don't think Lee Oswald ever knew Dave Ferrie. He might have been at some innocent thing, but I don't think he ever knew him. And Russo's the only guy. So what does Garrison do? Garrison has this preconception. He's already decided which way the plot went without any evidence. Dave Ferrie was first the getaway pilot and when that didn't work out, he's something or other. Just won't let him go, because the FBI squeezed him and threw him away and he's going to show the FBI what a real investigator is. So he just arbitrarily decided.

16

The Perils of LaBiche

Added to the wobbly Sciambra memo, the truth serum and hypnotic sessions of Perry Russo, and the origin of the name Clay Bertrand, there soon appeared a rash of charges pointing toward questionable investigative techniques used by the District Attorney's office.

NBC presented a one-hour show devoted to Garrison's investigation the evening of June 19, 1967. Two fellow inmates of Vernon Bundy's at the time of the preliminary hearing—John Cancler, known by the colorful name of John the Baptist, and Miguel Torres—came forward separately and claimed that Bundy had told them he was going to give perjured testimony against Clay Shaw "because it's the only way I can get cut loose [from serving a prison sentence]." John Cancler also claimed he had been approached by members of the D.A.'s staff to "plant" incriminating evidence in Clay Shaw's house. Miguel Torres told of a deal he had been offered by several assistant D.A.s if he would cooperate with Garrison and testify he had participated in sex orgies, for pay, at Clay Shaw's house and also identify Clay Shaw as the mysterious Clay Bertrand.

Both Cancler and Torres refused, although they were hardly in advantageous positions from which to buck the District Attorney; both were in the jurisdiction, serving time. Garrison and his supporters claimed these men must be discounted as reliable sources because they possessed records as burglars, and Torres had also been a heroin addict. Garrison and his supporters, on the other hand, would entertain no criticism of Vernon Bundy's testimony, although Bundy also carried the stain of thievery and dope addiction. Bundy had everything to gain by testifying against Clay Shaw and nothing to lose but his conscience. John Cancler and Miguel Torres were obviously not going to be rewarded with presents or offered deals by virtue of airing these accusations against the District Attorney. They could only expect to have the thumbscrews tightened.

Niles Peterson, one of the two people Russo testified had attended the assassination party with him, admitted he had been to a party at David Ferrie's around that time, but firmly denied ever seeing anyone there resembling Clay Shaw or Lee Harvey Oswald. Sandra Moffitt, the other alleged companion of Russo, came forth now as Sandra McMaines, the wife of a minister. She flatly stated she had not been to the 1963 party in question, adding she had not even met David Ferrie until 1965. She maintained she had been offered clothes and other accommodations by the D.A.'s office if she would return to New Orleans as a witness for the prosecution. Sandra McMaines lived for a while in Omaha and then moved permanently to Nebraska, which does not have an extradition agreement with Louisiana. She was thereby able to avoid Garrison's persistent attempts to return her to New Orleans.

The NBC show also highlighted the failure of both of the state's witnesses, Perry Russo and Vernon Bundy, to pass polygraph tests.

Alvin Beauboeuf, a close friend of David Ferrie's, who claimed he'd been offered $3,000 and a job with an airline by Lynn Loisel and Louis Ivon, both of the D.A.'s office, if he would cooperate in giving testimony that would further implicate Clay Shaw with Ferrie, contended he had been threatened with physical harm and was quoted as saying, "They've got some pictures of me that they said they'd hold over my head if I came out with this [charges of bribery]. They threatened to give these pictures out like they were going out of style if I came out in the open. . . . And also that I might make headlines as a—Ferrie's lover."

Yet another witness appeared claiming pretrial dirty work. Fred Lemanns, who had operated a Turkish bath in New Orleans, alleged Garrison had offered to aid in financing a private club if he would sign a statement maintaining he had known Clay Shaw as Clay Bertrand and that Shaw had visited his baths in the company of Lee Harvey Oswald. Lemanns admitted he had agreed to do this but now said he could not go through with it: "It wouldn't be right to swear somebody's life away and ruin the rest of their life on false testimony, no matter what was offered."

This was not a pretty parade of allegations to set before the District Attorney—in full view of the country.

Immediately after the NBC program was aired, the Metropolitan Crime Commission, under the direction of Aaron Kohn, dispatched a strong letter to Attorney General of Louisiana, Jack Gremillion, demanding an investigation of Garrison, his staff and his case. The response from the Attorney General was as quick as it was negative: "There is no authority within the law for such a procedure. I think this matter ought to be tried in the courts, not in the newspapers, press, or TV. I think Mr. Garrison ought to be allowed to try his case in the courts."

The state's higher authorities, to say nothing of the Federal government, continued to adopt a let's-see-what-else-he-can-come-up-with attitude, no matter how broad and varied the allegations charging a publicly elected official with all manner of extralegal tactics: bribery, intimidation, rigging and malfeasance in office.

Following hard on the heels of these unhealthy hints came the resignation of William Gurvich, a man who had worked closely with Garrison for five months and, having been privy to most phases of the investigation, could go along neither with it nor his conscience any longer. Gurvich journeyed to Washington at the request of Robert Kennedy and reported to the then senator his firm belief that there was no basis in fact for Garrison's investigation, his many charges, or the arrest of Clay Shaw. He then voiced this opinion publicly on a television news program. When he returned to New Orleans, he indicated he would be more than willing to go before the grand jury and tell them all he knew. He was subpoenaed, appeared before them and claimed the grand jury was not interested in hearing any criticism of the District Attorney or his staff. Instead, they soon indicted him for petit larceny, accusing him of stealing a master copy of Garrison's file, the Xerox paper of which was valued at nineteen dollars, thus bringing the charge under the jurisdiction of one Garrison-disposed judge, should it come to trial, instead of before a jury, which would have been the case if the value were set at twenty dollars or more.

This was the same grand jury that brought the indictment against Clay Shaw. It was called the LaBiche grand jury, after its foreman, Albert LaBiche, and the mention of that body brings shudders to most lawyers and knowledgeable folk in New Orleans. When you speak to anyone who appeared before it, the response is much stronger.

I was later told by William Gurvich, "There were twelve members of the LaBiche grand jury, hand-picked by Judge Bagert. Ten were white and two were colored. Of the ten whites, seven were members of the same athletic club. The same athletic club Jim Garrison used as a second office. All of them were Legionnaires. The two colored were not eligible to belong to either the Legion or the club. In the judge's chambers, behind his desk, is a large framed photograph, black and white, taken in the White House. In the center is John F. Kennedy, President. On one side is Judge Bagert in his Legion uniform. On the other side is Albert LaBiche, the foreman of the grand jury, in his Legion uniform. So he selected his Legion buddy as foreman."

Jim Phelan and I spoke of the LaBiche grand jury and of the dangerous homogeneity of the group. The imagination can easily picture the results of such a body, composed as it was, and activated at the same time Garrison's investigation into the death of the President was launched. James Alcock, defending charges of extreme bias against the LaBiche grand jury, said, "Whenever this jury or any grand jury is deliberating on whether or not to return an indictment, the assistant D.A.s leave the room." This would seem to be a pure technicality, in view of the highly publicized series of long and expensive lunches provided for the LaBiche grand jury, with drinks served, and often attended by Garrison or other members of his staff. Add to this the personal friendships of many of the jurors with both the District Attorney and Judge Bernard Bagert, who presided at the preliminary hearing, and the situation was perilously cozy. As another lawyer said, "So they leave the room for five minutes—big deal!" (It is also interesting that at the end of the LaBiche grand jury's six months, Garrison investigated every possibility in hopes of extending their term. This was too obvious a move even for New Orleans and he was advised to leave well enough alone.)

No one knows how many indictments, if any, the LaBiche grand jury refused to hand down in connection with Garrison's investigation but the indictments they and other grand juries under Garrison's direction did bring in are legion and they netted many who failed to cooperate with the District Attorney's office or who criticized him in any way.

Many of those indicted were first approached as witnesses for the state but refused to give the required testimony, starting with

Dean Andrews. There was also Kerry Thornley, a young man who had served in the Marines with Oswald and who was subsequently charged with perjury when he claimed he had not seen Oswald in New Orleans the summer of 1963 and could shed no light on Oswald's activities during that time. Layton Martens, who had been a close friend of David Ferrie's and refused to connect Clay Shaw with the ex-pilot, was also indicted for perjury. John (the Baptist) Cancler, was charged with contempt of court shortly after he appeared on the NBC program. David Chandler of *Life* magazine, who started out as a confidant of Garrison's and then became disenchanted as Gurvich later did, was also indicted for perjury. Two of the men who had prepared the NBC program criticizing Garrison's tactics were also shortly thereafter indicted: Walter Sheridan of NBC for public bribery, charged with offering Perry Russo gratuities and a trip to California if he would change his testimony and turn against the District Attorney; and Richard Townley of WDSU-TV, accused of public bribery and intimidation of a witness.

The theory behind these indictments, especially the charges of perjury, reads like this: Under Louisiana law, a convicted perjurer cannot testify in court; so, New Orleanians pointed out, Garrison was quick and clever to silence his adversaries by using this technique to prevent them from coming forward and presenting allegations under oath in the Shaw trial or any other formal courtroom procedure.

The indictments also carried another benefit. They tended to confirm Garrison's charges that a large ring of important citizens was involved either directly in the conspiracy or in sabotaging his investigation of it. Every indictment earned wide local and national publicity for Jim Garrison and his case. William Gurvich said of the District Attorney, "He believes everyone reads the headlines concerning arrests and charges but few people read denials or correcting statements."

The foregoing list of indictments reminds one that, as Dean Andrews said, Jim Garrison is given to pounce like a thousand-pound canary upon those who either refuse to cooperate with him or criticize him. The legend in New Orleans reads that you are either *for* Jim Garrison or *agin* him; there is no in between.

In the meantime, a large body of Garrison buffs had flocked to

New Orleans to assist the District Attorney in the pursuit of his theories. There were those on his staff who claimed that many of these fans only added to the confusion by leading the District Attorney down a series of blind alleys as they scattered crackpot clues here and there like so much confetti.

First and foremost of these Dealey Plaza Irregulars, often referred to as demonologists because of their morbid espousal of conspiracy and their vulturistic appetite for chewing up the Warren Report, was Mark Lane, author of *Rush to Judgment*. Called Garrison's guru by many, Mark Lane had made New Orleans home base for the greater part of the District Attorney's investigation.

There was William Turner of *Ramparts;* Vincent Salandria, a Philadelphia lawyer; Jones Harris, a civilian assassination devotee from New York; Penn Jones, Jr., editor of a small-town Texas paper, whose major contribution was keeping a death chart of all those whose demise could possibly be associated with the assassination, from Lee Harvey Oswald all the way to Dorothy Kilgallen, who had interviewed Jack Ruby. Then there was Harold Weisberg, who had written a series of books entitled *Whitewash;* Richard Popkin, author of "The Second Oswald," an essay that theorized Oswald had a Doppelgänger; Allan Chapman, a man dedicated to blaming much of our grief upon the Illuminati, an alleged worldwide conspiracy of intellectuals who supposedly control the television networks. There were others—photographic and ballistic experts, autopsy specialists—and to make it a completely mixed bag, there was even Mort Sahl, the satirical monologuist, who became hooked on Garrison and his cause and traveled about the country tub-thumping for him. It was Sahl who was responsible for Garrison's appearance on the *Tonight* show.

For some reason, though these people had flocked to Garrison like lemmings, many were missing now that the trial had come to fruition. Mark Lane was, however, conspicuously on hand. At first, during jury selection, he was not allowed in the courtroom because it was assumed he would be a witness for the state, but he was able to cover the day-to-day proceedings through a most attractive secretary-assistant, who occupied a seat adjacent to the prosecution table.

Jim Phelan told me he had bumped into Mark Lane and said to

him, "You gag at the smallest gnat in the Warren Report, but here in the Garrison-Shaw thing you're swallowing an elephant." Phelan was itching to testify. He wanted badly to aid in the demolishment of Perry Raymond Russo, and he was also not averse to giving Moo Sciambra a few good lumps.

17

One Lap Around the Pool

Back in the courtroom, this very same Andrew Sciambra, whose handiwork in the investigation was to be greatly evident during the trial, questioned a prospective juror for the first time. Sciambra, in his early thirties and the junior member of the prosecution, had been a boxer before passing his bar exams. Dark, good-looking, of medium height, always immaculately barbered and well dressed, Sciambra has what my mother would call "a fresh face," meaning there is an assertive team-pugnaciousness beneath the smooth surface that can easily be imagined manifesting itself. Sciambra, who will soon turn chunky if he does not begin watching his weight, has an assured walk, verging on the cocky; and his arms, in their swing, appear to be a mite short, especially for an ex-boxer. Widely tagged as "Garrison's boy" around town, Sciambra was called "Moo" to his face by nearly everyone. One version of the genesis of this nickname was given to me by an aunt of Sciambra's I met by accident in a cleaning shop. She explained that when he played hide and seek as a little boy, he could not pronounce "boo!" but used to pop around a corner shouting, "Moo! Moo!" His family and neighbors had picked it up and it had stuck.

Now, while questioning a jury candidate, his voice was oddly enough much softer than James Alcock's, with a barely discernible Southern accent and a small "s" thing, not quite a lisp but close to it. Moo Sciambra felt his way along carefully in the voir dire, not nearly as sure in his approach as Alcock.

As prospect after prospect was eliminated, the press began betting on the number of days it would take to complete the jury. Later that afternoon when I spoke to Irvin Dymond he grinned and said, "You're not the only ones betting. I tell you, Jim, it gets so boring, this jury selection, that Billy Wegmann and I take the sheets with the jurors' names printed on them. He takes one and I take another and we bet which sheet will have more fixed opinions of guilt or innocence. When we get bored with that, we start picking individual jurors when they're standing in line waiting to get on the stand, and we bet on their reasons for excusal."

Way late in the afternoon a 28-year-old credit manager named David Powe came up for questioning. Mr. Powe, who is single and lives with his mother and grandmother, is an extremely beefy pigeon-chested young man. A bespectacled high school graduate, he had about him a sort of chubby owl countenance and a certain tight earnestness that made it clear he wanted to become a juror. He'd read some magazine articles about the case and had seen Mr. Garrison on the *Tonight* show. Asked if he'd formed any opinion, he replied, "The only opinion I have is—I don't know." This was the right answer. When the state accepted him, the defense did also and he was sworn in as juror number eleven, taking his seat next to the other hefty young juror, Mr. Bainum. They were shortly thereafter dubbed "Tweedledum and Tweedledee" or the "Beef Trust."

Now the tension of finishing off the jury was apparent. With only one vacancy to be filled you could sense it: Make it one for our side!

Tension among those already chosen was also evidenced the next morning when Judge Haggerty announced that a request of one of the jurors to work out at the police gym had been turned down. He went on to say he would allow any of the jurors to order whatever exercise equipment they desired and this would be installed in a special room at their motel.

This announcement brought grins to the deputies and members of the press, together with speculation that because of their enforced celibacy—no conjugal visits permitted—perhaps one or more of the jurors were running out of cold showers and were in need of further preoccupation. That set the tone for the morning as side bets were made on which of the jurors had made the request. Most of us guessed it was Larry Morgan, the good-looking young aircraft mechanic. It turned out to be the Negro school-teacher, William Ricks.

Referring to this, one newsman remarked to another, "The poor bastards—what are they supposed to do for eight weeks?" "Read *Portnoy's Complaint,*" was the reply.

Questioned about the moratorium on pleasures of the flesh, a member of the Sheriff's staff cited the judge's guidelines that jurors were not permitted to discuss the case with each other or anyone else, at any time, for the length of the trial. This undoubtedly included the possibility of a certain amount of pertinent chitchat during sexual congress, had conjugal visits been sanctioned.

Nina Sulzer voiced a solution that would have enabled the jurors to keep their complexions clear, relieve stored-up tension and still not endanger violating the judge's guidelines when she said, "It could have been arranged without any legal challenge. All someone had to do was come up with twelve deaf-mute prostitutes." She then blushed considerably.

The strain of the voir dire upon the press also showed when, coming back from lunch one day, I noticed a blue cushion on the bench next to me with "Don McKee—AP" printed on it. Grins spread across the faces of many newsmen as they trooped in and spied this breakthrough in comfort. McKee was congratulated for his pioneering efforts, and the next day the benches resembled a pillow bazaar.

What of the defendant during this long stretch? I took lunch one of those last days with Clay and Nina Sulzer down in the small office assigned Clay. There was a discussion about the quality of food served, and I wondered why Clay did not sometimes go out for lunch. He explained it would require too much in the way of security precautions, leaving and returning. Although he lived at home alone all during the trial, with no security assigned to him, he nevertheless arrived at the Parish Prison entrance every day and was escorted up to the courtroom through a series of rear and extremely non-public passageways. He was released from the Criminal Court Building the same way, never exiting the courtroom into the corridor, except when he would be escorted briefly to the men's room by the two deputies assigned him.

It seemed to me if someone were seriously considering an attack upon him, it would be most logical to go after him at his house, either as he entered or left it. Or at some time in the evening when he was free to eat in restaurants or dine at the homes of friends. I could also not help think of the laxness of the guards in the late afternoon, in the event some fanatic wanted to stage a shoot-em-up scene in the courtroom proper. So there was Clay wide open in the evening and early morning hours, still not going out to eat a decent lunch for reasons of security.

Nina chided him for not hiring protection to watch his house. "Why?" he asked. "Well"—Nina shrugged with a wry smile—"after all, you've gone through this much—don't you want to stick around and see how it comes out?" "Yes," Clay replied, "but the expense of the trial has me in the hole so deep already, I can't afford to pay for protection." Nina thought for a moment, then said, "For God's sake, Clay, get a police dog, something." "Too much trouble, too long to train," Clay replied. He looked up at her with a grin and added, "What about a pet hamster?"

The twentieth candidate questioned on the eleventh day of the voir dire turned out to be juror number twelve. Peter Tatum, a maintenance mechanic for Kaiser Aluminum, was 43 years old but looked older, with his dark neatly combed hair graying down the sides and into the sideburns and his broad regular-featured face. Married, with a 19-year-old daughter, he appeared to be a solid, if somewhat stolid, citizen. Of Garrison's appearance on the Carson show, he remarked, "I seen part of that," which was surprising because in his conservative gray suit, white shirt and dark tie, he could have been vice-president of a small bank. He knew some policemen through his post of the American Legion but claimed that would not influence him in judging the case.

When Irvin Dymond took him over from the state, he asked, "Have you ever reached any opinion on the validity of the Warren Report?" Alcock quickly objected—this area of questioning had been ruled out—and the judge sustained him. Dymond argued that only the day before the judge had excused a man for saying he had faith in the Warren Report (I believe the man had offered the remark on his own, not in answer to a question). Judge Haggerty maintained his position and Dymond filed another bill of exception. This did not lead to unseating the juror, however, and with no peremptories left, Mr. Tatum was sworn in with not too much excitement on the defense's part, filling the panel of twelve jurors.

To celebrate the completion of the twelve, Jerry Cohen, Moe Waldron and I drove into town for lunch at the Roosevelt Hotel instead of eating at one of the several ptomaine taverns near the court building. We agreed the jury was somewhere between middle and lower middle. We also agreed that, in a matter of great intricacy, we would not particularly care to be judged by them. I told them that at a dinner party a night or so earlier someone had remarked the jury was in no danger of having the epithet "blue ribbon" attached to it, and this had reminded Clay of Oscar Wilde's quote when he was asked, "Are you trying to show contempt for this court?" Wilde's reply: "On the contrary, I'm trying to hide it."

Now, with only two alternates to pick, Judge Haggerty seemed to be even more lenient about excuses, often bringing up Mardi Gras of his own accord. By this time the panels of the eight Criminal District judges had been exhausted and now candidates' names were being drawn from a master jury wheel every day, subpoenaed and ordered to report the next morning. At the beginning of a court session the judge was allowing all those who would suffer pay loss or those who might have medical or family reasons for excusal to line up in front of his bench and give their reasons without having to be sworn in and questioned. This preliminary wipe-out sometimes used up three-quarters of those on hand and took as long as two hours. Soon even men who were afflicted by that newly discovered fatal disease "fixed opinion" were squeezing in the breadline to freedom.

Then along came dark-haired John J. Beilman, Jr., a slight nice-looking young man of 26, married and employed by the same microfilm company as juror number five, Herbert Kenison. Asked what his specific job was, John Beilman replied, "I'm a group leader." Urged by James Alcock to clarify what specifically a group leader was, this young man, who appeared to be extremely self-conscious, said, "A leader of men!" This earned chuckles from the assembled and turned out to be four or six men, according to the shift. This young leader of men wanted on the jury, even as an alternate, badly. The heaviest juror, Mr. Powe, of the team of Tweedledum and Tweedledee, got a tremendous kick out of Mr. Beilman and his determination to qualify, so much so that after a while he sat there cradling his chin in his hand, all grins and unable to look at Mr. Beilman for fear of laughing. This break in Mr. Powe's usual tightness of expression was heartening to observe; it was a relief to see anyone on that jury exhibit signs of personality.

Irvin Dymond questioned him at length. I believe the defense was suspicious of the young man's motive for wanting on and was looking for some out by which to have him excused for cause. This almost happened when the lawyer led him into the realm of probable guilt, possible guilt, reasonable doubt and beyond every reasonable doubt, which is enough to give anyone pause. Judge Haggerty soon entered into the discussion, attempting to straighten the man out on the finer points in this matter of semantics and the law, and Dymond challenged the young man for cause during this confusion. Alcock strongly objected, the judge sustained him, and Mr. Beilman was shortly thereafter sworn in as the first alternate. Only one to go. Half-hour, Mr. Shaw!

The court ran out of jurors in the midafternoon and was adjourned early, while deputies were dispatched with subpoenas for additional manpower. Judge Haggerty announced before recessing for the day that he'd had several requests from the press for information pertaining to points of law and the jury system in other states. He offered to let those who were interested come back to his chambers, so perhaps fifteen or twenty of us flocked back to a fairly large comfortable air-conditioned room to the right rear of his bench, furnished with a leather sofa, several chairs, easy and otherwise, a good-sized desk and a television set.

Judge Haggerty, now out of his official black robe, sat behind his desk, cluttered with papers and folders, and with those fascinating vibrating hands, which seemed to have distinct lives of their own, flipped through a pamphlet and told us Oregon required a vote of ten out of twelve for a verdict, that several other states required less than twelve but most called for a unanimous verdict, excepting Louisiana which required only nine out of twelve. The judge explained this was called a "bobtail" or a cut-off jury. If the vote should be eight to four the result would be a hung jury and a mistrial.

There had been a written motion filed at the end of court that day and the press was curious about it. Judge Haggerty explained it was a motion requesting a court order for the protection of a defense witness, Sandra Moffitt McMaines, who disclaimed attending the party with Perry Russo, in the event she should return to New Orleans to testify. It would, if granted, provide immunization from criminal prosecution from Garrison's office regarding any part of her past life in New Orleans (she had admitted to being quite a party girl) . The local *States-Item* had recently headlined, SHAW WITNESS AFRAID, HIDING—LAWYER. The story quoted her lawyer, who claimed she was more than willing to tell everything she knew but wanted to do it by deposition in Iowa, because of her fear of reprisals from Jim Garrison. This was not unwarranted in view of the long list of indictments handed to friends of the defense.

When a reporter asked the judge what he was going to do about the motion, he snapped, "How do I know, I haven't read it yet!" Asked to give the gist of the lengthy document, Judge Haggerty waved a hand in the air and said, "No, it would take me twenty minutes to read the damn thing."

A courtroom employee came into his chambers to say that Alvin Beauboeuf's lawyer, who had taped the bribery offer made by the D.A.'s assistants to Beauboeuf, was on the phone regarding a motion of his. (The defense had subpoenaed the tapes and there was some question about this.) To this Judge Haggerty said, "I don't want to talk to him over the phone, tell him to get over here!" The man returned shortly to say the lawyer was ill and could not appear in person. The judge shouted, "I don't care, tell him to get here on stretchers!"

After the jury was completed, the judge said he would adjourn court for the rest of the day to allow time for both sides to present oral motions and opening statements. At this point he would permit the press to go to the Rowntowner motel and take formal pictures of the jury, adding, "But no questions, I don't want you all talking to them." Someone asked why the pictures couldn't be taken right there at the courthouse. "Why?" the judge snorted. "I want the jury to go back to the motel and clean up, put on a shirt and a tie. I don't want 'em lookin' like the Scopes trial." (Many of the jurors had taken to wearing sports shirts and sweaters or regular shirts without neckties.)

Judge Haggerty announced he would call court from 9 until 5:30, not 6, as had been the case during the voir dire. "That's so we can catch Huntley-Brinkley and Cronkite—see what they say about us," he explained. "I've got this one set over here and I have a little one coming, a Sony."

He'd been given to understand that Jim Garrison himself would make the opening statement for the prosecution, that it would run approximately fifteen minutes. This was good news to the press, who had seen neither hide nor hair of the District Attorney since his brief drop-in visit many days before.

The judge finally took his leave; many of the press filed after him with further questions. He had put on a peppy, if brief, performance for them.

The following morning as I walked up the staircase to the second floor of the courthouse I spotted Perry Russo sitting on a bench in the corridor not far from the District Attorney's office. I put my paper cup of coffee down on the bench next to him and introduced myself. His grip was firm. He was immediately friendly on the surface but there was a subcutaneous layer of trouble frozen in his face.

I asked him how things were going. "Well, you know, I think the jury will be picked any hour now. And—ah, oh, I'll be glad when it's over with, all right." He half smiled when he said this, acknowledging with a certain irony that it was not going to be a picnic. "Yeah, I'll be glad when it's over," he repeated. We chatted briefly and he asked me where I was from. "New York. I'm covering the trial for *Playboy*." "Oh, *Playboy!*" he said, adding, "Sure —*Playboy*." I told him I was also planning to write a book on the case. He seemed interested and not at all suspicious at hearing this. "A book on it, huh? Well, say, why don't you give me a call sometime—after I'm through testifying, of course—" "Yes, I'd like to," I replied, thinking, You can count on it, mister! "Fine. You give me a call then. I'm not in the book, information has the number."

I told him I would, said goodbye and I heard myself wishing him luck, thinking how much he would need it and realizing I was not wishing him luck at all. He had been pleasant and personable and I did feel—I was going to say sorry for him, but the feeling was not exactly that. It was more—not wanting to be in his shoes, that was it.

The entire day was a disaster as one man after another was excused. After court several reporters were standing around in the hall going over statistics. There was a difference of opinion. One said he thought 1,417 prospective jurors had been exhausted; another had a figure something less than that. They turned to a third reporter, asking him what number he would file in his story. "Me? I'm just saying they've been through a whole shitpotful!" We wondered why it was dragging so. Someone came up with the rumor that Judge Haggerty was trying to break the Chicago Speck jury record of 1,532.

The next morning had to produce the last alternate or it was felt there just might be open revolt—if only to break the monotony. The perfunctory line-up of dismissals took almost two hours. Then, shortly after eleven, the second juror of the day to be actually questioned took the chair. He was Robert John Burlet, the 46-year-old president of his own crane service. Mr. Burlet had a rugged, stocky build, and appeared to be an outdoors man. He'd read no books on the assassination, seen very little TV pertaining to the case, and didn't try to analyze what reports he had seen. When Alcock asked him if he'd ever expressed an opinion, Mr. Burlet replied, "Oh, I'd read something in the papers and I'd say this, I'd read something and I'd say that." He claimed he could judge the case solely from the evidence produced in court. Mr. Burlet had a big open smile that flashed quickly off and on; he gave indications of a sense of humor. Alcock, in explaining the conspiracy law, said, "President John Kennedy could be alive today and the defendant could be sitting right where he is today." Mr. Burlet nodded, and when Alcock went on elaborating on this theme, the prospective juror said, "Yes, I understood when you explained it earlier." To this Alcock, in a display of good humor, replied, "Maybe I'd better stop while I'm ahead. I'll tender the juror to the defense." After brief questioning by Dymond, Mr. Burlet was sworn in as the second alternate at 11:29 on the fourteenth day of the voir dire.

An excited buzzing filled the courtroom, enough to cause the echoing of "Order in the court!" Judge Haggerty announced that those of the press who were interested could gather at the Rowntowner Motor Inn at 12:15 for picture taking. He admonished the jurors not to discuss the case among themselves and to discuss nothing with reporters; he added a warning to the press not to attempt to speak to the jurors.

As the fourteen men marched out, led by deputies, they were grinning, now that their number was complete. A newsman near me eyed them and said, "I wouldn't want them sitting on a traffic violation, let alone criminal conspiracy." And a woman spectator cracked, "My God, they look like a bunch of chiropractor's rejects!" Then I remembered Lou Gurvich's remark: "What's everybody squawking about the jurors for—just take a look at the *elected* officials in this town. That'll give you a clue!" When court was recessed until the following morning, Irvin Dymond and Eddie Wegmann walked down the corridor mobbed by reporters. Dymond scratched his head and smiled. "We could have done better and we could have done a hell of a lot worse!" Eddie Wegmann, from the look on his face, preferred not to comment.

The jury took more than their share of verbal abuse. They were not an especially stunning group but, after all, they were not the United States Olympic swimming team; they were a jury picked from the citizens of New Orleans. Who was to say they were not— at the very least—good guys?

Jerry Cohen had rented a car and, after several of our group had filed stories over the phone, we piled into it and made for the Rowntowner Motor Inn. The rear patio surrounding the swimming pool was jammed with cameramen and reporters. There was a manic high vibrating in the air. The tediousness of jury selection was over and now the Big Show was about to begin.

Judge Haggerty was in full command, ordering the deputies to set up chairs at one end of the pool and then—when the fourteen men appeared, all dressed up in their Sunday-go-to-meeting best and flanked by other deputies—arranging their seating like a seasoned public relations man. Judge Haggerty was looking pretty spiffy himself, in the event he just happened to be photographed, too.

The photographers began snapping the jurors—who sat stiffly at attention graduation-like—from every possible angle, kneeling, squatting, sideways, lying down and above from balconies adjacent to rooms surrounding the pool, as if they were the first human life to set down on earth from outer space. When they had been duly recorded for posterity and the judge indicated they would now be led into the dining room for lunch, one reporter asked if they could be photographed in motion. "Sheriff," Judge Haggerty called out in ringmaster style, "take 'em one lap around the pool." The fourteen men walked dutifully and self-consciously around the swimming pool in single file and then were led inside while the judge remained in the patio, making up to the press for the lack of conversation with the jurors.

Of the voir dire, he said, "Anyone who didn't want to be on this jury had an out. So you know anyone on there *wanted* to be on. I let the defense and prosecution try to figure out *why*. They've been playing mental chess with each other for the past two weeks." To questions about the Warren Report, despite his many statements that the report would not be on trial in his courtroom: "If the state wants to overprove its case, I can't stop that. If there's any objection, we'll have to call the balls and strikes as they come." Of all the questions put to him that afternoon about the technicalities of the trial, he seemed most interested in answering whether court would be in session Mardi Gras day. When he discussed this, his voice dropped to a conspiratorial tone that indicated the question had caught his fancy. "I'd like a recess on Mardi Gras day to come as a request from both sides. We will get out of holding court on Mardi Gras in a cozy fashion."

Someone asked if it would be possible to see the jury's accommodations. As long as the fourteen were at lunch, this was permitted. From the rush for the elevator, you'd have thought we were all going to have a peek at Mae West preparing for bed.

The Rowntowner Motor Inn is pseudo English-manor in feeling, an abundance of dark wood and as many crimson carpets and draperies as could be laid and hung. First we had a look at the exercise room, equipped with weights, a vibrator (this brought a few cracks from the press), a running-in-place track, card table and four chairs, chinning bar, red drapes and red carpet. Then we looked into two bedrooms, each one of which was equipped with three beds, looking to be three-quarter size, one cot and one bathroom. Everyone assumed that the jurors, since they were not being paid by the state, would at least have the luxury of a single room. Not so. Nine of them were stacked three to a room, plus one deputy who occupied the cot. The remaining five jurors were all in one larger room, and with a deputy that made six. Nor did the beds leave much in the way of walking-around space.

I spoke to a young Negro sergeant in charge of the jury, Matt Perkins. He displayed an engaging easygoing humor as he told about the communications problem. "The phone goes all night long. A wife will call up—you understand the jurors can't talk directly—and say, 'Tell my husband I miss him.' 'Your wife misses you.' 'Tell her I miss her, too,' the husband will say. 'He misses you, too,' I'll say. Then she'll say, 'Tell him I love him.' So I tell him she loves him and he says, 'Tell her I love her, too.' So I say, 'He loves you, too.' 'Tell him the baby misses him, too. Does he miss the baby?' 'The baby misses you, too,' I say, 'Do you miss the

baby?' 'Yes,' he says, 'I miss the baby, too.' " Matt Perkins broke
off with a laugh, "Oh, man, it's too much." He went on to explain
that all trial coverage was cut out of the newspapers. "You should
see the papers." Matt Perkins laughed. "They look like some kind
of cut-out puzzle! Like a kid would cut out paper dolls or
something."

Back downstairs, Judge Haggerty indicated he was thirsty and
would repair to the bar inside for a drink. Moe Waldron, Jerry
Cohen, Mike Parks, Roger Williams, Carl Pelleck, a few others
and myself followed him. The judge was in an expansive mood
and soon offered to lend his clubhouse passes to anyone interested
in zipping out to the race track. Several of the out-of-towners
introduced themselves. I followed suit, sticking out my hand and
giving my name. When I did this, the judge sat up straight and
said, "Kirkwood? Oh, yeah—you're the one from *Playboy!* Say, I
want to talk to you."

Now it comes, I thought, as his attention was diverted by another newsman, now I'm going to get womped for the Terry Flettrich show. And in front of my fellow newsmen. Serves me right, I
told myself, and I stood up straight awaiting my medicine. Finally
Judge Haggerty turned back to me, taking me completely by
surprise when he leaned forward from his bar stool and said,
"Kirkwood, huh? Somebody told me you were going to put in your
article that I had my hair styled before coming to court in the
morning!" My newspaper buddies all turned to look at me as I
made a few embarrassed toe passes at the rug, wondering what the
hell I would reply to that and also wondering who the spy was.
(My friends June and Dick Rolfe somehow came to mind.) I was
immediately taken off the hook when Judge Haggerty smiled and
added, "Well, listen, if you do, be sure and mention my barber,
Murphy of New Orleans, he'll get a great kick out of it. He's
named Barber of the Year, you know. Any time you want an
appointment I'll fix it up for you." I smiled and thanked him,
swallowing a sigh of relief. "You'll be sure and mention him, will
you?" I told the judge I would. When we finally left him at the
bar, it was agreed Judge Haggerty was "a friendly fella."

We decided to drive out to Lake Ponchartrain to a seafood
restaurant. All of us at luncheon that day believed, with varying
degrees of intensity, in the defendant's innocence. Yet spirits were
high, mine included. We were revved up for the trial—like kids

about to set off on an overnight hike. But that's not who we were. In fact we were adults on our way to watch the pillorying of a human being. Why with such relish? I wondered. For tomorrow, with the state presenting its case first, the testimony would be as brutal, as incriminating, as damaging and smearing as possible.

PART TWO

TRIAL

18

Standing Room Only

A warmish drizzle sprayed down in the early morning, but by time for court it was clearing to a mild splotched-sky morning. Roving bands of cameramen, ungainly television cameras hoisted on their shoulders like bazooka guns, loped from one entrance of the building to the other, determined to catch the arrival of all the stars, feature and bit players.

Upstairs the wide corridor leading to Judge Haggerty's domain looked like a Loew's theater lobby on Bank and Dish Night combined. Nina Sulzer, clipboard in hand and harassed in the most pulled-together manner, coped with a long column of roped-off press on one side at the top of the end staircase and a longer column of joggling, anxious spectators—the majority of them women, some of whom had taken up their posts as early as 7 A.M.—roped off at the other side.

A few V.I.P.s arrived. Melvin Belli, that silver-maned lion of the law who had defended Jack Ruby, barged his way past a bridling press corps with a party of five and swept in, as if he were surely trying the case himself. Mark Lane and party of three followed. Finally the individual members of the press were ticked off according to their publications. I managed a seat in the fourth row; the press was crammed shoulder-to-shoulder tight this morning.

By a quarter to ten the place was jumping; the anticipatory zizzing of excitement vibrated in the air, grew and swelled until the courtroom was filled with the hollow echo not unlike the sound of a YMCA gym during basketball practice.

June Rolfe, who wore her wig for opening morning, pointed out a beautiful streaked blonde with dark glasses riding atop her hair as Liz Garrison. She was a stunner; so shapely as she glided down the center aisle that it was hard to imagine she'd birthed five. With high cheekbones and smooth complexion (Camay girl standing in meadow gazing at race horse), she was not a sophisticated beauty, more a natural scrubbed one, on the order of Hope Lange—whom we all agreed to cast for the movie version. She took a seat in the spare jury box, along with some women friends of the judge and the wives, daughters, and friends of the various participating lawyers. Nena Dymond, wife of Irvin, a slim, dark-haired, extremely pretty woman with a soft South American accent was there with Shirley Wegmann, Eddie's peppy wife, who always looked as if she might have a pair of boxing gloves in her purse for any member of the prosecution team. (I learned later that Liz Garrison, years before, used to baby-sit for the Wegmanns with their charming redheaded daughter, Cindy, now 16.) This, before her marriage to Big Jim. I did not notice Mrs. Wegmann and Mrs. Garrison speak together during the trial, but Cindy and Liz would nod and say hello if they happened to meet.

Clay's lawyers, Irvin Dymond, the brothers Wegmann, and Sal Panzeca, were the first of the active combatants to appear. Then Clay came through the rear courtroom door to the left of the witness chair. The women on the spectators' side nudged one another and fell to whispering. Clay looked amazingly rested and fresh and was walking tall in a gray suit. Glancing over to the jammed press section, he flashed a full smile, moved to the railing and shook hands with several reporters. Someone farther back in the press section called out, "What's this—your cheering squad?" Clay smiled back and said, "I hope so." Then he took his seat at the defense table between Eddie Wegmann and Sal Panzeca, as the opposition—Jim Alcock, Alvin Oser, William Alford and Moo Sciambra—arrived.

A mile-high holiday mood stretched the seams of the courtroom when finally Jim Garrison, his massive six-foot-six frame draped in a well-tailored dark blue suit, strode in. His well-timed entrance brought a momentary heightened buzz, then a quick pull-down to a hush. When it was apparent he was not going to break into song or recitation, the sound soon increased to what it had been before he entered. Louis Ivon, one of his investigators, handsome in the slick Warner Brothers contract player style of the early 40's, was close behind Garrison. Several attractive secretaries—the District Attorney is not famous for employing uglies—legged in and out of the courtroom.

At 10 sharp, Judge Haggerty, hair never looking better, took the bench and the main event was under way. Two motions were argued out of the presence of the jury. A lawyer stated that his client, Alvin Beauboeuf, had waived his privileged communication classification with his previous attorney regarding the tapes of the alleged bribery offer made to Beauboeuf by two members of Garrison's staff, and Judge Haggerty signed an order to make the tapes available to the court.

Then came the defense motion requesting a court order to provide immunity from prosecution for Sandra Moffitt McMaines so she would agree to come to New Orleans and refute Perry Russo's testimony. Alcock strongly objected to this, maintaining the court was without authority to grant such an order and adding it would be completely foreign to the state of Louisiana. Dymond argued that Sandra Moffitt was an essential witness for the defense but she would not come to New Orleans without a guarantee of protection "because she is fearful of arrest." Judge Haggerty then said—and he did not appear to be speaking facetiously—that if she were fearful of arrest perhaps the only solution would be to put her in the Parish Prison for security. That brought an exchange of perplexed looks among the press. (No, Judge, that's what she's *afraid* of!) James Alcock took his cue from that and in a voice that was coated in oil and topped by a damp veiled threat, said, "The District Attorney's office does not intend to clamp her in irons as soon as she crosses the parish line." Alcock paused, then went on to add that if she did come to Orleans Parish and *were* to commit some infraction of the law, "We would not only charge her but we would be guilty of malfeasance in office if we did not charge her."

I could not help thinking, Well, that takes care of Sandra. Judge Haggerty refused to issue a protective order and told Dymond to take a bill of exception. "Now let's bring the jury down," the judge said, anxious to get on with it.

And down they came, ogling the packed courtroom as much as the spectators were ogling them. Jurors one, two, six and the first alternate were not wearing neckties; I wondered if the judge approved of them looking like "the Scopes trial."

After a short recess the clerk read both the preliminary hearing ruling and the grand jury indictment against Clay Shaw. Then Jim Garrison rose and walked slowly to a stand-up microphone directly in front of the jury. He spoke to the fourteen men in a deep, steady easy-on-the-ears voice with only the lightest brush-touch of a

Southern accent, telling them he knew they'd been imposed upon
but he would have to impose upon them further by delivering to
them a rather. lengthy opening statement. He then cleared his
voice and began to read the substance of what the state intended
to prove against Clay Shaw. The following is slightly abridged:

The State of Louisiana is required by law in all criminal trials
to make an opening statement to the jury. This statement is
merely a blueprint of what the state intends to prove. It has no
probative value and should not be considered as evidence in the
case.

The defendant, Clay L. Shaw, is charged in a bill of indictment
with having willfully and unlawfully conspired with David W.
Ferrie, Lee Harvey Oswald and others to murder John F. Kennedy.

The crime of criminal conspiracy is defined in the Criminal
Code of Louisiana as follows:

Criminal conspiracy is the agreement or combination of two or
more persons for the specific purpose of committing any crime;
provided that an agreement or combination to commit a crime
shall not amount to a criminal conspiracy unless, in addition to
such agreement or combination, one or more of such parties does
an act in furtherance of the object of the agreement or combination.

As required by the definition of criminal conspiracy, the state
will prove the following overt acts:

1. A meeting of Lee Harvey Oswald, David W. Ferrie and the
defendant, Clay L. Shaw, in the apartment of David W. Ferrie at
3330 Louisiana Avenue Parkway in the city of New Orleans
during the month of September 1963.

2. Discussion by Oswald, Ferrie and the defendant, Shaw, of
means and methods of execution of the conspiracy with regard to
assassination of John F. Kennedy—particularly, the selection and
use of rifles to be fired from multiple directions simultaneously to
produce a triangulation of cross fire, establishing and selecting the
means and routes of escape from the assassination scene, determination of procedures and the places to be used for some of the
principals to the conspiracy so as to establish alibis on the date of
the assassination.

3. A trip to the West Coast of the United States by Clay L.
Shaw during the month of November 1963.

4. A trip by David W. Ferrie from New Orleans, Louisiana, to
Houston, Texas, on the day of November 22, 1963.

5. Lee Harvey Oswald taking a rifle to the Texas School Book
Depository in Dallas, Texas, on or before November 22, 1963.

I noticed the overt acts first listed by James Alcock at the beginning of the voir dire had been diminished by one, namely, "A meeting among Mr. Shaw, Oswald and Jack Ruby, who killed Oswald, at the Capitol House Hotel in Baton Rouge in October 1963, at which time Mr. Shaw gave Oswald and Ruby a sum of money." That was out. The courtroom was deathly quiet as Garrison delivered his statement with complete matter-of-factness—no theatrics, no gestures, no changing of tone or raising the voice. Irvin Dymond leaned forward; Billy Wegmann leaned way back. Clay was making notes during this first part and, as always, smoking. The jury looked as if they were listening to the Gospel according to St. Jim. He went on:

The Criminal Code defines murder in the following terms: 1. When the offender has a specific intent to kill or to inflict great bodily harm.

The evidence will show that in New Orleans, in the summer of 1963, Lee Harvey Oswald was engaged in bizarre activities which made it appear ostensibly that he was connected with a Cuban organization, although in fact the evidence indicated that there was no such organization in New Orleans. This curious activity began on June 16th, when he distributed "Fair Play for Cuba Committee" leaflets on the Dumaine Street Wharf. This distribution took place at the docking site of the United States Aircraft Carrier, the U.S.S. *Wasp*.

Upon request of the commanding officer of the *Wasp*, Officer Girod Ray of the Harbor Police approached Oswald and informed him that he would have to stop passing out the leaflets and leave the wharf area. At this time, Officer Ray confiscated two pieces of the literature being handed out by Lee Harvey Oswald. One of these was a leaflet, yellow in color with black print, entitled "Hands Off Cuba!" The body of the leaflet contained an invitation to join the Fair Play for Cuba Committee in New Orleans. The other item taken by Officer Ray was a pamphlet entitled "The Truth about Cuba," published by the Fair Play for Cuba Committee, 799 Broadway, New York 3, New York. In conjunction with Officer Ray's testimony, the state will offer into evidence copies of these two pieces of literature.

The evidence will further show that in June 1963 the defendant, Clay Shaw, was present at a party given in an apartment in the French Quarter of this city. Among the guests at the party was David Ferrie, a man known as an accomplished airplane pilot. During the course of the party, the conversation among a small group of those present turned to President John F. Kennedy. In this group were David Ferrie and the defendant, Clay Shaw. The comment was made that President Kennedy should be killed and that the job could best be done by a rifle. At this point, the defendant, Clay Shaw, suggested that the man doing the shooting would probably be killed before he could make his escape. The defendant, after making his observation, turned to Ferrie and asked if it might not be possible to fly the gunman from the scene of the shooting to safety. David Ferrie replied that this would be possible. At this point, the conversation was turned to other subjects.

Later in June of 1963, the defendant, Clay Shaw, was observed speaking to Lee Harvey Oswald on the lakefront in the city of New Orleans. The defendant arrived at the lakefront in a large, black four-door sedan, and was there met by Lee Harvey Oswald, who had walked to the meeting point along the lakefront from a westerly direction. The defendant and Oswald had a conversation which lasted approximately fifteen minutes. At the conclusion of this conversation, the defendant gave Oswald what appeared to be a roll of money, which he immediately placed in his pocket. In shoving the money into his pocket, Oswald dropped several leaflets to the ground. These leaflets were yellow in color with black printing and dealt with Cuba. The color, contents and size of these leaflets were identical with the "Fair Play for Cuba Committee" leaflet taken from Oswald earlier that month on the Dumaine Street Wharf by Harbor Police Patrolman Girod Ray.

The evidence will show that on August 9, 1963, Lee Harvey Oswald was arrested by members of the New Orleans Police Department as a result of his becoming involved in a fight with several Cubans who were protesting his passing out "Fair Play for Cuba Committee" literature. This literature was confiscated by the New Orleans Police Department. The state will offer into evidence three of the seized items, one of which is a yellow leaflet with black print entitled "Hands Off Cuba!" This is the same type of leaflet taken from Oswald at the Dumaine Street Wharf on June 16, 1963, and also the same as the leaflet dropped by Oswald at the lakefront in the latter part of June 1963. The state will also introduce the bureau of identification photograph taken of Lee Harvey Oswald at the time of his booking.

A week later, on August 16, 1963, Lee Harvey Oswald was again distributing "Fair Play for Cuba" leaflets. Once again the distribution was done more as if to attract attention than to actually accomplish distribution. The actual distribution lasted only a few minutes, ending shortly after the news media departed. The state will introduce pictures and a television tape of this distribution, which took place in front of the International Trade Mart, whose managing director at the time was the defendant, Clay Shaw.

The state will show further that in the latter part of August or the early part of September 1963 Lee Harvey Oswald went to Jackson, Louisiana, a small town located not far from Baton Rouge, Louisiana. While in Jackson, he talked to witnesses in reference to his getting a job at the East Louisiana State Hospital in Jackson, Louisiana, and registering to vote in that parish, so as to be able to get the job. The state will introduce the witnesses who talked to Lee Harvey Oswald on this occasion.

The state will show that shortly thereafter, still in late August or early September 1963, the defendant, Clay L. Shaw, Lee Harvey Oswald and David W. Ferrie drove into Clinton, Louisiana—which is very close to Jackson—in a black Cadillac, parking the Cadillac near the voter registrar's office on St. Helena Street. While the defendant, Clay L. Shaw, and David W. Ferrie remained in the car, Lee Harvey Oswald got out of the car and got in line with a group of people who were waiting to register.

The state will introduce witnesses who will testify that they saw the black Cadillac parked in front of the registrar's office and who will identify the defendant, Clay L. Shaw, Lee Harvey Oswald and David W. Ferrie as the individuals in that car.

The state will introduce a witness who talked to the defendant, Clay L. Shaw, on this occasion. In asking Mr. Shaw for his identification, he was told by the defendant that he (Shaw) was from the International Trade Mart in New Orleans, Louisiana.

The state will introduce a witness who will identify Lee Harvey Oswald as the person he talked to in the registrar's office and who will also identify the defendant, Clay Shaw, and David W. Ferrie as the two men seated in the black Cadillac that brought Lee Harvey Oswald to Clinton, Louisiana.

The state will also introduce into evidence a photograph of a black Cadillac car that the witnesses will identify as either the same car or one identical to the one that they saw in Clinton that day.

The evidence will show that in the month of September 1963 the defendant, Clay Shaw, David Ferrie and Lee Harvey Oswald participated in a meeting in which plans for the murder of President John F. Kennedy were discussed and refined. This meeting took place in David Ferrie's apartment at 3330 Louisiana Avenue Parkway in the city of New Orleans. Shaw (using the name of Clem Bertrand), Ferrie and Oswald (using the first name of Leon) discussed details of the conspiracy in the presence of Perry

Raymond Russo, after Ferrie gave assurance that Russo was all right.

The plan brought forth was that the President would be killed with a triangulation of cross fire with at least two gunmen, but preferably three, shooting at the same time. One of the gunmen, it was indicated, might have to be sacrificed as a scapegoat or patsy to allow the other participants time to make their escape. No one indicated to Oswald at the meeting that he was going to be the scapegoat and there was no indication of any awareness on his part of such an eventuality.

They also discussed alternate routes of escape, including the possibility of flying to other countries. The defendant and David Ferrie agreed that as part of the plan they would make sure they were not at the scene of the assassination. Their plan for the day of the shooting was to be engaged in a conspicuous activity in the presence of as many people as possible. The defendant, Shaw, stated he would go to the West Coast of the United States. Ferrie, not as positive about his alibi, said he thought he might make a speech at a college in Hammond, Louisiana. As the state will show, Shaw made his way to the West Coast and Ferrie, after his long drive back from Texas, made his way to Hammond, Louisiana, where he slept, not in a hotel room, but on a bed in a college dormitory.

By a month after the meeting, Lee Oswald had moved into a rooming house in Dallas under an assumed name. By the following month when the time for the President's parade arrived, Oswald was on the parade route at the Texas School Book Depository, where a job had been found for him. By the night of Friday, November 22nd, the President was dead, Ferrie was driving through a thunderstorm to Houston, Texas, and the defendant, Shaw, was out on the West Coast. Lee Oswald, however, was in a Dallas jail ending up as the scapegoat.

As to the planning—the conspiracy—our jurisdiction is limited to New Orleans, although we will later offer evidence concerning the assassination in Dealey Plaza in Dallas because it confirms the existence of a conspiracy—

At this point Irvin Dymond rose in objection, contending Dallas was completely irrelevant to the case against Clay Shaw. Jim Garrison barely turned around, presenting not a word of rebuttal argument. That was handled by James Alcock, who claimed that what happened in Dallas was corroborative evidence and that the state was entitled to overprove its case if it so wished. Judge Haggerty (who had often said, "I don't care how much Jim

Garrison criticizes the Warren Report—we are not going to try the Warren Report in this courtroom!") quickly overruled Dymond's objection, remarking, "If the state wishes to overprove its case I cannot stop them." To which Dymond replied, with incredulity in his voice, "But Your Honor will have to make a 180-degree turn and reverse the voir dire. You did not permit us to go into Dallas." Judge Haggerty remained adamant, indeed making a 180-degree turn in front of all viewers. Dymond filed a bill of exception to this, while Jim Garrison stood placidly by, as he had during the argument, watching impassively, as if he'd known the outcome and it was a matter of minor disturbance, a mere nuisance raid— which it turned out to be. He then continued, every so often brushing a large hand across his forehead:

We will later offer evidence concerning the assassination in Dealey Plaza in Dallas because it confirms the existence of a conspiracy and because it confirms the significance and relevance of the planning which occurred in New Orleans. It is the position of the State of Louisiana that, regardless of the power which might bring about the execution of a President of the United States, whether it be initiated by a small group or the highest possible force, neither the planning of his murder nor any part of it, will be regarded in Louisiana as being above the law.

And so, with David Ferrie now dead and Lee Oswald now dead, the state is bringing to trial Mr. Shaw for his role—as revealed by evidence—in participating in the conspiracy to murder John F. Kennedy.

Returning our attention to the cluttered apartment of David Ferrie: The evidence will show that Perry Russo had been a fairly close friend of David Ferrie for some time prior to the meeting between the defendant, Ferrie and Lee Harvey Oswald.

The evidence further will show that Perry Russo first met Lee Harvey Oswald at David Ferrie's apartment shortly before the principal meeting between the named conspirators took place. At this meeting Oswald, who was cleaning a bolt-action rifle with a telescopic sight, was introduced to Russo by Ferrie as Leon. Perry Russo saw Lee Harvey Oswald at Ferrie's apartment at least once after the meeting of the conspirators. On this occasion Oswald appeared to be having some difficulty with his wife and he gave Russo the impression he was leaving town.

Russo also had seen the defendant Shaw, once before the meeting. This was at the Nashville Street Wharf at the time President Kennedy was speaking there in the spring of 1962. The defendant, Shaw, also was seen by Russo with David Ferrie subsequent to the assassination at Ferrie's service station in Jefferson Parish.

In connection with the testimony of Perry Russo, the state will introduce into evidence pictures of the defendant, David Ferrie and Lee Harvey Oswald, as well as pictures of the exterior and interior of David Ferrie's apartment at 3330 Louisiana Avenue Parkway, and other corroborating evidence.

The evidence will further show that the defendant in accordance with the plan, and in furtherance of it, did in fact head for the West Coast of the United States—ostensibly to make a speech —on November 15, 1963. He remained there until after President Kennedy's assassination on November 22, 1963, thereby establishing an alibi for himself for the day of the shooting.

The state will offer into evidence a ledger sheet of travel consultants and testimony which reflects the arrangements made by the defendant, Shaw, to go to the West Coast. This travel consultant firm—which in 1963 was located in the International Trade Mart—was the same firm which arranged for Lee Oswald to go to Europe, from which he went to Russia, several years earlier.

The state will show that Ferrie drove to Houston on the day of the assassination, departing from New Orleans on the evening of November 22—some hours after the President was killed and two days before Lee Oswald was killed. Ferrie drove, with two young companions, through a severe storm for the ostensible purpose of going ice skating in Houston. Upon arriving in Houston, Ferrie and his companion went to the Winterland Skating Rink, where Ferrie loudly and repeatedly introduced himself to the manager of the rink. Despite the fact that he had driven all the way from New Orleans to Houston for the purpose of ice skating, David Ferrie never put on any ice skates at all. While his young friends skated, Ferrie stood by the public pay phone as if waiting for a call. . . .

With regard to the assassination itself, the state will establish that on November 22, 1963, President John F. Kennedy and Governor John Connally, who was riding in the same limousine, were wounded as a result of gunshots fired by different guns at different locations. Furthermore, the state will show that President Kennedy himself was struck by a number of bullets coming from different guns at different locations—thus showing that more than one person was shooting at the President. The evidence will show that he was struck in the front as well as the back—and that the final shot which struck him came from in front of him, knocking him backwards in his car. Once again, since Lee Oswald was in the Book Depository behind the President, this will show that a number of men were shooting and that he was, therefore, killed as the result of a conspiracy.

The state, in showing that a number of guns were fired during the assassination of President John F. Kennedy, will offer, in addition to eyewitnesses, various photographs and motion pictures of what transpired in Dealey Plaza on November 22, 1963.

First, the state will offer an eight-millimeter color motion picture film taken by Abraham Zapruder, commonly known as the Zapruder film. This film, which has not been shown to the public, will clearly show you the effect of the shots striking the President. In this connection we will also offer slides and photographs of various individual frames of this film. The state will request permission from the court to allow you, the jury, to view this material. Thus, you will be able to see—in color motion picture— the President as he is being struck by the various bullets and you will be able to see him fall backwards as the fatal shot strikes him from the front—not the back but the front. . . .

The evidence will show that shortly after the assassination of President Kennedy, on November 25, 1963, agents of the Federal Bureau of Investigation interviewed Dean A. Andrews, Jr., in his room at Hotel Dieu hospital in New Orleans. As a result of this interview with Dean Andrews, a local attorney, the bureau began a systematic and thorough search for a "Clay Bertrand."

A man who identified himself as "Clay Bertrand" called Andrews the day after the president's assassination requesting him to defend Lee Harvey Oswald, who by then had been formally charged with the murder of John F. Kennedy. The state will introduce evidence in the course of this case showing that the defendant, Clay Shaw, and the "Clay Bertrand" who called Dean Andrews on behalf of Lee Harvey Oswald, are one and the same person.

The evidence will further show that some time during the year 1966 the defendant, Clay Shaw, requested the U.S. Post Office to deliver mail addressed to him at his residence at 1313 Dauphine Street to 1414 Chartres Street, the residence of a long-time friend, Jeff Biddison. This change-of-address order was terminated on September 21, 1966. During the period that the change of address remained in effect, the U.S. Post Office letter carrier for that route delivered at least five letters to 1414 Chartres Street, addressed to "Clem Bertrand," the name used by the defendant at the meeting between himself, David Ferrie and Lee Harvey Oswald in Ferrie's apartment in mid-September 1963. None of the letters addressed to "Clem Bertrand" were ever returned to the postal authorities for any reason. The period during which these letters addressed to

"Clem Bertrand" were delivered to 1414 Chartres Street preceded by at least six months the publication of the fact that the Orleans Parish District Attorney's office was investigating the assassination of President John F. Kennedy. In fact, it preceded the start of the investigation by the District Attorney's office. In connection with this evidence, the state will offer into evidence the U.S. Post Office forms reflecting the change of address initiated by the defendant and testimony showing the delivery to that address of mail addressed to "Clem Bertrand."

It will be shown that in December 1966 the defendant, Clay Shaw, visited the V.I.P. room of one of the airlines at Moisant Airport and that, while there, he signed the guest register in the name of "Clay Bertrand." Eyewitness testimony will be presented and the guest book which he signed will be introduced into evidence.

The State of Louisiana will ask you to return a verdict of guilty as charged against the defendant, Clay Shaw.

When Jim Garrison was finished—his reading of the opening statement had taken forty-two minutes—Judge Haggerty soon recessed court for lunch to give Irvin Dymond time to prepare his opening statement. There was a dandy hubbub as Jim Garrison made his way out of the court, followed by his aides, who were congratulating him, as were some of the press and many Ladies of the Court, who flocked after him as if he were their spiritual leader. These women, who now began regular attendance, soon became known as the "Hanging Ladies."

The Rolfes were looking like the parents of the class valedictorian at graduation and both inquired of me, "Well, what did you think of Jim? Didn't he do that well? You see, the man is really extraordinary . . ."

In truth, Jim Garrison had given a fine performance. His reading of the opening statement had been subtle, level and head-on, and the complete underplaying—the lack of any theatrics whatever —lent his speech a factual tone of complete conviction that made his accusations appear most impressive. With this delivery Jim Garrison made the charge against Clay Shaw chilling. He was not at all the bombastic, temperamental, flamboyant character I'd come to expect.

Outside in the corridor, a man from the District Attorney's office began handing out printed copies of Garrison's speech. He was immediately set upon, not only by members of the press but by spectators who wanted a souvenir. He ducked his head back and held the copies as far away from his body as possible to avoid injury; the cupboard was soon bare and fifteen or twenty people were left complaining that they had not gotten their copies. The man said there were more in the D.A.'s office, to come on down. I joined the mob and we trekked the length of the corridor into the outside office. Another man soon appeared at the railing holding out a handful of copies. They might well have been AT&T preferred, for all the clawing, grabbing, tearing and shouting.

I trotted downstairs to the defense office past the mob of spectators and reporters in the corridor. Clay Shaw sat behind his desk in an extraordinarily good mood. "What did you think of Big Jim?" I told him I thought he said his speech well. "Yes, I did, too. No overacting, just laid it out straight," Clay said. Irvin Dymond appeared briefly, then ducked into the adjoining office to pull his thoughts together for his opening statement, which he was going to deliver ad lib, the thought of which uneased me. I would want to be sure of my lines. The defense team, including Clay, was not unduly dismayed by the content of the opposition's opening statement: "There was nothing in it we didn't know about." Eddie Wegmann, of all of them, showed concern, but that was not at all unusual. Rosemary James said of him during the trial, "Eddie's face reminds me of a baby with the colic."

Not wanting to overstay my welcome with the defense, I left and rejoined the press corps, now sifting through Garrison's opening statement. It was not quite true that the opening statement contained nothing new. Eagle-eye Jerry Cohen pointed out a paragraph that hinted at a surprise witness and alluded to a party in the French Quarter in June 1963 at which Clay Shaw and David Ferrie supposedly spoke of killing the President. This was a different party from the one in September in Ferrie's non-French Quarter apartment where Perry Russo claimed he overheard Shaw, Ferrie and Oswald plotting the assassination. Someone else had come up with a party. We wondered who it could be.

When court resumed at 1:30, there was still enough excitement in the air to reach up to the pelican plaques. Almost everyone was on hand for the afternoon kickoff—with the notable exception of the District Attorney. It was incredible to me that he was not there to hear Irvin Dymond, as the defense lawyer stood up and said, "Your Honor, the defense knows that it is not necessary for it to respond with an opening statement, but we wish to do so." He then faced the jury and began speaking to them in his low growly voice. The following is an abridged version of his opening remarks:

We are not here to defend the findings of the Warren Commission, this is not the case at all. The defense has neither the inclination, the desire nor the money to do so. The Warren Commission interviewed 25,000 witnesses.

It is the defense's judgment to strike at the very core of the state's case—the alleged conspiratorial meeting between Shaw, David Ferrie and Lee Harvey Oswald. We will show you that this alleged meeting was not conceived until David Ferrie's death. That's when the roaches came out of the woodwork.

The defense has two courses of action to take. One, we can prove that Mr. Shaw was elsewhere at the time of the alleged meeting. But this would be impossible, since the state has never seen fit to set forth a precise time. And even if the state had set a time, Mr. Shaw couldn't be called on to go back three and one-half years and account for this time.

Secondly, the defense could prove who says this meeting took place lies. Perry Raymond Russo is a liar—a notoriety-seeking liar whose very name does not deserve to be mentioned among honest and just people. We can prove this.

When Irvin Dymond repeated that Perry Russo was a liar, James Alcock voiced an objection, claiming Dymond was going beyond the limits of an opening statement, that he was arguing his case. Judge Haggerty agreed with the state and so instructed the defense lawyer. Dymond denied he was arguing, and the judge told him to proceed.

We will begin with Russo's first entrance into this case. It was a few days after Dave Ferrie's death that Russo wrote the District Attorney and said he would be willing to tell him what he knew of Dave Ferrie, a fairly close friend of his.

The next day, February 24, 1967, Russo was interviewed by Bill Bankston of the Baton Rouge *State Times*. Russo told Bankston that he wanted to get down all he knew of the case and talked with Bankston for about forty-five minutes.

Russo did not mention Clay Bertrand, Clay Shaw, Clem Bertrand or any principals in the conspiracy. We will show this.

After this interview, three more newsmen interviewed Russo and he didn't mention Shaw, Oswald, Bertrand or a word of the conspiracy.

Then on February 25, 1967, Andrew Sciambra, an assistant district attorney in Orleans Parish, went to Baton Rouge to interview Russo. This lasted for three and one-half hours.

Three days later, Sciambra wrote a 3,500-word memo to the District Attorney. We will show you that nowhere in it was there mention of Bertrand, Shaw or a conspiracy.

We will show you that Russo was asked by Sciambra if he had ever seen Shaw. Russo's reply was that he had seen him twice— once at Ferrie's service station and a second time at the Nashville Avenue Wharf.

[At this point Moo Sciambra threw a quick sideways glance at Alcock, as if to say, Oh, shit, that effing memo is going to haunt me for the rest of my days!]

But shortly after, during the preliminary hearing for Mr. Shaw, Russo placed three meetings with Mr. Shaw, including the conspiratorial meeting.

Russo had many conversations with a reporter for a national magazine and at one time the reporter set up a meeting with Shaw for Russo. But Russo canceled out after the meeting had been arranged.

Russo told the reporter that he was afraid to go to the meeting for fear of Garrison finding out about it. Russo said he was afraid to get with Mr. Shaw and find out he was mistaken.

Then on May 28, 1967, this reporter said he noted to Russo the many inconsistencies in his testimony and replies. The reporter said Russo replied, "I can't argue with any of that."

But Russo said there is no way out for him without being caught. He told the reporter that if he sticks to his story, Shaw's lawyers will get him. And if he changes the testimony, Garrison will get him.

We will prove that another witness is totally unworthy. And we will present witnesses to whom Russo said he lied.

Concerning the overt acts referred to in the prosecution's opening statement, we will not try to dispute that Mr. Shaw took a trip to the West Coast. But we will present evidence that the trip was taken in the course of his employment and at the solicitation of the person who obtained speakers for a world trade conference there.

And we will get on the trip to Houston taken by Dave Ferrie. We will show that if Ferrie wanted an alibi, as contended by the state, that he went from a good one to one not so good.

We will show that Dave Ferrie at the time was on the staff of Attorney G. Wray Gill, who was defending Carlos Marcello. We will show that the case was prolonged and did not end until the day of the assassination. And we will show you that there is no way of telling when the case would end.

In closing, I want to remind you jurors that we are not trying the Warren Commission Report. I ask you not to let what happened at Dealey Plaza in Dallas obscure your view of this conspiracy case.

Dymond's remarks had been shorter by half than the District Attorney's and more impassioned in the depth of his unhealthy feelings toward Perry Russo and in his firm belief that his client was totally innocent.

Another brief recess was called, during which Dymond was congratulated by his followers. Jim Garrison lost a few points in courtroom decorum for not lending an ear to Dymond's oration. As one reporter put it, "All of us sat there paying solemn attention to Garrison's vast towering edifice of bullshit. The least Garrison could do was listen to Dymond's opening remarks."

Later I got to musing that perhaps Garrison's was purely a human reaction—not wanting to hear anything bad about himself. Still, after recess, and just as the assembled were settling into their seats, Jim Garrison strode in and took his place at the prosecution table. This made his previous absence appear intentionally rude, as if he'd merely been smoking in the lobby during a part of the play he considered boring. And now, with his own witnesses about to take stage and fascinate the audience, he was ready to occupy his seat once again.

19

The Country Folk

A different form of excitement took hold now as court was called to order and the name Edward Lee McGehee was called out. All heads craned around at the door as a balding man wearing glasses walked in, took the witness chair, and was sworn in. Mr. McGehee was a barber in Jackson, Louisiana, a town about 120 miles north of New Orleans. Under Alcock's guidance he identified a picture of Lee Harvey Oswald and testified that he had given Oswald a haircut in late August or early September of 1963. Oswald had been interested in securing a job at the Louisiana State Hospital, the barber said, adding he'd referred Oswald to a state representative, Reeves Morgan, and suggested if he were a registered voter he might have a better chance of getting a job. He testified that Oswald's car, parked in front of the barbershop, was old and battered and that a young woman sat in the front seat and what looked to be a baby bassinet occupied the back. (The Warren Report stated that neither Oswald nor his wife, Marina, could drive a car.) McGehee had never seen Oswald before or since, but he testified he'd mentioned to his wife upon seeing Oswald's picture the day of the assassination that "I recognized him from somewhere." The barber testified Oswald was neat and clean-shaven.

Dymond then took over. He was interested in the precise date of the haircut. McGehee said it was either late August or the first half of September. He remembered because the weather had turned cool. He was definite about it not being past September 15. (It was well documented that Oswald had departed New Orleans for Mexico City toward the end of September.) Asked how he remembered Oswald as being clean-shaven, McGehee replied, "Barbers notice that. When you give a man a haircut, you try to sell him a shave." The barber had testified under direct questioning that he'd never contacted the FBI or any other agency about Oswald's presence.

Dymond then asked, "Is there any reason that you waited five years to come forward with this information?"

The barber's reply was a snappish "No one approached me.",

To me, the next obvious question should have been: Who approached you to testify in this trial? I was disappointed that Dymond didn't ask it and instead excused the witness.

Reeves Morgan, the man to whom McGehee had referred Oswald, was sworn in next. He testified that Oswald came to see him in the latter part of August or early part of September; he'd advised the young man to get an application form and take a civil service examination, also suggesting it would not hurt if he were a registered voter in the area. Mr. Morgan said he did contact the FBI after the assassination to tell them he recognized Oswald as a man who'd come to see him about a job, but he claimed the FBI already knew Oswald had been in the vicinity of Jackson, that they thanked him for his call but that was the end of it. Reeves Morgan also recalled Oswald as clean-shaven and neatly dressed, and the weather as cool.

So far, Clay Shaw's name had not been mentioned, but the third witness of the day—John Manchester, the lean true-grittish town marshal of Clinton, Louisiana, a small town near Jackson— fingered him. Manchester testified under examination by Andrew Sciambra that in the summer of 1963 there had been a civil rights registration drive to get more Negro voters on the rolls. That summer, he said, there were many strangers and strange cars in town. It was his job to keep law and order and he was suspicious of outsiders. One day in August or September, he related, a black Cadillac pulled up and parked near the voter registrar's office. The town marshal claimed he had walked over to speak with the driver, who said he was from the International Trade Mart in New Orleans. "Do you see the man in this courtroom that you talked to?" Sciambra asked. The town marshal pointed to Clay Shaw.

When Dymond questioned the man, he asked the town marshal how long he'd spoken to the man in the driver's seat. The answer was "I'd venture to say two minutes." Dymond asked, "Before today and exclusive of the incident in Clinton, have you ever seen the defendant before?" The town marshal said he'd seen him two weeks previously, in this very courtroom, during the selection of the jury. Dymond wanted to know how it was possible to speak to a man for two minutes five years earlier and positively identify him. The town marshal replied, "I forget names, but I don't forget faces." Then Dymond got into the matter of when the town marshal had reported the essence of what he was testifying to right now. Manchester didn't remember. Dymond pressed him: "Was it after the preliminary hearing?" Manchester said he thought it was after Mr. Shaw was indicted. Dymond asked why he hadn't contacted the Warren Commission. John Manchester snorted, "I figured if they wanted it, they could come and get it." Now Dymond tossed in a question which was meant to discredit the town marshal with the Negroes on the jury: "Isn't it true the object of your presence at the voter registration drive was trying to keep Negroes from voting?" This brought Alcock and one or two other assistant D.A.s jumping to their feet, shouting, "Objection! Objection!" Manchester replied, "No, it certainly was not!" At that, Dymond excused him.

The fourth witness for the prosecution was Henry Earl Palmer, a fuddled man who had been the registrar of voters in Clinton for eleven years. When asked where his office was, in which building, he could not say. He struggled mightily with this problem until you could feel the embarrassment in the courtroom. He was obviously the registrar of voters, but he simply drew a blank on this one particular point. He testified that in the summer of 1963 there were a lot of out-of-towners in Clinton trying to get the locals to vote (one got a definite idea of his feelings about this effort) and that he had seen a black Cadillac outside the registration office. He'd seen the car parked there six times during the day—whenever he'd left for lunch or coffee breaks—and although he'd never been closer than fifteen or twenty feet to it, he said the man seated on the passenger side of the front seat had strange hair and eyebrows—"messed up," as he put it. He identified a picture of David Ferrie as this man. He described the man behind the wheel as being tall with white hair, broad shoulders and a ruddy complexion. The witness then identified Clay Shaw as that man. He went on to testify that he'd seen Lee Harvey Oswald in the predominantly Negro registration line and that in the afternoon he'd spoken to Oswald when his turn came up but had not registered him because he had no proof he lived in the area.

Palmer told Irvin Dymond he'd recognized Oswald's picture from the papers after the assassination. The lawyer asked if he'd also recognized Clay Shaw's picture. Sciambra quickly objected, but before the judge could rule the witness had replied, "I did not." Dymond then zeroed in on just how good a look he'd gotten at the two men in the black Cadillac. Palmer finally admitted he had not seen their faces, he'd only seen "the back of the head and shoulders of one and the profile of the other."

On re-direct Sciambra showed Palmer a photograph of Guy Bannister, the deceased lawyer many people said resembled Clay Shaw. Sciambra asked Palmer if he knew Bannister and the man said he'd known him in World War II. On re-cross, Palmer told Dymond he would recognize Guy Bannister on sight, but not if he saw only his head and shoulders.

I was hoping Dymond would then ask: And yet you recognize a man you had *not* known but only seen from a distance of fifteen or twenty feet five years ago and have testified that you did not even see his face—as *Clay Shaw?* But the witness was excused.

The last witness of the day was the most damaging. He was Corrie C. Collins, a Negro who had been the head of the Clinton chapter of the Congress of Racial Equality (CORE) at the time of the registration drive. Here was someone who would not be expected to corroborate the town marshal's story; they must have been on opposite sides of the fence, at least in the summer of 1963. Collins testified he'd seen the black Cadillac and identified Oswald, from a photograph, as the man who got out of the back seat and stood in the registration line, and he described the man behind the wheel as having a heavy build, gray hair and wearing a light-colored hat. Sciambra asked Corrie Collins if that man was in the courtroom and Collins pointed to Clay Shaw. He then described Ferrie by means of his eyebrows and hair and identified a picture of him.

When Dymond took over this witness, he was a much more persistent questioner. The lawyer wanted to know how he'd come to be a witness in this case. Collins said, "They came to me a few months after the defendant was arrested." He got Collins to admit he'd never volunteered any of the information to the Warren Commission or any other agency and asked him why he had not. "I felt if they wanted to know, they'd ask me," he replied.

DYMOND: When did you first see a picture of Clay Shaw?

COLLINS: In 1967 in the newspapers.

DYMOND: On the basis of a picture in the newspapers, you recognized a man you'd seen for only a matter of minutes at a distance of twenty to thirty feet years before?

COLLINS: I'd seen him here in this courtroom.

This verified the suspicion that all of the Clinton people had been brought to the courtroom to view Clay Shaw during the voir dire.

Now Dymond got him to admit that when he'd first seen Clay Shaw's picture he had not immediately recognized him. "I looked at the picture," Collins said, "studied it and began to place where I had seen him." Dymond wanted to know what were the main points of identification. Collins replied they had been Shaw's gray hair and the build of his shoulders. Dymond quickly said, "But you said he had a hat on?" Collins replied, after a pause, "Yes, but the hat didn't completely cover his head."

Dymond was warmed up now and he added, "Then you only saw gray temples?" "Yes," Collins admitted. Dymond further confused the witness by trying to get him to recall whether the car was to his right or left. Collins could not remember that, or which direction the car was pointed in, although he remembered it was on his side of the street. When Dymond insisted he remember, Collins said he could not do it "because I wasn't necessarily standing in the same position the whole time." Dymond returned to the fact that Collins had seen Clay Shaw in court during jury selection. "Yes," Collins answered. "And you had not seen him between 1963 and 1969?" "That's right," the witness said. "And you say it's the same man?" "Yes," Corrie Collins replied, and he was then excused.

As we all soon were. It had been a long day and it was good to be released from the courtroom.

The Rolfes were anxious to rub in the Clinton folk's testimony. "Well, what about that?" June asked. "Yes," Dick added, feigning a look of empathetic understanding at what I must be going through, "doesn't look good for Clay, does it?" I had to admit that if the witnesses kept clocking in at a steady rate, it did not look good. "You see, Jim [Garrison] just didn't make this up out of his own head," Dick said. (No, I thought. Jim Garrison must have *something!*) The Rolfes were never known *not* to belabor a point so I took my leave as graciously as possible. They dispensed small pained smiles that were meant to say, Cheer up, you've just been hoodwinked; we know this is hurting but you had to learn the truth eventually.

The Clinton people—soon known as the "Country Folk" because of their group homeliness—were not the steadiest clump of witnesses that had ever been trotted before a jury, but the very fact that they were such a mixed bag lent impressiveness to their testimony. Most of all, one could not help wonder how they got together, who first contacted one of them, and who took it from there, rounding up the others. A reporter told me he saw Corrie Collins drive off in a car with the town marshal. They were not playing the cobra and the mongoose now.

The jury this first day had listened to the Country Folk with active interest; from the seriousness of their expressions there was not much doubt they were impressed by the state's opening barrage.

Court started at 9 the next morning. Judge Haggerty invariably began the proceedings by asking the jury if they'd had a good night. Several of them would mumble and smile in return, a few would nod, and the rest would look at him, heads cocked, as if to say, Good night, indeed, locked up three-four-five to a room.

Another one of the Country Folk began the day. A second Negro CORE worker from the summer of 1963—William E. Dunn, Sr.—testified about the black Cadillac car and the man sitting behind the wheel. Sciambra asked what made him notice the man. "He was a stranger to me," Dunn replied. He then described the man as having "big shoulders, a big man, with gray hair." At that point he identified Clay Shaw.

The defendant reacted virtually the same to any moment of identification. Head up, he would look his identifier in the eye—not with belligerence or even disbelief—simply look at him.

Under direct questioning, Dunn went on to say he was not sure about any other passenger in the front seat. He said he noticed "one white boy" in the voter registration line and after looking at a picture of Lee Harvey Oswald, identified him as having been the one.

Under cross-examination, Dymond asked Dunn how he'd come to be a witness in the case. "The D.A.'s office got in touch with me about a year ago," was the reply. He also testified he'd come to court during jury selection for a look at the defendant. "Did the D.A.'s office ask you to look at him?" Dymond asked. "I don't know," the witness replied.

I was positive Dymond would ask the next obvious question: Then who *did* ask you to come to the courtroom to look at Clay Shaw? But the defense lawyer went on to concentrate upon Dunn's identification, asking if the man he'd seen in Clinton didn't have longer hair than Clay Shaw. The witness said he did not. Dymond pursued this question, wanting to know if Dunn would remember the length of a man's hair, since he'd seen the man only briefly five years ago. To this Dunn gave a marvelously all-inclusive answer: "Look, when a man's in town, I notice him, and I don't forget him." Dymond asked if the man in the car had worn a hat. "He didn't have no hat on," the witness said. Dymond immediately picked this up: "What if I told you Corrie Collins said the man was wearing a hat—" Alcock quickly objected while Dunn added, "I said he didn't have a hat." At one point Dymond asked, "Before seeing him [Shaw] in Clinton had you ever seen him before?"

DUNN: I can't remember.
DYMOND: Did he look familiar?

Dunn, for some reason, had extreme difficulty understanding this question and Judge Haggerty eventually asked the lawyer to rephrase it without using the word "familiar." Dymond: "Did he look like someone you'd seen before?" "No," replied the witness, "I'd never seen him before." A sigh rose in the press section.

Dunn had said earlier he'd recognized Shaw's picture in the newspapers when he was arrested and now Dymond asked why he hadn't come forward to make a report of this strange man he'd remembered seeing in Clinton the same day that Oswald was there. To this, William Dunn gave a reply that won him a few smiles: "I didn't think I had to report it. When I saw his picture he was already arrested—what am I gonna have cause to get him arrested again?" Dunn testified that Clay Shaw had worn a dark suit, but he could not remember what Lee Harvey Oswald wore. Asked why that was, he said he thought "the man in the car was the FBI." He was questioned further about the location of the car and finally released.

The Clinton people had a strong effect on the press and spectators and, one presumed, the jury at the opening of the trial.

Hugh Aynesworth of *Newsweek* told me a story that casts some light on these Country Folk. I later asked him to write down his impressions of a visit he'd made to Clinton right before the start of the trial. Excerpts from his account follow:

Sometime around mid-January I was in Dallas, running down a rumor that Clay Shaw's name had been found in old papers of Jack Ruby's . . . the wire services had used the story directly from the *Dallas Times-Herald* without checking. It said that in Ruby's papers was the notation "Opening for Shaw."

I got up there, found the guy who had the stuff and looked at the page in question. It said simply "Opening of *Show.*" On the same page were names and addresses of show business characters and contacts Ruby had. That is a perfect example of how irresponsible most of the press was in the matter.

Anyway while in Dallas I checked with a few well-placed contacts, informers and the like . . . and lo and behold, a guy I hardly knew called me and told me he could supply me with a list of all the witnesses Garrison was planning to use. Was I interested, he asked? Well, yes and no. I had run down about 75 to 100 similar "tips" and usually had found they were worthless—figments of somebody's vivid imagination or false. But at this point I felt Garrison had such an advantage I had to take a look-see.

There on a three page sheet were the names, addresses and planned testimony (capsuled) of more than 20 Garrison witnesses. Most of them I recognized, but a few were completely new. Most of the new were from the Clinton-Jackson area.

I had heard several months before, that Garrison's investigators were supposed to have found that Lee Oswald had sought a job at the state mental hospital at Jackson. Upon checking the dates and checking Oswald's whereabouts on those days, I found the odds about 100–1 that Lee Harvey Oswald could have been there. But, this was 1969 and after watching Garrison's behavior for better than 18 months, I knew that logic, fact or common sense had no place in Big Jim's strange world.

I asked Bill Gurvich . . . to go with me. About two-thirds of the names on the list were unknown to Gurvich also. In other words they had come forth more than five months after the preliminary hearing of Clay Shaw, and about six months after "the Giant" had bragged that he knew all the names, places and etc.

Gurvich and I drove to Clinton in his car, following a visit with a top Louisiana State Police official in Baton Rouge. We learned enough from the State Police official to let us know that the whole thing was a hoax, but we decided to visit several of the witnesses anyway—in the belief that if we could talk with them, and tape-record the conversation, we would probably find flaws in their stories. "It's for sure they'll never be able to tell the same wacky story twice," said Gurvich. This turned out to be true.

John Manchester, the town marshal, was the first witness we encountered. He was shocked that we knew that he was to testify. Manchester, a foul-talking, dirty and scruffy man who looked like the only way he could whip a man was to kick him in the groin, wouldn't comment on his testimony at first, but he kept saying, "Ain't no way that son-of-a-bitch (Oswald) coulda fired all them shots. Ain't no way."

Manchester told me he recognized Oswald at that time—the day Oswald shot Kennedy, adding, "And I told several people about it." I pressed him to give me the names of those people he had mentioned this to, but beyond a stammer or two, he couldn't come across. "You probably still run around with the same guys now you did then, don't you?" I taunted the skinny racist. "Damn right," he replied, "when I got a friend, he's a friend." He said he worked with and drank coffee with most of the same people in 1963 and 1968, but when I kept asking him who he mentioned seeing Oswald in Clinton to, he just grinned that brown smile and changed the subject. Once he said I reminded him of a guy he knew in the Air Force or the Army. "I got enough of that shit real fast," he added, "and I'm gettin' enough of these questions of yours too."

Some of his cronies were kidding Manchester that when Irv Dymond "got a hold of him, he'd shake loose and tell everything he knew." Manchester wiped mud from his cowboy boots and snapped, "Sheeit . . . ain't nobody gonna make me do nothin'." They told him he'd have to dress up when he appeared in court. "Sheeit . . . I'll wear just what I got on. If that ain't good enough for 'em, screw 'em," he said.

Gurvich, who is a well-known and respected referee at State Police (and other law enforcement) shooting matches, got to telling Manchester how Oswald shot Kennedy. Manchester said he couldn't believe it, that Oswald had help and that probably they "was plannin' the whole thing when they's up here that summer."

I kept talking to him about his early (November of 1963) identification of Oswald as having been there and he got angry and told me how he had "knocked the Hell out of a reporter" at a recent trial in Clinton. "He tried to come over that bar, towards the jury, you know, and I jes let him have it. He might still be pukin'." He added, "I don't mess around with these rabble rousers . . . the press. You or anyone else messes with me, I'll cut 'em a new asshole."

We went to see Corrie Collins, but were told he had left town. A deputy took us to his house and barged right in and sat down in the living room as Collins' father, Emmett "Snowball" Collins, looked at the three of us with fear in his eyes. It was just after dark and he knew we weren't there to watch TV. He told us his son now lived in Baton Rouge and worked at the Post Office there. The white-haired man of 70 told us he didn't know anything about the case and didn't know what his son knew.

We left and drove to Baton Rouge, where about 11 P.M. we just missed him at the Post Office, but we found that he was working there under an assumed name. We tried to find his home, but to no avail. We never found Corrie, but it was simple to see how he *had* to testify to what Manchester and the other scrub-nuts wanted him to. His father was simply terrified by three white men barging into his house after dark. In short, being a Negro in Clinton—a hotbed of the red-neck and the klan—is not much fun.

Henry Burnell Clark, a clerk at the Stewart and Carroll Store in Clinton, was supposed to have identified Ferrie and Shaw on the Clinton main drag. He didn't want to talk about it. "Go 'way, man," he winced. "I don't know what you're talkin' about."

We didn't get around to the others up there. It wasn't the most pleasant town to be in and we figured we'd come back another day. But Manchester soon called Garrison to complain about us and within days Garrison had sent Alcock to complain publicly at a press conference that Kent Biffle, Gurvich and I had been talking to witnesses. They weren't sure, said the little punk, Alcock, but there was a possibility that we were trying to bribe them. Of course, nothing ever came of it—except that Garrison dropped some of the witnesses.

Manchester, you'll recall, testified that he had spent two minutes talking to Clay Shaw that summer of 1963 and Dymond asked him how he could be so sure—to have only seen a man for two minutes five years before. "I don't forget faces," Manchester snapped. "I may not remember names, but I remember faces. It's my job to." More importantly, perhaps, three to four weeks after I'd spent one to two hours with the man discussing the very subject he was concerned with, Manchester did not recognize me when I went up to talk to him following his testimony on the stand. *"Newsweek,* eh," he said. "Yeh, I met a feller from there not too long ago, and . . ." One of the assistant D.A.s pulled him away—him, still not recognizing a man with a 12-inch scar on his face whom he had threatened a few days before. Quite a memory has mister Manchester!

Many people have asked me about the Clinton-Jackson witnesses. Were they mistaken? Who did they see? How could so many be wrong? And so on. I honestly cannot explain how it happened, though I have some small insight into how it could have occurred. First, I think John Manchester and a State Policeman . . . put it all together. I'm certain that there were many out-of-towners—FBI, press, etc.—during that 1963 Voter Registration Drive in Clinton. And, I feel certain every damn one of them was resented. And remembered. Maybe one of them looked something like Shaw or like Oswald. Funny though that nobody came forth after Oswald's face was plastered all over the world, November 22–24, 1963, when their memories should have been ultra sharp.

The rest of the morning, following the last of the Country Folk, was uneventful. Two women from the Louisiana State Hospital testified to Lee Harvey Oswald's alleged attempt to secure employment and his job application—which was missing. They were followed by a parade of New Orleanians, several of whom were policemen, who testified that Oswald had passed out "Hands Off Cuba!" leaflets in New Orleans in the summer of 1963 and to his subsequent arrest as the result of a street altercation. Dymond claimed much of this was irrelevant but the judge overruled his objections, and the defense lawyer took the usual bills of exception at every opportunity.

20

The Vernon Bundy Fix

When Judge Haggerty had taken to his bench after lunch and the jurors were seated in their box, the name Vernon Bundy, Jr., was called out. A 30-year-old Negro and self-admitted heroin addict, Bundy was considered by Garrison to be an important witness, being one of two who had testified at the preliminary hearing. Although by this time both Miguel Torres and John Cancler had claimed that Bundy told them he had made up the story so he might get preferential treatment, and it was known by those who followed the case that a few of Garrison's advisers had urged him to drop Bundy from the cast of characters, here he was again, two years later, wearing dark gray slacks, a white shirt without a tie and a black cardigan, ambling down the aisle of the courtroom, eyes a bit puffy, looking like a sleek thin cat who'd been through his share of back-alley survival scrapes and scraps.

Under James Alcock's direct questioning and after the preliminaries—address, occupation (clothes presser), and information about his attending a clinic and taking the methadone treatment in order to stay off drugs—Bundy repeated in a husky-hoarse voice his story that on a Monday in June 1963 he had taken two caps of heroin, a bottle of water, a soft drink, his cooker—"my outfit, as we refer to it"—along on a bus ride to the shores of Lake Pontchartrain, where he'd planned to give himself a fix.

"I was sitting on top of the steps of the seawall and was beginning to use my drugs, to empty two caps of heroin into the cooker . . . behind me I noticed a black limousine approaching. It was facing toward town on the other side of the street. A gentleman got out of the car and walked behind me, passing maybe thirty to forty feet from me. I didn't know if he was a narcotics officer or what. I didn't want him to run up on me with the heroin. I wanted to have time to throw the caps in the lake and let it dissolve. . . . I saw a man with a towel approaching from the white section of the beach. He came up to the gentleman already there. They must have stayed there only five or ten minutes, but to an addict it seemed like five or ten hours."

Alcock asked Bundy if he saw either one of those men in the courtroom. "I see one," replied Bundy. "This gentleman seated here." Vernon Bundy pointed to Clay Shaw, who sat in his chair, a cigarette in his hand, gazing calmly at his accuser. Alcock said, "Let the record show that the witness pointed out the defendant, Mr. Clay Shaw." Alcock then showed Bundy a picture of Lee Harvey Oswald and the young man identified him as the other man at the lakefront.

Bundy went on to finish his story, saying the two men talked for a while but the only words he could hear were from the man he claimed was Oswald. "What am I gonna tell her?" were the words. Bundy: "The gentleman here tried to make the smaller one quiet down." Bundy said the two men kept looking at him and he, in turn, kept his eyes on them. "The gentleman here," he said, once again indicating Clay Shaw, "gave the other gentleman what looked to be like money. He didn't examine it but put it in his back pocket. Some pamphlets or sheets—I didn't know what—fell out of his pocket. The gentleman here who came in the car said to me, 'It's a very hot day,' and adjusted his collar. He got into his car and drove off. The young fellow went back toward Pontchartrain Beach. I got my outfit and wrapped it in the sheets that the man dropped. It said something like 'Help Cuba' or 'Free Cuba.' The sheets were yellow and black and white and black."

Alcock then showed Bundy a picture of a car, which the witness said could have been the car Clay Shaw drove up in. It had taken Bundy approximately twenty minutes to run through his story on direct.

He was then turned over to Dymond. The defense lawyer, who had been expected to rip into Vernon Bundy, started off easily by questioning the witness about the methadone treatment and then asking how long he'd been a dope addict. "Off and on since I was thirteen," was the reply. Asked how he got money to support this expensive habit, Bundy replied that certain people in his family gave him money and he worked for the rest of it. Dymond then asked if it wasn't a fact that he stole regularly to pay for his drugs. Alcock objected and the judge sustained him, saying the witness did not have to incriminate himself. Dymond argued that Bundy had admitted in the preliminary hearing that he'd stolen, indicating he was attempting to impeach the credibility of the witness by contradictory testimony. "Aren't you a convicted burglar?" Dymond persisted. "I am not," replied Bundy, going on to qualify his answer. "It was a theft of a cigarette machine, and it was not opened—"

Dymond stopped him, but Alcock quickly objected, saying he wanted the witness to have the right to explain his answer. Judge Haggerty agreed and then Vernon Bundy, with an indignant tone to his voice, looked at Irvin Dymond and said, "As I stated before you interrupted me"—a burst of laughter in the courtroom and a call for order—"it was not a burglary, it was a cigarette machine from the Municipal Auditorium and it was opened by another party."

Now Dymond asked Judge Haggerty to have Bundy's police record retrieved. A recess was called and after the jury had filed up to their room, Bundy strolled over to sit in one of the jurors' chairs, where he smoked several cigarettes. Clay Shaw stood up and walked within inches of Bundy on his way to get a drink of water in the small corridor behind the witness chair. Neither looked at the other. I thought how difficult it would be, were I the defendant, to refrain from confronting my accuser.

After recess, Dymond read into the record that Vernon Bundy had pleaded guilty to theft on May 25, 1966. The lawyer then asked Bundy if it wasn't his testimony a few minutes earlier that he had secured money to support his heroin habit from relatives and from working. "That's right," Bundy said. Now the lawyer began reading from the transcript of the preliminary hearing. This brought forth an objection from Alcock, and a lengthy hassle ensued, during which Judge Haggerty told the witness he should not have had to give up his constitutional rights during the preliminary hearing, that he should have been so informed by the three-judge panel, adding that if *he* had been one of the judges, Bundy would have been so informed.

After a while, however, Dymond was permitted to continue reading from the transcript. Dymond: "You were asked, 'Where were you getting the money?' Your reply was 'By working and other little hustles here and there.' Do you deny that?"

Bundy: "No, I don't. I didn't understand the question. If I saw something around and no one was looking, I would take it. I didn't steal every day." "You did steal on occasion to satisfy your habit?" Dymond then asked. "Yes," answered Bundy. And that little detour was ended.

Then Dymond returned to the morning of his fix back in 1963. It turned out Bundy's family lived in a large house, twenty or twenty-five rooms, with three bathrooms. They took in eight or ten roomers, and he shared a room with his brother. He had taken a cap of heroin Sunday night, he said, and had saved the other two caps for Monday, adding, "I had planned to goof off." When Dymond delved into the trip to the lakefront and the arrival of the black limousine, Bundy suddenly made a request to the court, asking that he be allowed to give a demonstration in proof of his identification of Clay Shaw.

There was a brief pause while this request sunk in, then Judge Haggerty agreed and, with no objections from the defense, who must have been interested out of plain curiosity if nothing else, Vernon Bundy took over the courtroom as director and actor. Standing up from the witness chair, he asked to have Clay Shaw step to the rear of the courtroom. Whispers rustled through the court, all with question marks at the end, as Clay stood up with a quizzically bemused expression on his face. Several deputies fell into stride alongside him as he turned, passed through the gate at the railing and walked back toward the large entrance doors at the end of the center aisle. Bundy, in the meantime, stepped down off the witness stand, walked to Clay Shaw's chair and turned it sideways, sitting in it so that he faced away from the jury and in profile to Clay Shaw.

"Would the gentleman approach me?" Vernon Bundy asked, not looking at Clay but glancing down at the floor and a bit to his right as the defendant, flanked by the bailiffs, moved forward. "Here I am on top of the seawall with my cooker," Bundy said, leaning over and simulating this scene. Clay and the two guards approached him, Bundy glanced down and sideways toward Clay's feet, and the advancing party stopped when they had walked behind the witness. What, we all wondered, was the significance? We weren't to be told right away. Vernon Bundy asked to have the defendant repeat his part of the performance. Now, as Clay turned to walk back up the aisle, he gave a slight shrug and a grin, as if to say, Listen, I've gone along with enough already, why balk at this?

Clay, followed by the bailiffs, repeated his forward walk, once more passing behind Vernon Bundy, who again glanced suspiciously down at the defendant's legs and feet.

Vernon Bundy seemed satisfied and returned to the witness chair while Clay Shaw reoccupied his seat. When the courtroom had settled down Bundy said, "I watched his foot the way it twisted that day." Vernon Bundy wiggled his own foot. "This is one way I identified this man the next time I saw him." Bundy told of coming into the courtroom with an assistant district attorney and observing Shaw before he'd testified in the preliminary hearing, adding, "The twisting of his foot had frightened me that day on the seawall when I was about to cook my drugs."

Clay Shaw, because of his bad back, does have, at times, a labored, slightly stiff walk.

While the twisting of a foot might have frightened Mr. Bundy, there was another aspect of his experience on the seawall that did not seem to alarm him at all. And this Irvin Dymond got into, questioning him about the logic of a seasoned dope addict leaving the safety of his twenty-room home and taking a trip out to a public beach to give himself a fix, the harsh penalty for which he was well aware, and, then, to compound this recklessness, remaining on the seawall with his drugs and equipment within hearing distance of two strangers, one of whom he even thought might be a narcotics agent, when the rest of the beach, he testified, was virtually deserted. This, the defense lawyer indicated, did not add up. Anyone with common sense, especially with the suspicious self-protective nature of a veteran narcotics addict, would presumably have made fast tracks out of there—or certainly would have dropped, thrown into the lake, or swallowed the heroin.

The witness merely said he'd simply decided to go to the lake that Monday and goof off and that's what he'd done.

Now the defense lawyer asked Bundy if he'd known John the Baptist. Bundy, immediately on the defensive, said they'd been on the same tier in the Parish Prison but denied ever having a conversation with him. Dymond asked, "Do you deny telling him that you knew nothing of the Clay Shaw case, that you were going to say you did so you could get a better break on your sentence?" To this Vernon Bundy replied, almost like an angry child, "I didn't say *boo* to John the Baptist!"

The lawyer then asked if he knew Miguel Torres, the other

prisoner who claimed Bundy had spoken to him about false testimony. "No, I don't know him," the witness declared. "Do you deny," Dymond continued, "having told him you couldn't make up your mind about placing Clay Shaw on Esplanade [a street bordering the French Quarter] or the lakefront?"

"No, I didn't," Bundy answered. "I didn't even want the District Attorney's office to know about it. I had become friendly with a certain judge, he had helped me and got me to the hospital at Fort Worth, Texas, and I wanted him to know about it."

Bundy was soon excused. Again, one wanted Dymond to pursue the questioning. It would have been most interesting to hear Vernon Bundy relate precisely how he had appeared as a witness in the case, what judge he'd approached, if that were true, and how it progressed from there. If he had come forward by himself, had he done so upon seeing a picture of Clay Shaw in the newspapers after Shaw's arrest and had he truly remembered seeing this man on the lakefront for five or ten minutes all the way back in 1963, at a time when he was more interested in getting a heroin fix than anything else in the world?

Vernon Bundy stepped away from the stand in his cool-cat tucked-in gait, his eyes in squint position, first quickly brushing past the prosecution table, in sly declaration that he had not come apart at the seams, then shifting to the right and left as he passed through the press and spectator section. He was obviously pleased with his demonstration, which he had carried out with a showy display of bravado, and wanted to check the crowd's reaction to his act. It had been expected that he would be torn to pieces. Although hardly the most creditable witness, he had not been annihilated.

There was, by this time, not unanimous agreement among those in Clay Shaw's camp that Irvin Dymond was the ultimate defense lawyer. Quite a few had thought from the beginning that a high-powered trial lawyer from the East or West should have been brought in—a Lee Bailey or a Percy Foreman. According to one source, overtures had been made at one time to Foreman and the wind had it he was most interested and would have taken the case. It was Clay who had apparently balked at changing lawyers in mid-entanglement, remaining constant out of loyalty. There were those who thought this loyalty was misplaced and if he would not hang by it, he would most certainly end up convicted.

Now, after Vernon Bundy had escaped with his skin, there were low grumbles of dissatisfaction to be heard here and there, accompanied by grave head shaking. I was entertaining my own niggling doubts. I had heard Dymond's detractors, none of whom failed to praise him as a good trial lawyer. They would give him his due but they would go on to say that Clay Shaw needed a tiger, an infighter, a street fighter—no holds barred. This, on the theory that the situation in New Orleans was fraught with a cozy and stagnant insularity, that, after all, Irvin Dymond, the brothers Wegmann, and Sal Panzeca would undoubtedly continue their law practice in that city for the rest of their days, along with Judge Haggerty and, for a few years, the District Attorney and members of his staff. The defense team as constituted could therefore not afford to throw all ethics to the wind and incur undue enmity in the local courts, among the local judges, assistant district attorneys, policemen and local politicians. It was a point to give thought to, especially in view of the mass of retaliatory action already stacked up by Jim Garrison.

The defense had been dubbed the "Boy Scouts" by some New Orleanians and certain members of the press because of their dogged belief that right would out, no matter the extralegal tactics used against them by the District Attorney's office and, even more, despite proof so far to the opposite, that right had not aided in summoning any appreciable legal help from any branch of the Federal government, the Justice Department or the higher courts in the past two years.

So, during a recess, a trickling undercurrent of pessimism could be heard in the corridor outside the courtroom. Oh, God, it murmured, the Boy Scouts aren't up to it.

21

Tortured for Sixteen Years
by Fifty People

How badly the prosecution wanted a conviction and the risks they'd take to secure it were demonstrated next. The name of the game from the state's point of view was a neon-lettered big-blinking "Surprise!"

"Charles I. Spiesel," a clerk called out. Nobody had this name in his Shaw Trial Playbill, and all heads craned around to those large wooden doors underneath the clock as a dapper, balding little man marched down the aisle of the packed courtroom. Wearing a well-tailored pin-striped suit and the assured, almost righteous air of one about to perform his citizen's duty, he was sworn in. When he'd repeated his name and given his address in New York City, a breeze of hungry whispers spread throughout the court. Yes, here was a New Yorker on the stand and somehow this lent a certain nonpartisanship, which, in turn, would add a goodly amount of heft to his appearance and testimony.

Charles Spiesel spoke out in a loud clear voice in answer to preliminary questions regarding his occupation—accounting and tax work for a New York firm, a profession he'd been in for some twenty years. There was a definite no-nonsense tone to his voice that was impressive. This was no dope addict, thief, pimp, or pusher of pornographic films—here was a professional man.

Under direct questioning by James Alcock, Spiesel told of coming to New Orleans in May of 1963 to visit his daughter, who was attending Louisiana State University and also possibly to relocate in business in New Orleans, a city he had visited often. He went on to say he frequented a bar in the Quarter, LaFitte's Blacksmith Shop, and that one night in June he spotted a man he thought he'd flown with in the Air Force during World War II. This turned out to be David W. Ferrie. According to the witness, Ferrie, another man and two women invited Spiesel to accompany them to a party at an apartment in the vicinity of Dauphine and

Esplanade Streets. Spiesel said they climbed two flights of stairs and, after being let in by the host, he was introduced to all of the people present, ten or eleven men, including Clay Shaw. After a while, Spiesel said, the two women and the other man he'd arrived with left, and the remaining group, all men now, moved into the kitchen-dining area and sat around a large oval table, where everyone soon started knocking President Kennedy.

Spiesel: "Someone brought up the name of President Kennedy and just about everybody began to criticize him. Then someone said that 'Somebody ought to kill the son of a b!'" The witness said he did not know who said those words but he claimed that at first Clay Shaw seemed "amused" at the conversation. Soon another man voiced a desire to kill the President but wondered how it could be done. According to Spiesel, the talk continued for five or six minutes, and finally it was agreed that "It would have to be done with a high-powered rifle with a telescopic sight and about a mile away." Spiesel claimed Clay Shaw entered into the conversation when the talk got around to the difficulty of the killer's getaway, at which time he discussed the possibility of flying the assassin to safety with David Ferrie.

Spiesel maintained he'd been quite alarmed at the tone of the conversation, going on to add he had never seen Clay Shaw after this party but had bumped into David Ferrie two or three times. Ferrie, the witness claimed, had suggested that perhaps Clay Shaw could help him set up in business in New Orleans. Spiesel testified he'd phoned Shaw's office several times after the party but his calls had never been returned.

That was the essence of his story. Spiesel, it should be noted, did not volunteer endless reams of information in response to a question. He would usually answer without undue loquaciousness and then sit there patiently awaiting the next question. The courtroom had been completely quiet, and serious attention had been paid his story.

If James Alcock could have pressed a button and sent Spiesel careening out of the witness chair and back to New York at that very moment, no further questions asked, he would have been a most damaging witness.

Irvin Dymond began cross-examining Spiesel with a subtle undercoating of relish in his low easy voice. Dymond's first question was "Are you a certified public accountant?" "No," Spiesel replied. The defense lawyer soon got into his trip to New Orleans in the spring of 1963, asking Spiesel where he'd stayed upon arriving in New Orleans. "One of the hotels," Spiesel replied, "I don't recall." In what section of the city? Dymond wanted to know. Spiesel said it was probably in the French Quarter but he wouldn't be pinned down, adding he'd only stayed in the hotel two or three days or a week. Dymond kept him on this point until Spiesel, with a small patronizing smile, said, "If you give me a directory I'll thumb through it." Dymond then asked, "You mean you stayed in a hotel for three or four days or a week and you don't remember which hotel?" "No," Spiesel replied, not at all rattled. Spiesel said he'd then moved to an apartment for a month on Royal Street. Dymond wanted to know where on Royal Street. The witness said he thought it was probably in the 900 or 1000 block but he wasn't sure. From there, Spiesel testified, he'd moved to an apartment on Esplanade. Dymond inquired if he'd had a lease. Spiesel said no, it was on a month-to-month basis. Did he remember the landlady? The witness said he thought the owner was a doctor. How had he paid his rent? the lawyer asked. "Probably by cash," Spiesel said, adding, "If you want to check with the landlord, it's okay." But since Spiesel had not been too specific about who or where the landlord was, this might prove a formidable task.

Finally, Dymond got to the meeting at LaFitte's with Ferrie and friends. Spiesel could not recall the first or last names of either the other man or their two women companions. At this point the defense lawyer asked Spiesel if he'd ever tried to sell his story of the French Quarter party to any of the news media. "No," was the forthright reply. When Dymond pressed him, mentioning the name of a man from CBS-TV and asking Spiesel if he hadn't discussed appearing on a documentary program the network was planning, Spiesel admitted he'd been approached but firmly added he had not taken part in the program.

Dymond took a short pause and then asked, "How much did you want?" There was another brief pause before the question was answered. "I told him a couple of thousand," Spiesel said, not at all flustered at having been caught up in the fine points of cross-examination, merely indicating by tone that his time was not without worth.

Dymond, warming to his task and adding a slight dollop of

indulgence to his growl, went on to the party itself. Although Spiesel could remember much of the conversation, he could not recall the names of any of the other ten or eleven men present, with the exception of the defendant, Clay Shaw, and David Ferrie, of course, now deceased. Spiesel was clear that Clay Shaw had not been the party's host but he did not know who the host was, mentioning at one time he thought he might have been a schoolteacher. Dymond asked him to describe the architecture of the building. Spiesel said the building had a general look about it. "Give me a *general* description of it," the lawyer urged. Spiesel indicated it was not a really outstanding architectural job but Dymond was interested, even if it was not noteworthy. He finally elicited from Spiesel his opinion that the outside of the building was a light brownish color, either brick or some sort of stone. Questioned about the inside of the apartment, Spiesel indicated he could give a description of the kitchen-dining area but not the large living room. How large *was* the living room, Dymond wanted to know. "About eight by twelve feet," was the reply. "You call that large?" Dymond asked in a flat voice. Spiesel thought about this and then said perhaps it was larger. Dymond asked him to point out an area in the courtroom that would approximate the size of the living room. Spiesel did and when he'd finished, Dymond measured this off, saying, "Let the record show the witness indicated an area approximately twenty-three feet long and twelve feet wide."

Spiesel never appeared miffed when Dymond picked out contradictions in his testimony. On the contrary, he seemed to be entirely pleased to be sitting up there in the witness chair and if, finally, Dymond's tone was one of pure patronization, Spiesel patronized his questioner right back. Out front in the audience, we were all beginning to feel extremely happy that Spiesel had shown up. Boring he was not.

Finally, Dymond had Spiesel give a vague description of the kitchen-dining area, and then he pressed Spiesel to make a rough sketch of as much of the apartment as he could recall. When he finished the drawing, Spiesel mentioned it wasn't all that complete because he had not had occasion to go to the bathroom. Dymond showed the sketch to Clay Shaw and the rest of the defense team and had it passed around the jury. He then took the witness back

through the party and the entire conversation concerned with killing the President. After this, the lawyer asked if the witness had
noticed anything unusual about Ferrie. "No," Spiesel replied.
This was remarkable because anyone who had ever met Ferrie
spoke first of his bizarre appearance. Dymond continued along this
line, asking Spiesel to describe Ferrie's hair. "Reddish-brown."
"Was it well groomed?" Dymond asked. "Fairly well groomed,"
the witness agreed. "Did he have unusual eyebrows?" the lawyer
asked. "A little thinner than most men's, not unusual outside of
that," Spiesel said of David Ferrie, who, by wide acknowledgment,
had messy clumps of glued-on hair and thick pasted-on eyebrows
that rivaled those of the late John L. Lewis.

Now the defense lawyer went back over the testimony, returning
to LaFitte's and the witness's subsequent meetings with Ferrie.
Dymond appeared to be stalling. It occurred to me then that,
although it was after four o'clock, it was still not adjournment
time and I could not help thinking Dymond wished it were. The
defense lawyer next asked Spiesel what had been the reason for
selling his former income tax return business. James Alcock objected but Judge Haggerty permitted the question. "I'd had a
pretty good tax business, but it wasn't going too well," Spiesel
replied.

Finally, Dymond looked down at the defense table, paused
briefly, and then glanced back up at Spiesel. "Isn't it true," the
lawyer asked, "you filed a suit in New York in 1964 against a
psychiatrist and the City of New York, claiming that over a period
of several years the police and others have constantly hypnotized
you and finally harassed you out of business?"

Why, yes, Spiesel admitted without batting an eye, he had filed
a lawsuit and not only that, the suit was for $16 million.

The courtroom perked up at that; the press warmed to their
writing pads with slight time off for quick glances and raised
eyebrows that said, Oh-oh, what have we here? Moe Waldron was
all grins and Jerry Cohen's face was reddening in anticipation of
goodies to come.

Dymond's voice was now honey-coated in condolence with
Spiesel's problems as he asked why a psychiatrist and the police
would want to hypnotize and harass him. Spiesel really could not
say, but he casually pointed out that his father had done under-

cover work for the FBI and it might just be a communist conspiracy. ("Wheee," the woman sitting next to me whispered, "another conspiracy!")

After he had asked if it were true that Spiesel had filed his own $16-million lawsuit without aid of counsel and had furthermore acted as his own lawyer, to which he received a proudly affirmative reply, Dymond requested adjournment for the day, indicating he had new material regarding this witness and needed time to study it.

The new material was a copy of Charles Spiesel's lawsuit, which was arriving at that moment by air freight from New York City, a testament to quick and expensive investigative work. It was later reported the defense spent $4,000 to have a hurried but nevertheless exhaustive investigation of Spiesel's life and times. Although Clay Shaw had already been bled dry, the expense of this specific caper was well worth while.

Almost every morning I'd pick up the *Times-Picayune* and read the account of the previous day's happenings while riding in the cab to the courthouse. The next day, Saturday, I was amazed to read the report of Spiesel's appearance. Most of the story was devoted to the witness's testimony under direct examination. There was nothing outlining his vagueness regarding his hotel accommodations and apartment, very little about his inability to identify anyone else besides Shaw and Ferrie, or his equivocating testimony pertaining to the apartment in which the alleged conspiracy talk took place. His lawsuit and hypnosis were but briefly touched upon. There was nothing documenting his attitude or demeanor.

The headline read, SURPRISE WITNESS SAYS HE WAS INTRODUCED TO SHAW BY FERRIE. The subheadline was ASSASSINATION OF KENNEDY DISCUSSED, COURT TOLD. In the part of the story that made the front page there was this paragraph: "Dymond also established that the surprise witness had filed several suits, mostly alleging a conspiracy of one sort or another. Spiesel denied having attempted to sell his story to a television network." Twenty-eight paragraphs later, on the inside pages, the article went into slightly more detail about his lawsuit and mentioned the hypnosis, but had I not been present in court, I would have received quite a different impression of Spiesel and what had transpired.

This reporting so confused me that by the time I arrived at the courthouse I was warm under the collar, so much so that when I saw a reporter from the *Times-Picayune,* Clarence "Bumpy" Doucet, I approached him, shaking the newspaper in his face and demanding, "Did you write this?" I believe he thought I'd been bitten by a rabid dog. He backed off from me, saying he had not, and when I detailed what had riled me, he explained they had been short of reporters the previous afternoon or there would have been a fuller account. (And, I presumed, a more accurate one.) I liked Bumpy and later on felt embarrassed over my frontal attack. I was glad, however, to hear some of the other out-of-town newsmen express similar feelings over that morning's edition of the local paper.

The press section was packed much earlier than usual this morning in anticipation of the return of Charles I. Spiesel. Irvin Dymond, looking as if he'd breakfasted on half a dozen canaries, arrived and nodded good morning to James Alcock, who looked as if he might just be coming down with an Excedrin headache. Clay Shaw was beaming, as were Billy Wegmann and Sal Panzeca. Even Eddie Wegmann had a twinkle in his eye and his frown lines were not quite so deep. The jurors had had a good night, they said, and all was right in the courtroom of Judge Edward A. Haggerty, Jr.

The Ladies of the Court, hanging and otherwise, were all present, even on Saturday morning. One lady's arrival, in particular, we had all gotten accustomed to watching for each morning. We named her "Our Lady of the Hats." She possessed a wardrobe that would have made Joan Crawford appear a simple housewife. Elsie Dolin was her name and she made a smashing entrance each morning in an entirely new outfit and hat. Hat-hats, not just a little something to cover a lady's head, but something to sit up there like a wedding cake and be noticed. The lady herself was blond and striking, a handsome solidly built woman who put an extra tiger in her walk. She rarely if ever missed a day and to several of us, court was not really in session until she'd marched in betopped with a new creation, as she did this day, a little tiered something that defied description, except I wouldn't have wanted to be sitting behind it. (I believe she was a semi-Hanging Lady.)

Charles Spiesel himself, nattily dressed, strutted up and took the stand with as much evident pleasure at being back as we all felt at seeing him again.

Dymond began his cross-examination easily that morning, asking the witness if he'd discussed his testimony with anyone since leaving the stand the day before. "Only to say that I testified yesterday in court," Spiesel replied. "With whom did you talk?" Dymond asked. "Casual acquaintances. I don't know their names." The witness shrugged and added that he'd spoken to a few people at a bar in the Quarter, Lucky Pierre's, where he'd relaxed and played pool and had also called a friend from the Fontainebleau Motor Inn to say he was in town to testify.

Soon Dymond introduced into evidence a copy of Spiesel's complaint Number 32,001, marked U.S. Court of Appeals, against the Pinkerton Detective Agency and numerous other defendants. The lawyer then took his place in front of the jury and, speaking into a microphone, read portions of the suit, which claimed the defendants, during a period from January 1, 1948, to July 5, 1964, a total of sixteen years, had used a new police technique to torture him and conspired with others to torture the plaintiff in New York, New Jersey, Washington, D.C., New Orleans and various other places. Spiesel claimed these defendants also harassed, annoyed, tailed him, tapped his phones, and prevented him from having normal sex relations. ("What about abnormal ones?" cracked a reporter.) The defendants also kept him hypnotized for periods of time, caused him to make errors in his work because of their hypnotic control, wreaked psychological terror upon him, prevented him from making business deals and from borrowing money from public agencies, surrounded him with competitors in the tax return business, and hired "plants" to work in his office, who then acted intoxicated and annoyed and frightened his customers.

One of Spiesel's more interesting complaints accused the defendants of using disguises in their attempts to pass themselves off as his relatives for the purpose of gaining entrance to his home and also "to quickly pass by the plaintiff in public places."

The defendants also were accused of attempting to create the impression that Spiesel and his family were communists, attempting to link the plaintiff with various crimes, interfering with sign carriers advertising the plaintiff's business, conspiring to make Spiesel break the law, depriving him of his civil rights, mentally torturing, humiliating and financially ruining him. In a bar below Spiesel's office, near the building's main light switch, they also supposedly planted a man who enacted the equivalent of scenes out of *Angel Street*. Add this all up and Spiesel claimed the results forced him out of his own income tax return business in 1963.

At least.

During the reading of these accusations, Spiesel sat there with the air of one who had, after all, been mightily imposed upon but who was not going to let anyone get away with these foul deeds in the end.

The judge's lamp had been bent around earlier to shine down on Spiesel so he could verify the copy of his lawsuit. During a brief lull and with the harsh light still glowing down upon his balding head, I detected a slight twitch in his right eye and a tendency to press down hard upon the arm of the witness chair with the palm of his hand. I felt immensely sorry for him and was struck by a quick impulse to go up and crane the neck of the lamp, diverting the direct glow from him. But the cretin in me, the Shakespearean groundling drooling for more Bottom, soon rose to the surface when his testimony continued.

Dymond delved into the business of hypnosis, asking about various people named in the suit who had, he claimed, hypnotized him, and how he knew he was being hypnotized. To this Spiesel replied, "The best way I can explain it is to give you the general definition of hypnosis, which is to come under the will of a person but be aware that it is hypnosis."

At one point, after Alcock had objected to this line of questioning as redundant, Judge Haggerty asked Dymond, "Why are you going into this?" "Do you want me to tell you in front of the jury?" Dymond asked in reply, to which the judge answered a brisk no.

Dymond then asked Spiesel how many different people had hypnotized him. Alcock again objected and Dymond glanced up at the judge, saying, "My intent should be fairly obvious to the court." "You may proceed," said the judge. Dymond asked the question again. Spiesel thought a moment and then replied, "It's hard to say. Possibly fifty or sixty."

By this time reporters were all but spraining their wrists attempting to take down every possible syllable of this rich testimony. The following whispered aside took place between two members of the press:

FIRST REPORTER: Did he say hypnotized fifty or sixty times?

SECOND REPORTER: No—people.

FIRST REPORTER: Hypnotized by fifty or sixty different *people?*

SECOND REPORTER: Yes.

FIRST REPORTER: Jesus!

Dymond then wanted to know if Spiesel had ever been hypnotized in New Orleans. To this question Spiesel replied, "I believe I've been followed down by detectives." Dymond pressed for an answer about hypnosis in New Orleans until Spiesel finally said, "The point is, if I say yes you'll want to know the name of the person and I can't give it to you." Dymond then pulled his voice way down to a patently conspiratorial level and replied, "Suppose, then, I tell you I won't *ask* you for the person's name." Spiesel apparently thought that was fair and said, "From time to time someone has tried to hypnotize me." Again Dymond inquired how Spiesel knew when he was being hypnotized. The witness brought forth ripples of laughter when he replied, "After all this time, I'm an expert." Spiesel went on to explain: "When someone tries to get your attention—catch your eye. That's a clue right off." Now I could see several reporters covering their mouths with their hands or biting upon pencils.

On it went and the testimony did not get less bizarre. Dymond knew he had a show stopper and he wanted full value. This was not done as much to mock the witness, I believe, as to teach the state a lesson, to give them a sound spanking for the audacity and recklessness they displayed in their choice of witnesses. As the charade continued, James Alcock sat lower in his chair and his neck seemed to sink down between his shoulder blades. He had made as many objections as he possibly could—but now the cat was out of the bag and there was no stuffing it back in.

Dymond soon inquired if Spiesel had perhaps been hypnotized in May and June of 1963 at the time of the party he claimed he attended. "I don't really know if it did happen," Spiesel said, adding a gratuitous piece of information: "I've been coming down here since before that, since 1961. I'd come down twice a year. Once I came down to watch LSU play Ole Miss." Dymond then entered into the area of hypnotic illusions and the implantation of thoughts.

Now, after having testified for almost an hour about his suit, his allegations and hypnosis, Spiesel said, "You must understand this case may or may not go on trial in Federal court." He said he was aware that his testimony in the Shaw case would get extensive press coverage (amen, amen!) and added, "I'd hate to take a chance of having my case thrown out by having to go into the details"—he looked up at Judge Haggerty and blinked—"unless Your Honor orders me to."

Dymond earned chuckles when he asked in deadly mock seriousness, "You'd hate to jeopardize a $16 million lawsuit, is that right?"

Indeed he was right and Spiesel went on to explain the amount of the suit. The number of years during which he had been inconvenienced by the defendants added up to sixteen and he was well aware that the statute of limitations might well rule out seven or eight years, so he was "covering myself."

"Do you mean the damages to you are worth $1 million a year?" Dymond asked.

Spiesel replied, "That's what it amounted to."

Toward the end of this lengthy session, Dymond got Spiesel to admit that in 1965, when he'd made a trip to New Orleans, he thought he was being followed and had attempted to take depositions to this effect from the New Orleans Police Department. Said Spiesel, "At the time I was being followed around I was alone. I wanted to find out if the Police Department or the District Attorney's office was involved. But it was pretty well determined it was people from New York. I was puzzled who from New Orleans would be following me, since I knew no one here." Dymond also questioned him about whether he'd thought Aaron Kohn, the managing director of the Metropolitan Crime Commission, might also be involved. Spiesel said he had indeed and that Kohn asked him if he would accept a letter stating the Metropolitan Crime Commission was not tailing him. "I said okay," Spiesel said.

Dymond's final question was "Has anyone hypnotized you on this trip to New Orleans?"

Spiesel considered this for a moment, then smiled, cocked his head and said, "I'm afraid I would have to say no."

"Damn!" I heard a reporter mumble.

On re-direct, James Alcock tried to rehabilitate the witness by concentrating on his war record, honorable discharge and his tax business, which Spiesel claimed to have built up over a period of six or seven years. Alcock's final question on re-direct was "Have you ever been convicted of anything in your life?" "I have not," Spiesel replied.

Dymond, surprisingly enough, took him back on re-cross, asking, "Is it not a fact that fifteen suits were filed against you for bad tax returns?" "Yes," answered Spiesel, going on calmly to explain, "but they were part of the conspiracy against me."

It had been whispered around that the District Attorney's office must not have known about much of Spiesel's past activities or they would never have put him on as a witness. Now Dymond destroyed that theory when he asked, "When you conferred with the District Attorney's office about testifying in this case, did you tell them about these lawsuits and your having been under hypnosis?" "Yes, I mentioned it," Spiesel replied.

Dymond soon declared he was finished with Spiesel, who smiled at the judge, got down off the stand and had just passed the cheerless prosecution table—now only steps away from the swinging gate and freedom—when Dymond suddenly faced the judge and requested permission to have the witness lead the court to the building where the alleged party and conspiracy talk had taken place.

James Alcock objected strongly, saying it was improbable that the witness could possibly remember the exact place. Dymond insisted, saying Spiesel had gone into a description of both the inside and outside of the building. "Your Honor, it is vitally important to our case whether he can find this building and if he does, whether the apartment is there."

The judge soon agreed. "We will have to get a New Orleans Public Service bus to take the jury and we'll have to find out who owns the building and get the keys to go inside." Dymond smiled and crooned, "Let's see if we can *find* it first." Judge Haggerty then ordered the jury and all principals in the trial to be taken to the scene, the corner of Dauphine and Esplanade, stipulating that no testimony be given until the trial resumed in the courtroom.

With that the rush was on. Manic spirits were reminiscent of the last day of school in June. The corridor outside the courtroom rang with shouts of "How you goin'?" "Want a ride?" "See you down there!" and "Bring a box lunch!" Some of the Hanging Ladies risked their necks trotting down the marble hall toward the stairway in their high heels.

My Simon and Schuster friend, John Mourain, drove a few of us, including Bruce Eggler, a bright young student I had taken on to assist in research, to the Quarter in his car. Esplanade is a wide attractive street, divided in the center by a raised grassy stretch planted with trees (called the "neutral ground" in New Orleans), and it forms the lower boundary of the French Quarter. Dauphine, a much narrower street, intersects Esplanade and runs the length of the Quarter to the city's main street, Canal.

Court had recessed for this scavenger hunt at 10:30 A.M. By 11 the corner of Dauphine and Esplanade could easily have been mistaken for the scene of a major accident. Traffic was backed up for blocks and the natives of the Quarter—in holiday mood anyhow, for this Saturday was the beginning of the vast stream of parades that herald the active Mardi Gras season—were gathering on the neutral ground and the four corners in ever-increasing numbers: dogwalkers, bicycle riders, teenagers, old folks, and even a few hippies, two or three of whom had just been arrested half a block away and shoved into a police car, which immediately stalled and was given a rousing push-off by some of the crowd to the accompaniment of a boisterous cheering section. Most of the buildings in that area are laced with balconies, which quickly filled up. Soon the pedestrians were gawking up at the balcony folk, who were gawking down at them; many had no idea at first what the cause of the excitement was.

Clay's present house, oddly enough, was only several doors up Dauphine from the corner of Esplanade. Strange as it was, this seemed to be pure coincidence. Clay's place in no way fit Spiesel's description of the party apartment, and he had also testified that Clay Shaw was not the host. Still, there was something eerie about this mass of humanity gathering within sight of the red door on Dauphine Street.

Judge Haggerty, wearing a sporty cranberry-colored jacket, stood up against the side of a building, keeping close watch on the witness, Charles Spiesel, in his well-tailored pin-striped suit and now wearing an extremely dapper gray hat, a near-bowler, with a cigar jammed into the side of his mouth at a jaunty angle. Newsmen were aching to get their hands on Mr. Spiesel, but Judge Haggerty was intercepting all comers.

One kid of about nineteen approached a group of the press. "Somebody get murdered?" "Yeah," a reporter replied. "Yeah—

who?" the kid asked. "Him!" the reporter said, jabbing a finger toward Spiesel, who was not looking dead at all, but, as usual, extremely pleased to be on hand.

By this time photographers were swarming over the area taking pictures of Clay Shaw, who stood smoking and talking to his lawyers, friends, neighbors and reporters on the neutral ground in the center of Esplanade. When I walked up to him he grinned and said, "Isn't this wild—would you believe it?" I had to agree it was wild and it was hard to believe.

The crowd now numbered over three hundred. Everyone was present but the jury. Members of the prosecution team stood in front of a building on Esplanade across the street from the judge and the witness; I had seen them looking happier. Mark Lane was present, accompanied by the attractive young lady who took notes for him in court.

Finally, at about 11:30, the old New Orleans Public Service bus lumbered up. It had been detained, we were told, by one of the parades that had already begun snaking around the streets uptown. Soon the members of the jury were filing out onto the sidewalk. The crowd converged around them, the judge, the witness, Clay Shaw, bailiffs, and lawyers for both sides. Judge Haggerty turned to Spiesel and said, "Lead us wherever you wish, but don't say anything. We will put you on the witness stand later."

With that Spiesel looked across the street to a three-story brick building, the Dauphine Apartments, at 1323 Dauphine. He made for the entrance, followed by the judge, the jury, the lawyers for the prosecution, the defense team, various bailiffs, deputies and Clay Shaw himself. The press and all other spectators were kept from entering the building. They had been in the building a mere two minutes when they were led back out again by Spiesel, strutting like a bantam rooster. He now led them around the corner and into a four-story pinkish-beige stucco building with two balconies at 906 Esplanade. The group stayed in the building for twelve minutes this time before they trooped back outside onto the sidewalk.

The crowds surged in toward the principals. Dymond looked amused, as did others connected with the defense, and Clay himself was not looking troubled. Spiesel always presented a pleasant appearance, so it was difficult to tell what he was thinking. Judge

Haggerty again instructed him not to say anything until court resumed at two o'clock. He then ordered the bailiffs to take the jury to lunch. Spiesel, who had arrived with the judge, was now offered a ride by James Alcock. I would have liked to have been a fly on the inside of the windshield. Clay drove off with his lawyers and we all dispersed for luncheon.

The afternoon session was short, murky, and anticlimactic. Alcock asked Spiesel if he'd been able to locate the same or a similar building as the one described in his testimony. To this the witness replied that of the two buildings he'd led them into, the second one was either the one or similar to the building in which he'd attended the party.

When Dymond questioned him, the lawyer pointed out several differences between the sketch Spiesel had made of the apartment, along with his verbal description, and the actual building the court had now seen. Then he asked, "In respect to 906 Esplanade wouldn't you say that, unless structural changes have been made, you're mistaken?" Spiesel said he'd stick by his original testimony. It was quite obvious by now that the state did not want to prolong Spiesel's stay in the courtroom. So, in the early afternoon, he was excused and took his leave up the center aisle with a walk as jaunty as the one with which he'd propelled himself into the courtroom. There was still the trace of a smile upon his face.

Court was adjourned early. I could not help but toss June and Dick Rolfe a "Well, what about *that!*" June Rolfe snorted and Dick gave me a sick grin.

The following Monday morning, when minute clerk George Sullivan was recording the state-paid transportation voucher for Spiesel's round trip from New York, he turned to Dymond and cracked, "This is one the defense ought to pay for!"

Although no one knew exactly what testimony was forthcoming from here on out, the opinion was that the District Attorney's office must be fairly hard up for witnesses to have flown in Spiesel from New York. His testimony slapped a grin on the proceedings that was hard to erase. Members of the Fourth Estate were quick to catch the spirit. One newsman held up a pad upon which he'd printed, "P'SHAW—a farce in three acts by Jim Garrison." Limericks increased in considerable volume and graffiti appeared on the men's room walls down the hall from the courtroom.

Example: "Let's hang the guilty bastard!" Then written beneath it in another hand: "No, no—let's just elect a new District Attorney!"

I was curious to find out how the defense had got on to Spiesel. I soon learned through the courtroom underground that Tom Bethell, a young Englishman I'd recently met, had worked for Garrison for almost two years before coming to believe that the District Attorney did not have a case against Clay Shaw. Tom, who stands at a slouch with his hands mostly in his pockets and has a fascinating off-center gap between two of his front teeth, which gives him a self-conscious but delightful grin once he allows it to break through, later on explained the mysterious information leak to the defense: "I gradually became disenchanted. Sometime in August of 1968 I happened to bump into Sal Panzeca at the courthouse. We got to talking in general about what was going on and during our conversation I somehow let it out that I thought Clay Shaw was innocent. Panzeca said, 'Would you want to help us?' I told him I thought I would. Sal suggested we have lunch." Bethell grinned and shook his head. "I couldn't very well see sitting down in a public place with one of the defense lawyers, giving them secrets, so we got into Panzeca's car and drove around for a while and talked further. I finally gave them a list of the state's witnesses, which included a brief summary of their probable testimony. I'd written up this memo so I had access to it."

Tom Bethell told me the state eventually discovered there'd been a leak of some sort because several of their witnesses had been contacted—the Clinton people and Spiesel. Tom said there were only four other possible sources for the flow of this information: Louis Ivon, James Alcock, Moo Sciambra, and a man who'd gone under the name of Bill Boxley and had by that time been fired. When rumors of lie detector tests began circulating in the D.A.'s office, Tom was afraid he would be called upon to go under oath, perhaps before a grand jury, and swear he had not divulged secret information to the enemy. If he did and denied this, he feared that somehow during the trial someone might implicate him. He would then be a sitting duck for perjury charges. He was even deeper in tricky territory since he had indicated to the defense his willingness to be called as a witness.

His conscience, together with his fears of being caught, got the best of him and on January 14 he told Louis Ivon what he'd done.

Bethell claims Ivon's response was: "Tom, you realize this could mean your job?" This would seem to have been a remarkably mild reaction, considering the gravity of the offense. Ivon called in James Alcock, and Tom Bethell gave him points for being "extremely understanding." (This understanding might not have come direct from the heart. After all, they had a time bomb on their hands, a man who had been privy to the inside workings of the D.A.'s office.) They indicated if he did not go to the press and cause a major scandal, he would not be hurt; it was also suggested it might be a good idea if he left town to avoid being called by the defense.

Tom felt bad that he had not resigned from the District Attorney's staff after he'd given Panzeca the witness list, but just about that time the D.A.'s office suggested he stay on at the reduced pay of $200 a month, for which he would only have to put in two days a week. He was finishing a book on the New Orleans jazzman George Lewis, and it was a perfect situation, so he'd remained on the payroll until his confession.

It wasn't until January 21, the day the trial started, that Tom Bethell had a confrontation with Jim Garrison, whom Tom quotes as asking, "You don't think I'd try to convict an innocent man, do you?" He then went on at length about his duties and responsibilities as District Attorney.

Tom Bethell indicated a lingering dollop of affection for Garrison. He told me I must make every effort to meet the District Attorney, who, he said, was extremely well read, had an exceptionally retentive mind and could be, when he chose, "completely scintillating." Tom spoke with admiration of his sophistication, wit, humor and charm.

If Tom Bethell is anything, he is loaded to the gills with good will. He was also entirely naïve when he took representatives of the D.A.'s staff at their word when they claimed if he did not go public, he would not be harmed. He was to regret this trust.

Hugh Aynesworth was also partly responsible for the defense's coup with Charles Spiesel, a name which had also appeared on the list Aynesworth had come by in Dallas just before the trial. According to Aynesworth: "Ed Wegmann talked to me about this time and told me he had a similar list of 'witnesses.' We compared notes and they were the same list—except for a couple changes on mine. I briefed him on what we had learned—and suspected—in

Clinton and suggested he try to check out two others on the list—a San Francisco lab technician and Spiesel. Wegmann's feeling was that it was too expensive to check the out-of-state possibilities and I let it ride for a couple of weeks.

"Suddenly one night I awakened out of a nightmare and started to write Wegmann a letter. I had dreamed that a 'new Perry Russo,' much sharper, more urbane . . . had come in and sat down and captivated the jury, winning the case hands down. The more I thought of it, the more I knew that Garrison needed another meeting, another stronger one. A check on the San Francisco guy proved pretty conclusively that he was a nut and his background wouldn't reflect that he was anything as good as Russo. So it had to be Spiesel.

"I sent Wegmann a special delivery letter, asking that he consider checking out Spiesel and repeating that I felt a 'new Russo' was coming and it just might be Spiesel. Ed called me the day he got my letter and asked if I knew a good private detective he could put on Spiesel. I gave him two.

"The rest you know. Just before they took the dapper-looking Spiesel on cross, the information came through from New York about his various kooky schemes."

A chance meeting in the corridor of a courthouse and a nightmare. Sic gloria serendipity.

22

Perry Raymond Russo

The following Monday morning Perry Raymond Russo walked into the courtroom shortly after 9 A.M. He was dressed in a neutral beige-tan single-breasted suit, white shirt and a dark tie and appeared to be freshly barbered. You could almost smell the scent of cologne and the sweet aroma of hair tonic on his closely cropped dark hair.

He was the star of the show. The state knew it, the defense and the defendant, the judge and the jury knew it—and Perry Raymond Russo knew it. There were several possibilities: He would either be the sacrificial lamb—or goat—and, aiding and abetting his demise, talk his way into the corridors of his own bloody slaughter. Or he might crystallize with fear and shatter before all onlookers, simply fall apart. Or, somehow, he might remain standing, rather like one lone tree might be found after a hurricane (named Irvin) had wiped out the immediate area, perhaps with a limb or two torn off and its body bruised by the whiplashes of its own bark—but standing nevertheless. Or, he might just fight back for all he was worth.

Those of the press who had attended the preliminary hearing— most of whom were not overly fond of this young man—still had a high opinion of his steadfastness under fire. Even so, he had been in the driver's seat earlier; the defense had not known about him. Now two years had passed and the defense had not been idle; Perry Russo was no longer an unknown quantity or a surprise, as his predecessor, Charles Spiesel, had been.

There was speculation over Perry Russo's reaction to the prosecution's recent embarrassment. He was certainly aware of it and this must have done his nerve ends little good during the weekend.

So here came the star.

After the swearing-in, Perry Russo slipped into the witness chair past the ever-present squeaking-door microphone and finally faced front. His fear took out advertisements, concentrating in two target areas, the eyes and the mouth, especially the corners where the lips meet. This fear was not completely localized; it spread out over his face, just a zillionth of an inch beneath the tight mask of his skin, and it was completely conceivable, looking at him that morning, to imagine that a tiny scratch on the surface would release the pressure and allow the fear to ooze out. Terror is not an attractive emotion to witness and, no matter my personal thoughts, the sight of Perry Russo's discomfort made me ill at ease. At first.

James Alcock began his direct examination, calling the witness "Mr. Russo," as he questioned him about his current address, his past schooling, and his first meeting with David Ferrie. Very early on, Russo pulled a small something out of his pocket and either took a sip or a small bite of it, then put whatever it was back. During the early questioning he glanced very quickly at Clay Shaw once or twice; his eyes also flicked over to the jury as if he were on trial—as indeed he was.

Alcock gave him several photographs to identify: David Ferrie, Ferrie's apartment, Lee Harvey Oswald, etc. Judge Haggerty switched on the lamp near the witness so that he might see better. When he did this, Perry Russo glanced up at him quickly as if to say, Did you have to do that? He soon reached into his pocket again and this time took a very quick little taste of something. "Jesus," a reporter next to me said, "he's not drinking on the stand, is he?"

Alcock led him through his alleged meeting with Leon Oswald as a onetime roommate of Ferrie's and into the fateful party in September of 1963. Alcock called the witness "Mr. Russo" seven times before finally slipping into the more informal "Perry." From then on it was almost always "Perry," which was only natural; behind them were two years' knowledge of each other. Under direct examination Russo told approximately the same story he had detailed during the preliminary hearing. He had dropped in on Dave Ferrie after playing basketball—this time he left out his former companions, Niles Peterson and Sandra Moffitt—and there were eight or ten people there, Leon Oswald, three or four Latins or Cubans, a couple of young guys "and there was one well-dressed man."

ALCOCK: Can you give me a description of the well-dressed man?

RUSSO: He had on a deep maroon jacket, white shirt, I guess, and I am not real sure about the pants.

ALCOCK: Did he have on a tie?

RUSSO: No, not the way I remember him.

ALCOCK: Can you give me a description as to physical stature?

RUSSO: He was big, about six-four, six-five, wide-shouldered, distinguished-looking.

ALCOCK: Color of hair?

RUSSO: White.

ALCOCK: Was this man there when you first arrived?

RUSSO: Yes, sir.

ALCOCK: Do you see that man in the courtroom now?

RUSSO: I do.

ALCOCK: Would you point to him, please.

Perry Russo then pointed to Clay Shaw, who once again looked his accuser square in the eye, but not for long, because the point was not much more than the wave of Russo's hand in his direction.

Russo went on to say the defendant had been introduced to him as Clem Bertrand, and Alcock asked if he'd ever seen this man before. Russo replied he had observed the defendant at the Nashville Wharf when he had gone there to hear President Kennedy give a speech in 1962. Russo had arrived late and stood in the back. He was curious, he said, because he'd never seen a President before. When asked why he'd noticed Clay Shaw, Russo said, "The thing that drew my eyes away from the President to the defendant was that he was not looking at the President, he was looking around." He thought it funny that someone would not be looking at the President. When Alcock asked if Russo had noticed anyone else who was not looking at the President, the witness replied, "Not that I can recall."

(It seemed to me he should have said, No, just the two of us, because he went on to testify that despite his great interest in seeing President Kennedy he had watched Clay Shaw for eight or ten minutes. So although it had seemed odd to him that somebody was not watching the President, I wondered if Russo thought it strange of himself to be so diverted by a man he'd never seen before and had no idea he would ever see again.)

Alcock returned to the party and what took place, according to

Russo, after everyone else had left but Ferrie, Oswald, Bertrand (Shaw), and himself. The following is the exact testimony upon which the state based its conspiracy charge.

ALCOCK: And what was David Ferrie saying at the time he had the clippings [of President Kennedy] in his hand? Once again, only what was said in the presence of the defendant.

RUSSO: Well, he paced back and forth on the floor, he carried the clippings. There was a speech of some kind, of Latin or Spanish talking, going on a record. He didn't really—he just didn't say much at that time, except that he did walk around muttering about Kennedy.

ALCOCK: Now, getting back to the conversation that transpired at the time between—just the defendant, Oswald, and yourself, Ferrie and yourself present. What was said then?

RUSSO: Well, Ferrie, his habit was to walk up and down, and he was walking up and down telling how the projected assassination could be pulled off, the assassination of President Kennedy, and during that time he told them about this triangulation of crossfire where there would be [demonstrating] this is a habit he had, was sticking his hand up and showing a three-sided triangulation or a three-cornered triangulation, and he said of these three people, for two of them to escape one would have to be captured as a scapegoat or a patsy for the other two, and that perhaps there would be a diversionary shot or all three would shoot at the President somewhere in the middle and one of them would have to be the scapegoat. There could be what he called a diversionary shot and the other two would shoot for the kill or a direct hit.

ALCOCK: Did he mention the order of shooting at all?

RUSSO: He did say that there would be—He said the diversionary shot if fired would be fired to attract attention, and then instantly the police or whatever was around would look, and said the other two would shoot for the kill, and he said it would be just a slight delay but almost simultaneously.

ALCOCK: The last two almost simultaneously?

RUSSO: Well, except for the little small delay all three would be almost simultaneous.

ALCOCK: Referring specifically to the last two, were they to be almost simultaneous?

RUSSO: They were to be shot at the same time for the kill.

ALCOCK: What else was said, Perry?

RUSSO: Well, he told about as soon as the assassination was performed, he said that the escape would be by flight, said it could either—they could go either to Mexico, I mean to Brazil, or could go to Cuba, said if they went to Brazil they would have to stop for refueling somewhere and he said Mexico.

ALCOCK: And did the defendant at any time during this conversation make any statements?

RUSSO: Well, he—at that time, the defendant objected to that and said no, that wouldn't be possible because—

ALCOCK: Objected to what?

RUSSO: Objected to this—Ferrie called it availability, the availability exit would be to go to Mexico and then to Brazil, or to go directly to Cuba, and the defendant said that was not possible because if you had to go to Brazil you would need cooperation from some place to stop and refuel, and also the ability to fly out of the area of the assassination, and he said that wouldn't be possible with—instantly the police would be everywhere.

ALCOCK: As a result of his comment was anything further said by either Ferrie, Oswald or the defendant?

RUSSO: Well, Oswald told them to shut up, he said—

ALCOCK: Told who to shut up?

RUSSO: Oswald told Bertrand to shut up. He said, "Shut up, Ferrie knows what he is doing, he is a pilot."

ALCOCK: And then what, if anything, did Ferrie say?

RUSSO: What if anything—who?

ALCOCK: After this, did Ferrie say anything?

RUSSO: Well, he told about an alternative plan, that perhaps this would be the better way, this Plan B—he didn't call it that but he said an alternate plan—and he said what they could do was to make sure that they had alibis and were in the public eye at the time of the assassination.

ALCOCK: And what, if anything, did the defendant say to this?

RUSSO: Well, the defendant seemed—the defendant said that he could go on business for his company.

ALCOCK: Did he specify any particular location?

RUSSO: He said on the Coast.

ALCOCK: Did Ferrie say anything?

RUSSO: Well, Ferrie said he could make a speech at Southeastern—Hammond or Southeastern, I am not sure which—a speech at a college.

ALCOCK: Did Oswald say anything?

RUSSO: Oswald? No, he didn't say anything at that time.

ALCOCK: What, if anything, did the defendant talk about?

RUSSO: Well, he thought—in that exchange that I was just telling you about—he felt that Ferrie was a washed-up pilot.

ALCOCK: And was anything said— Did he make this comment?

RUSSO: I am not exactly sure of the words, because it was right before Oswald told him to shut up, because he said he knows what he is doing because he is the pilot.

ALCOCK: Was there a specific reference, Perry, to the number of people who would definitely participate in the shooting?

RUSSO: It had to be two or it had to be three. Definitely it was always one firing the diversionary shot. The three would be— Ferrie said one of them would fire a diversionary shot and two of them would shoot to kill the President. With the two situation, one would fire a diversionary shot and attract the attention, and the number two gun would shoot to kill.

ALCOCK: Was the type of gun or guns ever mentioned?

RUSSO: No, except that it was a rifle.

ALCOCK: Did you see any weapons at all on this occasion?

RUSSO: No.

Russo went on to say he was now unable to remember if anyone had accompanied him to the party or not. He could neither recall who left the apartment first, after the conversation, nor could he recall for sure how he got home himself. He said he thought he took a bus home.

Perry Russo told of having seen Leon Oswald twice more at David Ferrie's for brief periods of no more than five or ten minutes; the last time, Russo said, Oswald was about to leave town. Russo maintained he'd seen Clay Shaw once more, early in 1964, sitting in a car at a service station with David Ferrie.

Like an actor on opening night who is attacked by nerves, making his early lines rigid and his gestures shaky, and then after fifteen or twenty minutes returns to some semblance of natural performance level, so did Perry Russo warm up and relax once he'd entered the mainstream of his testimony. No longer did he take nips from the small bottle he kept in his coat pocket. His occasional looks to the jury were no longer so furtive, and his natural loquaciousness began rising to the surface.

During a midmorning recess, while Dick Rolfe was explaining to me what an excellent witness Perry Russo was (I often had witnesses and testimony translated for me by the Rolfes as if I had not been in the courtroom), I noticed Liz Garrison standing nearby. I decided to use my good friend Dick and ask to be introduced. He was most obliging. Dick Rolfe told Mrs. Garrison I'd written the article on Clay Shaw for *Esquire*. That did not seem to faze her one way or the other. She asked if I was covering the trial and I told her I would attempt an article for *Playboy* and hoped even to get a book out of it. I also mentioned I would like very much to meet her husband. She said she thought that could be arranged and she would speak to him—perhaps I could come out to the house some afternoon—and I should be in touch with Mr. Garrison's secretary. We spoke briefly of the trial, in generalities. She was soft-spoken and completely charming.

Before recess was over I returned to the courtroom and noticed Perry Russo sitting in one of the jurors' chairs; Clay Shaw, who had gone out the door to the left of the judge's bench, returned and in order to get to his chair had to pass within inches of his accuser. Russo glanced down at his hands; Clay Shaw looked stonily straight ahead as he grazed by the witness.

After recess, James Alcock, knowing full well the defense was going to exhume the now notorious Sciambra memo as well as produce James Phelan upon the witness stand, very wisely sought to shore up this gaping hole by tackling it on direct examination. He began by asking Perry Russo what he'd told Andrew Sciambra in Baton Rouge during that first interview.

RUSSO: Oh, I told Mr. Sciambra the first time I had met Shaw or Bertrand was at the Nashville Wharf.

ALCOCK: Did you tell him anything in addition to that?

RUSSO: I told him that the next time I had met him, I recollect it was at the gas station, and then finally I told him I had seen him up at Ferrie's apartment.

Actually Russo had not "met" Shaw/Bertrand at either the Nashville Wharf or the gas station and probably had not meant to imply that either, although I'm surprised the defense did not object to the use of the word. Oddly enough, Russo used "seen" the one time he claimed to have "met" Shaw/Bertrand at Ferrie's apartment.

If Russo had not originally mentioned the conspiracy meeting to Sciambra, and the state was now attempting to cover up, why didn't he just say, I told Sciambra about meeting Shaw at Ferrie's and hearing them conspire to kill the President, and I also said I'd seen him two other times. Why, still, the hedging—"and then finally I told him I had seen him up at Ferrie's apartment." The reason, one supposes, is that if Russo had voiced that claim, it would have made Andrew Sciambra either appear to have left all talk of conspiracy out of the memo purposefully or it would have made him out as incredibly stupid. So instead there was this halfhearted effort to salvage both Russo and Sciambra. It might have made much more sense to have sacrificed Sciambra, in this instance. Or Russo could have claimed he hadn't told Sciambra about the conspiracy because he was afraid at first to admit hearing such dangerous talk and not having reported it at the time. That would have made sense—certainly as much sense as this lukewarm attempt at credibility.

ALCOCK: Did you relate to him, Perry, essentially what you have related to this jury about the time that you saw the defendant at Ferrie's apartment?

DYMOND: I object to that as being too much a general question, asking him whether he related to him substantially what he told the jury.

JUDGE HAGGERTY: I will overrule the objection.

DYMOND: To which ruling, if the court please, counsel for the defense reserves a bill of exception, making the question, the objection, the testimony of the witness, the ruling of the court, the reason of the objection, and the entire record up to this point a part of the bill.

RUSSO [responding to the question which was read again by the court reporter]: Not in as great detail, but in essence, yes.

Another hedging answer.

Now Alcock led Russo into his meeting with Phelan and questioned him about what he'd told Phelan regarding the discrepancies between his testimony and the memo. At this point Dymond called for the production of the memorandum, claiming the defense was entitled to follow him on it. The memorandum was produced. In order for Russo to look it over and make his notations and corrections, and for the defense to study it (although they already had copies, as did many people connected with the case) , court was adjourned for the lunch recess.

It is interesting to note that there were three documents that literally fell into the hands of reporters—with any connections at all—who arrived in New Orleans to cover the trial. The first was a copy of the Sciambra memo. The second was an extract from Jim Garrison's army records showing his 1951 discharge for reasons of physical disability with a recommended 10 per cent permanent disability: "Cause of incapacity was anxiety reaction, chronic moderate . . . manifested by hypochondriasis, chronic, exhaustion syndrome, functional bowel symptoms, and psychogenic allergic manifestations." He was diagnosed as totally incapacitated for military service and moderately impaired for civilian life, with a recommendation for long-term psychotherapy. The third item on the list was a dirty picture featuring one of Garrison's Dealey Plaza Irregulars, a man known as a critic of the Warren Report. In the photograph he is nude, face grimacing, hands behind him (rumored to be tied behind him) , and sporting a full erection. Also present in the picture is a woman's hand holding a pin or needle to his genitals. It is not only a dirty picture, it is a filthy-dirty picture. I was asked if I would like a copy for my very own. Wall space being precious in my house, I declined.

During the lunch break you could hear many people saying things like: That Russo, he's pretty smooth now on direct, but wait until Dymond gets his hands on him—just wait!

After lunch, Alcock continued questioning Russo about whether the memo reflected their conversation accurately, to which he replied, "There are omissions and also some incorrect statements." He was asked if he'd pointed these out to anyone at any time and he replied he'd mentioned several glaring errors to James Phelan. Alcock indicated he would then like Russo to point out those errors to the court.

DYMOND: We object unless the document is first read to the jury and we will be glad to join the state in the offer in evidence [of the memo].

ALCOCK: I don't think it is necessary, but I don't think, I don't think there is a predicate—

DYMOND: The question is what is left *out* and the jury doesn't know what is left *out* if they don't know what is *in* it.

Judge Haggerty agreed with Dymond's objection and soon the defense and the state jointly offered the memo into evidence. Alcock then took his place in front of a microphone and, facing the jury, read this noteworthy document, which, according to Russo's testimony, Sciambra had based on exceedingly few notes taken during the interview itself.

MEMORANDUM

February 27, 1967

TO: JIM GARRISON
FROM: ANDREW J. SCIAMBRA
RE: INTERVIEW WITH PERRY RAYMOND RUSSO
        311 EAST STATE STREET
        BATON ROUGE, LOUISIANA

On February 25, 1967, I interviewed PERRY RUSSO at the above mentioned address. RUSSO was very cooperative and said that he was glad to see me as he had been hounded to death by the local news media. He said that he would give us all the help that he possibly could, and that he would furnish us with names of individuals who could be most helpful to us in our investigation.

He said that one of these persons is AL LANDRY who lives in Gentilly. He said that FERRIE was "in love" with LANDRY. He says in 1962 (the approximate month he cannot remember, but he says that it can be ascertained through LANDRY's mother) he went to LANDRY's house to try to locate him. He was told at the time by LANDRY's mother that FERRIE had taken LANDRY out of the country, and that she did not know where they were. RUSSO told me later on in the interview that FERRIE had taken LANDRY out of the country twice and this was the first trip. He said that later on he found out that FERRIE had taken LANDRY to Canada and to Mexico.

RUSSO said that he and LANDRY and a small group of other boys used to always pal around together and that it was common knowledge to everyone that FERRIE was a homosexual and RUSSO and his buddies were trying to alienate LANDRY from FERRIE. RUSSO said that LANDRY had some strange fascination for FERRIE and was greatly impressed by FERRIE's intelligence. He says that he is sure that FERRIE had LANDRY under some sort of spell from time to time. He said that what proved this to him was that in 1962 LANDRY took him to FERRIE's apartment out in Kenner and FERRIE was having a meeting with about eight or ten young boys who were in the Civil Air Patrol. FERRIE's mother was at the meeting and FERRIE introduced his mother to RUSSO. RUSSO said that he went to the meeting because LANDRY had told him that FERRIE was a great hypnotist and at this meeting FERRIE would demonstrate some of his hypnotic powers. RUSSO said that LANDRY could furnish us with the names of all the people who were at the meeting, and he could also furnish us with a lot of information about FERRIE for he and FERRIE put on a hypnotic demonstration and used LANDRY as his subject. He said that FERRIE stuck pins in LANDRY's body and LANDRY would not feel any pain. He said FERRIE gave a very long lecture on hypnotism and posthypnotic suggestions and demonstrated his power by using LANDRY as his subject. After the demonstration, FERRIE showed him and LANDRY five diplomas that he had and said that he had received his Ph.D. in two of these subjects. He also had various pieces of machinery in his attic and surgical equipment and bones which he doesn't know if they were human or animal.

RUSSO said after the meeting he and LANDRY went home and he did not see FERRIE for a while. He said a little later on he went to LANDRY's house to talk with him and LANDRY's mother told him that FERRIE had again taken her son out of the country. She told RUSSO that in her opinion FERRIE was a very strange and weird individual and that she had often told her son to stay away from him but that her son would not listen to her. She said that it was as if FERRIE had some strange power over her son. She asked RUSSO to help her to try to alienate her son from FERRIE. RUSSO said that he would try and do this.

RUSSO said that the next time he saw FERRIE was a few weeks later when he was standing on the corner of Decatur and Canal with a friend of his by the name of NILES PETERSON who presently drives a Yellow Cab, Number 792. FERRIE, LANDRY, and a Spanish guy or Cuban guy with a beard who could speak no English, and six or eight kids in khaki uniforms passed them on the street. He said the Cuban fellow was in green fatigues. He said FERRIE and LANDRY told him hello and FERRIE kept walking with the group, however, LANDRY stopped for a moment and told him that they were going somewhere but that he would get in touch with him in a few days. RUSSO asked LANDRY where had he been, and LANDRY told him that FERRIE and he had been to Mexico.

In a few days RUSSO contacted LANDRY and told him that his mother did not like FERRIE and that everyone knew that FERRIE was a homosexual and that he did not think that he should be associated with FERRIE. LANDRY said that he would think about breaking off his relationship with FERRIE but that it would be difficult. He said that FERRIE was teaching his group the art of fighting jungle warfare and that FERRIE's plan was to help liberate the South American countries. He said that FERRIE often referred to wiping out the rest of the BATISTA gang in Cuba. RUSSO said that he and several of his cousins all began to "bug" LANDRY about FERRIE, the C.A.P. jungle warfare, and the liberation of the South American countries. He said that this eventually got to LANDRY and LANDRY began seeing FERRIE not as much as he normally would have.

RUSSO said that one night he and LANDRY and TIM KERSHENSTINE who lives on 2061 Pelopidas, Phone Number 943–8490, and possibly NILES PETERSON were in the Intelect which is located on Bourbon Street and they ran into DAVE FERRIE. FERRIE said that he would like to talk with LANDRY privately and RUSSO told FERRIE that whatever he had to say to LANDRY he should do it in front of everybody. RUSSO then told LANDRY to tell FERRIE to take a walk and that he didn't want to be involved with him anymore. LANDRY then told FERRIE that he wanted to break off his relationship. FERRIE then told LANDRY that he would talk to him about it later and he then turned to RUSSO and told him that either he or one of his men would kill him for what he had done to him and LANDRY. RUSSO told FERRIE to just get away and stay away from LANDRY because he was no good for LANDRY. He said that LANDRY had told him that FERRIE used to hypnotize him and give him posthypnotic suggestions. He also said that FERRIE eventually confessed to him that he used hypnosis for sexual purposes.

RUSSO said that after this incident on Bourbon Street he said that he did not see FERRIE for about six months, and that one day he was driving his car on the Veterans Highway, and he noticed that he was starting to get a flat tire. He pulled his car into a service station and told the two young kids who were working there that he wanted to change his tire. About this time DAVE FERRIE came up to him and tapped him on the shoulder and told him hello and asked him where he had been as he had not seen him for some time. RUSSO then said that they exchanged casual remarks and pleasant conversation. RUSSO said that FERRIE was either the owner or the manager of this service station. He said that FERRIE then left and went and sat in a white or very light colored compact car and began talking with the individual in the front seat. RUSSO said that he then pulled his car right alongside of this compact car, and he looked at FERRIE and the individual that he was talking to in the front seat several times while he was waiting there for his car. After the car was fixed and he was about to leave the station, FERRIE asked him where was he staying because he wanted to come over and talk with him about a few business deals. RUSSO told him the address, and he said that a short while thereafter FERRIE came to his apartment. He said FERRIE brought over to the apartment some pornographic film that he had and that he wanted RUSSO to sell for him. FERRIE told him that he had just returned from Cuba and that he could get all of this kind of film that he wanted. He said that he could get more film out of Cuba very easily and if RUSSO could sell the film for him, they could all make money. He said that he would have to get $150 a roll for the film because it was pretty risky going in and out of Cuba. RUSSO said the film consisted of one man and one woman and that the story was essentially that of a woman cheating the man in a game of cards, and the man eventually beating her up and raping her for doing so. He said the man in the picture was either Spanish or Cuban, looked to be strong and rather husky and had black hair. He said that he had a patch over one eye. The girl was an American. RUSSO said that he took this film and sold it to someone who he believes eventually sold it to a seaman (RUSSO said that he would try and obtain this film for us). He said FERRIE then began coming to his apartment on an average of twice a week and that one time he came over to his apartment and told him that he had been working with chemicals and studying their effects on the human body. He said that FERRIE had told him that he had extensive knowledge about drugs and mixtures of drugs and how they would affect the human body. FERRIE showed him a drug that he said he concocted himself and that it was very similar to aphrodisiac but even better. He said that it would make a person extremely passionate and would enable him to forget all of his inhibitions and obtain a very free and loose attitude about love and sex. He said it would also erase any feelings of guilt that a person might have toward any type of sexual behavior that he might care to indulge in. He said that FERRIE told him that he had used this drug with different friends of his and this is how they reacted to it. He also admitted to RUSSO for the first time that he was a homosexual and he wanted to know if RUSSO would be willing to take the drug. RUSSO said that he did not care to take the drug. FERRIE also told him that he could get all of the heroin that he wanted but that he would not fool with it as it was too hot to handle and that he could concoct drugs that would serve his purpose.

RUSSO said that one day he and KENNY CARTER, a colored boy

who used to attend Loyola University and who he believes attends L.S.U.N.O., were in his apartment on Elysian Fields when FERRIE came in with two Cubans who were dressed in green fatigues. One of the Cubans had a beard and the other one didn't. Both of them were very strongly built, had dark complexion, and rough looking. Their faces were extremely tough looking. RUSSO said that they looked as if they could bend a bar of steel. He said that they were around 28 to 35 years old and that FERRIE introduced them, but he cannot remember their names. He said that they didn't say anything because they could not speak English. He said that FERRIE at this time started making remarks about Cuba and criticizing the United States. He said the people in Cuba are starving to death and they have no medicine and that he blamed the United States for this. He said that the United States is a barbaric nation and that no nation as powerful as the United States should be that barbaric. He also referred to the two Cubans with him as instructors in the manly art of jungle warfare. After this conversation FERRIE and the two Cubans left.

RUSSO said that he did not see FERRIE again until he went to his Louisiana Avenue Parkway apartment with KENNY CARTER looking for him. He said that FERRIE was there and he was with a Cuban guy in green fatigues who was younger and not nearly as powerful looking as the other two Cubans. He said that FERRIE introduced him to someone he called his roommate. He said FERRIE mentioned his name, but he can't remember it right now. He said this roommate had sort of dirty blond hair and a husky beard which appeared to be a little darker than his hair. He said the guy was a typical beatnik, extremely dirty, with his hair all messed up, his beard unkept [sic], a dirty T-shirt on, and either blue jeans or khaki pants on. He said he wore white tennis shoes which were cruddy and had on no socks. He said the roommate appeared to be in his middle twenties. RUSSO said that he went to FERRIE's apartment about five or six times and he can remember seeing the roommate about two or three times. He said that the roommate never talked to anybody. As soon as anyone would come into FERRIE's apartment, the roommate would get up and leave and go into another room by himself. RUSSO said that one day he tried to make conversation with the roommate by asking him where he was from, and the roommate told him from everywhere, and so he didn't try to talk to him any more because he appeared to be a real "punk." He mentioned this to FERRIE, and FERRIE told him not to worry about it because he was a funny guy, and he didn't like to talk to anybody, all he did was sit down on the porch in the dark and think and read books all the time. FERRIE told Russo that he had tried the aphrodisiac drug on his room-mate and it worked perfectly. He said that he and his roommate laid in bed naked, and he gave the drug to his roommate and his roommate became very passionate and aggressive and had inter-course with Ferrie. He said that after this was over, the roommate had no recollection of what he had done. He said that his room-mate was a perfect subject for this. He also said that his roommate did not get along with his Cuban friends and that this is the reason why Russo never saw the roommate with any of the Cubans or with anybody else for that matter. Russo said that as soon as he would walk into the apartment, the roommate would walk out without saying a word. Ferrie repeated that these Cubans who were coming to his apartment were jungle fighters and would help liberate South America. Russo said that he believes that Kershen-stine, Kenny Carter, and maybe Niles Peterson, and Landry would know more about the roommate and be able to recognize him. Russo said that it would be hard for him to pinpoint the time right now but that he knew that this was in 1963, and he believes it was somewhere between May and October.

Russo said that during the summer of 1963 Ferrie became obsessed with the idea that an assassination could be carried out in the United States very easily if the proper amount of planning was made. Every time Russo talked to Ferrie he told him more and more about how he was the kind of person who could successfully plan an assassination. Russo said that he never referred directly to J.F.K. and always used the President of Mexico or President Eisenhower as an example. Ferrie asked him, "How many times do you remember seeing Eisenhower riding in an open top automobile exposed to everyone without any protection whatso-ever?" He said the limousine usually drives around ten miles an hour and frequently stops at different points. Therefore, it would be extremely easy to shoot somebody. Ferrie said that the whole key to a successful assassination would be the availability of exit and the use of the mass confusion that would result from such a plot. Ferrie said that one person or a small group of people could sit down and plan the whole thing out and get out of the country after it was over before anybody knew what was going on. He said that he was the key to the availability of exit as he could jump into any plane under the sun and fly it out of the country to a place that would not extradite, such as Cuba or Brazil. He said even if for some reason the availability of exit were blocked, the people could still escape by making use of the mass confusion that would erupt. He said that he was sure that he could plan the whole thing very easily. Russo said that they got into many discussions about FERRIE's ideas on how easy an assassination would be and RUSSO said that many times he told FERRIE that it would not be as easy as he thought. RUSSO said that he remembered once going to the Nashville Street Wharf to hear J.F.K. make a speech and he remembers that he saw a Secret Service man guarding the President every five or ten feet. RUSSO said that he knew that these were either Secret Service men or FBI men because these were the only people not facing J.F.K. when he was talking. These people were looking into the crowd watching for any suspicious activity. FERRIE said that all of these complications could be worked out with the proper amount of planning. FERRIE said that a person could use the mob confusion to help him get away but that the person should not make the mistake of getting messed up in the crowd. FERRIE also said that another way that an assassination could be successfully carried out would be through someone very intimate to the White House who had sophisticated knowledge of medicine and chemicals and how they would cause the human body to react. He said with all the knowledge he had of medicine and its reaction in relationship to the human body, he was sure that he could commit a perfect murder and no doctor in the country and no autopsy report in the country could detect it. FERRIE said that he had extensive knowledge of medicine and chemicals and their effects on the human body. FERRIE said that he knew what the coroner and doctors looked for when they make their autopsy report and as a result of what they would find they would have to say that the death was a result of natural causes. FERRIE said that one thing that had to be remembered is not to physically disturb the apartment or the house because if the furniture were messed up, it may cause some suspicion as to the cause of death and further inquiry might result. He says murders are committed every day, that stupid doctors and coroners term natural deaths. FERRIE said that he knew of a type of drug which once it got into the bloodstream would cause physical reaction that would result in extensive brain damage or blood clot and eventual death. He said the physical reaction to this drug would be such that no doctor in this country would call it anything but a natural death. He said the chemical involved would dissipate without leaving any trace at all and the autopsy would say something like "blood clot." RUSSO said that in September and October of 1963, FERRIE got worse in his speeches about an assassination. He said that for the first time since he began talking about assassinations he began making direct references to J.F.K. FERRIE told RUSSO on several occasions that "We will get him" (meaning J.F.K.) and

that "It won't be long." Russo said that he hasn't spoken with
Ferrie since the assassination.

I then pulled out some pictures and I began to show Russo the
pictures asking him whether or not he could identify anyone in
the pictures. He picked out three people. I did not disclose the
names of any of the people whose pictures I showed him. I merely
said "Do you know or recognize any of these people?" The first
person he picked out was Arcacha Smith and he says that
Arcacha looks very much like the Cuban in the pornographic film
that Ferrie brought to his apartment and which he sold to a
seaman. He then called his brother, Steve, over to look at Arcacha's picture and asked him if that face was familiar to him and
his brother, Steve, said "Yes, it looks like the guy in the film."
Russo said he recognized the face because, "to be perfectly honest, I
looked at the film quite a bit." At this point he asked me if
anything he was telling me would be used against him. I assured
him that it wouldn't. The next picture that he identified was that
of Clay Shaw. He said that he saw this man twice. The first time
was when he pulled into Ferrie's service station to get his car
fixed. Shaw was the person who was sitting in the compact car
talking with Ferrie. He remembers seeing him again at the Nashville Street Wharf when he went to see J.F.K. speak. He said he
particularly remembers this guy because he was apparently a
queer. It seems that instead of looking at J.F.K. speak, Shaw kept
turning around and looking at all the young boys in the crowd.
He said that Shaw eventually struck up a conversation with a
young kid not too far from him. It was perfectly obvious to him
that Shaw stared at his penis several times. He said that Shaw
eventually left with a friend. He said that Shaw had on dark pants
that day which fit very tightly and was the kind of pants that a lot
of queers in the French Quarter wear. Shaw had on a corduroy
type jacket which was black with white stripes. The third picture
that Russo identified was that of Lee Harvey Oswald. When he
looked at the picture, he began shaking his head and said that he
doesn't know if he should say what he's thinking. I told him to go
on and tell me what was on his mind and that we would accept
this in relationship to all the information we had, and it may not
be as wild as he thinks it is. He then said that the picture of Lee
Harvey Oswald was the person that Ferrie had introduced to
him as his roommate. He said the only thing that doesn't make
him stand up and say that he is sure beyond the shadow of any
doubt is the fact that the roommate was always so cruddy and had
a bushy beard. He then drew a beard on the picture of Oswald

and said this was FERRIE's roommate. He suggested that I put a beard on OSWALD and not say who it was and show the picture to KENNY CARTER, LANDRY, KERSHENSTINE, PETERSON, and maybe a few of the people in FERRIE's C.A.P. unit who may have been up to his apartment. RUSSO was sure that they would say that that was FERRIE's roommate. He also said that we might show the picture to ROBERT LEMOYNE who lives in the vicinity of Nichols High School as he was in contact with FERRIE around that time. RUSSO said the more we talk the more comes back to me and he said that the name LEON really rings a bell. He also said that if he were hypnotized he may have total recall on names and places and dates. He said that he had been hypnotized like this before and it had helped him to recall and that he would be glad to do it for us.

RUSSO told me that he now works at the Equitable Insurance Company in Baton Rouge, Phone Number 926–5300. He said that the best time to reach him would be around 9:30 in the morning or 4:30 in the afternoon Monday through Friday. He says that on the weekends he usually leaves town mostly coming to New Orleans. I told him that we would be in touch with him.

During the reading Perry Russo kept his eyes glued to the copy he had in front of him, never once looking at Clay Shaw or the jury. Every so often he raised a hand to rub his forehead or eyes and perhaps smooth his hair. Clay Shaw's eyes remained focused on his own copy of the memo.

After a brief recess for James Alcock to refresh his throat with a glass of water, the prosecution attorney began going over the memo with Russo—now seated in the witness chair drinking a Coke from a can—for his corrections.

Russo has a problem pronouncing the letter "s" and a slight toothy mushiness to his speech, not unlike the late Humphrey Bogart. Many of his corrections were minor, but he went into great detail regardless of the importance. By now he was warmed up to the point of becoming a chatterbox. An example of Russo's ability to go on: "Toward the middle of the paragraph, 'Ferrie mentioned his name but he can't remember it right now. He said the roommate had sort of dirty blond hair and a husky beard which appeared to be a little darker than his hair.' A couple of things are not exactly right." Russo sighed. "The dirty blond hair and husky beard, exactly what I said, but I did mention husky trying to pick the right word to represent his facial growth classification but his hair was not dirty blond but more brown or black and the husky beard . . . well, when I talked with Sciambra I told him this guy had a growth of beard, call it a beard, and I didn't use the word husky. It was a growth of beard and he was dirty and probably at one time husky came in the conversation but it was possibly when I was pulling for a name or some type of adjective and to this day I haven't found the right adjective to describe the beard."

Perry had exhaled this almost on one breath before coming up for air. Most of the corrections were as lengthy as they were minor.

Toward the end of this session he got around to the important discrepancies. He corrected the sequence of when he had seen Clay Shaw, saying it had been at the wharf first and then the gas station. Now, still in murky terms, Russo circled the conspiracy party, which was now called a meeting.

ALCOCK: Perry, did you tell Sciambra about the meeting in Ferrie's apartment in mid-'63 between Ferrie, Oswald and the defendant?

RUSSO: At the end—not at the end of the evening but one hour before he left I talked with Sciambra—we were talking, going over things, and he took very few notes and it was a meeting [Russo evidently meant, I told him about a meeting] and he was more interested in Dave Ferrie and the quotes about he knows the thing could be done and "We will kill him and it won't be long," but I did mention in the meeting to Sciambra on the 25th, I think it was, the Saturday—

ALCOCK: Is that, Perry, the meeting you have related to the court and jury today?

RUSSO: Essentially but not in every great detail and actually there wasn't but a couple of questions after that about it.

Again this stretches credibility. Here was Russo being questioned by an assistant D.A. straight from Garrison, a man who was devoting all his energy, time and resources to investigating a possible conspiracy. Now, according to Russo, he tells Sciambra about a conspiracy meeting and adds, "There wasn't but a couple of questions after that about it." It makes one wonder how dull a conspiracy can be.

At the end of his direct examination Perry Russo was still elaborating, still hedging:

ALCOCK: Did you tell, did you tell James Phelan when you spoke with him that you had mentioned this to Sciambra?

RUSSO: I—the meeting lasted for three hours with Phelan in Baton Rouge right after the 20th of March, after the preliminary hearing, and I told him distinctly I had not mentioned the party to Sciambra in Baton Rouge and I told him that I called everything a *meeting* because I was involved with the Republicans to a great extent and I mentioned meeting and all of these guys got around and would be talking about shooting President Kennedy. [How much stronger a simple yes would have been.]

ALCOCK: Perry, prior to your coming down to New Orleans and speaking with members of the District Attorney's staff did you know the name or ever hear the name Clay Shaw?

RUSSO: I never heard the name of Clay Shaw and not exactly— when in that week, there was so much questioning and answers and after a couple of days in New Orleans and I heard someone mention that was Clay Shaw's picture.

ALCOCK: Up until that time, Perry, having picked this picture out, who did you think the person in it was?

RUSSO: The same way I identified it in Baton Rouge, Bertrand.

ALCOCK: Clem?

RUSSO: Clem Bertrand.

ALCOCK: I tender the witness.

That simple statement brought forth a wave of excitement, as Irvin Dymond cleared his throat and looked up at Perry Raymond Russo, who looked back at him, diverted his eyes down toward his lap, swallowed and brushed a hand over his forehead. The contest was on.

23

The Tea Party

Irvin Dymond started off extremely low key. There was a certain purr missing from the growl and his vocal production seemed to be more clear than usual as he elicited from the witness his current address, former address, occupation (Great Books of the Western World—sales and training), and the information that he had driven a cab off and on during 1967 and 1968, since the preliminary hearing.

Now the defense lawyer took a brief pause and then inquired in an easy half-humorous, half-serious tone, "Mr. Russo, are you sure this was Mr. *Sciambra* that you were talking to up in Baton Rouge?" Smiles and nudges in the courtroom but not from Perry Russo, who played it perfectly square: "Andy Sciambra? Yes, he identified himself that way."

DYMOND: And you recognize him in the court now?

RUSSO [glancing at Sciambra and nodding]: I do.

Thereupon followed a long petty exchange between the lawyers over how many errors Russo had found in the Sciambra memo (Dymond calculated twenty-five) and whether some of them were "corrections" and not admitted errors. Dymond wanted to know if it was Russo's contention that Sciambra had deliberately distorted what the witness had told him or that the Assistant D.A. had simply made that many mistakes. Alcock objected, claiming the witness wasn't qualified to answer that, whereupon Dymond commented the witness was disputing a memorandum of what he purportedly said and Dymond wanted to know on what basis. They went several rounds on that until Judge Haggerty suggested Mr. Dymond rephrase his question. The lawyer asked, "Did you clearly give this statement to Mr. Sciambra?"

RUSSO: We talked for about three hours. It would be hard to say whether it was clear. There was a lot of—in other words, to give you the physical aspect of how it stood, Sciambra sat there with a briefcase on his knees opened up and he had a bunch of photographs there, and he had a little pad, every once in a while he would write a little note on there, and most of the time he was holding the photographs, turned them all down, and pulled out and said, "Do you know this guy," and I would say yes, or I never seen it, or I would say yes, I remember him from somewhere or something to that effect, and he didn't let me see any of the notes taken, and I was sitting next to him.

DYMOND: Be that as it may, you did your best to state it clearly to him, did you not?

RUSSO: Oh, I would say depending on the questions, I don't know if it was my best.

DYMOND: You were not trying to *conceal* anything, were you?

RUSSO: He was asking me a question, and sometimes he would be asking the next question while I was trying to answer this one. A big deal was Ferrie's philosophy, I thought that it was important, I had to talk an hour and a half to explain that, he would listen but it was not all that exciting to him.

Dymond waxed incredulous at Russo's insistence that David Ferrie's philosophy was the "big deal." "Having heard these people conspiring to murder the President, and knowing the President had, in fact, been assassinated, you still, in 1967, thought when you were being questioned regarding an assassination conspiracy, you still thought the big deal was Ferrie's philosophy?" Russo clung to his original claim but he was hedging more and more, even with Dymond. In response to the question "In Baton Rouge, did you not then know that you had seen and heard three people plan to assassinate President Kennedy?" Russo replied, "Well, I don't know if I had seen or heard three people plan to assassinate Kennedy. I heard a discussion about shooting Kennedy as well as I had heard the discussion on the street about killing Judge Perez or killing Martin Luther King or killing someone else."

Perry Russo was not one to give a yes or no answer when a few hundred words would suffice. By the time Dymond got comfortably into his cross-examination of Russo, and despite the young man's extreme propensity for circumlocution, the lawyer indulged him, never raising his voice, never becoming snappish and not even requesting the judge to admonish the witness to confine his answers to yes or no—with, if necessary, a brief explanation after.

There was a certain dogged insistence by the defense attorney to receive an answer but this was achieved by repeatedly asking the same question over and over, to which Russo would respond by running three more times around the barn.

It had been easy to understand James Alcock's gentle but businesslike guidance of Perry Russo through his quiltwork of the past, but now here was Irvin Dymond following the same procedure on cross-examination. True, he would sometimes patronize the witness by pure incredulity of tone, but there was a frontal attack missing in his work.

By the midafternoon recess, we had been through three-quarters of a day of Perry Russo's talkathon. Jim Phelan, archenemy of Perry Russo and barred from the courtroom proper because of his upcoming testimony, was found warming a bench in the corridor, eager for a rundown of events inside. During a break several of us filled him in on the line Dymond was pursuing, and he shook his head sadly.

When court resumed, the lawyer returned to the alleged conspiracy talk and asked Russo if, in fact, he had failed to take the conversation seriously because it contained all the characteristics of a bull session. Russo admitted it had. Dymond lingered in the bull session area at length until Alcock objected, saying, "Mr. Russo's personal feelings about it aren't really relevant; it would be the feelings of the fourteen men to my left whether or not the conversation was serious."

The defense lawyer led Russo back to his identification of Oswald, trying to ascertain if he had truly fingered him as Ferrie's roommate from a photograph shown him by Sciambra in Baton Rouge or whether he had waited for positive identification until he'd been through a lengthy beard-sketching session in New Orleans. Russo was at his most indefinite during this prolonged display of verbosity.

I could not help eying the jury and spectators. Mr. Mason, juror number one, was engaged in some serious smoking, for lack of an activity. Next to him, Oliver Schultz, chin cradled in his right fist, appeared to be in dire need of a Dexamyl; Mr. Ricks, the young Negro schoolteacher, looked as if he might just snap his fingers and say, Come on, boys, let's pick it up! And so on down the line. The members of the Fourth Estate were restless and shifting on their cushions or the hard benches. The spectators displayed dyspeptic faces, as if they had actually paid for their seats only to find they'd already seen the show. The Hanging Ladies, up front in the preferred wooden pews ahead of the railing and spilling over into the extra jury box, were displeased that the guillotine was not in operation and even the deputies and court bailiffs seemed to be spelling each other in their tours of guard duty with much more frequency than usual. Yet nobody could take the chance of pulling up stakes. Although this lawyer cat was merely engaged in a lengthy play session, barely cuffing, claws retracted, with this witness mouse, no one wanted to miss the eventual big pounce and ensuing bloodshed.

Irvin Dymond began questioning Russo about the original letter he'd written to the District Attorney when he'd first come forth, and the novelty of the witness's brevity woke us all up in the following exchange:

DYMOND: Now, in this letter which you wrote to the District Attorney's office—I am speaking of the original letter you wrote before having interviewed Mr. Sciambra—did you make any mention of any conspiratorial meeting?

RUSSO: No, sir.

DYMOND: Did you mention the word "Leon," the name "Leon Oswald"?

RUSSO: No, sir.

DYMOND: Did you mention the name "Clem" or "Clem Bertrand"?

RUSSO: No, sir.

DYMOND: Did you mention the name "Clay Shaw"?

RUSSO: No, sir.

DYMOND: Did you mention the name "Lee Harvey Oswald"?

RUSSO: No.

DYMOND: I take it you did not mention the name "Oswald" in any form, is that correct?

RUSSO: No.

Dymond appeared to be picking up steam. Soon he returned to the meeting/party at David Ferrie's and questioned the witness endlessly about where he'd come from before arriving there and who might possibly have gone with him to the party. Russo replied in a shower of words about his life and times and activities—lots

of basketball playing—and the people in his world, but there was now no mention of Sandra Moffitt or Niles Peterson accompanying him that September evening in 1963. Soon the defense lawyer was reading him his preliminary hearing testimony in which he stated that both Niles Peterson and Sandra Moffitt were at Ferrie's with him. Why, now, Dymond inquired, was the witness unwilling to corroborate his original testimony and place them at the party? Was it because Russo had learned since the hearing that both of these people had denied being there?

Russo, however, had now warmed up to the point of feeling completely at home in the courtroom and, when pressed, came up with a charge against Dymond: "I said that only after you had forced me into the position, I said it." Dymond, surprised at this, asked, "I *forced* you to say these two people were definitely with you?" Russo remained adamant, claiming he had mentioned people who might have been with him, people he was associating with at the time, but that Dymond hadn't been satisfied with that answer and had pressed him for such a long time he had finally been forced to come up with those two names, now adding it had been a probable guess. To which Dymond replied, "You don't state a probable guess as a definite fact when you are testifying, do you, sir?" Russo: "You asked me over and over and I gave you an answer over and over and you still want the same question answered, and I am trying."

It was after 5:30 and court was adjourned. We wondered exactly what the District Attorney or his staff might say to Russo. For despite, and perhaps because of, his treatment by Dymond he had pulled the conspiracy meeting down to a probable bull session and he had indicated ambiguity surrounding his identification of Oswald. He had also subtracted, under oath, two people he had previously placed at the party with him. His relations with Dymond had been, compared to the expected fireworks, almost cordial.

Russo later gave me his reaction to the first day of his testimony: "You see, as versus the preliminary hearing and all the other times I was called as witness. All these other times, Dymond always sneered, snarled and spit his words out, called me by the last name and all kinds of stuff like this. This time he didn't. He was gentle as a baby. I couldn't believe it. I really couldn't. . . . Alcock even said something about it after the first day or Sciambra or one of them. Someone said, 'Looks like you're having a tea party, you and Dymond.' And I said, 'Well, look, I'm not gonna upset the boat. If he doesn't want to get mean, I'm not gonna get mean either and we just . . . ' you know. They said, 'Be a little stronger, you know, you're giving off a little too much, you know, like you're a witness for the defense. You're smiling back at Dymond and he's smiling back at you.' And so I said, 'Well, all right.' "

Among the press it was clear that Russo would perhaps spend an entire second day on the stand. It was surmised the defense lawyer had taken it easy the first day in order to draw whatever damaging equivocations he could from the witness, but going into the home stretch he would most certainly cry, "Banzai!" and the decimation of Perry Russo would be on.

Although Jim Garrison's absence from the courtroom was now the norm, it was noteworthy that he did not lend his presence to support his main witness, a young man who had left scattered behind him a two-year trail of doubts about his testimony. Had Big Brother been sitting there, maintaining direct eye contact with Perry Russo, speculation ran, the witness might not have elected to bob back and forth in a sea of ambiguity. There was little doubt that Garrison, having heard of the first day's equivocations and the almost tacit truce—forced or not—between Perry Russo and Irvin Dymond, would appear the following morning.

24

The Loneliness of the
Long-Distance Talker

Perry Russo had switched to a dark blue suit for his second starring appearance. Our Lady of the Hats had also, of course, effected a full change of costume. The courtroom was packed as Judge Haggerty took the bench and greeted the jurors, many of whom were dressing informally these days, with "I trust you gentlemen had a good night."

As to their nights, the jurors might have been cut off from many of life's ordinary pleasures but they were making up for this—and the lack of pay—by indulging in the one they were allowed: gluttony. Their eating habits at the Rowntowner Motor Inn were becoming legend. The tightness of their clothes lent testament to the tall tales of six dozen oysters followed by two sirloin steaks apiece.

As the jurors settled their increasing weight into their chairs, we looked for Jim Garrison to make his appearance, but he was nowhere to be seen.

Irvin Dymond began by asking Perry Russo if he'd given a complete account of the alleged conspiratorial meeting the day before under direct examination by James Alcock. The witness slipped into one of his shuffle-hop-hedge steps, but Dymond pinned him down and Russo admitted he could not think of anything specifically that had been omitted. The defense lawyer asked if Russo had contributed anything at all to the conversation at Ferrie's apartment. Russo replied, "No, I was most of the time going in and going back out . . . down the street a lot of times. I didn't hear the entire conversation." Dymond got him to reiterate he hadn't heard the entire conversation, only portions of it, and then, in his most casual come-on-you-can-tell-us voice, asked, "Now, Mr. Russo, referring to what you did hear of this conversation between the parties whom you say were Leon Oswald, Clem Bertrand and David Ferrie, was there ever any actual agreement to kill John F. Kennedy?"

Alcock objected to the question and Judge Haggerty sustained him, adding, "That is a question for the jury to decide."

DYMOND: I will break the question down, if the court please. [To the witness]: In your presence, did David Ferrie ever agree to kill the President of the United States, John F. Kennedy?

RUSSO: He said, "We will kill him."

DYMOND: He had said that many times before, had he not?

RUSSO: Right.

DYMOND: As a matter of fact, he had made that direct statement to you alone, had he not?

RUSSO: Right.

DYMOND: Did Leon Oswald ever, in your presence, agree to kill the President of the United States?

RUSSO: No.

DYMOND: Did Clem Bertrand ever agree to kill the President of the United States?

RUSSO: No.

[A reporter quickly printed a sentence on his pad and held it up: "Then what in Christ's name are we doing here?" It was true— one person does not a conspiracy make.]

DYMOND: Would I be correct in saying then that you never heard anyone actually agree to kill the President of the United States?

Perry Russo indicated he had finished paying his early morning obeisance to brevity when he replied, "Well, when you say 'agree,' it is a problem, that is the word 'agree,' you know, I mean, all I do is hear people talking about it—I don't know if they agreed or not. It would seem to me they were in agreement as far as certain things were concerned, I don't know if they actually—I can't remember either any of the three ever saying yes, this is how we will do it, let's do it this way."

Dymond inquired if the witness had ever heard anyone say, "We will do it." Russo admitted only David Ferrie had said, "I will get him" or "We will get him" and added that Ferrie had said this to him many times in the summer of 1963. Dymond was curious to learn if Russo had ever agreed that this was a good idea or if he had tacitly gone along with Ferrie. Russo replied that "I told him that it would be extremely difficult to do something like that, and that he didn't have much hope of success."

The defense lawyer then went into the character of David Ferrie, an aspect that Perry Russo was most interested in discussing at length and not without a generous portion of admiration. Russo gladly told of Ferrie's interest in philosophy, politics, religion, science, cancer and hypnotism.

When Dymond asked if it was his intimate knowledge of Ferrie that kept him from taking the conspiracy talk seriously enough to report it, Russo replied, "In other words, Dave Ferrie was a character. I was not indifferent to it, but almost, out of—somewhat I avoided the man mentally because he had a brilliant mind and he could sort of envelop and strangle a conversation or influence direction of thought because he might be able to prove it was wrong. And he did claim quite a few things that I didn't know if he backed up or not. He claimed he was in the Bay of Pigs to me, and I heard somewhere that he claimed that he was not. I don't know if he was in the Bay of Pigs. He claimed he flew down to Mexico and Cuba. These things I don't know, I could not test, but the problem with Ferrie was that along with the claims he had this appearance, he had no—it looked to me—no apparent purpose, but on the other side of the coin he did back up the things, things that just— When I came into contact with him, he did back these things up, he was well read in religious matters. He could quote book, chapter and verse on political stuff and things that I was interested in, and he did back himself up in this area, and he also had a medical lab. Now, I couldn't understand a man having a medical lab and not really knowing what he is doing down there, but he said he was a doctor or he had extensive knowledge in surgery and things of that sort, and what could he back up and what couldn't he, and I just pretended to be indifferent to his claims and talks and things like that. It just went in one ear and out the other, as far as validity, I didn't know which way to take it."

Take a breath, Perry.

It took quite a few more minutes of questions and distended answers to get Perry Russo to admit that in the four years between 1963, when he claimed to have heard the talk, and 1967, when he'd emerged into the limelight, he had not worried about the conversation, and indeed had been completely indifferent to it.

The witness then, on his own, offered a piece of gratuitous and contradictory testimony: "When Oswald was arrested, I told a couple of friends that I knew him, or it looked like I knew him. I thought it was the same guy." This despite reams of testimony the previous day about never having heard of Oswald before the assassination, his lengthy and troublesome identification of Oswald, and the hours spent drawing beards on his picture so that he could positively state he was Ferrie's roommate.

Dymond returned to the party, asking Russo for the names of any of the ten or twelve people who were there and had left before the alleged conspiracy talk took place. Russo could not come up with anything more definite than "There was a Julian, a Manuel."

Then Dymond veered back to Russo's identification of Leon Oswald in the Sciambra memo and his subsequent minor corrections of the day before, attempting to pin down whether the witness had described Oswald's hair as "dirty blond" or "brown" and if it was brown, was it light brown or dark brown or "just brown." James Alcock objected to this line of questioning as redundant (with the blessings of most of those in attendance), but the defense lawyer persisted, moving on to Oswald's beard. Was it a bushy beard or whiskers or just a few days' growth, and was it neat or messy or just slightly unkempt and was it darker or lighter or the same color as the hair on Oswald's head, and did it have spots or traces of gray and white in it? And did the sideburns extend down into the beard?

This went on to the point of saturation and thumping boredom. Russo's opinion, after painful circumlocution, was that Oswald had brown hair and an unkempt growth of three or four days' whiskers with spots where the hair had not grown in. He could not remember whether the beard connected to the sideburns.

Dymond next got Russo to admit, also based on the Sciambra memo and his corrections, to a two-year jump when the witness moved his alleged sighting of Clay Shaw and David Ferrie at a gas station from 1962, before the party, to 1964, which would have been after both the party and the assassination of the President. "That was a flat error on my part," Russo declared.

Had not the deputies and bailiffs surrounded us on all sides, there would have been a short round of applause at the terseness of this admission. There followed a complete recap of the interview with Sciambra, during which Russo remained steadfast in his insistence that Andrew Sciambra's notes would not have been sufficient to have revealed the true and complete content of what he'd told the Assistant District Attorney.

Court took the midmorning recess. On his way to the men's room down the hall, a smiling Clay Shaw said out of the side of his mouth, "Perry does go on, doesn't he?"

I learned during recess that the defense had been forced to order a complete transcript of the first day of Perry Russo's testimony. It ran to 248 pages and cost Clay Shaw over $900 to have it transcribed from the court reporters' notes and mimeographed in time for the defense team to go over it prior to the second day for purposes of catching the witness in contradictory statements. What, I wondered, if the defendant had been a pauper and could not have purchased this transcript—and could not have put out the $4,000 to investigate Charles Spiesel?

Soon after the recess, Dymond went puddle jumping from one area of questioning to another, areas in which he could either sniff out discrepancies in the witness's testimony, come upon small islands of illogicality, or sometimes make Russo appear to be either stupid, careless or completely forgetful. Still not raising his voice, the defense lawyer began to give indications that Russo's circumnavigation was causing him mild nausea and ever-increasing patience pains. Returning to Sandra Moffitt, Dymond elicited from the witness that although he had gone with the lady for five years, he could not state a specific address for her. "She lived at several places, she lived around Canal and Broad, she lived uptown, she lived different places." Pinpointing the year 1963, the lawyer drew from Russo the information that Sandra Moffitt probably lived at one place for the entire year and he still could not name the address. Dymond, amazement in his voice, asked, "You went with her for four or five years and did not know what street she lived on, Mr. Russo?" Russo explained that Sandra Moffitt always wanted to come to his house. This did not satisfy Dymond but he was still unable to obtain a specific address for Miss Moffitt.

He then asked Russo how many times he'd seen Ferrie in September of 1963. The reply was "Four or five times." He could not be specific about any one of the times. Back to the party and again the indefinite: Russo did not remember which week in September it took place, which night of the week, whether it was a week night or weekend, or how he got home from it. He thought perhaps he had caught a bus. When the lawyer asked, "Could somebody have given you a ride?" Russo replied, "Probably," and that David Ferrie might have given him a ride home, but he doubted it. "He was not the type to walk out with people he had around him."

With incredulity in his voice, Dymond wondered how Russo could possibly have forgotten "whether or not one of the three conspirators to kill the President of the United States rode you home from the conspiratorial meeting?"

RUSSO: I don't call them conspirators. No, I don't know who rode me home. I may have caught a bus or hitchhiked or not.

DYMOND: You do not call them conspirators?

RUSSO: I have never used that word.

After receiving that token gift from the witness, Dymond jumped to Russo's relationship with Ferrie after the assassination. Although in the Sciambra memo Russo was quoted as saying he'd never seen Ferrie after the President's death, he had corrected that and now testified that their friendship continued and he'd subsequently seen the ex-pilot five, six or seven times. Dymond wondered if Russo had seen fit to ask Ferrie whether he'd killed President Kennedy or whether he knew who killed him or anything about it. "I didn't see fit to ask him anything," Russo replied, displaying a woeful lack of curiosity. Dymond lingered over this for a while, unable to comprehend Russo's attitude, but the witness simply stated he had other things on his mind. Dymond: "Did he ever ask you, 'For goodness sake, keep quiet about what you heard up on Louisiana Avenue Parkway'?"

Alcock objected that the reply would be hearsay and Judge Haggerty sustained him. Dymond filed a bill of exception and then requested the judge to send the jury out of the courtroom while he got an answer to the question, contending that "Unless we do that, the Supreme Court has no way of knowing in the event of appeal what testimony we were deprived of." There was a lengthy debate over this between Alcock, Dymond and the judge, with Haggerty finally ordering the jury to leave the courtroom for the time it took the defense lawyer to ask, "At any of these meetings, wherein you saw David Ferrie and spoke with him, after the assassination of President Kennedy, did he ever caution you to keep quiet about what you had heard on Louisiana Avenue Parkway?" Russo replied no, and the jury was brought back.

The defense lawyer returned now to Russo's brief acquaintance with Oswald. Russo indicated Oswald appeared to be antagonistic toward him and because of that they'd not traded much conversation. The witness claimed he'd first seen Oswald polishing a rifle on the porch of David Ferrie's apartment, next at the party, and twice more briefly at Ferrie's after that. Dymond asked Russo whether after seeing television accounts of the assassination and pictures of Oswald, he had connected the two names (Lee Harvey Oswald and Leon Oswald) at all. Russo replied, "I told a couple of friends of mine that I knew him or I had known him." Dymond could not understand why, if Russo had done that, the identification of Oswald had been such a tremendous problem in Baton Rouge and in New Orleans. Russo claimed he had corrected the Sciambra memo to the effect that he had mentioned the name Leon Oswald.

If he had done that, why the labored beard-sketching session a few days later in New Orleans? It did not hang together, especially in view of Russo's testimony that the last time he'd seen Oswald he was clean-shaven. So he *had* seen Oswald without a beard. When you put all these ingredients together, they formed a dizzying stew of inconsistency, and Dymond was not averse to stirring it up over and over.

Before lunch, Dymond probed several other interesting facets of Russo's supposed relationship with David Ferrie. Here was a man he had known and seen from 1962 until 1965. Russo claimed that each had an open invitation to come to the other's house, an invitation both used freely. Despite this, Russo was unable, under extensive questioning by Dymond, to name any of Ferrie's roommates during that period, outside of the brief alleged residency of Oswald, a tenure unsupported by any other witness. The lawyer took him through an entire list of David Ferrie's close friends, most of whom knew one another and many of whom were alive and well and living in New Orleans—if under harassment by the District Attorney. Several had been certified roommates of Ferrie's for considerable periods of time, but Russo admitted knowing none of these young men. He could not name one person he had met at David Ferrie's, over a period of three to four years, other than Leon Oswald and Clem Bertrand and two Mexicans, a Julian and a Manuel, and one other briefly mentioned as "a guy named Tommy." Asked why he could not remember any of the names, Russo replied, "Nobody stuck out, it was just the same crew, if he was over at the house he was just with one or two people most of the time, none of these people ever amounted to anything." (If they had been the same crew, all the more reason for them to stick out, one would imagine.)

Perry Russo had met, *after* the preliminary hearing, one Layton Martens—under indictment for perjury now for refusal to cooperate with the District Attorney—who had been a friend of Ferrie's. The witness acknowledged, under Dymond's persistent questioning, discussing the case with Martens.

Russo admitted, with added lengthy explanations, saying to Martens that "This [case] is the most blown-up and confused situation I have ever seen," and "I have made most identifications on the basis of photographs alone."

Dymond confronted Russo with another alleged statement: "I am sure of the identification I made of Shaw but not 100 per cent. I want to meet with him to make absolutely sure, but I am afraid to. It could have been Bannister [who might have been Bertrand] or Lewallen [a roommate of Ferrie's who might have been Oswald]."

"No, that is absolutely false," Russo replied, going on to add, however, he would like to explain what he *had* said in line with this. Dymond agreed and Perry Raymond was off and running with what came to be known as the 100 per cent/1,000 per cent theory. Russo: "James Phelan made it a big point that he felt it [Bertrand] was Bannister. . . . Phelan made a big point of this, and I was talking to Martens about it and I told him essentially that I said I was sure 100 per cent, but I said in a case like this you have to be sure 1,000 per cent." Russo then told about Phelan setting up the meeting with Clay Shaw, adding, "And I told Layton Martens in a case as serious as this, you would have to be 1,000 per cent sure although it was impossible to be that, but I was 100 per cent sure. Does that make sense?"

Dymond pulled a "Russo" and avoided answering that question, countering with "Isn't it true that you asked this meeting with Shaw be set up?" Russo acknowledged it might have been he, but went on to say he finally told Phelan, "Well, that won't work because Shaw would have a wall that thick in front of him. It would serve no apparent purpose, the only way you could know a person is to have it unmolested and unharassed, and in the particular position he is in, it would just not be a free conversation."

Dymond moved to another area and asked Russo if he had told Layton Martens, "I was supposed to be given $25,000 by Garrison for helping him out, but thus far I have only received $300." When Russo responded with "All right, now, yes, I said that!" the courtroom perked up considerably. Even Dymond repeated, "You *did* say that?" But Russo dove into a long explanation, asserting a newsman had rumored he, Russo, was going to get $25,000. Russo ended with "*I* said *they* said I was getting $25,000." The press relaxed as Russo explained he had received $300 to cover three weeks' expenses in New Orleans around the time of the preliminary hearing and small checks for $45 or $50 or $60 or $70 in relation to Dean Andrews' trial and several other minor appearances. Then:

DYMOND: I want to ask you whether you made this statement to Layton Martens on the same occasion: "I am not real sure if they were plotting against Castro or Kennedy."

RUSSO: A qualified yes, very qualified.

DYMOND: Did you, first of all, did you make that statement, Mr. Russo, and then you may explain it!

RUSSO: Well, all right, yes, let me put it yes and I am going to say no afterwards. And I want to say yes, but it depends, in other words, Ferrie talked about Castro, too, you see, he thought . . .

Perry Russo was pleased to chronicle more of David Ferrie's philosophy, sparing few details. It seemed that if Dymond kept questioning Russo along any one line long enough without losing his patience or temper, he could eventually extract an answer from the witness that might not be 100 per cent satisfactory, but might give 80 per cent relief.

Soon Dymond jumped back to the conspiracy talk, asking, "Would your loyalty to David Ferrie have prevented your reporting it to the local authorities?" Russo replied he had no loyalty to Ferrie. Again Dymond asked if he would have reported it if he had considered it a serious threat to the life of the President. This brought a long speech from Russo about not knowing whether to take David Ferrie seriously or not, until Dymond finally cut him off by saying, "Now, I take it then that you didn't know whether they were just shooting the breeze, whether this was a bull session or what it was?" "Correct," replied Russo.

Dymond, not remaining long in any one arena, now veered back to the Sciambra memo and questioned Russo about Ferrie's homosexuality.

DYMOND: Yesterday you said that you had not said that Ferrie was a homosexual. Isn't that right?

RUSSO: I said that *Ferrie* had not said that.

DYMOND: Are you saying now that Ferrie never admitted to you he was a homosexual?

RUSSO: Oh, no.

DYMOND: Never? I refer to the same Sciambra memorandum . . . wherein you have given an account of Ferrie having told you he used an aphrodisiac on his roommate [Oswald] that aroused the roommate sexually and he had intercourse with his roommate. Is that correct?

RUSSO: No. The only—he said it worked like a—that is the nearest he ever came to saying it. I made a point of this down in New Orleans, probably, the nearest he ever came to saying that, but he didn't say anything about intercourse at all.

DYMOND: Is that another correction?

RUSSO [consulting the memo]: Right down on . . . "He also said that Ferrie essentially confessed to him he used hypnosis for sexual purposes." I said that is not correct, and another thing on page three. "He also admitted to Russo for the first time that he was a homosexual and he wanted to know if Russo would be willing to take a drug." And I said that is incorrect.

DYMOND: That is absolutely not correct?

RUSSO: Right, and, you know, I just say that—

DYMOND: Now, this statement which I shall read to you right now: "Ferrie told Russo he had been trying the aphrodisiac drug on his roommate and it worked perfectly. He said that he and his roommate laid in bed naked, and he gave the drug to his roommate and the roommate became very passionate and aggressive and had intercourse with Ferrie." Are you now saying that is an incorrect statement?

RUSSO: I covered it essentially with the first two, this is what— "Ferrie told Russo that he had tried the aphrodisiac drug on his roommate and it worked perfectly." That is about it.

DYMOND: Are you saying now that Ferrie did not tell you that he had intercourse with his roommate?

RUSSO: He said the roommate tried, that is the nearest he came. Now, he never said he *did*.

If David Ferrie gave a male roommate an aphrodisiac and it worked perfectly and the roommate attempted to have intercourse, it would seem to obviate the necessity for Ferrie to have declared that he was a homosexual. But as so much of the testimony in this case was left with threads hanging, so was this.

We were soon released until 1:30. Tension and speculation, mixed with equal parts of apprehension and disappointment, ran high over what had turned out to be a ping-pong match between Perry Russo and Irvin Dymond. It was apparent the cross-examination would be concluded in the afternoon session. There were still those who held firmly to the belief that Dymond was saving his big guns for the finish. Better to save the *coup de grâce* for the end and leave the jury with the ultimate impression of the witness—torn, bloody and shaking. There were others, and I was beginning to infiltrate their ranks, who were reserving judgment, who were starting to believe that perhaps Dymond knew exactly what he was doing in his approach to the witness, this on the basis that Russo, no matter how long-winded, was taking it easy on the defendant. He was not skewering him. By his very equivocations, his contradictions, his qualified admissions, the original spear of accusation had been loosened and was about to plop out onto the floor of the courtroom.

The *States-Item* was on the stands about the time we returned to the courtroom. The large black-on-pinkish headline read, DIDN'T HEAR SHAW, OSWALD AGREE TO KILL, RUSSO SAYS. Underneath was a smaller subheadline: "Ferrie Only One to Make Vow." Hmn, the mind said, not bad.

As court resumed for Perry Russo's last act, Irvin Dymond returned to the Sciambra memo and the preliminary hearing, again throwing Russo's earlier testimony in his face—that Niles Peterson had accompanied him to the party. Russo again charged Dymond: "I testified to that after badgering. You forced me in that position and I said the people I associated with probably were

Peterson and probably Moffitt." Now it seemed as if we might have a little fight.

DYMOND: By badgering you, you mean by asking you a number of times the same—

ALCOCK: I object—

DYMOND: If the court please, he used the terminology "badgering."

ALCOCK: I am objecting to this area because we have been over and over this and it is highly repetitious.

DYMOND: This is the first time I have been accused of badgering a witness.

ALCOCK: You used the word.

DYMOND: He used it first.

JUDGE HAGGERTY: Read the question and answer.

The court reporter read Russo's statement in which he first used the word in question. Alcock then said his objection was "not badgering but repetitious."

DYMOND: At this time I am objecting to the word "badgering." I have been accused of badgering and I want to know what it means.

JUDGE HAGGERTY: I think we all know what the word "badgering" means.

DYMOND: What does it mean?

JUDGE HAGGERTY: We can get the dictionary out. [Then to the witness]: What do you mean by "badgering"?

Russo repeated what he had said before, that Dymond kept asking and asking him and he had finally come up with those two names. To which Dymond jumped in with a most pertinent rejoinder: "Then if somebody will ask you something enough times you will give them the answer they want?" Alcock objected that Dymond was arguing with the witness, and Judge Haggerty sustained him.

Cool heads soon prevailed, to the disappointment of the spectators, as Dymond returned to the description of Oswald's beard and other well-trampled territory, over Alcock's objections. Dymond next inquired if Russo had been living in New Orleans at the time of Ferrie's brief arrest a few days after the murder of the President. Russo testified he was in New Orleans but had not known of Ferrie's arrest, to which Dymond commented, "And this is the same David Ferrie that was a close friend of yours and he had an open invitation to your home and you had an open invitation to his?" "Yes," replied Perry.

The defense lawyer proceeded to Russo's meetings with James Phelan. As background he led Russo to admit that he had, of his own accord, first contacted the Baton Rouge *State Times* and given various interviews before ever talking to anyone from the District Attorney's office and had also suggested that James Phelan contact him, after their first interview. Finally Dymond asked the witness if he denied making this statement to Phelan: "If Garrison knew what I told my priest in Baton Rouge after the Shaw hearing he would go through the ceiling."

Russo replied, "No, I don't deny making that statement but it needs somewhat of an explanation in context. I had told quite frankly many people this, and let me give you a little backup also. I told Phelan a great deal about colored versus black and white, something I mentioned today as to how I felt of the period of time from February 24, wherein I got involved, all the way up until the time he was there and also past that time actually. If you were at a basketball game or the fights you have a lot of vague memories and recollections that you have of that occasion, but from February 24 until that time my whole association in this case as the accuser of the defendant, or witness against the defendant, had been what I called a blank gray area and I would rather have—if I could pull myself out of it, and I went into a long explanation of that to him. Now, if you will repeat just exactly the statement I made—"

Dymond complied: "If Garrison knew what I told my priest in Baton Rouge after the Shaw hearing he would go through the ceiling."

"Essentially," Russo continued, "what I told the priest was that I'd like to be out of it, such a personal turmoil and upheaval in my own personal world and that it would not be the same whether Mr. Shaw was found guilty or not, that had no bearing, that my life would never be the same because there were so many news people, some with other motives such as WDSU and NBC, that not only reported the news incorrectly but quite often attempted to make news, things of this sort." Dymond asked why he presumed that would make Mr. Garrison go through the ceiling. Russo took out a handkerchief and mopped his brow. "It seemed like they had got me in a cross fire and I didn't want to name names and that if I could have avoided the whole thing, I'd rather not remember anything."

In relation to the meeting Phelan attempted to set up between Russo and Shaw, Russo testified he told the writer, "Don't take me serious, it's not possible," further explaining to Dymond, "It would be impossible because Garrison's office knew exactly well that Phelan was talking to me about it and they were tape-recording the conversations." When Dymond asked how Garrison obtained the tape recordings, Russo did not hesitate to say he'd informed the D.A.'s office that Phelan had called him, after which they had set up bugging devices and a tape recorder in his house. Dymond got Russo to admit there had been times when he and Phelan spoke outside his house *without* being recorded. As to the reasons for taping their conversations and for Russo's willingness to give so many interviews to Phelan—when the young man had been protesting he had been hounded by the press ever since the preliminary hearing—Russo commented, "The District Attorney's office was interested in how much and how far he [Phelan] would go." Russo claimed he was interested in how far Phelan would go, also.

Dymond read many statements that were attributed to Russo by Phelan. They were clearly painful to hear and reply to, because Russo knew full well Phelan would be testifying after him and, although he apparently did not want to deny them flatly, he was doing his level best to remove the incriminating stingers. A statement such as "I do not know the difference between reality and fantasy and I have told my roommate Steve about it and brooded about it" would be met by Russo with "That is accurate with some explanation." The explanation would be lengthy and rambling. When Dymond quoted Russo as saying to Phelan, "Everything you have commented on about my testimony has been bouncing inside my head and I am much more critical of myself than you are," Russo explained it by saying, "That was to make him think he was starting to get somewhere in breaking me down and my testimony . . ."

By the time a recess was called, the strain of testifying for such a long period was beginning to show on Russo. His eyes would not remain focused on their target for more than a few moments; they would dart from Dymond, up to the judge, over to the jury, back to Alcock. He had started out frozen by nerves, warmed up, hit a good steady stride and had almost taken over by sheer willingness to expound, but the marathon was taking its toll now. If he had been apprehensive about Garrison clobbering him, he was now trembling in anticipation of Dymond's sledgehammer. Dymond was exhibiting his own brand of restlessness. He had been most generous in his agreement to allow the witness to explain ad infinitum, but the emotional fee for holding himself in check was showing in his face that recess, and in his voice prior to it.

Judge Haggerty was looking displeased when he took the bench after recess. We soon knew why. "I would like to make one announcement before pulling the jury down," he said. "It has been brought to my attention that one of the news media people have seen fit to violate my guidelines. [A momentary shiver down my back as I thought, Could my little TV blooper have just now reached him?] When Mr. Russo—before he came back to take the stand—a newsman approached him and made some comment about his testimony. I am not going to do anything about it at this moment but if it comes to my attention again that my guidelines have been violated I am going to have that reporter's credentials, his admission credentials, taken up so he cannot enter this court-room. I hope it will not happen again."

Hugh Aynesworth later told me he'd muttered something to Russo about being a rotten liar. Russo, on the other hand, told me Aynesworth snarled to the effect, Hey, you got any dirty pictures to show me? This, in reference to pornographic films Russo had dealt with. Hugh, filled with unremitting anger over the state's case, had trouble reining in his temper.

Dymond questioned Russo now about an interview with George Lardner, a reporter for the Washington *Post*. "Do you deny you told Mr. Lardner you were willing to disclose weaknesses in your testimony for a price?" Russo absolutely denied it. When Dymond kept at him, Russo owned up to part of it, saying, "I discussed the approach to the cross-examining of me and what I would think would be weaknesses in my testimony." Dymond continued: "Did you make this statement: 'Garrison doesn't know what they are. I know what they are'?" Perry Russo earned some large grins when he replied, "That is absolutely incorrect. The District Attorney's office *does* know."

His delivery and timing on that were flawless.

Now Perry Russo was confronted with the most damaging

statements attributed to him. Russo had just finished telling the defense lawyer that he and the D.A.'s office had taped all conversations with newsmen to see how far they would/ go, when Dymond asked, "Did you have any reason to gather information for the District Attorney's office or to be taping your conversation with Sergeant [Lieutenant at the time of the trial] Edward O'Donnell of the New Orleans Police Department?"

Russo's face tightened as he replied in the negative. Russo had been sent to Sergeant O'Donnell for the purpose of taking a lie detector test. Alcock quickly objected but Dymond said he knew full well no evidence regarding the results of such a test was admissible; he was only establishing time, place and circumstance. It was then disclosed that a meeting had been arranged between O'Donnell and Russo "just to talk to the man," as Russo put it. Now Dymond started pegging the witness's own alleged statements at him, asking if he had not told Sergeant O'Donnell that he was under a great deal of pressure and wished he'd "never gotten involved in this mess." "That is correct," Russo said, adding, "And I went into great lengths to talk about the pressures."

"Is it not a fact," Dymond asked, "that in response to a question by Sergeant O'Donnell as to whether Clay Shaw was at the party which you have described, you replied, 'Do you want to know the truth?' and when he said yes, you said, 'I don't know if he was there or not'?"

"Uh," said Perry Russo, "with some explanation the statement is accurate." His explanation blamed all the newsmen who were around, pressing and telling him he was wrong and inaccurate, so "that it was hard to tell whether he was there or not."

"Is it not also a fact," Dymond continued, "that you stated to him that if you had to give a yes or no answer as to whether Mr. Shaw was at the party you would have to say *no?*"

"Again with the same explanation that I have given you," the witness replied.

"First of all, did you say that?" Dymond asked, indicating he was not going to stand for endless equivocation.

"Probably, maybe not those exact words you are quoting there but in essence the same thing," Russo replied, going on to mention the pressures but, outside of that, not dodging the answer.

"Is it not a fact," Dymond asked, "that when he asked you why you had come to court and positively identified Shaw at the preliminary hearing that you stated it was because Dymond, meaning me, turned you on, as you put it, by asking you whether you believed in God?"

"I told him something along that line."

"Did you tell him *that?*" the lawyer demanded.

Russo thought a moment before he spoke. "Yes." Another pause. "I said, and I might paraphrase it and it might ' ₁ lot quicker. I said you had gone for the juggler [*sic*] vein and that I didn't care to discuss that, and you asked me several questions I thought were out of line, or out of bounds, and you went into the examination of that area. . . . When I talked to him I told him essentially something along those lines."

There was now something extremely personal between Dymond and Russo as this young man went on to admit, when asked if the conversation at David Ferrie's apartment sounded like a legitimate plot to assassinate President Kennedy, that he'd said, "No, it did not." When Dymond inquired if he hadn't said it appeared to be another bull session, Russo made a minor correction: "I used the word 'shooting the bull.' I don't use the word 'bull session' that much." He admitted telling O'Donnell he wanted to meet with Clay Shaw and he did not deny telling the sergeant he wanted to know Garrison's complete case against Shaw because it would help him come to a decision. Russo's respect for the word of this police sergeant kept his hedging to a minimum and by the time the O'Donnell episode was finished, it appeared a major chalk-up for the defense.

Soon the lawyer jumped to an entirely new topic, asking the witness if he had ever been under psychiatric treatment. Russo admitted that, beginning back in 1959, he had been under the treatment of a Dr. Max Johnson on a consultation basis of twice a week for a period of twelve to eighteen months. Dymond asked if he hadn't had telephone consultations with the psychiatrist for quite a lengthy time after the active consultation period. Russo replied, "Well, not for a lengthy time, only when I had something I wanted to discuss with him." Asked if he'd ever talked to any other psychiatrist since 1965, Russo said, "Only as far as someone up at LSU, just discussing psychiatry. I have always been interested in psychology and psychiatry and psychoanalysis."

Dymond requested the court to bear with him a moment as he leaned over and spoke with the Wegmann brothers. As might have been expected the end of Perry Russo's cross-examination was tipped with a surprise.

DYMOND: Mr. Russo, have you ever attempted to commit suicide?

RUSSO: Never!

DYMOND: Do you know a man by the name of Mike Fitzpatrick?

RUSSO: Mike Fitzpatrick? Yes, sir.

DYMOND: You knew him in 1962, didn't you?

RUSSO: Oh, yes, sir.

DYMOND: Do you deny that in 1962 Mike Fitzpatrick came to your house, and when he got there your wrist had been cut and there was about a half-inch of blood and a spot on the floor?

RUSSO [raising his voice and his wrists]: Mr. Dymond, I don't have any scars on my wrist!

DYMOND: Do you deny that?

RUSSO: I deny that.

DYMOND: That is all.

Not quite time for Perry Russo to escape the barrel. Alcock took him back for a brief brushup on re-direct, asking him to identify various photographs of a microscope and test tubes purported to have belonged to David Ferrie. When Dymond objected that this was totally irrelevant, Alcock addressed Judge Haggerty: "Your Honor, I think that these will demonstrate to the court and the jury that when Perry Russo said Ferrie exhibited great knowledge in medicine . . . that these pictures will corroborate that testimony."

This appeared, in a way, to be a backhanded slap at the main body of Russo's testimony as far as credibility was concerned, as if to say that he may have been shaky about his identification of Clay Shaw and he may have gone overboard on the conspiracy bit, but he certainly knew what he was talking about when he said David Ferrie possessed a laboratory and a knowledge of medicine.

Alcock then attempted to clear up the reason for Russo's not having mentioned Clay Shaw in his many earlier press interviews. "Because I didn't know Clay. I was introduced to a man named Clem Bertrand," Perry replied, indicating that the same applied to his exclusion of Lee Harvey Oswald in his early interviews. "I had known a Leon Oswald and I maintain that to this point right now," the witness testified. The re-direct was brief, ending with a question by James Alcock as to the identity of the defendant. Russo's reply was: "The question is whether Clay Shaw and Clem Bertrand are one and the same? They are."

"No further questions," replied Alcock.

"All right," Judge Haggerty said, glancing down at the witness, "you may step down."

As Russo leaned forward preparatory to lifting off the launching pad, Dymond spoke up. "Your Honor, I have a few questions."

Perry Russo did his best to hide the oh-my-holy-God! he must have been feeling and eased himself back in his chair. The re-cross-examination was not lengthy; it could not have been. Tension showed signs of eruption and Russo's testimony did indeed end in a shouting match.

Dymond inquired if Russo had not been permitted to look at Clay Shaw through a one-way glass in the District Attorney's office on March 1, 1967. Alcock objected strenuously, saying this had not been brought out on re-direct (the law being that nothing can be touched on in re-cross that does not rebut what was brought out on re-direct). Dymond argued it *had* been brought out on re-direct, having to do with Russo's not knowing who Clay Shaw was on March 1. Judge Haggerty permitted the question and Russo admitted he had been allowed to view the defendant through a one-way mirror. Now the bad blood that had to be between them coursed to the surface:

DYMOND: Is it not a fact that when you were permitted to look at Clay Shaw through this one-way glass, you were told who he was?

RUSSO: I had been told that before, probably was told, or I heard the name at that same time also.

DYMOND: That was March 1? Right?

RUSSO: I had been told—I think if I came down to New Orleans on the 27th, I was probably told the next day or the day after.

DYMOND [his voice rising now]: But you did know his real name when you looked at him?

RUSSO [spitting out his answer]: His name to me is Clem Bertrand, I am not going to claim him as Clay Shaw right now!

DYMOND: Were you not informed by a representative of the D.A.'s office that you were looking at Clay Shaw through a one-way glass?

RUSSO [temper running high]: No District Attorney walked in there and said, "You are looking at Clay Shaw through a one-way glass," I am sure of that.

DYMOND: Did anyone inform you of the actual name of the man you were looking at?

RUSSO: I said that they did, someone did!

DYMOND: Now, is it not a fact that the interview which was conducted by Korbel and the other reporter on the steps of the courthouse was taken as you were *leaving* the courthouse that day?

RUSSO: Right!

DYMOND: Is it not a fact then that you did know the correct name of Clay Shaw when you—

RUSSO [shouting]: No, I didn't know Clay Shaw and I don't know Clay Shaw right now!

DYMOND [murder in his voice]: Let me ask the question before you answer it!

JUDGE HAGGERTY: Cut the screaming down. We can do better talking low. Let him finish the question and then you can answer it.

DYMOND: If you had been told this man's correct name when you were looking through the one-way glass in the D.A.'s office, and this interview was taken when you were leaving this building, why didn't you know his correct name by then?

RUSSO: Because I was never introduced to a man named Clay Shaw, I was introduced to Clem Bertrand and that is still the name that he goes under to me right now.

DYMOND [between his teeth]: You wouldn't be splitting hairs on this, would you?

ALCOCK [jumping to his feet, shouting]: Object, Your Honor!

JUDGE HAGGERTY: That is argument.

[Now the fight fans out front began a rumble they hoped might sustain the anger and override the judge's plea for cooler heads.]

BAILIFFS: Order, order, please!

DYMOND [voice still raised and insistent]: Do you still say you weren't told that was Clay Shaw you were looking at?

ALCOCK [riled to a cutting nasal pitch]: Objection! He has answered the question!

JUDGE HAGGERTY: He has answered the question. I sustain the objection. Cool it down, please, gentlemen. We can do just as well by keeping our voices down.

DYMOND: Your Honor, when somebody tries to talk when you are still asking a question you have to raise your voice to be heard.

[It went on a while longer and it was apparent that no matter what the questions, hostility would prevail. Now Dymond and Alcock wanted at each other.]

DYMOND: Isn't it a fact that you also did not mention anything about a plot, meeting or a conspiracy meeting?

ALCOCK: Objection! He has answered the question.

DYMOND: If the court please, the state went into this on re-direct.

ALCOCK: And he answered the question!

DYMOND: I would like to go into it now.

ALCOCK: He has *answered the question!*

DYMOND: Isn't it a fact—

ALCOCK [shouting]: Objection!

DYMOND: You have been overruled!

ALCOCK [squaring off]: I have not been overruled!

After Dymond had asked Russo if it was true he didn't mention anything to an interviewer about having known Lee Harvey Oswald after he'd testified he'd told friends that Leon Oswald and Lee Harvey Oswald were the same person, the judge spoke up: "Now I am going to intercede. He only answered the questions that were put to him, he didn't volunteer anything. That is what I understand."

DYMOND [getting to his feet]: If Your Honor please! We object to the court commenting on the evidence, we do, and we move for a mistrial!

JUDGE HAGGERTY: Well, it is denied!

Denied it was. Just as it was clear there could not be much more questioning of this witness without resorting to an out-and-out donnybrook. Dymond pressed for a few more answers and it was interesting that Russo threw in one gratuitous assist, even at this stage of their relationship. In reply to the question of sitting in on a conspiratorial meeting with a man whom he'd seen represented in the papers and on television as the killer of President Kennedy and not reporting it, Russo replied, "No, I never said anything about a conspiracy; I didn't sit in on any conspiracies."

James Alcock shook his head at that, as well he might.

The end of Perry Russo was mild.

DYMOND: You had your story to tell and you *told* it? Isn't that right?

RUSSO: That I knew Dave Ferrie, yes.
DYMOND: That is all.

For added punishment, Perry Russo was forced to sit in the witness chair while various photographs were formally marked and entered into evidence. It was like enduring a long operation, without benefit of anesthesia, only to pull yourself together and find you'd been strapped to the operating table. Perspiration glistened on Russo's forehead as the lawyers droned through the technicalities. When Perry Raymond Russo was finally released at 4:45 P.M. at the end of his second full day on the stand (the total transcript of his time spent in the hot seat fills 530 pages), his relief must have been dizzying. He made his way out, moving with that forced pulled-togetherness that one might achieve by inhaling through every pore in order not to disintegrate in full view of one's fellow man.

Clay Shaw regarded him closely as he stepped off the stand, passed the prosecution table and walked through the swinging gate and up the aisle to freedom. For the last two days it had been the trial of Perry Russo as much as it had been Clay Shaw's.

A woolly argument ensued after Russo's departure when the state attempted to enter into the record the preliminary hearing testimony of Dr. Nicholas Chetta, the deceased coroner who had administered sodium pentothal to Russo and interrogated the witness under that drug. Dymond objected because this transcript included lengthy portions of Russo's statements while under the influence of sodium pentothal. The prosecution claimed Dymond had "opened the door" on the question of Russo's sanity by introducing into the record his psychiatric treatment and maintained that Dr. Chetta's testimony would corroborate Russo's sanity at the time of the preliminary hearing. Dymond disagreed, saying, "In the first place, counsel is contending by asking a witness whether he has had psychiatric treatment that I have opened the door as to his sanity. You will probably get resentment from a lot of people in this courtroom if you questioned the sanity of each one who has consulted with a psychiatrist."

Judge Haggerty had something to say about this: "Well, to the layman, whether you believe it or not, to the layman a person who goes to a psychiatrist, they do think something is wrong with them; whether he is nuts or not, that is something else." Judge Haggerty had a way of stripping the issues down to the lowest common denominator.

Dymond insisted that Dr. Chetta's testimony, even if he were alive, would not be allowed, now arguing strongly against its introduction at this current trial. Judge Haggerty stated he would read the transcript of the preliminary hearing dealing with Dr. Chetta and announce his ruling the following morning.

We were released. It had been a long and trying two days. It was too early to computerize and digest the effects of Russo's two days on the stand. It was over, that was about all that could be said. Although only a spectator, I felt completely drained. The British Tattoo could have drilled above me that night and I would not have lost a wink.

25

"That May Make Me a Sloppy Memo Writer—But It Doesn't Make Me a Prostitute"

The next day's proceedings began in a fit of arguing over the admissibility of Dr. Chetta's testimony during the preliminary hearing. William Wegmann, making a solid debut for the defense, put up the major part of the fight against introduction of this evidence. Possessing a loud, clear, energized voice, he was sharp in attack this morning, claiming among other things, "The question is not whether Russo was sane in 1967—the question is whether he's sane in 1969!" He challenged the three-judge court that presided over the preliminary hearing, termed their rulings illegal, and called Dr. Chetta's testimony irrelevant at this time. Judge Haggerty eventually overruled the defense, saying, "Take a bill." After a bill of exception was filed, Alvin Oser, the large sandy-haired, crew-cut, knit-browed Assistant D.A. began reading the sixty-seven pages of Chetta's testimony to the jury. Oser's voice is not unpleasant but it contains a tricky built-in echo chamber that makes his words difficult to understand unless he strikes exactly the right pitch. If he spoke conversationally, it was all marbles and lost. It was when *almost* shouting that he made himself clear; too much shouting and the echoes collided, reverberating and defying translation. Initially it was refreshing to have a change of principals in Wegmann and Oser.

There was something lacking in immediacy, however, in this two-year-old testimony of a deceased coroner. The UP story in the New York *Daily News* reported, "Three jurors slept, Shaw napped and the judge's eyelids drooped during the session."

It was true, lethargy and restlessness soon took over, and by the end of the first ten pages a fair sampling of the press had slipped out of the courtroom and were, to borrow a phrase from Perry

Russo, shooting the breeze in the corridor. Hugh Aynesworth, passionately concerned as ever, talked about the need for someone to get down and slug it out in the gutter with Garrison's team. He liked Dymond but he was disappointed that the defense lawyer had not actually dismembered Perry Russo. If the Shaw-ites could have had their choice, the ultimate would have been smack out of Perry Mason, with the witness whipped and pummeled until he burst into a *mea culpa* confession of falsehood and deceit, then crumbled on the stand, eventually to be assisted from the courtroom, a mere shard of his former self. In relation to the damage wreaked upon the defendant over the past two years, there were many who would like to have viewed such a scene. I would not have covered my eyes.

On the other hand, considering the way in which Perry Russo had fudged, perhaps Dymond had known precisely what he was doing. Hadn't the witness himself admitted telling Sergeant O'Donnell he'd impaled Clay Shaw at the preliminary hearing because Dymond had "turned me on" by what Russo considered unnecessarily rough treatment? Dymond had been careful not to turn him on now. If the point to the trial game is winning, just as well to win calmly than to win with fireworks, especially if the fireworks might explode in your face. Russo had eventually testified that he had heard neither Clem Bertrand nor Leon Oswald agree to kill the President. No prima-facie case of conspiracy, therefore, had been established in the minds of many of the reporters, but who knew what had been established in the minds behind those fourteen impenetrable masks up front and to the left?

We trickled back into the courtroom toward the end of Alvin Oser's reading. The jury appeared to be in need of a brisk trot around the block. Liz Garrison, dark glasses atop her smoky blond hair, had arrived and sat in the row of chairs immediately behind the prosecution table. Her husband was missing, as usual. Perhaps, I thought, each night over dinner she gave the District Attorney a full account of what had transpired that day.

When Alvin Oser finished reading Dr. Chetta's testimony, the state called Andrew Sciambra to the stand in an attempt to patch up his memorandum. Now the session perked up considerably. Here we had one of Garrison's prime henchmen in the witness chair.

A defense objection boomed out every few minutes, voiced

either by Dymond or Billy Wegmann, as Alcock led Sciambra
through his explanation of the events surrounding the memo.
Sciambra's basic story was that the interview in Baton Rouge had
lasted about two and a half hours and that Russo's apartment had
approximated a fraternity house with people barging in and out.
He'd taken very few notes, perhaps two, two and a half pages, and
had not taken down everything Perry Russo told him. He had
displayed forty-some pictures for Russo to identify. He testified he
went directly from Baton Rouge to Jim Garrison's house, where "I
told the D.A. that Russo told me he attended a meeting—"

That was as far as he got. Dymond objected to Sciambra's attempt to insert hearsay evidence (in quoting what Russo purportedly said). Although Sciambra is an attorney himself and
should have been aware of the rules of testimony, he was often
stopped when he was about to repeat what someone had told him.
He continued his story about the memorandum, claiming he had
begun to dictate it on Monday, February 27, the date on the memo,
but asserting he had not finished dictating it until seven to ten
days later in what amounted to four or five sessions. Sciambra contended a memo he and Alvin Oser had dictated after Russo's
sodium pentothal session was completed first and more accurately
reflected the interview with Perry Russo, adding, "The sodium
pentothal memorandum includes the most important thing Mr.
Russo told me—"

William Wegmann sprang up and in no uncertain terms asked
Judge Haggerty to instruct the Assistant D.A. in the rules of
evidence to prevent him from introducing more hearsay.

Shortly thereafter court recessed. During the luncheon break I
was introduced to Pershing Gervais, the man who had formerly
been Jim Garrison's chief investigator but had resigned under
pressure when he was cast by the political opposition as Garrison's
Achilles heel. Gervais, before he went to work for Garrison, had
been discharged from the New Orleans police force after having
testified that bribes were handed out to policemen on a weekly
basis in their pay envelopes "like a fringe benefit."

Pershing Gervais swore that if he'd still been working for his old
pal Garrison, he'd never have allowed him to get mixed up in
"this bullshit Kennedy investigation." So here he was this day,
dropping by to see how the store was being run. Gervais, a tough

meaty man with a broad lived-in face, could easily be pictured as a fight trainer, towel slung around his shoulder, pumping up his boy for the big match. Several of us were discussing whether Sciambra would manage, in the jury's eyes, to glue together his memorandum. To this Gervais said, "Don't worry about all that bullshit that's going on in there—Sciambra and the memo—the state has the closing argument and that's all that matters in a case like this with that bunch of boobs in the jury box. They won't even *remember* Sciambra or anything else. They'll goddamn well remember the closing argument, though."

This was, for most of us, not an encouraging trial theory.

When I questioned Pershing Gervais about what he thought of Clay Shaw, the state's case, and the eventual outcome, he said, "Listen, kid, all of that bullshit doesn't mean a thing. Who's right or who's wrong—this is New Orleans!"

The afternoon session produced as much argument between the state and the defense as actual testimony, featuring one prolonged shouting match between Alcock, Dymond and Billy Wegmann. Nor did Sciambra, even while in the witness chair, overexert himself in attempts to restrain his temper. Under further direct questioning by Alcock, Sciambra admitted there were numerous omissions, errors and inaccuracies in the Baton Rouge memo, explaining they were the result of his attempts to *interpret* what Russo had told him. Sciambra wanted to go through the memo and explain each and every one of Russo's corrections. The defense objected, again claiming Sciambra would be inserting hearsay by repeating statements Russo allegedly made to him. Alcock argued that the defense, the day before, had used the Sciambra memo to impeach the credibility of Perry Russo and now the state should be able to offer its explanation of the twenty-six errors. To this Dymond quipped, "Sciambra is not on trial, Mr. Shaw is!" Alcock snapped back, "I didn't understand that yesterday!" indicating, of course, that Perry Russo had been on trial. Judge Haggerty called their arguing "legal mumbo-jumbo."

Whatever it was, it continued. Dymond and Wegmann spelled each other, popping up with objections every time Alcock began to question Sciambra about a point in the memo. Alcock insisted the state be able to continue its explanation of the errors. Dymond, now in an easy purring voice, said, "We don't want to keep them from explaining them." Judge Haggerty then asked, "How can he [Sciambra] do that without saying what Russo said?" Dymond, with a smile in his voice, replied, "I don't believe he can."

Eventually the judge ruled Sciambra could go through the memo and interpret how the errors got into it, over further loud objections from the defense. The jurors were now sitting up straight. The shouting alone was enough to keep them awake.

Sciambra was extremely cavalier in explaining his errors, maintaining most of them were unimportant anyhow. It was more than obvious that his nose was extremely out of joint from being constantly rubbed in his own memo. To Russo's claim that Sciambra erred in saying Ferrie used hypnosis for sexual purposes, Sciambra flipped, "Maybe I assumed he did, but the essence of this is correct, if not the word-by-word description."

Sciambra's flippant attitude, more than the content of his corrections, brought another objection from William Wegmann to the manner in which he was interpreting the errors. To this, Sciambra replied in a sullenly righteous tone, "I think I should be able to explain them!" Wegmann complained, "He's answering as an assistant district attorney." At this Judge Haggerty peered down from his bench at Sciambra and cautioned the ex-boxer, "Don't answer back from the stand." Wegmann also maintained Alcock was impeaching his own witness (Russo) and added that Sciambra was using extralegal privileges since he had been allowed to sit in on Russo's two-day cross-examination and had not been asked to leave the courtroom as had other witnesses. It was true; Sciambra was in the unique position of having been present during Russo's testimony and of being able to now shore up, or attempt to, any holes in his memo in accordance with what had been said.

"I can't tell him to rid his mind of what he heard yesterday," Judge Haggerty commented. Sciambra then continued with his corrections, telling how he came to write that Russo and Ferrie never spoke after the assassination. "What Perry said was they hadn't spoken *about* the assassination," Sciambra said, "so I put down they hadn't spoken." Sciambra's attitude was, So what, big deal, as he went on down the list.

Billy Wegmann took him over on cross-examination. He did not allow as much time for an answer as Irvin Dymond had allowed Perry Russo, nor did he allow Sciambra to linger in his explanations. Toward the end, Wegmann's *modus operandi* caused Sciambra to exhibit the enmity he felt toward the defense.

Wegmann at first concentrated on the date of the memo. Although it was dated February 27, Sciambra said it was not finished until seven or ten days later. Wegmann got him to look at a calendar for the year 1967 and Sciambra agreed it could not have been finished much before March 7, at the earliest. (If this were correct, Garrison would have given the memo, all typed up and mimeographed, to Jim Phelan in Las Vegas on March 4 or 5, *before* Sciambra had finished dictating it.) When Wegmann asked if he'd kept his original notes, Sciambra testified he'd burned them. Asked why, Sciambra explained that ever since the case began "we've had a problem of information leaking out of the District Attorney's office."

This should have been no surprise to Sciambra or anyone else. Many newsmen, writers and assassination buffs had been freely allowed to examine much of the evidence, in direct violation of the judge's guidelines. An outstanding example is Edward Jay Epstein, who wrote in his well-documented book *Counterplot* that shortly after arriving in New Orleans he had dinner with Jim Garrison and the following morning when he showed up at the Criminal Court Building, James Alcock informed him that Garrison had left word for Epstein to "start going through the evidence." He and Jones Harris, a New Yorker of independent means and a civilian Dealey Plaza Irregular, were then allowed to pore over six cardboard cartons of articles taken from Clay Shaw's house the day of his arrest. Alcock had told Epstein that even the District Attorney's staff hadn't yet examined all of the material. And now Sciambra was complaining about leaks in the office. At one point in his cross-examination he reiterated the outward flow of classified information and the way he put it earned a few chuckles. "There have always been leaks in the DA's office," Moo Sciambra said, adding, "at least, ever since I've been there."

Wegmann was a persistent questioner; he would not let up on Sciambra's *bête noir*, the memo. Wegmann finally asked how it was that "Some two years later you're full of corrections about what happened in Baton Rouge—yet seven to ten days after the interview you were full of errors, inaccuracies and omissions?" Sciambra replied that listening to Russo on the witness stand had refreshed his memory. Now Sciambra began to get surly. When

Wegmann inquired if it was his habit to state assumptions in memos besides the facts, Sciambra curtly replied, "Sometimes." Although he must not have known or cared how he was coming across, he stuck to his attitude and when Wegmann asked if he also chose to put down *his* impressions and interpretations of David Ferrie, rather than Perry Russo's, Sciambra shrugged and said, "Evidently I did."

He denied making a bet with Phelan whereby one of them would quit his job if the memo turned out to be deficient as Phelan claimed. The very mention of Jim Phelan's name brought about a severe narrowing of Sciambra's eyes and he finally could contain himself no longer and called Jim Phelan nothing more than a "journalistic prostitute."

By the end of his testimony, Sciambra was ready to step out in the parking lot and slug it out with someone, anyone. One of his last answers, when Wegmann would not let up, was a sullen "Well, that may make me a sloppy memo writer—but it doesn't make me a prostitute!" He was finally excused, leaving the stand in steamy distemper with his 3,500-word memo clanking noisily behind him.

Within minutes of resuming his seat at the prosecution table he was immortalized in the press section:

> On the stand Moo was far from a bore.
> He even called Phelan a whore.
> "Not so," Phelan cried.
> "This D.A. has lied.
> Read his memo and add up the score!"

Now the first of a parade of Texas witnesses was called. R. C. Roland, the compact, well-dressed, unctuous president of the Winterland Ice Skating Rink in Houston, took the stand and told of David Ferrie's visit to his establishment November 23, 1963, the day after the assassination. He claimed Ferrie, accompanied by two young men, had made a pest of himself by making sure his presence was known at the rink. The ex-pilot, Mr. Roland said, had not gone skating but had hung around the lobby and the telephone, making several phone calls and, Roland maintained, receiving one. He was happy to draw diagrams of the rink showing the location of his office and the public phones and throwing in incidental tidbits of information like "From one to three we gave lessons to Girl Scouts." Roland claimed Ferrie approached him at least five times to let him know he was still there. When Ferrie finally took his leave, Roland said, he made a point of saying he would be back later in the evening, but added, "He never returned." The witness was clearly enjoying the importance of his connection with the case. He was pleased to relate that an FBI agent had spoken with him for ninety minutes regarding Ferrie's presence at his rink.

Irvin Dymond, having enjoyed a breather during Sciambra's testimony, took Roland over on cross-examination and proceeded to extract an extraordinary blooper from him by asking when Andrew Sciambra had first contacted him as a prospective witness. Roland said it was about a year after the assassination, perhaps in November of 1964.

DYMOND: You couldn't be wrong by a year, could you?
ROLAND: No.
DYMOND: Or two years?
ROLAND: No.

This fascinating testimony placed the time of the contact two years before Andrew Sciambra went to work for the District Attorney. It would also have been two years before Garrison began his investigation. Dymond dropped no comment on this until, after questioning the witness about Ferrie's conduct and companions, he said in his most purry voice, "Mr. Roland, would you consider it unusual that you got a phone call from the D.A.'s office almost two years before they started their investigation?" At this Roland shrugged and replied, "So I was off on the time?"

There were snorts and head shaking in the press section as James Alcock took him back on re-direct. Certainly the time factor would be rectified as Alcock asked, *"When* did Mr. Sciambra contact you?" But Roland calmly replied, "Several years ago." He was invited to vacate the witness chair soon afterward.

It was time now for the state to come up with some solid incriminating testimony, and late in the afternoon they did. First, Richard Jackson, a well-dressed distinguished-looking Negro employee of the Post Office, testified he had handled a change-of-address card temporarily directing the delivery of Clay Shaw's mail from his own home to 1414 Chartres Street, the home of a long-time friend, Jeff Biddison. A small point of confusion resulted when it was ascertained that the card had no date indicating when the change of address had gone into effect, although there was a termination date, September 21, 1966. Under questioning Jackson testified both dates were usually to be found on change-of-address cards.

Richard Jackson was followed on the stand by a Negro letter carrier, James Hardiman. A soft-spoken man, Hardiman testified he'd been a letter carrier in the lower French Quarter for fifteen years. In 1966 he claimed to have delivered mail addressd to Clay Shaw to Jeff Biddison's house at 1414 Chartres. Asked by Alcock if he had delivered any letters other than those addressed to Clay Shaw to Mr. Biddison's home around that time, the postman indicated he had. When Alcock asked him what the names were, Hardiman said, "Names I'm not allowed to give out, but if you phrase your question so I can answer direct, I can say I delivered mail to Clem Bertrand at that address."

That testimony drew a gasp from the spectators. Folks sat up straight and attention was paid. June and Dick Rolfe quickly glanced around at me, foreheads wrinkled, either to express their sympathy or perhaps to see if I'd fainted.

It was getting late but Alcock continued with Hardiman, who said in reply to the question of how many letters he'd delivered addressed to Clem Bertrand, that there must have been several in order for him to remember and connect it up when the name Bertrand appeared in the newspapers. As well as he could remember, Hardiman thought the letters had been addressed in "a very nice handwriting, very clear," on personal-sized envelopes and probably carried local postage. When Alcock asked if Hardiman had ever received any of these letters back, indicating they might be wrongly addressed, the postman replied, "No, I don't recall ever getting any back."

Court was then recessed for the day. Hardiman's testimony, although hardly supportive of conspiracy, nevertheless was unhealthy for the defense, if only because of the apparent credibility of the man. Here was a witness who was a worker-bee with no apparent record of dope, thievery, arrest, or paranoia, a man who did not seem to be particularly delighted that he was testifying either.

The following morning, Irvin Dymond began his examination of the postman with a hint of distaste in his voice. The change in tone of a trial lawyer to suit the witness was illustrated now. Dymond was much more rapid in firing questions at Hardiman than he had been with Perry Russo—a technique reinforcing the opinion that his treatment of Russo had been well calculated.

DYMOND: How many letters did you deliver to 1414 Chartres for Clem Bertrand?

HARDIMAN: Enough of them that when the name came in the news I recognized it.

DYMOND: How many?

HARDIMAN: Quite a few of them. I know I handled several in a brown envelope, a woodframe type of paper.

DYMOND [without a pause]: Did they come in packets?

HARDIMAN: They were individual letters.

DYMOND: Would you say fifteen or twenty letters?

HARDIMAN: No, not that many.

DYMOND: Would you say ten?

ALCOCK: I object to this questioning.

JUDGE HAGGERTY: Sustained. Mr. Dymond, you cannot badger this witness.

DYMOND [keeping up the pace nevertheless]: As many as ten?

HARDIMAN: It's hard to say.

Dymond eased up slightly, asking if it were not a fact that he'd told Jeff Biddison there were less than five. "I didn't tell nobody any number," Hardiman replied. Under further questioning, Hardiman soon testified that the letters had been addressed directly to Clem Bertrand at 1414 Chartres. Now Dymond pulled a foxy courtroom trick upon Hardiman, who took the bait without hesitation and swallowed it shortly after the lawyer asked the postman if he'd ever had occasion to deliver mail to anyone else besides Bertrand and Biddison at 1414 Chartres and received an affirmative reply.

DYMOND: How about [to] James Biddison?

HARDIMAN: Could have.

DYMOND: Fred Tate?

HARDIMAN: I have, but it's hard to say what year.

DYMOND: How about Cliff Boudreaux?

HARDIMAN [without hesitation]: Yes, it hasn't been too long, after the first of the year.

DYMOND: Mr. Hardiman, would it make any difference in your testimony if I told you I made up that name?

HARDIMAN [completely unrattled]: Maybe you did, but I still remember delivering the mail to that address.

Dymond continued throwing names at Hardiman and the post-man snapped at another fictitious name. He testified he had approximately a thousand addresses on his route at that time and that he'd first talked to the representatives of the D.A.'s office about eight months before the trial, going on to add, "The first thing after this broke, some carriers were called into the District Attorney's office. Later on the Post Office Department made them subpoena the carriers."

Returning to the first made-up name for his last question, Dymond asked the postman when he'd last delivered mail ad-dressed to Cliff Boudreaux. The postman unhesitatingly replied, "Within the last six months." "That's all—excused," Dymond said with a grin.

If Hardiman hadn't been entirely discredited, certainly some of the starch had been taken out of his testimony. Another state witness who didn't quite pass the 1,000 per cent test. (Through a bit of sleuthing I later learned that Hardiman may have been in touch with the District Attorney's office regarding other matters between the time of the preliminary hearing and this current trial. Hardiman's son, Terry Gerard Hardiman, 20 years old, had been arrested in April of 1968 on a theft charge. As of March 1970, no action on the boy's case appeared to have been taken by the District Attorney's office.)

Irvin Dymond was congratulated by many who had long wanted the defense to fight back with whatever bricks, mud, sticks, stones and tricks were available.

Dr. Esmond Fatter, who had hypnotized Perry Russo, was next on the stand for over an hour, the greater part of which was devoted to a tug of war between Alcock and Dymond over the admissibility of any testimony relating to Russo's hypnotic ses-sions. Judge Haggerty in the end sustained the defense's strong objections when he ruled, "This testimony does impinge upon the hearsay rule. The state is trying to bolster the credibility of its witness [Russo]. But his testimony must stand or fall on his testi-mony to the jury. This would be corroborative testimony." As Alcock argued in opposition to this ruling, Dymond stood and began to speak, but Judge Haggerty soon settled the matter in good humor, saying, "Mr. Dymond, I think you have won. Stop while you're ahead." With that Dr. Fatter was excused.

The next state witness was a travel agent who handled Clay Shaw's train reservations for his trip to the West Coast in November of 1963. The trip was a matter of record, so there was little of note in this testimony, except that the travel agent was obviously a fan of Clay Shaw's. He explained that Shaw traveled quite often and was considerate enough to split his business between two agencies. He also offered a brief courtroom commercial for his business when he said, "Anyone leaving town—without their car—I can help them!"

Alcock asked for lunch adjournment early this day, saying the witnesses for the next few days were on their way to New Orleans "from a distant city." The distant city was undoubtedly Dallas. The Warren Report was about to be placed on the butcher's block.

26

The Darkest Hour

Irvin Dymond and the Wegmann brothers found themselves in a quandary at this stage of the game. As far as the trial
had progressed, there was not much question that a prima-facie
case of conspiracy involving Clay Shaw/Clem Bertrand and origi-
nating in New Orleans had not been firmly established. For all the
fringe testimony, only two witnesses, Charles I. Spiesel and Perry
Raymond Russo, claimed to have overheard talk that would
constitute a meeting of the minds to murder President Kennedy.
The credibility of both of these witnesses, no matter which side
one was on, was up for grabs. Therefore, if there was no firm case
of conspiracy involving Clay Shaw, the events in Dallas were
irrelevant. If that were true, it did not behoove the defense to
defend the Warren Report. Still it was manifest that the state was
hoping to further implicate the defendant not by his acts of
commission but by the alleged omissions and errors of the Warren
Commission.

In the defendant's appeal to the United States Supreme Court
in October 1968, his lawyers had asked that high body "Whether
or not this court should order the Attorney General of the United
States to defend the validity of the Warren Report to the President of the United States . . . against the intemperate and vitriolic attacks made upon it, the President of these United States, the
Chief Justice of the Supreme Court of the United States, and other
high-ranking public officials by a public prosecutor acting in bad
faith for no useful, valid, or legal purpose." Also: "Whether or not
the validity of the Warren Report is of such tremendous public
importance as to warrant the issuance by this court of an order
directing the Attorney General of the United States to become a
party to a case wherein the integrity of the United States, as well
as the President thereof, and the distinguished members of the

Warren Commission, is being attacked and impugned by a public prosecutor acting in bad faith."

The Supreme Court refused to take action in this case, so here was the defendant not only having to prove his innocence but forced into the position of defending the Warren Report's conclusion that Lee Harvey Oswald acted alone. How could an individual, unless he were John Paul Getty, possibly afford the battery of lawyers, interviewers, researchers, secretaries, medical, ballistic and photographic experts that would be required to bolster a report that had been under attack since the first copy was bound together? Nevertheless, Clay Shaw, now scraping the bottom of his financial barrel after two years of investigatory expenses aimed at disproving the state's case more than proving his innocence, found himself, with a staff of four lawyers, in exactly that position.

The majority opinion of the out-of-town press with whom I associated was to let the state dispute the report all it wanted; if a prima-facie case of conspiracy involving Clay Shaw had not been proven, the Warren Report could have nothing to do with the defendant. There were some who thought the best way to handle this was to offer no cross-examination whatsoever of the state's Dealey Plaza witnesses, on the theory that the events in Dallas were irrelevant to the case against the defendant on trial.

This theory of laissez faire turned out to be difficult to follow. For this afternoon proved to be what was generally regarded by attorneys for both sides, press and spectators as the all-time low in defense morale. Irvin Dymond stamps it the darkest hour of the trial.

When we returned to the courtroom after lunch, easels and stands were being set up in the area between the prosecution table and the defense. A mock-up stage model of Dealey Plaza was also on view.

The first witness called was Abraham Zapruder, a gentle, bespectacled, balding dress manufacturer who went to Dealey Plaza with his eight-millimeter Bell & Howell on November 22, 1963, hoping to get a few shots of Mr. and Mrs. John Kennedy as they passed by. He ended up with as gruesome and heartbreaking a piece of film as the world has ever seen. The shock of being witness and recorder to this event has not left Zapruder and doubtless never will. It has left the man humbled, as if he'd been witness to a holy—and terrible—vision.

Questioned by Alvin Oser, Zapruder told of the search, with his secretary, for a vantage point from which to film the motorcade. He was handed a photograph and identified himself and his secretary standing on a four-foot concrete abutment. When Oser indicated he would have Zapruder examine the exhibits on the easels, Dymond strongly objected that this evidence, all of it, was totally irrelevant to the case against Clay Shaw. The jury was sent upstairs and Zapruder was temporarily allowed to leave the witness chair as Dymond put up what we all knew would be a losing argument to prevent the state from "going into Dallas." The defense lawyer insisted there was no legal connection between the alleged conspiracy and the actual assassination. He reminded the court that Judge Haggerty had made many rulings regarding the Warren Commission and Dallas, pointing out as he made them that there had to be no connection between a New Orleans-based conspiracy and the actual death of the President. Judge Haggerty had also consistently maintained that no matter how badly Jim Garrison wanted to lay hands on the report, that document was not to be tried in his courtroom.

James Alcock argued for the state, contending that one of their witnesses (Perry Russo) had already testified to overhearing a discussion about triangulation of gunfire and the use of a rifle in the assassination, assuring the court the state's presentation of evidence would "be connected up and highly corroborative." Alcock insisted the jury must decide whether this additional evidence should be given weight. Dymond countered that it was the judge's reponsibility to decide what was relevant and what was irrelevant. Judge Haggerty, as was fully expected, ruled the state could overprove its case. The door to Texas was flung wide open.

The state's team eagerly undraped the easels to reveal an aerial photograph of Dealey Plaza and a survey plat drawn up for the Warren Commission, representing the topography of the area as of November 22, 1963. These were companion exhibits to the mock-up of Dealey Plaza. Zapruder was bypassed for the time being as Robert H. West, county surveyor for Dallas, Texas, and the man who had drawn up the plat for the FBI and the Warren Commission, took the stand and qualified as an expert in his field.

This was the point at which Dymond had to make his decision—whether to resist cross-examining these witnesses in an attempt to diminish their importance or whether token refutation of their testimony was necessary in the eyes of the jury. The jury—never so attentive as when these exhibits were undraped and referred to by Assistant D.A. William Alford in his questioning of the county surveyor—was alert to a man; not one chin was cradled in a hand. Many of the jurors leaned forward, craning for a better view of the aerial photograph and especially the mock-up stage setting of Dealey Plaza with its miniature trees, street signs, sidewalks and buildings, complete with a replica of the grassy knoll. Undoubtedly the intense interest of these fourteen men in this aspect of the trial made it difficult for the defense team to ignore Dallas. To the regrets of many, Dymond engaged in some minor cross-examination of the county surveyor. The troops from Dallas were on their way, and the defense could not simply let them overrun the courtroom without attempting to show up their testimony as far from flawless.

Robert West also happened to have been in Dealey Plaza on the fateful day. He testified to having heard four shots; it was his belief the shots came from the grassy knoll; he further told of seeing people running toward the knoll after the shots had been fired.

It was interesting that Jim Garrison made one of his brief courtroom appearances, I believe only his third, during the early part of the afternoon, now that the second phase of his show was under way. Well tailored as usual, in a dark gray suit, he was clearly proud of and impressed by his display of photographs, survey maps and the mock-up and lent them the importance of his rare presence. Jim Garrison actually remained in the courtroom for all of a half-hour during West's testimony.

During an afternoon recess, the defense team spoke with a few members of the press out in the corridor in an attempt to elicit the best solution for combating these efforts of the prosecution to damn Clay Shaw by a graphic reproduction of the assassination itself. Eddie Wegmann and Irvin Dymond were deeply distressed. They spoke of the enormous task of rebutting the mountain of testimony on its way from Dallas. Again many of us advised them to ignore these witnesses. Dymond shook his head and said, "Yes, but, Jesus—do you see the jury, you can't just—" He broke off, merely shaking his head again.

Shortly after the recess Abraham Zapruder took the stand again and, after placing a marker on the mock-up of Dealey Plaza representing his position, gave his eyewitness account of the approach of the motorcade and the assassination of the President.

When the motorcade turned onto Elm Street and began nearing him as it moved away from the Texas School Book Depository building, Zapruder said, "I heard a shot and noticed that the President leaned toward the left, toward Jackie"—his use of Mrs. Kennedy's first name was not irreverent but gentle and tinged with a sorrowful affection—"then I heard another shot. This one hit him in the head and he laid about the same way—leaning toward Jackie, falling down further." After the first shot, Zapruder testified, the President's hands went to his throat and he grabbed himself. Asked what he saw after the second shot, Zapruder, his voice becoming emotional, said, "I saw his head open up, blood and other things—I don't know what it was—brains coming out of his head."

Abraham Zapruder said he then stopped filming and soon found himself walking around, crying out, "They killed him, they killed him!" Finally, accompanied by his secretary, he made his way back to his office located in the Dal-Tex Building on the edge of Dealey Plaza. His secretary notified the authorities immediately, and Zapruder was soon taken to the Eastman Kodak processing office, where the original film was developed and three copies made. One copy was given to the Dallas police, another to the Secret Service and FBI, and a third was later sold to *Life* magazine for $25,000, with a rumored good-taste proviso that it not be shown publicly. (Zapruder donated the money to the Dallas Fireman's and Policeman's Benevolence Association.)

When Dymond questioned him on cross, Zapruder revealed he had not brought the film with him from Dallas but rather the District Attorney had been in possession of it and had given *him* the film when he arrived. Dymond objected to the film being introduced as evidence and maintained that the state had not established that this copy was, in fact, the same film Zapruder had taken five years before.

Judge Haggerty sustained the objection and the jury was instructed to leave the courtroom so the film might be run for

Zapruder's identification. A screen was set up between the prosecution and defense tables, facing the empty jury box and cocked slightly toward the witness chair.

As Alvin Oser manned the projector and the courtroom was darkened, those spectators on the right side of the room began squeezing and joggling to the left. They were admonished to be quiet and orderly but there was an insistent, almost panicky eagerness not to miss the first public showing of this widely heralded but little-seen film. The Ladies of the Court were most distressed; the majority of them were sitting behind the screen. Many crowded to the side of it, spilling over into the aisle and crouching down or kneeling, some on all fours, in their attempts to peer around and up at the white surface. The defense lawyers and Clay Shaw swiveled in their chairs and Judge Haggerty leaned forward from his bench. Those of us in the press section pressed to our left for a better view as the projector was turned on and the color film began to run off. Except for the whir of the machine, the courtroom was deathly quiet.

There came the motorcade, turning onto Elm Street, Governor and Mrs. Connally up front in the jump seat, the President, on the near side of the car to the camera, with Mrs. Kennedy in that now famous pink suit next to him, both of them smiling and waving, with the breeze blowing their hair and the trees in the background. The car is obscured momentarily when it passes the far side of a street sign. Immediately after it emerges into view, the President reacts to the first shot and his hands go to his throat as he appears to turn slightly toward his wife.

An intake of breath was heard in the courtroom, then a loud communal gasp when the President is hit a second time and his body jolts as the right side of his head literally explodes, sending a crimson halo of blood and matter spraying up into the air above him. Now short words and phrases filled the court: "Oh, God!" "Jesus!" "Ahhh!" Then the President is falling toward his wife, to the left, and disappearing out of sight down in the car. Next the total surprise—one had heard of it but had forgotten—of seeing Mrs. Kennedy rise up, twist around and scramble back across the trunk of the car, only to be grabbed by Special Agent Clint Hill and shoved back into the rear seat. Then the limousine is accelerating and the film ends as the car heads for the triple underpass.

The first showing was bloodcurdling; one could barely take it in. The only certainty, regardless of whether the President lurched slightly forward and then to the side or slightly backward and to the side, was the terrible spread of crimson above his head. When the lights were switched on there was complete silence as all of us who had viewed this testament to the savagery of man pulled ourselves together.

Soon the jury was brought back in. Zapruder was excused from the witness stand and took a seat with his comfortable-looking blond wife in the spectator section of the courtroom to the right. The film was set up for a second showing, this time for the jury.

The Ladies of the Court, most of whom had not had a good vantage point for the first viewing, began a mass migration to the left side of the courtroom. Although the judge warned them to move in an orderly manner, there was a goodly amount of pushing, shoving and grumbling over positions. Many of the press stood up, crowding close to the far left wall in order to have a more unobstructed head-on view. Three nuns in full habit crouched down in the center aisle, almost stretched out in prone positions on the floor, in an effort to see the film.

The jurors, to a man, were riveted to the screen; never had they appeared so completely fascinated. A few in the back row stood and all leaned forward as the lights were lowered once again and the slight regular whir of the projector was heard in the courtroom. Once more we witnessed the freakish tragic shot that snuffed out a life and changed the course of history.

The film was run off a total of five times that afternoon. The fourth showing was a meticulous frame-by-frame stop-action depiction, each frame remaining on the screen for seconds at a time. During this graphic, tense and tedious presentation, which lasted a half-hour, Clay Shaw and the defense lawyers moved from their table and stood to the side of Judge Haggerty's bench between the far end of the jury box and the empty witness chair. Clay alternately smoked and clutched his cigarette close to his chest. Standing with one hand braced on the witness chair, he appeared taut and grimly resigned that this gruesome document should be so patently used in an effort to convict him. His lawyers stood near him and watched with expressions of pained concern and brief glances at the rapt faces of the jury.

The spectators grew more cranky over their vantage points at every viewing. They crowded, chided one another, and pressed farther and farther to the left. At each showing the dreadful spread of crimson halo drew loud gasps. Mr. and Mrs. Zapruder sat quietly and virtually alone in the far right section of the courtroom, completely out of viewing range, staring not at the film but gazing rather sadly at the anxious, ill-tempered and, if not bloodthirsty, most definitely morbid craning mob of voyeurs who were glued to the screen as if it might illumine the mystery of the universe.

It was a black afternoon for the defense as the light outside the venetian-blinded courtroom grew dim in the early winter evening, enabling the images to stand out from the white screen with greater sharpness of detail and color than they had appeared in the earlier screenings. The film is extremely short, running less than thirty seconds and not without its share of jerks, giving a grainy, blurry view of the scene. It is the epitome of an amateur home movie. This is not to deprecate Mr. Zapruder's photography, it is simply a fact. He intended for it to be nothing more, and the idea that he was able to continue filming at all during the shots that suddenly exploded that day is amazing in itself. The nuances of detail, motion and expression are extremely difficult to pin down, and one can almost see in the film what one wants. The horror of that crimson haze spreading above the President's head is a certainty. And it is positive that he fell to his left. Having witnessed the film perhaps a dozen times in all, twice in stop-frame action, I would not want to say for certain, though, if he lurched forward or backward. Many of those in the courtroom thought they saw the President's head jerk back. There are those who claim this is not necessarily inconsistent with the Warren Commission's theory that the fatal bullet struck from behind, quoting ballistic experts who say a bullet builds up pressure traveling through tissue, so that at the point of exit there could be a backfire of pressure which would cause a backward motion. There are also those who say the sudden acceleration of the limousine could have caused the President to fall backward. One thing I would swear to—the crimson halo spreads above and slightly in front of the President's head, which would be consistent with a shot from the rear. But I am no expert, only an individual lay viewer.

During recess, small clusters of press and spectators hashed over the details of what they'd seen, instant experts all. Clay Shaw was usually greeted warmly by a few people, sometimes many, when he made his way down the hall to the rest room during recess. This afternoon when he passed by, he was accorded silence. Whether this was the hush of sympathy or a silence implying a probable guilt by association is hard to say, but it was noticeable and it was not healthy.

I introduced myself to Mr. and Mrs. Zapruder during the recess. They are a pleasant couple, she more talkative than her husband. He had not testified to the number of shots that rang out in Dealey Plaza and I was curious, now that the state was out to disprove the Warren Report. "Two shots, only two," Zapruder replied. His wife spoke up immediately: "Yes, he's always said two shots." We discussed the film briefly and Zapruder spoke of the intense horror it brings back to him even now, after all these years and the many times he'd witnessed it. Mrs. Zapruder indicated she had seen the film only once before this day, shuddering and adding, "It was gruesome, wasn't it?"

When court resumed, I noticed several of the jurors staring at Clay Shaw. There was a far different quality in their gaze now than the sort of curious offhand manner with which they had occasionally regarded him during the early part of the state's case. Despite its brevity and amateur quality, the Zapruder film is completely shocking to witness. The impulse is to make somebody pay for the horror it depicts. Lee Harvey Oswald is dead; still, payment is demanded, revenge is ached for. But—who? One could not help wonder if the fourteen men would be swayed to extract a toll for that tragic and freakish shot from the only person ever brought to trial for the brutal technicolor murder which had been run off for them in such graphic detail. There sat Clay Shaw in the defendant's chair, smoking as usual.

And if we thought we'd seen the last of the Zapruder film, we were mistaken. As the state was about to call its next witness, one of the jurors, young Larry Morgan, requested the film be run off again and that the screen be moved closer to them. This request was granted. Even though the film had been shown four times, there was an immediate surge for better positioning and Judge Haggerty held up the showing until everyone had made the cross to the left side of the courtroom. Although I was seated in the third row and within good viewing distance I could not bring myself to watch the film closely again. Instead, I focused on those spectators around me and the ladies and nuns hunched in the back and over by the far wall. Some of them were all smiles and giggles, nudging one another now that they had managed to get a bird's-eye view. A hungry look of salivating eagerness seemed to draw their faces to a point.

Suddenly there was something obscene about sitting there with pad and pencil in my lap, calmly watching the tragic moment of death come to the handsome and relatively young man who was John Kennedy. I averted my eyes at the very beginning as this beautiful couple came into view, smiling and waving at the crowds. And I thought how they were, at that moment, also coming into view of the cross-hairs of a telescopic sight. The realization that at that second death must have been the farthest notion from their minds struck me hard. The world ends so quickly.

I remembered being glued to my radio for what seemed ages the afternoon of November 22, 1963, waiting for word of the President's condition. Now, having seen the terrible impact of the fatal shot, it was obvious he could never have recovered. All the surgeons in the world could not have kept life in his body.

As I glanced to my left now in the courtroom, I saw one lady arch her neck forward, grasp her companion's arm and, eyes shining, whisper, "Now, now—here it comes!" This, followed shortly by the sucked-in vacuum of a gang gasp. I wanted out of there. But within seconds the film had ended and the lights were switched on, bringing to a close the fifth and final showing of the Zapruder film—that day.

Now the courtroom was filled with ghosts. I was taken completely by surprise when I realized the afternoon session was continuing. For me, the day was a dead duck.

The last witness of the afternoon—the planes were landing from Texas—had been a co-worker of Lee Harvey Oswald's at the Texas School Book Depository. Buell W. Frazier, a tall, thin, turtle-nosed country-looking young man, gave basically the same testimony he'd presented to the Warren Commission. He'd resided in Irving, Texas, outside of Dallas, where Marina Oswald was living in 1963 with her friend Mrs. Ruth Paine. While Lee Harvey Oswald stayed in a Dallas apartment during the week, he rode to Irving with Buell Frazier to see Marina and their baby daughter every Friday afternoon and returned with him Monday morning, except for the weekend preceding the assassination, when he claimed to Frazier he was staying in town to work on getting his driver's license. Buell Frazier's picture of Oswald was in keeping with the distant uncommunicative young man the world has been given to believe Oswald was. Although Frazier lived only half a block from Mrs. Paine, he had met neither Mrs. Paine, Mrs. Oswald nor their daughter, despite working with Oswald—they were both order file clerks—and the weekend rides. Buell Frazier testified, "He was more or less a loner, he stayed to himself." Alcock asked if Oswald had ever engaged him in conversation during their rides. "No, he didn't talk much, just not the talkative type. I don't believe in forcing people to talk if they don't want to. Some people are friendly and always have something to talk about. He was just the opposite." The witness went on to add, "I always could get some kind of comment on the weather, or his baby. And he talked about the kids in the neighborhood. They seemed to like him."

The night before the assassination, a Thursday, Oswald had asked Frazier if he could ride home with him to Irving. This was unusual, not being a weekend, but Oswald explained he wanted to pick up some curtain rods that Marina had bought for his apartment. He drove Oswald back to work Friday morning and testified Oswald had with him a brown paper package which he said contained the curtain rods (but supposedly concealed the stripped-down rifle). Buell Frazier last saw the package when Oswald walked ahead of him into the Book Depository building.

James Alcock asked what Frazier had done at lunchtime. The young man replied, "They said the President would come by at noon. You don't get to see a President that often." Frazier testified he'd stood outside on the front steps of the building. He claimed to have heard three shots and added, "They appeared to me to come from the triple underpass."

When the prosecuting attorney asked the witness if he'd seen Oswald immediately after the assassination, the young man replied in a matter-of-fact voice, "No, sir, I didn't. Several of us hadn't eaten lunch. So we went in and ate our lunch."

Was it possible to disprove the Warren Report by this kind of conflicting testimony? Zapruder claimed to have heard two shots and indicated he thought they'd come from his left, the area of the Book Depository building. The county surveyor, Robert West, thought there were four shots and in his opinion they had come from the grassy knoll. Now here was Buell Frazier, testifying to three shots, and saying he thought they'd come from the triple underpass. Three eyewitnesses, three varying numbers of shots, coming from three different directions.

Frazier, who appeared to be strangely untouched by his personal brush with history, was held over in New Orleans for cross-examination the next morning.

On my way out, I had a short chat with Clay, but the conversation was forced. The Zapruder film had destroyed all spirits. The defense lawyers passed us, proceeding down the long corridor toward the stairway with that bad-news gait that adds weight to the shoulders.

27

The Second Trial

By this Thursday evening, Mardi Gras season was in full swing with Insane Tuesday only days away. Both amphitheaters of the huge Municipal Auditorium were swollen with carnival balls every evening. Parades rumbled and snaked through the city each night and most afternoons, choking the streets and drawing thousands of shouting jumping-up-and-down spectators who clawed the air and one another in their efforts to catch the tacky little strings of colored beads and the shiny doubloon coins thrown by the costumed Krewes atop the floats. Police cars, red lights swiveling and sirens blaring, followed them up as marauding bands of joy peddlers, tourists, collegians (they wing in for Mardi Gras as they used to flock to the beaches of Daytona during Easter week), and hippies clogged the French Quarter, spilling off the sidewalks into the streets. The jazz bands blared until dawn, by which time the gutters were stacked high with beer cans and, upon occasion, a few drunken bodies.

The delicate and plentiful French Quarter balconies, now braced with timbers from below to withstand the crowded cocktail, dinner, and parade-watching parties, still sagged dangerously and sloped streetwards beneath the weight of the manic celebrants.

The madness I'd heard so much about gripped the city in a hairy palm. Fascinating as it was to observe, there was danger in it, the same danger and fascination one would feel in Africa watching a nearby herd of restless elephants. A change of wind, a shot, a lightning flash—and the mood could alter, you could easily find yourself the target.

The madness was exciting, though. It was also isolating. Now, as the city swelled and became a caldron of celebration, the vortex of all fleshly pleasures, it spun off and away from the United States, a great cruise ship drifting into a choppy Stygian sea. That evening, after battling my way back to the apartment across a parade route, I received a phone call from New York, and the distance to the far end of the connection definitely seemed transoceanic. I almost found myself asking, How are things back in the States.

Mardi Gras's derangement also infected the trial, which at best stretched credibility in American jurisprudence and only by means of a lengthy inheritance of standard courtroom procedure and physical setting managed to keep from bursting the boundaries into total insanity—a solid courtroom; a silver-haired judge who had not, despite his trembling hands, shown up inebriated and who managed to keep law and order even if some of the laws did appear warped; a jury and their box; well-groomed lawyers for both sides, none of whom had struck one another or stuck out their tongues or hurled an ashtray through the air; the press to the left, spectators to the right, with plenty of green-garbed bailiffs between to keep them from fighting or fornicating. The accouterments of sanity were there. It was the content—the flow of testimony and duality of purpose that trickled with madness, flashing off and on and lighting up the tilt sign—that made you want to keep ducking into a cold shower.

The following day, Friday, the Zapruder film was shown three more times in the courtroom, again over the violent objections of the defense that it was being used to prejudice and inflame the jury, whose focus and interest in it seemed not to have diminished with repetition. I switched seats in the early afternoon from the press section to the spectators' side to avoid seeing the President's head being blown apart once more. I took my place next to a tiny gray-haired lady in a gray flannel suit and wearing the tiniest pair of space shoes imaginable. By this time we'd been through Buell Frazier's cross-examination, a photographic expert, and several other witnesses, all related to the happenings in Dallas. After an hour or so, this lady touched my arm, the brush of a sparrow, and said in a soft voice, "Is Mr. Shaw here today?" I was surprised at first, then thought, No, why *should* he be here? Like a theater standby, he could have phoned in and checked with the stage manager to see if he was needed today. I informed the lady he was present and pointed him out, barely visible behind the easels, plats and aerial blowups that crammed the forward area of the court. Clay was gazing at this new parade of witnesses, none of whom he knew and none of whom even claimed to know him.

Craning to catch a glimpse of his white hair, the lady thanked me kindly.

If we thought the state's case against the Warren Report would make more sense than the case against Clay Shaw—other than a seriousness of purpose to convict—we were mistaken. This second phase of the trial was conducted in the main by Alvin Oser, he of the crew cut, knit brow and echoing voice, and William Alford, a tall soft-spoken man of great heft, a football lineman's build topped by a pleasant roundish baby face, a sort of well-groomed Ivy League Lennie from *Of Mice and Men*. Oser, whose attempts at sarcasm were archly heavy-handed and straight out of a high school debating team, came across as if he might just have brought it off if he'd been allowed several more rehearsals and some solid coaching. The intent was there. Alford, likably gentle, needed the speed-up signal; the distance between the stimulus and the response was somewhat attenuated. A majority of the Dallas witnesses turned out to be Warren Report rejects, cranks or eccentrics of one sort or another.

The witnesses' testimony varied as to the number, placement, direction and timing of shots, the movement of the President, and the reactions of the spectators at the scene. One lady from Dallas was asked at the end of her testimony, "Were you ever questioned by the Warren Commission?" Her reply was aired on a snort: "No, sir, I was *not!*"—indicating that if she had been allowed to speak her mind, she'd have settled the entire matter and there would not have been all of this confusion in the land.

The state's witnesses continued to backfire on them, not as spectacularly as Charles Spiesel, but backfire nevertheless. Special Agent Lyndal Shaneyfelt, a photographic expert for the FBI and a man of unimpeachable qualifications, who had not only examined the motion picture film and slides of the assassination but also had taken extensive part in the official re-enactment of the crime in Dealey Plaza ordered by the Warren Commission, was subpoenaed by the state as their witness. The state appeared to be pleased with this tall, thin, slightly graying man who possessed a scientist's approach, as they took him for nearly two hours through the Zapruder film, the timing of the camera, the individual slides by number, and the re-enactment in Dallas. Even Jim Garrison lent his presence to this expert witness for all of twenty minutes. The state then went on to concentrate upon omissions and certain facets of the re-enactment that did not conform exactly to the specifics of the original tragedy in Dealey Plaza. The prosecution did not, however, ask Shaneyfelt his expert opinion about the direction of the bullets.

On cross-examination Dymond sounded the missing and all-important question: "Have you seen any photographic evidence indicating that the shots came from anywhere but the right rear of the motorcade?" Shaneyfelt answered with a firm "No, I have not." He also explained that if a perpendicular line were drawn up from the President's head, the burst of pink and other matter would be seen in front of it and "going in a forward motion." Shaneyfelt turned out to be the defense's witness. The only advantage he afforded the state was to allow them to run off the Zapruder film once more for the jury.

The Perry Raymond Russo syndrome also popped up in a Texas witness. Roger C. Craig had been a sheriff's deputy in Dallas at the time of the assassination. He testified on direct examination, in contradiction of the Warren Report, that he had seen a slight Caucasian with sandy hair run down the grassy knoll approximately fifteen minutes after the assassination and jump into a light-colored station wagon, which was then driven away by a dark-complexioned Latin-looking man with black hair (the Cuban theory). Craig said later on at Dallas police headquarters that he'd identified the man who ran down the hill and jumped into the station wagon as Lee Harvey Oswald. Craig further testified he was in the same room with Oswald and quoted Oswald as saying, "That station wagon belongs to Mrs. Paine [the woman with whom Marina was living]. Don't try to bring her into this." Craig also maintained that Oswald leaned back in his chair at police headquarters and said, "Everybody will know who I am now."

On cross-examination, Dymond asked Roger Craig, natty in a sports jacket and black turtleneck sweater, if he'd related essentially the same story to the Warren Commission. He said he had. The Warren Report documents Roger Craig and his story as follows:

Roger D. Craig, a deputy sheriff of Dallas County, claimed that about 15 minutes after the assassination he saw a man, whom he later identified as Oswald, coming from the direction of the Depository Building and running down the hill north of Elm Street toward a light-colored Rambler station wagon, which was moving slowly along Elm toward the underpass. The station wagon stopped to pick up the man and then drove off. Craig testified that later in the afternoon he saw Oswald in the police interrogation room and told Captain Fritz that Oswald was the man he saw. Craig also claimed that when Fritz pointed out to Oswald that Craig had identified him, Oswald rose from his chair, looked directly at Fritz, and said, "Everybody will know who I am now."

The Commission could not accept important elements of Craig's testimony. Captain Fritz stated that a deputy sheriff whom he could not identify did ask to see him that afternoon and told him a similar story to Craig's. Fritz did not bring him into his office to identify Oswald but turned him over to Lieutenant Baker for questioning. If Craig saw Oswald that afternoon, he saw him through the glass windows of the office. And neither Captain Fritz nor any other officer can remember that Oswald dramatically arose from his chair and said, "Everybody will know who I am now." If Oswald had made such a statement, Captain Fritz and others present would probably have remembered it. Craig may have seen a person enter a white Rambler station wagon 15 or 20 minutes after the shooting and travel west on Elm Street, but the Commission concluded that this man was not Lee Harvey Oswald, because of the overwhelming evidence that Oswald was far away from the building by that time.

The most interesting aspect of Craig's testimony is a little item that came out on cross-examination when Dymond drew from Craig the information that he had come to New Orleans from Dallas in December of 1967 and had been employed at that time by Volkswagen International, a company owned and operated by Willard Robertson, one of the founders of Truth and Consequences, the group formed to finance Garrison's investigation into the death of President Kennedy. This disclosure lifted eyebrows a notch or two around the courtroom.

So the testimony went, over Friday and up until noon on Saturday, when we were let out of school early. Because of inclement weather, planes from Dallas were unable to land in New Orleans.

If Mardi Gras day is called Fat Tuesday, this Saturday and Sunday should have been tagged Fat Weekend, crammed as it was with brunches, cocktails, parades and more parade-watching parties. New Orleanians proved hospitable to a fault, and I touched all bases. When I would be introduced around, either by the host or hostess, often my reason for being in New Orleans was included with my name—"Here to cover the Clay Shaw trial." Many knew Clay socially, a few well, some not at all, although they were all certainly aware of him. I would be greeted by head shaking from the men and small shudders or distressed eyebrows from the women: "Isn't it awful what Garrison's done to Clay!" "Absolutely unbelievable!" "We can't get over it!" "Incredible— brutal!"

One woman, who'd known Clay socially and thought it was "a crime," said, "It must be a fascinating assignment—do you go to court often?"

"Yes, every day. I'm covering the trial," I added, in the event she'd so soon forgotten.

"Yes, but *every day!*" She called to her husband. "Darling, get Mr. Kirkwood a drink. He has to go to court every single day— Not on Mardi Gras?" she asked on a catch breath.

"No, not on Mardi Gras," I replied.

"Thank God!" she sighed, clasping my wrist as if we'd just made it into the lifeboat.

Many of the menfolk, after dropping their solid spoken support of the victim, would veer off quickly in another direction, as if by damning Garrison they were somehow aiding and abetting Clay Shaw. Rumors dropped like hailstones:

"Did you hear about the time he threw a drink in his wife's face at Brennan's?"

"You know he's got quite a rep for being a ladies' man. He used to make the rounds of the strip joints, and I don't mean to close them up—heh-heh!"

"The reason he picked on the assassination, he had to stay away from cracking down on the Mafia because, well, you know . . . so he had to get onto something bigger, as a dodge."

"As far as the hints he's dropped about Clay Shaw's—ah—pref- erences, well, there are rumors his skirts are not all that clean. If you know what I mean!"

I was consorting with allies and still disenchantment was setting in. If there was this considerable body of affluent citizens with a majority opinion of the defendant's innocence, why had not some of them coalesced into a concerted civic group to right the wrong they felt was being perpetrated under their very noses? They earned A for theory, but they were flunking practical application.

The trial was spoiling Mardi Gras and I decided to slap a temporary injunction against all further mention of it in social situations until the Lenten season began—only days off.

Sunday night was the capper of the weekend, as a new carnival organization, Bacchus, was to make its debut that year. With Danny Kaye flown in to reign supreme, the parade of Bacchus had been the subject of controversy for weeks in New Orleans. It was considered too commercial by many and criticized for installing a Hollywood celebrity as King Bacchus instead of a local professional man or some member of New Orleans society. Not only that, the newly founded organization had elected to have their postparade supper party and ball at the new convention hall across from the International Trade Mart, a splendid building on the banks of the Mississippi, one of Clay Shaw's last projects before retiring from the Trade Mart. Danny Kaye was also Jewish—God forbid!—another item to chew over. Cluck, cluck, cluck!

Sunday evening I attended a balcony party for the Bacchus parade on Royal Street. Quite a few guests were going on to the supper dance later and were in dinner clothes. They made a handsome group. Advance reports spread word that the Bacchus display would be the biggest and best, so I was there to relax, have a few drinks, and ogle the floats, the crowds, the marching bands, and the impromptu Negro street dancers, those peppy irrepressible dervishes who light up the night with their flambeaux torches. But the weather was freezing, and the parade was two hours late. This left more time for drinking as the crowd gathered on the balcony in what seemed dangerous numbers. We would take our positions at the wrought-iron railing, gawk over and down at the crowds below and crane our necks down Royal Street to see if we could make out by sight or sound the advance guard of the parade. Toes and fingers stiffened with the cold and inspired forays into the apartment proper for purposes of warmth and a refill.

As I left the bar, a man in his fifties approached me. Someone had pointed me out as a writer covering the Shaw trial. A solid, sensible, well-spoken man who turned out to be a civil lawyer, he was most interested and concerned. He'd met Clay Shaw but did not know him well; he was nevertheless outspoken about the wrong being done him. I agreed with him, but did not indicate a tremendous willingness to go into the matter in any great depth. Still, the more he spoke, the more I liked him. I finally thought,

Here's a lawyer, one who is obviously on the side of the angels, and as he talked on I decided to put the question to him. Prefacing my remark by telling him how often and from how many people I'd heard his exact sentiments voiced, I ventured: "Why doesn't everybody band together and do something about it then?"

There was a pause while he gazed down into his glass. "What can we do?" he asked.

I had not expected such immediate capitulation. "Well, God, hire a hall, form an organization, contribute money, get up some petitions." I could feel retroactive anger rising. "You're a lawyer—"

"A petition would go to the Governor or the Attorney General. They're thick as thieves with Garrison and what's more they're scared of Big Jim."

"But you're not?" I asked.

"No, I've never been thick with him," he snorted.

"No—I mean *scared* of him?" I asked. "Or are you?"

"Of course not, but what are you going to do? He's the District Attorney."

Yes, I thought, I had heard a rumor to that effect. He went on to explain Garrison had been elected by the citizenry to public office. That I had also known. This fact seemed to vitiate any recourse to charges of malfeasance in office.

"Well," I said, "yes, I understand. It's a good thing Hitler finally died of old age. Christ only knows what would have happened to the world if he'd lived to be a hundred!"

He laughed and placed a hand on my shoulder. "You don't understand New Orleans, you see—"

"Shit," I heard myself say.

He laughed again. "You may have something there."

I left the conversation impaled upon that lofty pinnacle, telling him I'd kill myself if I didn't get to see Danny Kaye and the Bacchus parade. By this time he didn't know quite what to make of me. "You're really taking to our Mardi Gras, eh?"

"Oh, yes," I told him, "I think it's the cat's ass."

Standing outside on the balcony, fingers and toes twinging with the cold, I watched the biggest, most opulent parade yet. The mechanized floats were so enormous they could barely make the turn onto Royal Street. The balcony was stacked seven or eight deep in from the railing. The weight of these bodies gave it a dangerous rake, so that I found myself sticking close to the walls of the building. The marching bands were on top of the music, blasting it out clear and loud. The tops of the floats with their costumed and masked Krewe members were only a little below balcony level, and they showered our party with strings of beads and shiny doubloons.

I stood back and watched these men and women in evening clothes, most of them natives of the city and not teenagers by any means, so their conduct could be ascribed neither to the novelty of the event nor extreme youth. I watched them reaching out as if for salvation, clawing and scrambling and tearing strings of beads out of one another's hands. I saw several beautifully coiffed ladies in gowns dive for the deck when a clump of beads would miraculously fall through this asparagus patch of extended fingers and land on the floor. I saw one man, in an elegant red-lined evening cape, stamp his foot down upon a woman's braceleted wrist as she was about to snatch up a doubloon. She withdrew her hand in pain, then knuckled him in the calf with her other hand as they both squealed and ended up on the wooden deck fighting over the shiny fake coin. Although the Krewes attempted to throw the beads in single or double strands, every so often a tangled weighty clump of them came hurtling through the air like a rock. An aristocratic elderly woman was struck in the eye with one such clump and was assisted inside for emergency treatment.

Yes, I thought, I'm really taking to Mardi Gras. And I censored myself for my boring one-track mind and my overrighteous insistence that everyone shape up, form ranks, and sing a brisk chorus of "Onward Christian Soldiers." For a second I thought I might just pack the hell up, take my leave of this City That Care Forgot and return to the United States.

28

Mad Tuesday

On Monday, the day before Mardi Gras, the name Clay Shaw went once again without mention in the courtroom. He was fast becoming the forgotten man at his own trial.

There was a guest inquisitor, however, in the person of the District Attorney, Jim Garrison, who for the first time in the twenty-four-day-old trial took part in the questioning of a witness. Mr. Garrison, well turned out in a light gray plaid suit, went about his direct examination of an eyewitness from Dealey Plaza with the same quiet authority he had displayed when delivering the state's opening address. The jury sat up straight in their chairs, ears cocked, eyes alert, as the District Attorney elicited from his eyewitness such descriptive passages of the assassination as "I observed his ear fly off . . . he just went stiff like a board and he fell left into his wife's lap. I said, 'This is it.'" The witness, William Newman, Jr., thought the shots had come from behind where he was standing, which would have been the area known as the grassy knoll as opposed to the Texas School Book Depository building. Newman also related that before the fatal shot but after the first one, "The President all the time stayed upright in the seat of the car. I caught a glimpse in his eyes and it was a cold stare like he was staring right through me."

Regis Kennedy, a retired FBI man, was the next witness. Kennedy had interviewed Dean Andrews in Hotel Dieu hospital after the assassination and had gone on a search for the elusive Clay Bertrand. He testified he had been unable to locate anyone by that name.

During a recess several of us speculated whether or not the Zapruder film would be shown to the jury again. I made a $5 bet with a local newsman that it would. Clay spoke to me briefly on his way to the men's room. "It's all fascinating," he said, adding, "but

I can't quite figure out where I fit in." I asked if he thought they'd ever come back to him. "I hope not." He grinned.

Herbert Orth, a photographic laboratory chief for *Life* magazine, took the stand next. Orth, it turned out, had some pictures with him. Outside of numerous black-and-white prints, he had made twenty-one color pictures and a hundred and twenty color slides from the Zapruder film. A quiet groan could be heard in the press section as Irvin Dymond stood up and issued one of his stronger objections. It was obvious the pictures would be allowed in as evidence and we were all extremely grateful that a luncheon recess was called before we would have to witness the graphic color slides.

The afternoon session began with Dr. John Nichols, an associate professor of pathology at the University of Kansas, who testified he had performed personally a thousand autopsies, supervised another thousand, and assisted in two hundred and fifty more. When he had qualified as an expert, Dr. Nichols testified he had studied the Zapruder film and the slides made from it. The magic word had been dropped and the state asked permission to show the film again. Dymond objected vehemently that another showing of the film to the jury would be completely irrelevant as well as damaging to the defendant, adding that Dr. Nichols had already testified he'd seen and studied the film. Judge Haggerty, who had said a day or so earlier, "They can show it a hundred times if they want," permitted the showing. Dymond filed a bill of exception, and I collected $5 while the rush to the left side of the courtroom broke out in full.

And so the Zapruder film was run off for the tenth time, inspiring one reporter to print upon his pad:

NOW PLAYING—CRIMINAL COURT BUILDING
THE ZAPRUDER FILM!
CONTINUOUS SHOWINGS—IN GLORIOUS TECHNICOLOR
(Bring the kiddies)

After the showing, the state, over vociferous objections by the defense, entered into evidence the black-and-white photographs, the color pictures and the color slides. The slides were then shown and proved to be as popular (and gruesome) an attraction for the courtroom spectators as the film. The fourteen jurors watched them with fascination, many of them leaning forward as the individual slides were clicked off. After the showing, during which a nun in the process of kneeling in the center aisle bumped her head against the side of a wooden bench and knocked her habit slightly askew, the jury was allowed to take the still pictures upstairs for a private viewing session, on the theory it would be easier for them to spread them out on their deliberating table than to pass them around the jury box singly.

A reporter said disgustedly, "I actually think if the state could get permission to exhume the President's body, they'd let the jury play with it."

During recess I found myself walking down the corridor alongside Andrew Sciambra. I figured, What the hell, I had not really gotten to know the members of the opposition, so I introduced myself, and we shook hands. "Kirkwood?" he said, his voice tinged with suspicion.

"Yes, I wrote the *Esquire* piece on Clay Shaw," I volunteered.

"Yes," he said, nodding his well-barbered young head. Then he suddenly jabbed a finger at my chest. "But what about that film?"

"Film?" I asked.

"The *Zapruder* film!" he said, adding, "What about that?"

"We've certainly seen it enough," I couldn't help remark.

"What about it?" he repeated.

Several answers flashed on and off in my brain: 1) I didn't see Clay Shaw anywhere in it. 2) I got a bigger kick out of your memo.

What I said was "I think you can see anything in the film you want to."

We now regarded each other with semi-guarded hostility. I wanted to ask him, Do you really believe Clay Shaw is guilty—I mean *really!* Or are you on a team and must you stick to the team's belief? I also felt an impulse to deliver an extempore fist to his face—based mainly on what I believed were the dirty tactics of the state. Neither was possible. We were both team men, diametrically opposed in every way, and there was nothing particularly civil we could say to each other. We nodded, more than spoke, goodbyes.

Dr. Nichols, a quietly pedantic man, went through lengthy testimony, giving the jury and the court his opinion of what had happened in the film and his interpretation of individual slides. Irvin Dymond had never objected so often or so strenuously, claiming the testimony was completely outside the realm of the doctor's qualifying credits. He had qualified as a pathologist and now he was testifying to what he had *seen* in the film and slides. Judge Haggerty continually overruled Dymond's objections, and Dr. Nichols went on specifying the pictures, at one time drawing sick grimaces from some of the press and spectators when, interpreting the slide that depicted the moment of the first shot, which entered the President's upper back and exited his throat (according to the autopsy report), he said, "President Kennedy is probably reacting to a pain in the neck."

When testimony touched on the area of the head shot, Alvin Oser asked the doctor what direction he presumed the shot had come from. Dr. Nichols delivered his and the state's answer: "Having viewed these slides and pictures and the Zapruder film, I find it is compatible with the gunshot having been delivered from the front."

Testimony was interrupted when the judge announced that one of the jurors had requested a recess. After court had reconvened, Judge Haggerty announced two of the jurors had been taken ill and court would be recessed until Wednesday morning, the day after Mardi Gras. Mr. Kenison, it was reported, suffered from a queasy stomach and Mr. Mason experienced high blood pressure. Perhaps, some of us in the press wanted to believe, the jurors were more sensitive than we had credited them with being, in the wake of all the times they'd seen the Zapruder film, topped off by the gruesome color slides. Perhaps the state had overplayed that part of its evidence.

Before adjournment, Judge Haggerty was happy to announce to the jury he had secured "a place for you all to see the whole Rex parade on Mardi Gras." He indicated they would be positioned on the balcony of a private home, accompanied by seven or eight sheriffs. He asked of them, "Please don't make a mockery or a joke just because we're trying to accommodate you." He then added, "If they throw doubloons at you, you can catch them." With that we were released for Mardi Gras.

I'd been berating myself for my churlish attitude over the weekend and I decided to throw myself into Mardi Gras day with as much abandon as I could summon up. It was my first and, from my growing feelings about New Orleans, it would without doubt be my last—so why not enjoy it?

The stores were still open, and I tore around buying a black Stetson hat, a black mask, and a Levi jacket. I already had Levi dungarees and a chambray shirt. I'd take part as a cowboy; uninspired, but better than running around in a suit, and certainly less damaging to the wardrobe in case I got falling-down drunk.

I was awakened at 6 A.M. on Mardi Gras morning by the sound of marching down in the streets below. I looked out of the window to see twenty-some Roman centurions—short gold tunics, leather-thatched legs, gold helmets with red brush plumes—striding up Royal Street. The little devils were starting right in.

A young hippie couple, both with long blond stringy hair and distinctly used clothing, slept on the school playground across St. Philip Street, on the far side of an iron grill fence from the sidewalk. They slept side by side, holding hands, their heads resting upon knapsacks. Two middle-aged drunks who looked as if they'd been bombed since their twenty-first birthdays staggered alongside the fence on comic rubber legs, one trailing the inevitable bottle of wine so beautifully disguised in its torn paper bag. They stopped, swaying back and forth as they sipped their morning vitamins. No sooner had they lurched off again, when one swung around, grasped the iron fence and vomited a geyser into the schoolyard, missing the young couple's heads by not more than three or four feet. Sleepers and drunks were oblivious of one another. The man who'd not thrown up congratulated his pal heartily with much back thumping and hand pumping. The one who'd been ill accepted the praise and, to show his appreciation, executed a courtly bow. This called for another drink and they were on their way.

After them came another, slightly younger, drunk with a gash over his left eye. He stopped, took his position on the curb between two parked cars, unzipped his fly and began urinating into the street. He glanced up, saw me, and swiveled around, spraying the hood of a Volkswagen with his stream, which did not ebb for a moment—such is the relaxation of a drunk—and as I clutched at the window, he staggered to the fence and proceeded to finish his task, wetting the school ground only several feet away from the sleeping couple, barely missing their legs. He zipped up and staggered off.

I thought of awakening Romeo and Juliet—they did seem to

have chosen a target area for their bower—but there were no more drunks in sight, only three young men dressed as nuns, striding along with arms locked, singing "Roll Me Over in the Clover." They stopped, genuflected and made the sign of the cross toward the sleeping couple, then carried on.

I tried to soak up an hour's more sleep but it was useless. The French Quarter was beginning to rumble and vibrate. Not that there were swarms of people abroad at that hour but there were constant bursts of activity as small bands trooped up Royal toward Canal Street. The morning was cold and energizing, spirits were high, and the revelers vocalized in preparation for full throttle to come.

So it was up, a little instant cowboy, then to the home of friends, where we dipped into a pot of coffee and then set off to catch the first parade of the day, the all-Negro Zulu Aid and Pleasure Club. The day was perfect, a crackling clear sky and nippy. What the weather lacked in warmth, the people of New Orleans made up for in pure caloric celebration. We trotted across to the rim of the Quarter, where the Zulu Parade was forming up in a small procession of rustic floats, open convertibles, in small jazz bands on foot, all in loose marching formation. Many Negroes were done up in mock blackface, grass skirts and top hats. As the Zulu parade moved off it had about it an easygoing homemade casualness, much different in feeling and spirit from the highly mechanized elaborate floats and grinding grand-parade determination of Comus, Rex, and Bacchus.

This year for the first time the Zulus were allowed to include Canal Street, the wide downtown commercial thoroughfare and dominion of the white parades, in their route. We tagged along to the strutting rhythm of the Olympia Brass Band. King Zulu the Great reigned nonchalantly supreme on a damaged float that had suffered the loss of its high crown when it struck the toll plaza of the Mississippi River Bridge on the way over from the west bank. King Zulu, a lighted cigar jammed in his mouth, had this to say: "The people's great! The weather's great! The parade's great! But most of all—I'm great!" Attaboy, King.

The Zulu parade had an extra added tiger's tail tacked on its rear as several trucks of Negro militants and an open car carrying a woman who identified herself as Queen Mother Moore rode behind handing out leaflets criticizing the Zulu Aid and Pleasure

Club for slandering the image of the black people and conforming to the Uncle Tom caricature. They claimed to be part of the official parade; the Zulus claimed otherwise.

Among the most sought after souvenirs of Mardi Gras are the gold-painted coconuts dispensed from the Zulu floats. It would not be wise to stay in the middle of a crowd when one is thrown; you could come up with a broken arm without any trouble at all—just reach. If you managed to emerge from Mardi Gras with a Zulu coconut and a Rex doubloon or two, you were considered hot stuff indeed.

Canal Street by ten in the morning was a surging, pressing mass of humanity—not reeling yet, but that was to come as the advance guard of early day drinkers could be seen toting beer cans, glasses and paper cups. I'd promised to stop by and see John Mourain and his family at a certain location on St. Charles Street, several blocks the other side of Canal from the Quarter. I soon found it difficult going unless I happened to be moving in the direction of the mob on any one street. I also found out who I was as people called out, "Hey, Lone Ranger." "Hiya, Lone Ranger, where's Tonto?" Yep, I thought, that's who I am, the Lone Goddamn Ranger. I finally made it to the designated area but I was unable to locate John for all the people. I did bump into Bill Block, a young law student who often sat with us in the courtroom. We struck up a conversation while waiting for John, his ex-wife and child to appear.

We agreed we would miss the regular showing of the Zapruder film; we also agreed the state's case, so far, was woefully lacking. Bill was extremely well versed in law, in the technicalities of courtroom procedure and in the intricacies of this particular case. The temptation to dig into our only mutual ground was too much and my embargo on trial talk was soon shot to hell. Suddenly Bill looked at me and grinned. "Do you know who I am?" he asked. "Bill Block," said I. "No, I mean why I'm here." "Law student," I replied. "No," he said, "I can level with you. I'm an attorney for the Justice Department in Washington. I'm observing the trial for them."

It was difficult to believe; he looked like a kid. "Sure," he said, "there are spies all over the courtroom—FBI, Justice Department—you name it." We spoke of other spies, the Rolfes, and laughed.

Now—planted in the gutter of St. Charles Street, gagging with people in wait for the Big Rex parade—we went at the trial hot and heavy. There we stood, gesticulating like fools, surrounded by fools.

"Jesus, if only the defense could ignore Dallas—let them saturate the courtroom, let 'em fly in three hundred witnesses from Dealey Plaza."

"Right. God, if only Dymond could . . ."

"And if only Garrison would . . ."

"And what about Spiesel and Russo—would you believe . . ."

"And Moo—write me a 3,500-word memo on today and forget to mention it's Mardi Gras!"

"Christ, it's a shambles, it's high farce, courtroom of the absurd—"

"With a little Grand Guignol thrown in!"

Laughter and knee slapping all around. Then our faces would suddenly congeal.

"What do you think about the outcome?"

"I think Shaw might just get it—poor bastard," Bill said.

"I'm afraid—"

"The jury!" we said in tandem.

We'd be jostled every now and then by a family setting up ladders for the kids to climb up, the better to see the parade, and dodging clowns, walking fireplugs, Frankenstein, Prince Valiant and a family of giant frog people—to say nothing of rolling beer cans. If Jack MacKenzie of the Washington *Post* hadn't come by, we might have stayed there all day. Jack was on his way up St. Charles, looking for the balcony that contained the jury. "What for?" we asked. "Going to hold up a big sign—VOTE INNOCENT!" He laughed.

By this time St. Charles was becoming impossible and impassable. The rumble and vibration had given way to full eruption. A particular crowd madness was in the air. The center of town was swelling—a combination of Times Square, Disneyland, and V-J Day with perhaps the end of the world thrown in for good measure. From ground zero to seven feet, there was little air space available. I decided to make my way back to the Quarter while I could. The cacophonous sounds of the Rex parade echoed from up St. Charles as I said goodbye to Bill: "Law student!"

Crowdaphobia is not a disease of mine, but the throngs began to get to me. There was a hidden danger in the pure mass and weight of this swaying, pressing—now teeming—sea of humans. There was also a 3-D reality lent to the scene by the sharp cold daylight and the relative early hour—now about 11:30—that added a magnified glare to the spectacle of thousands of bobbing heads, as far as the eye could see. Now we all seemed to be fighting our way down St. Charles in the freeze-dried sunlight as if pursued by a river of molten lava from some Louisiana Vesuvius that had risen up out of the swamps and blown its steaming lid. I suddenly felt I was being chased; but where to escape?

Looking past the crowds, past the sidewalk, I sighted sanctuary and, shoving and pushing, quickly ducked into an old damp barroom of more than average filth. Though crowded, it was not nearly as jammed as the streets. At least one could lift his arms and I did, hoisting a scotch. I glanced around, giving thanks for this dark odoriferous cave of safety.

Daytime drinking does not do well by me; I don't know why A.M. scotch proceeds immediately to the bloodstream, then shoots right up to explode in the head, but it does. I was instantly coursing with warmth, loose-limbed and feeling free. "Hey, bartender, set up one for the Lone Ranger!" A friendly geezer down the bar waved a hand. I remembered the Lone Ranger as a mannerly sort, so I waved a hand back and accepted the hospitality. The second jolt expanded my horizons even more, and I began developing a crush on Mardi Gras.

Once more into the fray. No fray now—my buddies. Jesus, I hadn't realized I'd invited so many! No glare either now, rather the warm glow of stage lighting. Bathed in the light of the Lord. "Hey, there, Lone Ranger!" "Hey there, Frankenstein, where you been?" And so on down the street, rubbing elbows with polar bears, a family of kangaroos, Count Dracula, King Kong, the great white hunter, several hundred clowns, two flying nuns, and almost every other get-up you could imagine and a few you couldn't.

I finally made it into the Quarter with a full can of beer in my hand, thrust there by one of your larger rabbits.

I decided to pay a Mardi Gras visit to the defendant. I knew he would be home. His lawyers had advised him not to go abroad on Mardi Gras day; he would be too easy a mark for some crackpot. I thought to phone him and apprise him of my arrival. Clay had a small magnified glass peephole installed in his red door so he would know who he was letting in. I advised him to be on the lookout for the Lone Ranger.

It was a battle getting through the Quarter—Bourbon and Royal streets were stalled by curb-to-curb people—but the farther down toward the edge of the Quarter, the thinner the crowds. Clay's house was on the last Quarter block of Dauphine so, except for the costumed latecomers heading for the scene of the action, it was relatively quiet.

When he opened the door, he allowed as how I made a good Lone Ranger, and we went into the living room. It was softly lighted and the quiet was extraordinary. After the hornet hum of the streets the quiet was something to hear, to listen to. Clay had a martini in front of him; I was running way ahead of schedule in that department, so I helped myself to his coffee pot. When I returned to the living room we raised our beverages and aimed an obscene Mardi Gras toast toward Clay's favorite "bugged" corner in honor of the District Attorney.

"So, what do you think of our Mardi Gras?" I acknowledged it was somewhat different from East Hampton, even on a Saturday night, and asked if he missed celebrating it. "No, not really. I suppose I've had my share of Mardi Gras." I could not help thinking, right then, that were I Clay, I would have had my share of New Orleans. I put the question to him. "I've always loved this town, I really have but—" The quick broad smile, then he cleared his throat and spoke in his pseudo-tough voice: "I don't know, Mac, I'll let you know how I feel in a week or so."

All the optimism in my born optimist's heart failed to pump life into the belief that he would be found innocent. But I could not, would not, convey this annoyingly persistent premonition to him. He's nobody's fool, though, and the cavalier manner in which his supporters quickly shrugged off a possible guilty verdict must have told him of our fears.

Clay went on to admit his feelings about New Orleans were mixed now and he would undoubtedly, if given his freedom, choose to get away for a while, take a long trip and brush the cobwebs off. We spoke of the jury and of their lengthened and strengthened attention span now that the state had gone into Dallas. Once again Clay indicated he was putting trust in the young Negro schoolteacher, Ricks, to lead them. He also repeated his wish that the second alternate, Bob Burlet, had a vote. Burlet did appear to be wide awake and highly attentive most of the time.

We touched on the Zapruder film, which Clay was greatly moved and shocked by. "I wouldn't be surprised if they let the jury take the projector and film back to the motel for evening showings," he said. Talk of the Zapruder film did it, brought that restless look to his eyes and introduced into his speech several "Um-hmns" that appeared without specific motivation, other than restlessness. So the conversation turned to general topics. I couldn't help commenting on the quiet again. "This house is an island of sanity. Any plans at all for the day?" I asked.

"Not a bit, I'm not going to budge. Willie Mae fixed some cold chicken, some other food. I'm going to stay put. I can use a complete day off."

The constant strain had bleached the natural color from his face, stamped it an unhealthy sallow gray. The half-moons under his eyes were an ominous dark gray. That and his constant smoking were the only outward signs of strain. His trial demeanor was the talk of everyone who stepped foot into Judge Haggerty's courtroom—friend, foe or neutral. His composure was so constant, his attitude so laced with the quiet authority of *who he was* that it verged on the superhuman. I'd mentioned this to him, could not help commenting upon it, as did the press, friendly and unfriendly, in their write-ups. I did not tell him how it was often interpreted by those who believed, or wished to believe, him guilty. Nor did I tell him that his behavior, at times, became irritating in its predictability, or that it was, at times, even boring. There were moments when one wanted him to stand up and say, Oh, now, come on, this evidence is a crock of shit! His behavior was sensationally unsensational.

After a while, we found ourselves sitting in silence in his living room on this Mardi Gras day. And it suddenly occurred to me we had no experiences in common to share—no life experiences, friends, or incidents predating his arrest. Our common ground was his predicament. We were bound to run short of topics because of this void. We could, of course, always fill in with talk about books, the theater, politics, the world scene, but that was like picking a category for a television quiz show. Still, it worked. Although, conversely, as we were now forming a solid friendship, we had the option of sitting quietly without *having* to fill the silence with words.

Clay was appreciative of my visit but he urged me, after I'd had a piece of cold chicken, to get back out into the celebration, saying, "Mardi Gras, the day we mask up and reveal our true selves. It's an experience. You mustn't miss it; get out there and soak it up!"

As I left the defendant, untrussed for a day of breathing free in his own lair, I felt a great affection for him and for his strength of spirit and, wanting to impart this to him, I gave him one of those self-conscious shoulder-squeezes and said, "The Lone Ranger says in a week or so all this will be over, then you can have your own private Mardi Gras."

"Right," he said.

And so I left the giant's castle, but the giant himself popped in and out of my mind at odd drunken moments during the rest of the day.

It was a day, too, and I gave as much of me as I could possibly release over to it. Most of all, I liked the way people looked at people. On Mardi Gras folk level with one another, eyes connect with eyes. There is missing that guarded gauze drop we keep unfurled right behind the eyeballs, making them opaquely inscrutable. On Fat Tuesday, none of that. You look, you like, you speak, you even touch. Not that we should all run around like maniacs the other 364 days of the year grabbing one another. Still . . . the looking, speaking, the freedom and directness of contact is extremely warming and unwarlike. If that part could be held over for 364 days, then one day of the year we might christen Mean Tuesday, a day in which we could go around snarling, shoving, bitching and cranking, as we do every ordinary working day now.

I was invited to Carroll Durand's, a charming New Orleanian stage designer who was giving a party for the New Orleans Repertory Theatre. On my way to her French Quarter apartment I came upon a platform built over the sidewalk and extending out into the street at the corner of Bourbon, across the street from New Orleans' famous gay bar, LaFitte's-in-Exile. All streets leading to this intersection were chockablock full as cheering, applause, whistles and catcalls thundered in praise of the annual drag contest—and it was a dilly. The nearby balconies sagged with revelers. Even the slanted roofs were solidly shingled with people clutching beer cans and drinks. A cowboy type emceed as one at a time the becostumed lads climbed the scaffolding, were announced, and then one at a time—sometimes two, if they happened to be the Dolly Sisters—pranced a fancy turn around the platform for the pleasure and approval of the crowd. The costumes were not lacking in ambition. There was a great glittering chandelier, a diaphanous butterfly, several other undefinable but exotic insects, and, of course, Mae West, a trio of sassy dancehall girls and a cowboy contestant in a dandy leather outfit, fringed chaps, boots, vest, hat, the works—only one item missing: when he turned around, the seat of his pants had been cut away, exposing his bare bottom to full view. This sight brought down the streets in wild cheering and applause. There was not even a blush upon his cheeks as he turned a full 360 degrees for all to see. This, I believe, is called "mooning the crowd." Prizes were to be awarded at the end of the contest but there was a long line of patient dress-ups waiting to climb the stairway to paradise and I was late for Carroll's.

Carroll has a good-sized balcony overlooking Royal Street, where much of the action was, and there is a fine up-and-down rapport on Mardi Gras between balcony and street: pegging back and forth of carnival beads and doubloons, occasionally food and beer—undoubtedly the cat would have made a few flights if it hadn't been kept inside—an ample share of "Come on up" or "Come on down" and late date making between mutual admiration societies. The scotch flowed like scotch should. I grew weary of my black mask, so Carroll, being a makeup artist as well as a scenic designer, applied a dandy black eye in subtle streaking shades of tender purple-red-yellow. This proved to be an excellent ploy for attracting sympathy once I hit the streets again.

After Carroll's party dwindled, a group of us, including Lloyd Burlingame, a close friend from New York, moved on to another and final parade-watching party—the wind-up—and once again the scramble for beads and doubloons, only by this time I was sozzled enough to catch the pointless point of it all. And eventually we ate, I think, but by this time Mardi Gras, the crowds and I were melting into a kaleidoscopic blur of drunken affectionate camaraderie. I remember later on we simply roamed the streets, which were tilting now a bit more than they had earlier, but still filled with the happy people, infinitely more woozy to match the tilt. Then vague memories of a packed Greek restaurant with a small band and Zorba-dancing and later on an upstairs Negro nightclub with a show runway suddenly supporting a Negro drag contest. They did it up with great style and humor—infinitely higher and wickeder camp than the street contest. I remember inhaling a dozen oysters at a seafood stand, then one last lap around the streets, now stepping over a few bodies—drunks, sleeping lovers, and the like—until the legs began to fill up with lead Novocaine and I was forced to throw in the towel, crooning love and undying friendship for the world at large, so filled with jen it was spilling out of my ears.

Heading home, weaving along a side street, attempting to stay out of the gutter, I passed small wooden cottages, not unlike the Conch cottages of Key West, when a middle-aged Negro man, perched on a stoop, stood at my approach and hailed me. "Hey, cowboy," he said, looping an arm around my shoulder, "do me a favor." "Sure," I said. "Give me a smoke." I obliged and lighted it for him. For this I was rewarded by a hug and, with his mouth close to my ear, a whispered "Do me another favor—let me blow you!"

Now this man was not a bum, he was well-dressed and, in a way, distinguished-looking in his middle years. I declined the offer. He hugged me to him. "Aw, come on, cowboy!" Then I thought of that old punchline that goes, in equivalent version: "Blow me! I shouldn't even be hugging you!" and I started to laugh.

I made my apologies and took my leave. But I got no farther than half a block when a form moved out from a wooden gate. The street light hit her face, illuminating a stunning high-cheek-boned almond-eyed Negro girl, a classic beauty in her late twenties. Her shape did not argue with her face. A yellow dress complemented her mocha coloring. She was all lushly there.

"Hi, hi, there," she said and her voice was low and warm, where I'd anticipated, for some reason, because of her staggering beauty, brittleness.

"Hi," said I.

"Well," she sighed, nodding her head toward the gate which led to a walkway and a back apartment, "want to come back, have a drink?" I was too far gone for a drink or anything for that matter but before I could reply, she gasped, "Oh, your eye!" and placed a graceful long-fingered hand on my cheek. The touch did it. I still did not reply but she took my hand and led me through the gate. Now we were in a narrow and darkened walkway between two cottages. She closed the gate, swung around and kissed me—just as an odor, the putrid smell of decaying flesh, flared my nostrils. "Honey," she whispered, as if it were sex talk, "before we go back, we got a dead rat around here somewhere. Help me to—"

"Sorry. Oh, sorry, I've got to go!"

And I was on my way out of the gate. The odor was sickening and I was in no shape to partake in a scavenger hunt for a dead rat.

"Chicken!" she said.

"Yes, sorry," I replied.

And so home and to bed, chuckling at this romantic coda to Mardi Gras 1969.

29

The Judge Takes a Stand

My hangover was beyond the aid of coffee, Alka-Seltzer and aspirin, though, of course, I tried them all. It required a complete transplant of the stomach and nervous system. Serious thoughts of not attending the trial were entertained. But, even in my shattered condition, I knew if I played hooky, some wildly bizarre incident would take place in my absence. There would be a mistrial, or Governor and Mrs. Connally, who had been subpoenaed by the state, would show up to either throw a sizable monkey wrench into the Warren Report or turn out to be hostile witnesses for the state. The Connallys had been due to testify Monday, but at the last minute they had not been called.

While shaving I managed, somehow, not to amputate my nose; I was able to dress myself, wobble down to the street and hail a cab.

Nina Sulzer laughed when she saw me tottering down the corridor to check in. "Ah-hah," she said. "Uh-huh," I replied. My old friend Sadie, badge pinned to that great sagging chest, lifted her hands in the morning ritual. "Sadie, take it easy on the frisk. Don't break me!"

Many members of the press were in the same tender condition. We could only look at one another, shudder and grin. It had not occurred to me to worry about the judge. But as he was announced and the door to his chambers opened, I thought, Oh-ho, *this* is going to be fun. But Judge Haggerty, whose hands were never the steadiest, appeared to be in as good shape as ever.

The opening early morning testimony could have been the devil's own work. Dr. John Nichols, the state's lugubrious pathologist, was still on the stand. The doctor was attempting to conduct an autopsy-in-absentia of the corpse by interpreting the Zapruder film and the slides made from it. He again aired his opinion that

President Kennedy had been shot from the front. Irvin Dymond soon took him over on cross, asking the doctor what his procedure would be in conducting an autopsy of a person who had died from a head gunshot wound. Dr. Nichols said if motion pictures were taken of the accident he would study them. He would also study the eyewitness testimony. Dymond's voice contained quiet scorn when he asked, "Ordinarily you wouldn't examine the victim?" At that juncture the doctor indicated he would even go so far as to perform an actual autopsy. Dymond pressed him on how he would go about this and before long the doctor was explaining, "If you try to dissect a fresh brain, it falls apart," and "You have to leave the brain in formaldehyde for about two weeks in order for it to harden."

"Oh, Jesus, no," a reporter moaned. And I was right with him.

After the autopsy details, Dymond asked Dr. Nichols if he considered himself a ballistics expert. The doctor proclaimed a degree of proficiency in this area. Asked to list his qualifications, Dr. Nichols replied he had attended a one-hour lecture on the subject and had conferred with ballistics experts. When Dymond asked for further experience and qualifications, Dr. Nichols replied, "I have created my own," explaining he had purchased a rifle and conducted experiments by shooting bullets into the wrists and ribs of cadavers. We were given some of the results but soon Dymond, who'd claimed the doctor was testifying more as a photographic expert than a pathologist, went on to question his training in that field. The doctor replied he'd had no formal photographic training but he wanted the lawyer to know he had received his first camera when he was ten years old and he'd started taking pictures right away.

Next Dymond asked the doctor if he had ever examined the clothing President Kennedy was wearing when he was shot. A small blip of the Spiesel syndrome popped up when Dr. Nichols said, "I'm suing the Federal government to obtain release of that right now." Dr. Nichols had testified he thought President Kennedy and Governor Connally had been struck by separate bullets because the doctor believed they were reacting to "a different stimuli." He later had rather ponderously added, "I'd like to correct the word 'stimuli'—that's the plural." When Dymond returned to the area of shots, timing and direction of movement, he asked the witness if he'd ever met Governor Connally. To this Dr. Nichols replied, "I've tried many times to get an appointment with Governor Connally, but Governor Connally rejects me."

Dymond sat up straight at this. "He *rejects* you?"

"Yes," Dr. Nichols testified. "He doesn't answer my letters."

The defendant was now dramatically and dangerously catapulted back into his own trial by the state's next and perhaps most inexplicable witness. In response to the calling out of "Mrs. Jessie Parker!" a tall, pleasant-looking, nicely dressed Negro woman, wearing glasses, walked down the aisle, through the gate and took the stand. Mrs. Jessie Parker was soft-spoken as she told her story under questioning by James Alcock.

For a time Mrs. Parker had been employed by Eastern Airlines as a hostess in their V.I.P. room at the New Orleans International Airport. She testified that on December 14, 1966, a man she identified as Clay Shaw had entered the lounge with another man, sometime between 10 A.M. and noon. "He [Shaw] and the gentleman passed a few words with each other, what they said I do not know." She related that Clay Shaw had picked up a pen and signed the V.I.P. guest book with the name "Clay Bertrand." Mrs. Parker maintained it had been her habit to look in the book after someone had signed it. The other man, she said, had not chosen to write down his name. James Alcock showed her the V.I.P. guest book and she identified the signature "Clay Bertrand," which happened to be the last one on the page. Mrs. Parker claimed the two had only stayed a few minutes, again saying, "He and the other gentleman passed a few words and left."

Although Mrs. Parker did not appear overly pleased to be in court (in the afternoon papers there was a picture of her arriving at the Criminal Court Building clutching her coat up around her face, whereas most witnesses had been only too happy to pose for photographers), she exhibited no outward signs of being a crank or vindictive. She'd told her story simply, with brevity and a certain quiet dignity. Even for those of us hurting for the defendant, it was refreshing to have a more or less normal witness take the stand for the state.

Because of her general character—and lack of apparent character quirks—Irvin Dymond was gently inquisitive when he cross-examined her. Mrs. Parker testified the V.I.P. room was seldom used, maybe one or two persons a day entered the lounge, sometimes there were no visitors. It turned out that entrance to the room was gained by a key. Mrs. Parker indicated there would have been four persons on duty possessing a key, among them a ground hostess and flight attendant, at the time she alleged Clay Shaw had entered. (She had earlier testified she'd been at the back of the room and heard the door open but by the time she'd walked to the front she had missed seeing whoever let the two men in.)

Dymond: "In other words these two men would have had to see one of four people on duty to get into the V.I.P. room?" She acknowledged this was true, although she could not remember anyone who was on duty at the time. The lawyer was interested in how she had become a witness in the case. "They contacted me," Mrs. Parker said, later adding: "When the District Attorney sent for me I was frightened. I didn't know what he wanted."

Asked why she recalled Clay Shaw and not the man he was with, she said the other man had not interested her, but she had admired the defendant's "pretty gray hair" and she'd particularly noticed his height, adding—just as the six-foot-six Jim Garrison walked down the aisle of the courtroom and took a seat—"You don't see many men that tall!"

The witness could not remember exactly when she'd been contacted by the D.A.'s office but thought it was in the summer of 1967. She told the defense lawyer that when she'd seen Clay Shaw's picture on television she'd said to her son, "I've seen that man before . . . at the V.I.P. room, Eastern Airlines." Dymond asked why she hadn't reported this to a law enforcement agency when the name "Clay Bertrand," along with the defendant's picture, hit the news. Mrs. Parker said, "It wasn't my business . . . I didn't want to get involved."

Mrs. Parker, it turned out, had also been brought to the courtroom to look at Clay Shaw at the beginning of jury selection.

DYMOND: Is it a fact you refused to identify him that day?

MRS. PARKER: Yes.

[This reply of Mrs. Parker's was completely ignored in the local paper's account of her testimony. In response to this question of Irvin Dymond's the paper reported, "Mrs. Parker denied this."]

Dymond then asked, "Isn't it a fact when they threatened you with a lie detector test, you then identified him?" Mrs. Parker said,

"Yes," adding, "They didn't threaten me, they asked me." When Dymond asked if she had, in fact, taken a test, James Alcock jumped up from his chair, demanding the results of the test be brought to the courtroom. When Dymond argued that the results of a lie detector test are not admissible in any court in the land, the prosecuting attorney shouted, "You opened the door, you opened the door!" I expected Dymond to shout, No, I didn't, no, I didn't! Judge Haggerty would not permit the test to be introduced.

Just before Mrs. Parker was excused, Dymond said to her, "In other words, these two gentlemen walked in, passed a few words, Clay Shaw [as Clay Bertrand] signed the book, and then they left?" That was her story.

The Rolfes immediately airmail-specialed one of their mm-humn-what-do-you-think-about-that looks?

As good a picture as Mrs. Parker presented on the witness stand, her story was strangely isolated and lacking in catenation. Though someone with a key had to have let the two men in, Mrs. Parker did not see this person, nor did the state deem it wise to check the duty schedule for December 14, 1966, locate and bring into court a corroborative witness who possessed a key to the V.I.P. room. There was also not a soul in the room, outside of Mrs. Parker, at the time of the alleged visit. Nor was there any apparent purpose for the defendant's purported visit to the lounge in 1966 other than to incriminate himself by signing an alias he had supposedly used in a conspiracy to assassinate the President back in 1963. If, as charged, the conspiracy had worked, wouldn't this co-conspirator have had the sense to drop this dangerous alias, the owner of which had been sought by the FBI, Secret Service and the Warren Commission, thanks to Dean Andrews. The signature, moreover, was the last on its page; if the signature had been forged after the fact, it would either have to be the first or last or it would not have fitted in on a lined page between signatures. And not only had the other man who was allegedly at the airport with Shaw failed to sign his name, thereby vitiating the possibility of another corroborative witness, but Mrs. Parker had not found him interesting enough to provide even a token description of the man.

By this time, despite Dr. Nichols' early-bird autopsy testimony, I was glad I'd not played hooky from school. I was soon to be even more grateful.

Shortly after Mrs. Parker's testimony, Richard Carr was rolled in, sitting in a wheelchair, and took the oath, remaining in his chair between the defense and prosecution tables. Carr, a crusty, outspoken homespun type and extremely happy to be on hand, was one of the most interesting and provocative of the Dallas witnesses. He was also accorded the distinction of being one of the very few witnesses in this trial to be questioned by Jim Garrison.

Carr gave a most fascinating eyewitness account of the events in Dealey Plaza. He had been positioned on the seventh floor of the new courthouse building facing the Plaza and as the Presidential motorcade passed the Texas School Book Depository he noticed a man across in the fifth-floor window with a light hat; he later saw this man down in the street. Carr testified he heard a single shot, then three more shots fired from a high-powered rifle. When his ability to specify the type of gunfire was questioned by the defense, Carr digressed into his wartime experiences, now telling of his outfit's landing in Casablanca, North Africa, and relating that only about thirteen men out of his entire battalion had survived.

Jim Garrison, in one of his few ad-lib courtroom statements, nodded at this and spoke in a serious voice shaded with the utmost conviction: "He's about as expert about the sound of a rifle as a man could be and still be walking around." (At which one member of the press, a group known for sticklership to detail, cracked, "Jesus, can't Garrison get anything right? He's in a wheelchair!")

Under low-key questioning by the District Attorney, Carr indicated that the shots had come from the area of the grassy knoll, and he pointed to the miniature picket fence at the top of the knoll on the mock-up of Dealey Plaza near him. The jury was again intensely interested in this testimony; they all leaned forward and several in the back row even stood up. Carr went on to give a detailed description of what appeared to be the getaway of the assassins. He claimed he'd seen three men come from the area of the Book Depository building and enter a Rambler station wagon. The vehicle, he said, was parked on the wrong side of a one-way street. Carr wasn't sure if the men had come from the building itself or from behind it. One of the three men appeared to be a Latin; they had entered the car immediately and taken off. A fourth man, he said, indicating this was the man he'd seen in the fifth-floor window, came across the street from the building and appeared to be in a "very big hurry," turning to look over his shoulder, "as though he was being followed."

GARRISON: Did you give this information to any law enforcement agencies?

CARR: Yes.

GARRISON: Did anyone tell you not to say anything?

Judge Haggerty advised Garrison, who was apparently not used to the rules of examination, that he was leading the witness. The District Attorney appeared stumped for a moment and then rephrased the question.

GARRISON: Did you talk to FBI agents?

CARR: Yes.

GARRISON: As a result of your conversation with the FBI—what did you do?

CARR: I done as I was requested. I shut my mouth.

Dymond soon had at Carr and as a result of his testimony on cross-examination, it became clear that if the FBI had indeed told him to keep his mouth shut, the advice was sympathetic and undoubtedly given to avoid embarrassment.

One of the defense lawyer's first questions to Carr was asked to ascertain when he'd learned the President had been shot. Carr was extremely candid in his reply, saying it had been a good hour and fifteen minutes before he'd known what happened, not only that the President had been shot, but that *anybody* had been shot. He said he was "aware something was wrong, but I didn't know what." Dymond's voice sounded a mixture of wonder and incredulity as he went on questioning this man who had specifically testified to the turmoil centering around the grassy knoll and the motorcade, to the number, quality and direction of the shots and virtually described the getaway of a bunch of assassins—without even knowing anyone had been hit. "Weren't you interested in what *caused* the commotion?" Dymond asked. "Yes," Carr replied, "I was looking to see what the commotion was." Apparently no one else at the scene had taken the trouble to clue him in.

The capper to this testimony came when Carr, who'd testified to being seven stories up in a building, suddenly told Dymond he had seen one of the bullets hit the ground and furrow through the grass. An astonished defense lawyer wanted to know—he had seen *what?* Carr said yes, "I saw the grass come up."

He had not seen the President's head blown off, Governor

Connally shot, or Jackie Kennedy crawling back onto the trunk of the car, but he had traced the path of a bullet as it furrowed through the grass.

Dymond excused the witness soon after this last bit of testimony and Carr was rolled out.

"Good Christ!" a reporter said in earnest anger, slamming his notebook down on his knees. "Where do they get them from?"

The afternoon session turned out to be a high old time and Judge Haggerty emerged the star, even though Clay Shaw, two of his lawyers and various members of the D.A.'s staff and the New Orleans Police Department took the stand.

In the summer of 1968 the District Attorney's office had authorized the release to the press of information contained on the fingerprint card made out at the Police Bureau of Identification on the night of Clay Shaw's arrest. The *States-Item* printed a photograph of the card July 30, 1968, and ran an accompanying article which quoted police officer Aloysius J. Habighorst as stating Clay Shaw had freely admitted he used the Clay Bertrand alias. The alias was typed out on the card, which Shaw had signed. Shaw had steadfastly denied ever using the alias, and claimed there had been no alias on the card when he signed it. The District Attorney's release of this purported incriminating evidence to the press was in strict violation of the pretrial guidelines; nevertheless this information had been widely circulated and highly publicized.

Now the state attempted to enter into evidence the fingerprint card together with the oral testimony of Officer Habighorst. Knowing he was in tricky territory, James Alcock wisely began by suggesting the jury be removed from the courtroom while the judge heard oral arguments pertaining to the admissibility of this matter.

Louis Ivon, Garrison's smooth-looking investigator, was sworn in and proved to be a somewhat groggy witness. Whether he wanted to discourage a lengthy session of questioning or whether he was simply having an off day of it was not known. He had been importantly present at Shaw's arrest, but when Dymond asked Ivon if he knew what an arrest sheet looked like, the investigator replied, "I may have seen them. I may have filled some out."

DYMOND: Did you examine the original Clay Shaw arrest form?

IVON: I don't know.

Dymond exhibited the form—which Ivon had actually signed—and asked where he'd filled it out. Ivon could not remember if he'd signed the arrest form or not, or the search affidavit. Only when shown his signature did this come back to him and then he was unable to recall when or where he'd signed them.

Now Officer Habighorst, natty in a snug-fitting dark suit and vest, was called to the stand. The good-looking police officer told James Alcock he had fingerprinted Shaw inside the Bureau of Investigation room the night of his arrest and that he'd not gotten the information he'd put down on the fingerprint card from Shaw's arrest record sheet, but from the defendant himself, including name, age, weight and, Habighorst and the state claimed, the alias Clay Bertrand. Habighorst detailed the procedure to Alcock and testified he had not threatened the defendant, not offered him promises of any sort in return for information, or abused him physically.

The policeman was cross-examined by Billy Wegmann, not Irvin Dymond. There was an interesting reason for the substitution.

Officer Habighorst's brother had been driving across a bridge several years previously and gotten into a contretemps with another motorist. They stopped their cars, argued, and then Habighorst's brother had taken out a gun, shot and killed the man. Dymond, who defended the brother, succeeded in reducing the crime from murder to manslaughter and the defendant had served four years in prison. It was widely rumored that Officer Habighorst thought his brother should have gotten off scot free, and his feelings toward Dymond were not friendly. In an attempt not to crank up an already hostile witness, Billy Wegmann handled the questioning.

Billy Wegmann, however, was not wearing kid gloves. His voice rang loud and clear and he did not permit time to swat flies between questions, nor did he allow the witness to dance rings around the answer. Wegmann headed immediately for a controversial area, wanting to know if Clay Shaw's lawyer, Eddie Wegmann, had been excluded from the B of I room when the defendant was being fingerprinted. Officer Habighorst said, "He was there for a time. If he was excluded, I don't know why." Was his attorney present, Billy Wegmann wanted to know, when Mr. Shaw signed the card? "Yes, sir," the policeman replied. "Are you sure?" Billy Wegmann pressed. Now Habighorst hedged: "I recall he was inside the door. I would say he was more inside the Bureau of Identification than outside the door in the booking area." Hammering at the police officer, Wegmann asked if it wasn't a fact he had seen the arrest register on Clay Shaw before he was fingerprinted. Habighorst denied this, repeating his claim that he'd received the information directly from Shaw himself.

BILLY WEGMANN: Was Mr. Shaw's attorney there when you got an alias?

HABIGHORST: He could have been. I don't know.

Judge Haggerty interrupted, asking the police officer how far the defendant had been from his attorney during the fingerprinting. "I would say twenty feet," Habighorst ventured. "As far as I am from Mr. Alcock." Judge Haggerty surveyed the distance and said, "That's about thirty feet." Billy Wegmann wanted to know if Habighorst had been speaking in a normal voice; the policeman said he could not say whether Eddie Wegmann had heard him or not. At one point, Officer Habighorst was completely thrown by the use of the word "subsequent" in a question and Billy Wegmann was forced to rephrase the sentence. Now the all-important questions:

BILLY WEGMANN: Did Ivon tell you that Mr. Shaw was not to be questioned?

HABIGHORST: I don't recall.

BILLY WEGMANN: Did you advise him [Shaw] of his constitutional rights?

HABIGHORST: No, I explained the booking procedure to him.

After a short afternoon recess, Dymond began to attack Habighorst's testimony by putting on the stand Captain Louis Curole, who had been on duty at Central Lockup when Shaw was arrested and had assigned a Sergeant Butzman to guard Shaw until his booking and fingerprinting were completed. Captain Curole testified that, as a rule, attorneys are *not* permitted in the B of I room with their clients. He went on to say Edward Wegmann had *not* been allowed to go into the room with Clay Shaw. He further testified that a copy of the arrest record is almost always sent to the B of I room and that this form would include any aliases attributed to the arrestee.

Dymond asserted that the credibility of Habighorst's version was now seriously in doubt in light of Captain Curole's testimony. Alcock objected strenuously but the judge overruled him. Judge Haggerty's face was, now tightening into a mold of absolute seriousness of purpose. His eyes were unblinking, as if he'd sighted a target that did not please him one bit.

Sergeant Jonas Butzman followed Captain Curole to the stand. He had been within five or ten feet of Clay Shaw all the time the defendant was in the B of I room. Butzman testified he had heard Habighorst ask Clay Shaw only one question and that was about the spelling of a name. Dymond's next question was "Did you ever hear the name Clay Bertrand mentioned?" "No," was the reply. The sergeant said he did not know if Habighorst had a copy of the field arrest form but indicated Eddie Wegmann had *not* been in the room at all.

The defense was picking up speed and called Police Officer John Perkins to the stand, again over Alcock's objections, but the judge, now pursed of mouth, quickly overruled him. Although Perkins was not on duty at the time of Shaw's arrest he was assigned to the B of I room. Questioned about standard operating procedure, the police officer testified he had never fingerprinted a person *without* the field arrest record. More damaging, he claimed that the fingerprints are applied to the card, after the arrestee signs the card, and the information is put on the card last of all.

Now Eddie Wegmann was called to the stand and questioned by his confrère Irvin Dymond. Eddie's face had never displayed such angry signs of colic as when he testified this day about Clay Shaw's arrest and the booking procedure. It was obvious he had much more on his mind than the specific testimony he was called to give this afternoon. Those were not acorns puffing out Ed Wegmann's cheeks. He was bursting with a sweeping blanket denunciation of the entire unspeakable injustice heaped upon his client from March 1, 1967, moment-to-moment, up until this very minute. If the jury had not still been playing poker in their waiting room upstairs, I think he might just have let it out in one ringing explosion. He snapped out his answers with bare civility to his own co-attorney in the case: No, he had not been allowed in the B of I room with his client. No, there had been nothing about an alias on any report sheet, no alias, in fact, had been mentioned that evening. He also testified about his meeting with Shaw in one of the D.A.'s offices after Clay had been told he was being charged with the crime and was being placed under arrest. Eddie Wegmann said they'd kept the conversation to a minimum because he had been warned the room might be bugged.

After Eddie Wegmann was excused, Sal Panzeca, the junior member of the defense team, was questioned by Irvin Dymond. Short, compact and snappy, Panzeca had been the first legal counsel to see Clay Shaw on the day of his arrest. He testified he'd told Louis Ivon and other members of the D.A.'s staff that Clay Shaw was not to be questioned and that he would, under no circumstances, answer questions. Panzeca also testified he believed the room they were in was bugged, that communication between him and Clay Shaw was mostly accomplished by writing questions and answers on a pad, adding, "I told him not even to say hello or goodbye to anyone."

Now Clay Shaw took the stand—the jury was still out—and in a firm, clear voice began his testimony regarding the circumstances of his arrest. The press and spectators granted him complete silence and attention. Here was the Big Boy himself. Clay stuck to the questions asked him, never volunteering more information than was requested, as he testified that he had obeyed the orders of his attorneys and spoken to no one. In no uncertain terms, he testified he had signed a completely blank fingerprint card, had not been asked about an alias, had certainly never told anyone he had used an alias, and that his lawyer, Eddie Wegmann, had not been permitted to enter the B of I room with him.

Under cross-examination by James Alcock, Clay got a laugh when he testified about giving information to an officer who typed up his original arrest sheet, before going to the B of I room. Clay said he had been standing three or four feet away from the booking officer and had not seen exactly what the man was typing. The judge asked, "Was there anything preventing you from seeing over the counter?" To this, the six-foot-four defendant replied in an easygoing voice, "No, that's never been a problem with me." The spectators and press laughed, and order in the court was called.

Clay Shaw also stood for no loose dangling ends. He had testified earlier that Habighorst told him it was necessary to sign the blank card in order to get bail, to which Clay said he replied, "In that case, I'll sign it." Now Alcock asked if Officer Habighorst had asked him any questions, to which Clay replied, "No." "You did not utter *one word?*" Alcock asked. Clay made no bones about correcting the attorney: "That was *not* my testimony. I said I was asked *no questions.*"

It was after the defendant was excused that the fun and fireworks began. Alcock sought to enter into evidence and before the jury—who had spent the afternoon upstairs—the fingerprint card and Habighorst's testimony. Dymond objected on the grounds that the witness testified he'd signed a blank card.

This brought forth the no-nonsense ruling of Judge Haggerty. He had been wound up by the preceding testimony of two lawyers, the defendant, and three members of the New Orleans Police Department, all in direct conflict with Officer Habighorst's testimony. Now he faced James Alcock squarely from his bench, saying he would not allow the fingerprint card *or* the testimony of Officer Habighorst introduced into the trial. He would hold to this ruling, no matter whose testimony was to be believed. Either way, the judge claimed a foul. Two policemen had violated Shaw's constitutional rights, he said, by not permitting the defendant to have his lawyer with him during the fingerprinting—in direct contravention of the famed Escobedo decision, which allows an arrestee to have his attorney with him at all stages of the booking, fingerprinting, and questioning process. Judge Haggerty also announced that Officer *Habighorst* (and when he hit the name of the officer, the judge hit it hard) had violated in spirit the effect of the Miranda decision by not forewarning Clay Shaw of his right to remain silent. The judge went on to say Habighorst also violated Shaw's rights by asking him the alleged question about an alias, adding, now that he was revved up and clearing his mind of feelings built up by this afternoon's performance, "Even if he did [ask the question about an alias] it is not admissible!" Judge Haggerty then spit out, "If Officer Habighorst *is* telling the truth—and I seriously doubt it!"

Alcock leaped up from his chair at this remark, his cheeks instantly crimson and his voice highly shrill and trembling with anger as he shouted, "Are you passing on the credibility of a state witness in front of the press and the whole world?"

Judge Haggerty jutted his head forward and said, "It's outside the presence of the jury, Mr. Alcock." He then sat back and spoke in a loud voice. "I don't care. The whole world can hear that I disbelieve Officer Habighorst." He gave Alcock a what-do-you-think-of-that look and then, as if to punctuate his feelings for all time and leave no doubt whatsoever, Judge Haggerty leaned forward once again and said, *I do not believe Officer Habighorst!*

Alcock was completely stunned. The entire courtroom was astonished. Finally the prosecuting attorney gulped down his amazement and immediately moved for a mistrial. Judge Haggerty, in a superb piece of underplaying, merely said, "Denied." Alcock announced he would immediately file for writs of review with the Louisiana Supreme Court to reverse Judge Haggerty's ruling. Haggerty's attitude was Go ahead, file away, file all the writs you want. With that he announced court was adjourned for the day, saying if no word was received from the Supreme Court by 8:45 the next morning, he would telephone the court in Alcock's presence. If the review should not be granted by 9 A.M., Judge Haggerty declared, court would resume on schedule.

Alcock's face was still a deep shade of persimmon as he strode out of the courtroom. The defense lawyers, who could not have been more pleased by this decision in their favor, were nevertheless so completely surprised they were barely able to exhibit their overt pleasure and could be seen merely wagging their heads in astonishment.

The press had something to skid down the hall about this afternoon. Although many claimed this was Judge Haggerty's token gift ruling for the defense, whatever it was, he had pulled off the gesture with complete bravado. It seemed to put roses in the judge's cheeks, clear the eyes and, even, steady the hands.

The Hanging Ladies, the Rolfes and the members of the District Attorney's staff all looked as if someone had broken the rules of the game.

I spent $5.95 of my own money that afternoon and bought a copy of my own book at Doubleday's, and I had the temerity to inscribe and send it back to Judge Haggerty's chambers the next morning.

30

Mom's Good Eats

Jim Garrison and the entire state team were present and sitting at attention the following morning, awaiting the Supreme Court's decision on their application for writs of review. When Judge Haggerty made his entrance, he appeared to have shifted into high gear. He had asserted himself and the act had agreed with him. He quickly informed the defense and the state that six out of the seven Supreme Court judges had signed a ruling denying the state's application. Without hesitation he said, "We will proceed with the trial."

James Alcock again argued at length with the judge to allow the jury, upstairs again this morning and out of hearing, to decide upon the credibility of Habighorst's testimony. Dymond cited the judge's statements of the day before when he'd claimed Shaw's constitutional rights had been abridged. Judge Haggerty was in no mood to waste time on this matter, saying, "It is not up to Mr. Shaw or his counsel to decide that his constitutional rights were violated, it is up to me . . . either Mr. Habighorst put the information on there without questioning Mr. Shaw or he got the information from Mr. Shaw. If he did admit it—which I said Wednesday afternoon I seriously doubt—then Mr. Habighorst did not follow the Miranda decision and advise him of his constitutional rights." Judge Haggerty concluded with "I have reconsidered and I will not change my decision. Bring in the jury."

By this time, a yellow slip of paper was making the rounds of the press section:

> The judge's attack was quite vicious
> On an officer named Aloysius.
> He implied that he lied
> And poor Alcock soon cried,
> "Goodbye, Al, we're sure gonna miss yez!"

The jury was brought down and James Alcock filed a bill of exception in their presence. When he was finished, Judge Haggerty said, "Call your next witness."

"The state rests," James Alcock replied.

Low crowd noises, the rustle of papers and notebooks, necks craning to look at the clock. It was 9:51 and the state had gone through approximately forty-five witnesses in ten days of testimony by this, the twenty-sixth day of the trial. Most of us could not believe this had been the total sum presentation of the state's case. We knew, of course, the state would have the right to call rebuttal witnesses, after the defense had put on their testimony. Still, it strained belief that this had been the answer to the refrain "He must have *something*."

Immediately, Irvin Dymond requested that the jury, who had been seated no more than three minutes after having been absent the entire previous afternoon, be removed from the courtroom again. After they had shuffled out, Dymond said, "The defense would like to file a motion for a directed verdict." Judge Haggerty nodded and then asked why the lawyer had requested the jury be excused. Dymond explained that if the case for a directed verdict were argued in front of them and the judge subsequently denied the motion, this might be interpreted by the jury as proof that the state had presented a prima-facie case of conspiracy against the defendant.

The defense lawyer opened his motion by citing the Louisiana conspiracy statute, which states the crime of conspiracy must include an agreement of a combination of two or more persons for the specific purpose of committing a crime, and an overt act in furtherance. As the fulcrum of the state's case against Clay Shaw was the testimony of Perry Russo, so was this the springboard of Dymond's motion for a directed verdict from the judge, which, if granted, would end the trial there and then and set the defendant free.

Irvin Dymond read extensively from Russo's testimony, his reply to Dymond when the lawyer accused him of sitting in on a conspiracy to assassinate the President and not reporting it to a law enforcement agency: "No, I never said anything about a conspiracy. I didn't sit in on a conspiracy." He then read Russo's replies to "Did you hear Shaw agree to do anything?" "Did you hear David Ferrie agree to do anything?" and "Did you hear Leon

Oswald agree to do anything?" The witness's reply to all three had been no. "I submit," the defense lawyer said, "that without an agreement to do anything you can't have an agreement or conspiracy." He kept his remarks centered on Russo's repeated references to the alleged meeting and talk as a bull session, adding, "I submit that at this time the President was unpopular and there were many loose bull session remarks made by many who disagreed with his policies. It would be ludicrous and ridiculous that these fit the description of conspiracy."

Dymond went on to the purported overt acts, claiming there was no dispute over Clay Shaw's trip to the West Coast and contending he had gone there only to fulfill a speaking engagement. Of Ferrie's trip to Houston, Texas, he claimed there was no connection between the trip and the alleged conspiracy, saying, "At the time of this act, the President had been shot and was dead." Dymond maintained the state had not even proved Oswald took the gun to the Texas School Book Depository when he said, "The witness [Buell W. Frazier] testified merely that Oswald had with him a package that Oswald said contained curtain rods.

"In closing," said Dymond, "we submit the state has proven no agreement or combination to commit a specific crime. And the state has not made out a prima-facie case. We urge the court to use the power vested in it by the Louisiana Legislature and direct a verdict of not guilty."

James Alcock presented a rebuttal argument, beginning with "The court knows that the conspiracy law is very broad." He insisted it was not a question of what worth Russo attributed to the words spoken at Ferrie's but rather it was a matter for the court and eventually the jury to interpret. Alcock contended Clay Shaw's trip to the West Coast "gained in stature" because Russo heard it would be used as an alibi; he claimed the same was true of Ferrie's trip to Houston. Alcock hit an interesting point when he charged that Dymond, on the one hand, wanted to strike at Russo's entire credibility regarding the alleged party and, on the other, wanted the court to believe Russo's testimony when he characterized the meeting as a bull session. "The state," Alcock said, "simply feels it has proven a prima-facie case." He asked that the jury be given a chance to decide for itself.

In the end, Judge Haggerty took the motion for a directed verdict under advisement. He granted a request for early adjournment so the defense could line up their witnesses, adding he would use his free time to read over the entire testimony of Perry Raymond Russo before making his decision. He called the jury down, careful to make no mention of the motion under consideration, and announced that they would be excused until the following morning.

When court was adjourned, before noon, there was serious speculation over the prospect of a directed verdict. Certainly there were many in the press who believed such a ruling was called for. Judge Haggerty's scorn for the state's testimony the day before lent a faint shred of hope to those who believed a directed verdict should be granted. He had also listened to the arguments that morning with all seriousness.

Now I will tell you a story on myself. After adjournment for the day, I was waiting at the bottom of the end staircase leading down from the courtroom for use of the pay phone. I heard the clatter of footsteps and turned to see Judge Haggerty walking down the stairs accompanied by two women. Immediately upon seeing me, he called my name, excused himself from the women, and walked to where I stood. He thanked me for the copy of my book, then took my arm in his hand—I could now feel the tension I'd seen in those fingers—and said, "Come here, I've got something for you, but I don't want you to say a word to anyone."

"No, I won't," I replied as we sidled over a few steps out of hearing distance of the man currently using the phone.

"Have I got your word?" Judge Haggerty asked in a low conspiratorial voice.

"Yes," I vowed, now thinking, My God, he's going to tip me off about the directed verdict, or a possible mistrial or—What I didn't know, but I was positive I was to be the recipient of top secret information in the form of an exclusive scoop straight from the judge's mouth.

"Especially," he went on, "any members of the press—that would not be good."

"No, no," I said, now worked up to sealing my pledge with a drop or two of blood. "I promise—not a word."

"All right," he said, still grasping my arm and now fixing me for a long moment with eyes which were clearly X-raying me for trust capacity. "Now, listen," he said as I held my breath, "in my chambers I've got a Zulu coconut and a Rex doubloon for you.

Give them to you tomorrow. Not a word, though, to any others in the press. I don't want them to feel slighted!"

I could not even respond; I was struck completely speechless—a Zulu coconut and a Rex doubloon!

With that he released my arm and gave me a slap on the shoulder. "See you tomorrow, Brother Kirkwood!"

I remained standing there. Picture of the author as undercover agent, outfoxing all members of the press. Secret Undercover Agent X-13 returning to Scotland Yard—with a Zulu coconut and a Rex doubloon, sir!

That day I had a bite of lunch with Clay Shaw. His feelings about a directed verdict were, of course, apparent. Mine were, too, but I could not dissemble with him about the possibility of its being granted. There was no doubt in my mind it would not come to pass, and I told him this.

Clay was anxious to know my reaction to his brief testimony the day before; he saw it as a dress rehearsal to his ultimate appearance before the jury, should the directed verdict be denied. He prefaced hearing me out by saying Eddie Wegmann felt he'd spoken too quickly, a little too brusquely. I told Clay I thought he had done fine. His voice was firm, loud and clear. I thought he should not attempt to put a governor on himself, by means of speed, pauses, or laying it on in any way that was not natural to him. The ease with which he spoke and replied to questions was not to be tampered with. My final advice, for what it was worth, was to listen to no one in regard to style—*content* perhaps, if that were necessary—but to follow his own impulses completely in the manner in which he testified.

Over lunch Clay told me of a long distance phone call the night before. In a trial of this sort, considering the source of much of the testimony, all lines must be kept open for the possibility of a tip-off to a witness's reliability. "When I got home from court," Clay said, "there was a message to call a number in Pensacola, Florida. Most important. A Mrs. ————. I tried but no answer. Before I went to bed, I thought, What the hell, I'd try again. I figured it might be— Well, who knows. I finally got the woman, who immediately thanked me for returning her call, then excused herself to get pencil and paper. When she returned to the phone, she explained she was originally from Alabama, but some of her friends had arranged for her to move to Pensacola, where, she said,

'They put me on welfare.' I don't know how this is done," Clay said, laughing, "but maybe we'd better look into it. Anyhow, she had a lovely, very genteel Southern accent, sounded like Amanda from *The Glass Menagerie*. After the preliminaries she got down to business, told me she knew I was innocent and was willing to help in my current trial. She knew this because two weeks before Kennedy was assassinated she had found out it was to happen. His murder had, she said, been committed by a member of the Kennedy family, though, of course, she went on to add, it had been ordered by the Vatican. She had a closetful of documentation with which to prove all this and she would ship it immediately in a footlocker. Who should she send it to? Well," Clay said, rolling his eyes to the ceiling, "I certainly didn't want it, so I told her to ship it to my lawyer, Eddie Wegmann. Poor Eddie." Clay laughed, adding, "Now, mind you, she sounded, her tone and manner, perfectly sane. No hysteria. Admittedly her content was to be questioned. But there she was in her lovely Southern accent telling me how Kennedy had been killed. At the end, she dropped a fillip. Although she had spoken in a perfectly calm, rational voice she said, just before she hung up, 'If I sound a bit upset, you must excuse me but in the past two weeks both my daughter and my lawyer have been murdered.' With that she signed off, cheerfully promising to send the footlocker."

Before our luncheon was finished, the afternoon paper was out, headlining, STATE RESTS; RULING DUE ON ACQUITTAL PLEA. Underneath on one side, a large photograph of Irvin Dymond faced a large photograph of Judge Haggerty. The way in which the page was set up indicated these two men just might resolve the trial.

"Not for a moment," I said to Clay Shaw, adding that it wouldn't be long, though. Bill Wegmann had said that morning the defense presentation could be wound up in four or five days, intimating there would be no more than twenty witnesses, including the defendant.

An open-house dinner was served up that evening by our Master of the Games, Moe Waldron, whose apartment was christened Mom's Good Eats because of the many meals the press took there, tossed together by Moe himself, one hand clutching a drink, the other throwing a smattering of everything available into the pot.

This evening's paella celebrated the wind-up of the state's case, and there were heated arguments over the judge's probable decision. By now the political scene in New Orleans was so patently claustrophobic in its lineage, so fraught with logrolling on all levels, I could not imagine Judge Haggerty granting a directed verdict, unless he were planning to step down off the bench and open up a shoe repair shop—preferably in Alaska.

By the time we'd had drinks, dinner, and a sing-along—invariably the ear-jarring capper to an evening at Mom's Good Eats, with Roger Williams of *Time* playing guitar and leading us when he was present—Jim Phelan was looking back on the spectrum of the state's case with all the Irish indignation in him. Pounding a fist down upon the table and shaking his head, he said, "Jesus, to try to rig a case like this with the world spotlight upon it is megalomania of the worst kind."

Jim asked me to walk with him as he was leaving. Though it was possible he would take the stand the next day, he was loath to say good night and pushed for a nightcap, which neither of us needed, at a nearby bar—actually the bar where Charles Spiesel claimed he had met David Ferrie. It was soon clear that Jim, for all his brusque exterior, was experiencing pangs of stage fright. He'd wanted rehearsals with Irvin Dymond, but there'd been no time in the lawyer's schedule. The rehearsals were not sought for purposes of content but for a way in which to get all of his testimony into the record. The hearsay rule is tricky and binding, and Jim was afraid he would not be able to repeat the main body of what Perry Russo had told him. Jim thought if he and Dymond had ample time they could have gone over his testimony point by point and discovered routes by which Dymond could lawfully extract the nuggets. I ended up advising Jim Phelan in the same manner he had advised Perry Russo. "Just tell your story, tell it the way it happened." I assured him Dymond would find a way. He was still fretting when we said good night on the corner. He would clearly not have a good night's sleep until he'd spoken his piece under oath.

31

Marina

The courtroom was packed for the Friday session. The crowd showed unmistakable signs of suspense as they awaited the judge's decision. Although I had not considered the directed verdict a serious possibility, I could not help thinking about it now. The courtroom would not settle down; press and spectators alike were seat jumping. Jim Garrison arrived a little before nine and went into the judge's chambers. He remained for only several minutes, then emerged unsmiling and left the courtroom. The jurors, unaware of the important decision about to be announced, were led in through the court and disappeared out the rear door on the way up to their deliberation room. Clay was smoking, as usual; when he turned to the press section someone called out, "What's it going to be?" Clay merely shrugged and smiled, turning front again.

At 9:07 Judge Haggerty took the bench. He switched on his desk lights, looked up and said, "I am going to make this announcement outside the presence of the jury. There will be a five-minute recess for the press's benefit after I make the announcement, so there won't be a rush for the doors." This statement further excited the crowd; it was indicative of a major news break. The courtroom was now hanging on his next sentence, which was: "The motion for a directed verdict is denied."

There was silence from the press, and a small smattering of righteous militant applause and whispered yeas of approval, enough for the bailiffs to call for order. Judge Haggerty quickly left the bench and returned to his chambers; by law, he was not required to give an explanation for his decision.

The Hanging Ladies were delighted; they chattered and buzzed, giving thanks that their picnic had been extended. As Clay later whispered to me (alluding to Madame Defarge), "I swear to God, if I see one of them starting to *knit,* I'll have her evicted from the courtroom!"

Now that the last and—as should be true in all good dramaturgy—shortest act was to be served up, the courtroom soon settled down, the jurors were returned to their box and Judge Haggerty advised the defense to call its first witness. Irvin Dymond replied, "Call Mrs. Marina Oswald Porter." All heads turned toward the doors as the widow of the man named the sole assassin by the Warren Commission entered the courtroom.

Marina Oswald Porter, now remarried to a Dallas businessman, walked down the aisle dressed in a gray wool dress with a white collar. Her eyes tentatively and somewhat apprehensively took in the scene, glancing from left to right as she moved to the witness chair and was sworn in. She was prettier than I'd imagined, with her broad face, light brown hair and wisps of bangs fringing her forehead. She had acquired a quiet poise as the widow of Lee Harvey Oswald, despite her slight nervousness at testifying.

As Dymond gently led her back to the summer of 1963, when she and her husband had lived in New Orleans, she replied to his questions in a soft voice with only a trace of a Russian accent. She often raised her fingers to her chin and sometimes placed a hand on her chest when speaking or considering an answer.

She had been called to contradict Perry Russo's testimony and, in a minor vein, that of the Clinton people. Asked if Lee Harvey Oswald drove a car, she said, "I've never seen him drive an auto." Asked if she'd known how to drive when she lived in New Orleans, she replied, "No." She smiled shyly and added, "No, and I still don't."

Such are the formal demands of the law, that she was handed a picture of Oswald so she might identify the man she could never forget. She went on to testify that Oswald had never gone around unshaven, that he was neat and wore clean clothes. Asked if he usually kept his hair combed, she said, "Yes," and then added, again smiling, "There wasn't very much to comb." She told Irvin Dymond he'd spent only one night away from home during their stay in New Orleans and that was spent in jail after a street scuffle over the Cuban leaflets he had been distributing. She said she'd never met or heard Oswald speak of David Ferrie, Clay Shaw, Clay/Clem Bertrand, Perry Russo or an entire list of people the lawyer read off to her. As far as she knew, Oswald had never been to Clinton, Louisiana, nor had she. She maintained that after he lost his job at a coffee company, he stayed around the house, or sometimes went to the library. She said he liked to read, sit on the porch and clean his rifle, sometimes play cards in the kitchen, or keep to himself in the bedroom. The picture she presented of their life together was an isolated one, threadbare and lonely—few friends, few activities, no apparent entertainment, none of even the small joys of living. Was there ever a picnic, one wondered, or even a movie they shared?

"What was the most amount of money he ever gave you?" Dymond asked at one point.

"A dollar." She smiled again and shrugged this time, explaining he paid all the bills. She mainly stayed home tending to the housework and their young daughter; she was also pregnant and carrying their second child at the time.

Her life with him must have been indescribably mean. She had been criticized (and was now by some of the press who'd come to know her in Dallas) for shrewdly hiring business managers and lawyers after the assassination. None of her alleged shrewdness came across in her appearance on the stand, but if their life together was as bleak as has been indicated, and not only by the widow herself, one cannot fault her for scrambling after whatever scraps she could salvage from the tragedy that was her husband.

When Dymond finished with her on direct, there was a recess. During this, she was introduced to Clay Shaw. They spoke briefly and then she sat in a jury chair, smoking and talking to Nina Sulzer.

Her attitude changed considerably during cross-examination by James Alcock, who actually, by keeping her on the stand for the rest of the morning, was able to damage the good impression she'd made in response to Dymond's questions. She admitted to Alcock that after Oswald had lost his job, he concealed this from her for a time and, pretending to go to work, left the house in the morning and returned in the afternoon. She did not know where he spent his time when he wasn't at home. She admitted he rarely told her what he did and acknowledged that at the time—the summer of 1963—she spoke very little English and this kept her from knowing what her husband's activities might be, kept her virtually in the dark, in this strange town, in a foreign country, with a child to look after and another on the way. At one point Alcock took

Marina back to her last meeting with Lee Harvey Oswald in a
Dallas jail after the assassination, asking: "Did he ever admit to
you that he shot President Kennedy?"

Her reply was surprising both in words and seeming casualness
of tone when she said: "No, he didn't. I didn't ask him that."

One wondered how it was possible to resist touching upon this
item, which had to come under the heading of *Topics of More
Than Routine Interest.*

As the morning dragged on, she grew restless and bored, even
sullen after a while. She began to mumble, to glance around the
courtroom and up at the ceiling. At one point she snapped out of
this lethargy when Alcock asked if Oswald had told her he'd fired
a shot at General Edwin Walker. She replied that he had told her,
but Dymond objected that the question was irrelevant. James
Alcock addressed the judge. "I'm checking the witness's credibility." "You're checking *what?*" Marina asked, obviously be-
wildered by the word "credibility." This got a sizable laugh from
the spectators. When Marina heard it, she glanced out front and
smiled too.

Soon, however, she was back giving vague answers such as "I
don't remember." "That was a long time ago, I don't recall." "I
don't think so." "I'm not sure." She'd been called to testify for the
defense, which she seemed happy to have done, but now it appeared she wanted no part of the prosecution. By the time she left
the stand, just before the lunch break, it was apparent she had
known little of Lee Harvey Oswald's life, outside the bleak realm
of their relationship and the time he'd spent in her presence. This
fit the state's contention that Oswald could well have known
David Ferrie without his wife's awareness. She had never even seen
her husband's apartment in Dallas when she'd been living in
nearby Irving with Ruth Paine.

Two of the afternoon witnesses had been closely associated with
Clay Shaw in business. Lloyd Cobb, the founder of the Interna-
tional Trade Mart and its current president, and Miss Goldie
Moore, Clay Shaw's secretary of nineteen years. Their testimony
on direct sought to refute the state's claim that he was in Clinton,
Louisiana, by establishing that the months of July, August and
September 1963 held a tremendously heavy work load for Clay
Shaw at the Trade Mart; the planned new building required a $12
million bond issue and there was a crash campaign under way to

obtain leases for tenants to support this issue. Lloyd Cobb, a solid-looking individual, testified Clay Shaw had only been absent from New Orleans one day during that period and that had been on September 25, when he'd been in Hammond, where his parents lived. Cobb added credence to the defense claims when he contended that at the time of the assassination Shaw had been on the West Coast to fulfill a speaking engagement, and his trip had been paid for by the organization that had requested him. In response to Dymond's questions, Cobb testified he had never seen Clay Shaw wear a hat or tight pants. Cobb had also been on the reception committee for President Kennedy at the Nashville Wharf along with Clay Shaw. "Was Mr. Shaw wearing tight pants that day?" Dymond asked. Cobb replied, "If he had been, I would have noticed it." Cobb described Shaw as a liberal and a man who, as far as he knew, had never used an alias.

On cross-examination, Alcock did his best with damaging innuendo when he asked Cobb if he'd often seen Shaw socially. "Clay Shaw and I were not social friends," said Cobb. "We had very little social contact. I may have had a drink with him after office hours." Alcock wanted to know if Cobb had ever been to Clay Shaw's apartment. "No," Cobb replied. I noticed one juror glance at another with a quizzically suspicious look.

The portrait of a secretary as a faithful, adoring employee was the essence of Miss Goldie Naomi Moore. Miss Moore, a black velvet hair band around her reddish hair, pink-bloused, lavender-vested and wearing dark glasses, with the white-white skin of a redhead, spoke softly, attesting to Clay Shaw's heavy work load, his one day out of town, on which she'd spoken to him by phone in Hammond, and his speaking engagement on the West Coast. He had been invited to make the Coast trip in connection with the International Trade Mart in San Francisco and had been paid to speak to the Columbia Basin Export-Import Conference in Portland. She had handled all his business correspondence and had never known him to use an alias or receive mail or phone calls aimed at Clay or Clem Bertrand. She testified he never wore hats and always dressed in conservative business suits. When Dymond asked if she'd ever seen her employer wearing tight pants, she replied "Never!" in obvious distaste.

Again Alcock attempted to activate the imagination of the jury to a Jekyll and Hyde split between the defendant's business and personal life by concentrating on questions similar to the ones he'd asked Lloyd Cobb. Had she ever been to Clay Shaw's apartment? No, she hadn't. Did she know many of his social friends? Miss Moore named a few, among them Mrs. Edgar Stern, Mrs. Muriel Bultman Frances Bogner and Jeff Biddison. Alcock delved into what he presumed might be an area of harmful insinuation when he questioned her about Jeff Biddison.

ALCOCK: Did you know they were close friends?

MISS MOORE: Yes, they were.

ALCOCK: Do you know where Mr. Biddison lives?

MISS MOORE: Not at present.

ALCOCK: Do you know whether Jeff Biddison ever lived with the defendant or the defendant ever lived with Mr. Biddison?

MISS MOORE: No, I do not.

When Miss Moore left the chair and walked past the defense table, she allowed her eyes to graze the defendant, and the message read, Oh, I hope I was helpful!

The defense next called to the stand a meteorologist for the U.S. Weather Bureau. Several of the Clinton people claimed they remembered the visit of Lee Harvey Oswald in late August or early September because the weather had taken a cool turn, one testifying to having shut off the air conditioning, another telling of a fire in the fireplace. The meteorologist gave the average daily high for the last fifteen days of August 1963 as 92.1 degrees and the average daily high for the first fifteen days of September of that year as 93.1 degrees.

And now a case of witness switching as Dymond called Robert A. Frazier, a ballistics expert for the FBI, who had previously been subpoenaed by the state but had been dropped when the FBI photographic expert Lyndal Shaneyfelt had backfired on them. The defense picked him up as a witness, and Frazier, a lean-faced, good-looking man, currently suffering from a mild case of laryngitis, was nevertheless put through an extensive series of questions by Dymond.

Robert Frazier had examined the Presidential limousine, the clothing the late President had worn, the clothing of Governor Connally, the bullet fragments recovered from the limousine, and the bullet found on the stretcher at Parkland Hospital. He had conducted tests using Oswald's rifle—firing and ballistics tests to ascertain if the three cartridges found on the sixth floor of the

Book Depository had come from this rifle. He had taken part in the official re-enactment of the assassination held in Dealey Plaza and also studied the Zapruder film and the slides made from it. Frazier was on the stand for the rest of Friday afternoon and for the majority of the next day. He firmly concluded "there was nothing inconsistent to preclude or indicate that the shots came from anywhere but to the rear and above."

Alvin Oser's laboriously distended cross-examination of Robert Frazier from Saturday midmorning until late afternoon proved to be a clear example of courtroom overkill, and the law of diminishing returns. Oser's voice and manner conspired in darkest suspicion from the minute he began questioning the FBI expert. He wanted to know first of all who authorized the removal of the Presidential limousine from Dallas to Federal jurisdiction in Washington so quickly (the car had been examined by Frazier in the capital within twelve hours of the assassination). Dymond objected that this was out of the realm of the witness's knowledge, and when Oser insisted this was important "because of the element of change—whose hands it passed through," Dymond stood up and said, "If the state wants to charge the Federal government with fraud, it should come out and do so!"

Oser did make some points early on when he concentrated upon the Warren Commission's failure to simulate the exact circumstances of the assassination in their re-enactment. The limousine used was not the same one but similar. More important, the firing tests by Frazier using Oswald's rifle were made, according to the FBI agent, for the purpose of determining whether a series of shots could be fired within six seconds with a high degree of accuracy. He had accomplished this by firing horizontally at a stationary target 300 feet away. Oser wanted to know why he had not conducted accuracy tests under the exact conditions of the alleged assassination shot—that is, from a height of 60 feet at a slow-moving target at a distance of 265 feet. This was certainly a logical question. Frazier replied he was following instructions for the experiments and conditions set forth by the Commission.

Oser had made his point, but, voice rising high in pitch to an accusatory whine, he was out to hammer the witness into the ground and rip the Warren Commission Report to shreds, instead of leaving a comprehensible area of general doubt open in the minds of the jury. Oser several times combined a series of five or six separate questions which he would propound to the witness as one, at which point Frazier would sit in total silence, until either Dymond objected or Judge Haggerty, on his own, would caution Oser to break the questions down and deliver them one at a time.

Oser was no match for Robert Frazier in style and poise. Frazier, obviously suffering from laryngitis, remained patient and cool, never failing to admit certain conditions were not equal to other conditions, and never claiming to have accomplished tests or experiments he had not concluded to complete satisfaction, never claiming knowledge of which he was not certain. The Warren Commission doubtless could have conducted a more painstaking investigation in certain areas, but Frazier came through as a man of high professional expertise and integrity who had carried out certain experiments and tests assigned him to the best of his ability. If the requirements of these tests could be faulted, why not call upon those who had set the standards and demand an explanation from them?

The more ferocious the state's attack upon the report, the more indicative, it seemed, that their case against Clay Shaw rested on a shaky pedestal. By attempting to prove a series of negatives regarding the report, they sought to establish the positive guilt of the defendant.

Alvin Oser's performance that Saturday was incentive for me to introduce myself to James Alcock during a late afternoon recess. All during the trial, he had not made himself unduly available to the press; in fact, he appeared to shun them. There was about him an earnest businesslike air that defied interruption, even when he walked down the corridor, but I took a chance, gave my name and extended my hand. Once his attention was secured, I was surprised by his change of attitude. Perhaps I warmed him up by telling him I thought he was doing an excellent job, adding, so as not to fawn completely, "with what you have to work with." He seemed to be appreciative of this, knew my name, connected me with the *Esquire* article and also asked, "Don't you have a current novel out?" I told him I did and he had even heard of the motion picture sale. I don't know why, but this surprised me completely. He regarded me without suspicion and I was grateful there was no mention of the Zapruder film. We spoke for only a few minutes— he was on his way to the District Attorney's office—but in that time he indicated it was a tough case and remarked he would be glad when it was over. I asked if he would speak to me at length sometime, telling him I was planning a book on the trial. He did not reply immediately but kept walking, then said, "Yes . . . yes, that would probably be all right. But not until it's over with." I told him I'd be in touch with him and we said goodbye.

When I returned to the courtroom, John Mourain, Bill Block and Bruce Eggler nabbed me and told their nun story. During recess, they had gone downstairs to the metal newspaper box containing the afternoon *States-Item*. John had put a dime in, swung the front window open and taken out a paper. Just as he discovered he'd taken out two copies, a nun approached the news vending machine with a dime. "Here," John said, "here, Sister, here's a paper. I took out two by mistake, just put a dime in." The nun took the paper, shot John a glance, said, "I'm not *that* honest!" and walked away with the dime in her hand. The three of them could not get over this. For the duration of the trial, every time they saw a nun enter the courtroom—and there were invariably two or three in attendance—they would shake their heads and say, "What about that *nun!*"

As court was about to reconvene, a marvelous middle-aged blonde, kewpie-doll face heavily made up, endless swirls and ringlets of curls piled atop her head and wearing a frilly-busy dress, pit-patted down the aisle. "You know who that is?" Rosemary James asked. I was about to say, Some classy ex-stripper, when she grinned and said, "Yolande Haggerty, the judge's wife." "Perfect," I replied.

Her appearance was completely fitting with late Saturday afternoon before the weekend recess, the last one this trial would know. Yolande Haggerty spelled Saturday night and maybe a little bit of Christmas. The defense's last witness of the day also upped the mood in the courtroom by completely charming the assemblage.

Mrs. Ruth Paine, a tall pleasantly horse-faced woman from Irving, Texas, who had befriended the Oswalds, Marina especially, is a near double in spirit, looks and voice of Carol Burnett. Wearing a handsome blue suit, a string of pearls and her dark hair in bangs above her wide eyes, she augured a breath of fresh air in an otherwise stale courtroom.

She told of her meeting with the Oswalds and again refuted Russo's description of Oswald as unkempt. She maintained that he was neatly dressed, that she'd never seen him with a beard or whiskers. She also cleared up the rumors of her station wagon being used as a getaway car when she testified it had been parked in her driveway at the time of the assassination (which she and Marina had learned about while sitting in the living room watching television) . She said it was she who had made a telephone call to the Texas School Book Depository in reference to finding a job for Oswald. Now she got into a bind with the hearsay rule as she began to describe what she had said and what was said to her during the phone conversation—over numerous admonishments that she could repeat what *she* said and what she had *done* as a result of what had been said *to* her, without directly quoting the other person. She finally threw up her hands and laughed, a big open laugh, remarking, "You've got me confused trying to get me to say what the man said without *saying* what he said." The courtroom responded with delight.

Later on, when she described the visit to her home of an FBI man who was looking for Oswald, she said, "I told him I hoped he would be discreet if he went to the Book Depository because Lee was afraid of losing his job and he said he would be—" This time, recognizing her own mistake although no one had objected, she cried, "Oops!" and slapped a hand over her mouth.

Her testimony was not all frivolous, as she added to the picture of Oswald as a loner and also displayed her compassion for his wife. She had driven the Oswalds to New Orleans in the spring of 1963 and had then come to pick up Marina and take her and her daughter back to Texas in the fall. She had never heard of any of the principals in this trial until the investigation of the assassination had hit the news, although she was candid about saying Oswald never spoke much of his friends or activities. She left her audience immeasurably cheered up, not particularly by her testimony, but by her presence.

When court recessed for the weekend, the defense let it be known to the press they would wind up their case the following week. I accepted a ride to the Quarter with the Rolfes; now that there was little time left, I was anxious to effect a meeting with Jim Garrison, and Dick Rolfe had assured me he would be able to arrange this. Oddly enough, June Rolfe loathed Ruth Paine. "Ahh," she exhaled, "she's nothing more than a clown!"

32

F–I–N–C–K

Monday confirmed the suspicion that this trial could not progress more than a day without tilting crazily in one direction or other.

The defense called to the witness stand Colonel Pierre A. Finck, a small pear-shaped man with thinning hair and enormous horn-rimmed glasses framing his eyes. Colonel Finck exhibited a slight European accent (he was born in Switzerland) as he disclosed he had been one of three pathologists who had performed the autopsy on the President's body and had co-authored the official autopsy report. With quiet pride he listed his qualifications as an expert in forensic pathology, stopping to address the jury: "That's f-o-r-e-n-s-i-c," he spelled, going on to add, "The word 'forensic' comes from the Latin 'forum,' which means the public place, the market place." He spoke softly but with great precision, mouthing each word as if someone might be taking notes. As it was, he could easily have been delivering a guest lecture—and pleased as punch to do it—on a subject that was dear to his heart. He was totally charming, if entirely quaint, on direct examination, often spelling out words for the jury, sometimes simple ones like r-i-o-t-s, sometimes a more uncommon word such as s-t-e-l-l-a-t-e (star-shaped). Once he used the words "tracheotomy" and "entry" in the same sentence, choosing to spell out e-n-t-r-y and leaving the jury to work on "tracheotomy" by themselves. He rarely neglected the jury for more than a minute or two, often addressing them, "Gentlemen, you will notice . . ."

Dymond first questioned Dr. Finck about the wound the pathologist had observed "on the right side of the neck of President Kennedy." Dr. Finck pointed out for the jury the approximate area of the wound, using Billy Wegmann as a model and a small ruler, measuring distances from the center of the back, from the mastoid, and the upper bony prominence of the right shoulder.

Dr. Finck felt and squeezed a good deal under Bill Wegmann's coat in order to be precise in his positioning, until Wegmann finally took his jacket off. When Dr. Finck had settled on his spot, Dymond asked him to mark Wegmann's shirt with a pen. Billy Wegmann executed a large turn-around take at this, as the doctor marked his shirt, and the spectators laughed in approval, already primed by the meticulous character of the doctor. Dr. Finck himself looked up at the sound of laughter and flashed an enormous wide smile that was immediately shut off.

Courtly of manner as he was, Dr. Finck was nevertheless firm about his opinions. He told Dymond he had examined the wound closely and identified it as a wound of entry, by means of the edges of the hole which were pushed inward and other characteristics. Dr. Finck had not been able, the night of the autopsy, to find a wound of exit, but had discovered an incision in the President's neck, a tracheotomy cut for breathing. The next day Dr. Humes, another member of the autopsy team, spoke with the doctors in Dallas and they confirmed performing the tracheotomy. Dr. Finck indicated this would have been medically consistent with the area which would have been the point of exit, and that the tracheotomy would have obscured the exit wound.

Dymond then asked Dr. Finck to discuss the head wound, offering himself as a model. Dr. Finck located the area of entrance and exit, speaking directly to the jury and giving no indication by the tone of his voice or by any vocal punctuation that he had finished a sentence. Only by observing him turn his head to counsel or the judge and fixing them with an owlish stare and silence was it apparent he was ready for the next question.

Dymond introduced into evidence a drawing prepared by Dr. Finck to illustrate lectures in demonstration of through-and-through or perforating missile wounds. Dr. Finck pointed out the lettered areas, explaining, "They are labeled A as in Alpha, B as in Brave, C as in Charlie and D as in Delta." Dr. Finck testified precisely and at length—keeping up his spelling bee, at one time even spelling o-u-t—as he described the shape, shatter and bone fragments involved, concluding with an answer to Dymond's question as to whether he had a definite impression about the path of the bullet. "I have," Dr. Finck said, "the firm opinion that the bullet entered in the back [of the head] and exited on the right

side of the top of the head producing a very large head wound."
Dr. Finck added it was also his opinion that the bullet had been
moving in a downward direction. At the end of direct examination, Dr. Finck was asked if his opinion had been affected by the
desires or at the request of anyone in the government. He replied,
"My opinion is an honest professional opinion."

Dr. Finck began well enough on cross by testifying that all three
doctors involved in the autopsy had agreed on the findings. But as
soon as it was apparent that Alvin Oser was out to discredit him,
Dr. Finck became confused, almost stunned, as if he had been
engaged to testify in the form of a lecture, to aid in this matter
any way he could, but with no idea his word would be disputed.
For a while it looked as if he might give Oser back some of his own
medicine when Oser asked why the doctors at Parkland had not
been phoned the evening of the autopsy instead of the next day,
by which time the President's body had been removed. "I can't
explain that," Dr. Finck said, going on to repeat the reasons for
the call: "We had a wound of entry and we had seen no exit and
we knew there was no bullet in the cadaver. There was a very
strong reason for inquiring [of the Parkland doctors] if there was
another wound." "Then why didn't you call the doctors at Parkland while the body was still being examined?" Alvin Oser inquired again. "I will remind you," Dr. Finck replied, "that I was
not in charge. I was called as a consultant to look at the wounds. I
wasn't running the show."

Ah, came the thought, he's caught on to Oser and he'll put up
with no further guff. But Dr. Finck soon testified he was specifically told by the Surgeon General of the Navy not to discuss the
case without first coordinating with the Attorney General (Robert
Kennedy). Oser asked Dr. Finck if "prior to writing your report
did you have occasion to view these [autopsy] photographs?"

"Yes, I did," Dr. Finck replied.

Oser then produced a report signed by Dr. Finck and asked him
to explain a statement that "Dr. Finck first saw the photographs
on January 20, 1967." When Dr. Finck said this was correct, Alvin
Oser asked why he had just answered that he'd seen them *before*
writing his autopsy report.

"I did not say I had seen the photographs before writing my
report in 1963," he answered. The court reporter was asked to read

the question and answer back and when Dr. Finck had listened to it he said, "I may have said I *didn't*—and was misunderstood. I am very firm on this point . . . I was there when they were taken but I did not see the photographs of the wounds before I wrote my report." Oser kept at him, asking why he said he had seen them if he hadn't. "I never said that," Dr. Finck insisted. "It was misunderstood."

Dymond interrupted, claiming Oser was arguing with the witness, but Oser persisted and now Dr. Finck, who had at one point said, "I'm afraid I don't follow you," made it clear he wasn't following him.

Oser asked if the autopsy photos and X rays were ever displayed to the members of the Warren Commission. Dr. Finck said that when he and the other two doctors appeared before the Commission in March 1964, "the X rays and photographs were not available to us in the preparation of our testimony." Oser wanted to know why. "I was told it was the wish of the Attorney General, who was then Robert Kennedy," Dr. Finck said.

As Oser continued to question him about the location of the wounds and the marks he'd made on Billy Wegmann's shirt, Dr. Finck began to be unresponsive to the questions. He would often volunteer added information but he was not comfortable answering yes or no, especially when it came to exhibits, drawings and sketches that were not of his authorship. At one point Judge Haggerty told the witness that he must answer yes or no—after which he might explain. Dr. Finck glanced up at the judge through his enormous horn-rimmed glasses; he actually looked hurt.

During the afternoon session Dr. Finck became even more vague in his responses. Oser must be given credit for his killer instinct; once he sniffed the possibility of trampling a witness into the ground, he did not let up. When Oser asked Dr. Finck why he had not dissected the path of the bullet through the track of the President's neck to discover if the wound had indeed been a through-and-through one, Dr. Finck said, "I did not dissect the track in the neck."

"Why?" Oser asked.

"We did not remove the organs of the neck," the witness replied.

"Why?" Oser insisted.

"We were told to examine the head wounds—I was told that the family wanted the examination of the wounds of the neck and the head."

"Why did you not trace the track of the neck wound?" Oser asked once more.

"As I recall, I examined the wounds—" Dr. Finck broke off, seemingly lost.

Oser demanded an answer by repetition: "Why did you not, as a pathologist, trace the path of the bullet?"

Dr. Finck paused, then said, "As I recall I didn't remove the organs of the neck."

Alvin Oser, now irritated and not without reason, addressed the judge. "Your Honor, I am going to have to ask you to have the witness answer my questions." Turning back to the doctor, he once more inquired, "Why didn't you trace the track of the wound?"

Another long pause from Dr. Finck, then: "As I recall I was told not to, but I don't recall by whom."

"You were not interested in the track?" Oser asked.

"I was interested in the track," Dr. Finck replied, repeating the sentence, except for the negative, by rote.

And on it went. Witness and questioner were completely mismatched chemically. Dr. Finck neither seemed able, nor did he care, to respond to the questions. He was not hostile, however, but his concentration and his meticulous attention to detail had deserted him.

Dr. Finck eventually admitted to Oser that the autopsy was not complete in 1963 and that later there was a supplemental report by one of the other pathologists and then, in January 1967, another report of the autopsy. Dr. Finck had not, oddly enough, been aware of the autopsy panel review that took place in 1968 until he'd received a copy of it in February 1969.

That afternoon Alvin Oser set up on easels two autopsy drawings illustrating the head and neck wounds. The sketches were grotesque; if they were meant to represent the President, they were even more grotesque, depicting him with bushy black hair, thin arched black eyebrows that appeared plucked, a mascaraed look to the eyes and made-up lips. An arrow ran through each drawing, one piercing the head, the other sticking through the neck. "In" and "out" were printed on the entrance and exit points of the arrows. They were totally impersonal and chilling to view.

One good laugh broke up the gruesomeness of the afternoon when, putting a hypothetical question to the doctor, Alvin Oser said, "If a bullet was fired from the sixth-floor window of the Texas Book Depository, sixty feet from the ground, and this building struck someone in the back—"

Irvin Dymond immediately interrupted, saying to the judge, "Your Honor, there is no evidence of a *building* striking *anyone* in the back!"

This earned a huge laugh, probably much more than it would have ordinarily, because of the afternoon's interminable purgatory of question and answer. Alvin Oser snapped, "Now you're being cute!"

It was hoped Alvin Oser would finish his cross-examination of Dr. Finck, but to everyone's chagrin he was held over for more questioning the next morning. It was also hoped that a good night's sleep might refresh Dr. Finck. And he did perk up slightly on the second morning, although it was doubtful if the impression he'd made the afternoon before could be bolstered in the eyes of the jury, if only because so much of the testimony was redundant. Sharp attention to details already muddied could hardly be expected. Dr. Finck remained on the stand longer than any other witness outside of Perry Raymond Russo, and a courtroom welcome soon wears out. Alvin Oser did not help to rivet the attention by indulging in a goodly amount of lint picking as in this exchange when he questioned the doctor regarding the thoroughness of the autopsy report and the amount of time spent on it:

OSER: Did you read over the final draft?

DR. FINCK: I did.

OSER: Do you agree with everything in the autopsy report?

DR. FINCK: Essentially, I do. I read the report and discussed it several hours.

OSER [as if this might well be an answer to the assassination itself]: Then why is Governor Connally spelled C-o-n-n-e-l-l-y and not C-o-n-n-a-l-l-y?

Irvin Dymond got a roar from the gallery when he slyly objected to the question on the grounds that "the witness is not qualified as an expert in spelling."

Judge Haggerty knew when he had a good thing and drew more laughter when he said, to the contrary, he'd remembered a lot of spelling the day before.

Dymond rehabilitated Dr. Finck somewhat on redirect; for some reason Dr. Finck replied to Dymond's questions more tersely and to the point. Oser was then again able to muddle him on re-cross. What Oser had done was to keep the witness confused and thereby spread that confusion to the autopsy itself—along with hinting at obstruction from unnamed high officials of a complete autopsy. This purpose was emphasized in Oser's last question before Dr. Finck was excused. Again harking back to the failure to dissect the President's neck, Oser said, "I believe you told Mr. Dymond earlier you were not taking orders from anyone . . . Doctor, you did take orders and didn't dissect the throat area?" "They were not orders," Dr. Finck said, "they were suggestions." "Now, Doctor," Oser said, and his voice was sheer innuendo, "there were admirals and generals present and you were only a lieutenant colonel." Dymond objected and the judge admonished Oser, saying, "We have been over that ground before." Oser indicated he was finished, and Dr. Pierre Finck was finally released.

We were given a short recess, during which I spoke to Dymond about the disintegration of Dr. Finck as a witness. The defense lawyer was saddened and said, "The doctor knows his job, obviously. He was just not used to cross-examination. The entire process was alien to him. Some people just can't operate on cross."

The Hanging Ladies were crowing about the discredited—in their eyes—autopsy report, as if Clay Shaw's fingerprints had actually shown up on the X rays.

33

The Return of the Fat Man

When court reconvened, instead of the expected James Phelan, still warming a corridor bench, fidgety as an Irishman at a dry wake, the name of Dean Andrews, Jr., was called out. This caused the biggest stir yet in the courtroom as Sal Brocato barked, "Order in the court!" and several other deputies echoed him.

Down the center aisle the little fat man strut-waddled, arms chopping out from his sides in that short clublike manner indigenous to those whose girth prevents a free hang of the limb. Wearing a dark suit and large dark glasses, he took the stand and was sworn in. He immediately tipped his glasses down on his nose and surveyed the courtroom scene: Yep, prosecution—oh, yeah, I know you devils—defense, uh-huh; press and spectators, okay. He smiled at the packed house—that's the way I like 'em, all systems go.

He tipped his glasses back up as James Alcock asked to have the jury removed. When they'd paraded out, Alcock told the judge that since Andrews was appealing his perjury conviction to the Louisiana Supreme Court, in all fairness he should have an attorney present to advise him of his answers—his statements to grand juries pertaining to this case already having gotten him in enough trouble. Andrews' law partner, a dark-haired horn-rimmed owlish young man named Michael Barron, whose ample size indicated his association with Andrews might be affecting his weight, appeared and pulled up a hard-backed chair right next to Dean Andrews, who, not wanting to allow for any dead air, had removed his dark glasses, tilted his head back, and was delicately administering eye drops. Dean Andrews got a laugh from the crowd, a sigh of patience from the judge and a small shake of the head from James Alcock.

Judge Haggerty, appearing to be friendlily disposed to Andrews, reminded the chubby lawyer, "The fact that you have been called as a witness does not take away your constitutional rights.

You don't have to incriminate yourself by your answers." The judge also advised the state it could not ask the witness in front of the jury if he had been charged or arrested for perjury. Alcock checked to make sure "the court isn't making a ruling that we can't go into the *subject matter* of the conviction." Judge Haggerty said he wasn't and, with those ground rules laid down, the jury was brought back in.

Irvin Dymond's direct examination lasted a brief twenty-five minutes. The defense only wanted one thing from Dean Andrews and they got it.

Dymond went straight to the phone call Andrews claimed to have received in Hotel Dieu hospital the day after the assassination and asked whom it was from. Dean Andrews leaned over to confer with his partner. When he straightened up, he said, "I decline to answer on two grounds, first the lawyer-client relationship privilege and second on the grounds that it may, might, would or could, tend to link me up with a chain of events that might incriminate me." He rattled off the last half of this sentence in syncopated style that made it sound like the scat verse to a rhythm song. He had the crowd with him already, acknowledging this with a sly grin. If he wouldn't say right then who the call was from, Dean Andrews was definite when Dymond asked if it had been from Clay Shaw. In a series of rapid-fire questions and answers, Andrews asserted he had never talked to Clay Shaw on the phone, had never met him, had never seen a picture of him until after his arrest and added that Clay Shaw was not now and never had been the Clay Bertrand to whom Dean Andrews had referred. To the question "Do you know who Clay Bertrand was or is?"—Dean Andrews replied, "I believe I do." Dymond didn't press him on this; he'd gotten the testimony he'd wanted to the jury and soon tendered the witness to the state.

It was clear from the beginning that Alcock was going to put Andrews through the long haul. He began by questioning him about his claimed office visit from Lee Harvey Oswald, and Andrews related basically the same story he'd given the Warren Commission, of Oswald appearing as a walk-in client with a Latin type, preceded by the visit of "three swishes." Alcock asked what he meant by "swishes" and after an admonishment from the judge, Andrews said, "They appeared to be homosexuals by the way they walked." As to what advice he'd given Oswald on that

first visit, Andrews claimed the lawyer-client privilege—this despite the fact that Oswald was dead and Andrews had never collected a fee from him for anything.

When the judge upheld his refusal to answer, Andrews grinned
and at one time tilted his glasses down and winked—at no one in
particular, simply winked out at the court. He would not testify
for long without salt and peppering his speech with a colorful
phrase.

Soon Alcock went into the area of the phone call Andrews
claimed to have received in the hospital on November 23, 1963,
asking him to defend Oswald.

ALCOCK: Did you recognize the voice?

ANDREWS: I had heard it many times.

ALCOCK: In the course of your legal practice?

Andrews conferred with his partner and came out of it refusing
to answer, claiming the lawyer-client privilege. Judge Haggerty
sustained him, to which Alcock said, "But he didn't claim it a
moment ago." Judge Haggerty: "If he didn't do it then, he's doing
it now." Dean Andrews looked as if he might break out in a
giggle.

ALCOCK [showing the first signs of frustration]: Did you get in
your mind that this was a human being?

ANDREWS [thinking a moment]: I believe I did.

Dean Andrews would testify off and on, then suddenly refuse to
answer, either on the grounds that it "may, might, would or could,
tend to link me up with a chain of events that might incriminate
me," or the lawyer-client relationship. James Alcock's face was
reddening as the judge constantly sustained Andrews throughout
the better part of the morning. Alcock claimed if Dean Andrews
denied that Clay Shaw was Clay Bertrand, the state had a right to
know who Clay Bertrand was. Andrews would lead him tantalizingly close: "I know a person who in the 1950s was *introduced* to
me as Clay Bertrand." He went on to say this took place at a "fag
wedding reception" held at a local bar.

ALCOCK: By whom were you introduced to him?

ANDREWS: Big Joe.

ALCOCK: Who is Big Joe?

ANDREWS: She's a butch.

JUDGE HAGGERTY: Speak clearly, is Big Joe a he or a she?

ANDREWS: She is a female.

When Alcock questioned the identity of Clay Bertrand, Dean Andrews said, "I know who he was. You know him, too." Alcock sighed and asked, "Would you mind *telling* me who he is?" At this point Andrews refused on the grounds of possible self-incrimination.

Soon Alcock sought to test the credibility of the witness by reading his testimony from the Warren Report and showing the discrepancies between what he was testifying to now and what he'd testified to in front of the grand jury. Dymond suggested Dean Andrews be allowed to familiarize himself with his Warren Report testimony during the lunch period; Judge Haggerty agreed and court was recessed.

Alcock fared no better with the witness in the early afternoon. He repeatedly threw Andrews' Warren Commission testimony in his face but when he pointed out an inconsistency and asked for an explanation, Andrews would repeat his peppy I-decline speech. Alcock's temperature was rising, as was his voice, now taking on the fine annoyed twang of a whine. The jury was sent out again and Alcock pleaded with the judge that when Andrews had testified for the defense about Clay Bertrand he had "opened the door" to a complete cross-examination by the state. Judge Haggerty claimed the witness was not an ordinary witness—that was certainly the very real truth—that he was already the defendant in a criminal matter and needed to protect himself. After further arguing, the judge even said to Alcock, "If you [the D.A.'s office] hadn't indicted him, he would not be in this position today [of having to decline to answer questions]. You got yourself in a legal bind. You people have caused him to be in this position."

Dean Adams Andrews, Jr., was enjoying the protection of the court and clearly relishing the ulcers he was germinating within James Alcock. The prosecuting attorney was persistent, however, in his arguments, once more appealing to the judge, claiming the door had been opened and that "Our client, the State of Louisiana, is entitled to confrontation."

"I feel sorry about your client," Judge Haggerty replied, "but I have to follow your client's *law*."

Jim Alcock would not give up and eventually Judge Haggerty called a recess to enable the state to research the law and come up with one that might change his mind to the extent of ordering a complete cross-examination of the witness. "If you show me I'm wrong I'll be happy to reconsider my position," said Judge Haggerty.

Alcock appeared to be up against a judicial stone wall. There was little doubt that Dean Andrews would be allowed to tease his way through the rest of the cross-examination until he was finally released by an agitated state. If this were to happen, although he had denied Clay Shaw was Clay Bertrand—the main revelation the defense wanted of him—his appearance on the stand might have been mistaken by the jury for a guest shot by yet another clown, and had he been excused without further ado, they might just have forgotten about him altogether.

James Alcock, however, wanted at him, perhaps to gather further conflicting testimony under oath for the District Attorney's office, enough to shoot for additional perjury charges. But in this trial the strange quirky country between intent and result was fraught with land mines. And so it was that after a long recess, we were called back to hear that both James Alcock and Judge Haggerty had been engaged in law research.

JUDGE HAGGERTY: In my research—and I am not saying this to take away from Mr. Alcock, but before Mr. Alcock came to my office I was about to send for him because I found . . . the following on page 376 of John J. McKelvey's *Law of Evidence*. This was published in 1907. It is an old lawbook but it is still good law. It states here, "The general American doctrine is that a witness who enters into a subject which is incriminating, must answer all questions relating to that subject. He cannot stop at will after having told part of the facts . . . it would be productive of grave injustice on many occasions if a witness could give such version as he chose as incriminating facts on his direct examination, and then be allowed to refuse to answer questions on cross-examination or when he saw on cross-examination that he was being made to put the facts in a different light, to stop short and decline to testify further."

Judge Haggerty then cited Alcock's source, *Wigmore on Evidence*, quoting from a Michigan case in 1869. After Judge Haggerty had read at length from Alcock's source, he announced his decision: "Considering what I have read and applied to the fact of the issue before me, I would state that when Mr. Andrews took the stand under subpoena, he could have at that moment, before he answered any questions put to him on direct examination by Mr. Dymond, he could have claimed his privilege of incrimination . . . but he chose not to do that at that time . . . I will now change my position after availing myself of research myself [two myself's, just to make clear who was running the show] and I will permit a full cross-examination of the witness, Mr. Andrews."

Dean Andrews at this point shrugged, took out a handkerchief and mopped off his face, while the judge said, "Therefore, bring the jury in." Before the jury arrived, however, Judge Haggerty slipped in this sentence: "Mr. Alcock, I might state before the jury comes down that I found it before you brought it to me."

Laughter in the courtroom. "Order in the court!" The laughter was due in part to the high spirits generated by the knowledge that there would be another full act of Dean Adams Andrews, Jr.

ALCOCK: Mr. Andrews, when you received this telephone call on November 23, 1963, did you have an image in your mind as to who the person was who identified himself on that occasion?

ANDREWS: Yes.

ALCOCK: Did you know him by any other name than Clay Bertrand?

ANDREWS: Gene Davis.

Dean Andrews went on to explain he had known Gene Davis for a year before he had met him at the "fag" wedding and been introduced to him by Big Joe as Clay Bertrand. He insisted he had only used the name Clay Bertrand as a cover for Gene Davis when he'd testified before Wesley Liebeler, counsel for the Warren Commission. When speaking to the FBI, he'd also done this because Gene Davis had had nothing to do with suggesting he go to Dallas to represent Lee Harvey Oswald and Andrews saw no reason to get him involved. Although he had kept up this pretext of having talked to someone named Clay Bertrand, he explained why he had given the testimony he had to the Warren Commission:

ANDREWS: At the time Mr. Liebeler was questioning me, it is just as it is in the courtroom, rapid fire. It was an informal meeting, I didn't place too much importance to why an insignificant person like myself would even be called. I answered the best I could at that time. I didn't deliberately lie. I might have overloaded my mouth with the importance of being a witness in front of the

Warren Report, but other than that I didn't deliberately lie. I think the only explanation I can give you is my mouth ran ahead of my brain.

ALCOCK: Do you recall telling Mr. Liebeler that you saw Clay Bertrand six weeks prior to the time that he questioned you?

ANDREWS: Well, I figured that wasn't material. You can call it a lie if you want, I call it huffing and puffing.

ALCOCK: Huffing and puffing under oath?

ANDREWS: Bull session.

When Alcock asked Dean Andrews if it weren't true that FBI agent Regis Kennedy had attempted to locate Clay Bertrand as a result of his conversation with Andrews, the witness replied:

ANDREWS: This is what I gathered. I was still under sedation, still using oxygen then, I believe. This is vague, way off in the distance. He appeared before me like a myth. I remember answering questions, I don't remember what they were . . . the only thing that I can recall is could I give him any better information, and I told him, no, call your man up, do whatever you want. If you want to think that I am a squirrel or I am not, be my guest, I cannot help you.

ALCOCK: And you didn't choose to help the FBI on that occasion by giving them the name of Gene Davis?

ANDREWS: I didn't choose to implicate an innocent man, Gene Davis, in something that I couldn't even recall what I said. All I was aware of was the importance, that it came after. It is just like I explained on direct examination. This man, Gene Davis, he makes the phone call . . . but all of a sudden it dawned on me that as a result of my calling those people [the FBI] I could involve an innocent party into a whole lot of humbug. At that time in the hospital under sedation I elected a course that I have never been able to get away from. I either get indicted or I get charged, or people interpret it different. And all it is, is just like I said. This is Gene Davis, I didn't want to get him involved. I started it and it has been whiplashing ever since. I can't stop it.

Dean Andrews then spilled the complete beans about the phone call. Gene Davis had called him to pass an act of sale regarding an automobile, and, Dean Andrews now testified, "I don't know whether I suggested— Man, I would be famous if I could go to Dallas and defend Lee Harvey Oswald. Whoever gets that job is going to be a famous lawyer, or whether in a conversation it came about."

"You mean," asked James Alcock, "you are now telling this court under oath that *no one* called you on behalf of the representation of Lee Harvey Oswald in Dallas?"

Dean Andrews replied, "Per se, my answer is yes, no one called me to say that."

ALCOCK: Why is it you called Monk Zelden on Sunday then and asked if he wanted to go to Dallas?

ANDREWS: No explanation. Don't forget, I am in the hospital sick. I might have believed it myself, or thought after a while I was retained there, so I called Monk. [Deadly serious] I would like to be famous too—other than as a perjurer.

[An outburst of laughter in the court. Clay Shaw, I noticed, was not laughing.]

BAILIFFS: Order in the court!

ALCOCK: That [to be famous other than as a perjurer] is going to be difficult.

ANDREWS [shrugging]: C'est la vie!

ALCOCK: Are you saying now that the call, as far as it regards the representation of Lee Harvey Oswald, is a figment of your imagination?

ANDREWS: I have tried to say that consistently, and nobody ever gave me a chance.

ALCOCK [after a few other questions]: Did you have a chance before the Warren Commission?

ANDREWS: They never gave me a second bite at the apple.

ALCOCK: You don't think they presumed you told the truth at the first bite?

ANDREWS: I don't think they believed anything other than Harvey Oswald might have been in the office. That is my appreciation of their evaluation of my testimony. I don't even know how they took the time and money to send somebody down to interview me.

And on it went. But now one got the feeling that Dean Andrews—regardless of his past contradictory statements, his circumlocution, his huffin' and puffin'—was purging himself of the whole bloody mess. It had been whiplashing and he was sick of it, as he soon said, "I got hooked with it. I elected to stick with it, and here I sit!"

ALCOCK: How do you know this, Mr. Andrews, that he [Gene Davis] had nothing to do with the assassination of President Kennedy?

ANDREWS: Just like I know you, Alcock, had nothing to do with it either.

ALCOCK: But you didn't give my name, did you?

ANDREWS [after a considerable pause]: No.

More laughter in the court. More order in the court.

When Alcock took Dean Andrews through his earlier varying descriptions of Clay Bertrand to the Warren Commission and FBI, the lawyer refused to go into detail, saying, "This is page after page of bull." To which Alcock said, "In other words, page after page after page of lies?" Dean Andrews: "If you want to call them that, that is your privilege." Dean Andrews would not veer from the course of total confession he had chosen.

By this time the judge appeared to have been struck by the distinct possibility that the entire matter of Clay Bertrand had been a charade, albeit a costly charade and not, in the end, a particularly funny one. As if to clear this up for once and for all, he asked Alcock if he might put a question to Dean Andrews. Permission was granted.

JUDGE HAGGERTY: Where did you ever get the name of Clay Bertrand in your mind?

ANDREWS: The only way I can explain it, Judge, is I tried during the time of [my interview with] Regis Kennedy to figure out some way to associate Gene Davis's phone call with what I had told Regis Kennedy. When it dawned on me that they would pounce on this man and cause an investigation—and I couldn't think of Clay to save my life, the only thing I could remember was Bertrand—I don't recall how long it took for me to put the two together. And I remember the fag wedding reception, Big Joe introducing me to a man I knew as Gene Davis, as Clay Bertrand, casually, and that is how I put the two together as a cover to remember what I was saying in relationship to the phone call.

JUDGE HAGGERTY: Not Joe Brown or Charlie Smith? Clay Bertrand?

ANDREWS [shaking his head]: Of all names to pick, I picked that one!

[An uproar in the courtroom, followed by "Order in the court!"]

ALCOCK: In other words, you went back in your mind thirteen years to recall that name on this occasion? Is that correct?

ANDREWS: It wasn't easy!

ALCOCK: I know it wasn't easy, but . . . How did you know Lee Harvey Oswald was even critical or interesting at that time?

ANDREWS: Out of TV in my [hospital] room . . . I saw him when he shot this guy Ruby.

ALCOCK: That was Sunday.

ANDREWS: The 24th.

JUDGE HAGGERTY [adjusting his glasses]: Wait a minute. Ruby shot Oswald, not Oswald shooting Ruby!

A roar of laughter, followed by a few claps of delighted applause. "Order in the court!" cried four or five deputies, as it seemed entirely possible this session might just turn into a Punch and Judy show.

After the tumult had simmered down, Dean Andrews made one of his most precise comments by reducing the entire matter to the simplest common denominator when he shook his head, sighed and said, "I can't give you any explanation, Mr. Alcock. Once you make a fool out of yourself, that is it, you are stuck with it."

For some reason Alcock continued with Dean Andrews, exhuming reams of previous testimony by the witness before the grand jury in regard to Clay Bertrand, descriptions, sightings, time and place—all of which Dean Andrews had now completely refuted. By now it was clear Alcock should not have forced Andrews to testify; the farce was becoming more apparent question by question, and when Alcock would not let up, Dean Andrews was not averse to telling the court he had told Jim Garrison the truth and other members of the D.A.'s office, but they had chosen not to believe him. He insisted again, as if he wanted to clear the matter up for all time, "Clay Bertrand is a figment of my imagination, or whatever you want to call it." He also said, "If I had my life to live over again, I would say his name was John Jones."

This also earned a laugh. I glanced at Clay Shaw. Although he sat with his back to me, I noticed his head bow ever so slightly.

When Alcock maintained that the chubby lawyer had even this day testified he'd met a person named Clay Bertrand at the wedding, Dean Andrews spoke as if Alcock were now being a little thick not to accept his explanation. He wound it up for one last time by testifying, "I was introduced to a person who I already knew to be Gene Davis, in a very casual manner, people half loaded, eating free sandwiches and getting all the free booze. I got there in the middle of the thing and Big Joe says, 'Meet Clay Bertrand,' just like that. I burst out laughing, I knew the cat—I mean I knew the guy was Gene Davis . . . I have been introduced as Algonquin J. Calhoun but people know me as Dean Andrews, know it is not my name."

When James Alcock had soundly set him up for more perjury charges, Dean Andrews was finally released from the witness stand. Before he left there was an aura of sad resignation about the little fat man.

Dymond did not touch him on re-direct. Later, when I asked why, he said, "Oh, God, Jim, I didn't want to subject him to any more. After what he'd done, I just didn't have the heart."

There was only time that afternoon for the defense to put on a notary public and qualify their handwriting expert. By then it was five o'clock. Judge Haggerty, as a result of Dean Andrews' testimony, it was said, requested a meeting in his chambers by counsel for both sides.

When court was adjourned, the sole topic of conversation was, naturally, Dean Andrews. Those of the press who were still pushing for a conviction, although their number was diminishing, and the Hanging Ladies, completely landlocked by their beliefs and stout-hearted to the end, viewed Dean Andrews the way June and Dick Rolfe did: "Oh, that Dean Andrews—what a card! Isn't he a clown? You couldn't believe the time of day from *him!*" They laughed and shook their heads, sighed and slapped their thighs, but behind their almost manic joy at the spectacle of Dean Andrews, their eyes were narrowly X-raying the rest of the press to ascertain exactly what we believed. Their persistence in maintaining total belief in the state's case, no matter the evidence, was beginning to turn rancid.

When I walked out into the corridor, Jim Phelan, now going into overtime parking on his hall bench, rose and came toward me, grinning widely and shaking his head. "Jim . . . Jim," he said, "I was sitting right there, right opposite the courtroom door when Dean came out. You know that little fat man walked directly to me, made a straight line, and says, 'Well, no matter what happens to me, Phelan, at least I can look you square in the eye!' " Jim Phelan slapped my shoulder. "How about that little fat man!" he said. He shook his head and laughed. "Jesus, I just love that little fat man today!"

We waited until the conference in the judge's chambers ended and the lawyers came out into the corridor. Dymond looked pleased. What had the judge called the conference for, we all wanted to know. "God, I'd love to tell you, but I can't. I honestly can't. I don't want to interpret the judge. I'm afraid I'll just have to say I burned my notes."

From another source I heard Judge Haggerty had been shaken by Andrews' testimony and because of it suggested to the prosecution that perhaps they should make a reassessment of their position in this case. The prosecution supposedly replied they did not have authority to do this, so on with the trial.

Dymond indicated that the defense would wind up its presentation in the next day or so, and the case would go to the jury soon after.

That evening over drinks at Mom's Good Eats, the talk centered around Clay Bertrand. If the name were indeed a figment of Dean Andrews' imagination—and no one could think of a reason in the world why he would claim so if it were not true; he could only be rewarded by further prosecution from the state, and he'd certainly done nothing to enhance his professional reputation as a lawyer—then how did the name Clay Bertrand jump from the imagination of Dean Andrews to the mail pouch of James Hardiman, how did it infiltrate the reminiscences of Perry Russo and how was Mrs. Jessie Parker able to see it signed into the guest register book at the Eastern Airlines V.I.P. lounge? The questions were as fascinating as the possibilities were frightening.

34

Counterattack

The next day might have been called the "Day of the Big Refute" as four major witnesses took the stand for the defense and contradicted the state's allegations.

No witness in the trial came to the stand cloaked in probity as much as Charles A. Appel, Jr., who had been with the FBI from 1924 until 1948, when he retired. Mr. Appel had qualified as an expert just before court recessed the previous afternoon. Now in private practice in Washington, D.C., he had testified as an expert graphologist in every state of the union except Hawaii; he was also famous for having broken the famous Lindbergh kidnaping case.

Mr. Appel, balding with fringes of wispy white hair, conjured up a picture of the elderly eternal scholar bent over a rolltop desk stuffed with documents. He came armed with large photographic blowups of the guest book signature as well as samples of Clay Shaw's handwritten "Clay Bertrand," for purposes of comparison. When Dymond had set them up in front of the jury, Appel methodically went over the signatures and pointed out the differences, letter by letter. As he testified, in a voice much younger than his years, I got the impression no one in court would doubt his veracity any more than they would accuse Mr. Chips of child molesting. When Appel was finished with the two signatures, Dymond questioned him as to whether he had seen other samples of Mr. Shaw's handwriting. Appel had and described them.

DYMOND: As a result of your test and examination, did you come to a firm opinion that these exhibits were different from the Clay Bertrand in the state exhibit?

APPEL: Yes, I did.

DYMOND: What is that opinion?

APPEL: The defendant Shaw did not write the entry in the book.

Appel was then tendered to James Alcock. There was not much that could be done to shake Appel. Alcock concentrated on the fact that Appel had worked from enlarged photographs of the signatures involved, rather than from the originals, although he had studied the originals when he arrived in New Orleans the day before. Asked whether his specialty of analyzing questionable documents is an "exact science," Appel replied, "That would depend upon what you mean by 'exact.' " Alcock: "I mean exact—such as mathematics is an exact science." Appel, the essence of mellowness, said, "No, sir, mathematics is the only exact science there is. In this case, certainly the comparison of design is most *scientific.*" Questioned about his testimony in past cases, Appel said he had never been proven wrong about a signature, although juries might have decided in opposition to his testimony.

On re-direct, Dymond asked Appel if he was being compensated for his services. "No," Appel said, "I'm appearing because I feel it a civic duty." Explaining he had done this in the past, Appel stressed that he does not usually take criminal cases but that occasionally there comes a time when "without my services an injustice may occur—I do it as a civic duty."

On re-cross, Appel was not in the least reticent about explaining his position, telling Alcock that he rarely appeared as a defense witness "unless there are some peculiar circumstances that convince me an injustice is being done." When Alcock pursued this, Appel said he'd been contacted by Lloyd Cobb of the International Trade Mart, for whom he'd done previous work. Cobb had asked what his fee would be. When Appel quoted $250 a day, Cobb said he felt the defendant didn't have that kind of money and Appel volunteered his services, because he felt an injustice might be in the works.

Jeff Biddison, a long-time friend of Clay Shaw's, took the stand next. Under questioning by Dymond he testified he had owned a black Cadillac in 1963, similar to the car the state claimed was seen in Clinton and the one Vernon Bundy described. Biddison maintained he had never loaned it to Clay Shaw in 1963, that he had used it in his own real estate business, and that Clay Shaw had his own car, a black Thunderbird. He had known Clay Shaw for twenty-three years, had never seen him dressed in tight pants, never seen him wear a hat, and had never known him to be acquainted with or mention Lee Harvey Oswald or David W. Ferrie. He explained that when Clay Shaw had gone to Europe in the summer of 1966, he had leased his house for him and had received mail for Clay Shaw at his office on Royal Street but not, to his recollection, at his home at 1414 Chartres. Dymond drew a smile from Biddison when he asked if a Clifford Boudreaux, the name Dymond made up for the postman, had ever lived at his house. Biddison replied in the negative, also testifying he had never received mail at his home or office addressed to Clay Bertrand. Jeff Biddison, a good-looking man in his forties, made a solid, straightforward witness.

James Alcock treated him with respect and did not attempt to sandbag him. The prosecuting attorney made it clear to the jury at the end of his cross-examination, however, that nothing but helpful testimony for the defense could be expected from Biddison:

ALCOCK: Were you subpoenaed to come here as a witness?
BIDDISON: No, sir.
ALCOCK: You came of your own free will?
BIDDISON: Yes, sir.
ALCOCK: Because of your friendship to the defendant?
BIDDISON: Yes, sir.

Excused. After Jeff Biddison came the Irish terror, Jim Phelan. There was blood in his eye for the state, especially for Moo Sciambra; sightings of nerves were present, too, for fear he would be hampered by the hearsay rule. James Alcock objected strenuously to much of his testimony as Dymond began putting Phelan through his paces, but the defense lawyer argued to the court that both Russo and Sciambra had been allowed to give their versions of meetings with Phelan, and now it was only right that Phelan should be heard.

His testimony, and the controversies between opposing counsel over it, was interrupted early on by the noon recess. Before court convened for the afternoon session, I spoke with Nina Sulzer. Now that the time was fast approaching for Clay to take the stand on his own behalf, Nina was fearful the prosecution had been working overtime on the graveyard shift, digging up skeletons from his past, perhaps a choice morsel from somewhere deep in his personal life that, while not indicative of guilt, might prove prejudicial to the eyes of the jury. Nina, usually so coolly poised, serene in the midst of courthouse chaos, showed the tension of concern in her eyes and a tightness around her mouth. I believe she wanted to enlist my aid in the hope I would throw whatever weight I might have with his lawyers in advising them to keep Clay off the stand.

Even realizing the state might resort to last-minute skulduggery—although I could not quite imagine Jim Alcock getting his fingers any dirtier than he'd already been forced to in the prosecution of this case—I had no doubt that Clay Shaw would be his own best witness, no matter what was thrown at him. I had every confidence that he could not possibly come off the stand without doing himself good. Although juries are advised that a defendant's choice not to take the stand should in no way be taken as a reflection of guilt, not one jury in a hundred could remain unaffected by a defendant's abstention from testifying in his own behalf. If he's so innocent, why not get up there and say so? What's he got to hide?

After lunch Jim Phelan continued his testimony, basically the same story he had given me on tape. Jim warmed to the task and, despite Alcock's frequent objections, was soon into the meat of his story, aiming much of it in his hoarse voice directly at the jury and also pegging a look now and then at Sciambra, who sat, still impaled upon his memo, at the prosecution table no more than twenty feet in front of the witness. Phelan soon began zinging the Assistant D.A. with more than looks, in such testimony as "Sciambra said in the memo Russo had seen the man [Shaw] twice. I pointed out Russo testified [in the preliminary hearing] he'd seen him three times. I said I presumed Mr. Sciambra was capable of counting to *three!*" A low chuckle throughout the court as the back of Sciambra's neck picked up a shade of color. Then: "I said [to Sciambra] it was absolutely incredible that a lawyer could go to Baton Rouge and interview a potential witness to the crime of the century, write a 3,500-word memo and leave out the *crime!* I said if he heard Russo describe the plot and came back and wrote one *paragraph,* he would have to mention the *plot!*" Although Jim Phelan had told this story many times—to me, to the members of the press at Mom's Good Eats—his voice still rang with incredulity, as if he were now relating it for the first time.

Phelan got it all in—the memo, the meeting Russo was interested in having with Shaw, his fear of reprisals from Garrison if he changed his testimony, his interest in securing a lawyer, and his doubts in identifying Shaw.

When Jim Alcock began cross-examining Phelan, he knew he had a slugger on his hands. There was a grim determination in Phelan's brusque voice that indicated if unduly molested he would battle to the end. He did not mince words with Alcock. When the prosecuting attorney wanted to know how Phelan got the impression that a conspiratorial plot was not involved in Sciambra's memo, Phelan snorted and said, "I didn't get the *impression*—it simply wasn't there!"

James Alcock did his best with Phelan, suggesting that the writer's role as a participant in the NBC broadcast was not so much a report on Garrison's investigation as an effort to wreck it. Alcock often received an explanation to a yes or no answer that was more damaging than the question required.

ALCOCK: Did you tell Russo he would be a patsy if Clay Shaw were found not guilty?

PHELAN: Yes, sir.

ALCOCK: Did you tell him that Garrison would turn on him?

PHELAN: Yes, with explanation. Garrison told me in Las Vegas that "I'm going to get a lawyer [Dean Andrews], a close friend of mine, and I'm going to wreck him."

Alcock's last question to Phelan was: "Were you aware in your conversations with Perry Russo that you were being led on?" "Absolutely not," Phelan retorted.

Now one of those strange non sequiturs, endemic to trials and this one especially, took place when the defense called Mrs. Jessie Garner, who had been Oswald's landlady the summer of 1963. She was called solely for the purpose of testifying that Oswald had been neatly dressed and beardless, and that she had never seen Clay Shaw prior to his arrest in 1967. When she was shown photographs of Oswald to identify, there was also among them a picture of David Ferrie. She suddenly and unexpectedly said she recognized him as a man who had appeared at her home shortly after the assassination. When Mrs. Garner, a small elderly Southern lady who spoke in a soft voice, passed this comment, many members of the press apparently did not hear it. I thought I had, though. She claimed many people, mostly Federal agents, were in and out of her home immediately after the assassination. Ferrie had arrived, she said, and after a few minutes she determined he was not there on official business and asked him to leave. She dropped that bit of information and for some unknown reason neither the state nor the defense pursued this odd morsel of testimony, which certainly, one would have thought, would have been extended by the state as proof that Ferrie had at least known or been interested in Oswald. I asked several of my press pals after court if they'd heard Mrs. Garner say Ferrie came to her apartment and they all looked at me as if I were insane. I later checked the transcript and also asked Irvin Dymond, who confirmed that she had, in fact, said it, indicating the defense would be the last to pursue that testimony.

I wondered why James Alcock, ever watchful, had not pounced on this. Perhaps it was simply too late in the game to open up a whole new can of peas.

Late in the afternoon, Lieutenant Edward M. O'Donnell, an assistant commander of the homicide division of the New Orleans Police, was sworn in and took the stand. Along with Charles Appel and James Phelan, he was one of the most impressive witnesses of the trial. For here was a man on the same side of the fence as Garrison and his staff, testifying most damagingly against them. Asked by Dymond if he'd had a conversation with Perry Russo in June of 1967, Lieutenant O'Donnell said that he had, and that Russo had told him Shaw was *not* at the mid-September party at David Ferrie's.

DYMOND: Did you ask him why he testified as he did at the preliminary hearing?

LT. O'DONNELL: Yes, I did. He told me that when he got to court he had every intention of telling the truth and you [indicating Dymond] turned him on by asking if he believed in God, and this was a sensitive point for him. After you, as he said, turned him on, he decided he was going to bury you.

DYMOND: Bury me?

LT. O'DONNELL: Yes.

O'Donnell said Russo had wanted to know Garrison's full case against Clay Shaw to help him decide what to do. O'Donnell asserted he had told Russo the only way to decide was to question his conscience and tell the truth. Lieutenant O'Donnell testified that after his interview with Russo he went immediately to the District Attorney's office and reported the content of his interview to Garrison and James Alcock. He also later wrote a memo detailing his entire conversation with Russo and gave it to Jim Garrison.

Alcock, on cross, brought up a later confrontation O'Donnell had with Russo in the District Attorney's office, in which Russo denied, in front of Garrison, having told O'Donnell that Shaw was not at Ferrie's apartment. Alcock asked O'Donnell if he had not asked Russo if he would like to hear a tape recording of their original interview. O'Donnell admitted he had *not* taped their conversation but had used this ruse in an attempt to get Russo to repeat his original story to the District Attorney.

At this point court was adjourned for the day. The prosecution team did not look happy. It had been a strong day for the defense. The state's case was decaying, as a woman spectator put it, "into something not very nice." The stench was in the air. Around this time I see written in my notes, "Clean fingernails are becoming important." There was something dirty about sitting in the courtroom, even as a non-active participant—almost a contagious funky element to the proceedings, so that simple physical cleanliness took on importance.

That evening I dined with Jim Phelan and Clay at the home of Mrs. Edith Stern, who had recently returned to New Orleans. Jim was relieved and delighted that his turn on the stand had gone so well. We toasted him and spoke of the good day's testimony. That's as far as the conversation went. Although we all felt a case against Clay had not been proven, there was no shouting for joy. We had our eyes on the stolid jury. We were getting up to the line and I believe it was superstition more than anything that kept talk of the unknown to a minimum. We were walking on eggshells, Clay Shaw above all. He had been informed by his lawyers he would be taking the stand the following morning.

We assured him he would be a fine witness. He assured us he was not nervous. We all, of course, could not have been more inwardly calm had we been about to undergo brain surgery.

How do you tell a man good night, have a good sleep, when the next morning he will take the stand after two years of guilt by besmirchment and finally testify before the twelve men who will determine his future? When Jim and I dropped Clay off we simply said, "Good night, have a good sleep—you're going to be fine!" I had kept a rumor from him, one that I took to bed with me. It would not have buoyed him to learn that courtroom scuttlebutt had the state planning to put on seventeen rebuttal witnesses.

35

Clay L. Shaw

The courtroom was standing room only the following morning. Liz Garrison, in a simple pink wool dress, her dark glasses as usual pushed up to rest atop her blond hair, was on hand. Her husband was not.

Lieutenant O'Donnell, presenting a no-nonsense authoritative appearance equal to a regiment of Canadian Mounties, was back on the stand for the completion of his cross-examination. Alcock questioned him only about when he'd first spoken to any member of the defense. O'Donnell said this had been after the start of the trial, a few weeks earlier. "No contact prior to that?" asked Alcock. "No," replied O'Donnell, after which he was excused.

There was a brief recess, but everyone remained seated. The jurors were wide awake and talking among themselves. Tension spiraled in the courtroom, and I noticed that now as the end neared, men and women of opposing beliefs kept their distance. This extended to counsel for both sides and to the press, although there were not many who still favored the state. I kept as far away from the Rolfes as possible, mostly to avoid aggravation, and like a member of some herd of wild animals sensing trouble, or a baby whale, stayed close to Jerry Cohen, Moe Waldron, Hugh Aynesworth, Rosemary James and my friends John Mourain, Bruce Eggler, and Bill Block.

There was one brief spate of interim testimony when Arthur Davis, an architect, was called. His signature had been the next to last one on the page in the V.I.P. guest book before "Clay Bertrand." Mr. Davis testified he had been in the V.I.P. lounge around noon the date of the signatures—December 14, 1966. A few other men had been there but he had not seen Clay Shaw, with whom he was acquainted. He testified he was relatively sure his was the last signature on the page when he signed the book. He was asked the defense's old standby question: "Have you ever seen

Clay Shaw wearing noticeably tight trousers?" Mr. Davis replied, "No," and was soon excused.

"Clay L. Shaw." The calling of the name rustled up a fine buzz but as soon as Clay, wearing a conservative dark blue suit, white shirt and quiet tie, stood up to make his way to the witness stand, the courtroom pulled down to immediate and total silence.

He was sworn in and Irvin Dymond began a direct examination that lasted no more than a half-hour. From the very first, Clay kept his eyes on the jury as Dymond asked him preliminary questions about his schooling, early employment, war record and association with the International Trade Mart. Clay's answers to these questions were succinct, although they allowed him a chance to warm up and provided him with the longest answers of his direct examination; for once Dymond entered into the area of refuting the charges against him, the defendant's answers by the nature of their simple denial could be nothing but short.

DYMOND [showing him a picture of Lee Harvey Oswald]: Have you ever seen this person?
SHAW: I have never seen him.
DYMOND: Were you ever acquainted with him?
SHAW: I was never acquainted with him.
DYMOND: Have you ever talked to this person?
SHAW: I never have.

And so it went, Clay keeping his eyes fastened to the jury sometimes for as long as four or five questions in a row before glancing back to counsel.

Although most of the jurors were watching the defendant, they lowered their eyes now and then, probably because he was regarding them so consistently. There was one exception. Larry Morgan, one of the youngest and usually the most high-spirited and open, barely looked at Clay. He occupied the end seat in the front row, closest to the prosecution table and farthest from the witness chair. He kept his eyes straight ahead; only once in a while would he look at Dymond, and his glances toward the defendant were rare indeed. His face, to me at least, registered a combination of boredom and rejection. I quickly scanned the rest of the men; they were paying dutiful attention.

I suddenly glanced toward the prosecution table; Jim Garrison was still missing. It had never occurred to me that the District Attorney would default when it came time to hear the man he'd held captive for two years reply to him. It was not merely a matter of manners. This absence suffered from a final lack of grace at the moment of ultimate confrontation. I would have thought he would be there out of just plain curiosity. It was incredible that he was missing.

The defendant, now answering deliberately but not slowly, kept a good pace as he denied he'd known Perry Russo, had ever been in Clinton, had ever driven a black Cadillac to the lake to meet with Oswald, had ever seen Vernon Bundy. Then Dymond asked, "Do you recall the testimony of the state's witness, Charles Spiesel?" Clay broke into an easy grin and replied, "Yes, I recall him." The jury, though, wore no smiles; in fact they were looking at Clay Shaw as if to say, What's so funny about that?

On Clay went, categorically and firmly denying this allegation and that, never forgetting the jury, neither speaking down to them nor begging their indulgence, simply telling them straight-on that he had taken no part in any of the evil machinations charged to him by the state.

When Dymond reached the area of the President's speech at the Nashville Wharf, even Clay got to answer the question "Did you ever wear tight pants?" "No," he replied with casual distaste. After Clay had testified about being on the mayor's reception committee for the President, his lawyer asked if, before that time, he had ever met the man he was accused of conspiring to murder.

SHAW: In the spring of 1962, Chep Morrison [a former mayor of New Orleans] was appointed by President Kennedy as our Ambassador to the Organization of American States in Washington. Mr. Morrison very kindly invited me to be present in Washington when he was sworn in and I accepted the invitation. I met the President then.

DYMOND: Did you ever have any ill feelings toward the President?

SHAW: Certainly not.

DYMOND: Were you a supporter of his?

SHAW: Yes, I believed in him.

I thought, What a much better way to put it than if he'd said,

Yes, I voted for him. Dymond took him through every major detail of the state's case, ending with:

DYMOND: Did you conspire with David Ferrie and Lee Harvey Oswald to murder President Kennedy?

SHAW: No, I did not.

DYMOND: Did you ever at any time want him to die?

SHAW: No, I did not.

There was a brief recess. There had been no startling developments on direct examination, which is par for the course. It is the cross-examination that invariably yields the unexpected. Nina Sulzer tried a smile at me from across the corridor; it was struck down by concern and she then held up a hand with her fingers crossed.

Clay Shaw was awarded good grades for his demeanor on the stand by most of the press standing around; but then most of them were rooting for him.

By now we were used to the recesses running to three times the announced length; Judge Haggerty cut this one short, however, and Clay was sitting in the witness chair with nothing to do but fondle his glasses as the judge urged the bailiffs to call those still lingering outside. Clay glanced up now and then, checking his audience as the spectators crowded back into the courtroom. No one wanted to miss the team of Alcock and Shaw. One of the local reporters assured me Garrison would put in an appearance for the cross-examination, but as the courtroom settled down and the rear doors were closed, there was no sign of him.

James Alcock began matter-of-factly with a long series of questions regarding Clay Shaw's trip to the West Coast (his alleged alibi) in November of 1963: when the arrangements had been made for his various speaking engagements, by what parties, when he'd left, how he'd traveled, when he'd arrived in Los Angeles, whom he saw during his day's stay there, his hotel and activities before moving on to Portland. When testifying about his time in San Francisco, Clay said, "And I was sheduled to speak at the San Francisco World Trade Building on November 22 [the day of the assassination] and, needless to say, no speech was given that day."

This early questioning, so filled with comparatively incidental data, smacked of a civil suit, perhaps an insurance case, merely

establishing time, place, date, and companions. Clay replied forth-rightly, again directing most of his answers to the jury. Larry Morgan was still not paying attention to the defendant, but where he had previously ignored Dymond, he now kept an eye on Alcock.

The prosecuting attorney seemed to be getting into an interest-ing area when he asked Clay if he'd ever known anyone who knew David Ferrie. "Yes, sir, I did," Clay replied. Ears in the courtroom pricked up.

ALCOCK: Did you know a Mr. Layton Martens?

SHAW: Yes, sir, I did.

ALCOCK: Did you know he was Ferrie's roommate?

SHAW: No, sir, I did not.

ALCOCK: Do you know a James Lewallen?

SHAW: Yes.

ALCOCK: Did you know he knew David Ferrie?

SHAW: I did not.

There had been no previous mention of Clay Shaw's knowing anyone who had known David Ferrie, outside of Perry Russo's testimony, and this revelation was interesting, particularly in the defendant's open admission. But Alcock left the topic without further questions, going on to Clay's previous ownership of 906 and 908 Esplanade, the former being the second building to which Charles Spiesel had led the court. Clay admitted he had owned the building for approximately three years before selling it, in 1952, he thought, years before any facet of this case transpired. In re-spect to 908 Esplanade, the building next door, Clay had sold it, he said, in 1962 or 1963 but had never lived there. Alcock went on to Clinton and asked Clay if he knew anyone who owned property there. It turned out Lloyd Cobb, the president of the Trade Mart, owned a farm outside of that town. Alcock asked if he'd ever been to Cobb's farm and Clay explained that Mr. Cobb usually gave a large annual party, that he'd attended perhaps three of them in the last ten years, but he also said to get to the farm, one did not have to go through the town of Clinton.

The questions and testimony were consistently once or twice removed from the crime with which he was charged and sometimes verged on trivia.

ALCOCK: Do you remember a press conference after your arrest where you called Lee Harvey Oswald "Harvey Lee Oswald"?

SHAW: I recall the press conference.

ALCOCK: Was there any particular reason why you would call Oswald "Harvey Lee"?

SHAW: No, it was purely a mistake. [And James Alcock was off that and onto the President's speech at the Nashville Wharf.]

ALCOCK: Do you recall having heard Perry Raymond Russo say that he saw you toward the rear of the crowd?

SHAW: Yes.

ALCOCK: Were you with anyone?

SHAW: No.

ALCOCK: You separated yourself from the rest of the welcoming committee?

SHAW: Only about five of the committee were invited on the platform. The rest were left to fend for ourselves.

ALCOCK: Do you recall what you were wearing that day?

SHAW: I had on a business suit. I don't recall the color or the color of the tie.

Returning later to the Nashville Wharf, Alcock asked the defendant if he recalled the names of any of the people on the reception committee who were on the bus with him. Clay's reply was "That's difficult to do. It's been six years ago." Clay lifted his glasses to his mouth, touching the piece that goes around the ear to his lips, while he thought. "I think some members of the City Council. I recall Mr. Fitzmorris was . . . Mr. *Garrison,* I think, was on the committee, and I believe he was on the bus."

Instead of questioning the defendant about knowing Oswald in connection with David Ferrie, Alcock chose an incident far removed:

ALCOCK: Were you present at the Trade Mart when Lee Harvey Oswald was distributing leaflets in front of it?

SHAW: Yes, I was.

ALCOCK: Did you view it?

SHAW [after asking if he could explain]: Someone came into my office—I think it was in the afternoon—and said some nut is distributing leaflets in front of the building. I said I would go down and look into it. But I got a long distance call that kept me busy for a few minutes, and by the time I got down there, Mr. Oswald was gone. But I talked to some cameramen and newsmen.

Clay was asked, at various points in the cross-examination, if he'd known individual witnesses for the state: Charles Spiesel, Vernon Bundy, Perry Russo, the Clinton people, Mrs. Jessie

Parker, et al. The defendant invariably answered no, after which James Alcock would ask if there might be any grievance that would have caused, say, Vernon Bundy, to testify against him. Again the answer would be a simple no.

As the questioning continued, it was almost as if they were two actors working on an improvisation in order to warm up for the actual confrontation scene to come—as if they merely were getting the feel of each other, testing voice levels, manner of speaking, basic approach—but saving the crux of the dramatic conflict until they were on the air, or the curtain was up. Testing—one, two, three.

So far the questioning on Alcock's part was syllogistic, with the primary charge, that of conspiracy to assassinate the President, omitted and the possible secondary links of connection exploited at length.

We waited for the whammy, as Alcock continued to deal in subtle innuendo.

ALCOCK: Do you recall during the trial when Mr. Spiesel took the trial group to the French Quarter that you stood in front of 906 Esplanade and then said you wanted to stand on the neutral ground rather than in front of the building?

SHAW: Yes.

ALCOCK: Why did you want to stand on the neutral ground?

SHAW: Because I wanted to stand on the neutral ground.

ALCOCK: Was it because you didn't want to call attention to those buildings?

SHAW: No.

ALCOCK: You just wanted to get away from them?

SHAW: That's right.

[At times there was no sign of a connective link and even the subtlest implication was missing]

ALCOCK: In the summer of 1963, did you have a roommate?

SHAW: No.

ALCOCK: Did you have a maid?

SHAW: Yes.

ALCOCK: What was her name?

SHAW: Virginia Johnson.

ALCOCK: Was she with you the entire summer?

SHAW: I don't recall. She left after Hurricane Betsy. Do you recall when Betsy was?

ALCOCK: 1965.

SHAW: That was when she left. She was with me until after Betsy.

ALCOCK: Have you seen her lately?

SHAW: No, I haven't.

On it went; now members of the press began exchanging glances which said, What is this, when's it coming?

Alcock voiced very few leading questions. He did ask if Clay had ever used the name Clay Bertrand—no; if he'd ever been to Dallas—yes; if he'd ever driven a car similar to Jeff Biddison's— no. Some of the questions were extremely conversational in tone. Alcock: "Do you remember how long it took you to make the thirteen samples of your signature used in court this week?" Clay Shaw leaned back in his chair and lifted one arm to rest on the back. "Oh, ten to twenty minutes," he replied. James Alcock: "Was this limp you have today with you in 1963?" Clay crossed his legs and said, "I have had a back condition from an Army injury since 1946. Sometimes it makes me limp. Sometimes it does not."

Now the suspense in the courtroom gave way to a certain rest-lessness, until:

ALCOCK: Were there any features on the drawing made by Mr. Spiesel that were familiar to you?

SHAW: No.

ALCOCK: You were checking [when Clay had examined it in court] to see if it concurred with your memory of the apartment?

SHAW: Yes.

ALCOCK: You made no marks on the drawings?

SHAW: No.

ALCOCK: No further questions.

A silence of pure stunned surprise. The cross-examination had lasted sixty-five minutes and Alcock had not even asked Clay Shaw if he'd conspired to assassinate the President. The Shaw-ites in the courtroom were delighted, although the end had come as such a surprise they could hardly display it. The press, even those pro-defense members, were disappointed in the lack of sensationalism extractable. The Hanging Ladies were dyspeptic.

Clay Shaw had barely taken his seat when Irvin Dymond rose and said, "The defense rests." A few minutes later Judge Haggerty recessed for lunch.

Outside in the corridor, Nina Sulzer was beaming. "I don't believe it. Wasn't Clay marvelous? Alcock, too!" She laughed. Father Sheridan wiped off his brow. The press were not stampeding for the phones. I believe they were trying to figure out an angle. I visited Clay briefly. If he was happy, he was also somewhat stunned. "I don't know," he said, shaking his head, "it just went off like clockwork, no curves, no—I can't get over it!" He looked down at his desk, then back up. "How did I do? Did I come over all right?" "Like gangbusters!" I told him.

In a way the surprise of his cross-examination should not have been a surprise; nothing turned out as expected in this trial. The anticipated bumpy stretches turned smooth; the good times were invariably torpedoed—as they were this day.

36

Flying Lessons

When I had taken my seat in the courtroom after lunch, my eye was immediately drawn to a cluster of assistant district attorneys and several Garrison buffs standing together between the prosecution table and the jury box. They were grinning, laughing even; there were a few backslaps exchanged and as I watched I expected an arm punch or two. I was, for some reason, riveted to them. Alvin Oser and Moo Sciambra turned and looked out at the press section, regarding us with a full scoop of derision, topped off by an irrepressible snicker. They reminded me of a bunch of high school boys who had just put a dead cat in the ugliest girl's locker and were now waiting for her to open it.

Yet the idea that dirty work might be afoot seemed impossible; things had been going smashingly well for the defense. One had only to think back to Dean Andrews, Charles Appel, Lieutenant O'Donnell and Jim Phelan. Even the defendant had come off unscathed. The courtroom was filling up. Still the gaggle by the prosecution table clung together, locker-room style. Their delight was virtually uncontainable. The door to the chambers opened and Judge Haggerty took to his bench as court settled down and the prosecution called its first rebuttal witness.

Emmet Barbe, Jr., was sworn in—a totally unfamiliar name, and it was possible he might be a surprise witness. He soon turned out only to have been a foreman of the coffee company for which Lee Harvey Oswald had worked in the summer of 1963. Barbe testified he had fired Oswald on July 19, 1963. Marina Oswald Porter had testified that her husband had not told her he'd lost his job until about August 25th, before which he had pretended to go to work. Alcock ended on that note, and Dymond declined to ask Barbe even one question.

Eugene Davis was next called to the stand—the man whom Dean Andrews claimed Big Joe, the "butch," had introduced to him kiddingly as Clay Bertrand. Davis, a man somewhere in his late forties, ran Wanda's Bar and Gene's Grill and once you saw him, that is exactly what you'd say he did. He testified he'd first met Dean Andrews at the Rendezvous Bar on Bourbon Street (the alleged scene of the "fag wedding"). Davis acknowledged that Dean Andrews had done some legal work for him from time to time, but he denied that he'd called Andrews shortly after the assassination or that Big Joe had ever introduced him as Clay Bertrand. Alcock's last question was "Are you Clay Bertrand?" Davis replied he was not. (Actually Dean Andrews had never said Davis was, only that Andrews used that name as a cover-up for the bar manager.)

Irvin Dymond was not friendlily disposed toward Eugene Davis. He appeared to want to make him out a shady character.

DYMOND: Did you send him [Andrews] any business?

DAVIS: I imagine I sent him some business.

DYMOND: Mr. Davis, this is a criminal trial and I would ask you not to *imagine*.

DAVIS: I would say yes.

The tone of Dymond's questioning struck a strange chord. Compared to the gentlemanly manner and kid gloves with which Alcock had questioned the defendant himself, charged with a heinous crime, Dymond seemed to be laying into a completely secondary witness as if he were dirt. The lawyer then turned his attention to the Rendezvous Bar.

DYMOND: What kind of a bar was it?

DAVIS: It was like other bars.

DYMOND: Wasn't it a bar that was frequented by homosexuals?

DAVIS [shrugging]: All types came.

DYMOND: But wasn't it predominantly frequented by homosexuals?

Eugene Davis turned, squinted up at the judge and asked if he had to answer the question, which was in itself tantamount to answering it. Judge Haggerty said he did. Davis turned back to Dymond and spoke in a barely audible voice: "It was." The defense lawyer inquired if they had wedding receptions there—a question that brought smiles to the courtroom as one imagined the happy couples, Fred and Sheldon, Sam and George. Davis denied the wedding parties but admitted they had a lot of birthday celebrations. When Dymond got around to Big Joe, he asked

Davis if it were possible that Big Joe would have referred to him as Clay Bertrand without Davis's knowing about it or hearing her. Davis replied, "I would say I wouldn't hear a word she said without she asked me for a drink." By that time Dymond had struck a miniature portrait of Eugene Davis, his life and times, and he was soon excused. I believe this could be called nullifying a witness.

It was at about 2:30 P.M. when the name Nicholas M. Tadin was called. Tadin, a balding, heavy-faced man, with more than his share of jaw, identified himself as a business agent for a musician's union. Tadin, who appeared from the first either anxious about his testimony or else to have a chip on his shoulder, went on to tell Alcock that he had two sons, both of them deaf, and that in the summer of 1964 his oldest boy, 16 at the time, took flying lessons from David Ferrie out at the Lakefront Airport. Alcock asked Tadin if he'd ever accompanied his son to the airport. "Yes, sir. Quite a bit," Tadin said, with undertones of suspicion. Alcock asked why and Tadin explained that a photograph had been taken of his son and a young lady who was going to be a nun and David Ferrie; the photograph had appeared in a Catholic publication. As a result of this, Tadin testified, he'd received a phone call which had disturbed him greatly. "Were you concerned about any particular individual?" "Yeah," said Tadin, "Dave Ferrie." (The call obviously warned Tadin about Ferrie's homosexuality.) Nicholas Tadin maintained he didn't know quite how to go about telling Ferrie of his concern, but one day he finally broached the subject while the two of them were sitting in the coffee shop. "Dave, my boy's a young kid and I don't know anyone out here—" Tadin interrupted himself to say this was not the truth and went on to name several people he did know, then continued with his conversation with Ferrie, in which he claimed he'd told the pilot he hoped nothing would happen to his son, because if anyone did anything to hurt him, "I'll come back and fracture his jaw and if I have to bring a two-by-four with me, I'll do it." Tadin said Dave Ferrie assured him his son would be all right. "He's a dear boy," the witness said of his son, "and he [Ferrie] was the only one ever paid any attention to him."

All this had to be leading up to something and the court soon found out what as Alcock led Tadin back to the summer of 1964 and an occasion when he and his wife had gone to the airport together.

ALCOCK: Did you see Dave Ferrie on this occasion?

TADIN: Yes, I did.

ALCOCK: Did you see him with anyone?

TADIN: Yes, sir, I did—Mr. Clay Shaw.

My stomach contracted. Reporters, who had been listening casually to the preliminary testimony of Tadin, now whipped open their pads. The Hanging Ladies licked their chops and nodded their heads—about time someone got down to brass tacks again in this case.

Tadin testified he had seen Clay Shaw riding around Bourbon Street in his car before spotting him with the pilot. Returning to the airport, he claimed he had parked his car and was on his way to look for Dave Ferrie when he saw the pilot and Shaw emerge from a hangar door. Tadin said he recognized Shaw, who walked to his automobile while Tadin approached Ferrie and asked, "Do you have a new student?" Tadin testified Ferrie replied, "No, he's a friend of mine. Clay Shaw. He's in charge of the International Trade Mart."

"Was your wife with you?" Alcock asked. "Yes, she was," Tadin replied, at which point the prosecuting attorney said, "Tender the witness."

Now Dymond was faced with the toughest task that can befall a defense lawyer—that of questioning a surprise witness about whom he knows nothing. Was there anything in the man's past that would make him hostile to the defendant? Did he hold a grudge against one of the defense attorneys? Had he some connection with anyone in the District Attorney's office? Had any member of his family ever been in trouble, thus making him vulnerable and easily persuaded to giving testimony?

The lawyer, at first, tried to pin down the time of Tadin's sighting. The witness said it was sometime between June and August 1964. The lawyer inquired how Shaw was dressed. Tadin said he didn't remember and when Dymond asked if Clay Shaw had been wearing a hat, Tadin replied, "No, I'm sure he wasn't. My wife made the remark 'Look at the beautiful hair he has on his head.' " The defense lawyer asked if Tadin had ever been introduced to Shaw on Bourbon Street. The witness said he had not met him, but had seen him riding around in his car. "What kind of a car?" Dymond inquired. Tadin said it was a Thunderbird; when Dymond questioned him about the color of the car, Tadin described it as "light cream or white." (Clay had a black Thunderbird.) Asked how many times he'd seen Clay Shaw in the Quarter, Tadin told of a specific instance: "One night I saw him riding around with four young fellows in the car with him. I saw him once or twice after that." Tadin's tone left no question about what he thought of the sight of Shaw with four young fellows. Could this possibly be connected with his previous concern about his son?

Dymond wanted to know when Tadin had first contacted the District Attorney's office. "This morning," was the reply. Asked if he had been reading the newspapers and watching the television coverage, Tadin said he had, indeed.

DYMOND: Were you aware of the preliminary hearing?

TADIN: I sure was.

DYMOND: Did you know Dave Ferrie was one of the parties?

TADIN: Yes.

DYMOND: Did you know Clay Shaw was a party?

TADIN: Yes.

DYMOND: Did you know the question had arisen whether Clay Shaw knew Dave Ferrie?

Tadin testified that was the thing that disturbed him, the statements that Shaw did not know Ferrie. He said he'd told a few friends about the knowledge he had to the contrary, adding, "They got on me, said I better get down there."

DYMOND: Can you explain why you did not come forward during the preliminary hearing?

TADIN: It bothered me, but like a lot of people, I didn't want to get involved.

DYMOND: Did you want to get involved this morning?

TADIN: Yes.

DYMOND: Why did you want to get involved this morning—

Tadin began to answer, but the defense lawyer continued talking. Alcock objected, claiming Dymond wasn't allowing the witness to respond. Dymond explained he had not finished asking the question. End-of-the-trial tension blew this up into an argument and Judge Haggerty had the jury removed while "this critical point," as he put it, tongue in cheek, was argued. During this time Judge Haggerty dropped a remark to the effect "I know Nick [Tadin] a long time—we went to school together." (The wonder, in that case, was that Tadin had not contacted the trial judge with his information.) Irvin Dymond explained he had intended to ask, "Why did you want to get involved this morning when you didn't want to get involved two years ago?"

The jury was brought back in and Dymond put the question to Tadin, who explained that Wednesday night he'd been watching the television coverage of the trial, which included the comment that Shaw claimed not to have known Ferrie. "Hell," Tadin quoted himself as saying, "that's not true and I'm going to tell it."

Dymond, in his most level voice, asked Tadin if he ever lied. "Yes, sir," Tadin replied, "I guess we all do—but not in this case."

"That's all," Dymond said.

Alcock asked Tadin one question on re-direct: "Mr. Tadin, have you ever lied under oath?" "No, sir," was the reply. The witness was excused and a midafternoon recess was called.

The recess was a memorable one. The case had been going so well for the defense and now, at the last minute, here was this damaging testimony. True, it was not concerned with the major charge of conspiracy, but coming as it did so close on the heels of Clay Shaw's firm denial—still ringing in the courtroom—of knowing Ferrie, it reflected seriously upon the total credibility of the defendant.

If Tadin were to be believed by the jury, whose attention could not help be snagged by the drama of this last-minute surprise testimony, then there would be every reason to believe that the defendant had lied about his association with Ferrie and therefore attribute sinister connotations to the *reason* for the lie. As Judge Haggerty had remarked during the voir dire, "If you believe a witness has lied in one instance, then you have the right to disregard the entire testimony of that witness."

Outside in the corridor, merry jigs danced in the eyes of the opposition. Now it was perfectly clear what had been at the source of the joy the prosecution had exhibited earlier. The Rolfes were attempting to catch my attention. The Hanging Ladies were nearing orgasm. A nervous-looking woman—one presumed it was Mrs. Tadin—was seated on a bench by a window next to Mr. Tadin, guarded from a curious press, several members of whom would have approached her and her husband, had not Alvin Oser been standing there, satisfaction stamped on his face, blocking the Tadins off from all comers.

The out-of-town Shaw-ites—the gang from Mom's Good Eats—were gathered together attempting to rationalize Tadin's testimony or, failing that, at least trying to interpret its relative importance. Jerry Cohen's face was red. "Jesus," he said, shaking his head, "what a rough break! Jesus!" he repeated again. One heard such sentences as "Where did they come from?" "Christ, what timing!" "Who dug *them* up?" "I wonder if Dymond or Wegmann's had a chance to run a check on them?"

As we were hashing this over I suddenly thought about the oddity of a 16-year-old deaf boy engaged in flying lessons. Could a deaf person, I wondered, ever qualify for a pilot's license? Not that I doubted the boy had taken flying lessons—that would be easy to check—but there was a strangeness. How could he communicate with the control tower, how could he receive landing instructions, how could he hear other aircraft or the sound of his own engine if it were missing? When I voiced these questions, Hugh Aynesworth and several others suggested I transmit them to Dymond. I walked back into the courtroom. The defense lawyers did not have the luxury of relaxing during this recess; they were in a serious huddle in the working area of the court. While I scribbled a note and found a deputy to deliver it to Dymond the recess was ending.

By the time I returned to my group there was a dramatic clutch at the doors of the courtroom. Hugh Aynesworth and one of Garrison's supporters, a strong critic of the Warren Report, were squaring off. Hugh had hold of the man's shirt, right below the collar. Paula, Hugh's wife, held her husband in check, attempting to restrain him, and several other newsmen were gathered around as Aynesworth and the demonologist exchanged grinding unpleasantries between clenched teeth. They were soon joggled through the doors by the incoming crowd and the deputies' security frisk broke up the group before a punch was thrown.

I sat next to Paula, who was shaking she was so livid. Hugh's face was drained of color. They both loathed the man, who happened to be the individual in the tasteless nude photograph so freely accessible to trial buffs in New Orleans. The argument had come about because Aynesworth thought the Tadins were a last-minute dirty trick and took exception to the prosecution's gloating.

Now I heard Paula muttering under her breath as she dug around furiously in her purse for something. "Ah!" she said, coming up with a safety pin. She'd soon folded it up neatly in a piece of paper, had another reporter write the man's name on it, called over a deputy, and in her down-South accent and with a sweet smile asked, "Would you please be so kind as to deliver this to Mr. ——— up front? Thank you ever so much."

Word of her prank spread quickly from row to row, so that by the time the man in question had received Paula's anonymous valentine, opened it, stared for a long time at the safety pin, and then turned around with narrowed eyes to see who had sent it, he was met by a dozen pairs of eyes, wide with facetious innocence.

Soon Mrs. Tadin, a medium-attractive brunette who would have looked years younger than her husband had her face been allowed the freedom to relax, was on the stand. Her rather strident nervousness threw her into a pinched, ageless category of worrisomeness. She did not appear pleased to be in court.

Matilda Tadin testified that she made it her business to be at the airport every afternoon when her son took a flying lesson. Alcock walked behind Clay Shaw, placed a hand over his head and asked if Mrs. Tadin had ever seen the defendant before. She replied she had and went on to specify: "We were waiting for Dave [Ferrie] when they [Ferrie and Shaw] came out of a hangar. They were walking towards us. I passed a remark to my husband about how distinguished a man Dave was with." Mrs. Tadin said her husband told her who the man was, to which she replied, "Oh, no!" There was something more in her reading of that expletive than she gave words to. She testified Shaw walked past them and disappeared out of sight while Ferrie stopped to talk. Alcock asked if she'd spoken to Ferrie. "No," Matilda Tadin replied, "my husband spoke to him."

When Dymond took Mrs. Tadin over on cross-examination, she told the defense lawyer that she and her husband always made a point of being at the airport when their son took a flying lesson. Dymond wanted to know the relative positions of the two men as they emerged from the hangar. Mrs. Tadin said Shaw was walking to the side and slightly behind David Ferrie. The defense lawyer asked if Clay Shaw could have been as much as three feet behind the pilot. Mrs. Tadin said that was possible. Questioned about what Shaw was wearing, she could remember nothing except his hair and face. "I remember he was a distinguished-looking person."

Dymond also questioned Mrs. Tadin about her knowledge of the case. She admitted knowing of the criminal proceedings against Clay Shaw from the time of the preliminary hearing, but she had refused to come forward until this time, explaining, "I didn't want to get involved. I wouldn't be here today if my husband hadn't made me come." Dymond ended with Mrs. Tadin, concentrating upon the point that she had waited two years to come forward and even then had appeared on the very last day of the trial.

Alcock had only one question for Mrs. Tadin on re-direct: "Are you telling the truth?" Mrs. Tadin hiked her coat sweater up over her shoulders and then snapped, "Of course I'm telling the truth!"

Although it was only four o'clock, Alcock asked for an early recess, explaining some of his rebuttal witnesses were "snowbound in the East." Judge Haggerty agreed to adjourn court until Friday morning, telling the jury he would undoubtedly deliver the case to them for their verdict the following afternoon.

I spoke with Eddie Wegmann briefly after court; he shook his head over the Tadins and admitted that they might well harm Clay irrevocably. Brutal timing, everyone agreed. Clay, oddly enough, was the most sanguine, at least on the surface. And whatever surface he presented to us, to me, was not to be scratched. The terrible burden of the outcome was his and one respected whatever attitude he chose to display without questioning it. The knowledge that very soon now the case might well be over, the verdict in, the unknown known, had my mind completely locked. The Tadins kept running through my head. The possibility of even more surprise witnesses who had been "snowbound in the East," the closing arguments that could be so all-important to the jury, and the mass enigma represented by those twelve unreadable men crammed the brain and allowed for no peace.

37

No Further Witnesses

February 28 dawned crisp and clear, one day before the second anniversary of Clay Shaw's arrest.

The Criminal Court Building was jumping. In-for-the-kill spectators were lined up on the far side of the staircase as the press was passed in. Inside, Clay Shaw came to the railing to speak with several newsmen; I walked up to wish him well. He looked at me and sighed. "Well, we've gone through it as best we could. Any mistakes that have been made are done and in the past." He grinned and shrugged. "No use worrying over them." Again I awarded him the Purple Heart and the Croix de Guerre.

The first rebuttal witness called was Dr. John Nichols. The press could not believe the temerity of the state. But, surely enough, Dr. Nichols took the stand and proceeded to rebut the testimony of Dr. Finck and FBI agent Frazier. William Alford dragged him through the well-trampled territory of the autopsy, with Dr. Nichols again testifying lugubriously over the strenuous objections of Irvin Dymond that the man was expertising merely from what he had culled from viewing the Zapruder film.

Dr. Finck had testified the bullet that passed through the President's neck had not struck bone. Alford now brought this up to Dr. Nichols, who gave his opinion that a shot would have to have been fired at a "lateral angle of twenty-eight degrees" in order not to have fractured the cervical vertebrae. The contention implicit here was that a shot from the sixth floor of the Texas School Book Depository would not have been fired at that angle. This was, of course, pure supposition taken from the relative position of the President's head and body as viewed in the Zapruder film, but the mysterious "twenty-eight-degree lateral angle" was used later on in the day to such an extent by Alvin Oser in his part of the state's closing argument that it began to get laughs in the courtroom. Dr. Nichols had brought several drawings he had made, all of which illustrated his "twenty-eight-degree lateral angle," but when Alford attempted to enter them into evidence, Dymond objected, saying the drawings represented simply what the witness wanted them to represent. Judge Haggerty sustained the objection.

When Dymond took Dr. Nichols over he asked, not without a touch of the facetious, "Are you the same Dr. Nichols who was suing the government?" Dr. Nichols corrected the defense lawyer's tense: "I *am* suing the government right now." Dymond got right down to Dr. Nichols' rebuttal of the autopsy with a quick series of pertinent questions.

DYMOND: Did you ever examine the remains of President Kennedy?

DR. NICHOLS: No.

DYMOND: Did you ever see the X rays of the President's body?

DR. NICHOLS: No.

DYMOND: Have you ever seen the autopsy photos?

DR. NICHOLS: I have not.

DYMOND: Now, Dr. Nichols, is it a fact that you were a student of Dr. Finck? [This was new information.]

DR. NICHOLS: I attended three lectures which he gave and to that extent I am his protégé but he has refused to talk to me about this matter. I went to Washington to see him, but he rejected me.

Dymond ended his cross-examination of this doctor who had now been rejected by Governor Connally, the Federal government, and Dr. Finck.

The next rebuttal witness was a photographer from the coroner's office. He had enlarged a picture of the area known as the grassy knoll taken in Dealey Plaza at the time of the assassination. He had concentrated upon the right top corner of the picture, and when asked by Alvin Oser what he saw, he testified, "In my opinion . . . a man." Dymond objected strongly but the judge ruled the man had qualified as an expert and could testify as to his opinions. When Oser asked the witness what else he discovered in this picture, the photographer said, "He appears to be holding something."

Having seen the photograph, Dymond asked the witness in a voice laced with incredulity, "Are you testifying under oath in this courtroom that you are certain this is a man?" The witness replied, "I think it's plain to me." Then, as if this weren't strong

NO FURTHER WITNESSES   423

enough, he added, "I'm definitely sure." Dymond then inquired, "And he's holding a *gun?*" The photographer replied, "I didn't say that. I can't be sure. I don't know what he's holding." "But," Dymond asked in mock seriousness, "this is definitely a man?" The answer was affirmative and Dymond said, "That's all."

Oser passed fourteen copies of the blowup to the jury, who studied them for approximately five minutes as Judge Haggerty cautioned, "Don't discuss this with each other. Don't tell each other what you see. You can do that later."

I happened to see a copy of the photograph during the recess when I walked up to the railing to speak to a pressman—several Ladies of the Court were also examining a copy—and if what I saw in that photograph was a man, he was not an earthling. There is a light blur visible. I could not tell whether the light blur was holding a gun or not. That this photograph was introduced to rebut the Warren Report's theory that the President was shot from behind was sheer quixotry on the part of the state.

Jim Garrison was on hand to take active part in questioning the state's next and last rebuttal witness as the name Elizabeth McCarthy Bailey was called out.

The rear doors to the courtroom opened and a vision in aquamarine—dress and wide-brimmed hat to match—appeared, paused a moment, mouth in a half-smile and tugged over to the side at the prospect of the packed courtroom spread out in front of her, and then made a slow walking-from-the-hip Mae Westian entrance down the center aisle. Mrs. Elizabeth McCarthy Bailey, a fading blond beauty in her sixties, immediately perked up the courtroom. God only knows what she was going to testify to, especially when the District Attorney himself asked her to give her full name.

"Elizabeth McCarthy Bailey," she said, with a fierce Boston accent, immediately apparent from the one word "Mc-Kathy," and then went on to add, "but I use my maiden name in my business." One could sense, from the way the Hanging Ladies alone were sitting at attention, that the courtroom was expecting some manner of lurid testimony, and we were all disappointed—and surprised—when her business turned out to be "an examiner of questioned documents, called a handwriting expert."

Jim Garrison led the woman through her qualifications. "I have an A.B. degree, an M.A. degree and LL.B. degree. I have studied handwriting, erasures, typing, anything that goes to make up documents." She informed the court she had testified in thirty-eight states in the last thirty years and in three foreign countries.

An interesting courtroom slip occurred next when Garrison asked what famous cases she had participated in. Dymond immediately objected, and Judge Haggerty sustained him, saying, "Yes, I stopped you from going into the Lindbergh case with your expert!"—thereby, of course, bringing that information to the attention of the jury.

Dymond soon got to question Elizabeth McCarthy regarding her qualifications:

DYMOND: You stated you received an A.B. degree. Is that related to handwriting?

ELIZABETH MCCARTHY: No.

DYMOND: You stated you received an M.A. degree. Is that related to handwriting?

ELIZABETH MCCARTHY: No.

DYMOND: You stated you received an LL.B. degree. Is that related to handwriting?

ELIZABETH MCCARTHY: No.

Dymond asked the witness when and if she had taken a course in handwriting. She replied, "I took a course for three or four years around 1930." The defense lawyer inquired if it had been a formal school. "No," replied Elizabeth McCarthy, "but the man who taught it has written three or four books." She later explained that "as new problems come along, I have consulted with experts."

Elizabeth McCarthy Bailey was soon accepted by the judge as a qualified expert, and Jim Garrison began his questioning. He got right to the point, and after asking the witness if she'd studied the signature "Clay Bertrand" and the defendant's signature of his own name, Elizabeth McCarthy soon said, "It's my opinion that it's highly probable that Clay Shaw signed the name Clay Bertrand."

June and Dick Rolfe swiveled around and checked out our row to make sure we hadn't missed this.

Jim Garrison inquired of her reasons in reaching this conclusion, to which she replied, "I find all Mr. Clay's [sic] unconscious writing habits in the signature Clay Bertrand. He is a very facile writer with a light pen. All of these characteristics I find in the questioned exhibit. This is an unusually agile writer. The signatures are reasonably similar. In addition, I find similarities in all of the letters except the capital B. This may not be unusual. It's not unusual in this case to write in a different fashion than normal." She went on for a few more sentences, referring to Clay Shaw as "Mr. Clay" again and ending with "For all these reasons, because I don't find appreciable variance, I have concluded that the signatures are the same."

She had given scant specific evidence, whereas Charles Appel had gone over each letter. Garrison tendered the witness to Dymond, who inquired when she had first been retained in this case. "Yesterday," was the reply. Under further questioning Elizabeth McCarthy Bailey testified she'd arrived in New Orleans the night before, had first seen copies of the signature at that time in her hotel room and had viewed the originals only this morning. She had spent four or five hours studying the evidence and had not enlarged any of the signatures.

"What equipment did you use in reaching your conclusions?" Dymond asked.

"I'll show you," Elizabeth McCarthy replied, digging down into her purse and coming up with a pair of binoculars. "This binocular."

A reporter next to me had been busy writing and when he heard this he looked up, but by this time she was replacing the binoculars in her handbag. *"What* did she use?" he whispered to me. "Binoculars," I told him. "Binoculars?" he repeated. "That's what I *thought* she said." He started to write and then looked back up at me. "You mean regular binoculars that you use . . ." His voice trailed off. "Yes," I replied.

DYMOND: I see, are you being paid to testify?

ELIZABETH MCCARTHY [laughing]: I hope so, it's my business. Mr. Garrison didn't mention a fee. He told me just to submit a bill.

DYMOND: You do expect to charge a fee, don't you?

ELIZABETH MCCARTHY [laughing again]: Naturally, that's my business.

The witness was soon excused and performed a slow undulating exit with just as much style as she had exhibited upon her entrance.

"No further witnesses," said Jim Garrison.

The state and the defense handed the judge statements stressing points they believed should be included in his charge to the jury. Judge Haggerty announced that once the jury had retired for their verdict they could neither examine the evidence exhibits nor have any testimony read back to them. I had always heard of juries calling for part of a transcript to be read to them and mentioned to someone nearby that the judge's statement seemed unusual. "This is Louisiana!" was the reply.

Judge Haggerty announced that closing arguments by both sides would be presented at the beginning of the afternoon session, and then he adjourned court. Walking out into the corridor, I heard one of the Hanging Ladies say, "Thank goodness for those Tadins." I could not get the possible effect of their testimony out of my mind.

I popped in quickly to see Clay in his office. The realization that we were into the home stretch hit me and I wanted to see how the odds-on favorite to lose was making out, because, believable or not, the betting odds were stacked for a guilty verdict. Clay said, "Well, here we go, this is it, eh?" "Yes, this is it." Irvin Dymond and the Wegmann brothers were in and out; I knew Irvin was going to be busy working on his closing speech to the jury, so I soon left.

Jerry Cohen, Moe Waldron, Paula Aynesworth, another fellow from the Los Angeles *Times* and I went to lunch at the Rowntowner Motor Inn. It was my choice in the hopes we might catch a glimpse of the jury in their natural habitat and perhaps gauge their mood, if that was possible. The choice was a bad one. The jury was not eating in our dining room and the service was brutal.

I was suddenly struck by an intense attack of pessimism that descended upon me like a noxious cloud. Jerry, Moe, Paula and I could always joke; I suddenly found myself unable to say a word to them, outside of a side comment that I would like to strangle the waitress. Jerry and Paula were as concerned about Clay as I was, but they were putting up a front. Moe was, I believe, the only one among us who was quietly optimistic; Moe also played his cards close to his chest.

As we sat there and were finally served our food, I could do no more than pick over my plate, as my brain picked over the Clinton Folk, James Hardiman, Jessie Parker, Perry Russo, Vernon Bundy, the Zapruder film and the Tadins. Pershing Gervais also returned to mind and his theory of the importance of the closing arguments

—all this shrouded by the vast mystery represented by those twelve men in the jury box.

I went numb, at first, and then I felt a hotness behind my eyes. Good Christ, I thought, I think I'm going to cry! No, not in front of my friends, all of whom were making small talk, carrying on like Londoners in the Blitz. I was further sickened at my lack of control and, I suppose, by what we are taught is, or should be, our manliness. The surprise of this shameful attack added to the panic. I told myself I was experiencing this sensation because of my impotency to do anything about what might well turn out to be a bum rap. That did not help matters. The heat was increasing. Something had to be done and immediately. I quickly excused myself to go to the men's room, where I promptly threw up.

When I returned to the table, Moe Waldron, with the perception of the Dalai Lama, said in a gentle throwaway voice and without even looking at me, "Don't worry, Jim, it's going to be all right." What I supposed to be my hidden emotions were clearly dripping down the front of me like a gallon of red paint.

38

One Candy Bar

When court resumed, Irvin Dymond filed his second motion for a directed verdict, maintaining that the undisputed testimony of Dean Andrews showed there was no such person as Clay Bertrand. There was not even time to make a bet on the judge's ruling this time, it was denied so quickly.

James Alcock began his argument for the state at 2:28. He started off by thanking the members of the jury for their time and patience. Moving back and forth in front of the fourteen men, he spoke in a clear voice with unflagging energy that lent conviction to his assertions. "The state carries the heavy burden. It must show proof beyond a reasonable doubt. At the outset of this trial, we made an opening statement in which we outlined what the state intended to prove during the course of the trial."

Now Alcock's tone changed, the niceties were over, and one could feel the attack about to commence.

"The defense counsel also made an opening statement in which they made a promise . . . a promise to show that Clay Shaw not only did not conspire with David Ferrie or Lee Harvey Oswald, but that he never knew David Ferrie or Lee Harvey Oswald." Alcock looked down at the floor, then back up at the jury. "That promise was broken. It was shattered and the pieces were left lying in the dust of Clinton, Louisiana."

The prosecuting attorney then pointed to Clay Shaw, who sat listening intently, smoking a cigarette. "That man was proven a liar and unworthy of your belief. If he lies on one material issue, you can disregard all of his testimony." When Alcock pointed to the defendant, Clay looked him right in the eye, not with hostility or comment of any sort in his expression, merely looked him in the eye, as if to say, Yes, I'm Clay Shaw, that's me.

Alcock claimed the Clinton people had nothing to gain by coming forward. "They were not seeking publicity or notoriety."

He went on in detail through the testimony of each one, not at
boring length, merely picking the most salient points and high-
lighting them. In the midst of this he touched on Jeff Biddison's
automobile, saying, "The state is not wedded . . . to the proposition that the black Cadillac belonged to Jeff Biddison, a friend of
the defendant's . . . but it is known that Biddison had a Cadillac. We're not saying necessarily it was Jeff Biddison's automobile.
No one ever got the license number of the car to let us say
positively." From his tone I thought Alcock might add: But it was.
When Alcock had finished with the Clinton Folk, he again turned
and pointed at Clay Shaw. "The defendant is discredited, he is
proven a liar and unworthy of your trust!"

Now it was time for Vernon Bundy. Alcock began by saying, "I
do not apologize for Vernon Bundy or any other witness. You take
your witnesses as you find them. It would be nice to have all bank
presidents as witnesses. But that is not possible. You don't find
many bank presidents who associate with the likes of Lee Harvey
Oswald." He went through Bundy's story, touching on Clay's
"limp," going on to say the defendant admitted he had a limp in
1963. Finished with Bundy, Alcock once more pointed a finger at
Clay Shaw and reiterated, "When the defendant states he knew
neither of these men [Oswald and Ferrie] this proves he was a
liar, and unworthy of your trust."

The first few times he referred to the defendant, Alcock pointed
directly at him, arm thrust out and eyes following the line of his
aim. Clay Shaw met each accusation with a solid return look that
was a challenge in itself. After a while, Alcock's accusatory thrusts
became more perfunctory and toward the end they often went
unaccompanied by even a glance.

"Again the state does not apologize for its witnesses . . . including Charles Spiesel." James Alcock related the crux of Spiesel's
testimony, making specific mention of certain points that co-
incided with Perry Russo's testimony—the hostile sentiment, the
use of a high-powered rifle, and flying the assassin to safety. Asking
why Spiesel had remembered the defendant, Alcock answered his
own question: "Because he's not the type of person you can
forget . . . his physical stature, his hair, his general appearance.
Clay Shaw is not easily forgotten once you've seen him." Alcock
also touched on the coincidence of Spiesel having led the court to
a building that had at one time been owned by the defendant:

"The probabilities of that happening again are almost incalculable." Alcock then warned the jury that Dymond would undoubtedly spend a good deal of time on Charles Spiesel, and he wanted them to keep in mind that "he has never been convicted in his life. He has a responsible job in New York and his employer permitted him to leave his work to testify. He told you of his education and his military service. Charles Spiesel was telling the truth!"

The state's attorney next entered the testimony of Perry Raymond Russo. Alcock told the jury, "I don't deny Russo characterized it [the party at Ferrie's] as a bull session, [but] the only characterization that's important is *your* characterization!" He hammered away, insisting that everything that had been said in the conversation at Ferrie's had been carried out. Toward the end of Alcock's discussion of Russo's testimony, the prosecuting attorney's voice rose in pitch, at times cracking with the intensity of emotion he was conveying to the jury. "Mr. Dymond will say that this case will rise or fall on Perry Russo's testimony. Essentially, I agree." Alcock claimed Russo's testimony that he had seen the defendant at the Nashville Wharf was corroborated by the defendant himself, when Clay Shaw admitted being there.

It was corroborated, but it had nothing to do with the conspiracy charge, yet Alcock made it sound important in testing the believability of Perry Russo.

Alcock also maintained that Russo's testimony was corroborated by the mailman James Hardiman when he testified that he'd delivered letters to Clem Bertrand at Jeff Biddison's address at a time when Clay Shaw was not staying at his own home.

Next James Alcock claimed that Mrs. Jessie Parker of the V.I.P. room was telling the truth when she testified to seeing Clay Shaw sign the guest book as "Clay Bertrand." He reminded the jury that two handwriting experts had been called in and they disagreed, but Charles Appel had come into the case with a "fixed opinion," feeling an injustice was about to be done. The state's witness was being paid, said Alcock. "She did not have a fixed opinion."

When he arrived at the Tadins and their testimony, Alcock admitted he was disappointed they had not come forward with their knowledge of the case earlier, but he did not want that to detract from the importance of their testimony, which placed David Ferrie and Clay Shaw together at the Lakefront Airport.

Alcock turned back to Clay Shaw and said, "This man was proved to be a liar again and again and he is unworthy of your belief."

Toward the end of his argument, Alcock touched briefly on Oswald's former landlady, Mrs. Jessie Garner, and now mentioned her testimony that David Ferrie had shown up at Oswald's former apartment directly after the assassination. "How did David Ferrie know where Lee Harvey Oswald lived in New Orleans?" Alcock asked.

Before concluding, Alcock mentioned Marina Oswald and said she had known little about her husband's activities and, indeed, had been kept in the dark by Oswald when it came to what he did and who his friends were.

Noting that he would not go into the testimony of the defense witnesses at this time, but would be back with a rebuttal argument after the defense had presented their closing statement, Alcock declared, "I think the state has proven its case . . . that the defendant is an absolute liar . . . that he is absolutely guilty. In this case I ask for a just verdict and I hope that verdict will be guilty as charged."

The time was 3:50. Alcock had spoken for approximately an hour and twenty-five minutes. There was a recess. Out in the corridor, the consensus was that James Alcock had done an excellent job, with what he'd had to work with. If he was faulted at all it was for his attempted rehabilitation of Charles Spiesel. Alcock had thrown himself into the task with energy and all serious conviction. No matter what the jurors were thinking of the case, it was obvious from their faces that they respected the prosecuting attorney's courtroom ability. Even feeling as I did, I had to admire Alcock's talents, if not the use to which they were put.

The recess was a long one. When we returned to the courtroom we understood why. The Alvin Oser Art Gallery had been set up. Easels stood at attention, the surveyor's plat and the mock-up of Dealey Plaza were back with us. Color photographs taken from the Zapruder film were attached to one easel, which also featured the large aerial photograph of Dealey Plaza; a three-by-four-foot blowup of a page from the autopsy report was affixed to the witness stand and an enlarged photo of the bullet found at Parkland Hospital was even tacked to the judge's bench.

The sight of all this brought groans from the press. We knew we were in for another high school debating round on the failings of the Warren Report. This would have been far less objectionable to many of us if only the state would come up with an alternative that would hold water.

Alvin Oser, the bright relishing glint of attack on the enemy shining in his eyes, began his part of the state's closing argument a little after 4:30 in the afternoon. His strong point, and certainly that part of the single-assassin theory most open to critical speculation, was the timing of the shots—supposedly three—that gunned down the President and wounded Governor Connally in such a short flash of time. There are probably many who consider Lee Harvey Oswald's feat of accurately aiming and firing the two shots that struck the President (leaving aside, for a moment, the possibility of a third shot, hit or miss) in something less than six seconds remarkable, and Oser concentrated on this aspect at first, to cast suspicion on the Warren Report.

Still, a refutation of the Warren Report scarcely placed conspiratorial blame for the crime in the lap of Clay Shaw. The big question hanging over the courtroom was: How did the jury feel about the alleged chain of connection?

Six Seconds in Dallas, a book by Josiah Thompson, subtitled "A Micro-study of the Kennedy Assassination Proving That Three Gunmen Murdered the President," puts forth conclusions contrary to the Warren Report with much more effectiveness than any demonstrated during the Shaw trial. Vincent Salandria had assisted Josiah Thompson and is given credit by the author for his contributing knowledge. Salandria was also advising the prosecution in opposition to the Warren Report, and it was therefore puzzling that their presentation lacked cohesiveness and clarity. This failing was not the opinion of one or two of us but a majority opinion of the attending press. I believe part of this was due to Oser's attitude of complete ridicule and his heavy-handed use of sarcasm. Of all the attorneys participating in the closing arguments, Oser resorted most to theatrics—and to such an extent that the eye was constantly drawn to the performance rather than the substance of his lines.

At times Oser raised his voice close to the level of a temper tantrum as he stalked back and forth in front of the jury, and in the process he managed to make entire phrases unintelligible; at other times he would lean in close to the first row of jurors and lower his voice so it was barely audible. When he spoke of the autopsy, his voice was a sledgehammer of scorn as he continually referred to Colonel Finck as a "quote pathologist unquote." His derision was as thick as the icing on a cake and just as sticky. The colonel, no matter what one thought of the autopsy, was an accredited pathologist. Oser brought this courtroom overkill to almost every phase of the case he touched upon, finally calling the FBI re-enactment of the assassination "the monumental flop investigation re-creation in the history of the world!"

At times he thumped against the autopsy work sheet of the President's head with a pointer, causing a newsman to whisper, "Jesus, I wish he wouldn't do that!" He placed a toy red car on the mock-up of Dealey Plaza and otherwise was busily engaged in working his act with a maximum of props. He named Dr. Nichols as the only expert witness who testified with an opinion based on a complete viewing of the Zapruder film. (Many other witnesses had studied the Zapruder film, among them FBI agents Frazier and Shaneyfelt and Colonel Finck. Their opinions were based on more than the film—all three of these experts had examined the evidence firsthand—so that Oser's statement would seem to have been a self-defeating remark, but he issued it proudly.)

If there was any doubt that the state would show the jury those frames of the Zapruder film depicting the President's head wound, it was soon dispelled when Oser set up the slide machine and ran them off once more—it was, incredibly, the tenth or eleventh viewing. But this time there was no surge to the left by the press or the spectators. The Zapruder film had clearly been overexposed.

Heavy reliance on eyewitness testimony from Dallas did not cloak Oser's theories with credibility; the testimony in itself was so split by divergencies that any thoughts of it only added to the general confusion.

Although Governor Connally has contended that he was not hit by the same bullet that struck President Kennedy in the back, but by another shot which had by necessity to have been fired outside of the minimum time it would have taken for the *same* gunman to have fired a second shot, the state had not, in the end, chosen to use the Governor and his wife as witnesses. One would have thought the Governor's testimony, had he not changed it, would have been most helpful in bolstering the state's contention that there was more than one rifleman working Dealey Plaza that day.

District Attorney Jim Garrison entered the courtroom and took a seat as Alvin Oser wound up by claiming that the wounding of Kennedy and Connally by separate bullets, the head wound of the President coming from the front, and the "twenty-eight-degree lateral angle" made it clear that there were "three people with three guns." He added, "It is mathematically and scientifically impossible for one person with one gun to perform the results that happened in Dealey Plaza." He concluded: "And where have we heard the word 'triangulation'? It seems strange that a triangulation of gunfire was talked about and discussed in the conspiracy, and agreement was hatched in the presence of the defendant—Clay Shaw!"

At the end of the hour we had spent with Alvin Oser, the defendant's name had finally been mentioned.

It was nearly 6 o'clock when Oser finished. There would have to be a recess, if only to clear the courtroom of all the exhibits—photographs and easels, mock-ups and sketches—that now crowded the space. Judge Haggerty announced a dinner break from 6 to 7:30. Irvin Dymond would give the defense's one and only closing argument at that time, followed by whatever rebuttal argument the state wished to indulge in. It was understood that Jim Garrison would deliver the final words on behalf of the state.

The strange technicolor twilight glow that suddenly makes us aware of living in a color world spread through the courthouse as lights were switched on and advertising signs outside on Tulane and Broad Streets penetrated the wide marble corridor with their flashing rays of blue and red and green. Reporters disappeared into the pressrooms to file their stories. The building was soon cleared. No one wanted to dawdle over dinner and miss getting a seat for the big evening show.

I made my way down to Clay's small office. There he sat behind his desk. "If I could ever use a martini"—he grinned—"it's now." We spoke for a while. Father Sheridan was in and out as were Nina Sulzer, his attorneys, a few other friends and reporters, all nervously checking on him. No one stayed long enough to settle down and look him in the eye; no one wanted to transmit the terror of a possible adverse verdict.

I would like to have stayed and spent the dinner hour with him, but I could not do it. Although my deep funk of the luncheon recess was past and I was now able to go about my business without the threat of tears or vomiting, I was still infected by pessimism. Not the best of liars, I would have found it difficult to tell him I knew he would be turned free in a matter of hours, when I did not believe it. My eyes would be the dead giveaway. You had to make any token comment about his freedom and be able to divert your attention immediately to other matters.

Jim Phelan and Bruce Eggler appeared. By this time there was only an hour left and we decided to go out in search of a hamburger. Before leaving Clay's room, I asked if there was anything I could do for him, anything I could get him. He leaned back in his chair and thought for a moment. He suddenly swung forward and smiled. "You know what I'd really like, Jim? I think I'd like a candy bar—if you can find one someplace?" "Sure," I said and quickly made my exit.

Jim, Bruce and I walked several blocks up Tulane to a small luncheonette. One harassed cook-waitress was attempting to take care of the eight or ten of us in there, among them Judge Haggerty's minute clerk, George Sullivan, as silver-haired as the judge.

My cheeseburger had no taste—it could have been made of cardboard and painted and I would have chomped it down. My nerves were switched to numb, suspended in anticipation of what seemed the most important decision I'd ever awaited.

When we'd finished eating we stopped by the counter to speak with minute clerk George Sullivan, a man who had spent the best years of his life in a courtroom and who was retiring after this trial. A wise old bird, it was said. We asked his opinion of the outcome. He hesitated for a moment, then told us he thought the judge would give the case to the jury that evening, even if it ran into the late hours. We asked him again. George Sullivan looked down at his plate, then up at us and leveled: "I've been betting lunches for conviction—" Before we could comment, he quickly added, "—on the basis of the jury. Alcock and Dymond both wanted a different class of man for the jury and when it got down to the line, Alcock won out. From juror number four through fourteen, every man who got on wanted on. By that time, the rules were laid out. There were only two reasons to be on it. A morbid streak, which might well lead to a morbid verdict—or those who want so badly to be a tiny part of history. In the latter case, their moment in history would be extended much more by conviction of the accused of this crime of the century and on through subsequent appeals, than by acquittal." He paused. "At least that's the way I see it. But I'll tell you something, this is one of the toughest juries to read I've ever come up against."

The walk back to the fortress was not the most carefree stroll of my life. There were signs of heightened activity outside the Criminal Court Building: batteries of television and newspaper cameramen speckled the sidewalks in front of the large mobile television units, with their night lights blazing, parked at the curb. Spectators and reporters pulled up in cabs and private cars. Small clusters of people hung about the steps as we climbed up and entered the building.

Opening the door to the Sheriff's offices, I suddenly remembered the candy bar. It had slipped my mind completely, no doubt as a result of our chat with George Sullivan. I tore out of the building, down the steps, and trotted several blocks on Tulane toward town until I came to a small motel. There was a candy vending machine in the lobby—a nickel machine, and you know the size of a nickel candy bar these days. I wanted to buy two but I had only a nickel and a quarter in change and there was no one at the desk. I settled for a nickel Baby Ruth about the size of my thumb. I hurried back and ran up the steps, now lighted and swarming with people.

I entered Clay's small office—he was still sitting behind the desk—and presented him with his closing-night present. What a sad-ass token! He took it, smiled and thanked me. Then we had to laugh. It was now time for him to leave with his guards for the courtroom upstairs. He stood up and said, "Well, it's been a high old time, hasn't it?"

The top floor of the Criminal Court Building bristled with the skittishness of an opening night, but not a Broadway opening night. The spectators waiting to be let in jostled and shifted like displaced persons at one side of the staircase. It reminded me of opening night of the high school senior class play. Perhaps it was the setting—the marble corridor was not unlike a corridor to be found in an institution of learning; the various courtrooms strung along it were the classrooms; the impressive paneled doors of the District Attorney's office at the far end certainly led to the principal's office; the assistant district attorneys now emerging from it and clicking down the hall with their briefcases and sheafs of paper were his instructors, our teachers. There was also the novelty of being inside this building at nighttime with artificial lights that gave it an entirely different look, a strangeness, the same strangeness of a special occasion one felt in a school building at night.

Once back inside the courtroom, pressed shoulder to shoulder with my fellow writers in the fifth row, I found that my nerves had been replaced by the pure electricity of the event itself. This was it, the culmination to thirty-four days in the courtroom, to say nothing of the two-year procession getting there. Trial history was being made this evening and we were all part of it. And so I psyched myself up, rapped with myself to the point where I could say, Yes, no matter what happens I am here, I will observe, inhale this happening so I can tell of it and perhaps help by the simple fact of being alive and wide open to the event.

39

"... And Don't Make a Mistake"

Clay was seated at the defense table; counsel for both sides was present and accounted for. The wives of all the principals were also on hand. This was a big family night. Clay rose and stepped back to the railing to speak with his two cousins, Suzanne Day and Mrs. Tulip Atkins. He was standing to the side of the gate when the jury was led in from the dinner break; they walked single file and solemn-faced down the aisle and passed through the gate, no more than three feet from the defendant. Clay kept his eyes on them. Not one of the jurors glanced his way.

Irvin Dymond began, as Alcock had, by thanking the jurors and asking for their indulgence. Emphasizing that the law allows the defense only one closing argument with no rebuttal, Dymond made certain the jury understood that just because the defense would not be heard from again did not mean they had nothing to say. It only meant they were not permitted under Louisiana law to return in rebuttal. (This rule supposedly balances the advantage given to the defense in presenting their testimony last.)

The defense lawyer claimed the Shaw trial was unique in his experience. Contending it was based upon "innuendoes, veiled accusations, and hints of guilt and wrongdoing," he maintained that a criminal trial is no place for innuendo and, throwing a glance at the prosecution table, added, "If the state means to charge the Federal government with fraud, deceit, dishonesty and every other dishonorable word you can mention, let them come forward and do so ... the Warren Commission is not on trial. This case is against Clay L. Shaw."

Dymond's argument, though backed with as much inner conviction as Alcock's, smacked more of an informal man-to-man talk with the fourteen men. He took his time, allowed for pauses, indulged in the freedom of time for thinking, consulted his legal pad of notes, and did not keep up the pace the prosecuting attorney had maintained. Nor did Dymond's closing statement suffer from this approach; his relaxed style lent his words the ease of complete confidence in his subject.

"I am an American," the lawyer said, "but I cannot, will not accept the idea that the Warren Commission and the Federal government engaged in one giant fraud as the state would have you believe. I cannot and will not buy it." He informed the jury he would be the first to admit the Warren Commission did not do a perfect job. He paused, taking a long look at the fourteen men, who were paying him the same attention they had accorded Alcock. "Have you ever stopped to think how inconceivable it is that the Federal government, the Secret Service, the FBI, the Dallas Police, the Justice Department, the doctors at Parkland, the doctors at Bethesda, that entire group in the autopsy room, would all get together and try to make Americans believe that one man fired that gun from the sixth-floor window of the Texas Book Depository? What earthly reason would there be for doing that? If there is one, I don't know it. I call on you as intelligent, mature men to decide if it's possible that this many people right down the line could be parties to this fraudulent scheme, yet more than five and a half years later not one person has come forward and said, 'I want to tell the truth, I told a lie'—not one!"

Dymond wanted no mistake made about who was on trial. He told the jurors that although they were not lawyers it did not take a lawyer to decide the difference between a contest over the validity of the Warren Report or a contest over whether Clay Shaw sat in an apartment with David Ferrie and Lee Harvey Oswald and plotted to kill the President. He implored them to keep in mind at all times that "a verdict for Clay Shaw does not constitute a stamp of approval on the Warren Commission Report."

Using an easygoing soft-sell brand of humor to chip away at the state's case, he reminded the jury that Garrison's opening statement had heralded the FBI agent Robert Frazier as a ballistics expert who would testify as an expert state witness. "But when they got him down here they obviously didn't like what they heard and we decided to use him." Dymond went on to say that, after vouching for the expertise of Frazier, "the state now comes before you and says his re-enactment of the assassination was a monumental flop."

The defense lawyer moved on to Dr. Pierre Finck and said he thought Dr. Finck suffered somewhat on the stand because of his language difficulty but added he doubted if anyone could "question the professional integrity of that little doctor." When Dr. Finck was turned over to the state, Dymond cracked, "they pounced on him like a mountain lion on a chained goat!" A smile crossed Dymond's face and he shook his head. "I was quite amused to hear Mr. Oser this afternoon describe Dr. Finck as a 'quote pathologist.' Had he forgotten the testimony of Dr. John Nichols to the effect that he was a student under Dr. Finck at the Armed Forces Institute of Pathology? And then Dr. Nichols takes the stand and contradicts the testimony of Dr. Finck and Mr. Oser sees fit to adopt Mr. Nichols. It seems peculiar to me that the good Dr. Nichols would pay money to be taught by someone who knows less than he does." Dymond told the jury there were many men who sought to rise to fame and fortune over the dead body of the President and, referring to Dr. Nichols, added, "It looks as though we might have another member of the club." He noted a final distinction between these two doctors when he said, "Dr. Finck did not come to his conclusion by looking at the Zapruder film or firing slugs through the wrist of a cadaver. This little doctor from Switzerland is one of the men who actually performed the autopsy on the body of our President."

He went on to the FBI photographic expert Lyndal Shaneyfelt, saying the jury might have forgotten by this time, but Shaneyfelt had been the state's expert witness, that they vouched for his credibility by putting him on the stand and when he testified, along with Dr. Finck and Agent Frazier, that in his opinion the President was hit by two bullets fired from the rear, then the state pulled an about-face and chose to ridicule his testimony. "There you had the testimony of three expert witnesses—add to that about three thousand more people and I'll tell you how many lips had to be sealed to defraud the American people!"

Dymond was soon interrupted by Alcock when he commented that the Warren Commission had interviewed 25,000 witnesses. Alcock claimed he was going far afield in his argument and the judge sustained his objection. Dymond took it well and went on to say, "The state has put on quite a pageant in their attack of the Warren Report. They brought before you a handful of hand-picked witnesses, some of them mercenaries, some of them wanting to get their names in the paper, others whose motives we'll never know—brought them here to dispute the findings of the Commission." He paused and a gleam came to his eye as he looked over the jury. "One of you gentlemen, during the voir dire, told me you'd seen the movie *Rush to Judgment*. Anyone who has seen this movie will recognize the state's presentation and may well mistake it for a rerun of *Rush to Judgment!*"

This got a gentle laugh from the press section, which drew annoyed glances across the aisle from several Hanging Ladies, as Dymond went on to reiterate that "Clay Shaw has been brought here for no other purpose than to create a forum for the presentation of an attack on the Warren Report."

The defense lawyer's voice rose in volume now when he commented that there were certain things in the state's case that hit him between the eyes: "One of these and one of the most obvious acts of desperation, one of the clearest indications of how the state feels it must grasp at straws that I've ever seen in my life—and I'm referring to the *guts* the state has in standing before you and trying to rehabilitate and ask you to accept the testimony of the witness, Charles I. Spiesel." Dymond shook his head, almost sadly, then looked up at the jury and asked, "I'm sure you remember Mr. Spiesel?" A few more smiles from the jury, and a good-sized laugh from the spectators. The defense lawyer shook his head again. "This poor little paranoid bookkeeper, who came down here to New Orleans thinking people were following him, hypnotizing him, causing him to lose his sexual potency. What kind of a good faith prosecution, what kind of a legitimate presentation would try to get up here and con you gentlemen into buying that man's testimony?" Now Dymond's voice exhibited outrage. "My God, gentlemen, this is a court of law, a court of justice! You don't ask a jury of men to consider testimony of that type in deciding the fate of one of their fellow men! It is incomprehensible, it is beyond pardon!" He pulled his voice down, adding, "Mr. Alcock seemed to indicate he thought I might try to attack the memory of this poor little man. I'm not trying to attack his memory at all. I think Mr. Spiesel thought he was telling the truth—he's the most obvious paranoid case I've ever seen in my life."

Perry Russo earned a large share of the defense's closing argument, and Dymond began by looking the jury square in their collective eye and saying, "Mr. Alcock is dead right! I *will* tell you that the case stands or falls on Perry Russo's testimony and I'm amazed they will admit it."

When the defense lawyer spoke of Russo's contention that Dymond had forced him into saying Sandra Moffitt and Lefty Peterson accompanied him to the party, he stepped back a pace and asked the jury, "You've sat here for some thirty-eight days and heard me examine and cross-examine witnesses, and I ask you, Have you ever seen me badger any witness or force any witness or blackjack any witness into saying what they didn't want to say?"

Dymond maintained that Russo changed his story solely because Sandra Moffitt and Lefty Peterson denied having been at the party and that Russo was caught in a lie. He reminded the fourteen men that if they thought any witness had testified falsely on a material fact for the purpose of misleading them, they were entitled to disregard all of that witness's testimony. Even if they believed every word of Russo's testimony, he went on, they could still not find Clay Shaw guilty of conspiracy. The defense lawyer then picked up a transcript of Russo's testimony and read excerpts from it, concentrating on the "bull session" aspects, the witness's denial that he ever sat in on a conspiracy, and his assertion that he did not hear the various parties say they would murder the President. He read at length from the transcript and when he finished, he summed up the testimony of Perry Russo by saying, "That is why there is no way on God's earth a guilty verdict can be rendered."

Dymond then proceeded to the Clinton people. He questioned their failure to come forward until some five years after the alleged happening. He called their identification of the defendant the result of picking him out of "a one-man line-up," and pointed out the discrepancies in their testimony: "One said he wore a hat, one said he didn't wear a hat, and the one who said he had a hat identified him by his gray hair. One said he wore a white shirt, one said he had on a dark shirt." Dymond reminded the jury the Clinton people had remembered the time of the alleged visit because it was a cold day, one even testifying to a roaring fire. The lawyer brought up the U.S. Weather Bureau records, commenting,

"During this period there was only one day when the high was under ninety degrees and it went down to eighty-nine or eighty-eight that one day."

Noting the solidity of Lloyd Cobb as a witness, Dymond called him one of the leading citizens of New Orleans and said it was unthinkable that he would take the stand and perjure himself on behalf of the defendant. He also spoke of Goldie Moore's corroboration of Cobb's testimony that there was no possibility of Clay Shaw having gone to Clinton during the period of time in question.

The defense lawyer was at his best when attacking the opposition's case, however, and this he did with relish when he lashed into the testimony of Vernon Bundy. "Mr. Alcock said he would not apologize to you for having put Bundy on the witness stand. Well, let me say that now I, as an officer of the court, *will* apologize to you for your having been subjected to that. Gentlemen, the fantastic story that this convicted thief, this admitted liar, this inveterate and veteran narcotic addict told on this witness stand is worthy of *Alice in Wonderland.*" He reminded the jury that Alcock maintained Bundy had two things in mind when he went out to the seawall—"shooting those narcotics and avoiding the law." The lawyer hammered away at the folly of Bundy's having left the safety of his twenty-five-room house to carry his dope out to a public place and shoot it. "The state will get up here and say he didn't want his mother to find out. Would Bundy rather be caught by his mother [who knew of his habit] or the police?" Dymond asked. He reminded the jury Bundy had testified there was a vacant mile of beach on either side of him and yet the state asked them to believe Clay Shaw would pick the exact spot where Bundy was sitting to meet with Lee Harvey Oswald, with whom he was supposedly engaged in an assassination plot.

Dymond left the testimony of Vernon Bundy soaking in a pool of scorn and went on to the mailman James Hardiman. "I cannot in all sincerity stand here and tell you I think he was lying. I think he thought he was telling the truth, but I can say he was 100 per cent flat dead wrong." The lawyer suggested that the key to the postman's testimony was the fictitious name he'd made up when he asked if Hardiman had delivered mail to a "Cliff Boudreaux" and the postman replied that he had and recently.

"Well," said Dymond, tapping his forehead, "that name came from right up here—just like the name 'Clay Bertrand' came from Dean Andrews' head."

A laugh in the courtroom. In the jury box, Mr. Hebert, the retired fireman, smiled so broadly he was forced to put a hand to his mouth. Dymond remarked it wasn't necessary, however, to rely on tricks of cross-examination to refute the state's case. He introduced Jeff Biddison's testimony, which completely contradicted that of the postman. Dymond indicated he thought the state had cast veiled aspersions on Biddison's testimony by nature of his long friendship with Shaw. The lawyer asked the jury, "Don't some of you men have friends of twenty years' standing, but does that mean you'd get up on the witness stand and raise your hand and tell a lie for them?"

Regarding the alleged use of the name "Clay Bertrand," Dymond summarized it this way: "Can you believe by any stretch of the imagination that if Mr. Shaw had actually conspired to kill the President that he would still be using the name 'Clay Bertrand' in 1966. If so, I think the state is wrong in trying to send him to Angola [the state prison]—they ought to send him to Jackson [the state mental hospital]."

To counter the state's contention that Clay Shaw's trip to the West Coast was an "overt act," Dymond went over the letters and testimony that proved the trip was made to fulfill speaking engagements that had been solicited by others. He concluded: "If you are here in New Orleans, why are you going to the West Coast to get an alibi for a crime that's committed in Dallas? Once again, gentlemen, it does not add up."

A deepening layer of incredulity coated the defense lawyer's voice when he spoke of the V.I.P. guest book. "By this time," he said, "it's December 14, 1966, President Kennedy murdered, the name 'Clay Bertrand' made public by the Warren Commission and played up in the New Orleans papers because of Dean Andrews, and Clay Shaw goes out to the airport and goes into the V.I.P. room for no purpose other than to sign his name 'Clay Bertrand'! Once again, gentlemen, that would be the act of a complete lunatic, if you are to believe the state."

Speaking of the two handwriting experts, Dymond said he did not know too much about the professional qualifications of the state's witness but he could certainly vouch for the professional reputation of "the old gentleman we put on the witness stand." The defense lawyer asked the jury, "Can anybody make any man on this jury believe that the state hadn't tried to confirm Jessie Parker's statement by an expert in the field of handwriting before they called this woman yesterday? . . . The answer is they had to have tried other experts and could not get one to say what they wanted him to say—that's the reason they finally found a last-minute killing." Dymond concentrated on Charles Appel, referring to him as "one of the foremost handwriting experts in our country," and maintaining he had conducted a scientific, proper and thorough examination. When the defense lawyer mentioned Appel's many years with the FBI as head of their handwriting analysis, he said, "Oh, I knew when we brought him down here we were going to step into a buzz saw as soon as he said 'Federal Bureau of Identification'—as you know the state's going to make you believe we have a bunch of bogeymen, a bunch of real culprits in the FBI and the Secret Service. Be that as it may, gentlemen, this man hasn't been with the FBI since 1948." Dymond insisted that Appel had not appeared in New Orleans with a "fixed opinion," but had come down without pay and was willing to testify in the interests of justice. "Mr. Appel gave you a firm opinion that that was *not* Clay Shaw's signature," the lawyer noted. "The lady wouldn't go that far, she said there is a great probability it is."

After consulting his notes for a few moments, Dymond said, "I think this is an appropriate place to mention Mr. and Mrs. Nicholas Tadin, the two witnesses that took the stand yesterday evening—as a team—and stated to you they had seen Clay Shaw out at the Lakefront Airport in the company of David Ferrie . . . Gentlemen, you'd be justified in asking me whether I think these two people are lying or whether I think they're mistaken. I think they're probably mistaken. I don't know why they should lie, but I will say this—whatever the husband is doing, the wife is doing the same thing. That poor woman [she was due for lenient treatment, thus meriting an adjective] was scared to death when she got on that witness stand. 'I came here because my husband told me to.' " Dymond nodded in agreement with her predicament. "And frankly I don't blame her, if a girl had a husband walking around talking about hitting people in the jaw with two-by-fours, I can well understand her fears."

Dymond then touched upon an interesting facet of the defense's basic case: "First of all you must realize, it has to be clear to you, that this case would have been much safer to defend by saying Clay Shaw knew David Ferrie. Don't you know we realized there was always the possibility of someone coming forth like this and claiming to have seen them together? No doubt about that. But our defense, gentlemen, has been based on truth. It has been based on truth from scratch and Shaw did not get up there on the stand and I did not get before you and tell you he knew David Ferrie because he didn't know him. The point I'm making is that if he did know him, our defense wouldn't have been any different—it would have been a lot safer."

Returning to the Tadins, he said, "Were you to even consider the testimony of these two Tadin people, what do you have to do then? You have to accept the testimony of Perry Raymond Russo—and, gentlemen, if you can accept that, it is beyond me. If you don't accept that, what difference does the Tadins' testimony make?" Dymond went on, once more, to question Clay Shaw's common sense in allowing himself to be seen at a public airport less than a year after the President's assassination with a man he had supposedly conspired with. He now used one specific member of the jury when he said, "I'm sure some of you gentlemen know something about this Lakefront Airport [Larry Morgan worked there as an aircraft mechanic], that had Mr. Shaw been out there with Ferrie, at a crowded airport, that other people wouldn't have seen them and come forth, is inconceivable." He finished with the Tadins by mentioning their failure to come forward until the last day of the trial, adding with a shake of his head, "I cannot buy their testimony!"

Dymond then returned to the prime target area, Perry Russo, and hit upon every possible inconsistency in his testimony. The defense lawyer drew his biggest laugh of the evening when he paused at one point, wagged his head, grinned and said, "Gentlemen, I hate to beat a dead dog, but here it comes—the Sciambra memorandum!"

Hefty Mr. Powe and quiet Mr. Hebert of the jury smiled at this; the other members looked to the spectator and press sections to see what the cause of the laughter might be.

Now Dymond pulled down to his most anecdotal level and spoke to the jury as if they were all lounging around the men's locker room together. "You know," he said, bending toward them, "when I was sitting here listening to the arguments of the other counsel, I leaned over to Billy Wegmann and I said, 'Billy, my God, I thought of something, we gotta be stupid.' Billy said, 'What?' I said, 'Sciambra claims that Russo told him about the conspiracy meeting and identified a picture of Clay Shaw on the 25th of February and Clay Shaw wasn't arrested until March 1st.' Billy said, 'Damn, you're right.' " Dymond stepped back from the jury, held his hands out in front of him and said in his loudest voice yet, *"Where were they, gentlemen?"* Then a drop back to his conversational tone. "Does that answer the question about when Perry Russo mentioned anything about this? If it doesn't, the D.A.'s office sure dragged its feet from the 25th of February to March 1st in arresting a man they claimed conspired to assassinate the President of our United States!"

He delved into the great omission in the memo and this time the analogy was, "It's like a man going lion hunting, shooting a lion and a rabbit, then coming back and writing a story and leaving out the lion." Now Dymond posed a question to the fourteen men and gave them a choice: "I hesitate to bore you with a reading of this entire Sciambra memo, so rather than do that, rather than eat up your time in that way, I'm going to ask you if there is any man on this jury who has any doubt as to whether anything about a conspiracy meeting, Clay Shaw, Clay Bertrand, Clem Bertrand, is in the memo? If you have any doubts, I'll read it to you *word for word!"*

Dymond allowed for a brief pause, sighed and said, "Apparently you don't." We sighed also, sighs of pure relief.

Before leaving the memorandum forever, he pointed out the contradiction between the time Sciambra said he finished the memo—seven to ten days after beginning it on February 27—and the date Garrison gave it to Phelan to read in Las Vegas on March 5. The time span did not jibe. "Not according to my arithmetic," said Dymond.

Dymond's brain had to be striking on all pistons now. Fifteen or twenty times during his argument, he either prefaced or concluded a statement by saying, "The state will get up after me and tell you . . ." "But, keep in mind . . ." etc. He did this now when he spoke of the many damaging statements Russo had made to Phelan. "Oh, I can hear the state now, getting up and screaming

to you that Jim Phelan was an employee of the National Broadcasting Company, part of the Eastern Establishment, that horribly
sinister outfit, just wanting to destroy his case."

Jim Garrison had just entered the courtroom. He strode quietly
down the aisle to the prosecution table at the beginning of this
sentence, perhaps accounting for Dymond's use of "his case." The
lawyer continued. "The state will try to destroy Mr. Phelan's
testimony in that way. Thank goodness we have it backstopped,
backstopped by someone whom they have no way of destroying
and that is one who is traditionally one of their own prosecution,
Lieutenant O'Donnell." Dymond concentrated on the similarity of
Russo's damaging admissions to both men. When he mentioned
Lieutenant O'Donnell's statement that Russo had told him he had
every intention of telling the truth in the preliminary hearing
until Dymond "turned me on when he asked if I believed in
God," the defense lawyer questioned the jury once again: "Would
I make you mad if I asked you if you believed in God . . . would
it be enough to make you get on the witness stand and lie, to send
an innocent man to the penitentiary?" In his summation of the
state's star witness, Dymond spoke in a quietly grave voice: "I
submit to you that Perry Russo is not a normal individual."

Now approaching his wind-up, Dymond reminded the jurors
where the entire Garrison investigation had originated. "It all
came from the mind of Dean Andrews," Dymond said. Again
anticipating the state and throwing an affectionate adjective to
the man in question, Dymond said, "Gentlemen, if you have ever
heard any vitriolic screaming, any debasement of a witness, any
criticism of an individual, you are going to hear it when they get
up here in rebuttal on Dean Andrews. Let me say this, this little
fat man with the peculiar manner of talk got on that witness stand
a ruined lawyer, bared his chest, said, 'Do to me what you may,
I'm going to tell the truth now.' And I don't think there's a man
on this jury who does not think he told the truth. This man has
lied before, there's no doubt about that, no question in the world,
but believe me when he took that witness stand and did what he
did, he rose, in spite of his faults, to heights that may not be
attained by many people in this courtroom."

If Irvin Dymond could be faulted anywhere in his closing
argument, it would be in this Ode to Dean Andrews, and the

extraordinary praise of that last sentence, which was rewarded by a small derisive chuckle from even the pro-Dymondites in the audience. James Alcock had earned the same reaction with his attempted rehabilitation of Charles Spiesel.

Dymond now dropped his voice and spoke only to the jury. "Gentlemen, after Dean Andrews came out with the Clay Bertrand story, we had the Warren Commission Report and along with the Warren Report, came the scavengers, came those who would like to make a living out of it, those who would like to pick it to pieces at the cost of undermining the confidence of the American people in their very government. And that, gentlemen, is when the fur began to fly. Andrews had started it, Russo wanted to get into the news, with the aid of a little hypnosis, a little sodium pentothal, and what other prompting we don't know, came forth with the story you heard at the trial. . . . Newspaper reporters gathered from every corner of the globe. I dare say it has been one of the most highly publicized cases in the Louisiana legal annals, possibly the annals of any state. And, gentlemen, I tell you now that the entire world is waiting to find out whether you twelve men can convict a man on this *Alice in Wonderland* situation, on a group of facts that were scrambled together. If you check back and just remember when each of these witnesses showed up at the D.A.'s office, you have to wonder, *What did they have when they started?* They had practically nothing, nothing except Russo.

"They're waiting, gentlemen, to see whether a man can be convicted in a situation such as this, in a production such as this, where a patsy was picked in order to provide a forum for an attack on the Warren Commission and the Warren Report. You've seen the extent to which the state has gone in attacking the Warren Report here. Gentlemen, for a while Clay Shaw had become the forgotten man. You had to actually stop—for days—and remember who was on trial! I just hope that you will not permit the issue to be confused by this big production. *Rush to Judgment* would have been a lot easier and a lot cheaper—but don't let it confuse you. Just remember what this man is charged with, remember the state, by its own admission, says its case has to stand on the testimony of this liar, Perry Russo, a man who is an admitted liar from the witness stand. Separate these two issues and there's no way you can go wrong. If our law permitted, I think that in doing this you wouldn't have to leave this jury box to return a verdict of not guilty.

"The state is going to come back before you and wave the Dallas flag again, going to talk about the Zapruder film again. That's a horrifying film and that's the reason I squawked about you seeing it ten times. I'd never seen it before and I was shocked and horrified by it. But don't let that make you lose sight of the basic issues in this case."

The defense lawyer then uttered the last sentence of his two-hour presentation: "The twelve men who pass on this case are actually going to create history in our country. Gentlemen, I implore you not to make a mistake. This man is as innocent as any one of you fourteen men sitting here on this jury. To find him guilty, you have to believe an admitted liar. I don't think you can. I'm confident you can't."

Irvin Dymond paused briefly and there was the slight tremor of hope and fear in his voice as he said, "I ask you to vote your conscience, follow the law—and don't make a mistake."

40

Ask Not What Your Country
Can Do for You . . .

A badly needed recess. Court had begun at 9 that morning, and it was now 9:40 in the evening. The air in the courtroom was stale from constant refiltering through the lungs of the packed crowd. By now the smog of cigarette smoke drifting from the working area permeated the entire courtroom. The pure sweat of the attorneys, the sweat of the effort to win, the sweat of tension among the press and spectators and, I'm afraid, the stench of the entire case hung in the air—deadening it. We were jammed ten and eleven to a row, where we'd usually been nine, with room for at least a shoulder move. A restless, itchy fatigue took hold. The entire group was wilting fast. By rights, we all should have been sent to the showers.

The corridor provided some relief. There was general agreement that Dymond's closing argument had been perfectly geared to the jury at whom it was aimed. It had been a man-to-man logical, low-key, heartfelt presentation, and the defense lawyer was soundly praised for it.

Back in my seat, surrounded only by friendly press folk, there was talk of betting. I would not bet on the verdict, but we soon organized a jury foreman pool. We wrote twelve numbers on twelve slips of paper representing the seating arrangements of the men, chipped in a dollar and each picked one from a hat. I drew the impassive-appearing, always well-groomed Mr. Tatum, seated nearest the witness chair. Although I knew I would not win, I would have been hard put to pick the foreman had I been given a choice. I probably would have considered the corpulent Mr. Powe, young Larry Morgan, or Mr. Ricks, the Negro schoolteacher. For seniority, Mr. Hebert, the retired fireman, would have been my choice, but I somehow did not think seniority would count with this group.

I had not realized that all phases of the state's case were due a rebuttal, but when court resumed, Alvin Oser stood up. His rebuttal, mercifully, took less than fifteen minutes.

The Assistant D.A. claimed Dymond had talked a great deal about the state's lawyers being un-American and added, "But not one word about our [Dealey Plaza] witnesses and what they said on the witness stand."

Dymond stood up immediately and interrupted Oser: "The purpose of rebuttal is to speak about what I *did* say, not to speak about what I *didn't* say!"

Oser continued, at one point asking, "And what about the twenty-eight-degree lateral angle?" This earned a ripple of snickers and would have earned him a custard pie had the ammunition been available. From the looks exchanged in the press section it was apparent that at least half a dozen had the impulse to stand up and shout: Yes, what *about* the twenty-eight-goddamn-degree lateral angle?

When it came time for James Alcock to give his rebuttal, this earnest, hard-hitting bulldog ventured into the nearest thing to evangelist oratory we'd seen during the trial. His voice was now strident, at times cracking with emotion—the emotion of persuasion and wanting to win—as he refuted the defense lawyer, now stepping in close to the jury, now ducking back from them, using his hands more than he ever had and using them well to emphasize his points.

He delivered scorn in equal measure right back to Dymond, with such sentences as "His answer to Clinton—the weather, sixty degrees and raining!" As if to say, If that's all he can come up with to destroy the testimony of all the Clinton people, that's pretty sad.

Alcock flipped the defense lawyer's words back in his face when he touched on the character of the state's witnesses. "Something struck me, as Mr. Dymond said, right between the eyes. The state finds its witnesses where it can. Has Charles Spiesel ever been convicted of perjury? No. Dean Andrews has—twice before a grand jury . . . and they have the gall to put Dean Andrews on the stand!"

In the nearest Alcock came to overt "dirty pool" he circled the personal life of Clay Shaw when he said he found it almost impossible to believe the defense had not put on one character witness to testify for the defendant. He maintained that Lloyd Cobb and Goldie Moore "were careful to say they did not associate with the defendant after working hours." And then he dipped into sinister innuendo: "You have the picture of a man who lived a Dr. Jekyll and Mr. Hyde existence—a respected businessman by day, by night consorting with people like Ferrie and Lee Harvey Oswald."

The prosecuting attorney, keeping his voice and energy high in his last few active minutes of final pleadings, touched on Bundy, the mailman, Mrs. Jessie Parker—"She took an oath on this stand and said she saw him sign the book!" He claimed again that the defense's handwriting expert had a "fixed opinion," that Nicholas Tadin had recognized the defendant from having seen him on Bourbon Street and positively identified him. Speaking of Mrs. Tadin, he admitted she might have been nervous but contended, "She wouldn't lie on the stand under oath." Alcock did precisely what Dymond had predicted when he spoke of Jim Phelan and "the NBC scavengers, who tampered with the state's case because"—and now he ducked a step toward the jury and pointed a finger at them—"they didn't trust *you,* a jury composed of a cross section of the community, to decide."

James Alcock, who had so ably ramrodded the state's case and without whom the presentation engineered by Jim Garrison would have trickled down the drain, now faced the fourteen men, his voice cracking from pure residual strain, and concluded, "Whatever your verdict is, it is yours—you have a right to a verdict that concurs with your conscience . . . I am asking you for a just verdict and I plead that that verdict will be guilty—as charged."

The jurors' respect for James Alcock was spread over their faces like a mudpack. He had spoken less than a half-hour. And now, if rumors of the finale were true, we were to be accorded a valedictory address by the District Attorney, who had lent his personal benediction to the case no more toward the end than he had his presence at the beginning.

And, indeed, here came Jim Garrison, in person, immaculately turned out as usual. In fact, he was the only person in the courtroom who did not look frayed at the edges. No Dial soap for him. But then he was the only one present who had not put in a full day. It was five minutes to eleven when he stood and turned to face the jury. Holding the pages of his closing statement in his large hands, he was the quintessence of soft sell.

If you had listened word by word and not strung them together for connective sense, you would have believed you were listening to the Bible or a simple translation in laymen's terms of the science that permitted our flight to the moon. Putting the words into sentences, however, made the spine prickle in recognition of the subtle and insistent villainy of persuasion Jim Garrison was injecting into the jurors' brains. He was pumping them up with the authority, not necessarily to send a guilty man to prison for "the crime of the century," but investing them with the divine power to save the United States of America. He was tempting them to punish The Government, to slap the wrists of Power in High Places by delivering a token verdict of guilty—but a verdict that would hardly be token to the defendant. I find it a completely shocking statement, a monument in the art of the smooth con job, but one delivered with the low-key assurance of complete truth that, of course, raised the level of danger in it to frightening proportions.

Jim Garrison brought his ample backside to rest on the edge of the prosecution table, thereby adding ease of body to the complete ease of delivery, as he said:

May it please the court. Gentlemen of the jury:

I know you're very tired. You've been very patient. This final day has been a long one, so I'll speak only a few minutes.

In his argument, Mr. Dymond posed one final issue which raises the question of what we do when the need for justice is confronted by power.

So, let me talk to you about the question of whether or not there was government fraud in this case—a question Mr. Dymond seems to want us to answer.

A government is a great deal like a human being. It's not necessarily all good, and it's not necessarily all bad. We live in a good country. I love it and you do, too. Nevertheless, the fact remains that we have a government which is not perfect.

There have been indications since November the 22nd of 1963—and that was not the last indication—that there is excessive power in some parts of our government. It is plain that the people have not received all of the truth about some of the things which have happened, about some of the assassinations which have occurred—and more particularly about the assassination of John Kennedy.

Going back to when we were children . . . I think most of us—probably all of us here in this courtroom—once thought that justice came into being of its own accord, that virtue was its own reward, that good would triumph over evil—in short, that justice occurred automatically. Later, when we found that this wasn't quite so, most of us still felt hopefully that at least justice occurred frequently of its own accord.

Today, I think that almost all of us would have to agree that there is really no machinery—not on this earth at least—which causes justice to occur automatically. Men have to make it occur. Individual human beings have to make it occur. Otherwise, it doesn't come into existence. This is not always easy. As a matter of fact, it's always hard, because justice presents a threat to power. In order to make justice come into being, you often have to fight power.

Mr. Dymond raised the question: Why don't we say it's all a fraud and charge the government with fraud, if this is the case? Let me be explicit, then, and make myself very clear on this point.

The government's handling of the investigation of John Kennedy's murder *was* a fraud. It was the greatest fraud in the history of our country. It probably was the greatest fraud ever perpetrated in the history of humankind.

That doesn't mean that we have to accept the continued existence of the kind of government which allows this to happen. We can do something about it. We're not forced either to leave this country or to accept the authoritarianism that has developed—the authoritarianism which tells us that in the year 2039 we can see the evidence about what happened to John Kennedy.

Government does not consist only of secret police and domestic espionage operations and generals and admirals—government consists of people. It also consists of juries. And cases of murder—whether of the poorest individual or the most distinguished citizen in the land—should be looked at openly in a court of law, where juries can pass on them and not be hidden, not be buried like the body of the victim beneath concrete for countless years.

You men in these recent weeks have heard witnesses that no one else in the world has heard. You've seen the Zapruder film. You've seen what happened to your President. I suggest to you that you know right now that, in that area at least, a fraud has been perpetrated.

That does not mean that our government is entirely bad; and I want to emphasize that. It does mean, however, that in recent years, through the development of excessive power because of the Cold War, forces have developed in our government over which there is no control and these forces have an authoritarian approach to justice—meaning, they will let you know what justice is.

Well, my reply to them is that we already know what justice is. It is the decision of the people passing on the evidence. It is the jury system. In the issue which is posed by the government's conduct in concealing the evidence in this case—in the issue of humanity as opposed to power—I have chosen humanity, and I will do it again without any hesitation. I hope every one of you will do the same. I do this because I love my country and because I want to communicate to the government that we will not accept unexplained assassinations with the casual information that if we live seventy-five years longer, we might be given more evidence.

In this particular case, massive power was brought to bear to prevent justice from ever coming into this courtroom. The power to make authoritative pronouncements, the power to manipulate the news media by the release of false information, the power to interfere with an honest inquiry and the power to provide an endless variety of experts to testify in behalf of power, repeatedly was demonstrated in this case.

The American people have yet to see the Zapruder film. Why? The American people have yet to see and hear from the real witnesses to the assassination. Why? Because, today in America too much emphasis is given to secrecy, with regard to the assassination of our President, and not enough emphasis is given to the question of justice and to the question of humanity.

These dignified deceptions will not suffice. We have had enough of power without truth. We don't have to accept power without truth or else leave the country. I don't accept either of these two alternatives. I don't intend to leave the country and I don't intend to accept power without truth.

I intend to fight for the truth. I suggest that not only is this not un-American, but it is the most American thing we can do—because if the truth does not endure, then our country will not endure.

In our country the worst of all crimes occurs when the government murders truth. If it can murder truth, it can murder freedom. If it can murder freedom, it can murder your own sons—if they should dare to fight for freedom—and then it can announce that they were killed in an industrial accident, or shot by the "enemy" or God knows what.

In this case, finally, it has been possible to bring the truth about the assassination into a court of law—not before a commission composed of important and powerful and politically astute men, but before a jury of citizens.

Now, I suggest to you that yours is a hard duty, because in a sense what you're passing on is equivalent to a murder case. The difficult thing about passing on a murder case is that the victim is out of your sight and buried a long distance away, and all you can see is the defendant. It's very difficult to identify with someone you can't see, and sometimes it's hard not to identify to some extent with the defendant and his problems.

In that regard, every prosecutor who is at all humane is conscious of feeling sorry for the defendant in every case he prosecutes. But he is not free to forget the victim who lies buried out of sight. I suggest to you that, if you do your duty, you also are not free to forget the victim who is buried out of sight.

You know, Tennyson once said that "authority forgets a dying king." This was never more true than in the murder of John Kennedy. The strange and deceptive conduct of the government after his murder began while his body was warm, and has continued for five years. You have even seen in this courtroom indications of the interest of part of the government power structure in keeping the truth down, in keeping the grave closed.

We presented a number of eyewitnesses as well as an expert witness as well as the Zapruder film, to show that the fatal wound of the President came from the front. A plane landed from Washington and out stepped Dr. Finck for the defense, to counter the clear and apparent evidence of a shot from the front. I don't have to go into Dr. Finck's testimony in detail for you to show that it simply did not correspond with the facts. He admitted that he did not complete the autopsy because a general told him not to complete the autopsy.

In this conflict between power and justice—to put it that way—just where do you think Dr. Finck stands? A general, who was not a pathologist, told him not to complete the autopsy, so he didn't complete it. This is not the way I want my country to be. When our President is killed he deserves the kind of autopsy that the ordinary citizen gets every day in the State of Louisiana. And the people deserve the facts about it. We can't have government power suddenly interjecting itself and preventing the truth from coming to the people.

Yet in this case, before the sun rose the next morning, power had moved into the situation and the truth was being concealed. And now, five years later in this courtroom the power of the government in concealing the truth is continuing in the same way.

We presented eyewitnesses who told you of the shots coming
from the grassy knoll. A plane landed from Washington, and out
came ballistics expert Frazier for the defense. Mr. Frazier's explanation of the sound of the shots coming from the front, which was
heard by eyewitness after eyewitness, was that Lee Oswald created
a sonic boom in his firing. Not only did Oswald break all of the
world's records for marksmanship, but he broke the sound barrier
as well.

I suggest to you, that if any of you have shot on a firing range—
and most of you probably have in the service—you were shooting
rifles in which the bullet traveled faster than the speed of sound. I
ask you to recall if you ever heard a sonic boom. If you remember
when you were on the firing line, and they would say, "Ready on
the left; ready on the right; ready on the firing line; commence
firing," you heard the shots coming from the firing line—to the
left of you and to the right of you. If you had heard, as a result of
Frazier's fictional sonic boom, firing coming at you from the pits,
you would have had a reaction which you would still remember.

Mr. Frazier's sonic boom simply doesn't exist. It's a part of the
fraud—a part of the continuing government fraud.

The best way to make this country the kind of country it's
supposed to be is to communicate to the government that no
matter how powerful it may be, we do not accept these frauds. We
do not accept these false announcements. We do not accept the
concealment of evidence with regard to the murder of President
Kennedy.

Who is the most believable: a Richard Randolph Carr, seated
here in a wheelchair and telling you what he saw and what he
heard and how he was told to shut his mouth—or Mr. Frazier with
his sonic booms?

Do we really have to actually reject Mr. Newman and Mrs.
Newman and Mr. Carr and Roger Craig and the testimony of all
those honest witnesses—reject all this and accept the fraudulent
Warren Commission, or else leave the country?

I suggest to you that there are other alternatives. One of them
has been put in practice in the last month in the State of Louisiana—and that is to bring out the truth in a proceeding where
attorneys can cross-examine, where the defendant can be confronted by testimony against him, where the rules of evidence are
applied and where a jury of citizens can pass on it—and where
there is no government secrecy . . . Above all, where you do not
have evidence concealed for seventy-five years in the name of
"national security."

All we have in this case are the facts—facts which show that the defendant participated in the conspiracy to kill the President and that the President was subsequently killed in an ambush.

The reply of the defense has been the same as the early reply of the government in the Warren Commission. It has been authority, authority, authority. The President's seal outside of each volume of the Warren Commission Report—made necessary because there is nothing inside of these volumes . . . men of high position and prestige sitting on a Board, and announcing the results to you, but not telling you what the evidence is, because the evidence has to be hidden for seventy-five years.

You heard in this courtroom in recent weeks, eyewitness after eyewitness after eyewitness and, above all, you saw one eyewitness which was indifferent to power—the Zapruder film. The lens of the camera is totally indifferent to power and it tells what happened as it saw it happen—and that is one of the reasons 200 million Americans have not seen the Zapruder film. They should have seen it many times. They should know exactly what happened. They all should know what you know now.

Why hasn't all of this come into being if there hasn't been government fraud? Of course there has been fraud by the government.

But I'm telling you now that I think we can do something about it. I think that there are still enough Americans left in this country to make it continue to be America. I think that we can still fight authoritarianism—the government's insistence on secrecy, government force used in counterattacks against an honest inquiry—and when we do that, we're not being un-American, we're being American. It isn't easy. You're sticking your neck out in a rather permanent way, but it has to be done because truth does not come into being automatically. Justice does not happen automatically. Individual men, like the members of my staff here, have to work and fight to make it happen—and individual men like you have to make justice come into being because otherwise it doesn't happen.

What I'm trying to tell you is that there are forces in America today, unfortunately, which are not in favor of the truth coming out about John Kennedy's assassination. As long as our government continues to be like this, as long as such forces can get away with such actions, then this is no longer the country in which we were born.

The murder of John Kennedy was probably the most terrible moment in the history of our country. Yet, circumstances have placed you in the position where not only have you seen the hidden evidence but you are actually going to have the opportunity to bring justice into the picture for the first time.

Now, you are here sitting in judgment on Clay Shaw. Yet you, as men, represent more than jurors in an ordinary case because of the victim in this case. You represent, in a sense, the hope of humanity against government power. You represent humanity, which yet may triumph over excessive government power—if you will cause it to be so, in the course of doing your duty in this case.

I suggest that you ask not what your country can do for you but what you can do for your country.

What can you do for your country? You can cause justice to happen for the first time in this matter. You can help make our country better by showing that this is still a government of the people. And if you do that, as long as you live, nothing will ever be more important.

When Jim Garrison finished, there was an impulse from part of the spectators' section—led by the Hanging Ladies—to applaud. It was stifled, however, but it was unmistakably there.

The press sat in unbelieving silence. Clay Shaw's name had been mentioned once. The use of the late President's words so near to the end—"I suggest that you ask not what your country can do for you but what you can do for your country"—was so blatantly designed to appeal to the emotions, as if the corpse of the President were reaching from the grave to enjoin Garrison in his plea for vengeance, that we were stunned by it.

The District Attorney had spoken for twenty-five minutes; it was now 11:20. There was a short recess. Jeff Sulzer, Nina's good-looking husband, a psychologist, stood in the corridor. I walked up to him. "What did you think?"

Jeff shook his head. "I didn't hear all of it. I had to leave."

"Why?" I asked.

"There were so many American eagles flying around the courtroom I was afraid I'd be shat upon!" He was not smiling.

When we returned to our seats, Judge Haggerty announced that he had offered to let the jury return to their motel and retire for the night, so they might begin their deliberations refreshed in the morning. They had assured him they were ready to start on the case regardless of the late hour.

Before reading his charge to the jury, the judge also let it be known the front doors were now locked. I wondered what that meant; could anyone possibly absent himself from the courtroom at this point? Yes, someone could. I noticed that Jim Garrison was now apparently locked out. As usual, he had said his piece and left. His wife, Liz, was there, however, wearing a skirt and a beige cardigan with little decorative patches sewn on and a small green kite stitched in the middle of the back. Her dark glasses were still perched up in her hair.

In his charge to the jury, begun at 11:30, Judge Haggerty once more outlined the crime of conspiracy as defined in Louisiana and advised the jury of the verdicts they might return. He slurred over the charge, reading it quickly, or perhaps it only appeared that way because of his voice, which was tired and showing faint signs of laryngitis.

The judge finished a few minutes after midnight. It was now March 1, exactly two years to the day since Clay Shaw's arrest. Judge Haggerty instructed the jurors on their deliberations—first they were to pick a foreman—and as they were finally excused to file upstairs and begin their task, he released the two alternates, young John J. Beilman, whose wife had been spending a lot of time lately sitting opposite him in the courtroom, smiling and signaling to him, and sturdy, solid Robert Burlet, whom the defense would have preferred on the working jury. The judge advised them that they would be presented with gilt-edged certificates from the New Orleans Bar Association and himself, adding, "I'm going to get you and the other jurors excused from further jury duty for the rest of your lives!"

Both men, smiling broadly, stepped from their chairs to the side of the jury box and walked between the prosecution table and the defense toward the gate in the railing. Clay Shaw, still seated, was turned around slightly in his chair as both men, grins still upon their faces, extended their arms and shook hands with the defendant. They made a right turn, passed through the gate and proceeded up the aisle to freedom. They had not shaken hands or even glanced toward the prosecution table.

The *States-Item* said of this remarkable little incident, "At this point Clay Shaw may have gotten a tip or preview of what was yet to come."

Yet we later learned that Burlet and Beilman had been asked by their fellow jurors to mark down on slips of paper what their verdicts would have been had they been allowed to vote and to leave the slips with a deputy.

They had both marked guilty.

41

The Verdict

As soon as the jurors had disappeared through the back door to the left of the judge's bench—it was now about 12:06—Judge Haggerty retired to his chambers for the long wait, which turned out to be not so long at all. He was joined by his wife, Yolande, a few of the Hanging Ladies, a few friends, and a nun or two.

Clay remained seated at the defense table, smoking for a few minutes. It was obvious no one in the courtroom knew quite what to do. We were a crew without a captain, suddenly becalmed in a vacuum. Certainly there would be no verdict returned immediately, so there was no reason to stay inside the courtroom. Gradually members of the press and some of the spectators stood up and straggled out. Clay rose, walked toward the jury box, then turned and came over to the railing. I walked up to speak to him. Words, at that time, were only to fill the silence, they had no meaning of their own, there was no impulse behind them which governed their choice. A few other newsmen came up to wish Clay luck. He nodded and smiled and when he wasn't speaking he hummed a tuneless little tune which also had no relation to any formal piece of music. I mumbled a few hollow words of reassurance to him, then drifted out of the courtroom into the corridor.

Groups were clustered, not near the courtroom doors as usual, but strung out down the lighted corridor as far away as the center stairway. Suddenly, Nina Sulzer was standing in front of me, a completely foreign look upon her face, a look so strange I was forced to ask, "What?"

"Oh, Jim," she said, "I didn't have the heart to tell Clay—" She broke off and I could see her forcing back tears.

"Nina, what?" I asked.

"—that he'll have to spend at least this one night in jail?"

"What do you mean?"

Now the tears were slowly oozing out to rim her eyes as she explained that it would take until at least tomorrow to arrange bail and that after the verdict—although there was no mention of what it would be, there was no doubt in her mind it was going to be guilty—he would be taken immediately to the Parish Prison, where he would spend the night. She was apologetic but said there was nothing she could do about it and her quandary was whether to tell Clay.

"No, don't bother him with that now," I said. "No," she agreed and moved away.

Rash thoughts of post-verdict reactions now struck me—leading a courthouse riot, kidnaping the defendant in the midst of the confusion from under the talons of the law, smuggling him to New York and sanctuarying him in St. Patrick's Cathedral. Make a Federal Case out of him—anything but capitulate to this Louisiana Witch Trial. I caught sight of Nina Sulzer talking to Clay's pretty young cousin, Suzanne Day, in front of the courtroom doors. Suzanne's face signaled distress. I walked on down the corridor and spoke briefly to Jerry Cohen, who had a hunch the verdict would not be long in coming. I, somehow, felt that, too.

When I turned back toward the courtroom, Suzanne Day was seated on a bench, huddled over, sobbing her eyes out. Two women were comforting her. I stayed away.

Suddenly there were louder individual voices heard above the fragmented buzzing of the groups in the corridor and the dash was on to the courtroom. I joined in and found myself jamming through the doors, engaged in a good deal of ungentlemanly the-hell-with-your-neighbor pushing and shoving. Within seconds there were approximately twenty of us squeezed through the doors and standing in the center aisle about to take our seats when we saw all those still inside the courtroom looking at us for the answer to the panic. We looked at them, they looked at us. A few shook their heads, indicating nobody had announced anything.

Almost everyone straggled back out into the corridor. I passed several groups, dropped a word or two here and there, and then spoke briefly with John Mourain, Bruce Eggler and Bill Block. The smell of the entire building began to get to me. I thought I might just go outside and inhale a breath of fresh night air. My father used to have an expression, which I was not overly fond of, but which came back to me now: "Think I'll take a walk to wash the stink off."

As I approached the staircase I heard a loud voice, a man's voice: "The jury!" By the time I'd turned around another rush was on. It was still not an hour since the jury had gone upstairs, but I could not take the chance that it was a second false alarm. I skidded across the marble floor and elbowed my way through the doors with the best of them. The deputies were helpless to restrain us.

Something was definitely afoot. The attorneys up front were on the alert. Deputies ducked in and out of doors to the left of the judge's bench. And now someone came out of the judge's chambers. Clay was sitting erect at the defense table. People were still crowding in the courtroom as Judge Haggerty quickly walked in from his chambers and took the bench.

The jurors had, indeed, reached a verdict and were on their way down. I looked to my right and thanked God Rosemary James had slid in and was seated next to me. I quickly shot a glance back to see Jim Phelan, Jerry, Moe and my other friends all quickly pushing into their seats. I glanced across the aisle to the spectator section. Gail Baumgartner, outside of Father Sheridan, Clay's most loyal attending friend during the trial, hands clenched in front of her chin, eyes closed, sat praying and crying at the same time.

The rear door next to the witness chair was opened and here came the jury—first Mr. Mason, Mr. Schultz, Mr. Ricks, Mr. Ordes—in they walked, single file, looking drawn and tired and as solemn as ever. There was not a smile to be seen. I had always been told an acquittal jury is a happy jury, a convicting jury is a serious jury. I'd also been primed that an acquittal jury will usually toss a glance toward the defendant as they return to the courtroom, to the person they have just set free. Not one of them looked at Clay Shaw.

(Oh, Jesus, don't let it be! Oh, Jesus!)

And then it was all over so quickly—with unbelievable, untheatrical swiftness. I turned and glanced at the clock, just a few minutes after 1 A.M. When I looked back, five or six deputies were gathering around Clay, flanking him, obscuring him from sight, as if at the given word they would be positioned to pounce upon him.

As soon as the last juror was seated, Judge Haggerty asked, "Gentlemen, have you reached a verdict?"

Mr. Hebert, the senior member and their foreman, mumbled something. I took it that he said, "We have." He handed a slip of paper—such a small piece of paper—to George Sullivan, who quickly passed it up to Judge Haggerty. The judge, one hand making a pass at his glasses, glanced at it, then handed it back to minute clerk Sullivan, who had bet lunches on a guilty verdict.

Sullivan read, "We, the jury, find the defendant, Clay L. Shaw, not guilty."

A roar—a wild cheer—exploded in the courtroom.

Later, in the massive post-verdict confusion, after the courtroom had been hastily cleared and the defendant, oddly enough, had been spirited down the back passageways to the Parish Prison one last time, the courthouse steps were flooded with lights while cameras whirred away, TV reporters grabbed at any and every principal emerging. As we walked down the steps Judge Haggerty appeared with his kewpie-doll wife, Yolande, blond hair done up in intricate ringlets. He was besieged. He looked happy and tired, and proudly told the newsmen—with five or six microphones jammed into his face—that he'd predicted Mr. Hebert would be the foreman and that he'd had an idea the verdict would not take long. Asked if he was surprised at the verdict itself, he said, "No," but would not elaborate. When a reporter questioned him about what effect the trial might have upon the Warren Report, the judge replied he had no idea, adding, "The Warren Report was not on trial, Clay Shaw was."

Around the side of the building, near the garage entrance of the Parish Prison, a crowd of around a hundred people, spectators, reporters and cameramen, all waiting for Clay, were kept back from the gates by deputies. Suzanne Day and Gail Baumgartner, still weeping, were being interviewed by television reporters, full lights and cameras in action.

Suddenly the large gates twenty or so yards up a drive from the sidewalk were opened and the sound of a siren, whining from way back inside the Parish Prison, wailed to a nearing scream as headlights loomed toward us and a sheriff's car, lights atop flashing, came forward, picking up speed as it approached. Newsmen swiveled their lights and cameras around, aiming at the car, and as it came down the drive, Clay Shaw could be seen in the middle of the back seat, alone—two deputies sat up front—a huge smile broadening his face, one hand held up in a benediction wave. The light beams streaked out in circles and the siren now shrieked a warning to stay away. In a moment the car dipped off the drive into the street, swerved wildly to the left and sped away.

"Christ, what an exit!" someone shouted. The crowd laughed, a few even applauded.

It had, indeed, been a classy egress. It had also been a day. In honor of it—many of us got blind drunk.

PART THREE

ENCORES

42

Garrison Rides Again

A phone call from Clay awakened me the next morning. The weights had been lifted from his chest; he could breathe free. Pick any euphoric adjective—it fit. A press conference was scheduled for early afternoon at Eddie Wegmann's and he would pick me up on the way.

Jeff Biddison, Jim Phelan and Clay—all beaming—pulled up in Jeff's car later on. They could hardly wait to hand me the *States-Item*, which featured on the front page a large sketch of Clay and an enormous printed white NOT GUILTY on a black background. Boxed and starred beneath it was the following editorial:

GARRISON SHOULD RESIGN

District Attorney Jim Garrison should resign. He has shown himself unfit to hold the office of district attorney or any other office.

Mr. Garrison has abused the vast powers of his office. He has perverted the law rather than prosecuted it. His persecution of Clay L. Shaw was a perversion of the legal process such as has not been often seen.

Mr. Garrison's conspiracy case was built upon the quicksands of unreliability and in the end it did not stand up. A 12-man jury found unanimously that Mr. Shaw is innocent.

Clay L. Shaw has been vindicated, but the damage to his reputation caused by Mr. Garrison's witch hunt may never be repaired. It is all too shameful.

This travesty of justice is a reproach to the conscience of all good men and must not go unanswered. Mr. Garrison himself should now be brought to the bar to answer for his conduct.

Mr. Garrison should be the object of our scrutiny. His handling of the Shaw case, we believe, merits the closest examination by the state and local bar association.

This newspaper has been constrained from comment on the case by the guidelines which Mr. Garrison himself has consistently ignored. We have had to bite our tongue in the face of the injustice that unfolded before us.

But that is the case no more. The jury has spoken. Clay L. Shaw is innocent. And Mr. Garrison stands revealed for what he is: a man without principle who would pervert the legal process to his own ends.

The editorial, we agreed, was strong, unequivocating and—about time. They had finally stood up to be counted, but it was rather like placing a bet on the long shot after the final track results had flashed on the tote board.

Within forty-eight hours both New Orleans papers were to pull the most shocking about-face in the history of stand-taking.

A well-stocked bar was set up in the lower half-level basement playroom of the Wegmann house. The place was jammed with cables, lights, microphones, cameras, rejoicing members of the press, a few friends and some of those who had been involved in the case. William Gurvich was out of the hospital, a bit weak but happy to be on hand. Eddie Wegmann's colic had completely disappeared and I could see his face and features for the first time. It was actually a happy face, now that it was unglued and back in place after two years of angst. Irvin Dymond said to me that day, "I'll tell you, if I'd gotten as personally involved in every one of my cases as Ed was in this one, I'd have ended up in a sanitarium—no *way* of surviving!"

After cheers and applause at his entrance, Clay had a drink shoved in his hand and sat on a sofa, flanked by Eddie Wegmann and Irvin Dymond, with Billy Wegmann and Sal Panzeca standing nearby. The seated trio looked like three bears who'd just discovered the largest honeycomb in North America. Lights, mikes and cameras were turned on and many of the press sat on the floor in front of them as the questions began. The Rolfes, June and Dick, had the nerve to show up and were freeloading at the bar. I actually admired their chutzpah.

Here was Clay Shaw speaking off the top of his head on the second anniversary of his arrest. His composure and lack of vindictiveness were almost maddening:

Q.: Mr. Shaw, how do you feel?

SHAW: I feel wonderful, of course. Two years ago today I was arrested, and two years ago Sunday I said I would be vindicated. It has been a long time, but it has happened; and the fact that it has happened as it has happened is, I think, a tremendous indication of the strength and validity of the judicial system and, particularly, the jury system as it is employed here.

Q.: Did you ever lose faith?

SHAW: No, I won't say I lost faith. There were dark times, of course, during these two years; but really I feel that there is something in juries that has an almost mystical way of getting at the truth of matters. And I think this jury did exactly that.

Q.: What about Jim Garrison? Can you say anything about how he came upon your name, why did he pick you to prosecute?

SHAW: I wouldn't undertake the mental processes of many people, and Mr. Garrison is one I absolutely refuse to understand. I don't know.

Q.: Do you think Mr. Garrison should resign?

SHAW: That is a matter for Mr. Garrison and his conscience. I won't comment on that.

Q.: Do you believe Mr. Garrison simply used you in order to get the Warren Commission testimony on trial?

SHAW: In large measure, yes.

Q.: Do you think he [Garrison] didn't believe you were guilty?

SHAW: Yes, I think he did not.

Q.: What are your plans for the future?

SHAW: I hope to be able to sort of pick up the strings as much as I can as of two years ago today. That means writing, traveling . . . but mainly, writing. There are a couple of plays I hope to do.

Q.: Don't you have a house you are restoring?

SHAW: Yes, that has been part of the pattern of my life for ten or fifteen years, as you know. So I will continue working and finish this restoration.

Q.: Do you plan to write a book on your experiences?

SHAW [smiling]: Quite possibly.

Q.: How has this affected you, Mr. Shaw, these past two years?

SHAW: Well, you can't give a definite answer to that. It's been a horrifying nightmarelike experience. It also on a purely practical level has been disastrous financially because these matters—investigators—cost a great deal of money. On the other hand, adversity of this sort has deepened my life somewhat. I have met many people I would not have met otherwise, some of whom are in this room. While I might not go so far as to say I would go through it all to have met them, nevertheless, having done so, it is a positive factor in the whole experience. It has been a very bad time in many ways, but there have been some good things.

Q.: Over the past two years, you have been heard to say you had nothing to worry about. What were your thoughts when the jury was out deliberating?

SHAW: I said I had nothing to worry about, and yet you don't know what twelve men will decide. You can never tell the inter-actions of twelve people upon each other. And, of course, I had to consider the possibility that they might have returned an unfavor-able verdict. But when I took that into account and was prepared for it if it should come, I was not really worried in the sense that you use the word.

Q.: How do you mean prepared?

SHAW: Psychologically prepared. Had there been an unfavorable verdict, it meant an appeal in another court, another year, two years of the same kind of thing I had been going through. But I was psychologically prepared that if that was what had to be done, that was what had to be done. . . .

Q.: Philosophically speaking, what do you think this all proves, Mr. Shaw?

SHAW: It has proven the dangers and strengths of our system. The danger is that a district attorney—prosecutor—has altogether too much power; and while this is generally not used to its fullest, it can be. It has been in the past two years.

The strength of the system is the corrective fact, that when this kind of power is abused, there is always a recourse to the judicial forum and to a jury.

I've been struck by a number of things that might be of interest to you. And I think one of these things is that I am surprised that the press has not paid more attention to.

You are all aware of the fact that a group of private business-men has contributed money to the public prosecutor to go out and investigate someone. This appalled me when I first read it in the paper. I didn't have any idea I would be involved in it.

But I was appalled to think that a public official would accept funds from two or three rich men to investigate anybody or any-thing. I think this is one of the most vicious things I have ever heard of.

If you think about it, you can see the door it opens in wild and bizarre abuses of power. Suppose two rich fellows didn't like Rosemary James [the television reporter]. But I can't imagine anybody not liking Rosemary [laughter]. No, let's suppose they did, and they went to the District Attorney and said here's a considerable chunk of money and we are going to give you a chunk of money every month until you find out the truth about whatever it is. . . . We might say there was a murder in the French Quarter, you know, and Rosemary James lives in the French Quarter.

But why has there been no comment in the press that this hideously vicious thing has been allowed to happen? I don't know. . . . I don't think there is any Louisiana law forbidding it, is there? I don't think the framers of the laws ever considered the possibility. . . .

Q.: Mr. Shaw, what possible reason could Mr. Garrison have had in charging you with conspiracy to assassinate the President?

SHAW: I said before that I was not going to try to explain the workings of Mr. Garrison's mind.

Q.: Mr. Shaw, did it ever occur to you during the proceedings what it might be to be really poor?

SHAW: It has occurred to me many times.

Q.: I mean someone who could not afford the likes of Mr. Dymond and Mr. Wegmann? [Laughter.]

SHAW: No, it's a very valid question. I don't like to joke about it. The thought has rarely been absent from my mind during the two years what would have happened if I had been friendless, absolutely poor—as I will be soon but am not at this time—and not in a position to defend myself. And you can't help thinking that maybe this has happened more often than any of us realize. Yes, that has been very much in my mind.

Q. (to Dymond): Is there any way of determining how much money the District Attorney has spent on his investigation?

DYMOND: It appears there would be some records available on it. I also suggest that he be asked about it. . . .

Q.: What were your feelings about the District Attorney's closing statement, Mr. Shaw, particularly your feelings as they might apply beyond the confines of your own case? In other words, were you worried or frightened at all about this?

SHAW: No, I wasn't worried or frightened. I thought it interesting, as a matter of fact. For while it dealt mostly in generalities which had nothing to do with the evidential qualities of the case, much of what he said is quite true.

He said, for example, that justice doesn't happen without some attention being paid to it and that, if free men are to remain free, we must be ever vigilant about justice. He pointed out the dangers in a society—any society—of power and authority preventing justice from happening. That is a true statement. The only thing I found wrong in the statement was that Mr. Garrison had mixed up the cast of characters. [Laughter.]

No, he was St. George, and the dragon was the Federal government. But actually the fact of the matter is the District Attorney of the Parish of Orleans was authority, was oppression, and I and my attorneys were representing justice and humanity. So I endorse his statement completely—with a change of the cast of characters.

Q.: A few months ago, you were quoted as saying you thought this was a tragedy without a villain. Now do you think there is one?

SHAW: I'm not going to be vindictive and talk in terms of villains. The thing has happened, and it has not ended here, as I say, but I will not say this man is wicked, this man is black, this man is that.

After the press conference there was some good solid drinking done. Before Dick Rolfe left he assured me he would do everything he could to bring me together with Jim Garrison. Indications were the District Attorney would not be all that accessible, especially to writer types.

That afternoon Jack Sawyer from Station WYES-TV, the National Educational Television Network, called to ask if I would appear on a half-hour program on Monday devoted to the trial, entitled *Press and Prejudice*. I agreed and suggested that Jim Phelan and Hugh Aynesworth might be interesting to have on hand also. The program was set up and prominent ads were placed in the *States-Item* over the weekend and on Monday. We were to tape the program around 7 in the evening for a 9 P.M. air time.

Sunday morning the *Times-Picayune* also came out with a brave editorial; it, too, was prominently boxed and situated on the center of the front page:

JUSTICE, AT LONG LAST
(AN EDITORIAL)

Acquittal early Saturday of Clay Shaw of a charge that he conspired to kill President John F. Kennedy brought a just end to a prolonged and greatly publicized criminal prosecution.

Jim Garrison, Orleans Parish district attorney, it seems to us, prosecuted Shaw to prove that conclusions by the Warren Commission placing responsibility for the president's assassination were incorrect. . . .

Beyond question, in our opinion, the district attorney was entitled to question the Warren Commission's finding. His selection of the Orleans Parish criminal district court as the forum in which to vindicate his own conclusions, we believe, was improper, unjust and an unfair reflection and burden on the community which he was elected to serve.

The background of most of the witnesses placed on the stand by Mr. Garrison's staff in attempts to prove his point has been so well publicized that it is unnecessary to delve here into their records and personalities. That the district attorney brought some of them to New Orleans to testify was almost unbelievable. That they were not believed by the jury is obvious.

Since Mr. Shaw was named a defendant this newspaper has remained editorially silent. To have taken any other course might have prejudiced the case. Now that the matter is behind us, it seems appropriate for us to speak out about it. We don't think charges ever should have been preferred against Mr. Shaw on the basis of the unreliable verbal statements and flimsy documentary evidence which were available to the district attorney. That these charges were unanimously rejected by the 12-man jury, we believe strongly, should renew and rekindle faith in the Louisiana jury system.

Sunday afternoon Moe Waldron of the *Times* threw an open-house farewell for the press and victory celebration for the defendant at Mom's Good Eats. Terry and Leonard Flettrich, Jeff and Nina Sulzer, Jerry Cohen, Hugh and Paula Aynesworth, Mike Parks, Jim Phelan, Bill Block and his young and pregnant wife, Judy, John Mourain, Rosemary and Jud James, Doc Queeg of the UP and perhaps twenty others were there, including some of the local newspaper fellows, who were indulging in a goodly share of drunken crowing over the local editorializing. It got a bit thick after a while and I could not help commenting that although the editorials were indeed called for and appropriate, it was surprising that the papers had been able to restrain themselves for a period of two years, since they now asserted, "We don't think that charges ever should have been preferred against Mr. Shaw . . ." and "We have had to bite our tongue in the face of the injustice that unfolded before us." Certainly this was one of the great tongue-biting jobs in the history of journalism. And if the *States-Item* truly felt "constrained from comment on the case by the guidelines which Mr. Garrison himself has consistently ignored," why compound Garrison's violation of the guidelines by printing his many shocking and unfounded allegations, such as the Clay Shaw finger-print card and other highly suspect "evidence"? To these questions the newsmen pleaded innocent and reminded me that the policies of their papers rested with Ashton Phelps, president and publisher, and George Healy, Jr., executive editor at that time.

The next afternoon, I was walking down Royal Street in the late afternoon on my way home to get dressed for the television program when Marge O'Dare, who works for Jeff Biddison in his real estate agency, stuck her head out the door. "What about the latest—do you believe it?"

"What?" I asked.

"Garrison's rearrested Clay!"

I laughed, waved a hand at her and went on my way. "No, wait," she called, "it's true!"

"You've got to be kidding!"

But I could now tell by her face she was not. I stepped into her office and she told me a warrant had been issued that afternoon for Clay. He had already gone to the Criminal Court Building with Eddie Wegmann and Irvin Dymond in answer to a bill of information filed with the clerk of court charging him on two counts of perjury stemming from his testimony during the trial. The counts were based on two simple sentences: "No, I did not know Lee Harvey Oswald" and "No, I did not know David W. Ferrie." The bill of information was personally signed by Jim Garrison. Bail had been set at $1,000; Judge Malcolm O'Hara, however, authorized Clay released on his own recognizance.

Struck completely numb by this news, I quickly went home and phoned Clay. "I don't believe it!" I told him.

"I don't either, but he's done it."

"What does this mean?"

"Well," Clay said with a sigh of resignment over finding himself still trapped in this Kafkaesque whirlpool, "the case will be allotted to a trial judge in a day or so, and then we begin all over again, I suppose. Fighting to quash the whole thing and appealing and—I can't believe it!" There was silence for a moment. "Then if we have to, I suppose it means another trial."

There was not too much time before I was to be picked up. It was agreed that we would gather at his house after the taping, watch the show together, and then attempt to make some sense of this newest insanity.

Jim Phelan and Hugh Aynesworth were as baffled and shocked as I was. Rumors were abroad that Clay's most recent charge was only the first in a series of arrests and citations to come flying out of Garrison's black book of grievances. Aynesworth, who had been of great help to the defense as a source of information, was leaving on a plane that evening for his home in Houston, and Phelan, who had most definitely aided in the destruction of the state's case, was leaving for the coast the next day. Both figured they were getting out not a minute too soon. Although I was certainly not a favorite of the prosecution, it was presumed my involvement in the case had come relatively late to matter. The only citation possible for me was a contempt of the court's guidelines, possibly for the *Esquire* piece and more likely for my brief but gratuitous remarks on the Flettrich show.

So here, at the television station, were the three of us piling into our chairs and strapping small microphones around our necks, ready to sound off and earn a heightened degree of enmity for ourselves. The show was hosted by Larry Johnson, whom I had worked for in an industrial film in Detroit years before; I'd also appeared on a two-hour talkathon of his during the trial, but I'd been careful not to put my foot in my mouth. This evening he gave us free rein and we took it. The outrage of these newest charges against Clay spurred us on to speak in candor of the trial. Jim and Hugh, both about to pull up stakes as they were, did not treat Garrison kindly. I was not exactly strewing rose petals at the mention of his name either, but knowing this show would be watched by many on the D.A.'s staff, if not the Big Boy himself, and hoping to effect a meeting with Garrison, I was careful not to slander him outright. I limited my comments to the completely bizarre aspects of the trial and saved my anger and outrage for the perjury charges leveled that day.

There was a certain last-train-from-Berlin feeling in the studio after the taping. Jim Phelan was most apprehensive, expecting someone to serve us with papers at the studio door. We reminded him that the show would not be aired for another hour, so the storm troopers had most likely not been dispatched yet.

A high wind was blowing, and the low-flying rain clouds skimming the city made for fine cloak-and-dagger weather. As we got into Jeff Biddison's car for the ride back to Clay's, Jim Phelan swore a pickup truck was following us. He sat scrunched around in the back seat, never taking his eyes off it. "See—look, it turned at that corner, it's still right behind us. I tell you!" The truck did not disappear until we'd almost arrived at the red door on Dauphine.

Once at Clay's, we were given drinks, and although he was still shocked at the perjury charges, he was making a joke out of the outlandishness of it all. When I questioned him about his equanimity at finding himself once more upon the firing line, he said, "Well, listen, you stew an old bird in a pot for two years and that old bird gets tough."

We watched the program with Clay, who appeared pleased at the stand we had taken. We downed a quick nightcap with Hugh, who then left for the airport to catch his plane. He wished us luck and indicated we might be needing it.

If we had been shocked by the new charges, we were, I believe, even more stunned by the *Times-Picayune*'s account of the event. It was accorded headlines: SHAW IS CHARGED ON PERJURY COUNT, but the story was treated as a pure news item, giving the time of Clay's appearance at the Criminal Court Building, the formalities at the clerk of court's office, the amount of bond, and adding a few personal comments such as "Shaw was smiling as he emerged from an elevator on the second floor of the courts building" and "Edward F. Wegmann, one of Shaw's attorneys, said that Garrison appears to be challenging the credibility of the jury system. 'This is what it amounts to,' said Wegmann. 'F. Irvin Dymond, who served as Shaw's chief defense counsel during the 40-day trial, was asked his opinion of Garrison's action; and speaking into a television microphone, he said: "The Federal Communications Commission wouldn't let you tape mine!" ' "

On the story went. As we read it, all we could do was swear, shake our heads and think back to the brave editorials of outrage only the day before. Toward the end of the account, there were other hints that the post-verdict outrage over Garrison's conduct was not likely to be long-lived. On Saturday the American Bar Association had issued a statement saying it would urge an investigation of Garrison's tactics by the local bar association. Now there was this word: "Howard W. Lenfant, president of the New Orleans Bar Association . . . said Garrison is not a member of the NOBA, so, 'We have no jurisdiction over him whatsoever.'" Another paragraph read, "Kohn [Aaron Kohn, managing director of the Metropolitan Crime Commission] pointed out that the MCC has in the past asked State Attorney General Jack J. P. Gremillion to investigate Garrison, but to no avail. Gremillion said Monday he had no comment on the matter."

As an added fillip, the Mayor of New Orleans, Victor Schiro, was quoted as being happy over Clay's proven innocence. But the story added, "The mayor declined to discuss either the conduct of the trial by District Attorney Jim Garrison or Truth and Consequences, a group of businessmen which has been financing some of Garrison's operations. 'I don't intend to become an armchair strategist and a post mortem authority,' said Schiro. 'As far as I am concerned, the matter is closed.'"

It was clearly not closed in the eyes of Jim Garrison.

After coffee the following morning, Phelan and I were still feeling the jolt of the *Times-Picayune*'s retreat from bravery. I phoned Mr. Ashton Phelps, the publisher, and explained that Phelan and I had covered the trial and that after having read the editorials in both papers over the weekend, we would appreciate a few minutes of his time. Cordial but wary, he finally agreed to see us around 11:30.

The new plant housing both New Orleans papers is modern, spacious and immaculate. Mr. Phelps's suite of offices could belong to a movie executive: plush, light and airy, with wall-to-wall trophies and awards. We were kept waiting no more than five minutes. After introductions, we complimented him on the new plant and then went on to speak of the trial and the three-ring circus it was. Mr. Phelps—color him gray—sat nodding in metered agreement, knowing full well this was only the warm-up. He made me feel as if I were about to knock him up for a loan. We went on to praise him and the papers for their strong editorials, and when this seemed to produce something less than total ecstasy, we added the compliments of our out-of-town press brothers. At this point, Mr. Phelps said, in a grave voice, that of course we realized they had been constrained by the judge's guidelines from speaking out before the verdict. This brought us to the target area. There were no guidelines in effect now, we noted, and we were positive he was shocked by Garrison's newest charges against Mr. Shaw. Yes, Mr. Phelps was indeed surprised, he said in a voice that pronounced the words but did not harbor the emotion. We were sure the national press would exhibit *their* surprise in print and we hoped the *Times-Picayune* and the *States-Item* would also continue editorially along the same road they had traveled the previous weekend. They would, of course, wouldn't they? Mr. Phelps, hands folded across his front, leaned back in his chair at a slight angle. "Well, of course, you have to realize . . ."

Mr. Phelps went on briefly to speak of—what, I couldn't really tell, except that the yellow flag of surrender was obviously on the way up the pole. At one point we mentioned the impression we had received from that morning's coverage of the perjury charges issued by a District Attorney whom the paper had so recently decried and even demanded a resignation from, and yet now there had been no comment, no denunciation of this further injustice, which certainly came close to encircling the defendant with double jeopardy. Mr. Phelps nodded again, saying that, of course, a newspaper's policies were not decided upon rashly, there would be a meeting to discuss possible future editorials regarding the District Attorney.

Jim and I exchanged looks of quiet hopelessness. After the fiasco the District Attorney had wrought, after the twin editorials castigating him for it, now a *meeting* was required!

We soon found ourselves standing in a hallway, with Mr. Phelps looking at his watch, then extending a hand and saying how nice it was to have met us. From his tone, I would not have been surprised if he had offered to drop us off at the airport on his way to lunch. It would only be an hour or two out of his way.

Deciding to try George Healy, the executive editor, we entered the large room housing the city desk, where we found several of the reporters who had covered the trial. They were as jarred as we were over the perjury charges. We soon met Charlie Ferguson, who'd written the *States-Item* editorial, and told him what a pungent and concise piece he'd written. He thanked us and indicated he was ready to pen another as soon as he was given the go-ahead. We believed him—it was the go-ahead that was in doubt.

We soon found our way to George Healy. He was more outgoing than Mr. Phelps had been but, even so, his attitude about the vindictiveness of the District Attorney was tinged with almost humorous amazement, as if he were saying: Yes, how about that? I mean, that takes the cake, doesn't it? Well, you just can't figure that Jim Garrison!

He was on his way to a luncheon appointment downtown and offered us a ride. On the way to his car, we repeated basically what we'd said to Ashton Phelps. Healy's replies, although not overly direct regarding future editorial policies, indicated the paper couldn't very well *ignore* the matter from there on out. He would certainly do everything possible to further implement a program of keeping a watchful eye on the D.A.

I now decided to try to see Garrison and asked to be left off at the Criminal Court Building. "After last night?" Phelan asked. "Sure, he might even be more interested in seeing me," I said and told Jim I'd see him later at Eddie Wegmann's office.

Entering this building, neither an architectural favorite nor a repository of happy memories, especially this day, I strongly felt the lack of companions. I had intended to go straight up to the D.A.'s office but, finding myself in need of a warm-up, I walked instead into the Sheriff's wing and searched out Nina Sulzer. We embraced and then exchanged phrases of shock, disbelief and disgust over the perjury charges.

Sheriff Louis Hyde came by, congratulated me on the program of the night before, and added that everyone thereabouts had looked in on the show. Nina asked what I was up to, and I told her I was going to attempt to see Garrison. She and Hyde shook their heads in a way not designed to encourage me in this pursuit. It was confirmed that I did not rank high on the current popularity charts in that vicinity, and I soon learned that a warrant was out for Tom Bethell, former researcher for Garrison. Bethell was in hiding, but not for long. New perjury charges were also being drawn up against Dean Andrews—and this was reportedly only the beginning. District Attorney Jim Garrison was not taking the jury's verdict lying down.

I made my way to the D.A.'s offices upstairs at something less than a trot. The inside waiting room was buzzing. A few Sheriff's deputies were on hand with several prisoners, a group of Negroes discussed a false arrest with a lawyer, several assistant D.A.s who had not been associated with the case were in and out, and one of Garrison's bodyguards—I did not know his name but had seen him escort the D.A. in and out of the courtroom—recognized me as I stood at the switchboard and said, "Oh, hello. Saw you last night." I almost said, "Thank you," but realized no compliment was intended. I merely nodded.

I told the switchboard operator that I wanted to see Jim Garrison. I was asked my business and simply said, "I'm writing a book and I want to see him." "Wait a minute, please." The girl left the switchboard, disappeared down a hallway and returned with the word that he was not in. I asked to see his secretary, Lorraine, of whom I had heard. The girl disappeared once more, returned and said she was not in either. When would either of them be in, I asked. Not sure, best to call back later.

In the corridor I saw a small group of local newsmen, including Rosemary James, bunched up outside the clerk of court's office. They were waiting for Tom Bethell to appear with his attorney; he had been charged with "unlawful use of movables"—which translated means handing a list of the state's witnesses over to the defense.

Later in Eddie Wegmann's office, Jim Phelan and I learned that each count of perjury was worth one to ten years, bringing the total possible sentence to the same twenty years required for the offense of criminal conspiracy. So the defendant faced the identical sentence, only on charges that, by their very simplicity alone, were much more difficult to defend. How do you prove you don't know someone? Where can you secure corroborative witnesses to testify to a lack of acquaintanceship? To such a witness there is one question: "Have you been in the defendant's company every minute of the last ten years?" That brings the contest down to a simple declarative denial by the defendant as opposed to God only knows how many witnesses who might come forward now to attest that Clay Shaw had known either Ferrie or Lee Harvey Oswald.

That afternoon Jim Goode called up with word that Mark Lane had phoned *Playboy* in Chicago, claiming I had slandered both Lane and the District Attorney on television. I replied that the shock I had expressed at the trial and the perjury charges had not been couched in libelous terms. Goode nevertheless advised me to take it easy, explaining that Lane had friends on the magazine. I felt obliged to tell Goode, "This article can't possibly turn out to be a valentine to Jim Garrison. There's no way." "No, but you don't have to go overboard," he replied.

The next day I received another phone call from Goode, this time apprising me of an upcoming $10 million libel suit against *Playboy* as a result of Garrison's allegations in his lengthy interview published by them. Goode's point was that it would not be wise for the magazine to print an article that unduly attacked Garrison, who would be appearing as a co-defendant when the case came to trial. Again he urged me to tread softly. At this point I really should have said, Look, it's obvious there's a rather substantial problem—shall we call it quits? For some reason I didn't. I was committed to turning in an article and I decided to fulfill my part of the agreement. As courteously as possible, I suggested that there be no more warning phone calls. It was not helping to set up friendly karma around the typewriter.

43

The Jig Is Up

For two and a half weeks after the trial I remained in New Orleans—a period of total depression. The tentacles of the District Attorney stretched out in slow creeping vengeance while the town lapsed into ennui as it became clear the newspapers had allowed themselves one showy Fourth of July burst of bravery and were now fizzling back into their soggy everyday brand of laissez-faire reporting. The Louisiana Bar Association hedged over its lack of jurisdiction; the Attorney General and the Governor, both with their ostrich necks jammed down into their own waste matter, were gagging on a few scandals closer to home in Baton Rouge than the District Attorney of New Orleans. There had been talk of petitions of recall for Garrison but so far there had been no sign of anything more than—just talk.

Attempting to write the *Playboy* article was a debilitating task. Why write about an injustice when you have the feeling nobody gives a damn if the perpetrators are apprehended and put out of commission?

Each day I had to drag myself out of bed and sit for hours in a cluttered stupor amid mountains of newspaper clips of the trial and my own copious notes. I believe I was attempting to make sense of people and their reactions more than I was trying to decipher the trial. Perhaps it was a delayed reaction to the strain of the actual courtroom proceedings, a letdown from having been so keyed up for those forty-some days. My appetite disappeared; I went for days without shaving or picking up around the apartment. After a week I began to worry. Although no hypochondriac, I suddenly imagined I might be coming down with hepatitis.

A victory celebration had been planned by Irvin Dymond at his country place across Lake Pontchartrain in Covington, Louisiana, for Saturday, March 8, despite the perjury charges. I drove over with a charming and attractive young painter, Noni Lyons, a friend of Clay's. It was a twenty-seven-mile drive straight ahead over the white concrete causeway stretching across the lake into seemingly endless mists out of a Fellini film. On the far side of the lake several large homemade NOT GUILTY post signs guided us to the Dymond house. Almost all the friends of the defense were on hand. Yet for all the games, drinks and anecdotes exchanged, and the warm hospitality of Nena and Irvin Dymond, the party only sporadically jolted me back to life.

Clay himself appeared weary of the whole thing, even of the cast of characters, despite his fondness for everyone present. There was a faraway look in his eyes, and his smile appeared to be more a social nicety than an expression of pleasure at being there.

A few days earlier I'd sent a copy of my book by messenger to Jim (and Liz) Garrison, with a note saying that although they were aware of my sentiments regarding the trial, I was not a hatchet man and genuinely wanted to meet with him. Monday brought the beginning of a series of phone calls from Dick Rolfe, saying he'd been in touch with Garrison, who'd received the book and the note and would, indeed, see me—in a few days. Dick informed me he'd told Garrison about me, that I was different from the rest of the hostile press (whatever that meant) and that as long as I was writing about the trial, perhaps Garrison should grant me an interview. "He wants to know if he can trust you," Dick added. I laughed and wondered why he should have to *trust* me—I didn't entirely trust *him*—but I did want to meet him.

Another phone call brought word that the meeting was set up for two nights hence, the night after Garrison was to appear on a half-hour program with a local newscaster, Alex Gifford, who also happened to be a friend of his, to discuss the trial. The Rolfes would pick me up at 8 in the evening and drive me out to Garrison's house. I was very much looking forward to this.

I naturally tuned in the television program the next evening. A few nights earlier, Gifford had taped a half-hour with Clay and was oddly ill at ease with him; the interview was downright dull. This evening, however, the newscaster was completely at home with the District Attorney. Jim Garrison, still looking puffy, appeared to be highly tranquilized. There was a dryness about his mouth and speech that one could feel. His eyes at times made a strange slow-blinking roll up into his head and then to the left. Composed he was, and his voiced lack of rancor at the adverse verdict was disarming. At times he did not respond at all directly to the queries put him and simply ignored questions he did not care to answer, filling in, instead, with exactly what he wanted to get off his chest, cryptic and otherwise. His voice, as usual, was low and pleasing to the ear in its mellifluousness—the perfect lulling tones of a psychoanalyst, undoubtedly a great part of his mesmeric appeal. Here is part of what Garrison had to say to his constituents that evening.

GIFFORD: What is your reaction to the verdict in the case?

GARRISON: Well, Alex, my reaction is not greatly different than it was the night it came in. It is this essentially. I was not depressed, nor was my staff, because we felt we had accomplished a great deal in bringing out an awful lot of material that had been suppressed by Washington and by the Federal government. On the other hand I must say, in all candor, I did not turn cartwheels when the verdict came in for the defendant. . . . We were disappointed because such hard work had failed to communicate a point to an awful lot of people.

On the other hand I, as a prosecutor, one of my shortcomings, I suppose, is that I tend to put myself in the position of the defendant perhaps too often and I was conscious of being able to put myself in Shaw's place and feeling how relieved I would be if I were Clay Shaw.

GIFFORD: A number of people have said that the verdict has repudiated you as a public official. . . . Do you plan to resign?

GARRISON: Well, first of all, we've been in office six and a half years. And this is, as far as I can recall, the first major public interest case that we have lost. There may be one other but I cannot recall. Six and a half years is an awful long time to go without losing a public—you know, a major case. We finally lost one.

GIFFORD [laughing]: You lost a big one, didn't you?

GARRISON [smiling]: We lost one in a goldfish bowl. Everybody saw us and maybe it's a good thing psychologically, in that sense. The point is that, ah—ah— I must say that I certainly was surprised that within twenty-four hours the newspaper was calling for my resignation after I had gone six and a half years without losing a major case and we finally lost *one*. Six and a half years and not a single murderer—well, not a single person charged with murder had walked out of the courtroom. Which I thought was a pretty fair *country* record and [shaking his head], darn it, we lose *one* case and the next morning I'm called on to resign!

To make a long story short, my reaction is that, for the first time in many many months, I find myself thinking about running again. Because the last thing I'm going to do is to resign under any sort of authoritarian pressure. I did not fight the Federal government for two and a half years to resign or leave this office simply because the newspaper thinks I should.

GIFFORD: You now have charged Clay Shaw with perjury, claiming he lied under oath when he denied he did not know Lee Harvey Oswald or David Ferrie. Now Clay Shaw's attorneys are citing this as proof positive that you have crossed the line from prosecution to persecution. How do you feel about that?

GARRISON: My answer is that if Mr. Shaw's attorneys are honest, it seems to me that this was an eminently fair prosecution from the outset. For two years I refused to mention his name except to say that he has to be presumed innocent until he's proven guilty. I say the same thing—he has to be presumed innocent. I've said it again and again. We leaned over backwards to have the fairest possible trial.

The mind could not help yaw at the memory of the District Attorney proselytizing about the conspiracy and his evidence from New York to California on the radio, television, in scores of magazine and newspaper interviews, and in the hundreds of press releases he issued bolstering his case. He continued:

GARRISON: It's not a matter of persecution when we charge someone with committing perjury; it's my duty to charge people if there is an indication that they lied under oath. I would be committing malfeasance if I failed to charge someone when there was an indication that they lied under oath. Ah—we did not use all of our witnesses, but if we just took nothing more than the witnesses that we had at the trial, you know yourself that there were a number of witnesses who testified to seeing Clay Shaw with Lee Harvey Oswald.

[Already he is publicly bolstering his perjury charges against Clay Shaw.]

GIFFORD: Mr. Garrison, some people would suggest this: that the jury, by their verdict, said they didn't believe these people. Would you say that's a fair statement?

GARRISON: Ah—you cannot conclude that. This was a complex case and the primary reason for the jury verdict was not in that area, actually. Some journalists have talked to members of the jury, which is perfectly all right when they have come in with a not-guilty verdict and—this was not a matter about which they felt any concern at all.

GIFFORD: You suggest you will have new witnesses at the perjury trial.

GARRISON [with high energy]: Oh, yes—yes!

GIFFORD: Why did you lose the case?

GARRISON: Well, we lost the case for two reasons. It should have been won. We lost it because of some bad—in retrospect, some bad tactical decisons which I made and, ah—we lost it because of the tremendous difficulty of presenting a—what was essentially a domestic espionage situation in an Anglo-Saxon courtroom. I can analogize it by saying Jack Kennedy was killed by what was, in effect, a domestic espionage operation and to try to present that in an American courtroom is the nearest thing in the world to trying to carry, ah—water in a sieve. If you were to read a novel by Len Deighton or even a James Bond novel and then consider yourself trying to present it in terms of evidence, you could see that there may be many things that you know in terms of probabilities but that you do not actually have much evidence there and this was our problem.

So that was one of our main problems. I made the decision that, ah—despite the fact that this was obviously, in effect, a coup d'état —ah, a plan of assassination which was originated in Washington, D.C.—not in New Orleans—in *Washington!* And New Orleans was just a part of the force. Ah, and in spite of that and in spite of the fact that, ah—that, ah—well, that a number of individuals that we referred to were genuinely involved in the assassination, we were forced, because of the restrictive rules of evidence and because of a rather ancient statute, essentially a nineteenth-century statute, to present an espionage operation in ancient terms. So I can't even, ah—I can't even be mad at the jury, because, my God, I found myself putting myself in their place and I found myself being up there in their jury room and saying, What is this—the Three Stooges [Oswald, Ferrie and Shaw] ah—how could these three guys accomplish such a grand design as this? And I was conscious all the way through. So you had the structural failure and, ah—there wasn't too much we could do about that.

GIFFORD: You almost seem to be saying that had you been on the jury you would have found the man innocent.

GARRISON: I would say this: that I would have had a great deal to debate about, Alex. But because there was—we don't have to prove motive in conspiracy, because that is the nature of conspiracy. You never know much about it. Otherwise there's no use having the conspiracy statute. But I would say that were I on the jury I would be concerned about the lack of motive. So in that sense you're correct.

Now one of the bad decisions I made and it's like having been wrong once or twice before. I've made a few bad decisions and one of my bad decisions was not to use all of our witnesses. For example, so much was made after the preliminary hearing about the fact that Vernon Bundy—who in my judgment is a totally honest man—so much was made about the fact that he'd been in trouble before that I made the decision that none of our witnesses who'd ever been in trouble before would be used. Ah—in retrospect, I would say this was an unfortunate decision because some of these witnesses connected up the plan for the assassination in a rather substantial way and—what I did was cut off a piece of our case and it was my fault and nobody else's. And it's a shame because nobody ever worked harder than Jim Alcock or Al Oser or Andrew Sciambra and, ah—the fault is mine.

GIFFORD: I think you're hitting on something which I've heard from many of the people who've supported you most strongly from the beginning of all this. They were frankly disappointed in the trial. They felt Jim Garrison was going to pull some trump card out. He's got an ace up his sleeve. And apparently there was no trump card, no ace.

GARRISON: That's a good question and I can answer it very shortly. There never was any possibility, in my judgment, of bringing out the involvement of the—what I referred to as domestic espionage in a court in Louisiana. This is the kind of thing that could be brought out at a Congressional hearing where—or there's the Foreign Affairs Subcommittee of the Senate—but not in a court in Louisiana trying a Louisiana case under Louisiana statutes. There was no way to even begin to introduce it. In other words, Alex, the possibility never existed of going into that. Now I can tell you this, just in a few sentences, and I'll make it very brief. There is no mystery about why John Kennedy was killed, and there is no mystery about the group that killed him. John Kennedy was killed by a section of the Central Intelligence Agency, more particularly a part of the Plans Division of the Central Intelligence Agency, which is why the United States government immediately turns the other way and starts talking about the weather when you bring up John Kennedy's assassination, which is why they've concealed all the evidence.

[Later on Gifford asked Garrison what started him after Clay Shaw in the first place.]

GARRISON: Ah—what started us in the first place was, ah—we came across this, ah—within seventy-two hours after the assassination, more by accident than by talent—I certainly don't claim to be a talented investigator—ah, we found that the evening of the assassination a man by the name of David Ferrie, a strange and very brilliant man had made an all-night trip to Texas under the most peculiar circumstances and, ah—when we questioned people at his apartment what he was doing there, nobody could explain, so we had a stake-out waiting for him to come back to see if it had anything to do with the President's assassination. Ah—to make a long story short, we arrested him when he came back and turned him over to the FBI, which took about twenty minutes. They said they didn't want him. So, you know, we said, well, you know, that they looked into everything, which wasn't true, but we thought so . . . but subsequently, about three years later in 1966, when I was talking with Senator Russell Long, he mentioned that he didn't feel completely satisfied about the assassination investigation. I was astonished. I said, "You mean to say you think there still might be something else to it?" and he said, in effect, yes. So that started me thinking and I thought, Well, the first thing we'll do, we'll call in David Ferrie and ask him some more questions. So we did and his answers were so unsatisfactory! He drove all night through this driving thunderstorm to go duck hunting and—he had no guns with him—and, ah, it's exceedingly difficult to go duck hunting without guns, even in *good* weather! So you might say my curiosity was aroused and it began from there.

The question, of course, had been: What started you after Clay Shaw in the first place? Clay Shaw's name was not mentioned in the answer, nor was Clem/Clay Bertrand, nor Dean Andrews. It was also interesting to note the change in David Ferrie's purported reason for driving all night to Texas in a driving rainstorm—from a trip to go ice skating with the emphasis on the fact that Ferrie had not even put on skates, to duck hunting, without guns.

His performance on television primed my curiosity even more. I was eagerly looking forward to seeing the Jolly Green Giant in his own den the following day, surrounded by his artifacts, his wife and cubs.

I went so far as to take a haircut that day; I even went to Murphy the Barber, the judge's hair stylist and also Garrison's barber. I was talked at non-stop for two hours and twenty minutes while I was clipped, fussed over, anointed, set, baked, brushed, combed out and anointed again. I was talked at so much my nerves began to twitch. He was not Barber of the Year, he was the Long Distance Talker of the Year.

So there I was at 7:30, all dressed up and ready to go. I had the temerity to have my tape recorder tucked in its case. At 7:45 the phone rang. It was Dick Rolfe, saying he was sorry but he had some disappointing news. Jim Garrison had come down with a terrible cold and was afflicted with almost total laryngitis. I volunteered to do *all* the talking and noted that on television the night before he'd given not the slightest evidence of laryngitis. Dick skipped that and asked if I didn't think he'd given a splendid performance. I replied that he had, although I hadn't *understood* much of what he was saying. "Well," Dick said, "that's why you have to meet Jim in person, talk to him. He's really fascinating." "Yes," I replied, "well, I'm ready, that's been my point for weeks." Dick asked how long I was going to be in town; I told him only another week. He would be in touch with Garrison in a day or so and as soon as he was better, we would most certainly get together.

The rest of the week was pure swampland as I struggled to find a focus and point of view, a twist even, that would enable me to funnel the trial down to 10,000 words for *Playboy*.

In an attempted manic fit to snap myself out of this quicksand, I sent a dozen red roses to Jim Garrison in condolence of his laryngitis but received no reply. There were several phone calls from and to the Rolfes. Jim Garrison was now, Dick said, afflicted by a virus that appeared to be hanging on—and on and on. June Rolfe, during one call, informed me that "Liz read your book and was wild about it, thinks it's the greatest. She said she told Jim to drop everything and read it immediately." I believe I then offered to hop a cab, go out to his house and read aloud to him.

I had to go to Cincinnati to appear on a television program March 17. I knew I would go direct from there back home to East Hampton. The jig was up in New Orleans; the sap was drained out of me. I was listless and disenchanted, unable to work or play.

There was one more call from Dick Rolfe, who said Garrison's virus was lingering on. Again there was a mild query about whether Garrison could trust me. I was short on patience by this time and replied that, for God's sake, we were both grown men, he knew what my point was and if he was as bright, intelligent, charming and witty as I'd heard tell, what was the big worry? He would certainly not say anything that would provide me added fuel with which to singe him. "I just want to get the feel of the man," I told Dick. "I'm more than ready to be charmed. I would like very much to find something in the man I could admire." The upshot of it all was "Jim promises he'll see you the next time you come to New Orleans."

There were farewells with favorites—Clay, Irvin, Eddie, Nina, Rosemary, but it was salvation getting on that plane. Much as I dislike flying, I'd have taken off in a crippled B-29 with a defective landing gear, just to escape New Orleans. Actually my only disappointment was not meeting Garrison. Despite his refusal to see any of the press, I had decided he would see me, and my failure rankled.

Even as I was winging the hell out of there, I decided I would come back and accomplish my goal.

44

The Prisoner

Although the article was extremely difficult to write, I managed to finish it in happier surroundings, and I sent it on to Jim Goode at *Playboy* about three weeks after my return. It was entitled:

P'SHAW
A Farce in Three Acts
by Jim Garrison

(Reviewed by James Kirkwood)

It was not long before my agent called with word that the magazine had declined to print it. The news was not exactly unexpected and I was depressed for a few days. Before embarking on this somewhat lengthier account, there were loose ends to clear up in New Orleans, the apartment to dispose of, the perjury charges to check on, many friends to see and that promised meeting with Jim Garrison. I had certainly had the pleasure of personal contact with the defense as well as their confidence. I now wanted to speak with some members of the opposition, a cross-sampling of jurors, and perhaps a few witnesses. I'd made certain overtures shortly after the trial, but wounds were too open, nerves too frayed, fear too apparent. It was now almost two months after the verdict and, presuming that tongues might be loosened up a bit, I flew back to the City That Care Forgot on Saturday, April 26, 1969. Although the drive into New Orleans from the airport did not raise a lump in my throat, there was that certain indefinable pulse of familiarity which manifests itself upon the return to the scene of an important event, pleasant or not.

Clay looked much better. His face was tanned and there was a relaxation of speech and manner, now that he was no longer under constant public scrutiny. He was shocked, however, that the citizens of New Orleans had all but forgotten the disgrace Garrison had wreaked upon himself and the city. There seemed now to be a detectable wave of underground support in New Orleans for the District Attorney, as if he had been handed a bad deal at the trial—had, in some devious way, been blocked by the law, by agencies of the Federal government, the national news media, and an entire dossier of sinister organizations. It was clear there would be no petitions of recall or impeachment or charges of malfeasance by any higher state authority. The newspapers, the Attorney General and the Governor, the Mayor, the Louisiana Bar Association—all were going about business as usual. The only rumor of action on any front concerned the Metropolitan Crime Commission, headed by Aaron Kohn. They were having meetings, gathering material, considering some sort of citizens' petition.

Clay, badly in need of income, was supervising the renovation of an old building in the Quarter into luxury apartments. It seemed likely, because of the brutal financial drain on him, that he would be forced to sell his carriage house. (He has, in fact, since sold it.)

Not wanting Garrison to use him as a "hangover" case in his upcoming campaign for a third term re-election, Clay indicated he would like to go ahead with the perjury trial as soon as possible. It was my opinion the perjury charges would be extremely difficult to beat, and I told him so.

Jim Garrison himself had been lying low, giving no interviews, issuing no pronunciamentos. Monday I nevertheless phoned the District Attorney and was not surprised to find him not in, at least to me. I spoke with his secretary, Lorraine, and requested her to please ask Jim Garrison to set up a time for us to talk. She promised to get back to me. I had decided not to go through the Rolfes, if I could help it.

Miguel Torres, one of those who alleged the D.A.'s office had attempted to bribe him, had recently been released from prison and had indicated a desire to meet Clay Shaw, the man he'd been asked to testify against. A meeting was arranged and Clay had been most impressed by Torres, by his native intelligence and his bravery in defying the District Attorney. I asked Nina Sulzer to see if Miguel Torres would speak with me. An appointment was set up for him to come to my apartment.

The following day I stopped by Dean Andrews' office and asked

if he would give me a taped interview before I left town. He agreed. When I inquired about his most recent perjury charges, he grinned and said, "They aren't going to fuck with the fat man here. They'd better not or it'll be their asses." He also informed me he was running for judge in neighboring Jefferson Parish. Yes, sir, your honor! That would be one court worthy of the Marx Brothers.

Another phone call to Garrison's secretary. She said she had relayed my message to her boss and he would be in touch with me. I half-jokingly told her that I had put up with all the delays and cancellations I cared to and now I meant business. I knew his home address and might just take a cab out to his house and drop in on him, if it came to that. She did not seem amused.

Besides making phone calls, I also received one from a friend who worked at the Criminal Court Building with the information that my return to New Orleans had not been met with delight. It was explained that a RAP (record of arrest) sheet had been obtained on me. (My only arrest was for growing seven marijuana plants in a spare bedroom. "In a window box," the press had reported, but actually the arrangement had not been that quaint; they'd merely been in earthen pots.) It was strongly hinted that I'd better watch my step and it would not be at all unlikely for someone to "plant" marijuana on me or in my apartment for reasons other than my smoking pleasure. From another source I heard that although *Playboy* had decided not to publish the article, someone there was not averse to circulating it on a more selective basis, and a copy had been sent to the District Attorney, to whom it was less than complimentary.

Later that afternoon when I picked up my phone to make another call I heard two men talking. They had gruff voices and appeared to be disgruntled with each other as they discussed certain technicalities. "No, the other line." "Have you got the jack!" "No, for Christ's sake—yes, there you go." "All right, check the goddamn—" At this point there was a silence, after which one man said, "Someone's on the line." A pause. "Who's on the line?" he demanded.

"I am," I said.

"Who are you?" came the question.

"Who are *you?*" I asked.

"I said," the man repeated, "who's on the line?"

"Who are *you?*" I asked again.

"Listen, I asked—"

"Listen yourself, goddamit, it's *my* line. That's why I'm on it. Why are *you* on it?" Silence. "Who is this?"

"Phone company!" came the abrupt reply as the other man said, "Jesus Christ!" and they clicked off.

Suddenly I was not feeling too frisky about being back in New Orleans. I don't know if my phone was tapped or not, but if those two were employed by the phone company I advise you to unload your AT&T fast. The following morning the top part of the mailbox downstairs had been pried open; there was mail in most of the other boxes, but mine was empty. During the trial, this had happened several times. After the first such incident I received a phone call from my lawyer, asking why I hadn't signed and returned the contracts for this book. I explained I'd never received them. They'd been mailed, I learned, several days before the box was jimmied. I never did receive them; other mail and a royalty check or two were also missing. Duplicate contracts had to be made up. Now the box had been pried open again. It could have been a simple mailbox thief. But all these items together did not combine to weave a warm security blanket.

A twinge of going-home struck me, I can't deny it. Still, I could not very well back down in view of my criticism of the cowardice and inertia of others. I decided to stick it out for a while and satisfy my curiosity as much as possible. There were no thoughts, however, of taking up *permanent* residence in New Orleans.

Miguel Torres came to my apartment the first of that week. A slight, dark, amiable-looking young man, he was working long night shifts at a Royal Castle eatery. I offered to make coffee. Yes, he would like some—with sugar and milk.

I had not completely unpacked and the apartment was cluttered with my things: tape recorder, typewriter, cufflinks on the dresser, portable radio, luggage, clothes, etc. I was out of milk and said I'd run down to the corner store. Miguel was immediately on his feet. "I'll—I'll come along with you, Jim."

"No," I said, "I'll be right back."

"Well, yes, but I'll come along."

"No need. Won't take me two minutes."

"Still, I'd feel better if I came with you."

I was about to ask why when I realized that Miguel had served time as a burglar and, as a matter of fact, had a reputation around town for being one of the better men at the trade before he'd gone to jail. He wanted to spare me concern at the thought of leaving him alone in my apartment. There was something extremely touching about his offer to accompany me. Finally our eyes met and I said very quietly, "I really would rather have you stay here, Miguel. Make yourself at home, use the phone or whatever." He caught my acknowledgement of his position and my trust, shrugged, smiled and said perhaps he would make a phone call.

When I returned and we'd sat down opposite each other with coffee and the tape recorder between us, Miguel told me his story. He'd begun stealing when he was a kid in Cuba.

TORRES: I think 99 per cent of the kids steal a little bit, but when I became, when I was 17, that's when I first started doing these things, stealing heavy, you know, and doing things like that. When I was 18 I started robbing with pistols. To show you how foolish I was, one time I had a .32 revolver with a .22 bullet—and the bullet kept falling out. [Miguel laughed and slapped his leg.] So I wrapped *paper* around the bullet and I stuck it in there so it won't fall out and I ran in a place and said, "All right, nobody moves. This is a holdup, everybody. I don't want to hurt nobody, give me all that money." And if I'd pressed the trigger, Jim, it probably would have killed me, because it would have blown up in my face. You see how stupid I was?

Miguel Torres had moved to the United States with his family in 1952. He'd gone to prison for the first time in 1959 for armed robbery. When he came out, through contacts he'd made on the inside, he began pushing heroin, although he did not use it himself. He'd made good money, but eventually discovered that his middleman was cheating, so he began cutting and testing the stuff himself and soon became hooked. At first he told himself he didn't have a habit, only a mild yen, but after a while he could not go without a fix for long without experiencing nausea, the cold sweats and other symptoms of addiction. To support what became a real habit he began stealing heavily.

TORRES: I was just wide open. I didn't care what happened. I'd walk in houses like it was my own. I'd walk by a house and I don't see a car in the garage, sometimes I even *see* a car in the garage, there'd be two cars—because even little signs tell you people ain't home. When they leave the light on the porch I know they're not home. Sometimes they leave the light on the porch and I know they're *home*. It's a little something about it that you can tell, I don't know how, but—you know right away whether somebody's home or not. And I used to walk in there and take whatever I know would give me fifty, sixty, seventy dollars, and that would be going on all day. Two or three times a day. Until I finally wound up in the penitentiary.

Miguel Torres was sent away to Angola, the State Prison, for nine years. He told a bloodcurdling story of withdrawal from drugs while in the Parish Prison and equally frightening tales of life in the big place. Then one night, after he had been in for about three years, he was called out to the control center and told he had a special visitor.

TORRES: It was seven o'clock in the evening. And it was very unusual for a person to get a visitor at that time of night, unless something happened in his family, or an attorney made a special trip. And I went up to the control center, and there were these two people sitting there. Well, I didn't recognize any of them because I'd—well, I never did meet them before. . . . One of these men was Lynn Loisel. They called him "Pete the Heat." He was an undercover agent a while back. In '58 he busted a lot of people, you know? And the other one . . . I'm pretty sure it was Ivon. He was an assistant D.A. And when I walked up to them . . . they asked me what was the thing I wanted the most. And I told them—and I told them—*matches!* That's a silly question, you know. You can't ask a prisoner what do you want the most. *Freedom.* So Loisel—this is his exact words, I never forgot the words. He said, "Well, I'll tell you, Miguel, we come from the D.A.'s office and you know Jim Garrison is a very powerful man. Now," he said, "you're doing nine years here and you've got three years with the Feds. Now he can cut you loose altogether if you cooperate with us. If not, the boss is very powerful and he will be sure to make you do all this time. So the best thing you can do is cooperate with us."
   Now at the time, I didn't know what they had in mind, see? I—in my mind was this. You see, in the joint [prison] they got a

lot of drugs. Lot of bad things happen. And the thing that came to my mind was, these people might want me to be an undercover agent in here. You see? To boss some kind of a deal. And I knew a lot of deals that was going on. So I said, "What you all want me to do?" And they told me, "We're investigating the President Kennedy assassination. And we believe there's a conspiracy. And we want you to cooperate with us." I said, "Man, I don't know anything about this here." They said, "Well, you don't have to know anything. Just cooperate with us and we'll be sure the boss cuts you loose. You can be going to Florida and we'll give you an ounce of stuff where you can lay out on the beach and *blasé*." That's a word they use—*blasé* means to lay out.

So I had no choice, Jim. I had to tell them, "Yes, well, I'll go with you to New Orleans, man," because if I refuse right there and then I was—I fear that they—and if I *went* with them, then I had some kind of stepping stone, you know, something to hold on to to see what they wanted.

So . . . about a week later they came and got me on a writ of habeas corpus. It was a fictitious writ of habeas corpus. It was for a simple robbery case that happened in 1966. And I'd been in prison since '64, you see. So they came and got me. It was in the evening, about 6 o'clock, and they drove me to New Orleans. We got there about 9:30, 10 o'clock. They took me to Garrison's office. He was sitting in the chair and Bill Gurvich was there and he introduced me, we shook hands, you know. Sit down, Miguel, sit down. I sit down. They sent for some beers. I didn't want to drink beer because I was afraid. I figured maybe they wanted to get me a little dizzy.

So this is what Garrison told me personally. He said, "You do what my men tell you to do, and I will do my best to see that you will be out of prison—as soon as it is possible." So I said, "Yes, sir, I'll do anything that you tell me to." They asked me a few questions and they showed me a few pictures. We stayed there about an hour. Different people. I don't remember seeing Clay Shaw at the time. But they showed me pictures of all kinds of Cubans and different people. Anyway, a week later they sent for me.

Q.: Where were you in the meantime?

TORRES: In the Parish Prison. They brought me to the D.A.'s offices and Numa Bertel was there. And he wanted me to let them hypnotize me. And I told them, "No, I can't do that." He said,

"Well, if you let us hypnotize you—" Oh, by the way, a deputy brought me down there and Numa Bertel threw me in a little room, a little office, and closed the door. And he said, "You spoke with the boss already. And you already know what's going on. Just do what we tell you to do." So I said, "What do you want me to do?" He said, "Well, what I want you to do is let us hypnotize you." And this is his exact words: "Let us hypnotize you and you will not remember anything until later, when we will ask you some questions."

Well, right away I got suspicious, Jim. I know something about hypnosis. I know what it can do to a person. So I told him—no. "I can't do that, man." And he got mad. "Man," he said, "you make a deal with the boss and now you want to turn back. You're going to get the boss mad and the boss is going to fuck you around. Because he can fuck you. He can *help* you, he can also *fuck* you." . . . So I told him, "No, I'm sorry, man, I've got to think it over." So I went back to the Parish Prison.

A few days later they sent for me again. And this time it was Mike Karmazon . . . an ex-football player [and assistant D.A.]. When I got to the office I had an attorney, his name was Kimball. He was there. Now he had been there awhile. I don't know what went through between these people, but we went to the office and we sat down. Kimball told me—he's not a fool, he's afraid, I can tell he was nervous because of something. I don't know what Karmazon told him, but they knew each other from way back. But I knew he was nervous. So he sits next to me, he tells me, "Do anything he wants you to do, do anything he wants you to do." So I said, "All right, what do you want me to do, Mr. Karmazon?" He said, "Well, you know Clay Shaw, don't you?" "No, I don't know Clay Shaw." "You know Clay Bertrand?" "No." He said, "Yes, you know him, sure you know him. You used to go to his house. Remember the parties you went to? Where sex orgies used to take place? He used to give you money and he used to whip you and you used to do the same to him and all that?" I said, "No, sir." He said, "Oh, come on, Miguel, you going to tell me—"

But now, you see, I'm looking at my lawyer and I'm looking at Mike Karmazon. I know—this is what I'm *supposed* to say. See? But I can't do that, Jim—you know? So I said, "Mr. Karmazon, I'm sorry but I've got to have time to think." He said, "Take all the time you want. When you get ready, call me and we'll get together." I said, "Okay." So my attorney got up and he left and Mike Karmazon took me and he walked me down the hall to the Parish Prison. And he told me, "Man, don't forget to call. Let these people know that you want to talk to me here. Talk to me, when you get ready." I said, "Okay." That was the second time. Another thing that happened that I can't—oh, yes, yes, yes. The lie detector test. They came and got me one night.

Now, Jim, I tell you, I never been hypnotized. But this night, after the deal was through, I felt as if I had been hypnotized. It was a funny feeling, with the lie detector test, the polygraph machine. He set me down and he said, "We're just going to ask you a few questions, just answer me and everything will be all right." He asked me a bunch of questions. About Cubans and about Clay Shaw and if I knew him and this and that and the other. Now when I took this polygraph test, I don't know the purpose of it. . . . I thought they did it to see if I knew all these people. But it is also possible they did it for their own protection. You know, for their use, to say . . . that they gave me a test, a polygraph test, to see if I was clear and then they cut me loose. So that's what I figure they did that for.

Q.: Was this test right in the Parish Prison?

TORRES: No, this was in the D.A.'s office. They didn't do anything in the Parish Prison, Jim. Whenever they wanted me they took me out to a private office and that's how—all this time, when Loisel came to visit me a couple of times he came to the Parish Prison. And the only time I met Garrison was that time when I came in, when he let me know that he was the man and that these were his henchmen and that all I had to do is whatever they tell me and he will take care of the business. That's the only time he came up front . . . the only kind of a message I got was—the boss wants you to do this or the boss wants you to do that.

And then the news broke loose all over the papers. Some newspapers got wind of it . . . they found out there was an investigation going on. And that's when the news broke loose. They started to put the pressure on me. "Come on, you got to testify, man, you've got to—*Clay Bertrand!*" And that's when I really got scared. . . . Through a friend of mine, I told him, "I want you to get Sal Panzeca." Because I know Sal Panzeca, see? "And I want you to get him to come and see me."

So he came and I told him what these people wanted me to do.

"Man, these people want me to testify against a man that I don't even *know*." And he said, "Well, just hold on and let me see what I can do." And then later on we got together and—you probably know the rest of the story after that. I went on TV, you know, and I told the people that—what these people wanted me to do. I had interviews with different reporters and I told them what it was.

Q.: That was the NBC show?

TORRES: Yes . . . and it wasn't only me, it was another man, John the Baptist. . . . Now this man here, John the Baptist, he had a burglary charge on him. It was a bum rap. They had no burglary charge, they put this on him. You see, because they wanted him to break into Clay Shaw's house. And he refused to do that when they told him what it was. So when he refused, they charged him with burglary and they got him convicted and they gave him eighteen years . . . and he's either in the Parish right now, appealing the case, or he's in Angola. . . . They took him one night, Loisel and another one, I think it was Ivon, too, the same that got me. And they wanted him to go to Clay Shaw's house and . . . put some things in there. He refused. So they got him. They took him right in and booked him.

Q.: And you met Vernon Bundy?

TORRES: I met him in the Parish Prison. Man, man, man! I was in the hospital in the Parish Prison. . . . And this man comes in here. And I look at him, you know, he's walking up and down. He's not sick . . . he's just nervous. Walking up and down . . . And I'm not saying nothing to him. Because I know how it is in prison. You know, people get nervous like that. So all of a sudden he sits down, he says, "Man, I don't know what to do, I don't know what to do!" I said, "What's the matter?" He said, "Man, these people got me, man. If I don't do what they tell me to do, they're going to send me to the joint. And they're going to do me in over there." Well, right away, when he says "do me in," I know that the only way they can do him in is if—the man turn somebody in. You know, or he set somebody up. So I say, "What you gonna do?" He says, "Man, the only thing I can do is tell these people what they want. Do what these people want me to do."

And at the time—I mean, I did not know, Jim, that he was involved in *this* deal, you see? But I knew that he was going to do what these people were *telling* him to do. And later on, when I see

him, what he was doing, then I seen the truth, you see? Boy, ain't
this something, man! Too much!

Miguel and I spoke for several hours. He told me of his several
skirmishes with the grand jury as a result of his refusal to cooperate. He never once alluded, even in an offhand way, to the guts it
took to defy the District Attorney. He related his experience only
as a problem that had to be faced—and had been, through his
tenacity and the efforts of a lawyer, Burton Klein. He'd built up a
good record at Angola and had later been recommended for
parole, despite what Miguel felt were efforts from New Orleans to
quash it. He had then been released to serve a Federal term on a
previous narcotics offense at Texarkana. There, too, he'd earned
parole after fifteen months and had been released. At the time of
our meeting he'd only been out of prison a little over a month.

I wondered if he worried about Garrison causing him any
trouble.

TORRES: Well, yes. . . . What I worry about is that they try to
grab me and put something in my car. In my pocket or in my car.
And charge me, you know? That's one of the reasons I didn't want
to come to New Orleans. But I say, man, if he's going to get me,
he's going to get me. Here or anywhere else. So I'm not going to
run from him. I'm going to come right here where I belong. He's
not going to run me out of the city. And if it happens to me, Jim,
I'll try to overcome it some kind of way. . . . About two weeks
ago, this girl that I—her father's a detective. I knew her a long
time ago, I used to go out with her. But she knows a lot of detectives and they're connected together. She told me to be careful,
because I might get shot in the back. I said, "What do you mean,
girl?" She said, "Be careful, you're gonna be shot in the back—
when you're alone." And I said, "Well, if I'm gonna be shot, let it
be that way." You know? It doesn't hit me. I don't want to die. I
love life. But I'm not going to lose any sleep over it, Jim. Somebody might just tell me so I'd be all right, you know. Or it could
be true. I don't believe anything until it happens. [Miguel
laughed.] Well, it would be too late then.

Miguel ended up speaking of his job, his parents, his new girl
friend, his ambition to move on to a better job and his philosophy

of this new constructive life he was leading. One comment particularly struck me: "I can tell you one thing, Jim. When I came to your house, you know, and I was standing down there by the—and you caught me just right. You said, 'What a beautiful day!' Oh, jeez—every day is beautiful for me now—I'm beginning to learn to live, man."

I would be very much surprised if he got into serious trouble of his own making again.

45

Reasonable Doubters

The only person who refused me an interview during this second visit to New Orleans was William Ricks, the Negro schoolteacher. I reached him on the phone, explained that I'd covered the trial and was writing a book on it, and hoped to speak to a cross section of jurors. He was guarded from the first hello, explained he'd refused to see all newsmen and didn't want to break that rule now. I reminded him that I wasn't a newsman but merely a free-lance author and that nothing he said would be printed in the papers, only in a book that would not come out for a year or so. To this he replied, "Well, I'm thinking of writing a book myself, so that wouldn't work out."

Although I did not badger him, I did my best to persuade him to agree to a meeting, but he became more adamant the longer we talked. To my surprise I found myself becoming annoyed, almost angry, even while acknowledging that he had every right to his privacy. I had to smile when I finally capitulated, thinking, as Dr. Nichols had often stated in his testimony, that I had been rejected.

Time for another call to the District Attorney's office. No, Jim Garrison was not in, his secretary, Lorraine, told me, and then asked, "Hasn't he been in touch with you?" No, he hadn't. "Well," she explained, "he said he would be." I asked her to please remind him again and clicked off.

I then placed a call to Sidney Hebert, the jury foreman, and although he didn't sound overly delighted at the prospect of an interview, I promised not to take up more than fifteen minutes of his time, it would be painless, I'd come out to his house and . . . an appointment was set up.

Mr. Hebert, a retired fire department captain, lives in a small, tidy, almost antiseptically clean tract house way the hell and gone from downtown New Orleans, on a street in a development that took the patient cab driver half an hour to pin down, once we got to the area, and ran the fare up to something near ten dollars. Mr. Hebert and I settled in the living room while Mrs. Hebert remained back in the kitchen with the television going, except for one brief appearance.

Mr. Hebert revealed himself to be a completely conscientious man. He had taken his duties as a juror with the utmost seriousness. He also regarded the time spent on the jury as extremely pleasant, an experience he will always remember.

HEBERT: I'll tell you, everybody—I've never met a finer group of men. . . . The colored were just as nice as the white. And we all stayed together like old family. More or less a family. You got so used to one another. And we all had our little jokes, and it was a pretty jolly time. We played cards and of course we saw movies that Judge Haggerty had gotten. He also got us a place where we could view the carnival parade from a balcony. Of course we were surrounded by security.

Q.: Somebody said a couple came by and held up a printed sign that said, INNOCENT! Did you see that?

HEBERT: No, I didn't, no. I heard some young kids hollering up, "The fruit is guilty! The fruit is guilty!"

Q.: Jesus!

HEBERT: Personally, I don't know Clay Shaw. I've seen the man's picture in the paper because he's a prominent citizen. He was head of our International Trade Mart for years. And the only thing that I knew was that he was a respected citizen. As far as his personal life, I don't know anything about it. Whether the man is what they say he is, I don't know. I don't judge a man by what I hear. I mean if I know a man personally then I can judge him. But I never met Clay Shaw, I never spoke a word to him. The only thing is I saw him in the courtroom day after day and when the verdict was rendered I walked out and I never spoke to a soul. . . .

[As to the downfall of the state's case, Mr. Hebert put it this way]: Actually the whole case rested on the testimony of Perry Russo. And his testimony didn't prove a thing to me. He had too many conflicting statements . . . and he was supposed to have had witnesses with him there, Sandra Moffitt and Lefty Peterson. They didn't show up, I mean for what reason I don't know. I imagine if they'd paid them a little bit of money they'd show up. . . . But maybe they didn't want to perjure themselves. Maybe they weren't there or something.

Q.: Can you tell me about your being elected foreman and the verdict?

HEBERT: Well, I was the oldest man there . . . When we went up to the jury room I said, "Well, the first thing you've got to do is elect a jury foreman." And then one of the younger fellows spoke up and said, "Well, I think the senior member should be the jury foreman," he says. "Mr. Hebert's the oldest," he says, "I think he'd make a good foreman." So they all said yes and I was elected.

Q.: What happened after that?

HEBERT: Well, I told them . . . "You know this is a serious case. It's not only local, national—but international." I said, "What you decide today will have a great meaning . . . all over the world, all over the United States." I said, "Now you can't let your emotions or anything else influence your decision. . . . All you can go by is what you heard from the witness box." I said, "I want you all to think about it awhile and try to review all the testimony you've been through for the last three weeks." And I said, "When you get ready for a vote, you let me know and I'll poll the jury."

So they sat down and—thinking, talking, thinking. I said, "Well, the only thing you can go by is what Perry Russo said—as far as a conspiracy." I said, "Overt acts, even if they can be proven—first you've got to prove conspiracy . . . that's the first thing you have to prove. If you couldn't prove conspiracy, the overt acts had nothing to do with it." . . . So, after they all thought awhile, I guess—I think we were up there about fifty-five minutes, all told—I said, "Let me know when y'all are ready to be polled . . . we'll take a vote." So we had a little hat that somebody had found up there. They all put their ballots in there. I said, "Just write your name on a slip and put it in there." I said, "We'll poll the jury." So—not guilty, not guilty, not guilty, not guilty. I said, "Boys, you wound up with a pretty good—" In other words they were all in accord.

Q.: And there was actually no juror who was holding out for anything but an acquittal?

HEBERT: There was never a dissent among any of the twelve.

This version of the jury's unanimity was later contradicted by other jurors. I told Mr. Hebert that Mark Lane had gone on television—I had not seen his appearance but it was described to me—and claimed that the two alternates had marked guilty. Mr. Hebert replied, "They may say that—I mean, not having anything to do with it, you understand?" He was not anxious to pursue this. Mark Lane also maintained he had asked many of the jurors to grade witnesses in the case on a scale of 1 to 5 for credibility, with 5 the highest. He claimed the Clinton people had earned 5. Mr. Hebert informed me he'd talked to no other reporters or writers but me, adding, "He [Lane] never talked to any juror that I know of."

Mr. Hebert felt certain Lee Harvey Oswald had been in Clinton but he wasn't overly impressed with the testimony of the Clinton folk: "Whose black Cadillac it was, and who was in there—one guy said he had a hat on, one guy said he didn't have any hat on, one guy said he had a white shirt on, another guy said he had a coat on—I mean there's too many conflicting witnesses. They didn't get their stories together before they went up there."

Q.: Well now, how do you feel about the perjury charges?

HEBERT: To be frank with you, I don't know whether he knew the men or not. But I've never seen a witness like Mr. Shaw. He looked the jury in the eye and answered every question as quickly and as accurately as he could. And you see, Perry Russo—I was trying to catch his eye quite often and he would not look at you. He was a shifty-eyed witness, in my opinion. I mean, I don't know, maybe the guy just didn't want to look our way, but very seldom he glanced at the jury. . . . I always—I looked at every witness. I tried to fathom—I mean I can look at a guy and tell if he's telling the truth or not, you know. Because that's what you've got to go by, the credibility of a witness. I mean, after all, the man, he had a lot at stake. I mean, it's not just a felony trial or anything like that. It was a serious charge. And more charges could have grown out of it, too. If that was proven, you see . . . Now Russo's not a dumb bunny, he's a smart boy. But I think he was trying to gain notoriety. Now the thing that got me, was why did Perry Russo wait until after David Ferrie was dead to come out with all of this? Why didn't he come forth before David Ferrie died?

Mr. Hebert had many other pertinent questions. He had clearly been paying strict attention and using his powers of logic. He was adamant about the jurors' complete silence as far as discussing the case during the trial. He admitted it had been difficult but maintained nobody had broken this strict rule of the court. He smiled when he spoke of the Sciambra memo, Dean Andrews, Alvin Oser's performance, and especially when we discussed Charles Spiesel, saying, "He led us on a merry chase." He admired James Alcock and was surprised that Jim Garrison had not taken a more active part, although he did not in any way express displeasure with Garrison.

At one point he brought out a neat envelope containing his trial souvenirs, various clippings, a printed something from the motel, and an eight-by-ten glossy photograph of the jurors, signed on the back by most of the principals. He handled these mementos with gingerly regard for their worth. When he pointed out the signatures, he said, "Judge Haggerty signed it. Clay Shaw even . . . and Jim Garrison!" Garrison's signature was directly next to Clay's.

Mr. Hebert folded up his souvenirs with great care and replaced them in their envelope. He spoke again of his fondness for his fellow jurors, especially for Larry Morgan, one of his roommates and a boy the same age as his son. He also passed a remark that would not have pleased Mr. Garrison, who, despite the adverse verdict, claimed he had proven the Warren Report to be a pack of lies. Said Hebert, "In fact, I didn't think too much of the Warren Report either until the trial. Now I think a lot more of it than I did before this trial."

Oliver Schultz, the 39-year-old employee of the New Orleans Public Service who had so often sat in the box with his head cradled in the palm of his hand, lived in a house very much like Mr. Hebert's. He turned out to be a friendly fellow as we sat in his kitchen drinking coffee while the television set was tuned to a wrestling match and a canary and a parakeet added their two cents.

Mr. Schultz, too, looked back on his jury days as being most pleasant.

SCHULTZ: Yeah, well, we ate—you ordered what you wanted and you got it. But it took a little while to prepare it, but we just waited and—just fooled around a little bit till they come. . . .

We had a special dining room and if they had a party or something like that and we couldn't use that, we had to go out in the big dining room and—we had one long table away from everybody. But it was pretty nice.

Q: Were any of your fellow jurors cut-ups? Any of them with great senses of humor?

SCHULTZ: Oh, you mean comedians in the crowd? Well, they had one colored boy, Ricks, he was kind of a clown all the time. Pretty lively. And I mean, for being a Negro, he didn't—I mean wasn't nothing to him, you know? Like one joke, he said when it was over he was going to go lay in the sun, put his palms and his feet up so he could get a suntan. I mean he wasn't—he was a Negro and he *knew* he was and that was it. It wasn't like he was a—you know, how some of them would take it if you called them something like that. But I was in the room with one, you couldn't ask for better companionship, you know? . . .

Q.: Your deliberations were apparently very simple, weren't they? Was there much discussion?

SCHULTZ: Well, we had a little discussion, wasn't too much. But we all had about the same opinion, that it wasn't enough to convict him. As far as—you know you had to have—beyond a reasonable doubt. Well, to me, I still had *plenty* of doubts. I mean one way or the other. But we all had about the same opinion.

Q.: What did you think was the main part of the state's case that let it down?

SCHULTZ: Well, I thought—beginning with Perry Russo. That was his main witness. And when he could come up with that idea that it could have been a bull session. I mean to me, if I was going to conspire to kill somebody I sure wouldn't let somebody in and out like he claimed he was walking in and out, especially on a party. And especially if it was a drinking party. I mean anybody would be liable to be saying something, you know? To my opinion, I couldn't see him walking in and out like that.

Q.: How did you feel about the Sciambra memo?

SCHULTZ [laughing]: That was something. He tells him one thing and then when he went and wrote the report and reads it back, he's debating that he didn't say this and he didn't say that. Kind of confusing, too . . . I thought that there lawyer was a real clown—the one that made up that name?

Q.: Dean Andrews?

SCHULTZ: And like he said—the one that took us down on Bourbon Street. He was another one.

Q. [gathering Mr. Schultz meant Esplanade Street]: Spiesel. How did you feel about the Clinton people?

SCHULTZ: Yes, that first bunch to come up there. I mean they had nothing to gain by it, but . . . hard to say one way or another. I couldn't say it. I mean right now I wouldn't swear to nothing no more. After being on that jury. I mean, because the way they can twist you around. I mean, they'd probably catch *me* in a lie. That was one reason why I guess I was on that thing, because I didn't want to lie. I was the eighth man on that jury [Mr. Schultz was actually the second juror chosen] and I can't see how in the world people could have a fixed opinion that didn't even hear a thing about it. I mean, what you read in the paper. I mean, you can get an opinion one way or the other, and the next day it's another way. In other words, you would still have a mixed opinion. So how could they have a *fixed* opinion is beyond me. I say, I couldn't go along with that because I was a-scared that they could have twisted it around and got me for perjury.

Q.: How do you feel about Mr. Garrison now?

SCHULTZ: I think he done his job. I mean, he had to back up the state when they convicted him—I mean, put that indictment against him.

Q.: But he was the one that *did* that. [No reply. Mr. Schultz just grinned.] How did you feel when they got into the whole Dallas thing?

SCHULTZ: I think it was trying to—with that Warren Report again. I mean that's what it seemed to us, the whole thing was nothing but the Warren Report. And they wasn't supposed to use none of that Warren Report.

Q.: How did you feel about seeing the Zapruder film?

SCHULTZ: It was amazing that he got it so good, you know. I mean, with all the confusion you'd figure he would throw the camera to someone else. It's a pity that somebody else didn't get some close-ups like that. Of course, nobody wasn't expecting nothing like that to happen.

Q.: What about the reaction of people you know at work and neighbors?

SCHULTZ: Well, they rode me for a while. But, like I told them, I said—they were telling me stuff that we didn't know, when we was upstairs. They said what was going on. And I said, "Well, you all knew more what was going on than we did." [Oliver Schultz laughed.] . . . Well, after—what I explained to them, you know, that you had to have it beyond a reasonable doubt. Well, naturally, they all agreed. And they said, Well, in that case you couldn't do nothing else but that—not guilty. That one little clause in there, that makes a big difference.

Q.: Did you think Mr. Garrison in his closing remarks wanted to use Mr. Shaw to get at the Warren Report?

SCHULTZ: I think like *he* thinks. I think somebody higher up had more to do with that and what I thought that he was trying to do was bring him to say—you know, bring out some more names or something, you know? So he could convict these other ones, bring them down here and convict them. I thought this whole case was— trying to get the higher-ups. And I still say it's higher-ups that had more to do with it than just the fellow that shot him, you know.

Q.: How did you feel when he said, "Ask not what your country can do for you but what you can do for your country"? Did that impress you very much?

SCHULTZ: Yeah. . . . And I thought they was going to bring his [Kennedy's] wife down. Who could be more a witness than his own wife? Sitting right in the car with him. Seems to me that she would be more interested in that case.

So Mr. Schultz, by his own admission, was convinced someone else had been involved. Still this man, who came across exactly as I would have imagined after only having seen him in court— friendly, simple and unsophisticated—reminded me of Clay Shaw's remark about the jury system: "They have an almost mystical way of getting at the truth."

David Powe of Tweedledum and Tweedledee agreed to come to my apartment and arrived in a drenching downpour, sopping wet, except for his spirits, which were high, as were his energy and curiosity.

David Powe is a big man, taller than I'd imagined from seeing him in court, with the look of an owlish administrative sergeant. He did not appear to be at all put out over trekking down to my place in the rain. He soon accepted a scotch and water and agreed to let me switch on the tape recorder.

Q.: How did you feel about being on the jury from the beginning?

POWE: Nothing to feel, really. Now let me ask you a question, before we get onto the questions. I don't mind sitting here talking, but before we get into the questions—can we get to the real core here? [Mr. Powe put his drink down on the coffee table, sat up straight, looked me square in the eye and spoke in a loud voice.] What's in it for me? Because I tell you, I got what I hope to be a book and probably will wind up to be articles and I don't want to sit here and blow that either. Now, if we can get together—fine. I'll be glad to sit here and tell you exactly what I'm writing, go right down through it and tell you where I think the case blew up, tell you what I thought about, what I considered to be the key witnesses and which way they were going but, ah—I'm mercenary and I'm very crude and vulgar. I want something out of it. I spent thirty-one days on that jury. I didn't get a thing financially out of it and now I'd like to recoup the losses.

Q.: Well, ah—What are you thinking of?

POWE: Depends on how far you want to go. I mean, do you want the Reader's Digest Condensed Version or do you want the Unexpurgated Grove Press Version?

Q.: You're obviously talking about money—right?

POWE: Right. Definitely!

Q.: Let's see. I don't know. I never paid anyone for an interview. But that doesn't mean I wouldn't. Ah, this just kind of pulls me up short.

POWE: Well, you know, as I say, I'm very abrupt. I'm crude and vulgar and—

Q.: No, let's amend crude to read candid.

POWE [nodding]: Okay. All right. Fine.

Q.: I don't know. What would you say?

POWE: I have no idea. But I figure this. I think that the book is going for—what's it going to sell for—$5.95, $6.95, depending upon the thickness of the volume? I have no doubts . . . I don't know how soon it's coming out. I imagine it would be shortly, though.

Q.: Well, I guess—You seem to be talking about a *lot* of money, like a percentage?

[David Powe did not disagree. He was not about to give up on a deal.]

POWE: I have no objections to sitting down and saying what went on. There were a couple of things that went on in the deliberating room that amazed me because I just didn't think they would happen. But I would think that if we could get together, that you would not only have enough to go into your book, but you'd have enough possibly to come up with an article for a magazine, as you did on Shaw. What I'm trying to do . . . I'm trying to put down what I thought, what I felt. Where I felt the thing started going in the other direction. I liked to change my mind a couple of times. Where I went back the other way and just sit there and re-evaluate the whole situation, try to get it all down. And what went on when we left court. You see in the movies and they talk about all these things in the movies, about what juries say. Man, that ain't so. That ain't so!

We then spoke of his writing and I told him I thought he should go ahead and write an article based completely upon the jury, their personalities and reactions. I finally found it necessary to say it would be hard for me to make financial concessions to him. He said, "Oh, yeah, I can understand that." After a long silence, I told him I didn't want to pick his brain and asked, "So, what we are going to do—have another drink and forget about it?" We shared a hearty laugh over that, and he said, "Well, I don't know."

I thought at this point he might request me to turn off the tape recorder, but we somehow got onto the subject of Judge Haggerty.

POWE: Judge Haggerty, he's a good man. I'd like to know what he thought. Because, of course, he's been through all this before. He's seen these things and he knows all the tricks of the trade and I'm quite sure he knew where those boys were going before they ever took off with their questions. . . . I think he was fair. I thought he did very well. There were times when he really fooled me. There were times where I thought he wasn't really paying attention to what was going on, but he caught everything. Every time they asked him a question, he caught it. I don't know that much about judges, but he apparently was doing well enough so that nobody asked to have him removed. . . . This trial had a lot of things to it that I—I'd sit there and I kept waiting for them to get into things that they never got into or I would wait for them to ask questions that they didn't ask—that's one thing. *I* wanted to ask questions. I wanted to jump up there and say, Let *me* ask a question. Or, Let's go one step further with that. And then I said, Well you better not ask any questions or we're going to go through this whole damn thing again. Somebody's going to jump up there and say, Well, that's all, let's get rid of that man. Or let's get rid of the whole damn jury. And I don't believe you could have found another fourteen . . . I think that frankly both sides were hoping and praying that the jury was going to be influenced by what it had read pretrial, either in the newspapers or books . . .

We spoke of Mark Lane, who had contacted Powe shortly after the trial concluded and asked him to rate the credibility of witnesses. I mentioned that I found something strange about Lane, in effect, fighting the verdict. To this, Mr. Powe laughed and said, "I don't find anything strange about it." Powe had also been contacted by a reporter from the Washington *Post*. "He [the reporter] just couldn't understand the number of people he met [in New Orleans] that just wouldn't go with the verdict. I said 'No, 99 per cent of the people that I've talked to believe that Shaw's guilty.' "

I expressed disbelief and said I thought that reaction was astonishing.

POWE: No, not really. It's not particularly Clay Shaw. It's anybody. If it was David Powe or Jim Kirkman [sic]—it's not a man, it's a name and it's not really a name any more. It's the government.

Q.: It is the government, isn't it?

POWE: They feel like the man would have been proven guilty if the government had said, Okay, take whatever you want out of the Archives, take whatever you want.

Q.: They could have gotten Governor Connally, but by this time they said, Oh-oh, it's not turning out so well. . . . I can't believe you can get Chief Justice Warren and the entire Commission and the CIA and the FBI and the doctors. These men are so disparate; you couldn't get a group of men to agree on the time of day, let alone conspire to hide evidence. They're as different as you and I and the jury was. You can't do that.

POWE: It could be done.

Q.: It's a huge job.

POWE: Depends on what the ultimate goal is. What is the ultimate goal?

Q.: The only one that had anything to gain was Johnson.

POWE: You can hear some good stories on Mr. Johnson, too [laughing and slapping his knee]. You can hear some tremendous stories there. [Suddenly.] I would still like to know where Clay Shaw's name came from.

Q. [after a pause]: Where his name came from?

POWE: It was not brought out in the trial. . . . How did his name get in the hat to be pulled out? This frankly is the question that is being asked. If he's not guilty, why pick Clay Shaw? Why not pick somebody else?

I was staggered that a man could sit on the Shaw jury for more than a month and still be asking these questions.

We then spoke of Jim Garrison and I mentioned my surprise at his lack of attendance. David Powe did not think this was surprising at all, ending with the comment: "I think this, if you held the election tomorrow, he'd be re-elected."

Q.: It's amazing to me.

POWE: Not to me.

Q.: Well, I'll tell you something. In my opinion, if this had happened in Cleveland or Chicago or New York, he wouldn't be.

POWE: O.K. But you've got a different atmosphere there. You have a lot of people who feel that Garrison's done an awful lot of good for the city and they're going to vote for him on that. I walked down Bourbon Street coming down here. . . . Every time you spend three or four months off Bourbon Street and you walk back down, there's one more joint gets closed up and it's now a perfume shop or a gift shop or a hot dog stand and, of course, I attribute this to Garrison, who closed up so many of the places several years ago and took their license . . . without a liquor license in this town, forget it. You're completely out. You have a lot of people who still remember this, remember he fought so long to get the place cleaned up. As I said earlier, we have a lot of people who still believe—the man on the street still says, well, he

[Shaw] was guilty. They didn't prove it, but he's guilty. The public is funny.

Q.: In the eyes of the nation it was a catastrophe for him [Garrison].

POWE: The nation doesn't have to re-elect him, only Orleans Parish. And I don't know who's going to run against him. If James Alcock would run, I might vote for Alcock. Who's going to run against him? Southern politics are something else, especially Louisiana politics. Earl Long used to be re-elected every damn time he ran. And it was the strangest thing . . . The day of the election, nobody voted for Earl Long and when the votes were counted, Earl Long was always elected. I've got the feeling it's going to be the same thing with Jim Garrison. Nobody's going to vote for him, he's made a complete ass of himself, but when the votes are counted, he'll be elected.

David Powe, at one point, shook his head and blurted out, "I could see what was coming and I wanted on this jury. I wanted on it something ferocious. . . . But I didn't think they would take me."

We spoke of some of the other jurors and touched on the lack of segregation in their living accommodations, which I found happily surprising. Powe said one of his best friends on the jury was Warren Humphrey, a Negro, explaining his theory this way: "I'm a little bit strange for this climate and for this part of the country and sometimes I get into some big arguments on this thing. I was always taught that you didn't judge a book by its cover. You didn't say it was a bad book because you didn't like the cover. You had to read it. And I always thought, If we're giving this consideration to a book, let's at least extend the same courtesy to a human."

I asked, "How did you feel about the perjury charges?"

"I don't know . . . I guess there were a lot of people that were glad to see it. I don't know if you'll get a jury. But who knows how people are going to think? They may say, Well, this is perjury, this is not conspiracy, okay! And, after all, if we're getting ten dollars a day—after all, the first boys didn't get *anything*. So who knows how people are going to think?"

The papers had publicized the possibility of jurors in Orleans

Parish being paid in the future, as a result of the Shaw case. Mr. Powe's statement appeared to hint that if jurors were being paid by the state, this might be an incentive in delivering an attractive verdict.

"Still, some said the perjury charges seemed like mad dog tactics, after the jury's verdict," I told him.

Powe laughed. "Hell, man, I always say, All's fair in love and war. Let's go, let's see what he's got!"

We spoke for perhaps another half-hour, of Garrison's probable ambitions, of the upcoming elections, of the trial, the principals, and eventually of other possible jurors that might be interesting to speak with. Powe urged me to call Larry Morgan. "He's not as mercenary as I am. I don't believe." He suddenly sat up straight, looked at me and smiled. "Although probably, in an indirect way, you got what you wanted from me."

"Yes, I have."

"Right!" He laughed.

If I had not had an engagement, I'd have gladly taken him to dinner. David Powe is an original, in his own amiable, contradictory way. I believe, if there were any possible way to manage it, he'd be in the jury line-up for the perjury trial. David Powe likes to be where the action is.

46

A Large Dose of Tyranny

The following day marked the beginning of a maddening and unexpected game of ring-around-the-rosy with Judge Haggerty. I arrived at the Criminal Court Building in the early afternoon and stopped off at the District Attorney's office on the way. Once more Jim Garrison was not in, at least not to me. Finding Judge Haggerty's courtroom empty, I sent my name in and was soon summoned to his chambers.

His greeting was warm. "Well, Brother Kirkwood!" he said, extending a hand. "Welcome. What can I do for you?" I told him I'd like to tape an interview and he appeared to be extremely amenable. At mention of the trial and what I might want to speak with him about he suddenly said, "That Shaw—he looks to me like a Mongoloid-Negroid. Doesn't he strike you that way?"

"No," I said, defusing my tongue and swallowing my amazement at the thoughtless crudity that would permit the trial judge to speak in such terms to someone he knew might easily quote him.

"Well, he does to me—a sort of Mongoloid-Negroid!" he said, shaking his head and agreeing with himself, as if he'd coined an exceedingly apt and original description. "Yes"—he nodded again—"a Mongoloid-Negroid."

I prayed to Christ he would not repeat the phrase. I found it distasteful in the extreme and was already experiencing a sledge-hammer blow of shame for remaining mute, but I was learning in this new spin-off of my writing career to keep silent. Give people free rein, let them talk and they will eventually pay more by their own exercise of speech than they would if chastised.

Just as he was juggling the flame in an effort to connect with a Salem, he happened to mention that he'd allowed all the participants in the Shaw trial to smoke in the courtroom. Had I remembered that? Yes, I had. "That's because," he explained, "a lot of them were very nervous. Especially with an important case like this, they needed some sort of nervous release. Now, me, I wouldn't need that, but I figured they did," he told me. I could not help thinking, Then why did you almost light your nose instead of your cigarette?

Out of thin air he mentioned, "The jury didn't believe the Tadins." He shook his head. "No, they didn't go for the Tadins." His manner seemed to indicate regret at this.

There were several people in and out of his office and again he asked specifically what I wanted to talk to him about. I told him that since I was writing a book on the case, it would be interesting to have an interview with the presiding judge. There were several phone calls and documents brought in for his signature, and I suggested it would perhaps be better if we could speak alone, when he was finished with his day's work. He agreed, and I was to come by next afternoon for a taped discussion with him. He spoke of a filmed interview he'd given to one of the television stations before the trial and promised to have it run off for me. The interview had not been aired because the station, the judge indicated, believed it violated the pretrial guidelines—set down by Judge Haggerty.

Before I left, the judge dug through some ill-kept scrapbooks, all dog-eared and faded, jammed with loose photographs and memorabilia, some from his early Navy career and one photograph in particular of a muscular young man. "Ever see that picture of Clark Gable?" "No," I replied. "You never saw that picture Clark Gable gave me?" "Nope," I said, setting him up for the punch like a good Brother Kirkwood. "Hell, that's not Gable, that's me!" he said, giving me a playful swat on the arm. "But a lot of people think I looked like him, I'll tell you that!" I did not entirely agree, but I did admit he looked to be in damned good shape. And he did. He also presented a card to me with his brother's picture and credits. Dan Haggerty, a lookalike for Ed, was gearing up to run for election as Clerk of the Criminal District Court, to replace their father, Edward Haggerty, Sr., who was finally retiring at an advanced age, after having been clerk for many years. Somebody once told me, "The number of Haggertys working in the Criminal Court Building and in other city and state jobs has never been accurately ascertained."

Early that evening, while I was getting cleaned up to go out for dinner, the phone rang. A man's voice asked, "Is Jim Kirkwood there?"

"This is Jim Kirkwood."

"This is Jim Garrison."

I thought someone was putting me on and as I was considering who this might be, he said my name again and I recognized the deep mellifluous voice. Surprise shattered my cool. "Oh, hello, there!" I heard my voice echo off the walls of the apartment close to a shout.

"You're extremely persistent, aren't you?" he asked.

"Well, yes, I guess so."

"You're one of the most persistent reporters I've come up against."

"Well—"

"Why are you so set on meeting me?" he asked, not sternly, but with simple curiosity.

I would not have believed my reply if I hadn't heard it myself. "Well," I said, "I've heard an awful lot about you."

He had the good grace to chuckle faintly as I regained some semblance of logical speech. "That is, I've heard many interesting things about you personally. That you have a good sense of humor and—I simply want to meet you. I'm curious. I'd really like to just talk to you, get the feeling of you."

"I think that could be arranged," he replied.

"Fine."

"I haven't been talking to reporters lately."

"I know. But then, I'm not really a reporter."

"Tell you what. I'll give you a non-interview. Would you settle for that?"

"Yes," I replied, wondering exactly what a non-interview was, but acknowledging it certainly would not include a tape recorder.

"You're a very good writer," Jim Garrison said.

"Thank you."

"I haven't read your book yet, but I know you're a good writer."

"I hope you will read it."

"Yes, I will. I'm not in the habit of accepting books and not reading them."

He went on to explain he had been extremely busy. When we got back to our meeting, I said the sooner the better. I would make myself available when he had free time and suggested lunch. The date was set for the next day at noon. I was to call his secretary midmorning, and she would tell me where we were to meet. I thanked him, and we said goodbye.

The following morning I had an interview with Aaron Kohn, the managing director of the Metropolitan Crime Commission. He and Jim Garrison had been friends and allies, early on in the District Attorney's career. Their relationship had altered drastically, and now they were archenemies. Indeed, Garrison had gone so far as to have Kohn thrown in jail upon occasion.

Kohn, in his late fifties, is a serious man with neat sparse gray hair and a prominent nose that gives direction to his handsomely intense face. I asked him if the talk I had heard after the trial about a petition to recall Garrison was accurate.

KOHN: Yes, well, it was our crime commission that made a statement that we were forming a committee to evaluate the availability of evidence which could be used to support a petition for the removal of Garrison as District Attorney—under provisions of our state constitution, which specify very specific but very limited causes of action for such removal. The constitutional authority also provides that the removal of an elected official of the state can be accomplished in a variety of ways. For various reasons it appeared that there were only two reasonably within likelihood. One was through the filing of a petition by twenty-five citizens and taxpayers with the Attorney General of our state, Jack Gremillion. The utility of this method is, of course, substantially reduced by the fact that the State Attorney General has been asked by us before, publicly, to investigate the accusations of alleged crimes on the part of the District Attorney and his staff. And the Attorney General has consistently refused such requests or ignored them. Therefore even though the law would require him, upon receipt of such a petition, to initiate a removal action, we've had our experiences with Mr. Gremillion and he can make sure that the action is so non-vigorous that it would be ineffectual. Therefore we eliminated this as a reasonable likelihood of impartial government handling under state government.

That left us with only one possibility that seemed to have some fair chance of success if the evidence which would be produced would back up such a move. And that is the constitutional authority for twenty-five citizens to file a petition in a civil district court of Orleans Parish, asking that court to undertake a removal action and also asking that court to appoint an attorney to prosecute it before the court. And this is what we had come to the conclusion as the most potentially useful vehicle for possible removal. However, since then this committee, which consists of volunteers in the community, members of our crime commission, has been devoting some time to it. I've been devoting quite a bit of time communicating with people, who during the past couple of years have been involved in the making of accusations against Garrison or his staff. Not only with reference to the Shaw trial, and the alleged conspiracy to murder President Kennedy, but also in other matters. . . .

We're having great difficulty in getting people who—in the heat of the affair, when Garrison was indicting them, accusing them publicly, now that the Shaw trial is over, and the community has become silent on the subject—they seem to be very reluctant to cooperate. Not all of them. Don't misunderstand me. But part of our difficulty, part of the time-consuming delay that is now involved, has been our attempts to get these people to make formal statements which could be evaluated as potential testimony in a courtroom within the framework of what is and is not admissible. . . . And it's a foot-dragging process. It's a very difficult one.

Q.: You certainly would have no trouble getting the petition signed by twenty-five people?

KOHN: No, there'd be no trouble getting it *signed*. But it would be irresponsible to ask people to sign such a petition unless we were in a position to give them reasonable assurance that when the court proceedings following that petition were held, that what is alleged in the petition—since the petition must allege a public official involved has been guilty of acts which under our state constitution are the basis for removal—can be proven.

Q.: Does that come under malfeasance in office?

KOHN: Well, not actually. Malfeasance is not one of the terms used at all. There are a number of areas that might be applicable to what we now know about the Garrison pattern of conduct. They include high crimes and misdemeanors. Favoritism in office.

What might be called tyrannical conduct. . . . Gross misconduct. And I might mention that gross misconduct becomes very difficult to define, in anticipation, in view of a recent decision of our own State Supreme Court involving our similar efforts to get a judge who was a former very close friend of Garrison's also removed from office . . . What we alleged and what was proven constituted in our opinion gross misconduct. But the State Supreme Court found that although it was misconduct it wasn't *gross* and therefore refused to remove him.

Q.: Where does bribery fit in?

KOHN: Well, that has to be under the broad category of high crimes and misdemeanors. As you know, part of the challenge of compiling what might be ultimately sound proof of allegations upon which removal could be based is that so many of the people who Garrison drew into this matter and who were the targets of his compulsive drive to prove afterwards something he prematurely claimed to exist—and that is the conspiracy—that so many of them were people with past criminal records, people who were obviously emotionally unstable, persons who are either known to be or reasonably suspected to be homosexuals, narcotics addicts, convicted burglars, and therefore people on whose evidence alone it would be reasonably anticipated that a court would have considerable doubt. And therefore it means building up enough confirming proof to make such direct testimony as they might give believable. And I mean these are among the things that make the construction of proof so tenuous.

Even Garrison's own conduct, its inconsistencies, his flamboyance, the fact that he has had a number of lawyers who are assistant D.A.'s who have given affirmation to the things that he has done. We have to anticipate that those who were a part of what he has done would be witnesses confirming anything that he might allege or deny. Then it's quite difficult for a court to take the testimony of five lawyers and put it alongside the testimony of five emotionally disturbed or criminally convicted persons and to balance credibility. So we're still trying to see if we can't induce the persons who have direct knowledge, who might contribute that which would be admissible in the total proof production in court—people like the lawyers for some of these people who are not necessarily credible, but who have direct knowledge. People of that kind. And these are among those who have been most difficult to commit to cooperation. . . .

Q.: When I was here before it sounded like maybe the ball might get rolling.

KOHN: Well, I'm still not sure it won't. But I'm just saying there are problems. There are people who were vehement and indignant just a matter of weeks ago, who today are evasive and avoiding when it comes to trying to produce what they were saying and accusing then. They were defending themselves then. They no longer are on the defensive. Now they have a different viewpoint when it comes to being on the aggressive, and doing something about Garrison. . . . And again this gets down to something fundamental you were talking about—maybe when you were here before—and that is this business of fear. Real and imagined fear.

Q.: I know, it's almost like fiction to me—to come down here and gather up all these bizarre elements that went into this case. It's almost as if, being a fiction writer, if I had written this, I think my editor or publisher would have said, God, I'm sorry, you've just gone way off the deep end there, you've got to bring some of this back into more or less normal perspective.

KOHN: I think you're describing pretty much how I envisioned it as it was happening, and still do as I look back on what did happen in this history of Garrison's, both official handling as the District Attorney—and his script-writing handling as a voice through the news media. To me he's always been a man of imagination—who set out a broad plot at the very beginning, when he first announced he had solved this thing, a broad plot but hadn't yet decided on his characters, and how they were going to act. When the public bought his rough script, he then started to write his book. And permitted each character, as he reacted, to write the next page for him. The mistake, of course, was that he sold the book as a text, as an historic text. But actually he was writing fiction. And this has been its history. And it's consistent with Jim Garrison. I think I mentioned to you, when the British Broadcasting Corporation interviewed me . . . and I told them then I thought it was going to prove to be a fraud, because this is the way Garrison has functioned. Prior to it, in other matters. And it wasn't until more recently, however, as pieces fell together including some past documentation of his medical record—it seems as though fraud wasn't exactly the right term. Actually he is an emotionally disturbed person, who is compelled to act deceptively in order to preserve his own fundamental ego.

I often also think that as we hear all the very useful loud noises being made right now about organized crime, and the destructive influence of organized crime on the administration of justice, how inadvertently organized crime might be responsible for this vastly destructive thing that went on beginning early in 1967 and is not yet over—the Garrison prosecution investigation and the John Kennedy assassination plot, so-called—and that it was all started really as a result of that very ego quality of Garrison's when he wandered into unsupportable controversy over the question of whether organized crime existed in New Orleans. Here was this great white knight on a white charger, an image he had projected for so long, unreal with reference to his own personal character and personal habits, personal morality. Nevertheless the kind of thing that the glibness of news media projection can do for an individual, that is, create a nonexistent individual. And then he tries to fit this image he suddenly discovers has been created for him . . . and this is what Garrison had done.

Aaron Kohn laid out a theory that I had heard from several other sources, the fulcrum of which is the existence of organized crime in New Orleans. A strong branch of the Mafia is firmly entrenched in the Mardi Gras city. It owns bars, motels, vending machines, sightseeing tours, and, apparently, quite a few politicians. The head of the local Mafia is reputed to be Carlos Marcello, described in the confidential records of the New Orleans police as "one of the most notorious underworld figures in the country."

Frank Occhipinti, a partner with Marcello and his brother in several business ventures, built the house that Garrison lives in and, in fact, lives right next door to the District Attorney. Occhipinti also happens to own the Rowntowner Motor Inn, which happened to be picked as the domicile of the jurors in the Shaw case and is also a favorite and almost nightly watering hole of Judge Haggerty. The coziness between the Occhipinti family, the Marcello family and Jim Garrison gives off a heady odor indeed. The FBI knows all about Marcello and the Mafia in New Orleans, the Internal Revenue Department and the police know about him and the Immigration and Naturalization Service has been trying to deport him for years. In fact, Jim Garrison would seem to be the only person in town who denies the Mafia's existence. He once described Carlos Marcello as "a respectable businessman."

Such indifference would be ludicrous if it weren't so damnably blatantly frightening. If the man who denies the existence of organized crime is the very man elected to fight same, you have a situation rather like an exterminator refusing to acknowledge the existence of termites. One would think he should get into another business. And this is precisely what Aaron Kohn believes Garrison did—the other business being the investigation of the assassination of President Kennedy.

KOHN: He was under considerable attack at the time from our Crime Commission about a pardon he had forced the Governor to grant, which the Governor admitted he should not have granted, and would not have granted other than owing Garrison political favors, for an employee of one of the Cosa Nostra—connected joints on Bourbon Street. And then Garrison lied about why he did it. He lied about it, was caught in the lie, perhaps for the first time since he had been in office. He had been in office by then over four years. There was a television editorial ridiculing him, making him look silly . . . In the meantime a grand jury probe was started to investigate organized crime . . . and there were a great deal of inconsistencies . . . Anyhow, there was all this pressure . . . Oh, and incidentally, the press is on the neck of the D.A.'s office all the time. So it was right at this time, the fall of '66, this is when Garrison's assistants, particularly Charles Ward, start leaking to the press, confidentially—when they heard we were trying to probe into what he's doing in these other matters—"Well, he's working on a very important thing. Tremendously important." And then a little bit more. "Has to do with the Kennedy assassination." And this was all being leaked out. Incidentally, all the press representatives up at the Criminal Court Building knew that he was working on this before the States-Item story broke it. In January of '67. You remember he also made statements when things started getting hot that the press handicapped him by breaking the story. The fact is his office had leaked it to all the news media prior—at a time when he's under pressure about organized crime. So it may well be, and again it would not be inconsistent with the pattern of Garrison, because he has said to me so many times, "The best defense is an *offense*." . . .

He's a man who easily feels threatened. No matter how unreal it might look to other people, to him he is alarmingly threatened. And it may well be that he engages in extravagant diversions when he's threatened. If, in fact, this thing was tossed into his life by Russell Long on that air trip that he talks about, this may have become for him an opportune suggestion for diverting massive attention away from his vulnerability in the organized crime area.

Q.: Because he has stated flatly that there was no organized crime—

KOHN: He completely denounced those who said there was [organized crime] as having ulterior motives. . . .

Every time you tried to do anything thereafter, about the inadequacies of the performance of Garrison's office, his major purposes and objectives, and that is the investigatory and prosecutive responsibilities in dealing with the real and present crime problem . . . it was always then attacked as being an attempt to handicap his efforts to accomplish this thing of worldwide importance. And I can tell you, the record is clear, of his accusations against everybody that was critical as being a part of a conspiracy and we were included, a vast conspiracy of the "Eastern Establishment" and the Federal government to keep him from proving that the Warren Commission report was wrong.

Mr. Kohn spoke of one letter that had broken off relations between Garrison and the Metropolitan Crime Commission when they pressed him further about organized crime in New Orleans.

KOHN: I think you'll find that letter very interesting because it's a paranoid letter. He said, in effect, Who the hell do you think you are to ask me questions like that? It's none of your business whether I do or don't do anything. Whether I do anything is a matter for my own decision. And then he went on to say, "From now on I will absolutely refuse to accept any kind of communication from the Crime Commission." This was in December 1966. "And I'm instructing my entire staff to return all letters unopened." And they've come back here unopened!

Now this prosecutor, a public official, is paranoid. To back away from his entire function, from all communication! Not just Garrison, the man, but the District Attorney and the total District Attorney's functions—to refuse to accept any information about any crime going on in the community, about any criminal in the community!

Q.: All of that seems to be such a part of supportive evidence in the petition to have the man removed.

KOHN: I agree. And of course this would be used. But even a good many of our judges around here are afraid of Garrison. We've got to give them—we realize that if anything is to be done, in the face of the tyranny of this man, which is only in part real, but which is perhaps 80 per cent in the eyes of the beholders, that we're confronted with a real touchy situation. The battle between the Crime Commission and Garrison is a matter of public knowledge. It hasn't changed popular belief in his hates, which is what, really, his supporters believe in. They don't believe in Garrison. They believe in the things he vocalizes for them. He vocalizes popular hates. Hate for Washington, hate for the Supreme Court, hate for law enforcement structures. And therefore he is their man. . . .

It is frightening. . . . You must remember that a corrupt governor like Jimmy Davis was re-elected. That a man like Earl Long was re-elected. Let's not forget the mayor of Boston, who went to prison and was then re-elected. . . . Garrison could be elected to the United States Senate. And make this combined clever intellect with destructive emotional disturbance felt on the national scene. . . .

You probably see it in my face as I talk. My concern is so deep about this because I have long had the feeling that I have been sitting at the ringside of the evolution of Mussolini, Adolf Hitler, any tyrant who has successfully taken over total control of a massive part of society. With the cooperation of that society. I no longer see this as a matter of Garrison and New Orleans. I see it as the problem which repeats itself through the history of man, civilized man. The willingness of the public, given the right personality, the right demagoguery, and a sufficient amount of almost insane compulsion to use these qualities—they can be led to slaughter. And I'm watching it happen. And I don't see this any longer as Garrison and New Orleans. To me, for a long time now, it has been the problem of tyranny fed by public popularity.

After our talk, although I harbored admiration for Aaron Kohn and the long, seemingly endless and frustrating battle he was putting up, I felt weighted down with dismay that there would be no petition, no charges filed. I could smell it.

The Metropolitan Crime Commission is in the same building that houses Irvin Dymond and Eddie Wegmann. I dropped by for a talk with Irvin and used his phone to call the District Attorney's office and find out where I was to meet Jim Garrison for lunch.

His secretary came on the line and informed me something unforeseen had come up and Mr. Garrison had to cancel our luncheon appointment. If disappointment can be manic, mine was. "Listen," I said to her, "will you tell Mr. Garrison that if he does this once again, I'll haul him into court and sue him for breach of promise." "What?" she asked. "I mean it," I repeated. "I'll haul him to court and sue him for breach of promise! I've got some pull, too. Now, will you give him that message?"

For the first time I got a laugh from her, as she promised she would relay my threat. She would do everything she could to set up another appointment and would get back to me. "Just in case—I'll get back to *you* tomorrow," I said.

Dymond sat behind his desk laughing in his low growly way and shaking his head. "He'll never see you, Jim. Forget it."

"Yes, he will."

I arrived at the Criminal Court Building that afternoon for the interview with Judge Haggerty to find him huddled over his desk, shuffling papers and folders about. I was as warmly greeted as before, but there was a distraction about him. He seemed to be using the disarray of his desk and barking at his patient court reporter, Donald Theriot, and his new and equally patient minute clerk, Mike Steubben, in a manner that was indicative of a delaying action. He was soon summoned out to his courtroom on official business and told me to make myself at home. I did so by taking out the tape recorder and setting it up on his large desk.

When he returned, there was more shuffling about through papers on his desk and a few lengthy phone calls. I noticed he kept brushing his hand nervously across his mouth and sometimes, across his forehead. He apologized for the delay, explaining he had several extra matters to attend to. I sat there for a while, until things finally calmed down and there appeared to be no other activity to keep us from talking.

"Brother Kirkwood," he suddenly said, brushing his hand across his mouth again, "I would rather not give a taped interview."

"Really? But yesterday you said you would."

"I know I did. But—I talked to some friends last night, and a lawyer, and I think it would be better if I didn't."

He was earnestly apologetic, but just as earnestly set against the tape machine. "I tell you what. We'll handle it like this. You make out a list of questions you'd like to ask and submit them to me. I'll look them over, study them, and then we'll have our talk."

"But I'm not going to ask you any questions that—"

"I'd rather do it that way. Just make up a list, you know, whatever you want to ask me about and I'll look them over." He started to summon his court reporter, so I could dictate my questions, but I said I'd rather do it myself—that would, at least, give me time to think up a few pertinent questions, as long as I was to be limited. He apologized again and chattered on in a most friendly manner as I gathered the tape machine up and put it back in its case.

47

The Red Pepper Gun

To assuage my day's failures I stopped by Bill Gurvich's office to speak with him. Bill is a charming man, good-looking, graying, mellow, with a tough skeleton of resolve beneath his amiability. I asked him how he figured the perjury charges against Shaw.

GURVICH: Well, knowing Garrison, I can picture just about how he felt when that verdict came in. Because no one was more confident of a conviction than Jim Garrison was. Now, I can't say that so much toward the end, because I wasn't around. But from what I got, the information I received from other people, certainly indicated he was enthusiastic, as optimistic as ever. He has his fears, he has his sick moments, he has his unpleasant moments, and this depends on when this sickness of his takes over. If some little thing happens—I could see how little things affected him. So, I tried to visualize how he was reacting to this loss. And as well as I know him, as well as I *think* I know him, I still can't vividly see him because it's just—God knows what he went through! Just— you know, it's indescribable. Unimaginable. You just can't imagine how he reacts!

Q.: I've heard about a couple of funny episodes you had with Garrison, when you were still with him. What about the FBI raid?

GURVICH [laughing]: This would have been about February '67. Garrison was convinced that his home and office phones were bugged, the phones of all staff members were bugged, everyone's phones were tapped. He used to pick up the phone and before dialing he would say into the mouthpiece, "Fuck Hoover!" You know? Like, when Hoover hears this he's really going to get mad but he can't say he's mad without admitting he has a bug. So this paranoia became so intense that he told me he was planning to raid the local FBI office here. For the purpose of confiscating tape recordings to prove that he was right. He further said . . . he knows that each FBI office has a secret recording room, that within this recording room—wherever it was in New Orleans in the Federal Building—we would find the machine and the tapes and when we'd confiscated them and made them public we would prove that the government was trying to torpedo his investigation into the death of the President. I told him I'd never heard of this recording room but anything was possible. I said, "How are we going to do this?" He said, "I have a warrant and I have a judge who'll back it up." I said, "When and where?" "Well, we'll do it late at night. They'll only have a law student, a phone answerer, a clerk—he'll be studying and we'll hit him with the warrant, he won't be able to use the phones or anything else." I said, "Well, that would be the best time, late at night, but," I said, "knowing these agents, they never work alone, what if two or three of them check in while we're searching for this room?" He said he didn't know where the room was, that we'd find it behind a panel in the wall, or behind a file or something. We'd have to move all the furniture and go around beating on the walls trying to find this room—that doesn't exist. And he said, "Well, you're really going to come in handy, Bill, because you're a ballistics expert." . . . I wanted to know how that would work into the deal. "Well," he says, "we're going to have red pepper guns." "What's a red pepper gun?" I laughed. "And where do you get them—at the A and P?" "No," he said, "a red pepper gun, you know." Well, I didn't know but I figured it was some kind of chemical mace that you spray but he only referred to red pepper guns and told me to get some. "If I know what it is, I'll get it," I told him. "But—a *red pepper gun!*" "You spray it on them and it immobilizes them for a few moments," he told me.

Q.: If he had a warrant, why would he need a red pepper gun?

GURVICH: Who knows? In case they came while we were there, I suppose. And so he had this big plan and talked about it the next day. And there were other people who asked to go along. They wanted to be along for this historical search and seizure. God knows what he'd have found—communist records, maybe some white slavery records, but certainly nothing on Jim Garrison.

Q.: Did he ever explain the red pepper gun?

GURVICH [laughing]: No, he just assumed I'd figured it out.

The whole thing died out, just like a lot of other plans. One day it was one thing, the next day he'd talk to somebody and it would be another big deal. I wanted to go along and see what would have happened. It would have been hysterical.

Q.: There are stories about a mysterious picture deal.

GURVICH [laughing again]: There was a fellow named Raymond Marcus. He wrote a book called *The Bastard Bullet*. It's about Exhibit—is it 299? The strange bullet that did all the damage. He came in the office and he had some large blowups of what he said was the picket fence area in Dallas, in Dealey Plaza. And these photographs would support what Garrison was saying about multiple assassins. Behind the fence. Behind the wall. So these photographs had been enlarged so many times that they looked like a checkerboard—they were black and white squares. Which was the printer's screen, enlarged. You couldn't distinguish anything. I joked with them when they showed it to me, and I said it looked like a Purina checkerboard sign. So Garrison called me over and said, "Look!" He had a pencil and a magnifying glass. He says, "Look at this, Bill. You can see a *man*." So I looked in the glass, he was holding the glass, I looked over his shoulder, I saw nothing. I said, "Jim, I don't see—what—maybe I—." Then he had to come back and focus *his* eye on it again and he said, "Well, it's right *here!*" But then *he* couldn't find it. So he says, "Wait a minute." He says, "Raymond, where is that again?" So then Marcus came over, and we're all standing behind the desk now, looking for this—whatever it is. And Marcus—it took him a few seconds to find it, and then he put his finger on it, pointed a pencil toward it, and then Garrison took the pencil from Marcus, held the glass—now he saw it too, because the pencil is pointing toward this area. Then I looked at it. And I said, "Well, I see the pencil and your finger," and I kidded him again. I said, "Your nails are dirty, Garrison." I said, "I don't see anything." So Marcus said, "Well, the reason you don't see it is because it's enlarged so many times you're too *close* to it." So he took it—it would have been about sixteen by twenty inches—across the room and he set it in the middle of the sofa, which would put it somewhere between ten to fifteen feet from Garrison and me.

Q.: Was that in his office?

GURVICH: Oh, yes. "Now do you see it?" I said, "No, it's still Purina to me." And Garrison said, "I don't see it either, Raymond."

I lose it when you move it." Well, then it isn't so obvious if you can't see it all the time. If you have to get to the originator or the printer or whoever he is to point it out to you each and every time. So Marcus says, "Well, we're still too close to it." By this time Jim Alcock had come in. I didn't know where he was going to go now—this was the largest room in the building, other than one of the courtrooms. So Marcus says, "Give me five minutes and look out the window." He left and we waited. We raised the blind in five minutes and we looked out from the third floor there, out onto Tulane Avenue, sort of facing in a northerly direction. And lo and behold, standing across the street, at about 5 in the late afternoon, during the peak hour of traffic, is Raymond Marcus. On the opposite side of the Avenue, holding up this Purina sign! . . . And I could read his lips: "Can you see it now?" That's what he's saying. And it was worse than ever. But now not only were we three, Alcock, Garrison and I, looking at it, but every other son of a gun, everyone passing down Tulane Avenue in their cars was slowing down, staring at this stranger who was holding this checkerboard sign and saying to a building, "Can you see it now?" And we would see people look at him and then people look up toward the building. But we're standing inside of a dark building and they can't see us.

Well, there was a used car lot there. And one of the salesmen, being a little shady himself, I imagine, wondered who the hell this character was in front of his property, holding up a sign, talking to the wind. *"Can you see it now?"* So he came out and he looked at the front of the sign, looked at the back, and looked at Marcus. I figured any minute there's going to be an altercation there. Then in the middle of the block is a barbershop, which was maybe fifty or sixty yards from where Marcus was now standing. And one of the barbers—I guess it was an idle time of the day—came out and stood in the doorway in his white uniform and was smoking. As he glanced down the street he took a second look, a double take, at this man. He stares at the guy and he's looking up too, you know like this: Well, who the *hell's* he talking to? And then he disappeared and went back inside. But that was the story about Raymond Marcus.

There were others that were bringing in photographs. Another fellow brought us one that immediately upon looking at the photograph, of the picket fence area, you immediately saw a Latin-type guy with *sunshades* and *earphones!* Well, man, you didn't—if somebody saw it in the photograph then everybody else around there originally saw it. And it was just so obvious you know that it had been put in there. It was a fake. But well done. Very well done. It never was used. But I always thought Garrison would use it because he usually used anything anyone gave him or anything anyone said.

Bill Gurvich told stories of other goose hunts he'd been sent on. Garrison had dispatched him to Dallas on the theory that David Ferrie's role in the assassination had been that of getaway pilot and that he had been perched in a small plane with the engine running at the end of a runway on the afternoon of the assassination, waiting to fly Oswald to safety. Gurvich, a pilot himself, had flown from airfield to airfield, checking records and showing pictures of Ferrie to all available personnel. Finally, at one airport, White Rock, a mechanic said *maybe* he'd seen the man at one time or another, he wasn't sure. Garrison had every gasoline voucher from that airport for a period of three months Xeroxed and checked—a total of more than 4,000 vouchers.

GURVICH: The control tower operators in Dallas told me, "Well, a plane at the end of a runway with motors running? Only if he was taking off, otherwise we wouldn't permit him to be there." And then, I knew these engines are air-cooled. How long can you stay on the ground with engines running without them overheating? How much fuel do you consume? What about other planes taking off and landing? And if you wanted to be that conspicuous, why don't you just hold up a sign saying, "Lee Harvey, here I am!" and hang it on the plane.

Then one day by accident, in New Orleans, I am told that David Ferrie was in Federal court in New Orleans at the exact moment of the assassination. And I immediately figured, This is impossible. So I checked. And lo and behold, it was indeed true.

Q.: In the face of the obviousness of his gullibility to believe anything—all the wild schemes, the manufactured clues—what about the loyalty of the people who have stuck with him? They're not all stupid. What about Alcock?

GURVICH: The most common theory as to why they stay is that's their employment, they have notes to pay, they have families to

feed. Well, I always felt, like, if that's what you have to do to feed
your family, how the hell can you go home and *face* this family?
How can you eat with them? And persecute a man, put him in
prison possibly for twenty years because some insane boss has said
so—when you know the truth. That makes you equally as guilty.
Because you were a party to it before it happened, before the
conviction, before the trial, and one's as guilty as the other. You
cannot be an accessory before the fact. You're a principal. You can
be an accessory after, but if you're an accessory before, you are, in
fact, a principal. They stuck with him. I think they were afraid to
leave. Because if they left, and they were attorneys and had been
up there in criminal work, in all probability they would go into
private practice and specialize in criminal work. Something they
had been close to and were best suited for. If they did this, they
certainly, to be successful, would have to be able to get along with
the District Attorney.

Those who haven't stuck, have been seriously hurt by him.
Especially in a city like New Orleans, where things are done
through wheeling and dealing and payoffs, more so than on
ability, you have to get along with the man. Because you can earn
your fee, not in the courtroom, but earn your fee by getting your
case postponed, getting the case reviewed, or getting the case—just
dismissed. You can get a larger fee for having it dropped than you
can for defending. Because it's worth it, really. No embarrassment,
no fear, no nothing. I think one reason is that they didn't have the
guts to try it on their own. And had Garrison won this thing, in
all probability he would have been bigger than ever. Because how
many more years would it have taken for the truth to be *known?*
And by then, how many people would remember?

His assistants would immediately suffer. The day they left they
would have been on his list. And he does have quite a list. He's a
very vindictive person. As you wrote in *Esquire,* as I said to you
once before, he's extremely dangerous. And people might be
convinced that he's *somewhat* dangerous, but they haven't yet seen
exactly how much. I think the day will come when they will see,
get a better idea of the extent he will go to.

So you have the fear of leaving because they couldn't practice
law successfully with the D.A. fighting them all the time. Also,
some of these people were convinced that this guy would win and
go up the ladder as far as he wanted—almost to the position of

God. And that if he did, if he became Governor—remember, the Governor can name the Attorney General. There's judgeships, he can name judges to unexpired terms. Or newly created judges. And all these guys would line up, you know, with judgeships, maybe a criminal judge, they could practice civil law—they're fixed for life. And they were all looking ahead. Greedily. The hell with Clay Shaw, or any other individual. . . .

Q: What about your leaving? Did you have a real tussle about—so-called defecting? Or did you simply have to do it?

GURVICH: Well, in April and May '67 I talked to two lawyers from town. Both of whom were friendly with Garrison, both of whom knew Garrison, both of whom were good friends of mine, both of whom had once worked for Garrison. One of whom at the time was *still* working for Garrison. And I told them that I thought it was all a fraud, I was convinced it was, and I had been involved in it now for four months, so I was going to get out. What did they recommend? What did they suggest? They said, "Well, you can get out very quietly." I said, "After what this guy has got me involved in," I said, "man, I just—I want everyone to *know* I'm out of it and I'm sorry I was ever associated with it." "If you do that," they said, "you will be called a defector." And I said, "Well, that sounds bad but it's not half as bad as what they will call me when the truth of this investigation is known." So that was in April. We discussed it again in May, and then June 8th, or the 7th of June—I had an occasion to tell the story to Bobby Kennedy. I told him. Immediately after that, Bill Moyers with *Newsday* up in Long Island—I guess he got the story from Kennedy—comes out with it. I'm in New York City, and he comes out with my meeting with Kennedy, which was confidential and private. I haven't told it to anybody, so who else told it? And when I came back home I couldn't get into the office, you see. But I was definitely going to quit anyhow.

Q.: How did you happen to get to Kennedy?

GURVICH: Through one of his emissaries. I was asked if I would see the Senator. I didn't know for sure what he wanted to see me about, what he had to say. But I went, I paid my own way. They offered to buy my ticket, but because it was Kennedy and because Kennedy was on the other side—although I didn't believe in Garrison any more at this point, I was still on his payroll and I'm a firm believer in loyalty. That's why I never—they wanted me on

NBC on the white paper, but I said, "Regardless of how I feel or what I believe, I am still working for him, I haven't resigned, therefore I can't say anything against him."

So when I saw the Senator it was quite obvious he was more interested in hearing what I had to say than he was in telling me anything.

Q.: In other words he contacted you?

GURVICH: Yes. I talked to his emissary at the Royal Orleans Hotel.

Q.: What was his reaction to what you told him?

GURVICH: I don't think he ever thought the guy had anything. And I've never really discussed our meeting with anyone. He's dead, it was confidential—whether he honored it or not, I don't know. But basically what I told him was, the exact words were, "Senator, Mr. Garrison will never shed any light on your brother's death." What he wanted to know most was, and I'll quote him, "Then why is he doing this?" At the time, I told him I did not have the answer to it. That if I had the answer to that I'd have the answer to the whole damn thing. Was it political? Was it insanity? Was it for money? Was it revenge? What was it? But I don't believe anybody could actually say at the time. I didn't try. I just simply said, "I don't know. I wish I did."

[After his return to New Orleans, Gurvich had volunteered to go before the grand jury and give them the substance of his charges that Garrison's investigation was a fraud. This is tantamount to jumping into the lion's den stark naked.]

GURVICH: I publicly said I would volunteer, but I was subpoenaed . . . before the LaBiche grand jury. And they were not interested in hearing what I had to say. They kept me waiting eight and one half hours the first time. And offered two rebuttal witnesses, Turner and Yacci, before I testified. *Before* I testified. And then I was told that, you know, they were going to indict me.

Q.: Who was handling the jury for the D.A.'s office?

GURVICH: Alcock and Burns. They denied my constitutional rights a dozen times or so. It's all recorded. I deliberately had them do it over and over again so it would be recorded. . . . It's so ridiculous, to me and to most attorneys. It's an archaic idea to have this grand jury thing so secret. Because the secrecy of the grand jury is to protect the witness. And if the witness doesn't care, then don't keep it a secret. . . . If the witness wants to testify in secret and not be named as a witness or an informer, then he should be protected. But if he doesn't care and makes it public, well, then the hell with it. Who could care less? . . . I tell you, Jim, I had—I still have a hell of a fine record in this city. I've done many things, given my time to charitable organizations, and was really interested in the community. I don't have one blemish on my record. Truthfully, I've been highly respected among professionals in all walks of life. And suddenly I quit a man, and I make terrible accusations. Who came forward and wanted to hear it? I said things about policemen up there, but did the police department ever contact me and say, "Just what is it, Bill, these people have done? Whether we believe you or not, we sure want to hear about this." Nobody. No Federal, state, no city, no private— nobody. Because they didn't want to get involved with anyone or anything that opposed Jim Garrison. I couldn't find a friend. I saw people I knew for twenty years avoid me in narrow spaces, at coffee stands, turn their backs or walk away.

Q.: What do you think are the chances of Garrison's being reelected?

GURVICH: It's hard for me to give an unbiased opinion. I must say this, that I have fears he will be. Because it's New Orleans, because it's Louisiana. And as one of the U.S. attorneys said on television last night, he has never seen a more corrupt state than Louisiana. He was down here investigating crime and rackets, syndicated organizations. It's true. You see, I think if they dug up Huey Long, they could run his corpse. If they could get it all together, they could run his skeleton for public office. Legal or not, I think he would win enough votes. This is what New Orleans and Louisiana need. They need things like this, this is all they've ever been accustomed to. They thrive on it. It's a continual Mardi Gras, never stops. And this is part of the circus, the festivities.

[Gurvich had been critically ill in the hospital with bleeding ulcers during the trial. I wondered how he would have felt about testifying.]

GURVICH: I wanted to very badly, because I have yet to have a chance to say anything under oath, in public. I had a chance before the grand jury—I thought. Their minds were made up about me because Garrison had told them all about me. As for the trial, I had been told by Judge Haggerty, long before the trial, that I wouldn't be able to say much. He admitted he knew I wanted to

say a lot and had a lot to say. But then he's like that old Indian—
he speaks with a forked tongue. He'd tell me that he was convinced I was right, Garrison was cuckoo, and then tell Jim it's too
bad they've got rats like me running around. I knew this. He's a
politician and he was going to play both sides. But he told me I
wouldn't be able to do this and wouldn't be able to do that. So I
knew my testimony would be very limited. His mind was made up.
He wasn't going to let anybody get up there and say too much to
hurt Jim Garrison. Because if Jim Garrison came up smelling like
roses, Garrison would have to support Haggerty when he ran for
office. And any members of Haggerty's family who run for office.
And they don't want any opposition. No one has really tested
Garrison's strength yet. . . .

Q.: How do you figure Garrison and his motives out? Have you
come to any definite conclusion?

GURVICH: He's not a well man. He's not—you know, if you start
figuring out why he does this and how he reacts, you really know
you're admitting that you, too, are crazy. Because how do you
figure out an insane man? Without being a qualified psychiatrist?

When I left Bill Gurvich, I got to thinking about him and
Aaron Kohn, Eddie Wegmann, Irvin Dymond, Clay Shaw himself
and other New Orleanians similarly inclined in their attitudes
and efforts toward bucking the District Attorney. I could not help
likening them to left-behind American soldiers on a Japanese-
infested island during World War II. They had as much chance to
unseat the District Attorney as a few strays, dug in in caves or
hiding out in the forests, would have of taking that island back
from the enemy.

48

Look Up, New Orleans

Time spent with Dean Andrews, attorney-at-law, is guaranteed therapy. He really should have his own television program. He was not overly eager to speak of Garrison or Clay Shaw, but he held forth most agreeably with an outpouring of jokes and anecdotes about his life and times in the City of Perpetual Manipulation. As bad fortune would have it, the newly purchased batteries for my tape machine were dying of packaged old age during our conversation, so when I returned to my apartment I found Dean Andrews sounding like a faraway chipmunk on a Benzedrine kick. The tape was totally untranslatable.

He told marvelously colorful courtroom tales, but I would be doing him a disservice to paraphrase him. His dialogue is uniquely his own and should not be tampered with.

Typical of the easygoing informality that inhabits his law office, Dean Andrews peered over his dark glasses at me in the middle of one joke and asked, "Jim, you don't mind, do you? It saves me a trip down the hall." I said I didn't mind, although I was not sure what I was not minding until Dean Andrews hoisted his bulk out of a chair, walked to a wash basin in the corner of his small office, unzipped his fly and relieved himself while delivering the punch line to his joke.

On to Mayor Victor Schiro. I was greeted by various staffers at the Mayor's handsome offices in the extremely modern Civic Center, where I was handed literature and a bio of the Mayor, given coffee and finally ushered into Mayor Schiro's luxurious private office.

Scheduled to retire the following year after nine years as Mayor and a total of twenty years in New Orleans elective politics, Schiro came over as an amiable professional politician—a short balding man with bright beady eyes, a bright manufactured smile that has,

I would imagine, been tried out before many mirrors, and a pencil-thin black mustache, the kind that the movies glue on characters who usually turn out to be shifty. Mayor Schiro, rather than shifty, is a cagey, diplomatic, and public relations-minded politico of the old school.

During our talk three of his administrative assistants sat behind us, all chiming in from time to time, and toward the end, we were joined by a fourth. I was given a copy of the *Annual Report of the Mayor/City of New Orleans/1968–1969*, which had appeared in a special Sunday section of the *Times-Picayune*. It turned out to be as much a testimonial to Mayor Schiro as it did a report, featuring forty—count 'em, forty—different pictures of the Mayor: the Mayor alone, with Spiro Agnew (a picture one New Orleanian referred to as "the daily double"), in his American Legion hat with Hubert Humphrey, with Governor McKeithen reviewing the Berlin troops during the *Volkfest,* climbing a fire ladder, in a baseball cap with some little leaguers, in a cowboy hat greeting Rex, King of Mardi Gras, in a jockey's cap in the Soap Box Derby—and always with his trademark pencil mustache slashing across that white toothy beam of professional charm.

The Mayor was not all that disposed to talk about Jim Garrison. He was, however, never less than diplomatic. He agreed the trial had been big news, adding, "But we could have done without it. It didn't help our image. I always felt about it, Let's bring it out, let's get it over with. I'm glad it worked out as it did and I'm happy that it did."

Q.: Did you have any feeling about Mr. Shaw's—

MAYOR SCHIRO: I've known Mr. Shaw in business since his connection in international relations and the Trade Mart. And he's always been a very outstanding personality in that field. All I know is from that standpoint. I knew nothing about his personal affairs. I've never had any contact with him on that basis.

Q.: What do you think this case did to the community?

MAYOR SCHIRO: Well, I don't think it gave us any publicity—any *good* publicity. It didn't help our image at all. It was not a good spotlight. We like to be known for jazz, for our jazz festival, our shipping, international programs, things of that kind.

Q.: Isn't the fact that Garrison will probably run for election again extraordinary?

MAYOR SCHIRO: It isn't extraordinary at all. These things are very normal. Why would it be extraordinary?

Q.: The trial was a catastrophe for him.

MAYOR SCHIRO: It split opinions. Some people still believe he had something. Some believe he had something he couldn't prove, there were some who believed it was a ridiculous fiasco. He hasn't been rejected by this community by any means.

Q.: He has been rejected by the national—

MAYOR SCHIRO: Yeah! But they don't vote for him. [Laughter—actually it was more of a cackle.] Can't vote for him because they're not registered! This man has had quite an image here. He's a handsome man, a typical movie Mr. District Attorney. The people here do not cast him aside like those far away who just read about him.

Q.: There has been a lot of criticism of people in politics, in important positions in New Orleans, for allowing Garrison's investigation to continue for two years. How do you feel about that?

MAYOR SCHIRO: Well, what do you do? When does the public get in there and try to run the District Attorney's office? Or the courts? I mean, they did the right thing, they said, Let's wait and see. I took that position.

Q.: Yes, that's what I was talking about.

[I questioned him about the local newspapers. We spoke about the editorials and the silence following Clay Shaw's rearrest. This evoked a response that spoke volumes about the taste and sensitivity that governed New Orleans.]

MAYOR SCHIRO: That's strange. You see, the case is completed. Now this is nit picking—right? So I think that's when they should have come in. If they had anything to say, that was the time to say it. But the newspapers here don't work that way. They hit me. Oh, boy, they hit me twenty-four hours a day. I can go to the bathroom and you'll read about it. "The Mayor went to the bathroom. Somebody saw him, the dirty little sneak, he went right into the bathroom and took a crap, right in the middle of the taxpayer's dollars!" Any other mayor, you'd go to the bathroom and they'd say, "Well, what do you know? The smell in the city's so fragrant. Maybe it was because the Mayor went to the bathroom!"

Believe me, it's sometimes just that bad! That kind of conveys to you how I've been fighting this thing. . . . Oh, that Garrison—

he's a charmer, he's a charmer. He gets on TV and he's pretty doggone good.

Q.: What about the fear people have of him?

MAYOR SCHIRO [looking at me in wide-eyed surprise]: Well, now, I don't know that anybody really has any fear of him. At all. I never get that impression.

Q.: I do.

MAYOR SCHIRO: You do—really? Well, we don't have any fear of him *here*. In fact, I just had him down to the annual celebration of our third anniversary. I had him come down as District Attorney and sit right at the head table with us. . . . [I had not meant to imply Mr. Garrison would *bite* anyone.] But I see no fear. I don't know what there would be any fear about.

When I mentioned the Governor's oft-quoted remark that he would not criticize Garrison because he knew all of his enemies ended up being buried, Schiro said, "Oh, well, McKeithen. That's what I'm telling you. He's a colorful person. He says all sorts of colorful things. But when you break 'em down, there's no real basis for it, except to get a little laugh. That's all—a little humor."

Jim Garrison had been an assistant city attorney under Mayor Schiro when the Mayor had first taken office. I asked the Mayor if he'd backed Jim Garrison for election as District Attorney. He was quick to say he had not endorsed Garrison. One of the men seated in back of us spoke up: "Well, your organization sure helped get him elected." Mayor Schiro then said, "I'd made a statement that I thought the people should choose their own District Attorney, not the Mayor's choice. So I had to stay out of it. But I put my organization to work for him. We put him in. My organization worked for him, went to the polls for him, talked to the people, raised a little money."

This would seem tantamount to endorsing him. I asked Mayor Schiro if he'd back Garrison in the upcoming election. The Mayor replied, "I don't know. I'll tell you this, I'd have to see who the candidates are first."

Toward the end of this delightfully superficial interview, Mayor Schiro suddenly exploded in a burst of civic pride mixed with outrage over criticism of New Orleans. I was honored to be on hand for this scene, triggered by a question I asked about the amount of money poured into Mardi Gras every year, money that might be used for more important and worthy projects. He said, "Every city has something they associate with! Because of our tradition—many years of French, Spanish and Latin atmosphere— we built up this Mardi Gras as a tradition. It's just like you going to church for twenty, thirty, forty, fifty years. This is part of your life. These people sacrifice all year to have that one night of glory, or one week of glory. And you just don't wash away tradition just because—that money is their money. This pleasure is their pleasure and they're not about to say, Let me use it to give John Doe an education. That's the bad angle, in a way—the selfishness. But then, what does it do for the city? It brings millions of people here, that's what it does! Wherever you go all over the world— Mardi Gras. In turn, we're able to do more for this fellow [the aforementioned John Doe] because of what this generates, than if we gave them this little pittance of money. They're doing the job indirectly."

Mayor Schiro suddenly reached for something and thrust a small metal badge at me. "This means, *Look Up, New Orleans!* I'm tired of hearing people tell what's wrong with this city. This city is great! This city has the greatest potential in the world, and you cannot sell your liabilities. You must sell your assets. Nobody's buying your bills and your troubles. They're buying your poten- tial and your opportunities and your inspirations, and I just got damn tired of these newspapers and TV people saying what's wrong with New Orleans. Nothing's wrong with New Orleans! So I coined this—*Look Up, New Orleans!* [Which sounded to me faintly dirty.] . . . They'd have you believe the port is dying on the vine, going out of business. [It is.] We have to prepare for the changeover to containerization, that's all. We need capital ex- penditures, this is what the fuss is all about. We've got to modern- ize to meet our competition. They'd have you believe everything's falling apart, the city's dropping dead. Actually we had the biggest Mardi Gras we ever had in our history. We had a Jazz Fest and it was oversubscribed and—and over*everything!* We have another one this June. And we added a Food Fest. It's going to grow. And next year—a Film Fest. You see? We brought the American Legion here, the Elks. We got the Super Bowl away from Miami. We snatched it right out of their hands. Every city in this country, including Los Angeles, would like to have the Super Bowl Game. It's a $50 million project. So I'm saying, *Look Up, New Orleans!*

After I said goodbye to the Mayor, one of his assistants followed me out into the hall and asked if I wouldn't like to have an eight-by-ten picture of the Mayor. "Is he smiling?" I asked. "Why, yes he is," came the reply. "Then I'd like one," I said. We went to a public relations office, but they were fresh out of pictures of the Mayor. "They're very popular," one secretary told me, adding that a new shipment was on its way and suggesting I stop back in a day or so for one of my very own. I got the notion a huge freight car loaded down with eight-by-ten glossy prints of the Mayor might be groaning toward New Orleans at that very moment.

I dropped off a list of questions at Judge Haggerty's chambers and left word that I would return the following day. I did not go without my daily phone call to Mr. Garrison's office. Mr. Garrison, I was told, was in with the grand jury. I refrained from asking what—or who—was cooking. His secretary said once more she would get back to me, but by this time she knew she did not have to worry about communications being broken off. My phone call was a daily routine.

I then phoned juror Larry Morgan, the 24-year-old aircraft mechanic, and he agreed to speak with me. The Morgans live far from downtown New Orleans, miles away in neighboring St. Bernard Parish, and I got seriously lost en route to their modest house, lower on the income scale than the homes of Mr. Hebert and Mr. Schultz.

The Morgans' small living room was sparsely furnished: one sofa, one easy chair, a folding play pen and a little sit-in cart for their 8-month-old son, Troy. There were no rugs on the floor but there was one good-sized painting on black velvet prominently displayed on the wall, a Mexican moonlight cactus scene. A Siamese cat frieze, mother and kitten, sat atop the large television set. The small house loudly proclaimed: young people starting out.

Larry Morgan was somewhat formal when we first began to talk but then he relaxed. As to how he happened to get on the jury, he had this to say: "Well, when I went up there—my daddy always told me to tell the truth. I said this is one time I'll tell the truth—and it put me in a bind from then on."

He, too, had obviously enjoyed his time on the jury. He spoke of the food, the outings, the movies they were shown, the card games and the comparative ease with which the jurors got along. He liked the judge, although he felt at first he was disposed more to rule for the defense but after a while he'd evened out. (This was definitely a minority opinion from all those I spoke with.)

I asked Larry Morgan what he thought the weakest part of the state's case was, and he said, "Well, the whole thing. I was surprised, I just couldn't picture the type of case the state put on. The caliber of witnesses was really unbelievable for the seriousness of the case. That's my opinion. . . . After it was all over, it was like—wow, what happened! What—that's it? We just couldn't imagine the state had brought up a case against Clay Shaw—absolutely nothing! Or what was, was so wishy-washy that the judge said you have to have a reasonable doubt, beyond a reasonable doubt. There was just no possibility, there was no question but what the jury would find Clay Shaw innocent."

For a young good-looking man who appeared to be fairly intelligent and possess a sense of humor, I found Larry Morgan to be strangely detached, almost isolated, and sometimes contradictory.

Q.: Didn't you find the Zapruder film an emotional experience?

MORGAN: Well, it was a very—as far as the fact, did it upset me any? In a sense, no. I'm not a brutal sort of person but the effect of the film didn't bother me any. It was something more or less unusual to see, something you don't see every day. That was the only thing. It was a human life being taken, not that it was the President or anything to that effect. It was just the actual viewing of a person's head exploding, not that it had anything to do with the President. Emotionally—no, it didn't upset me.

Q.: When Clay Shaw was testifying, you didn't look at him. I noticed that particularly. Why was that?

MORGAN: I did that on several occasions. It was mainly because I wasn't interested in him as a person. I was listening to his point of view—seeing what he had to say. But it didn't make much difference whether I looked at him or not as long as I could hear him. I'd seen him day after day. I knew what he looked like. I didn't have to look at him.

Despite his earlier professed amazement at the weakness of the state's case, Morgan still said, at one point, "I think Garrison had something to go on. There's something still to this and whether Clay Shaw's involved in it I don't know. I'm sure myself that there's more to this than anyone knows about."

When I asked Morgan what he thought of the Tadins' testimony, he said, "In my opinion, I think they were telling the truth. But it had no bearing on the fact that Clay Shaw was involved in the conspiracy. The fact that they identified him with David Ferrie—well, fine, that's all it was. He knew David Ferrie. I concluded even though there was a good possibility he knew David Ferrie, they still had to prove beyond a reasonable doubt in my mind whether both of them were involved in conspiracy. The rest of the trial didn't do that."

When I mentioned the rumor that the two alternates had voted guilty, Morgan was surprised. He had been the one who asked them to mark down what they would have voted and leave the slips of paper with a deputy. But in the excitement after the jury was dismissed, he'd forgotten all about his request and failed to collect them. He'd not heard this rumor, as reported by Mark Lane, and said, "I didn't read the newspapers before I got on the jury and I haven't read them since. It's probably bad that I don't, but I could care less what goes on in the world. I should be ashamed of saying it, but it's the truth. You can't believe half of what you read and a quarter of what you see, I guess."

When I brought him back to the alternates again, he said, "It sure would surprise me. They were just like the rest of us. I can't believe it. They saw what we saw. I'll have to call Bob [Burlet, an alternate] and ask him. I can't believe it."

Just as I decided I probably wouldn't learn anything new from talking to any other jurors, Larry Morgan dropped a tidbit that intrigued me when he described what had taken place in the deliberating room.

MORGAN: There wasn't much discussion. Basically all of us felt the same way. In fact, we decided to take a concealed vote at first. No names, just mark down the verdict on a slip of paper. Well, when it came down to that, it was a split second and I had the paper and pencil and the decision written. When we took the reading, we had one guilty, the rest not guilty.

Q.: One guilty?

MORGAN: Yes. Well, we asked who it was, if he wanted to—to tell

why he thought the man was guilty, discuss it. Because the judge
had said if you can be shown you are wrong and someone else
might be right, you can discuss it, you can change your decision.
Well, he decided he had been wrong. It was a misunderstanding
on his part. He'd misunderstood what had been said in the
courtroom.

Q.: As far as the judge's charge?

MORGAN: No, in one particular instance, he'd misunderstood. He
believed it to be another way. I don't remember exactly how it
was. Anyhow, when we had a discussion, he said, "Well, wasn't it
so and so?" We said no, it was this way. He said, "Well, I understand and I'll change." It had to do with the Clinton people.

Q.: But the Clinton people didn't have to do with conspiracy.

MORGAN: No, it was more or less identification. It was a misunderstanding. It didn't have anything to do with conspiracy as far as
that was concerned.

Q.: Can you say who it was?

MORGAN: No, I don't want to say.

49

The Uninvited

Bob Burlet was talkative. Here was the man Clay Shaw and his lawyers would have traded for any other juror to have on the voting squad. In the courtroom he presented a picture of a wide-awake, vigorous, totally interested natively intelligent man.

I found Mr. Burlet in the small office of his CNT Crane Service Company. Stocky, muscular, balding with an open face, large brown eyes and a quick smile, Bob Burlet is 46 and the father of five sons. He was immediately friendly and responsive to questions.

He had been extremely surprised that he'd been picked to be an alternate. He'd attended an import-export school years ago and Clay Shaw had spoken to his class several times in his connection with the International Trade Mart. Clay had made a good impression on Burlet and because of this he thought the state would not accept him. He had been quartered in the motel room that held five jurors plus a deputy and I discovered something new about the accommodations when he said, "Well, it was pretty crowded, but ours was the only room with a window in it, you know? All the other jurors used to come down to look out the window." I had not realized the other rooms had no windows.

Bob Burlet, a good-natured man, also expressed fondness for his fellow jurors: "I'll tell you, I think this was an outstanding jury. Not because I was a member . . . But I think they were intelligent. More intelligent I guess than the appearance they made." The more I spoke with him the more certain I was he had not marked his slip of paper guilty. After a while I asked Mr. Burlet if he'd had a pretty clear idea of what the verdict would be.

BURLET: Yes, I thought the verdict would be not guilty. And I told the men that I didn't think they'd be there too long, you know.

Q.: Larry Morgan said that you and Beilman wrote down your—

BURLET: Yes. Did he tell you what we put down? Not guilty. I mean, *guilty!*

Q.: He didn't know that. Somebody else had said that.

BURLET: Somebody else? I figured somebody would tell him. I put on there guilty and I think—what's his name, Beilman?

Q.: Yes.

BURLET: He put on there guilty because I put on there guilty.

Q.: Now why did you do that?

BURLET: I don't know. I thought there would be more would vote guilty. And after the discussion, would vote not guilty. As far as him being guilty, in my mind I think he did have—now whether it was a bull session like Perry Russo said it was, or whether it was really a conspiracy to kill the President, I don't know. The prosecution never made that plain. But I do think that something was involved in that.

Q.: I'm surprised to hear that, especially when you say you had an idea what the verdict was going to be.

BURLET: Yes, it was going to be not guilty. It didn't make any—in other words . . . when pressure's put on the original jury, they would have to really stop and think. Well, when they went upstairs the guy told me to put something down and I put guilty. You know? Not thinking of anything, or not having any weight on me. You follow my thinking on this deal? [Not really.] I just put guilty—it didn't make any difference. And I think a couple of the jurors put more in that than what they should have. After the thing was over with. Because—who's the blond-haired fellow? He and I got to be real close. He felt bad about the verdict.

Q.: One of the jurors?

BURLET: Yes. And I told him, I said, "Listen, I'd have voted the same way." He said, "But you put on there *guilty.*" I said, "Yeah, but I didn't have to—it didn't make any difference."

Q.: You mean he felt bad about what you had put down?

BURLET: Yes. Because—he was on the border. And what I thought they were going to do—

Q.: I heard that there was one juror that voted guilty on the first ballot.

BURLET: Yes.

Q.: Would that have been him?

BURLET: No. He didn't vote guilty. One juror did vote guilty though. I thought there'd be more. And I thought they would—

what they did when they went upstairs. I think they told you they discussed the case, instead of voting. If I'd had anything to do with it, I'd have asked whoever the foreman was if we could vote first.

Q.: I understand they didn't talk about it much, that they took the first ballot after they got the foreman. And one voted guilty.

BURLET: No, they discussed it. What's his name, the fireman? The smoke eater?

Q.: Hebert?

BURLET: Hebert. He called me up that morning, that Sunday morning, right away. And I asked him if they discussed it or did they vote right away. He said they discussed it about half an hour. Then they voted and one voted guilty.

Q.: I wonder which one that was?

BURLET: I know—I wouldn't want to—they didn't tell you?

Q.: No, I only heard that the last time and I didn't ask. [Which was a lie; I had asked.] But it doesn't make any difference who—

BURLET: No, it doesn't make any difference as long as they came up with not guilty.

Q.: Which one was it though?

BURLET: Did you—what jurors did you interview?

Q.: Hebert, Schultz, Larry Morgan, Powe, you, and I'm seeing Ordes.

BURLET: Yes.

Q.: Who was it?

BURLET: Well, it was one of the ones you interviewed already.

Q.: It was?

BURLET: I'll narrow it down to that. And they didn't tell you, so I don't think I should tell you.

Q.: Okay. Then there was a real doubt in your mind?

BURLET: I got the—I think there was something. He [Shaw] was definitely involved with Oswald and Ferrie as far as my way of thinking. And I think, on this perjury trial, I don't think they should have any trouble. . . . Because there's too many connections—not to even know Dave Ferrie and Oswald, like he claims. Why would Jim Garrison pick a man on the street and say, Okay, you're the man? I mean, that doesn't make sense to me. And there were so many other witnesses, too, that said they were with him. They were together, you know?

Q.: How did you feel when you heard the verdict?

BURLET: I come home in a cab. And I hurried and turned the

TV on, and waited till it came on. Like I say, I thought about that not guilty—I mean the guilty—that I put on the paper, you know. And I told my wife that. And she said, "Well, I think he's guilty, too." She said, "If you'd have voted *not* guilty, I wouldn't talk to you." I said, "Well, maybe the man is guilty, but they didn't prove it in the courtroom though—beyond a reasonable doubt."

Q.: It still surprises me because I remember when you left, you shook hands with Shaw and you were smiling. How did that work out?

BURLET: I'm glad you asked that question, because I want to get that straight. I read it the next morning in the paper. You know where I was sitting? Now to get out of that place I had to walk down that aisle and past Clay Shaw's back, the desk right there where they were sitting. Clay Shaw, Wegmann and the rest of them. I had to walk down that aisle. There were a lot of people by the prosecution's desk at that time. I had to go through a lot of people to get out. So when I was going out, Mr. Shaw himself turned around and put his hand out, for me to shake it. And he thanked us for being attentive and being good jurors and he said also—I think he said—that he was sorry that I wasn't one of the ones to be—you know, to vote on him.

Q.: Little did he know! . . . If you'd been on the voting jury what would you have done?

BURLET: I think I would have voted guilty at first. I'd have put on there guilty. And after discussion, I'd have changed my vote. Just like that one man.

Bob Burlet went on to say he thought Garrison and Alcock had a good case, enough to convict—"If the testimony wouldn't have been like it was. And that's my honest opinion." He also had some suggestions which he believed would have helped the state: "Let Mr. Garrison bring out the affair there at Clinton. Put Mr. Alcock on the Dealey Plaza, the Dallas deal. I think he would have done a much better job than Mr. Oser. And Mr. Sciambra, try to keep Mr. Sciambra out of the picture as much as possible. He'd messed it up enough."

He added that he had voted for Garrison before and would again. "I think he's a good D.A. Not knowing any of the inner things about him. They say if Garrison wants to get you he's going to get you. I don't know anything about that. Being an outsider. But as far as the man himself and his job, I've never saw anything that would make me say, No, I wouldn't vote for him."

Bob Burlet, as friendly and agreeable as he was, had turned out to be a complete surprise. Now the verdict did not seem to be the complete walkaway it had first appeared. Also the number of jurors who believed Clay had known Ferrie and Oswald was surprisingly high; in fact, almost every one indicated there was a good possibility of their acquaintance—mild tremors in the stomach at thoughts of the perjury trial.

I felt I ought to seek out one more juror in hopes of finding out which man had voted guilty. I was extremely curious about this, especially since Burlet mentioned it had been one I'd already interviewed.

Charles Ordes, black-haired, black-mustached and recently turned 39, lives in a small house on a residential block closer to the center of town than any of the jurors I'd visited. He was working night shifts as a supervisor for Continental Can and I caught him in his pajamas shortly after he'd awakened in the early afternoon.

He, too, was most friendly, offering coffee and indicating a willingness to talk about the trial. But, as with most of the jurors, his statements were laced with paradox and sprinkled with ambiguities.

"I kept waiting for the state to present a case," he told me. "I don't think they had enough to get this far. I was surprised that it was even presented on this evidence. I was just waiting for something to happen. I just kept waiting, you know, something's gonna come up. I just can't see where they had a case. I feel the grand jury should have stopped him."

Yet within a minute, at the mention of Perry Russo, Mr. Ordes had this to say: "He was under terrific strain . . . but I think he was perfectly honest in everything he said. I believed him. To me, it was like he stated. I think it was Dymond called it a bull session. Because it may well have been this. So I thought if I was in his place and unless this was absolutely the truth, he [Russo] could never fabricate a story like this. This is what I thought."

Mr. Ordes expressed surprise only at the timing of the perjury charges. He could not understand why they had not been brought right at the conclusion of the trial. He thought there was a distinct possibility that Clay Shaw had known both Ferrie and Oswald. On the other hand he said of Clay Shaw as a witness, "He impressed me like he was telling the truth. I believe him . . . he wasn't nervous and I could believe him from what he said." Still, a few minutes later he said, "I think maybe he could have been involved in the conspiracy had there been one. But none of this has ever been proved. The possibility's always been there. And I think it's an unusual fact that he is supposed to have known Ferrie and supposed to have known Oswald, supposed to have been together. There's some connection here . . . but as far as proving it is something else. I could never say that he actually did what was presented. But in my mind the possibility could be there."

Although Mr. Ordes had maintained that the grand jury should have stopped Jim Garrison from bringing the case to trial, he nevertheless said of the trial's outcome, "I think that shouldn't hurt him, is the way I feel. Because I think he thought he had a case and he presented it and he didn't have one. And if this is going to hurt him, as far as any re-election is concerned, me personally, it wouldn't bear any weight on the case."

Now the cumulative effect of talking to these jurors—puzzlements all—began to dizzy me slightly and I thought I'd best head directly for the mystery I hoped to uncover. So I asked Mr. Ordes about their deliberations.

ORDES: We had a little discussion about who was going to be the foreman, a little discussion about setting up procedure, so one person could talk at a time and we all could understand . . . and then we had a little discussion about the case itself. We tried to pick it up and carry it on through, you know. But that was it.

Q.: One of them told me about the first vote. There was one guilty—based on a misunderstanding of what the Clinton people testified to?

ORDES: Yes. Everybody at least expressed their own opinion, this is the way they felt. Nobody influenced them. Other than this one boy with the Clinton case. He was under the opinion he was guilty just on their testimony alone.

Q.: That's strange to me, because the Clinton people didn't testify to conspiracy. That had nothing to do with it.

ORDES: We all discussed it, and gave our points of view of the people from Clinton. He could see that—yes, this was right. How could you ever convict a man on the evidence that was presented? Even Garrison himself on television stated several times that with the evidence that was presented, he himself would have had to go the same way—

Q. [deviously grasping at straws]: Somebody told me that Schultz was the one who was confused about the Clinton people.

ORDES: Let's see, it may have been Schultz. . . . But I don't think so. It was—the professor, the schoolteacher. Colored boy.

Q.: Ricks?

ORDES: Ricks. Ricks was the one.

According to Ordes, it had not been one of the jurors I'd interviewed (as Bob Burlet recalled), but William Ricks, the one juror who refused to speak with me. I remembered so well that Clay Shaw and his attorneys had often expressed the optimistic opinion during the trial that Ricks might well be leading the jury for the defense. Nina Sulzer had also indicated this belief. Putting this together with the one consolidated regret they felt—that Bob Burlet had not been on the voting squad—I thought of a definition I had once read: "Logic is a way of going wrong with reason."

Although I had tried to contact several other jurors and had not been able to reach them by phone, I decided there was no pressing need to speak with any more of them. It was all too confusing, too mind-rattling. And I could only shudder at the thought of an eventual perjury trial.

The day after I dropped the questions off at the judge's chambers, I made my usual phone call to the District Attorney's office. Mr. Garrison's secretary, Lorraine, indicated she had good news for me. By this time I felt a rapport with her, and I believe it was returned.

"Mr. Garrison will see you at ten o'clock Saturday morning."

"Fine. Where?"

"At his office, here at the Criminal Court Building."

"For real? I hope this is a firm date."

"That's what he said."

"I'd really like it in writing," I said, "but I suppose that's impossible."

She was certain he would keep the appointment this time and we rang off.

Thus filled with anticipation once again, I set off to see Judge Haggerty. The judge was in his chambers and he was, as usual, friendly in his greeting. He had not, he said, had a chance to look over the questions. I displayed mild annoyance at his continued procrastination.

"You know, Judge, if you keep on doing this—I mean you *were* the trial judge and you were important to the case, so I'll have to write something about you. I'll just have to write about how you kept dodging me."

"No, no. I'll look at them over the weekend and then we'll get together."

"What about this afternoon? There's nothing tricky in there."

"I'd rather have a chance to study them. Besides, I have to attend a function this afternoon."

"The first of the week then. Do you promise?"

"Yes, of course. No problem. You have my word."

As I was about to leave, the judge called me back. "Say, Brother Kirkwood, I got a thought. What are you doing this afternoon?"

"Nothing. I was planning on spending it with you."

"Tell you what. The District Attorney's office is having a crayfish party, to celebrate their seventh year in office, the beginning of their eighth. I'll take you out there."

I hesitated. I would certainly be walking into the enemy camp, but that wasn't the reason for my hesitation. I had an appointment with Jim Garrison the following day. I didn't want to jeopardize it by meeting him at a large party and end up only exchanging a few words with him over a drink.

"What do you say?" the judge asked.

"I'm game. But do you think they'd appreciate—well, an outsider? You know what I mean?"

"The hell with them." Judge Haggerty laughed. "I'm taking you. They told me to bring anyone I wanted. I'm taking you. You're my guest. Ever had crayfish?"

"Yes."

"You know how to suck the heads off?"

"No."

"We'll teach you how to eat 'em right!" The judge suddenly laughed and slapped a hand down on the top of his desk. "Hey, you know what I'm going to do? I'm going to take you up to Moo Sciambra and say, 'Now, Moo, I want you to write a 3,500-word memo on the crayfish party for this fellow *but*—I don't want you to leave out the *crayfish!* " He roared with laughter. "What do you think of that?"

"Whatever you say. You're the judge!"

"Yeah, that's what I'll do." Judge Haggerty had an hour's work to finish in his chambers. He gave me the name of the restaurant and directions to it, saying he'd see me there at 4 o'clock.

I returned to my apartment to get cleaned up, vowing that when I spoke to Jim Garrison at the party, I would not let him abort our meeting the following morning. I pulled up to the combination restaurant-bar at 4 on the nose and parked in the large adjoining lot. Members of the D.A.'s staff, many of whom I recognized, arrived in a steady stream and entered a separate building containing a banquet room. By 4:30 I had seen no sign of Judge Haggerty and decided he might well have arrived early and be inside. Although I would rather have walked in with the judge (and Cassius Clay), as long as I had not been invited personally, I decided to search him out.

I was sure there would be a hundred or so people milling about having drinks, so that I might make a more or less inconspicuous entrance. I stepped inside the building and walked down a narrow corridor until I came to a door. There were loud voices and laughter behind it. Taking a good healthy breath, I opened it and stepped inside.

Except for a few waiters and a bartender or two, everyone in the room was seated. Four or five long banquet tables were spread out quite a distance from the door, jam-packed with members of the District Attorney's staff, their wives, girl friends and, I imagined, a few secretaries. I took several more steps into the room and quickly scanned the tables for Judge Haggerty.

Within seconds there was not a sound to be heard.

One, two, then three and four and soon nearly everyone had turned and seen me. It was suddenly as if the sound track of a movie had been cut off. There I stood. Now almost all eyes were on me. I was hoping the judge, wherever he was, would stand up, shout out, "Brother Kirkwood!" and I would be rescued from this uncomfortable spotlight that seemed to be beating down upon me. But there was not a sound. I could not locate Jim Garrison either. The silence continued.

Several one-liners occurred to me.

Like: "Well, how do you like the act so far?"

Or: "I suppose you're all wondering why I've asked you here!"

Or: "All right, god damn it, this is a stickup!"

Instead, my eyes swept the room for a friendly and familiar face until I reached the table to my far left. There I spotted Andrew Sciambra. His eyes were narrowed at me and at the exact moment I saw him, he winced, ducked his head down, turning the other way and putting a hand up to his cheek, as if to say, Oh, shit, look who's here!

The quiet continued, although I wasn't positive why, since I'm sure the majority of them did not know who I was and could not have cared less. But it persisted, perhaps spiraling from the nucleus of silence coming from those who did know and disapproved. Several seated near Sciambra caught his reaction; they snickered, looked at me, then back to him. Sciambra kept his face averted. His rudeness embarrassed and angered me.

So I did the first thing that came to mind. I walked directly—in ringing silence—to his table and stood next to him. I now noticed Alvin Oser seated across from him.

"Hi," I said.

"Hi," Oser replied, glancing at Sciambra, who was still turned away from me.

At the nearness of my voice, Sciambra swiveled around and regarded me coolly. "Hi." I extended a hand. Sciambra looked at it as if it were a dead cat, then at me. I kept my hand extended.

He finally took it and said, "Hi." I just stood there, thinking at least he would say, Sit down, Have a drink, or Go fuck yourself! He said nothing.

Eventually I said, "Is Judge Haggerty here?"

"I don't know, I haven't seen him," Sciambra said.

"He asked me to meet him out here."

"Oh," was the reply.

I waited a beat or two longer, thinking now he would surely say, Sit down, he should be here soon, or—something. After I'd stood there long beyond the bounds of human pride at this reception, I said, "Well, then I guess I'll go outside and wait for him."

"Okay," said Sciambra, thereby earning him the Charm of the Month Award.

I left the room, red-faced, I admit, in total silence. I waited in the parking lot, standing between two cars, like some refugee, until 5 o'clock. No judge. I phoned his chambers from the bar in the adjoining building. No answer. I drove off feeling a fool.

The only consolation was that I hadn't seen Jim Garrison and therefore would be able to meet him afresh the next morning.

50

Jim Garrison

Saturday morning was cloudless and dazzling in its clear sparkle, the kind of Saturday kids would turn in their parents for. I was up early, breakfasted, and drove to the Criminal Court Building, arriving about 9:45. For a few minutes I stood in front of the building, soaking up the sun and thinking how the beauty of the day contradicted the need for such a building. I climbed the long flight of steps.

The darkness inside was immediately ominous. The absolute quiet was equally scary—and surprising. There was not a sound to be heard, not a person in sight, no movement at all. I had never seen the building, or even imagined it, in such a tomblike state, so completely cleared of human activity or presence.

As I crossed the foyer toward the marble stairs, the sound of my own footsteps echoed loudly off the walls and multiplied down the corridors, making me stop for an instant to determine if I was the sole cause of the echo. The elevators were not even in operation. They stood at anchor, gaping open. The doors leading to the Sheriff's offices were closed, but I could see through the venetian blinds hanging on the far side. There was no movement to be seen even in there, no sound to be heard.

As I clacked up the long circular staircase, I could not help thinking how much I would have preferred a luncheon meeting at Brennan's, say. At least the ground would be neutral. Here, I was entering his circle of authority. I was in enemy territory—without witnesses. I thought of phoning the Swiss Consulate for a neutral observer and smiled to myself at the idea. Walking down the corridor past the empty criminal courtrooms toward those massive wooden doors with JIM GARRISON, DISTRICT ATTORNEY slapped across the top, I lost my smile. From the break in the light between the doors it appeared they might be locked. No, perhaps that was only the regular catch that keeps the doors closed. Wrong. I grasped the handles and they were not about to open.

"Son of a bitch!" I said. I knocked several times loudly and turned away in disgust.

It was unbelievable that he would cop out again. I could not believe he would summon me to the Criminal Court Building on a Saturday morning at 10 A.M. for a no-show. On second thought, perhaps he possessed a perfectly honed perverse humor that would enable him to devil me out of town in pure annoyance. I sighed and thought, Well, hell, at least I can document my efforts to see the bastard! That will make a story of sorts in itself. Jim Garrison was equaling Howard Hughes in accessibility.

I decided to wait at least a humiliating half an hour so I could really give it to him good; there could be no mistake in that event about his intentions. I set my briefcase down upon a bench, complete with tape recorder, and simply roamed about the corridors. After a while I decided the marble floor would make a fine surface for a soft shoe, so I dragged out an old routine and practiced. I suddenly thrust myself into a courtroom musical and tried the vaulted ceilings for sound, belting out a few favorite songs—the voice carries beautifully in the Criminal Court Building—and conducting myself like a certified disturbed person.

After twenty minutes or so of fantasizing, I decided to leave. I picked up my briefcase and, just for the hell of it, tried the doors again. Locked. I turned and started to walk away when an attack of tongue-in-cheek madness struck me. I swung around, dropped the briefcase to the floor, and hurled myself against the doors.

I pounded both fists against them, beating on the wood and shouting in my loudest voice, "You son of a bitch, you'll pay for this! I swear to God, I'll have your royal District Attorney's ass for this little gambit, you sadistic son of a bitch! You'll be out of office so goddamn fast for this it'll make your goddamn giant head spin." I hurled a few less tasteful epithets at him and then realized fun's fun, I would only injure my hands if I kept up this assault.

I picked up my briefcase and started to walk away when I heard footsteps approach the door from the other side. My God, I thought, somebody actually heard that little scene. Turning around, I froze, just as the lock clicked and the doors were very cautiously opened, no more than several inches. A face plastered with suspicion peered out. It belonged to a deputy or guard I had never seen before. "Yes?" he said.

"Oh!" I replied.

"What is it?" the man asked, taking in this crazy bearded interloper.

"I had an appointment."

"An appointment?" he asked.

"Yes."

"An appointment with who?"

I hesitated to say, "With—ah, the District Attorney."

"With Jim Garrison?" he asked.

"Yes."

"Today?"

"Yes, at 10 o'clock, in his office."

"Today?"

"Yes."

"He's not here."

"Has he phoned or anything?"

"No."

"Oh." He started to close the doors. "Ah, does he ever come in on Saturday?"

"Sometimes, yes, to pick up his mail."

"I'll wait a while longer."

"What's your name?"

"Jim Kirkwood. Ah, will you tell him if he calls?"

"Tell him what?"

"That I'm here, waiting."

"Oh, yes, I'll tell him." He closed the doors and locked them. I couldn't blame him. He undoubtedly had heard my complete performance. I went to a bench and sat down quietly. After several minutes, I heard footsteps inside again, approaching the door and then stopping. The guard was apparently listening. In a few seconds the door opened again and the man said, "Maybe it would be better if you waited in here." I suppose he thought it would be better to contain an insane person than to let him roam the building on the loose.

I arose and stepped into the District Attorney's outside reception room. The man pointed to a chair and asked if I'd like to read a paper. I thanked him, sat down, and was given the morning

Times-Picayune. The man left to sit in an adjoining office with the door open and in a position allowing him to keep an eye on me.

There was barely time to finish reading an article on the front page when I heard a faraway voice coming from down the hallway leading to the various inside offices of the District Attorney. As the voice grew closer I recognized the deep tones of the District Attorney. I sat up straight in my chair. He had been talking to someone, but he stopped speaking before he came into sight from the hallway.

And suddenly there he was, a true giant of a man. He approached the railing which separates the waiting area and a desk that houses the receptionist and phones. I stood up and stepped toward him.

"You must be Jim Kirkwood," he said, extending his hand.

"And you must be Jim Garrison," I said, attempting what I hoped might be a small indication of humor and gratification at our long-delayed meeting. He did not appear to respond as we shook hands and said hello.

The District Attorney looked much better than he had in the courtroom. Some of the puffiness had disappeared from his face. His size alone does nothing to relax one at the outset. He invited me in, swinging the gate open, and I followed him down the hallway past several small offices. They were all empty, save for one, which Andrew Sciambra occupied. He was standing, facing the door. We exchanged a combination nod-sneer and I thought, Wouldn't he have to be hanging around today!

I was suddenly sure that this was a setup. I was to be confronted with somebody or something that would prove a lever for propelling me to the airport immediately.

As we entered Garrison's large well-appointed office, the District Attorney mumbled, "I really don't know what there is for us to talk about. I don't want to discuss the Shaw case." He then told me to sit down and make myself comfortable. He walked behind his massive desk and sat down facing me. He was rather less delighted to see me than I was to see him. I decided to express my pleasure at meeting him and did. We spoke of the weather, which was perfection.

Garrison was impeccably dressed in a well-fitting mustard-colored sports jacket with a small checked pattern and lighter slacks. He wore a yellow shirt and a tasteful yellow and mustard-colored tie. It was a fine country-club-for-lunch outfit.

We passed a few more amenities, during which I felt he was eying me to determine what kind of animal I was. I, in turn, was more aware of deciphering his mood and basic attitude toward me than performing an instant character analysis. We were sniffing each other out, there was no doubt of that.

We soon fell into conversation. Was I, in fact, going to write a book? Yes, trials fascinated me, especially this trial. Finally Garrison said, "In my fight to bring this case out into the open—" He paused, glanced down at his desk, then back up at me. "You see, most people don't realize we're living in a totalitarian state. Most citizens of this country live—we live—in the world that *appears* to be, while those in power live in the world that *is*."

"How do you mean?" I asked.

"I mean, there's a difference. Especially those hiding behind the intangibles of power in the government and the military complex and the CIA. When you recognize and deal with the intelligence apparatus in this country, you're encountering the world that is. If you don't, you're living in the world that appears to be. Even I only came to this conclusion recently—the difference between the world that appears to be and the world that is." Jim Garrison looked directly at me when he spoke, again in those low pleasing tones of complete, as well as easy, authority I'd heard in the courtroom. "If you don't realize there's a clandestine operation going on in this country, you'll be removed. Because you're then living in the world that appears to be, not the world that is."

He had clearly repeated these words to make certain I grasped his point. I told him I found this a most interesting theory, so interesting I would like get it down on tape, explaining that my handwriting was something less than satisfactory. He did not look askance at my presumption in bringing a tape machine to a non-interview, but merely waved the suggestion aside, saying, "Perhaps later. Not now."

He repeated what to him was a hard fact: We were living in a totalitarian state. Whether I knew it or not, whether the people knew it or not, he knew it.

"If we are living in a totalitarian state," I replied, "most citizens don't or can't believe it because in that event there's usually one man in power, one figure to point to as a virtual dictator, and there's no one now in our country to fit that description."

"No," he replied, "there isn't, I agree. And that's where it's even more insidious, when the country is ruled by a power *group*." In answer to my questioning look, he said, "The industrial complex and the Pentagon, both of which want desperately to keep the war going in Vietnam. Those—along with certain clandestine organizations—make up the power combine ruling this country now. That is the world that *is*."

At about this time, Moo Sciambra, wearing white slacks and a sports shirt, stepped into the office. "Hello," he said.

"Hello," I replied.

"You know each other?" Jim Garrison asked rhetorically, nevertheless going on to give our names. "Andy Sciambra, Jim Kirkwood."

"Sure," Sciambra said, shaking my hand. "How you been?"

"Fine," I said, then thought I could not ignore his rudeness of the day before. "Except I felt like a lousy mattress when I walked into the crayfish party." Smiling faintly and coloring slightly, he asked why that was. "My reception," I said, leveling with him, "wasn't all that warm. I somehow didn't feel everyone was happy to see me."

He ignored this, saying, "The judge was looking for you later on."

I sat down as the two of them then embarked upon a veiled private conversation in front of me.

"Were you successful in contacting the . . . individual?" asked Garrison.

"Yes." Sciambra nodded.

"Is he here?"

"No, I'm going to get him."

"You are?"

"Yes, I'll pick him up and bring him over."

"Then it was successful?" Garrison asked.

"Yes."

Sciambra went on to mention Ivon, the one man invariably included in allegations of skulduggery involving the D.A.'s office. Sciambra had been in touch with Ivon and was either picking him up, too, along with the other "individual" or was going to meet him someplace.

Again the possibility that they might have a little surprise in store for me struck home.

After Sciambra left, Garrison and I resumed our conversation, soon touching on Clay Shaw and the Warren Report. I informed him that although I had never cast myself in the position of defender of the report, I most certainly believed Clay Shaw was completely innocent.

"I can easily understand that belief—in your position. I can understand others believing it. But I have information that does not permit me to believe the same." Then out of the blue he asked, "Are you familiar with the Trade Mart building?"

"Yes," I replied. "Matter of fact, I had drinks up at the top of the Mart only a few nights ago."

"No," he said, "I mean the *old* Trade Mart building—the layout of it?"

"Well, yes," I said, having no idea what his point might be. "I've seen the old building, passed it often."

"Do you know who had offices there?"

"Well—"

He got up from his desk and walked to a large city directory, the size of several phone books. "I think it might be very interesting for you to have a list of all those who had offices in the old Trade Mart building." He called Moo Sciambra in and asked him to photostat the page in question. "I want Mr. Kirkwood to have a copy, and I'd like one myself."

Sciambra left with the book. I'd noticed that Garrison's mouth appeared to be dry, from the way his lips tended to stick together. He spoke only a few more sentences when he acknowledged this and excused himself to get a glass of water.

Left alone in the office, I swung around in my chair to see what was behind me. Stacked in a corner were several large blowup photographs of the grassy knoll and picket fence areas in Dallas. It was like seeing part of a set after the show had closed. I could not help recalling Bill Gurvich's story about his experience with similar blowups. Prominently featured on the wall opposite the D.A.'s handsome desk, was a horizontally oblong framed painting/sketch/photograph—I couldn't be sure—of a naked young lady lying on her stomach, displaying a deep tan except for the white strip across her buttocks where her bikini had shielded her and another narrower strip of white circling her upper back to her breasts. The office itself is noteworthy for its soft lighting and general comfort. It is a pleasant room to be in.

Garrison had no sooner returned when Sciambra entered and handed him two sheets. Mr. Garrison made a mark on one and gave it to me. He had encircled "International Trade Mart" in red. It was a sheet from the city directory, taken up mostly with a listing of the offices in the old Trade Mart building on Camp Street. Although the year was not apparent on the page, I imagined it was either 1966 or 1967, the time of Clay Shaw's arrest or prior to it, before the occupancy of the new Trade Mart building overlooking the Mississippi.

"Just take a look," Garrison said, "at the list of offices. This is not a coincidence, this is very meaningful."

I glanced at the list as he said, "The Cordell Hull Foundation! You know about that, of course." I noticed a short penciled arrow pointing to office 536, "The Cordell Hull Foundation." There was one other heavy pencil line ending in an arrow pointing to office 509, "Latin American Reports, Inc. publs." These marks had been on the original page. "I think you will find the list of offices extremely interesting," the District Attorney intoned.

There was never any doubt that the Trade Mart housed many consuls, many foreign trade organizations, as well as such offices as Hiram Walker, Inc., Distillers, Morton Salt, Chase Bag, Films Afloat and General Gas Corp.

"What do you think of that?" he asked seriously.

I did not reply. I was speechless that in 1969, after the trial, Jim Garrison was handing me a page out of a public city directory several years old and treating it as if it were new, secret and highly suspect evidence. I could feel my face tightening. In a way I took it as an affront to whatever intelligence I possess, if not a blatant implication of my gullibility. I simply sat in silent disbelief. "Keep it," he said. "Look it over when you have time. I believe you'll find it most interesting." He also mentioned he was glad he'd had it copied for himself. I was hoping he would not press me on this page, for the only remark I could have made would have been: Are you quite mad, sir?

To my great relief, he dropped the subject and returned to Vietnam. "John Kennedy was killed because he was against the war in Vietnam. There is no doubt about that."

While he let this sink in, I could not help recalling his many statements, both spoken and in print, accusing the anti-Castro Cubans, together with the CIA, of turning their wrath at the lack of air support for the Bay of Pigs to Kennedy. This was *the* iron-clad theory—previously. Now it was Vietnam.

Garrison explained. "John Kennedy was killed because he was ending the cold war rapidly. He was in the process of bringing about an entente with Russia. Ending the cold war meant a tremendous loss of power to a number of highly placed individuals and to some extremely important corporations, along with the Pentagon. They would not stand for it. For example, now we have close to 550,000 soldiers in Vietnam. Back in August of 1963 we only had 15,000. And these were not even combat troops, they were only advisers. By October 1, 1963, John Kennedy had brought back 1,000, leaving only 14,000 U.S. personnel in Vietnam. One of his last orders was to reduce it by another 1,000 which would bring it to 13,000. They killed him before that order could be carried out. He'd given orders to McNamara that by 1965 there would be no U.S. troops in Asia.

"If you'll remember, one of the first things Johnson did was to escalate the war and it's been escalating ever since."

Garrison spoke further of Vietnam, criticizing Dean Rusk's statement that we were in Vietnam to contain the Yellow Peril. "We were in Vietnam even *before* China had a nuclear capacity, so that is essentially an old tired line." The District Attorney snorted. "I became so disgusted over Vietnam that I quit the National Guard." He shook his head and sighed. "Only two years ago I spoke at a university, urging the students to do their duty in the service of their country. I was not on to the truth—again, the world that appears to be as opposed to the world that is—at that time. Now I look back in horror at what I told them."

I agreed with him that the war in Vietnam was a brutal, senseless and disgraceful chapter in our history and would be looked back on in years to come with shocking incredulity that it was allowed to happen, adding, "Had I not put in my three years and were I eligible, I would not attend this war. If I had children old enough to fight, I would urge them not to."

Garrison agreed with me and we spoke briefly of the college youth of today, not only of their protest but of their intense interest in politics and the course their country is taking. I expressed disappointment that I had not been as aware of important issues when I was their age. We agreed again.

Now Garrison took the President's murder one step further. "Not only was John Kennedy assassinated because he was opposed to the war, but look at Martin Luther King and Robert Kennedy. Do you think it's coincidence that these three men, all assassinated, were all against the war in Vietnam?"

"I can't say."

"You can't? I can. It couldn't just be a coincidence that the three assassins were all lonely psychotics who just *happened* to hit their marks without fail and that all three men just *happened* to be against the war. The coincidence is too much. And if Senator Fulbright continues his opposition of the war, continues vociferously, then there will be a little accident between Washington and Arkansas and again it will be hailed as the work of some poor loner with a distressed childhood and good aim. But that will not be the case. How many times does it have to happen before people wake up!"

Jim Garrison is a persuasive exponent of syllogistical logic: (1) all three men were anti-war, (2) all three were assassinated, therefore (3) all three were assassinated because they were anti-Vietnam and undoubtedly by a conspiracy of individuals who were warmongers.

The District Attorney spoke again. "There is a great problem determining what reality is in our time, in our government. But I have determined it and that's what makes me go on fighting for what I believe is right and against this totalitarian complex of power. I have found that the assassination was much more complicated than anyone believed and that a corner of it—I've never pretended it was more—existed in New Orleans. And that's what I've been pursuing."

Garrison had, in the past, claimed to have complete knowledge of the entire plot, who, how many, where, when, and how. But this, too, had changed, along with the reason for the assassination.

Now he spoke briefly of the three principals he had been concerned with as conspirators. He called David Ferrie a "brilliant individual and a crack pilot." "Oswald," the District Attorney said, "was a bright person, not stupid or a loner as so many people have claimed."

"Then he must have been an excellent actor," I said.

Jim Garrison smiled at me as if I'd figured it out. This brought him to his quarry. "Look at Clay Shaw, a most agreeable personality—bright, warm, charming, knowledgeable, without being creatively brilliant. He could always move in all circles, no matter where it might be. He would fit in anywhere. Again, I don't think he is creatively brilliant, a mastermind. He would always be somebody's lieutenant." The District Attorney went on to imply Clay was in the secret employ of some government agency. "Most likely the CIA," he said, adding, "you see, and there is the motive, and it hurt our case that this could not be proven in court. Although motive is not a necessary part of the conspiracy law, still it's—people want to know, what is the motive? But because of the clandestine quality of the operation we could not prove the motive angle, which seemed to be missing in the trial." He paused and nodded his head. "Clay Shaw is a smart man. He's smart."

Jim Garrison insisted he was only doing his duty in bringing the case to trial and reiterated it was the nature of the clandestine government power forces, such as the CIA, which could not be brought out in the open, that made the case impossible to win. "I was really glad myself," he said, "when the verdict came in. I felt relieved for the defendant."

"I don't believe I would have," I told him. "Not if I really *believed* he'd had a part in killing the President."

This somehow brought us to Robert Kennedy. Jim Garrison admired him greatly. I did, too, commenting that I would have voted for him. "I think he would have made a surprisingly fine President; I believe he had grown and mellowed." We discussed this and the happy quality that is the freedom and willingness to learn and change from what one learns. We were in total agreement about Robert Kennedy.

Garrison then shook his massive well-proportioned head. "Although I don't believe in capital punishment, I believe I would want Sirhan Sirhan put to death."

I felt exactly the same. Perhaps our agreement led to his next statement. "I believe even Clay Shaw would have to say he'd been given a fair trial."

I smiled and said, "I believe he feels the *verdict* was fair."

"I never entered into any pretrial statements that were prejudicial to Shaw. The only thing I said, and I said it time and time again, that Shaw was to be presumed innocent until proven guilty."

I could have given him damaging quotes and disclosures of evidence until I was blue in the face. Or he was blue in the face. Now, I thought, here's an enormous area—thousands of miles' worth—of disagreement. But I do not earn high marks as a nonpartisan debater. Emotions rise to the surface, coloring the face, constricting the throat, glazing the eyes. Still, I felt I should voice a token comment. I mentioned the lengthy *Playboy* interview, which certainly bolstered his case.

To this Jim Garrison replied, "Eric Norden, whom I admire, dropped a lot of that information in. Certainly the last page of it was mine, but a lot of that information was dropped in."

The *Playboy* interview was a question-and-answer proposition between Norden and Garrison. I have been told it was all taken from tapes of their conversation. It would be highly irregular to drop fictitious words into print and pass them off as quotes from Jim Garrison's mouth.

While I was contemplating questioning him further about this, he returned to Vietnam, speaking of the crime it was and the $80 billion it was costing and concentrating on how much the military and industrial complex would suffer if the war should end. "The poor whites and Negroes were being sent over so the middle class could stay here in college. And when that system was opposed, there was trouble. The Kennedys and Martin Luther King opposed this system and they were put out of the way."

The longer we spoke, the easier his manner became. I could easily understand the man's power of persuasion. When he looks at you, he is not looking beyond or past your ear, nor do his eyes leave you for frequent scouting trips around the room. He focuses a full 100 per cent upon his subject. In moments of reflection there is that odd slight bulging of the eyes, followed by the upward roll and the lift of the eyebrows I had noticed on television and the dryness of his mouth, often attributed by New Orleanians to the taking of some sort of pep pill, such as Dexamyl. These characteristics accomplish one thing. They make the observer focus even closer upon Jim Garrison, the way in which a slight tic can be particularly mesmerizing.

He spoke of his own career with a complete ease that lent his utterances the ring of truth. "You know, Jim [I believe I had asked him by this time not to call me Mr. Kirkwood], I really dislike public life. I don't enjoy backslapping, pumping hands, making public appearances, or making speeches. I don't like that stuff at all. In fact, I've avoided it almost completely for two years now."

He may not have engaged in politicking—backslapping and hand pumping—but I doubt if any other city official in the country, outside of the Mayor of New York, had been heard from in press releases, on the radio and television, in magazine articles and in addresses to various groups as consistently as the District Attorney of New Orleans in the past two years. And here he was sitting opposite me and calmly denying his proven magnetic field of publicity and public relations.

Garrison continued in this vein. "I hadn't even wanted to run for District Attorney originally. I also didn't think I had a chance of winning. I did it only because of the previous holder of the office, Dowling. Cases were fixed or not prosecuted or—I'd worked in the D.A.'s office and I respected it. I thought I could do something to help put it right again, where it had badly disintegrated."

"Are you going to run again?" I asked.

Garrison fingered a pencil, then looked up at me. "I haven't come to a firm decision, but I probably will. I don't think I'd want to hold office for four more years. I think I'd like to serve only two more—bringing my tenure as District Attorney to ten." He smiled an easy warm smile. "Probably because no one else has ever done it."

Again I asked if I could switch on the tape machine. "No, this is fine," he said. (I should perhaps explain that my seeming addiction to tape machines is not an obsession with gadgetry. It merely allows the complete ease of enjoying an interview without having to fret about misquoting and without distracting the subject by presenting him the picture of hunched shoulders over a cramped hand feverishly making love to the page.)

"What would you like to do after your reign as District Attorney?"

"I think I'd like to return to private practice. I've always been concerned more with defending the individual than prosecuting him. My natural bent is to defend." He spoke of private practice and within a minute or so informed me, "We've never lost a murder case in all the years I've been in office, not one."

This, to me, made his previously avowed proclivity for defending the individual slightly contradictory. If he'd been D.A. going on eight years, that meant eight years of prosecution. Where was the defending?

Again he began speaking of the real world as opposed to the world that appears to be, of the importance of people detecting what was illusory and of the importance of his fight against the concealment of evidence by the government. But as much as I was enjoying Jim Garrison's company and undivided attention and even the contradictions, I could not let them all fly over my shoulder. "Could I ask you a question?"

"Of course," he said.

"If, as you say, you believe so strongly in what you're doing, why *not* aspire to higher political life? You've slugged away at this long enough and hard enough, why not go on slugging, if you feel so strongly?"

He merely shrugged and replied, "I simply don't want any other political or public office. It's not my nature." He laughed. "I'm not the flamboyant character I'm made out to be, not at all. I loathe the word flamboyant. As I said, I really don't enjoy public life."

"You may not enjoy it and you may loathe the word flamboyant but you certainly have a natural style and flair for it. There's no getting around that. You can't deny it."

Jim Garrison hunched his shoulders, indicating if he possessed these qualities that was just the way it was, he certainly didn't work at it. There was, at this point, a look exchanged, together with a smile that, to me at least, acknowledged my interpretation of his professed dislike of the spotlight as a put-on. If so, I enjoyed the moment.

When Jim Garrison smiles or laughs, he is not presenting the social trappings of a professional. These expressions are motivated from within and he is enjoying them. To react any other way, I believe, he would consider beneath him, a cheat. Herein another contradiction. The leap from the small honest reaction to mendacity on a gargantuan scale. One is improper, the other entirely permissible and performed with outrageous aplomb.

I could not have our talk conclude without saying, "I was terribly surprised—as I know Clay Shaw was—at the perjury charges."

In a very low quiet voice he said, "It's my duty, the duty of my office. It's the only possible thing that could have been done. What else could I do?"

In a very small quiet voice I replied, "Forget about them."

A small smile, which I was unable to return.

"Tell me about your writing career? You used to be an actor?"

After I gave him a brief rundown, he paused for a moment, then said, "I've had ambitions along that line, but I don't know if they're strong enough. It's a difficult field—writing."

Andrew Sciambra rejoined us about this time, taking a seat across from me. We spoke of Tennessee Williams, who had in the past frequently taken up residence in New Orleans when he was about to plunge into a new work. Sciambra said he'd often seen him in bars in the Quarter. "There's a very saddening thing about authors in America," I remarked. "Seems like they reach a certain degree of success, the good ones, they enjoy a period of vogue and then the tide turns and everyone, the critics and spreading on to the public, feels compelled to dump on them. The worst of it is when a man, for example Williams, comes up with something less than his best work, Christ, the black crepe is dragged out, the coffins are opened up and the word is spread in print by columnists and critics and on panel shows that he's finished, his talent has dried up like a river bed and he will undoubtedly produce nothing but garbage until he shuffles off. What a destructive thing for a working author to hear and read about himself as he rises each morning to face the blank pages. Why can't they simply say this play or that novel is not up to par, even say it stinks to high heaven, but not damn the man's talents for all time to come!"

"You feel strongly about that, don't you?"

"Yes."

"You like Williams' writing?" he asked.

"Yes, and what a body of work he's produced. If he doesn't write another word, he's earned a solid and extremely high place in American theatre."

"You know," said Jim Garrison, "there's one small perfect gem of an American classic—"

"I'll bet I know which one you're referring to," I interrupted.

He looked slightly annoyed. "I haven't even—"

"*The Glass Menagerie,*" I said.

Now he looked slightly amazed, glancing to Sciambra and back at me. "How did you know I was going to say that?"

"Just a hunch," I told him. "I feel that way about it. It *is* a contemporary classic, a gem. So simple, so perfect in its simplicity and its compassion—"

"And poetry," Jim Garrison added.

We moved on to television and the utter predictability of most programing. We both spoke with admiration of the Smothers Brothers, who had recently been in the news over their departure from one of the major networks in a dispute over censorship. Sciambra approved of them, too.

We then got on to Mort Sahl, who had been an aficionado of Garrison and who was, not surprisingly, admired by Sciambra and the District Attorney. I remembered Sahl when he first began as a terribly clever satirist but had not seen him perform lately. This led us to Lenny Bruce, a man vastly underrated and misunderstood while he was alive, who used vulgarity and prejudice as a mirror to our national hypocrisy and who was anything *but* prurient. Again, total agreement. And so we delved further into the field of entertainment, into books we liked, plays, a film or two. Our tastes were similar. I found both Garrison and Sciambra to be interested in the arts and entertainment and fairly knowledgeable.

Now we were rattling on, speaking with all guards down, perhaps not as old friends but certainly as friends, although we were, in fact, enemies, holding a most enjoyable symposium. I found this perverse and intriguing.

Around 1 o'clock—I'd been there over two hours—Jim Garrison indicated he would soon have to excuse himself. Knowing I planned to include his closing speech to the jury in the book, I said, "I thought your closing speech was fascinating."

"You did?"

"Yes, absolutely fascinating."

"I'm glad."

"I would like very much to have a copy."

"Fine," he replied. A copy was soon produced which he signed in red ink, "From Jim Garrison to Jim Kirkwood." When he stood up and handed it to me, he smiled and said, "This has been a most friendly interview. I've enjoyed it."

"So have I." I was telling the truth. I also wondered if we would trust each other the distance it takes a rattlesnake to strike. I shook hands with my old buddy Moo Sciambra, then with Jim Garrison. "God, you're tall," I said. "Oh, give my best to your wife. I spoke with her during the trial several times. She's extremely attractive."

"I will. The next time we get together I'll have you out to the house to see her and meet the kids."

"Good, I'd like that."

"We'll do it."

Sciambra stayed in the office while Garrison walked me down the hall, through the gate and to the outside doors of the D.A.'s office. Just as I was about to leave, I turned to him and said, "You know, it's amazing, we agree on almost everything—Williams, *The Glass Menagerie,* Vietnam, Bobby Kennedy, Sirhan Sirhan, the Smothers Brothers—everything but Clay Shaw. I still believe he's completely innocent."

"I know. But no matter what you believe, at least I think you realize now that we run a good office here, an honest one."

I could not answer that. But, after a pause, I said to him, "You know what I can't help thinking? Knowing Clay very well and having spent this time with you—I know if the two of you ever spoke privately, you'd get along like a house afire. You really would. You'd enjoy each other immensely. This has occurred to me often, even before I met you. I know you'd be fascinated with each other. I'd like to see it happen."

"I agree. He's a charming man, I'm sure. I'd like to talk to him and will, if it should ever happen by accident." Jim Garrison smiled at me now, put a paw on my shoulder and dropped the capper and a great clue to his undeniable charm as he said, "But you realize, we couldn't very well take a table for two at Brennan's. That would just confuse hell out of people!"

51

All the King's Men

The following afternoon I met with James Alcock in his office at the Criminal Court Building. The motives of many of Garrison's underlings can be pieced together and understood. But James Alcock, the brightest of them all, represented more of a question mark. He had prosecuted the Shaw trial as if his life depended on it, with apparent total belief and with all his considerable courtroom talents. Had he known the case was a fraud? Had he gone ahead and prosecuted it, knowing that? If so many on the outside had come to know the truth, if even that divining jury had caught the scent, how could an intelligent man on the inside from the very beginning *not* know?

Brown-haired James Alcock, studious-looking with glasses framing his blue eyes, spoke with me on tape in an outgoing, unsuspicious manner.

Born in New York, Alcock had lived in Hawaii, California, Oklahoma and Fort Worth, Texas, attending the same high school with Lee Harvey Oswald's brother, Robert. He had later moved to New Orleans and after a hitch in the service had returned to enroll at Loyola University, where he eventually graduated with a law degree in 1963. He had been with the District Attorney's office and Jim Garrison since that time.

The color of Jim Alcock's face had been a barometer to his emotions during the trial; now I had only to watch for the rush of blood to his roundish persimmon cheeks to discover how much of a conscience he possessed for his part in the Shaw case.

Q.: You actually worked on the case from the very beginning, didn't you?
ALCOCK: Right.
Q.: In the investigatory phases, as well?
ALCOCK: Well, I didn't do too much investigation on the case. I

think I did initially, more than toward the later stages of it. As a matter of fact, I was with Bill Gurvich in Texas when they brought Clay Shaw up here that day, the day he was arrested. I recall coming back just before he was arrested. I wasn't here during the Perry Russo episode, going to Baton Rouge and bringing him down, putting him on sodium pentothal. But once the case was accepted, after the defense starting filing pleadings and going to Federal court, I almost exclusively was engaged in the legal end of it. Rather than the investigative end . . . And I did, as Gurvich has announced, I did go into the office and attempt to talk Jim out of charging Clay Shaw. But I didn't know of the existence of Russo, and I didn't know what Russo had to say, and when he said that—of course, I didn't know who Russo was, his background, or I didn't know he'd been on the sodium pentothal or hypnosis or anything—of course that changed my opinion.

It appeared that James Alcock did not want to be overly associated with the investigatory phase—the murky work—and one could not blame him. There are people who believe that, if witnesses were coached, inducements offered, and stories fabricated, Jim Alcock was not brought in until the dress rehearsal, until the character in question was familiar with his lines. I believe Alcock would have wanted it that way. But can you have it both ways? Can you be engaged in bolstering suborned testimony and walk away at the end without certain nasty stains on your fingers?

Jim Alcock was candid about the state's preferences for jurors, saying, "We didn't want necessarily a completely blue-collar jury although we would have gone more with a blue-collar jury than a white-collar jury. It turns out it didn't make much difference, we didn't get any of them. . . . It's more or less a guessing game— you really don't know what kind of a juror you want. You know there's some you definitely do *not* want. Of course, I didn't want any—I'm reluctant to use the phrase—'uptowners,' but I didn't want any people on there that might have been engaged in business with Shaw, the International Trade Mart, or been familiar with Shaw's background, which certainly was of some status. . . .

Q.: Yes. Because it seemed the state wanted a less sophisticated man.

ALCOCK: Right. That's true. I don't deny that.

Q.: And I suppose you want people you can persuade.

ALCOCK: That's what it's all about. If you don't feel you can persuade them, no sense having them on the jury. . . . I can see that some people might—you know, begin to question the state in attempting to get the lesser intellectually qualified juror on there, but again, we had our case to try and I thought that, as a judgment of mine, that we'd be better off with those kind of jurors. And we didn't get—we got several of them—and you know, I don't want to characterize the jurors, but I think it was a fairly good cross section of the community and as it turned out, Shaw couldn't have asked for anything more. . . . But I still think in the final result—I'll never forget, when we were in Federal court in this case, and I wrote a brief in support of our position [to come to trial] and my last line was something to the effect that the United States Supreme Court had exhibited great confidence in the jury system, I only ask this court to do as much. I remember I had a chamber conference with Judge Ainsworth of the Fifth Circuit Court of Appeals. He said, "Are you really sincere?" I said, "Yes, I am, because I've been out in the District Attorney's office for five years and I've tried many cases. And I can't recall any of them where the verdict was really way out of bounds." It's surprising the way that—I guess it's the way group consensus works, that they really—they're hard to fool. Although you might not get the shake of the dice that you think you should get. Nevertheless, I think in the main it's by far the best [system].

[The foregoing seemed to indicate James Alcock thought even the Shaw jury could not be fooled.]

Q.: How did you feel about the case coming to trial?

ALCOCK: Well, I was glad to see it come to trial because it was like a millstone around my neck. I mean I knew that I would be trying the case, would be the principal attorney. I also knew that it would be an awful lot of work to prepare and actually go into trial. Of course, being human, I wasn't too anxious to do all that work. But these were the only real reservations I had about going to trial. Once I saw it was finally going to go, and once I got busily engaged in preparing, I was glad to see it come and get over with.

Q.: Can you often tell when you're watching the jury, which way they're going? The press couldn't, we couldn't tell what they were absorbing or thinking or—

ALCOCK: No, you're right. Some of them I can recall looking at during the trial, no matter what happened, like this one juror—again I don't want to mention his name lest you put it in the book—he'd be mad at me. But no matter what was said by either side, no matter what the witness said, he'd be looking off in the other direction. And I couldn't understand it either. In many cases I've been able to tell which way the jury was going. I think generally you can when you've got a case of shorter duration. Now, in this case, frankly I couldn't . . . I couldn't read this jury.

Q.: Another thing about this—

ALCOCK: Although I wasn't surprised at the verdict.

[This completely unsolicited remark surprised *me*, certainly indicating Alcock did not think he would win. Later on I returned to this subject.]

Q.: Did you hold out much hope for a guilty verdict, right there at the end?

ALCOCK: Well, you see, I hate to answer this question because I don't want it misconstrued. I don't want anybody to think I did not have confidence in my case, that I do not think we should've tried Clay Shaw. Because I think we had to try Clay Shaw. But I was not confident of a guilty verdict. . . . Maybe again this is a matter of sensing things. I told you I couldn't really read this jury too well, but I could read them well enough to know they were not going to convict him. And I'll never forget—and I won't mention the juror's name—when Shaw was on direct. And he was very imposing and very articulate and very calm, exhibiting anything but the traits of a guilty man. This juror looked at me and he shook his head. And it wasn't like, Well, he's lying through his teeth. It was like, Sorry, but you're wasting your time. So—but that was just one juror. But I just—and again I hope you're not misconstruing it, but when they left, when they came back with the verdict, my wife was there and I told her, "We're not going to win this case." In fact, I wasn't the least bit—I mean I wanted to win, naturally, and I thought that we'd put on—I thought we'd done everything we could. Let's put it that way. But I wasn't the least bit surprised. And I wasn't surprised by twelve to nothing. If I'd been surprised by twelve to nothing, I would have polled the jury. . . . The only thing that—it didn't change my mind, but gave me a flicker of hope, was the fact that I'd heard the two alternates were for guilty. But even that didn't really change my mind, because I just felt—just something. I'd been with this jury for forty days and I knew the case and I'd tried it personally. And I just felt that, although I thought they listened attentively to my arguments, they did the same to Dymond. I just didn't believe closing arguments were going to do it. So I just felt that we weren't going to win the case.

[James Alcock spoke of Clay Shaw as being an unusual defendant several times. He was obviously intrigued with the man he had prosecuted.]

Q.: If I were a trial lawyer I think there would be many times when I would want to talk to the defendants. I'd be curious to know what they were really like. Did you ever have that impulse?

ALCOCK: Right. I would say I had that impulse. In this case. In fact I enjoy talking to the defendants. They'll be brought into the dock in other cases and I will have convicted them. After the case is over. Or they were acquitted, whichever the case may be, and I'll talk to them. Because I enjoy it. You get a different perspective and you get their side of the story. But again, that's the run of the mill defendant. That's not a Clay Shaw. But I would have liked to have spoken to him and talked to him and got—not necessarily his side of the story but—because his side has got to be opposed to your side. . . . But really this is a situation that had to be prosecuted and so in a way I guess it's just as well that I didn't get to talk to him. . . . And in a way I really didn't want to. Because the man is a charming individual. And he's very—his manners are very gracious and I think it would be very difficult to consider him in the light that you do most defendants, especially after you spoke with him.

Now, of course, he's got the homosexual aspect. But I have never personally—of course I'm not a champion of homosexuals by any stretch of the imagination. But I've personally never had any feelings one way or the other. I don't—you know, what the man wants to do is his business. And I think this is something that we—although I know many people thought we behaved improperly in this case, there were many times that we could have interjected that. And I purposely did not interject it. Although I was pressured—well, not pressured, but many people kept asking me, "Why don't you interject the homosexual?" And I said, "No, it has nothing to do with the case." I think I could've gotten it in on the Clay Bertrand thing, since Bertrand was allegedly a contact for homosexuals in trouble. I probably could've gotten it in that way. But I just didn't think it was relevant in this case.

Q.: I think most people, because of the innuendoes in the pretrial publicity over the past couple of years, expected it. I did. I think everyone was delighted that you didn't do it. And I think if you had it would have backfired.

ALCOCK: Positively. Well, let me say this. Although I've tried to make myself magnanimous, to a certain degree I didn't do it because I thought as an individual it wasn't fair. . . . But also being a trial lawyer and being concerned with trial tactics, I knew there was a great possibility that the thing would really boomerang. And they'd say, Well, look at this. They can't get him for this so they're going to bring his personal life in. As it turns out, you can't get much worse than twelve to nothing, but still I thought as an individual I didn't want to do it. And secondly, as a trial lawyer, I thought it had a real possibility of boomeranging. So you're right, you had both aspects. . . . As a matter of fact the only guy that brought homosexuality into it at all was Dymond when he had Eugene Davis on the stand. Kept talking about a homosexual bar, trying to impugn this man's character as a homosexual. And then, of course, he's *defending* a man who's allegedly a homosexual. I've got no proof he *is* a homosexual. I'm just saying.

Q.: Well, of course, there was the Sciambra memo—right?

ALCOCK: The memo. But, of course, *they* [the defense] wanted the memo read. I mean this was [Alcock's face colored and he exhaled a deep breath]—I'll never get over having to defend Sciambra's memo writing!

I asked Alcock what he thought were the main weaknesses in the state's case. He politely replied he would just as soon not discuss them. We then went to the difference between witnesses and the way each side handled them—Dr. Finck, for example.

ALCOCK: Finck had obviously testified very few times and it's very easy of course on direct examination to testify. You've got a friendly questioner who's going to lead you *without* leading you, you know? You know what he wants and you're going to give him what he wants. But then you get somebody on the other side picking your story apart. And a good cross-examiner generally doesn't just let you repeat what you did [on direct] and let you go chronologically down the line. He'll pick out something here and get you on it and then pick something over here and then go back over here, and it confuses you if you've got it sort of memorized. So I think this may have been Dr. Finck's trouble. . . . And yet many witnesses during trial are much better on cross, because the lawyer for some reason will get under their skin and, boy, they'll heap it on. You see, this is the reason—say like when I had Phelan on cross. Now Sciambra had some personal dealings with Phelan and they weren't too happy. As a result, of course, Sciambra wanted me to really go after him. And he had reams of stuff for me to ask him. But when I saw the drift of the situation, Phelan is no ordinary witness. Shaw was no ordinary defendant. This is an intelligent man and he's strictly *not* on your side. It's just like an expert that's against you. Every chance they get they're going to bury you. So the best thing you can do with a witness like this is catch him on a couple of points and then let him go. I think this is the test of a good trial lawyer.

Of course, I've said how good I think Dymond is. But I think Dymond tried on a couple of occasions to get a little bit too much out of witnesses on cross. In other words he'd pass that point of diminishing returns. Like Spiesel. Now he destroyed Spiesel. Why he had Spiesel go down to the French Quarter and look for this apartment? As it turned out he picked one that may or may not be significant, but it did rehabilitate him a little bit. Certainly not completely. But I think Dymond would have been better off if he'd let him go. Because he completely destroyed him with his lawsuit.

Q.: What about putting him on as a witness in the first place?

ALCOCK: I'd rather not go into it.

Q.: Okay, I don't blame you.

ALCOCK: Because, you know, we've got the same situation, although it's not the same case, we've got some of the same issues. I'm not saying he'd be a witness, but I'd rather not. . . . Believe me, I'd like to have gone through the floor during some of the cross-examination!

[We soon touched upon Perry Russo.]

ALCOCK: He was under actually much more lengthy and much more searching and much more severe cross-examining in the preliminary examination than he was in the trial. . . . I almost get to the feeling where perhaps Russo said, God, this whole thing is derived from what I've said. When you get down to it the case does rest upon me, and if I'm not 100 per cent sure I'd better soften the blow a little bit. Again, I have nothing to base that on. I don't say that's what he did. But I know the boy found himself in a tough situation. Not tough, I mean, but he was—either you're 100 per cent sure of yourself—you take a man of Shaw's stature and this almost seeming incompatibility with what we were alleging, you become a little bit wary and say, Well, maybe I'd better kind of vacillate here a little bit. Equivocate. And maybe I can soften the blow. I don't think that's what he did, but—in effect at least he did.

Q.: I had a great respect for his ability to qualify his answers. He's very bright that way.

ALCOCK: Yes. I'll tell you, though, I think that might have been part of his downfall in front of a jury. The boy was a compulsive talker, for one thing. You couldn't ask him a question—and anything that related to Ferrie we had to go through this— Well, this guy was an amazing man, this guy, you know? I think the jury got tired of qualifications that were so long. It looked like he couldn't just answer the question. Of course, Irvin, he was doing the right thing. Ask him a question, let him go on. Ask him another, let him go on. The jury's got to see that—actually, it's not too normal for a witness to do that. I know any time I talk to a witness before trial I'll tell them, "Answer the question. Be truthful, answer the question. But don't volunteer a lot of other things." Many times I've tried cases and witnesses have done that, and all they do is give you more ammunition to cross-examine them with. So it's not the best thing to do. Although the qualifications were sometimes adroit, I think he overdid it. That hurt his credibility.

Q.: Everyone has mentioned the fact that Garrison didn't attend the trial as much as expected. I would have thought when Perry Russo was on the stand—not necessarily that he would question him, but he would sit there and keep his eye on him. It was remarkable that he wasn't on hand.

ALCOCK: Well, I think that—he did exactly what he said he was going to do. In other words he delegated the responsibilities in this case and I think—and I'm certainly not throwing any bouquets my way or the way of the other assistants who tried the case—I think he thought he had competent counselmen there and that they were going to try the case and he wasn't going to try it. Therefore he wasn't going to sit there and second-guess. Actually, although we might have wanted him there occasionally for a little moral suasion, it's better to try a case without your boss there, really. Because, you know, if he's looking over your shoulder he might be saying, Why did he do this? or Why did he do that? So in some respects we didn't mind that at all. Others, of course, I might have wanted him there a bit more.

Q.: How did you feel about the press coverage?

ALCOCK: Grossly unfair!

Q.: You did?

ALCOCK: If there was one consensus among those who attended the trial—and I'm not referring to the press people but the non-press people—this consensus was that what they saw in the court-room and what they read in the newspapers were entirely two different things. It was to me the most biased presentation of a case I've ever seen.

Q.: Really? I know a lot of people who felt it was the other way around.

ALCOCK: I mean it. Now, of course, there were certain people I knew were going to be like that to start with. I think the *Newsweek* guy—Aynesworth. He filed five or six stories in the Pitts-burgh papers. God, those things were absolutely malicious, not only malicious but totally inaccurate. I mean if you're going to be malicious, at least be accurate. . . . But I felt the coverage in this case and on Channel Four was absolutely devastating. In fact I went up to the news director just before the closing arguments and I said, "Are you going to make a closing argument for the de-fense?" He said, "What are you talking about?" I said, "You've been making one for six weeks." And I was really mad . . .

Q.: Well, take Aynesworth, for instance. He really felt strongly about this. But in all honesty, why did he feel so strongly? He felt—and I know it's not diplomatic to say but I can say it to you—he felt like it was a rigged case, from the beginning. And he felt outraged. And I've felt that way, too.

James Alcock listened quietly as I spoke of others in the press and their feelings. He did not respond to the charges of rigging, except for a heightened coloring of his cheeks. But he believed strongly the press had been unfair, speaking of the coverage at length. As to the basic validity of the trial, he said:

ALCOCK: This is something that really amazed me when the newspapers came out after the trial calling for Jim to resign, saying he should never have tried Shaw. Well, this Federal court, I can remember their decision, they said the state had every right to try this man. Actually they had a *duty* to try this man. And the United States Supreme Court went along with it. Judge Haggerty, twice refusing to grant directed verdicts, went along with it. I just never could understand it. I think during the course of the trial, we did everything in our power to give him a fair trial. We didn't inject the homosexuality, we didn't inject, that I could see, any non-relevant issues and try to becloud the minds of the jurors. Additionally, we had other witnesses who were to testify and might have been devastating and might have held up. But after appraising their background and going into their story, we just decided that they weren't telling the truth. Or if they were, it was just— So I really feel the characterization of the office was unfair. And the characterization of Jim was unfair. And I know people made great capital of sodium pentothal and hypnosis—these mysterious things. Again, and I hate to fall back on the Boston Strangler, but boy, what they did in that case! They put everybody—they put DiSalvo under sodium pentothal. They put many witnesses under sodium pentothal. Many were hypnotized, many took lie detector tests. . . . Everybody uses it. It's not as if it's— And I can honestly say if I felt otherwise I wouldn't have tried the case, that the only reason Jim subjected this boy to these tests was, as he put it, "to objectify his testimony." I don't know, you probably never met Dr. Fatter . . . but there was no way you could look at this guy and say he was trying to plant a story. To me these charges were totally baseless and in some respects I was sorry we didn't get an evidentiary hearing in the Federal court. Because many of the allegations made in the pleadings were totally false. And I thought somewhat reckless. I mean these things like following Shaw around. We never followed him after the first day we arrested him. Tapping his telephone, tapping the defense lawyers' telephones—that's all a lot of nonsense. I know they had to make it look bad to catch the court's attention, but I think those things are completely unjustified. Because absolutely none of that went on.

I don't know if you're familiar with some of the stories that—like John Cancler was supposed to have said. That's totally ridiculous. Can you imagine us having him plant evidence? . . . They had this other man, this burglar Torres, said we'd offered him a month's vacation in the Bahamas and something like a couple pounds of heroin. I mean that's just totally absurd. And I just think the charges leveled against us by the press have been really unbelievable.

Q.: Well, it gets to be that very dirty game of everybody pulling out all stops to back up their beliefs.

ALCOCK: Yes, but, it's really unfortunate, because it's really—you know, they besmirch your character personally as well as the office. When you talk about the office, you're not just talking about some entity in space. You're talking about people that occupy the office and have families and go home at night. I wouldn't want any of that sort of nonsense on my conscience, and I just don't believe that—I know no one else in the office would. So I always felt it was really unfair.

Q.: Well, I think in all honesty—

ALCOCK: I can't—does Shaw really believe all this stuff?

Q.: Well, he's remarkable. I know you've seen him on television where he says he doesn't feel hatred. He doesn't, which is incredible. If I'd gone through two years of that and—

ALCOCK: That's another thing, you know. The two years was a result of *their* actions. Not ours.

Q.: Yes, but that's like trying to avoid a painful operation for two years. The amputation of a leg when you don't agree the leg is malignant. Nevertheless I'd be pretty annoyed by it. I think he was greatly surprised and shocked by the perjury charges. I was, too, and I'll tell you why. It seems like after two years, it was hell for the defendant. As long as it wasn't conspiracy, it just seemed like mad dog tactics to hit him with this. And I felt badly about it. Also, I don't happen to believe he knew them. But that's my belief. He's a bright man, you see, he's not a stupid man no matter what you say. When he was first questioned, I think in December of '66, and asked if he had known Dave Ferrie and Oswald, he must have known something important was up.

ALCOCK: I don't know if he was asked that much in December. I don't. I don't think the question was very—

Q.: I think he was asked if he knew them and I think he was told what it was about.

ALCOCK: He may have been, I'm not sure. I didn't question him. I think Sciambra did. But I didn't think it was that detailed. . . . You know again, what's always—I wish he had taken that lie detector test. We might have resolved the whole darn thing.

This statement—Jim Alcock's out-of-the-blue brand of "Ah, shucks" simplicity—threw me for a minute, really threw me, so much so I forgot to mention that his lawyers had agreed to let him take the test after a night's rest. This condition was turned down. Also, Perry Russo's failure to pass a lie detector test did not prevent them from using him as their main witness. So the state's reliance on lie detector tests remained questionable.

Q.: But, you see, in spite of being called up to the District Attorney's office and asked certain questions—obviously if it had to do with Lee Harvey Oswald, it had to do with the assassination. And he never called his lawyer. Now, I think if he had even known *any* of the participants, being a bright man he would certainly have called up Eddie Wegmann and said—

ALCOCK: Well, maybe being a bright man, he just might have used the reverse psychology. . . . I think that you just can't put Shaw in the mold of the usual defendant now, or the usual man who commits a crime. You can't say he was necessarily reacting the way they would. And I agree with you that, if we were talking about a run of the mill burglar or armed robber, if we started questioning him: What about—what were you doing on such and such a day? he would automatically and instinctively say, Well, look, I want to talk to my lawyer. But it doesn't necessarily follow in the case of Clay Shaw.

A little later in our taped interview, I asked Jim Alcock if he would prosecute the perjury charges. At this question, his cheeks bloomed pink and, glancing down at his desk, he spoke in a low voice. "I don't know. I wasn't here the day the charge was made. I had nothing to do with the charge. I was kind of hoping for a rest." He caught my expression, which could be classed in the rueful smile category, and added, "Not that I'm opposing the charge, because I do believe the man lied. But, I tell you, now I don't know what the defense is doing. Man, I'd be up in Clinton looking for the Federal people who are up there, any Federal people up there. They ought to be able to get someone to say who that was if it wasn't Shaw. You know what's always fascinated me. And I've looked for it and looked for it. Remember the testimony was that a woman took him [Oswald] up there, the first time they went to a barbershop? Man, I'd like to know who that was. Because I have got no doubt that he [Oswald] was up there. None whatsoever. He was definitely up in that area. Now whether he was with Shaw—I think he was, Shaw's side think he wasn't. But I would sure like to know who that woman was. Because you know, it couldn't have been his wife."

Sciambra came into the office, and it was clear James Alcock had matters to attend to. We soon ended our interview, but then Alcock walked me out into the hall, and we stood talking by the stairs for another fifteen or twenty minutes.

Now that he was not on tape, he was much more informal, more relaxed, although he had certainly been friendly in his office. Our conversation took on the ease of a bull session as we both leaned against the staircase railing. I, too, loosened up and spoke about other members of the D.A.'s staff. Although Alcock had admitted that defending Sciambra's memo was a task that caused him considerable pain, he nevertheless praised Sciambra: "He's never had any money. He came up the hard way. He was a boxer and put himself through school by hard work. He might not be a great memo writer, but he's honest. I believe him."

When I indicated I found belief difficult at best, Alcock asked: "Why would we have brought Russo up here if there'd been no mention of conspiracy? We weren't all that interested in Ferrie's habits."

"Why was that all Sciambra wrote about then? It was all *he* seemed interested in documenting."

Again Alcock's face colored and he joked about Sciambra's talents as a writer. To me it was really no joke, nor was, despite the buffoon he is, Dean Andrews' figmentation of the name Clay Bertrand. At the mention of Andrews, Jim Alcock said, "If Dean

Andrews really made the name Clay Bertrand up out of thin air—then Shaw must harbor some bitter thoughts about Andrews, because that's where it all started."

When I spoke of my meeting with Garrison, Alcock expressed nothing but soaring admiration for the man and awarded the District Attorney high marks for humor and charm. Now Jim Alcock's curiosity came to the fore as he inquired how well I knew Clay Shaw, if it was true he had a good sense of humor, how he'd taken the trial and how he'd endured the entire ordeal. "I'd really like to talk to him sometime," Alcock said, after I'd spoken of Clay. "You know," he went on, "Shaw got me during my closing argument. He really did. In most cases when I point to the defendant and I'm accusing him, the defendant will look down or glance away. But not Shaw. He held his head up and looked straight at me. If you want to know the truth, after a while I tended only to point in his general direction."

"I noticed that."

Jim Alcock's next question particularly struck me, posed as it was in a casual offhand manner which indicated genuine concern: "Tell me, ah, does Irvin Dymond—does Irvin feel bitter toward the office?"

"He feels incredulous—about the perjury charges."

Toward the end of our conversation, I felt enough at ease with Jim Alcock to spit up my opinion of the perjury charges again. His face reddened once more as he emphasized he'd had nothing to do with the charges, that he hadn't instigated them, that he only worked for the D.A. Now I put forth this hypothesis: "You know what I made up in my mind?"

"No, what?" he asked.

"I think you believed Clay Shaw was not guilty but that you prosecuted the case to the best of your ability because it was a job to do. You were employed by Jim Garrison and you did his bidding. I can't believe *you* believed."

Now his face colored mightily. He looked down at his hands which grasped the railing, then back up at me. "Well, you know, Jim, I can't—what can I say?"

He glanced away and shrugged. But he did not deny it.

When we said goodbye I had to admit I liked him personally. Yet I was annoyed at myself for this, because if my theory was correct and he'd prosecuted the case knowing Clay was innocent, how much worse than if he'd believed in the defendant's guilt.

Were not Garrison's aides just as culpable as the men who performed the actual dirty work at Dachau and Belsen, men who claimed they had only been following orders and were therefore not guilty of the atrocities they had so ably carried out?

52

An Evening with Perry Russo

      The following morning I awoke with the distinct feeling that my time in New Orleans was running out. The depression of being immersed so long in this brackish matter was shrinking my spirits again, as it had immediately after the trial.

      The promised interview with Judge Haggerty was set for the afternoon, but as I phoned up to make plane reservations to New York for a few days later, Perry Russo kept reoccurring to me. Had it not been for him, there would have been no trial. When I'd introduced myself in the corridor, he had said to give him a call, but that was before his testimony. I wondered if he would speak with me now. I decided the chances were slim indeed, but I would give him a try.

      He'd mentioned that his phone number was unlisted, but it could be had through Information. I rang up and was told the phone had been disconnected. This strengthened my belief that he was incommunicado. After a series of phone calls to various contacts in the Sheriff's office, I managed to get his last known address.

      I drove out the wide street known as Elysian Fields until I came to the number I'd been given. It was a small stucco two-family residence. There was a name on the downstairs bell but none for the top apartment. I rang both bells repeatedly. No answer. Walking up the steps to the second floor, I found only a small hallway and a door with no name. I knocked. No reply. Back downstairs, I heard voices coming from the back yard. Following the driveway, I encountered a middle-aged man and asked if Perry Russo lived there. He spoke in Spanish and said he did not understand English. In my halting Spanish, I asked the question again. The name did not appear familiar. On a chance, I showed him an envelope with Perry Russo's name written on it. (I had typed out a note, in the event I found the correct address and no one home, asking him to phone me.) The man recognized the printed word and, again speaking in Spanish, told me he lived upstairs. I asked if he were home. The man replied he was probably at work. I thanked him and said I would leave my note. The man came around to the front and watched while I went upstairs, stuck the note partially under the door and returned. As I was getting into my car, the man called to me, saying Russo was indeed home and pantomiming that he'd peeked out of the window.

I returned to the second floor. The note was gone. I knocked. "Who is it?" a voice asked from behind the door. I gave my name, and the door was soon opened. Perry Russo stood there in a pair of shorts, his black hair tousled and my opened note in his hands. "What do you want?" he asked. I reminded him we'd met at the courthouse and said I'd like to talk to him. "Well, I don't know what there is to say," he said. Then: "Come in. Let me just put some clothes on." I entered and apologized for waking him up—it was almost 11 o'clock. He said, "No, that's okay. I have to get up anyway. Sit down, I'll be right back."

He disappeared into a bedroom off the living room and I sat down on a black Naugahyde sofa. The apartment was dark and sad-looking, with the barren, unsettled appearance of just having been moved into. The largest object, a huge wooden console housing a record player, radio and, I believe, a television set—I'd say six feet long—stood against the wall opposite the sofa. A black Naugahyde chair, a black Naugahyde ottoman, and a walnut coffee table made up the rest of the furniture. Piles of records were scattered on the floor next to the console. Two wooden Spanish-style candle holders and a wrought-iron candle bracket were attached to the walls, which otherwise were bare—no pictures, paintings or other decorations at all.

The bareness and the darkness—ill-hung gold drapes were closed over the windows—made the apartment seem cold, despite the warm weather. I shuddered. This was the apartment of someone going it alone.

Perry Russo, bare-chested and combing his hair, soon emerged from the bedroom in a pair of pants. The pallor of his body skin was deadly white contrasted with the darker coloring of his face. He appeared larger, heftier in semi-dress than fully clothed. The mounds of his pectorals sagged slightly. He apologized for his appearance, saying he'd overslept, then asked, "Do you like music?"

"Yes."

"Good," he said, moving toward the console. "Do you know Mahalia Jackson?"

"Yes."

"Do you like her?"

"Yes."

"Good, so do I. I've got this new record of hers. It's great. Do you want to hear it?"

"Ah, not right now."

He mentioned the name of the song, which I don't recall, and, fumbling for a record, insisted that I really had to hear it. I shrugged and he opened the top of the console, placed the record on and fiddled with switches. The disc dropped, and Mahalia Jackson began belting out a bluesy-religious song. After a few seconds and still standing by the set, he asked, "Isn't she great?"

"Yes," I replied.

"Oh, well," he said, switching it off, "I guess you don't have to listen to the whole thing. It's too early for that."

Jim Phelan had told me and testified in court that as soon as he'd entered Russo's apartment, Russo would switch on a record for a few seconds, then invariably display a lack of interest in playing the entire piece of music. I had to smile now. As he walked away from the machine, I noticed a small red pilot button glowing at the lower end of the console. I could not get over it. His naïveté in so obviously pulling this stunt—knowing I'd sat through the entire trial and heard of this precise maneuver not only from a witness but detailed by Russo himself—was totally refreshing. My spirits were immediately hypoed. I was enjoying the routine thoroughly. I felt as if I were in East Berlin, engaged in espionage work.

"So, what do you want to talk to me about? I mean, I don't see there's anything to say, really," Russo said, looking at me with rhetorically quizzical brown eyes. He knew there was a lot to say.

I explained I was writing a book, and it would be interesting to get his impressions of how the trial had affected his life, adding, for the District Attorney or any of his staff who might care to hear, "I don't want to pump you about your testimony—any of that. It's old hat now, anyway. Just to get your personal reactions, the effect it's had upon you." Russo listened as I told him about my meeting with Garrison and Alcock, praising them as much as I could without making a farce of my declarations.

Perry Russo, still protesting that he didn't really know what-all there was to say, nevertheless agreed to talk with me. He told me he'd gone into partnership in a clothing boutique and had to tend to business, so he couldn't do it then. I invited him to dinner that evening, and I thought for a moment of dropping a little item like: "I can't make it now either. I have to meet a guy at the corner of Esplanade and Royal at noon. I'm trying to get rid of an ounce of stuff and I think I've finally made a contact." I would then show up at the appointed spot with a bag of fig newtons and later sue for false arrest. It was agreed I would phone Perry Russo at his shop around five and we'd make arrangements for meeting that evening. I thanked him and left, stifling the impulse to say, Oh, don't forget to switch that thing off.

I'd been given to understand that Judge Haggerty would be available that day at 1, so I arrived about 12:30. The courtroom was a portrait of lethargy—unbelievable that this was the same bristling jam-packed theater of the absurd I'd sat in for so many days. One man dozed in the left jury box, two elderly country-looking codgers and a woman sat in the far right spare jury box opposite him. A Negro couple, the man sleeping with his head resting on the woman's shoulder, slumped down in the spectator section. Five rows behind them sat two Negro women, one of them nursing a small baby. Two other couples lounged idly on the other side of the spectator section; near them a large woman was sleeping. A deputy drowsed against the railing.

The Special Anniversary Fire Sale was over; business at the old stand was back as usual.

I walked back to the judge's chambers where a young assistant district attorney sat on the sofa, nervously anticipating his first in-court trial appearance. Two other men waited to see the judge. Haggerty's minute clerk and court reporter were fielding phone calls. The judge had been due in court at 10 that morning; it was now almost 1 o'clock; he had not been heard from and no one knew where he was. We all sat shooting the breeze for half an hour or so until Judge Haggerty finally breezed in. He was bedithered. His glasses were broken, the air conditioning was not working, and his car was on the fritz, which partially accounted for his absence.

Besieged with messages from his minute clerk and court reporter and pressed on business by the assistant D.A. and the two men, he was not in the calmest of moods.

He greeted me with the usual "Well, Brother Kirkwood!" but the implication was: Oh, you again! I reminded him of our appointment.

"Well, I'll tell you, I've decided to do it this way. I'll dictate my answers to your questions to my clerk. Then I'll go over them, correct them, and you'll have what you want."

"That's not what I want," I said. "I want to talk with you, take you to lunch or whatever."

"But if I dictate the answers it's the same thing—you've got your information."

"It's not the same to me. It's too dry, not personal enough. It's just not interesting—no fun, either," I told him.

The judge, who was being urged to get into court and attend to those people who had dozed off after waiting since 10 o'clock, looked at me and sighed. "Brother Kirkwood, I admire your tenacity—no, *irascibility*, that's what it is."

"I'm getting pushy in my old age," I replied. "Look, I've spoken with Garrison, I even had a long taped interview with Jim Alcock. If he got to a question he didn't want to answer, we just skipped it."

"That's different," the judge snapped. "He's not an elected official. I am. I come up for election in 1972."

"Yes, and if you don't give me an interview, I won't vote for you."

By this time he was being helped into his robes and was on his way out of chambers. "I have to attend to court now. I'll dictate the answers."

"I'll wait here," I told him as he rushed out with the two men after him.

"God damn it, he's driving me crazy!" I said.

One of his employees, who shall remain anonymous, laughed and said, "He's driving *you* crazy? You should *work* for him."

With that I was left alone in his chambers. After an hour or so he returned, not overjoyed to find me still there. After taking off his robes, he quickly began pawing through a stack of mail, saying, "The only thing I want to find is my Federal income tax refund check—that's it." Those magic fingers fluttered over the official debris on the top of his desk. "I still want to dictate my answers," he said.

"After getting me out to that crayfish party and not showing, the least you can do is let me take you to lunch. That was a dirty trick."

"No, I was out there."

"Not when I was."

"I was a little late, but I went out there, looked all over for you. Somebody—I forget who—said you'd been around."

"Sciambra probably."

"Oh, yeah." Judge Haggerty laughed. "Moo Sciambra—he told me."

After considerable hedging, he admitted he still had not read my questions.

"You—*what?* After all this time. Oh, come on, now! Damn it!"

"I've been busy."

"Not that busy."

"I've had a lot of things to do."

"All right, I'm going to give you one more chance. I want to see you before I leave town."

"When are you leaving?" he asked, with genuine interest.

"In a couple of days. And I want to take you to lunch *alone*. I probably wouldn't even pursue it except for your rotten treatment. And if you don't come through—then I'm really going to let you have it. I'm not kidding."

Which, of course, I was. But not completely.

Judge Haggerty, with grudging good humor, agreed to lunch two days hence. I was to phone at noon and he would decide upon a restaurant.

That evening I drove to Perry Russo's boutique shortly after 6 o'clock. I went inside and found Perry dressed mod in yellow-gold bell-bottom slacks and a red sleeveless fishnet shirt. The clothes in the boutique had the very "in" look of Greenwich Village '69 about them.

We got into my rented car, which he suggested driving, saying he had a couple of errands and it would be easier because he knew the town better than I did. The weather had turned cloudy and a muggy Southern drizzle fell. As he drove off he noticed the tape machine lying on the floor of the car. "What's that?" he asked.

"A tape machine."

"Does it work on batteries?"

"Yes."

"Well," he said, "why don't you turn it on now, while we're driving. Save time that way."

"Sure," I said, pleased at his suggestion.

While I took it out of the case and plugged the microphone in, we spoke of the upcoming local elections. Although the primaries were months off, several large billboards had already appeared. Charles Ward, Garrison's next-in-command assistant D.A., had taken several signs proclaiming simply, ELECT CHARLES WARD. They did not specify to which office. He was waiting to see if Garrison was going to run; if so, he had in mind the city council or a judgeship. (He was soon to quit the D.A.'s office and run *against* Garrison.)

RUSSO: Yeah, I even have one sign in the office that says, "Elect *Clay Shaw* for District Attorney." [He laughed.] Somebody gave it to me at the Encore, a lounge in the Quarter. I went there one night and somebody spotted me and ran up to me. They just happened to have it in the back of the bar.

Q.: Shaw's quite a guy. I think you'll probably meet him sometime. Wouldn't you want to meet him and talk to him?

RUSSO: This is the only thing. I'm sure he holds a great deal of bitterness, if he really is sincerely and truthfully and he knows he was not anywhere and all this kind of stuff and not a part of it—then I'm sure he's very bitter. See, I would be.

Q.: I'd be so bitter you wouldn't be able to find me. But he's not. I did a profile in *Esquire* on him, I've gotten to know him well and actually he's not bitter. He's been very philosophical about the entire two years. Tell me, how did this whole thing affect your life?

RUSSO: Well, the initial effect was news people always around . . . so many of them and I couldn't believe some of the things. They were knocking at the door at all hours, always calling, wanting in, wanting this, wanting a statement, as if I were important. I'd be kind of pretentious to think that my opinion made a difference to anybody. And that was the first shock. After that, widespread publicity just didn't help personally at all. People all had different ideas. Some felt Clay Shaw was innocent, there were some felt he was guilty. Verdict or no verdict, it doesn't really change 'em a great deal. Accordingly, people took sides and in taking sides they generally lumped everybody together. If they thought Clay Shaw was innocent, then they thought Garrison was a no good D.A. and Perry Russo was a liar. If they felt Clay Shaw was guilty, then I was telling the truth and Garrison was a good D.A. And this really doesn't follow. That don't come as a consequence of Clay Shaw being guilty or innocent. . . . But the court ruled, the jury said he was innocent, that conspiracy had not been proven. And that's the way it is, you know. That's all there is to it. It's all over as far as this particular charge is concerned. Now if he does anything—like sues or whatever he can do, I don't know legally. If he does anything like that, then that's a story of a different color, but as he stands now, he's innocent of the charge of conspiracy. He wasn't involved in killing Kennedy.

Q.: Were you surprised by the perjury charges?

RUSSO: Well, I'd talked to Ivon [of Garrison's staff] that same day, it was accidental. You know, about all this humbug by the *States-Item* and *Picayune*. That's a bunch of bullshit—Garrison's malfeasance in office. If he was malfeasant in office the day of the verdict, he was malfeasant the day before. Right is right. Clay Shaw is innocent, Garrison is malfeasant—it just doesn't work like that. That same day I read the editorial and heard all the hurrah and humbug on television, which was only right. Clay Shaw should have his say. He's waited a long time to have it. Then there was the editorial. I called up Ivon and said, "Louis, what's going on here, what are you all gonna do, are you all gonna fight back?" He says, "We haven't begun to fight." Now this is round one in the afternoon. Then later on at the 6 o'clock news I heard Clay Shaw had been rearrested and charged with perjury.

Q.: Seemed to me when the serious charge was over, they'd forget about it. But apparently not.

RUSSO: I don't know why they wouldn't. Of course, some people say Garrison is on a witch hunt, that he's out for some odd reason to persecute Clay Shaw, which may or may not be the case. . . . The question is, who are the perjurers? He chose to charge Clay Shaw with perjury, he could have turned around and charged the other seven or eight or however many others there were involved. He could have charged *me*. Like you say, I thought it would be dropped, that Clay Shaw would probably sue me or sue Garrison or do whatever he could do. Because Dymond's a good attorney and Dymond would know what he could do under the circumstances. Clay Shaw did say he had some things planned. He didn't go into big detail about it, just said he did have some things planned.

[Russo pulled up in front of a house in a residential section.]

Q.: Some people say the perjury charge was to keep Shaw from taking action like that.

RUSSO: It could have been. I doubt it though. I do feel something, there was some reason for it. I tell you what you could do. I'm gonna run inside, why don't you check the machine, see if it's recording all right. That'll give you something to do for a few minutes.

I could not help looking after Perry Russo and grinning as he trotted up to the house. Here was the star witness, a young man whose main problem had been his harassment by the press, now driving around in the rain with a scribbler he didn't know from a bar of soap, holding a microphone jammed up to his face and advising me to check the machine to see if it was recording correctly.

I did and it was. Within a few minutes Perry was back in the car and we were on our way to the main post office to drop off some mail.

Q.: Did you feel great relief when your testimony was finished?

RUSSO [laughing]: Yeah, oh, yeah! You see, I figured Dymond was gonna start on me something awful. And, boy, it was getting about the second day, right before he said, "Through with the witness," or whatever he said, and I figured he was gonna light into me any minute. I was just waiting for it. The more time passed, the more questions he asked, just fucking around, just asking bullshit questions. And I figured it's coming, just be prepared, because they must have a catalogue that thick on me. Which I'm sure he did—although he really didn't get into that stuff. All he done was get me pissed off. Other than that, I was surprised, to tell you the truth. You see, as versus the preliminary hearing and all the other times I was called as a witness. All these other times Dymond always sneered, snarled and spit his words out, called me by the last name and all kinds of stuff like this. This time he didn't. He was gentle as a baby. I couldn't believe it. I really couldn't. . . . But anyway, I was relieved when that was over!

Q.: I could see your nervousness easily at first but then it was like when you got warmed up, like an actor on opening night, very tense, because you don't know what the hell's going to happen, what the audience reaction is going to be. Then once you got into it, you relaxed more.

RUSSO: I can tell you, I had a nervous little habit and I kept doing it over and it was just something to occupy myself. I had a little bitty bottle of Tips [a breath freshener] I kept putting on my tongue.

Q.: A lot of press people who'd been down for the preliminary hearing were anticipating a knockdown dragout, a little blood-shed. They were all very amazed. It was almost like a mutual respect society.

RUSSO [laughing]: Yeah, I guess it was.

Q.: Like, you don't murder me and I won't murder you.

RUSSO: That's what it amounted to. Boy, I was glad when he didn't. Because I know, I felt I could pour it on, you know. You can always add in an extra word as a witness and nothing can be done to stop what you've already said. . . . You see, Dymond had to make several decisions and he made 'em correctly evidently. Such as which approach would he take, like with me, for example. Should he go into a brutal or vicious attack and see if he could get me upset and hope that I'll say something that will violate what I'd said before? Or should he take it soft and gentle? Now what-ever provoked him to take it soft and gentle, I don't know. I really can't say, but he did. And I felt a lot better because of it. I don't know if he got what he wanted. I don't know.

Q.: He certainly got the verdict he wanted.

RUSSO: Well, he got the verdict, yeah, the long-run thing.

Q.: How did *you* feel about the verdict?

RUSSO: Well, I tell you. I'm sort of passive about things like that, you know. I mean that's the way it is. I wasn't shocked and yet I wasn't depressed either. I wasn't just sitting around saying, Jesus, I wish it had gone the other way. Clay Shaw maintained he was never at David Ferrie's apartment all along, ever since '67. He said that and, ah, and I'm sure he was, he was there. That's all there is to it. But if the jury felt that he wasn't there, then that's the way it is.

I felt bad, you know, personally, for Garrison. All this malfeasance, impeachment—all that. It just didn't follow. . . .

Q.: It was kind of a token grandstand thing the newspapers did, because they certainly haven't continued.

RUSSO: No, they haven't continued, that's for sure. But I'm sure they will when election time comes around. But that's their prerogative. They have a right to support or not support if they want to. . . . Boy, I'll tell you if I'd have been Clay Shaw and I'd been sitting where he was sitting for so many days, I'd have snarled at everybody that came up there.

Q.: I would, too.

RUSSO: I would have been a bitter bastard, that's for sure. . . . I'll tell you what I felt was just totally unfair. Now probably it could work both ways. The news of this was just unfair. Not so much a person's conclusions. You might have a conclusion—Garrison doesn't have a case, he's a big phoney, blah-blah. Not so much that. I'm talking specifically about Phelan, Sheridan, Townley. They just didn't try and report the news, they didn't ask me any questions. Well, Phelan did. Now Phelan was a little more sincere than Sheridan and Townley. But Sheridan and Townley, they were after Garrison's goat, they didn't care whether Clay Shaw was innocent or guilty. It didn't make any difference if it took making Clay Shaw innocent to get Garrison. Get Garrison, get him. And that, just to me, that stinks. It's not fair, period. . . . Walter Cronkite [of CBS] played it fairly, although Garrison didn't believe that. I did. He said the net results of the Garrison investigation is yet to be proved, which it surely was at that stage. And that Garrison himself will prove it or not prove it and then it would go by the wayside. I think that was fair enough, although I heard Garrison say something against Walter Cronkite. I thought that was kind of fair.

There was a long pause now, during which we drove in silence through the light rain falling with only the muted sound of the windshield wipers. Then he asked, "Ah, what is Clay Shaw doing now?"

He listened with interest while I told him Clay was restoring an old building into apartments. I mentioned that he intended to go on a lecture tour, if he could get enough bookings, to help recoup some of his losses.

RUSSO [suddenly looking sideways at me]: Say, wait a minute. You mentioned something earlier, just struck me. Did—*you* wrote the article in *Esquire?*

Q.: Yes.

RUSSO: Oh, well, you're a bad egg, too!

Q.: No, I'm not. Why?

RUSSO: Well, that's the impression I got. I'm almost sure—it was *Esquire.* I went up to the D.A.'s office one day. I was sitting in Sciambra's office or Bethell's office, somebody's office. Somebody came in and asked or said, "Read this!" Sciambra, I'm sure. What, in essence, was your point?

Q.: Mainly a profile on Clay Shaw.

RUSSO: Oh, yeah, that's right. About a taxicab driver and so forth?

Q.: Yes.

RUSSO: Yeah, that's right. I remember that. [Glancing over at me again.] It *was* you, then. And so, anyway, I read through it. You read it, you feel pathetic toward Clay Shaw, what a pathetic situation! [Laughing.] And, oh, I heard some nasty words about you. Oh! That's a bad guy, one of the bad guys! . . . It doesn't affect me as far as my own—I'll cooperate with you, but I did hear some nasties. And when you said *Esquire*—cause it's the only place I can remember, being in *Esquire.* You talked a great deal about his finances. On how the cab driver would let him ride free. It was a well-written article. . . . Well, Sciambra was the one, you know. He was rapping on about you something fierce. . . . Oh, yeah, I remember Sciambra lighting into the article something awful. Bad words up at the office about you and—"Yeah, but he didn't report all the *facts.* He didn't say *this* and he didn't say *that!*" And all that kind of humbug. I read the article and it was well written. And I felt sorry for Clay Shaw. Man, the guy's busted financially.

Q.: What did you think of the jury—not the verdict, but the jurors themselves?

RUSSO: Just to show you how ironic the situation is, knowing the guys on the jury— I don't know him personally, but remember the girl I introduced to you in the store?

Q.: Yes.

RUSSO: Well, that's Gerald's wife. He put up the capital because I have no money. And her uncle was on the jury. Now for me that was grounds for a mistrial.

Q.: Really?

RUSSO: But I had never met the man, I don't think. Maybe at some little function there at her house or something like that. Perhaps. But I never met the man, you know. Now I'm not sure of his name. I think his name was Schultz.

Q.: Oh, yes, Oliver Schultz.

RUSSO: But I'm not real sure of that. Was there a guy on the jury named Ira—first name Ira?

Q.: No, Oliver.

RUSSO: Could have been Oliver then. You know, and that was grounds for a mistrial. I thought that if they did come in with a verdict of guilty, then I probably would have had to say something about that to somebody. [Jesus, no, Perry. Don't start up again!] You know, because that might have affected it, because this guy might have been gung-ho in the jury room or something, say to every juror in there, No, you're all wrong. I know he's guilty, and all that kind of stuff. But evidently it didn't have any bearing whatsoever. I wouldn't even recognize the guy, I don't think.

Q.: Could you tell what they were thinking on the stand?

RUSSO: Oh, some of them seemed bored. Well, one guy in there, I just didn't like him, you know? I'll tell you who it was—you know, physically. This guy was on the row nearest Dymond and he was balding a little bit. He just kept looking at me all the time. The rest of them yawned and looked every which way, but he kept looking. And he was the second guy or the third guy from the left.

Q.: That must have been the one who turned out to be the foreman—Sidney Hebert.

RUSSO: This guy just kept staring, looking, looking like that. I got a little self-conscious. Alcock told me a couple of times, he said, "If you get a chance"—this was the first day—"slip in back in '61, '62, '63"—this is when I associated with several Negroes from Xavier High School, St. Augustine, Loyola—"slip in for the jury a little of that." [Obviously referring to the Negroes on the jury.]

We used to bum around, play ball. Oh, we had a great time. We integrated the Royal Castle [lunch counter] one night, you know. We had a sit-in!

Perry pulled up to a franchised eat-in-or-take-out fried chicken spot. I suggested a real restaurant, where we could have drinks and a leisurely meal, but he declined, saying he didn't go for all that "fancy fuss business." We ordered our fried chicken at a counter, then sat down at a formica-topped table in the corner. It was his suggestion that I turn the tape machine on while we were eating.

Q.: How did you find your friends during this whole time? Were they fairly loyal?

RUSSO: Well, I found out who my friends *were*. Some of them— well, the biggest thing—I didn't lose any friends. I lost people I could have made friends out of, you know? Shying away. A guy couldn't play baseball for me because I was Perry Russo. . . .

Q.: What about your family?

RUSSO: My mother's dead. My brother—he and I don't see eye to eye about much of anything.

Q.: Is he older or younger?

RUSSO: He's three years older. He teaches, got his doctor's about a year ago, two years ago. If anything, this trial gave him reason to try to get a little closer, but he—like the north and south poles. My old man, ever since my mother died, he and I don't see eye to eye either. He doesn't talk about me—period. So, you can't alter that.

Q.: When did your mother die?

RUSSO: She died January 31, 1963. That's one of the reasons Dave Ferrie used to come over to the house. My old man was convicted on income tax evasion in September of '62. At that time he knew my mother—now I didn't know it—but he told the judge that my mother had terminal cancer. And so she was dying, so the judge said, "I'll hold off on the sentencing." I think, I don't know if this is true or not. So anyway, she died January 31. My brother was married and away, he was with his family. That left three of us, she died, that left two of us, and he went to jail in April of 1963. From April to October he was in jail, serving six months out of a year in Texas. During that period of time I literally went wild. I had civil rights movers over, Dave Ferrie was over, anybody came over. It didn't make any difference, we had one party after another. You know, the more the merrier. We had gangs of people, all the time, people sleeping over all night long, just—you know, party, party, party. I had no responsibilities, until the old man came back, right after Kennedy got shot.

q.: Was that a reaction to your mother's death and your father's trouble—just going wild for a while like that?

russo: I don't know, to tell you the truth. Never did think of it that way. I just went wild. See, my old man wasn't a real good guy. He plays a role, this Catholic stuff and Jesus, I mean, "Kill the black bastard" and all that kind of stuff. . . . And I told him, I said, "Now I don't know where you can go to church on Sunday and go to communion and go to confession on Sunday—and then I hear all *this* racket?" I've never seen eye to eye with him. Integration, that's my number one probe. Whenever I get around, I stick it to him.

q.: How often do you see him?

russo: I haven't seen him but maybe once in the past—probably I saw him at the voting polls, you know, Nixon's election. Just bumped into him, said hello, and I went and voted. And I saw him about a year ago at his house. I had to go for some papers over there on Dave Ferrie. You know, some stuff he'd left around. And I asked him if I could go in and he said, "For what?" I said, "To get some papers," and he said, "How long you gonna be?" I said I'd be an hour, so I went in.

q.: Do you feel badly about this situation with your father?

russo [shrugging, brushing it off]: No, we're just separate. He can go his merry way and I'll go mine. Doesn't affect me that way much. But it did at one time. That's probably one of the reasons I went to a psychiatrist, you know? . . .

q.: Of all the people you got to know at the D.A.'s office, who did you feel closest to?

russo: Well, I tell you. Many people I respected. But I was never real close to any of 'em. Louis Ivon—very conscientious sort of person. And he's the kind, likes to follow the book. I thought he was always a good guy. Alcock was business. Sciambra [Russo pronounces it "Shambry"]—Sciambra didn't exactly level with me. So I lost a little bit of respect over a period of time. Garrison, I didn't have that much contact—in the beginning, yes, quite a bit. But after a while, I mean there was no reason for me to see him. Everything could be handled by other people. But the person I respected most of all was Charlie Ward. . . . Now I told Phelan, if it's really true that Garrison's down to his last nickel and he doesn't have a damn thing except *me*—which isn't much, you know—I said, the one person I hope doesn't really go under, that he could serve the city of New Orleans, would be Charlie Ward.

Q.: What about strangers, the reaction of strangers?

RUSSO: Well, I got some crazy ones. The general reaction from friends of mine, the people I'd generally associated with, they just wondered where I was at. I'd get the same thing every night. . . . My own sex preferences doesn't have anything to do with it. Whether I was all straight or all gay, it wouldn't make any difference to them. They like to play this role of whips and belts and chains and belts—you know, playlike? And Clay Shaw allegedly entertained those kinds of desires, so therefore, who am I beating up now and all that sort of stuff? They'd just rap on. And I got a lot of that, but that didn't really bother me. A great deal. It's just a funny joke and a way of talking, I guess.

Q.: I should think there would have been a lot of that kind of reaction because of knowing Dave Ferrie.

RUSSO: I didn't get that much reaction, because he was such a clandestine type of personality. He didn't come over at 7 o'clock at night, it was 2 in the morning. And someone comes over at 2 in the morning, there weren't many people around.

Q.: No, I mean the fact that in the preliminary hearing and trial it was brought out that you'd been to his house many times, he'd been to yours. People would say, Well, I wonder what was going on?

RUSSO: Right, yeah. I got that—sure. . . . You fight an avalanche on that. . . . I'm sure that may be what Clay Shaw said.

Q.: Everything was said about Clay Shaw, too. Everyone said, Oh, God, what they're going to do to him in the trial, dig in or make up things about his personal life!

RUSSO: Well, I heard Garrison say this in the office. I heard him void [sic] certain things, you know, talking to some of the assistants. I knew they were sexual things. But you see the problem is—now I'm talking for myself, not for anybody else—me, as a witness, and some of the others, too. Now we had not the greatest background in the world. And I kept telling them. That's what I feared most from Dymond. . . . [Laughing.] Because I'm not the cleanest saint that's ever been around, that's for sure.

Q.: Well, nobody is.

RUSSO [laughing again]: Well, but—you should know some of the things I've been in. Boy—oh, boy! . . . If I probably got a little bit too nasty with Dymond on the stand, if I said something too bad, really way out of the way, he could have pulled this little book from underneath there and asked Wegmann, "Go get file twelve." [Laughing and shaking his head.] I'm sure they had a big old thick book.

Q.: The state must have known everything the defense knew, didn't they?

RUSSO: Oh, well, I told them everything. Now I'm sure they know everything there is to know about me. Because in advance I told them. I said, "These are the things that I did." And I said, "Anything else other than that—I *didn't* do." And they kept saying, "They can't bring that out in the courtroom," and that made me feel good. But the one that kept telling me that was *Sciambra*—and that *didn't* make me feel good! [Laughter from both of us.]

Perry Russo now appeared anxious to get back to his house. He made ready to leave, but I hadn't quite finished eating. "That's okay, finish," he said. "I do want to take a quick spin over to the house." He'd been trying to phone someone and said he must have the wrong number, indicating the right number would be found at his apartment.

Q.: Did you feel in the end you were the key witness?

RUSSO: Turned out to be. When the state rested its case—I figured I was it. [Laughing.] I figured I had been.

Q.: Until then, did you even think they were coming up with some others?

RUSSO: I thought I was just the lead-up. Yes. It had to be. You know, Sciambra told me, "Just wait till the first day, it's gonna be all over the first day." Talking about the state's witnesses that first day, the Clinton people. I said, "Oh, that sounds good, that'll take the pressure off me. I'm going to be anticlimactic to the whole thing. Forget me!" And he said, "You don't need to worry about a thing from Dymond. Because when Dymond sees what happens the first day, he's going to be so thoroughly demoralized, they won't

worry about you, you won't be all that important." So I believed it,
you know. I figured that way. Evidently the first day they didn't
demoralize *anybody*—least of all F. Irvin Dymond! . . .

[Back in the car, Perry spoke again of the changes in his life
brought about by his involvement in the case.]

RUSSO: I gave up all kinds of things. That's the way it has
affected my life. It affected my life sexually, you know. It affected
my life party-wise, and it affected my life drinking-wise. All these
things. I went asexual for a while. Because you couldn't figure out
who you were having sex with. Do they work for this guy? Or do
they blabbermouth to that guy?

[I asked Russo what he thought reflected most damagingly
upon his testimony. He mentioned Phelan's name and went on.]

RUSSO: And then I had some second guesses about a couple other
things. You see, it was my decision, my suggestion the day before I
went onto the stand, that—about the Sandra thing and Peterson
being at the party. To say that I wasn't sure if they *were* there. I'd
stated oppositely a couple of years before. But this was something I
decided. I told Alcock, I said, "This is the way I feel about it.
Sandra says she wasn't there, Peterson—" He didn't say anything.
If Peterson would *tell* me he was there I wouldn't know if I'd
believe him. And I know him for fifteen years. So I said, "I'm just
gonna say I'm not sure." And I went through, reading through the
transcript of the preliminary hearing. And I looked for the questions that I could hinge it on, so I had something to say why I'm
changing my mind a little bit . . .

About this time Russo said, "Hey, well, why don't we drive
around a little bit on the way home? No hurry. Okay?" This was
fine with me. The rain was coming down hard now, making
driving anything but relaxing. But still he put off going home;
perhaps, I thought, he has a few things he wants to get off his
mind, without having them on record at the D.A.'s office. We
spoke at length of the Sciambra memo. Russo laughed at mention
of the corrections and errors, which he put at seventy-six. I corrected him, saying I thought it was twenty-six. He laughed again
and concluded his remarks on the Sciambra memo by saying,
"Now, the memorandum—it's just bad literature!"

RUSSO [suddenly]: You know what gets me in the whole retrospect on this thing. It just bugs me. A couple of times I wasn't

being leveled with. I mean I wanted to be right down the middle
and play it fair and square and all that kind of stuff. Now this I
didn't realize until I heard Clay Shaw—or read his statements.
Clay Shaw said he was called up on subpoena to Garrison's office,
which he showed up—some little bullshit thing. After eating a
sandwich and being there a couple of hours, Ivon or Sciambra said
this to him: "We know that you knew Dave Ferrie in September.
You collaborated with these people and conspired to kill President
Kennedy. We have three people that will say you did. What do
you say to that? Will you take a lie detector test?" . . . Now at
that stage the three people had to have been Perry Russo, Sandra
Moffitt and Niles Peterson. . . . The *three* got me. . . . And
they hadn't talked to Sandra or contacted Peterson yet. Purely on
the basis of him refusing to take a lie detector test, they arrest him.
Either they were ready to arrest him on the basis of other information or they weren't. But not because of these *three* people, one of
which is me. But these other two, you see, they had never been
consulted. And that—that bothered me a little bit. . . . They
shouldn't have done that, until they at least investigated because—fuck, I might be a crazy man. I might even be fucking poor
Dave. And they should check out everything I say before they go
around indicting people.

Russo had his own set of standards and measures. Limited as
these might be in weighing the majors and minors of the case, he
nevertheless prescribed circles within circles within circles in his
rulings upon pertinent matters involving his concept of right or
wrong.

At one point, in a strange roundabout apparent admission that
the Garrison case against Clay Shaw was completely defective, he
got into his theories on politics in general.

RUSSO: I do feel that *something* went on in Dallas that—you
know—but Oswald didn't shoot the President dead. There were
other people involved and maybe Oswald didn't do anything at
all. But I just don't know what the fuck's going on with that. It
was nothing to do with Clay Shaw, really. Maybe it taints the
Federal government. The Democrats! I love to taint those bastards
any time I can. Dymond asked me in the preliminary hearing—big

point, was I anti-Kennedy? I sort of soft-pedaled that one. I mean I wasn't violently anti-Kennedy but, boy, I'll tell you, I didn't want Kennedy in the White House. And I didn't want to see him, didn't want to hear him. I didn't want any Democrat in the White House. Quicker we got a Republican, I don't care if it was Rockefeller or Goldwater—it didn't make any difference. Get a Republican in. I wanted to soft-pedal it. I guess it would look bad if I was violently anti-Kennedy. Whenever I hear things violently anti-Democrat I entertain them, love to hear them. It's exciting to me that people are getting fed up with the Democrats. I am just thoroughly satisfied to hear things like that.

Q.: That doesn't seem to go with your rather liberal leanings.

RUSSO: Well, that's the thing, you see. I try to persuade my Negro friends that the only true course for them is the Republican party. For several reasons. One—and I don't want to get into philosophy, because I know it's not the kind of thing you're interested in right now—but liberalism, the economic liberalism we have right now, all it eventually means is a mortgage on the future. And that means eventually somebody's going to have to pay it and eventually the mass is going to get poorer and poorer. Therefore, the mass is going to be the one that pays. So poor people are going to be the one that pays it. . . . And it's because of the economic policy that we don't have some of the things that Negroes want now and are justifiably entitled to. . . . How can you get it with the Democrats? The Negro who will vote for a Democrat, chooses to register as a Democrat, talks with his stomach. The Negro who votes for a Republican, chooses to register as Republican, talks with his mind. The mind—it's like a child versus an adult. The child will do anything it wants right now and not realize the consequences. . . . I'm sort of a pragmatist when it gets down to that, any kind of a way you can eliminate the Democrats—good! Get rid of them. . . . And another reason for it is that I happened to grow up—after the age of twelve or thirteen—opposite of my old man. He's a Democrat, I'm a Republican. He's a segregationist, I'm an integrationist. I grew up like that around all the marks of a conservative Democrat—segregation, white supremacy, Anglo-Saxon, and a few other goodies. . . .

Q.: How do you feel about Nixon?

RUSSO: Oh, Nixon's a tremendous man. Going to be a great President. He's thinking economically first of all. He's also thinking humanistically . . . and trying to secure some programs that are within sanity. . . . Though he hasn't been a very dynamic, vociferous President that we've had in the last two clowns. But we don't want one. We're tired of all that bullshit. We don't need a Jackie Kennedy. We need a Pat Nixon that stays, like a wife should stay, in the White House. First a wife and then a First Lady. We don't need any Lady Birds, any Jackie Kennedys. And we don't need Jack Kennedy. Although Jack Kennedy brought forth the crowds, standing up on their feet and cheering—just doesn't thrill me. We need thought now. And not so much mouth.

Toward the end of this political run, he pulled up in front of his apartment. We had no sooner entered the living room when he said, "Let me just—just for a second—I want to turn this on. I just want you to hear this one record."

He walked straight to the console, put a record on for no more than thirty seconds, said, "Oh, well, you don't have to listen to the whole thing," and turned it off. I noticed again that the small red pilot light remained on, so I said, "You know, when I came here this morning, you went right over to that console and turned it on for a minute. I thought about the testimony, you know? About taping Phelan and everyone."

After a small nervous laugh, Perry said, "Oh, no. I'm not taping you. No, *you* got the tape machine. Now I want to put your mind at ease. I should put your mind at ease about that. We did tape Phelan and we had this thing set up—"

"I don't mind," I said. "I'd just like to know it. Because when I tape you, you obviously know it. That's all. But now there's no reason to be worried about it, because the trial's over with and—"

"Right," Russo said. "Well, anyway, they wanted Phelan bad. I think it was because of—Sciambra wanted him bad. And Garrison wanted Sheridan bad, too."

We spoke more of the press now, but I was positive I was being recorded and felt slightly annoyed at being dissembled to about it. Otherwise why play no more than a scratch of the record and why was the pilot light on? It had not been on when we entered the apartment. But it glowed like the Star of the East even though the machine had supposedly been turned off.

Russo soon returned to the time of his entrance into the case, saying, "I was just thrilled by this, you know—guys knocking at the door and editors calling, like I was a big-time Charlie or something."

We spoke of Garrison's token attendance at the trial proper. I told Perry many people were surprised that the District Attorney had not appeared during his testimony to make him feel Big Brother was keeping an eye on him.

RUSSO: Right. Well, there's been a lot of speculation like he's holding something over on me or he's threatened to send me to the bottom of the river or something, if I didn't go along with this. Or they were paying me off or—which is a big joke. I don't know why he didn't. Maybe, you see, I'm that way, too. I don't like competition, I really don't. I've got some sort of basic inferiority sense about that. And if it gets down to the real competition, some crucial thing for me is on the line, I prefer not to be around. I generally like to go and mope off to myself. That's just the way I am. I don't know if that's the same thing the way he is. Or not. I know I like to be that way. I like to go be off alone. When I sink I like to sink alone.

We talked about Russo's impending lawsuit against *Time* magazine. They had called him a drug addict; it was apparently a mistake, but it had appeared in print and Perry had filed suit.

RUSSO: Donald Hess wrote it and he's from the Houston office. I've never met him. What he said was, he remembered three things. It was a drug addict, a convict, and a homosexual. David Ferrie was a homosexual. Vernon Bundy . . . was the convict. And I must have been the drug addict. It was a deductive thing.
Q.: Is your lawsuit a big one?
RUSSO: $450,000. They called and apologized about it on top of that. They said they made a typographical error—of a whole *paragraph!*

Perry Russo rarely went for more than five or ten minutes without returning to Dymond, whom he often referred to as "Old F. Irvin!"—with definite admiration. "I'll tell you something about Dymond," Russo said. "Dymond's a professional. During the preliminary hearing—off camera, in other words, when the jury wasn't there, he wasn't such a bad joe. He'd talk to Alcock. During the preliminary hearing he even said hello to me. You know? But Wegmann was not. Wegmann was just a bad egg. . . . He looked like you just stabbed him in the back. . . . He was uptight about it. . . . But Dymond, he really was a reasonably nice guy. Of course, he has a natural sneer. I remember at the preliminary hearing he would sneer and smirk, twist his face. He was a character. He really was."

I eventually asked Russo how he felt about the climate of fear surrounding the District Attorney's office—while reminding myself that his reply was going to be heard by Big Brother.

RUSSO: Well, I never have really thought about the fear bit, you know. Phelan and some others, I think they felt that I felt that if I changed my testimony any way whatsoever, that I felt I was going to be crucified to the state by Jim Garrison. And I really didn't feel that way. Oh, they have reason to believe that, because I said, you know, I said it would be my ass if—if I said what you said—what happened. I said Garrison would send me to the state. I think that was really what I felt about it. . . . If I were Clay Shaw I would start thinking about reprisals. I don't know what he's going to try and do, try to sue me maybe. . . . Maybe the Truth and Consequences people. But I never did fear that. I don't think there's a great climate of fear down here. The law—you know the respect for the law. There's an attitude about the law that—I haven't traveled much so I can't compare it. But police brutality, for example, received a little notoriety every once in a while. People really don't give a fuck about it. So a guy gets his head smashed in, so what? Big deal. I don't really care. I fear a mob more than I fear anything else. I love to see the heads crash in a mob. I don't fear Garrison—I don't think. If he charged me with perjury tomorrow morning it wouldn't shock me at all. It really wouldn't. If he decided he was going to go be friends with Clay Shaw and Dymond and they're going to work out a little deal or something and charge me and seven other people—big deal. I'd have to go scrape and scrounge and get some kind of bond. And it would just be life like it always was. It wouldn't affect me a bit.

But the thing—him [Garrison] indicting people afterwards. Now this Clay Shaw indictment. . . . Purely from the point of view of maybe—bad taste. That might have been it, you know?

That might have been a poor play. Because when I lose on a baseball field, I just say, "I lost." And walk off.

[We went on to speak of Clay Shaw and out of that came a most revealing comment by the state's main witness.]

RUSSO: When I thought of it, I mean I feel sorry for Clay Shaw. *If* Clay Shaw's innocent. And if Clay Shaw's *not* innocent, I don't feel sorry for him.

Q.: Yes, but *you* would be the one that should know!

RUSSO: Well, you see, conspiracy and conversation. Let's suppose I'm lying and I know it. Let's suppose I'm not lying. Let's suppose he's lying. That still doesn't make him guilty. You see? By any stretch of the imagination. If I'm not lying, and he *is* lying—or maybe he's forgotten about it, or whatever. Then it could be just a nonconsequential conversation. . . . Could have just been making mild conversation. Even if he were there, or if he had forgotten. Or perhaps he was lying.

Q.: Well, it's hard to imagine someone having been there and really not knowing if someone else was there or not—or what they said. You know? I don't mean to knock you, but—

RUSSO: Oh, sure. No, I have no . . . Okay, let me ask you this. Now you believe Clay Shaw was innocent?

Q.: Yes.

RUSSO: Clay Shaw said he was not at Clinton, Louisiana. Yet put New Orleans all together—who was? I mean those people weren't lying, not *all* of them?

Q.: I don't know.

This conversation, more than any we'd had, reminded me of Russo's courtroom testimony. He would nibble around the edges in a tantalizing fashion, dart in at the kernel, circle it, dance back, then, when you got right down to the line, remain mute, or change the subject, or even tacitly admit that perhaps he was mistaken, and swing over to someone else's testimony. *If Clay Shaw is innocent?* Incredible that Perry would profess not to know in his own mind—thus leaving an even wider margin of doubt in the credibility of his tale. When we emerged from a conversation about the Zapruder film, again he made a gratuitous comment that appeared to contradict his entire position in the case: "I thought that [the Zapruder film] would have much more impact on the jury. Of course, Clay Shaw said that night on television that his faith in the jury system had not been dimmed." Russo sighed and smiled. "Well, I don't think mine has been either. The jury system must be pretty good. I always thought I'd be better off with a judge, if I were charged with murder or something. But that—the jury must have paid off pretty well."

Shortly after this, Russo excused himself to go downstairs and use his neighbor's phone to make a call. As soon as he'd gone out the door, I scooted over to the console and tried the various knobs to see if I could extinguish the pilot light. The inside of the machine looked to me about as complicated as the instrument panel in the cockpit of a plane. I turned and flicked and switched and nothing would douse that damnable red light. Just as I heard footsteps downstairs, I reached around in back of the set and unplugged the entire shooting works. I had just enough time to hurtle myself back across to the Naugahyde sofa when he entered. I glanced at the pilot light, and it was now dark. I couldn't help smiling as Perry returned to his chair. The smile didn't last for long when it occurred to me he might well notice the light was out. If he did, he gave no sign of it as we slipped back into our conversation.

Russo told me about the time he posed as an insurance salesman and knocked on Clay Shaw's door in order to make sure of his identification for members of the D.A.'s staff. After this account he suddenly said, "But now listen, I had amnesia for a while, just a little—couple of weeks. I don't know when it was, though. I got whipped up on. Some guys just banged—beat the shit out of me. I had amnesia for about a week; I didn't know what the fuck was going on. I've been in about ten fights. All of them knockouts. I got knocked out nine times and I knocked out Lefty once. Number one kayo artist—down for the count, man."

I told him that I'd never been knocked out.

RUSSO: Oh, man, I have. I must have a glass jaw. But these guys—you know, I mean I don't create any enemies, but for some reason or other I get involved in a situation where I shouldn't be involved. And these guys picked up a wrench, smacked me up, crushed the bone in the back of my head. [Baring his teeth.] These teeth are all screwed up because of that. They proceeded to make a new person out of me.

[Then] But you know my initial impulse? I felt sorry for Clay

Shaw. Now if the whole world is gonna look at this man and condemn him and everybody's going to be against him, I don't like to see anybody go it alone, you know? That's a feeling I don't like. Cause I've had to go it alone many a time and I don't like that feeling myself. . . . And deep down I guess—and I'm being really sincere about this—deep down I guess I was plugging for Clay Shaw. But which kind of a way—it's kind of goofy. I'm the one pointing a finger at him and saying, "You're a bad guy," and then turning around and saying, "Well, I hope nobody does anything because of it." The bad evil, the bad thing of it all is that now Clay Shaw is innocent, there are some people who don't believe that he is. . . . You know, I saw Clay Shaw once, this is the only time I've ever seen him, except in the courtroom. [At a look from me, he added] Before—you know up to 1967, all the way up to now. Was once. And that was at the Royal Orleans Hotel. He was walking out with a couple of women, or one woman and a man, I think it was. And evidently they were reporters, bugging the shit, same old story. Tell it 4,000 times, tell it 4,001. And he legitimately looked sad. This was about halfway between the preliminary hearing and the trial. And I legitimately felt sorry for him. I thought of blowing the horn and waving, but I know he'd turn around and say, "Fuck you!" . . . I mean there's nothing I could say to him. What can I say? I thought of blowing the horn and saying, "Well—" You know? But it just—I just rode on. I was driving a cab that night. And there's not a thing I could've said to him.

Q.: You'd get a very pleasant surprise if you met him. He wouldn't be hostile to you.

RUSSO: Well, it's hard to imagine. I can't imagine it. There's no way in the world I could—now someone else could penetrate him. Eddie Wegmann perhaps could penetrate him. But, Jesus—I'm the man. Like Judas Iscariot, walking up there, the kiss of death. I go up and knock on his house—the next day he's in all kinds of trouble. He feels he's not guilty. I feel he's wrong. I never did say I thought he was *guilty*. But I feel he was there. And because of all this he began to think first of all, it's misidentification, which he initially said. Somebody's making a mistake. And secondly, after being filled in with some goodies by all the defense investigators and the notorious news media, he feels I'm lying or a psychopath. Something along those lines. And I say, How in the world can you talk to a man or get at him? Jesus Christ, you can't just go talk social small talk. There's nothing we have in common. And we can't answer each other honestly.

Q.: I think he could. . . .

RUSSO: Well, from all the impressions I get—I mean I can judge a person. That's bad to say, because it makes you sound like you're a damned simpleton. I know a little bit more about Clay Shaw, you know, than what a person would know just by looking. I mean I've been around the man a little bit. So *I* think, anyway. Now one reason I felt sorry for him on this Royal Orleans thing is financially. Because they had told me at the D.A.'s office the defense were putting out a pretty good sum of money for research, not only to investigate me but other witnesses, too. And that he was having to go back to work. To pay for these things. I looked at him there and he had on a baggy pair of—he had a suit on, but his pants were baggy, you know. And I said, It's either from a loss of weight or because he can't get the correct fit. If you have $500 you can get your tailor to cut 'em, otherwise—and I just felt sorry for him. That's one touchy point with me, is money. When the lights are turned off because I can't pay the electricity bill, something's wrong. I worry about that. Cause I've sort of been on my own since '65.

Q.: How old are you now?

RUSSO: Twenty-seven.

Q.: Well, you're still young, you've still got a lot of future ahead of you.

RUSSO: It's just that every dollar always meant something to me. But I don't drink that much and I don't go out that much. If I socialize, I socialize here. And some of this stuff is not mine, some of it I'm paying for. I get my kick out of music. That's the one thing I really dig—music.

And that poor bastard, Jesus, he's retired, finished his life, had a brilliant career, somewhere along the line accomplished quite a few things, multilingual, ready to tour, travel around the world. And everything's just rocking on good. And all of a sudden— chung! And that's what it is. I mean, there goes the retirement money, there goes the cash investments, there goes his reputation, his name and—some people, oh, quite a few, think that he still was involved.

Q.: How does it feel, when you get involved in something like this, all this publicity? In a way you become a celebrity.

RUSSO: How does it feel to be a celebrity?

Q.: Yes.

RUSSO: Well, I tell you, at times—you know, Dymond was correct when he said that I was a publicity seeker. That's a bad word to use, but it isn't really. I'm not a hound for it. But at times I really enjoyed it. Because, well, I began to be comparative in my judgment about myself. You know? That I looked good or I didn't. I said, Well, Jesus, man, I shouldn't have said that, that's kind of stupid, you know? Or, I'm sounding like a damn simpleton when I answer the questions. I could have answered it much better. I have seven years of college, speak two languages, and I'm supposed to have a fairly good education. And I could speak a little better than that. I criticized myself. Not a publicity seeker, that's a bad word. I became—well, judging myself or something. But at times I enjoyed it. At the very beginning I thought it was unique. And then it began to weigh on me, the role I was playing. I was always, you know—the role I was playing was Emile Zola's "I Accuse." Remember that? All right, the role I was playing is the accuser. And I was always reassured all the way along the line, up until the time they said, "The state rests its case." Hmn, rests its case. [Russo grinned, cocked his head and said]: What happened to the *rest*? . . . I used to question them, the D.A.'s office, about what else they had. And—oh, they were playing footsie with me then, trying to keep me happy.

[Russo soon dropped a little item that made me wince.] And I got disgusted for a while and I just stayed away from 'em [the state] for about four, five months. I was really disgusted with Sciambra is what it amounted to. Before they had another hearing and somebody called me. I always let 'em know where I was, you know, but I got disgusted for a while. Really disgusted. Now, if somebody [like Phelan] would have come up *then*, I probably would have chimed in along with them. . . .

Q.: Does the time seem longer than two years—the time this thing's been going on?

RUSSO: Time seems as though it's just been my *life*. You know, in other words, this is my life. I tell you one thing—if Clay Shaw had been convicted, then I would've been freed from the state. I would have been freed then. And then I'd had all my own—I mean, nobody owned me. I wouldn't owe anything to anybody. Then I would have approached Clay Shaw. You see what I mean? Now I know he'd gotten out on appeal or something, you know, for another fuckin' year. If it takes that long. Then I would've gone and spooked his house until he walked out . . .

Q.: Really? What would you have said to him?

RUSSO: I don't know, to tell you the truth. I'd have talked to him though, then. Cause then I would've figured he has nothing to lose to talk to me. Before the trial he had a lot to lose if he thought I was playing him for a sitting duck, or a fool. . . .

But let's suppose he's convicted now. His wall of prejudice is gone. . . . He can tell me all the fuck he wants to tell me. He can plead with me, if he wants to plead, which I wouldn't expect of a man of his personality. . . . So now I'm the one that would be receiving information. And it would be sincere information on his part, at least something I'd analyze. Okay, now, a wall of *bitterness* might rise up, but that I could handle. That wouldn't bother me as much. . . . Very big deal. He has a right to be. Even if you are guilty, you have a right to be pissed off. But the wall of prejudice would have been eliminated because there's nothing more you can do to him. Because you've already witnessed—you've sent him to jail.

Q.: I would think it would be harder to face somebody when you have sent them to jail than it would be if he was acquitted.

RUSSO: Well, let me just throw this out to you, Jim. . . . The rest of the guys, you know—even Clay Shaw himself—quite a grand majority of you all think I'm lying.

Q.: Um-hmn.

RUSSO: But there was a party there that night. Sometime in September. And there was a guy that looked just like Clay Shaw there. Now, whether or not the hypnosis made me say it was Clay Shaw or Clem Bertrand, or whether I said it beforehand, is academic to me. But there was one there, and I was there. And there was a rowdy bunch of people, ten or twelve or eight people. I was there. Now the only reason that I would approach him afterwards is because damage had been done in a contested thing. And he believes that he wasn't there. At least he stated that. And I can psyche him out. I would sit down with him because there's nothing more I can do to him because I have done it. I could sit down with the bastard and talk. And he could talk to me. So he says, Okay, you can't even help me any more. Because now the appeal's gone and new evidence is not even allowed—which I know always *would* be allowed. I told this to Phelan and let me get this point across. I told him even twenty years from now if I felt differently about it, I would say it. If I felt Clay Shaw wasn't there and perhaps it was so-and-so from down the street, that I would say it.

Perry Russo and I soon went for a short ride to pick up cigarettes. We were feeling quite at ease with each other, I believe. There was certainly a willingness to talk on his part, matched by a willingness to listen on mine. I was on my way to a solid conclusion as a result of psyching him out, and he was soon to fill in the complete picture for me. Oddly and annoyingly enough, I found him, once I was able to perform a huge suspension of judgment on the morality of what he'd done, strangely likable in a—to use his language—fucked-up way. Soon we were back in his unlived-in apartment. Beer was offered and accepted. Perry had already eaten his way through a cantaloupe.

Q.: What would you like to do eventually, if you had your druthers?

RUSSO: Well, my inclination always was and still is politics.

Q.: Really?

RUSSO: Political life. I love to speak in front of audiences, you know. And my whole philosophy, the political thing about me—a lot of action. I like things like that, I like movements. I used to like acting, you know? I was never very good.

Q.: I'll bet you were.

RUSSO: I like to read a lot. And I appreciate music, certain types. But that'd be the thing I'd want to be, would be in politics. Because it holds an appeal. I read a lot about Hitler, I've read a lot about Hitler and Huey Long—that type personality. They have a charismatic nature to 'em that really, you know, you try to psychoanalyze 'em—they feared the mob. But yet they used the mob. They were really paranoiac about a mob. I guess you have to say that Hitler was. That man really just feared the mob something awful. I don't know too much about Huey Long because you read so much biased material down here. You can't get too clearly to the facts.

[The talk turned to his father again and to religion. He said he was raised a Catholic and added]: It's a sick faith. . . . I went to Loyola. I was at Tulane for two years, '59 to '61. During that period of time the hectic world began to collapse. That's when I started going to a psychiatrist. I was fighting with him [his father] most of the time, is what it amounted to. And nobody could take my defense. And shit, my older brother—but he didn't the fuck come to my aid. He couldn't care less about a relationship like that, went his own merry way. My first year at Tulane I armed myself mentally with the philosophies of Hume and Descartes and Spinoza and Nietzsche and some of these others. And some bitter attacks on the Catholic Church, you know. I used to relish reading this kind of crap. And so I was all loaded for him. When he wanted to start, I'd bang into it. So he began to surmise that Tulane University was a bunch of Communists and left wingers and integrationists and nigger lovers and a few other goodies, you know? So he abruptly said, "You can't go to Tulane any more, you'll go to Loyola or you'll get out." So in my third year he pushed me over to Loyola. Which I didn't have any choice. I went over there and fought Jesuits for about—well, I went there for four years. I fought them. Oh, I used to burn 'em up. I read a lot of Hume. And they weren't even allowing the students to read it. I read it, used to tell 'em, "Excommunicate me!" The Jesuits were sick. They warp people's minds.

Q.: When was the last time you were a practicing Catholic?

RUSSO: Oh, at about fifteen, sixteen. I quit about then and I—officially said to myself, I quit. I quit—it was a sex thing. This is a crazy little thing. When I was in my teens—I used to masturbate a lot. . . . I was going to Catholic grammar school and this one priest bugged me. He was trying to be conscientious and scrupulous and all that kind of stuff. And this one guy told me—he was a perverted little bastard, he had to be—he told me, "If you ever have impure thoughts in your mind, in your home, and you're taking pleasure in it," he says, "and someone should come knock at your door, like your buddy Tommy, want to go play baseball, and your train of thought stops, and you go out to the door and say, 'Well, Tommy, I don't want to go right now,' and you go back and resume it—it counts, two sins." . . . Two mortal sins. Because you've taken two different periods of time. Now, I went to confession seven days a week, communion seven days a week, and confession—I went for four hours. I didn't go once. I would go and when I was finished, I would go and get back in line. Because I knew I'd committed about fifteen million sins. I knew I'd had this many thoughts in the past hour. One time I went to this priest and I got so tired, I was just run down. It was about age fifteen. I went to this monsignor—a grouchy old priest—and I said, "I want to make a general confession." . . . He said, "You want to make a general confession? You couldn't have done anything that bad?" I said, "Well, I've done quite a few bad things." He said, "How long since your last confession?" I said, "About fifteen minutes." And he started laughing. He said, "Well, what did you do?" . . . I said, "I committed twenty million mortal sins that I didn't tell the last priest about." He laughed and laughed and laughed. . . . But any religion I have, I get it out of just—music now. . . .

This discussion led to David Ferrie. Perry told me in detail of his weekly black masses. The chalice featured animal blood, the wafer consisted of some kind of raw flesh, instead of cake or bread. The next eight or nine pages of the transcript of our conversation are a virtual monologue on David Ferrie: "He wore a little black toga, solid black. He wore nothing underneath. And he would start in preparation for it, burn incense. Which always puts you in a goofy mood anyway . . . he called it the American Eastern Catholic Orthodox Church . . . he was evidently the only priest in it. . . . After all the ritual, shouted ritual . . . it ends up and it's a brutal thing, a sadistic quality to it—bloodletting, chicken killing, stuff like that. All kinds of crazy things going on."

Perry detailed Ferrie's theories about committing the perfect murder, described his efforts to train young recently graduated Boy Scouts to invade Cuba, his habit of showing up at any place at almost any time, and he ended up with his alleged homosexuality.

RUSSO: He never mentioned he was homosexual . . . the only thing he did say was that he tried this drug on his roommate, which he showed me, which he suggested he *try* on me. I told him to go fuck himself. And he wanted to try it on my baseball players. I told him to go fuck himself again. And this drug—what it did was it made a guy drowsy and then the guy became aggressive.

Sexually. And he said—and this is the only thing Ferrie ever said—"He tried to make love to me."

Q.: What about being the life of the parties and everything? Didn't he ever try to score? I don't mean with you, but with other people?

RUSSO: No. Unless maybe he got his kicks just looking, being around people. He was always gregarious—of course, I had my own reasons to believe *why*. Because, I mean all the guys around him were always young, vibrant, athletically inclined and stuff like that. I mean—why not? But he never made a proposition to me. And this guy, Al Landry, the guy I originally met Ferrie through. . . . Last time I saw him before he [Landry] went in the service, he said Ferrie used to blow all the guys after he'd hypnotize them. Which I felt that anyway. He was a strange sort of person.

Q.: He ever hypnotize you?

RUSSO: He tried.

We next spoke at length about his sodium pentothal and hypnotic sessions under the auspices of the District Attorney's office. He apparently did not remember much of what went on while he was "under," except the last hypnotic session, which brought Perry to the date of his mother's death. I asked him his reaction to this.

RUSSO: I had a guilty reaction. I suffer from a guilt complex. And that's why I'd hate to be wrong, as far as Clay Shaw was concerned, because I didn't—twenty years from now if I thought differently I'd tell somebody. I wouldn't give a fuck if Clay Shaw was dead or not. It means something to me. And on the day my mother died—at seven in the morning—the doctor calls up and says, "This is it, you better come down." And so I came down. And see, I'm patient. And nothing much bugs me. Sex bugs me. Money bugs me. But that's about it. And I'm patient, I can wait, you know. Wait and wait. And I waited, and she wouldn't die. At the last gasps of breath, you know, the body's struggling to keep life, and she wouldn't. And I sat, I stayed there . . . I felt she'd be better off dead. . . . About eleven o'clock I said, "I can't take it any more." . . . So I went across the street and got something at the Rexall, something to eat, and I went back. And I said, Maybe she's dead now. And she wouldn't die. And about ten

minutes of one, I said, Die, die, you bastard, die! I was hoping
she'd die, you know. And I was not right to say that, you know?
You should never say—then I always felt guilty about that. . . .
But I kept that with me for a long time, that I wished her dead.
. . . I was closer to her than anybody. My brother, I resented him
because of—he didn't take his share of the fight with my old man.
See my old man . . . he cut my allowance off, he took the car
away. . . . I had to get money from my mother when she was
alive, then after that I had to get it anyplace I could get it. He
just took it out, bang, bang, like that. Cut the rug from under
your feet. I don't know any sorrow about it, because I'm better off
away from him. He doesn't upset me, doesn't affect me, any more.
He used to. . . . I've been mentally independent since I'm fifteen,
cause nobody really could affect the way I was looking at things.
At least about social things.

Q.: Money's a great pressure, isn't it?

RUSSO: Oh, yeah, man.

Q.: You said you were bugged by sex. And money. Why sex?

RUSSO: Well, you see, the past two years have been a bad stretch,
a bad streak for me. Because two things I really lived for were sex.
And money to get sex. That's the only two things I ever lived for.
Or to afford me things that would be conducive to having sex.
Some sort of hedonist—something—that might be my religion.
But that's the only thing. Everything else I can do without. That's
part of my breaking point. When I don't—aren't satisfied inside, I
begin to worry, get depressed, despondent. And then to plan
things—I plan sexually. You see? I want a new car—sexually.
That's the only reason I want a car. The only reason. Because I
have no pretense about dress or education or color TVs or anything—doesn't really make any difference. The only thing that
makes any difference to me is good times at night. One good night.
Or a long period of time. And that's my—that's my real hangup.
. . . You know, I read all these crazy fucking novels and my mind
does tricks. Not tricks, but I love to fantasize. If I had a house
built, this is the way I'd want it, you know? A camera deal, films
in the back. Used to have a library. Love that stuff. Film—I had
some good sixteen millimeter. Ferrie gave me one in fact. I don't
have that one around any more. But beautiful sixteen millimeter—good pornography. Hard-core stuff. . . .

There's one thing else that always turned me on and that's

mobs. They turn me on. That's when I'm a little bit crazy, I think. Because mobs do turn me on. They have a strange fascination for my— I read once a long time ago, a fascist has certain things that are just notably attached to a fascist personality. And one of them is a liking of columns, structures, tidiness, symmetry in things. If a person did like that, in a psychological test, you might deduct that he had inclinations along those lines. And I tell you, bridges, buildings turn me on. At least they're conducive to putting me in a good attitude. . . . And this, of course, along with the mob stuff. I like mobs.

Q.: I thought at one point you said you were frightened of them.

RUSSO: Oh, yes, sure.

Q.: But you like them?

RUSSO: Yes, I like them. I love to see 'em. I never want to be one, never want to be a part of it. And I don't like to—whenever I get in the middle of a mob or something, I'm squirming. I'm generally a reactionary. I'm against whatever they're for. I don't like an unbridled mob to have its way.

Q.: But vicariously—you like to watch?

RUSSO: Oh, yes.

Q.: What does Mardi Gras do to you? Or is that a different kind of a mob?

RUSSO: No, it's the same thing. I know—not because of the Clay Shaw thing—I never did ever think I was going to get shot. That was for sure. But I always keep my back to the wall. I guess it's something psychological with me. But I don't like to walk, for any length of time, with people behind me. I don't like to be crowded, unless I'm against the wall so that I can watch. Three different ways, 180 degrees. . . . There's just a certain fascination in a mob. I used to have records. I don't have 'em here, they're over to the other apartment. Records of Hitler speaking—hear the mob shrieking. Beautiful sounds, beautiful! I didn't even understand the German, but I knew the inflection in the voice and what he could do with people. And I have some Martin Luther King records. He was a charismatic type of person—magnetic. I'm not trying to say I'm that way, but I sure—for some reason or other I always end up leading. Whatever group I'm involved with. Always end up that way. I was always supposed to be a nutty personality, too. But I always end up the leader. Of something. Baseball—I'm the fucking chief. And even the store, you know, fuck it, I shoot all the shots. I mean, I put up $130 in the thing so far, my cousin's put up $10,000. And I call the shots. I know what I'm doing, too, you know. I'm not a bungler. I do a good job.

Around this time Perry Russo made a trip to the kitchen for a final beer. We were into the last act of An Evening with Perry Russo—it was now after 11 and the curtain had gone up around 6—so I quickly slipped over to the console and plugged it back in. I figured I should sign over and out officially.

Toward the end I asked him, "If you had a message for Clay Shaw, what would it be?"

RUSSO: If I had a message for Clay Shaw? Well, if I had a message I'd first tell Dymond, Congratulations. Because I would hate to write him a note—Congratulations! Would look like I was playing for him. But he did do a good job. Clay Shaw—I just don't know what I could tell him. Just like, you know, he's won, he's innocent. You know, what would Judas Iscariot tell Jesus Christ? I mean, what could you tell him? Can't go up to him and say, "Well, how's tricks?"

Q.: Yes—"I'm sorry I planted one on you."

RUSSO: Yes. I mean, let's start all over, let's go back to February 25th. Something like that, two years ago. But there's not much you can really say. I would hope that everything turns out—as he sees the truth, what he knows is true, and what's not true. As far as the defense is concerned, I just really don't know how the fuck they're going to get around this [the perjury charges]. One day I'm going to get a chance, I'm going to meet Clay Shaw. And I'm going to shoot the shit with him a little bit.

As I was preparing to leave—it was now midnight—Russo suddenly said, "I wish in my heart I knew that Clay Shaw really wasn't—didn't really know all of these people. You know, he didn't know me or all these other people."

It was too late to kindle up a debate but I did suggest once again that Russo should really be the one to know. I also wondered why, if Clay Shaw and Russo had met at Ferrie's, Clay Shaw did not recognize him and say, "Oh, hi," when Russo went to Shaw's door to identify him for the D.A.'s office.

RUSSO: As far as him distinctly remembering me, I don't think he would. You see? Cause shit, a guy of his importance, as he was with the Trade Mart and the Trade Missions. Shit, he was a confidant of Chep Morrison [former Mayor of New Orleans] and—well, he knew President Kennedy. He knew all the bigwigs in trade and probably a lot of Latin American, South American presidents. Stuff like that. Who the fuck am I? He probably wouldn't have remembered me from that point of view.

Q.: If you remembered him, there's no reason for his not remembering you.

RUSSO: No, no, that doesn't work. He's six foot four, 225 then . . . I'm six foot. I fade into the walls just like a blender and—

Q.: Oh, no.

RUSSO: Well, I do, really. He doesn't. So remembering him is a lot easier than remembering me.

We finally exchanged good nights. It was my idea to leave. We both maintained that we had enjoyed the evening. For my part, I had certainly found the six or so hours fascinating. But I was worn out. Time with Perry Russo had taken an extra toll of energy, spent controlling the riptides that held my tongue in check so many times when I could easily have become argumentative, when I could have highlighted massive inconsistencies, when I could have leveled with him and spewed out what I thought about his testimony and the entire case. But what use would that have been? I had not sought him out in an attempt to get him to recant. I was intensely curious about what kind of a boy-man he was. I wanted to know who and what lived inside. There is something strivingly, sadly likable about Perry Russo's desire to be congenial. There certainly is elasticity to him; I appreciated his non-rigid behavior toward me, as an outsider and a disbeliever.

One thing I feel strongly. If Perry Russo had, by chance, been given a banquet by his baseball team at the time of Ferrie's death, or if he'd been awarded a plaque as Southern Louisiana Little League Coach of the Month—it would not even have had to be "*of the year*"—chances are slim he ever would have contacted the newspaper in Baton Rouge and stepped into the ring of the Garrison investigation. There is such a craving for attention, for some little bit of importance, in this young man. It's human and understandable, and most of us feel it, whether we admit to the yearning or not.

Perry Russo had leaped into the enticing pit of notoriety and had been trapped in it by his own sweet tooth—and by a most persuasive manager-showman, the District Attorney.

53

The Judge

Two days later I had lunch with Judge Haggerty. Even this final appointment was not come by easily. There were several phone calls that morning leading up to it and eventually a half-hour wait in a broiling gas-station parking lot kitty-corner from the Criminal Court Building, waiting for the judge to emerge. When he did hit the sidewalk he bumped into his brother, Dan, Administrative Clerk of Court for their retiring father, Edward Haggerty, Sr., and next up for election to that office after the senior's thirteenth consecutive term. They stood gabbing by the steps for another ten minutes.

Finally the judge crossed the street and got in my car; his was still on the blink. We drove down Broad to a small but good steak restaurant, often the lunching spot of the grand jurors. He was well known there and effusively greeted by the lady manager and the help. We ordered drinks and fell into easy conversation. The judge was never anything less than good-natured.

JUDGE HAGGERTY [shaking his head]: Whatever sentiment existed in this city for that man [Clay Shaw], which apparently it did because you had a wave of all the reporters here, not one of 'em objectively. You asked this question [it had been on the list]: what did I think of the local press coverage? I thought it *stunk*.

Q.: The local press?

JUDGE HAGGERTY: Yes, and I thought the outside press *stunk*, too. They didn't give him [Garrison] half a chance—when he made a good point. Take Spiesel for instance. Here's a man got a record in the service, got a couple of degrees, he's competent, he's made money. All right. Of all the places in the city where did he take them? He took them to the apartment that Shaw [once] owned and lived in the back. That's not bad, damn it. So nobody played it up. You can have the biggest damn fool in the world, he can see an accident out there, but his eyes are still good. So they made him the funny little man with being hypnotized out of his sex and all that stuff. But not once did they get the fact that he did go down to the place where he was. Nobody played it up.

Q.: Don't you think it would be easy for him to know, to have investigated, or have found out where—

JUDGE HAGGERTY: They didn't. He just got in town. The stupid so-and-so's didn't even have time to bring him down there to acquaint him with the place. If you follow me on that. If it would have been *me* I'd have taken him down there first, and reacquainted him where Shaw lived and where his apartment was. [Laughing.] Hell, there's nothing wrong with that, refreshing the memory of your witness. On that one incident they didn't give him anything. . . . If they hadn't had that suit against him they couldn't have torn him apart like they did. Somebody tipped their hand. Like me playing—you trying to bluff and you get somebody to tell you what I got.

Q.: True, if they hadn't gotten that information on the lawsuit, he'd have made a good witness.

JUDGE HAGGERTY: That's correct. Now, you take this fellow, Nick Tadin. I told you I went to Aloysius with that little fellow. [There was nothing little about fifty-some-year-old Tadin's appearance on the stand; neither his build, nor his mouth.] He was one or two grades behind me. Now they should have built that kid up to show— Now here he is with two sons, one particularly, taking flying lessons. And his wife and him are so concerned they go out and meet him and then he gets this terrible phone call advising him that Ferrie apparently is a queer, so they double their efforts—"God, what's going to happen!" And here it's so logical. Why did they go out there? They had a good reason, it's not spurious, not made up, it's not a false deal. He's with his wife, they see Ferrie, they ask him, "Is that another student of yours?" "No, he's not a *student,* he's the Managing Director of the *International Trade Mart!*" . . . But the jury, I asked one of them, they said they couldn't buy that because he waited too long. Well, I didn't want to get into an argument with the juror, but I said, "Look, the fact that you know that Shaw knew Ferrie and you [Tadin] say, 'This man [Shaw], this man, this is terrible. He's lying to that jury right in their face and I don't believe he should get by with that, so I am going to tell the D.A.' " Tadin and his wife did, he had to talk her into it—if you remember one of the questions—she didn't want to do it. But he told her to, he forced her to do it.

The judge indicated again that the jury had chosen not to believe the Tadins. The jury might not have, but the judge clearly believed them. From his defense of them and Spiesel it was quite obvious where his sympathies lay. Next up from the judge was a spate of dialogue that I found particularly shocking.

JUDGE HAGGERTY: I'll tell you, if Garrison were to put a one-page ad, put a one-page ad—let me give you this idea—"*I Need You!* The Kennedy implication is not involved. It's a question, can any person—no matter how big or little—can he stare a jury in the face for two hours and now be snickering—*snickering* is the word—because he got by with it. He took a calculated risk, said, 'I'm gonna get up there and lie for two, two and a half hours, that I do not know Ferrie.'" Now that's the one thing I'm talking about. Not whether he's in the conspiracy, not whether he knew Oswald. *Ferrie!* Because I'm about to tell you what Dymond said. He said, "Ed, between you and me, if we wrestle with that problem, that's the biggest problem we've had since we got the case. Number one, whether we explore the fact that he's a queer. Number two—" That's what we're talking about, not about whether he's gonna admit he knew Ferrie. I didn't ask him that question, because that would be too damn— But they decided their strategy and I said to them, I said, "You can take it for what it's worth, but I read in either Illinois or Michigan, where a man, a queer, was accused of a brutal murder and the defense attorney got up on voir dire examination of prospective jurors and admitted, 'This man is a queer. We're not going to try to hide it, but he did not have anything to do with this murder and if you find out that he's a queer—and we admit it—but that fact has nothing to do with this murder. Would you convict him because he's in this poor state of being a queer?' And they said, 'No.'" I told Dymond that. Now, me, *I* wouldn't admit it. Of course, he beat the case.

Judge Haggerty appeared to be fascinated with the homosexual element, often introducing the subject into the conversation.

When the judge said he would not have admitted it, I asked him why he thought the trial had remained relatively clean in that respect.

JUDGE HAGGERTY: Oh, they got into it a couple of times, remember? With Perry Russo saying he wore tight pants and when he looked at you, he looked down at your—and he's got his eyes down there. Here's another thing, as a writer, you should know, being around as much as you—*queers know queers!* In New Orleans particularly. You might have a fly-by-night group coming in here, but if he's in town one or two nights, he'll find out who to meet or where do they meet and all that stuff. They've got a clique better than the CIA.

[We ordered another round of drinks and a fine lunch, steaks all around.]

JUDGE HAGGERTY: These people [the defense] can't hold this case up like they did with me, with these pleadings. They can't go into pleadings now on the perjury thing. They're trying to give everybody the idea that it's *res adjudicata* [a case that has been decided]. It's not *res adjudicata*. It's a completely different crime at a different time. The fact that this jury didn't buy Tadin's testimony— Now let me get back to this ad. And Garrison, the subject came up to do this, and he said, "It would be a damn good idea." Now it's up to the people of New Orleans: You owe it to yourself, to your country, if you know anything about Clay Shaw being in company with David Ferrie, being seen with him, talking to— You didn't come forward before because you didn't want to get involved in an assassination deal with the Kennedy family. Whatever your reason may be, *that reason is out the window now!* [Judge Haggerty looked at me with eyes particularly gleaming.] And don't be surprised if he don't do it!

Q.: No, I wouldn't be surprised.

JUDGE HAGGERTY [leaning into me]: I suggested it, just offhand. At this party we had, the same day down there. I missed you by five minutes.

Q.: I waited. I told Sciambra, when I was talking to Garrison. He was very friendly then, but when I walked in to the party, it was like a lousy mattress had just been dragged in.

JUDGE HAGGERTY: Well, they know you were pro-Shaw, they said that you'd been conned by Shaw, or something.

Q.: No, I wasn't conned by him at all, by anyone.

JUDGE HAGGERTY: That you were very much pro-Shaw and that if you were pro-Shaw, you were against him. Well, that figures.

[Eventually we touched on the art of jury selection.]

JUDGE HAGGERTY: You try to get an intelligent jury in one case, you try to get a stupid jury in another case. Another case you try to get a cross section. You try to get some laborers or something. A sex case, an offense like that, you'd want Jewish people on a case like that. You get a theft case, stealing money, and the defense wouldn't want a Jew. You get a crime of passion, the defense wouldn't want a German. They would, in a passion case like that, want an Italian or Irish because they're soft-hearted. Then certain cases you'd like to get an older jury because they'd say, Oh, my goodness, there but for the grace of God goes me. I remember my peccadilloes and my indiscretions of my youth, and there goes me. And they'd say, Oh, let's give 'em a break. Germans—no! Irish—yeah, Italian—yeah. Germans—no! So you do know if you've been practicing law.

Q.: In this case, it was obvious that the state wanted the least—

JUDGE HAGGERTY: Yeah, when they took that first juror, that Negro, Mason, the first guy they took.

[I don't know exactly what the judge meant by that, and I'm not sure an investigation would have been entirely flattering.]

Q.: When I was talking to Alcock, he said, "Yes, we wanted the least sophisticated jury." I suppose that's because of Shaw's background.

JUDGE HAGGERTY: That's right. You see, the businessmen of the world, they're educated, they're very tolerant of queers. They've been in business enough to know. Well, that's life, we have to accept it. The jury didn't get too much on that queer angle. They didn't make the *cause célèbre* out of it that *I* would have. I *would* have if I'd have been the prosecution.

Q. [as long as Judge Haggerty obviously wanted to concentrate on this angle]: Is it true the state couldn't bring in any of Clay Shaw's personal life, because it was irrelevant, unless the defense brought in character witnesses?

JUDGE HAGGERTY: That's correct, and you notice in the closing arguments Alcock said he [Dymond] didn't put one character witness on, with all these big shots, all the people he knew. The only man, they didn't even ask *him* his character, that's this Lloyd Cobb.

Q.: But in trials they can slip a lot of things in. You might have sustained an objection, but the jury hears—

JUDGE HAGGERTY: Well, when Shaw himself was on the stand. "Mr. Shaw, are you a homosexual?" They object: "It has nothing to do with the case." "I'm testing his *credibility*. If he says no, I intend to prove that he is." Certainly it's permissible. Certainly it is! I'm surprised they didn't.

Q.: Except if they had done it, it might have boomeranged on them. . . . Everybody might have said, Jesus, that's really getting dirty now.

JUDGE HAGGERTY: They could tie it up by showing that Ferrie was a queer. And Oswald, he's a switch hitter. He went three or four different ways, I understand. [I should have asked the judge what the three or four different ways were; I'd been given to believe there were only two.] And the purpose, there would have been a good purpose. It wouldn't have been irrelevant or immaterial, because it would have been another link in the chain to show that he would have occasion to be in the company of Ferrie and Oswald. Just by being a queer. And the fact that these weirdos, these homos, were talking about knocking off Castro and the President. Ferrie—I never met the character. . . . He, ah, he, you know there are some rumblings that he did not die of natural—you inject a certain solution into a man, knowing that he suffers from something else and you know that's going to cause something to make it look like apparently—look like a suicide. He left some notes, you know.

Q.: Did you find the jury—

JUDGE HAGGERTY: I want to show you a letter I got from Sidney Hebert, the jury foreman. . . . I picked him to be foreman, did you know that? . . . I also predicted the jury would be out in an hour.

Q.: Did you predict the verdict, too?

JUDGE HAGGERTY: I didn't predict that to anybody. I would not have been surprised if he had been found guilty.

Q.: From having watched the jury, I thought there was a good chance they would.

JUDGE HAGGERTY: Those women that were there every day. They

all thought he was guilty. . . . Actually, you take a trial that unfolds every day, it's better than anything you got on Broadway. You got the wits being matched against each other. You know somebody's trying to get out this, the other one's trying to keep it back. You have worthy adversarial opponents. You're trying your best [it was inevitable]—like they didn't want Clay Shaw to admit he was a queer, they tried to keep it out. Now all the places where he could have been with David Ferrie in this city or else-where—how many people do you imagine in this city have seen them together? Would you say hundreds? [I made no reply; I had already stated when we'd talked in his office that I believed Clay Shaw had not known David Ferrie.] Well, let's see, you want to go down this list of questions? . . .

They're going to pursue this deal, on the perjury. They're going all out on that. . . . They could come back and convict him on this. He gets a sentence in the penitentiary because he lied. And here everybody believes he had nothing to do with the case. And still he lied. Now he must have a reason for lying. What his reason was, I don't know. I am personally convinced that—from people I've spoken to and what I've heard over two years—I am convinced that Shaw knew Ferrie. I am convinced.

Q.: A lot of people think Garrison is doing this to hold some part of the case over through the elections. Do you think he would like to come to trial as soon as possible?

JUDGE HAGGERTY: I think he's out digging for witnesses right now. More than before, more than Tadin. . . . And that advertising deal, don't be surprised if you don't see that, because he felt it might be an unusual approach, like you put something in the want-ad section: "Will the person who saw the accident at Eighth and Ninth Street on such and such a day—I'm the attorney for the people and we're looking for witnesses." Well, this would be a bit different. A whole page—everybody in the city's going to see it!

There was something highly unethical about the trial judge of a man who had been unanimously acquitted, now seeming to cheer on the further prosecution of the former defendant. Having heard Judge Haggerty's sentiments, I certainly hoped the perjury case would not be allotted to him. As we were digging into our steaks, I could not help thinking that perhaps the judge had a point when he'd shown such hesitancy in speaking with me. Colorful he was, in his own solid brand of moral Babbittry, but the more he talked man-to-man the more astounded I was that he'd conducted the trial as well as he had. The judge soon returned to his hunch about the jury.

JUDGE HAGGERTY: I thought it was a jury below average intelligence from what you would really ordinarily try to get. . . . I tell you, the night before, when the jury was in there at the Rowntowner eating, I said, "Now if we wind this thing up tomorrow, do you fellows feel like I should put you to bed and let you get a good night's sleep and then you could come down fresh and start your deliberations?" "No, sir, we want to go right through." So I knew—I had a suspicion that their minds were made up before they even heard the arguments. Now they hadn't heard Tadin at that stage. He testified the morning of the last day, didn't he? Tadin and his wife. . . .

Now we had a couple of prospective jurors by the name of Shaw. Did you know that?

Q.: No.

JUDGE HAGGERTY: Yeah. Three. They were colored. [Laughing.] S-H-A-W. I made a notation. I would have asked, "Are you related to the defendant?" [Laughing again.] I was more or less in training. I'm not afraid to shoot from the hip, as they call it.

Q.: You said in court during the voir dire that the Warren Report was not going on trial.

JUDGE HAGGERTY: That's correct.

Q.: But it did, didn't it?

JUDGE HAGGERTY: It did. I will admit that. For this purpose. Garrison was trying to bring to the public the fact that the Warren Commission were told to go out and produce this and get this. And anything that didn't correspond to what they were told, if they got it, it was disregarded. Now, that's not the way you investigate the death of the President. That's not the proper way to handle something. You say, Go get it, whether it's good or it's bad. This Commission Report—I've never read it.

Q.: Every once in a while I'd be sitting there and there'd be questions I'd either want Alcock to go on and ask and the same with Dymond.

JUDGE HAGGERTY: Well, they took a calculated risk. That was

their biggest decision: whether to come out whether Shaw was a queer. [Here we were again.] I think more than that was their decision, steadfastly to the bitter end, vehemently, not just casually, *vehemently* to state under oath that he did not know David Ferrie. You know, I charged—in my charge to the jury—that if you believe any witness either for the state or for the defense was deliberately lying or perjured himself about a material fact in the case, then you have a legal right, not a duty but a right, to disregard his entire testimony as not being worthy of belief. Now if you had a juror that would have reminded the other jurors, "Do you remember the judge's charge?" "Yeah, we remember it." "Remember that part where he says if we believe that any witness either for the state or the defense purposely, deliberately, looks us in the eye and lies to us for two hours, we have a right to disregard his testimony? Now, if we disregard his testimony, we gotta believe the other people. If we believe the other people, we gotta convict him." That's how easy it is.

Q.: How did you feel about the mailman?

This brought still another accusation of another witness being "a queer." Not the mailman, I hasten to add. The judge rapped on about this for a while. I was getting to believe Judge Haggerty had what amounted to an obsession about "queers." Now it almost became a game. I would try to think of questions that could not possibly lead to the subject and sit in fascination while Judge Haggerty eventually worked back to it. I was, as the discussion wore on, fascinated that the judge would bolster the state's witnesses, in almost every case. He had done this with the Tadins several times, and his attempt to rehabilitate Charles Spiesel was even more astonishing. Now I asked the judge about the credibility of Vernon Bundy.

JUDGE HAGGERTY: You know, when he told you this man had a peculiar twist to his foot—"Let me be seated here and let Mr. Shaw walk in." It was down like this, with the peripheral vision that he may or may not have. He said, "Look-it." He pointed his hand and said, "Look, see the way he throws his foot out." Sure enough, Shaw threw his foot out that way. He said, "That's why I remembered." It's amazing! . . . Like I tell you, you get up and say, We don't choose our witnesses. We'd like to have the presi-

dent of Loyola and Tulane and what have you. All right, we take
the witnesses who were there. We don't want Bundy, but he
happened to be there. . . . Supposing Garrison, as a result of
some endeavor on his part, could get hold of twenty or thirty
witnesses in this perjury trial? Don't you think Dymond and
them—they know the score. They know they might be able to
parade twenty or thirty substantial citizens to the effect "Why
certainly I was there, saw 'em, I was there for a couple of hours."

Now followed a prime example of Judge Haggerty's ability to
veer back to the queer angle, regardless of what we were talking
about. I asked the judge how it would be possible to find a jury for
the perjury trial, when it had been almost impossible to seat one
for the conspiracy trial. By now the publicity had quadrupled,
saturating the community like some self-multiplying ooze from
another planet.

JUDGE HAGGERTY: Like you mentioned, if you didn't want to get
on there, you could have very easily gotten off, very easily. . . . I
think the honest man was one of the fellows that said, "I don't
have a fixed opinion, I have a *mixed* opinion." Now I was quoted
in some article that said I thought he was the most honest. In fact,
I congratulated him for being so honest. But to me, like you'd
hear one thing one day and—now *queers!* [I almost laughed.]
As you know, I've been exposed to them, not too many. But you
do have some intelligent queers, god damn it! And whereas a
bunch of Irishmen, like me, they'd go and have a drink, or somebody would say, Let's go across the lake or make out we're fishing
and have a little party—somebody get the broads. Something like
that. To me, that would be okay. These intellectual bastards,
when they're all together, sex is out of the picture. They don't talk
sex, so what do they talk about? Okay, you got world affairs.
They're up to date on world affairs—*Czechoslovakia!* [I don't know
why, but that choice, out of the clear blue, struck me as wildly
funny.] They have stimulating conversations concerning these various things. "Isn't that terrible, what he's doing?" [To what—Czechoslovakia?] I've met many. Most of the queers I've met have been
intelligent people. I don't know whether it comes with intelligence. But I sure have met a lot of them.

I had a professor at Loyola University, a captain in the Navy.

He came home one night, his wife and three daughters were engulfed in a fire in the family, all of 'em burned to death. From that moment he had a violent aversion to women. He became a queer and taught me at Loyola. I was on the debating team, representing the school. He invited me over to his pad. All the liquor! Any of these queers, whenever you went to their pad, they're loaded with liquor. You can believe they got five hundred or a thousand dollar—they got liquor galore. Because that's their first move. They invariably get into something cool and charming, a pajama robe or something.

[And so it went. Until we finally reached the subject of the District Attorney.]

Q.: Jim Garrison's been pretty bold about pointing his fingers at a variety of people. How is it nobody ever came after him?

JUDGE HAGGERTY: I don't believe I told this to anybody. I may have, I may or may not. When he wrote a letter to the Federal Communications Commission—why he got involved in it I don't know—he stated—I got a copy, I've got the duplicate original—and he practically states that Shaw refused to take a lie detector test. I get Charlie Ward in the office. I said, "Charlie, did you see this?" Well, he got out of it. Charlie Ward didn't want to fool with that. He was trying to protect whatever little semblance of sanity he had because he was hoping to run for D.A. or councilman at large. . . . You see, some of these fellows are so angry, like Bill Gurvich, Hugh Aynesworth. They were in from the beginning. . . . And to think on such flimsy evidence that they would proceed to put this man on trial—whether he's a queer or not—and a whole motive is to get a forum in court, under oath, where he can lambaste the Warren Commission, irrespective of whether Clay Shaw is involved. And that's what they were concerned about. And they said it was dirty pool. Well, Garrison sure got enough national publicity out of it.

Q.: As you were saying, about your guidelines?

JUDGE HAGGERTY: He [Garrison] violated them more than anyone else. When I showed that letter to Ward, I said, "Charlie, aren't you up on your law to the effect, the Supreme Court decision, that if you comment in advance of trial, particularly the D.A. or any of his assistants, that a person refused to take a lie detector test there are cases right on point that that's reversible error." . . . In other words because people read it and see that Clay Shaw refused to take a lie detector test. That's prejudicial against him. Well, if he was innocent, why didn't he take it? I've got a copy of that I could give you. That in and of itself, it shows you the whole theory behind Garrison. It was not ever leading up or possibly looking for a conviction. He wanted to blast the Warren Commission and he did find some reasons. Now—you can say what you want—they got people all over the United States that still think it was worth while for him to attack the Warren Commission. He was big enough to do it. Damn it, he did it.

After Judge Haggerty spoke at length about the Warren Commission, during which he revealed his thorough skepticism over the report's single-assassin theory, he told me a great deal about his family and background in the Irish Channel section of New Orleans. He was a good storyteller with a fondness for acting out dialogue. Toward the end of our luncheon he mentioned the preliminary hearing, of which he was critical, despite his obvious feelings for the state regarding the recently completed trial.

JUDGE HAGGERTY: I'm second senior to Bagert and everybody asks me, "Judge, how come Benny Bagert didn't select you and Brahney, the next two senior to him?" I said, "I don't know." I'll tell you, now that the thing's over I'm glad he didn't select me. Cause I disagree with many of the rulings. In fact, I would have ruled there was *not* probable cause. I would have. And he permitted all kind of hearsay evidence to go in. Because it was a preliminary hearing. The rules of evidence don't change because it's a preliminary hearing. It's the same goddamn rules of evidence. He made a lot of mistakes just between you and me. . . .

[On the subject of the LaBiche grand jury]: That was Judge Bagert's grand jury . . . it was the LaBiche grand jury where Al LaBiche was foreman. Now that has been attacked in my court and in many other courts by the claim that Judge Bagert picked his crones [*sic*] from the New Orleans Athletic Club and the American Legion.

Q.: That's what I heard.

JUDGE HAGGERTY: I belong to the club for over eighteen years— up till two years ago. All my buddies have left there, they don't go there. They got mostly Jew people—that play cards and gin rummy and it has no attraction for me. I still belong to the American Legion, pay my dues. But you can't belong to the post unless you belong to the club. I'm going to get back into the club. It's just a political help to belong to it. . . . Bagert, he had about seven or eight friends of his from the New Orleans Athletic Club and the American Legion, and a lot of people were suspect that of all the people in this city, why suddenly— Well, it did look bad!

Judge Haggerty spoke more about his earlier life and times and explained with clarity and enthusiasm points of law about which I questioned him. His knowledge of the law and his respect for it, to me, are his most engaging qualities. I would trust his interpretation of the law more than I would invest any dependence in him as a man outside the law. From the pure singular chemistry he exudes and from what he'd told me about his Irish-Catholic childhood, I was able to picture his entire life with clarity and in 3-D. He is a total product of his environment.

When I drove him to pick up his car and we said goodbye, for some inexplicable reason I felt a certain nostalgia about Judge Haggerty. Even the use of the word "nostalgia" does not make logical sense—but that's what I felt.

The next day, the day before I was to leave New Orleans, I received a phone call from Jim Garrison in response to a letter I had written after our meeting in which I invited him to spell out his political and assassination theories in a statement I would be glad to include, uncut, in the book.

He was friendly and warm-sounding on the phone. "I've been thinking about your proposal, but I think I'll leave it as it is. It's a matter of the population explosion. With 200 million people I don't really feel I can be a bellwether or prophet, warning of the dangers facing our country." He paused. "That would be like dropping a BB in the middle of the Atlantic Ocean at midnight."

I told him I was sorry he wouldn't include his philosophies in my book. Again we told each other how much we enjoyed our meeting. Jim Garrison ended up saying, "I'll talk to you any time you're down here. Have a good trip."

54

An Epilogue—But Not the End

There were farewells with many friends and a goodbye dinner with Clay Shaw, as outwardly unflappable as ever. I sensed, however, that he retained a sickening knot of disgust and hurt that the monstrous charade he had battled his way through was continuing.

Several things have happened in New Orleans since I left.

Nina Sulzer was fired from her job with the Sheriff's office. No reason was given.

Alvin Oser was awarded a judgeship. It is now Judge Alvin Oser. I can hardly wait until one of those heavy paneled doors reads, JUDGE MOO-MOO SCIAMBRA.

The campaign for District Attorney went into full swing in the late summer and fall of 1969. Mr. Garrison was soundly opposed by both local papers, who endorsed his most viable opponent, Harry Connick, a former Assistant United States Attorney. Dubbed "The Phantom D.A." in an editorial by the *States-Item,* Jim Garrison remained unusually silent, participating only marginally in the primary campaign, claiming a bad back and refusing to debate with the other candidates. He knew the Shaw case would be thrown at him, but at least if he did not enter the ring, he would not have to stand there with egg dripping down his face.

A Garrison aide delivered a letter to one station shortly before air time, setting forth the D.A.'s reason for refusing to appear on a panel program with the three other candidates. The letter read:

If you will recall, Channel 8 sponsored a program after the Shaw trial in which a panel consisting of Hugh Aynesworth of *Newsweek* magazine, James Phelan of the *Saturday Evening Post* and a free-lance writer by the name of James Kirkwood, who just completed a book criticizing my investigation, engaged in a one-sided diatribe of our investigation and my office.

Because your station was flooded with calls protesting the unfairness of the show, I responded by applying to your station for equal time to answer these charges. Needless to say, I was disappointed when I was refused equal time. Because of the above set of facts, I decline to appear on your station.

The following statement was read on the air by the management of the station several times during the program, which featured an empty chair representing the missing District Attorney:

The Channel 8 management wishes to state that the program mentioned in Mr. Garrison's statement was a national press analysis of the Clay Shaw trial. Viewer response to the program was generally favorable. In response to Mr. Garrison's request, WYES–TV offered him a personal appearance in a 30-minute press interview program in the week following the program under discussion. Mr. Garrison did not respond to the invitation.

And so Jim Garrison played it cool during the preprimary battle—until the very end, when he suddenly swung into the picture with a reported $50,000 Madison Avenue cozy-slick personal commercial barrage that drew great attention and a wide listening audience exactly because of his previous scarcity.

According to one local publication: "The first words out of his mouth were a tongue-in-cheek parody of the most frequently voiced criticism of him—that he is crazy; that he is afflicted with delusions of grandeur and suffers from a persecution complex."

"I am opposed in the race," the District Attorney said, "by Harry Connick, Ross Scaccia, Charles Ward, and the New Orleans *Times-Picayune*, the *States-Item*, *The New York Times*, the Federal government, the CIA and the FBI . . ." and several other agencies and publications.

Thus he announced his position—the brave lone crusader, pitching himself in sacrifice between the evils of the Establishment and the common people, threatened by the encroaching tentacles of the Federal government. One of his quotes was a far from modest reference to his own martyrdom: "To have wisdom, you must suffer. You must be a victim of the system."

In one of his last medium-is-the-message appearances he introduced his family to the viewing audience. During this warming episode he cradled his little daughter in his arms, squeezed her to him and murmured, "Who's nutty?"

The outcome? After wreaking disgrace upon himself, his office and the City of New Orleans, Jim Garrison went on to win a smashing majority in the November Democratic primary in a field of four candidates, avoiding even a runoff. This is tantamount to election, since Democrats make up 98.6 per cent of the registered voters in New Orleans. So he was guaranteed a return to office for his third four-year term. He ran exceedingly heavy in the black and poor white communities. It is widely agreed that his great popularity among the Negroes rests upon the stand he took in his trumpeting attempt—regardless of whether it came to naught—to solve the murder of President Kennedy, one of the white men most revered in black America.

His appeal to the poor whites lies in his constant and vociferous cries of "Foul!" directed at the Federal government, its many agencies, and the highly sinister Eastern Establishment. Add to these specific issues Jim Garrison's movie-star mystique, his unerring cleverness in aiming the correct beam of appeal to each corresponding classification of voter, and a phenomenon rises out of its own ashes. At his victory celebration, he was asked to what he attributed his wide public endorsement. Jim Garrison, with easy charm, replied, "Maybe it's my sex appeal."

Questioned about what he intended to do about Clay Shaw now that he was returned to the catbird seat, Garrison looked directly into the television camera with those bulging hypnotic eyes and said, in his lowest and most serious tone, "He goes to trial. He goes to trial."

After winning the primary, the District Attorney went into the hospital for back surgery. Of this Clay Shaw wrote me, "I believe it's a slipped disc—I trust from carrying around his conscience. I have offered to defray the costs of an operation. But not on his back—a frontal lobotomy."

Just for an added fillip to this grotesque panorama, the good Judge Haggerty was arrested December 17, 1969, in a vice raid during a stag show in a motel room on Tulane Avenue, several blocks from the Criminal Court Building. Thirteen others, including three women, were hauled in at the same time and later three employees of the motel were arrested for alleged participation in arranging the party.

Judge Haggerty attempted to flee when the police broke in but was dragged back, subdued, knocked to the floor of the motel room and handcuffed by the arresting officers. Someone had tipped off the news media, and Judge Haggerty's embarrassment was recorded under the full glare of television lights, cameras at the grind.

He was charged that night on four counts: simple battery on the police, resisting arrest, conspiracy to commit obscenity, and soliciting for prostitution. The judge suffered a scraped head in the fracas. The police let it be known they had received advance information that the motel room had been rented for staging an obscene show. Persons entering the room were charged $5 to watch stag films. They alleged that an additional charge was to be extracted later on for "live entertainment."

Judge Haggerty arrived at his courtroom and assumed the bench the following morning. Questioned by a reporter as he entered the Criminal Court Building, he smiled wanly, posed for a photograph and said, "Oh, well, the world's not coming to an end."

Clay Shaw sent on the local newspaper clips with this note attached:

Dear Jim,
You just *thought* you were finished with your book. But these characters down here won't let you end it. This should be worth a 20,000 word epilogue.

Apparently Channel 6 had been tipped off to the raid, for they have some really fantastic live TV coverage of the affair. Including three plainclothesmen wrestling Haggerty to the floor, pushing his face into the expensive carpeting and handcuffing his hands behind his back. By contrast, MY arrest was as dignified as a high pontifical mass!

There are interesting theories about Judge Haggerty's collision with the law. The room had been staked out by the police hours before the raid and the press had been tipped off. It was difficult, therefore, to believe the judge's presence was not known, especially since there are indications that an inside informant was present, thus obviating the need for a search warrant.

The charges were reportable to the District Attorney's office. Speculation was high for days over the probable official response. On January 1, 1970, the *Times-Picayune* reported that the following specific charges had been filed by the District Attorney's office against Judge Haggerty:

Willfully and unlawfully soliciting, inciting, directing and transporting Janelle Vincent, 21, Wanda Norman, 39, and Jean Clemens Shipp, 32, with the intent to commit prostitution. The penalty is a fine of not less than $100 or imprisonment for not more than six months or both.

Resisting arrest by police officers P. Melancon, R. Pence and Richard Siegel. The penalty is a fine of not more than $1,000 or imprisonment for not more than one year or both.

Unlawfully exhibiting and displaying lewd, lascivious, filthy and sexually indecent motion pictures with the intent to appeal to the purient [sic] interests of the average person. The penalty is a fine of not less than $100 nor more than $500 or imprisonment for not more than one year or both.

New Orleans wondered who could be out to get the good judge and why. To enrich the irony, who should be named to preside at Judge Haggerty's trial but one of the men who had tried the state's fiasco in front of Judge Haggerty—newly appointed Judge Alvin Oser. This was quickly remedied, however, when Haggerty's attorney filed a motion to have Oser recused as judge in the matter because, the attorney claimed, having signed one or more of the arrest warrants, Oser would be called by Judge Haggerty as a material witness in the trial. The case then fell into the hands of Judge Matthew S. Braniff, a close friend of Haggerty's.

Judge Haggerty was found not guilty of obscenity, soliciting for prostitution and resisting arrest in a one-day trial held on January 26, 1970, before Judge Braniff, who said, "The court finds that a private party in a motel room rented by an individual who invited friends is the same as if the party was given in his home." Judge Braniff refused to accept into evidence a film projector, seized stag films and an electronic transmitting device.

Since the trial, however, there has been a strong body of public opinion, including the voices of the Metropolitan Crime Commission and various civic organizations, demanding the judge's removal from the bench—enough to cause an official probe into Haggerty's behavior by the Judiciary Commission of Louisiana. This move could result in a recommendation to the State Supreme Court that Judge Haggerty be removed or voluntarily retired.

As if the judge's predicament weren't epilogue enough to the events in New Orleans, yet another bizarre charge was in the air—this one involving Jim Garrison. During the primary campaign things had got so dirty that Garrison, in a free-for-all bout

of mudslinging, was accused in a widely spread whisper epidemic
of molesting a 13-year-old boy at the New Orleans Athletic Club.
The rumor persisted and *The Grit,* the annual satirical publication of the New Orleans Gridiron Club (made up of members of
the city's press corps) printed on Friday, November 7, 1969, four
individual photographs of Jim Garrison with the following four
captions: "Urh . . ." "Well . . ." "Huh . . ." and finally, *"Now
They Tell Me* . . . you can't play handball in the steamroom of
the NOAC."

The rumor was carried one step further when, on February 23,
1970, Jack Anderson's syndicated Washington Merry-Go-Round
column headlined in certain papers—the column was not carried
in New Orleans—the following: JIM GARRISON ACCUSED OF
MOLESTING BOY, 13. The story read:

> The Orleans Parish grand jury is investigating a charge that
> New Orleans District Attorney Jim Garrison sexually molested a
> 13-year-old boy at the city's posh Athletic Club.
> The allegation, based on statements by the boy's father, was
> filed by the New Orleans Crime Commission with grand jury
> foreman William J. Krummel, Sr. A November 5, 1969, letter from
> Crime Commission Director Aaron Kohn to Krummel, detailing
> the charge, has now been obtained by this column.
> Krummel, on the record, would concede only that he received
> the letter. Nevertheless, an authoritative official source confirmed
> that the grand jury was "looking into it."
> Garrison has denied the charge, the same official said. The
> controversial DA's friends said he was a "devoted family man."
> Persistent efforts by this column to reach Garrison for comment
> failed.
> The allegation was made by a prominent member of the New
> Orleans "establishment" whose brother is one of the most re-
> spected men in the South. To spare the young man embarrass-
> ment, we will leave out the names.
> Kohn, as director of the privately financed Crime Commission,
> has often been at odds with Garrison. He would confirm for the
> record only that the text of the letter obtained by this column was
> authentic.
> "On a Sunday in June, 1969," the Commission letter to the
> grand jury states, "at the New Orleans Athletic Club, District
> Attorney Jim Garrison conducted himself in a manner which, if
> true, would be in violation of Louisiana criminal laws."

The laws in question punish "Indecent Behavior with Juveniles" and "Crime Against Nature, Attempt," the letter went on.

The letter then states that the father spoke to three men about the incident and all three had "separately and independently communicated" the father's accusation to Kohn. This column read the allegation to the father, who confirmed it with a minor addition.

"In brief," said the letter to the grand jury, the father "alleged that on a Sunday in June, 1969, he and his two teenage sons were swimming in the nude at the New Orleans Athletic Club.

"Garrison invited them to the Slumber Room to relax and take a nap. In that room, Garrison twice fondled the genitals of the younger son, 13 years old (name omitted by this column). The elder son (name omitted), then age 19, openly denounced Garrison at the club.

"It is hoped that your grand jury will see fit to call before it for testimony without the presence of any of Mr. Garrison's staff the three men spoken to by the father himself and the sons," said the letter.

Under Louisiana Law, the "indecent behavior" count carries a maximum year in jail and 500-dollar fine. A "crime against nature" carries a 2,000-dollar fine and five years in jail, but merely an "attempt" cuts the penalty in half.

There is an irony in the charges. Garrison has frequently brought the element of perversion and sex into his own cases. He made his name by cleaning up prostitution in New Orleans.

In his most famous national case, the prosecution of Clay Shaw for conspiring to kill President Kennedy, Garrison's office made much of Shaw's alleged homosexuality. The jury threw out Garrison's conspiracy charge, but Shaw remained marked with the sexual stigma.

The irony of this turnabout is completely classic, so rich that even the most extravagant fiction writer would not have dared conjure it up. As if the tides were not changing enough, Clay Shaw struck another blow at the perpetrator of this case when, only days before the first anniversary of his acquittal, he filed a $5 million damage suit against Jim Garrison and others. These included Perry Raymond Russo, Dr. Esmond Fatter, who hypnotized Russo, and three members of Truth and Consequences of New Orleans, Inc., the private fund that helped finance Garrison's investigation —Joseph M. Rault, Jr., Willard Robertson and Cecil Shilstone.

The suit, filed in Federal District Court, contended that the conspiracy charge brought by Jim Garrison against Clay Shaw was "in furtherance of his scheme and that of the defendants to conduct an illegal, useless and fraudulent investigation of the assassination of President Kennedy."

While these latest developments involving Judge Haggerty and Jim Garrison might stretch the Yankee imagination, they seem to be entirely in keeping with New Orleans. Dirty politics, demagoguery, skulduggery, character assassination, rigging and all manner of corruption in high and low places are to the people of the region an old and accepted Southern custom, a status quo entertainment deeply entrenched and equaled in popularity only by television. In this free-for-all political soccer field called Louisiana, there is only one unforgivable ingredient—boredom. God forbid it should be boring. And those in elected and appointed posts do His bidding and make sure the fun and games don't pall.

The prime keeper of the games people play in Louisiana politics at the moment, of course, is the District Attorney of Orleans Parish. I believe him, gamesman or otherwise, to be totally ambitious. I would be surprised if he does not have, and not necessarily at such *odd* moments, dreams of the Presidency. In the early stages of his career Jim Garrison fell in love with crusading. His forays caught attention. The public spotlight warmed him all over, stirred up fires that have never waned. He soon became mesmerized by his natural talents for the performing arts, his almost eerie skill for attracting publicity, and his mastery of the high con. The glow of his first successes burgeoned within him, pushing him over the line into a quiet and deadly brand of megalomania.

Where do you go from District Attorney of New Orleans? You must push onward and upward and spiral out over the country. That cannot be done by closing up bars on Bourbon Street, fighting the local judges or even taking on the State Legislature. Is it possible to find an issue of great national import—and preferably one of wide international speculation as well? Through the odd quirk of fate that Lee Harvey Oswald had spent the summer of 1963 in New Orleans, the Kennedy Assassination dropped into his lap. There had to be one positive on which to begin. This positive was Jim Garrison's devotion to conspiracy. He is completely conspiracy-minded. He believes in them. If, through the crosscurrents of his charm, his peculiarities, and his talents, he has been able to perpetrate fraud upon others, he has no less managed to defraud himself by drawing the blinds on the logical reasoning processes that might have stabilized his wilder fantasies and helped set him back on course.

Is he, then, basically a corrupt public official? No, that's far too petty a characterization. He is far more dangerous than that. In his megalomania he has deified himself beyond all singing and telling. Therefore his beliefs, and his desires to believe, become holy canons not to be tampered with by mortal man. He will stand for neither interference nor criticism. Therein lies his paranoia, curled up like a snake ready to strike out at the slightest move that might be interpreted as being counter to his interests.

The classic fault, the horror inherent in this quick, witty and charming individual, is his unshakable belief that the end justifies any of *his* means.

The key adjective to Jim Garrison is "reckless." Recklessness knows no choice of victim. It can strike the innocent as well as the culpable—no matter—depending upon the drift of his mood, the direction of the wind, or the chance dropping of a name—say, "Clay."

By this very recklessness in attacking the Warren Report through the prosecution of an innocent man, Jim Garrison has performed a great disservice to any further investigation into the assassination of President Kennedy. Although there are many who believe Lee Harvey Oswald must have had assistance, the task of proving this theory will be infinitely more difficult should evidence emerge in the future. He has cried wolf at a lamb, and that cry will be remembered.

Involvement in this matter has had a profound effect upon me. Putting together this account has been a most difficult task. Fiction, although certainly no less bizarre, is dessert in comparison. Without being too melodramatic, I sleep lighter now. Something in the subconscious keeps popping up in my mind like the blips on a radar screen and makes me wonder who might, at that very dark and quiet hour, be hatching plans against some unknowing soul whose charted course will be abruptly altered by ambition, timing, chance, and misplaced desires. I read the newspapers more closely. I ask questions—at the risk of appearing stupid. I keep track of what my congressmen and senators are up to and I have even taken to letting them hear from me upon occasion. For the first time in my life I know who my local electees and officeholders are and I have begun to attend local meetings concerned with current problems. I make it a point to investigate the individuals pro and con the issues and attempt to understand what their motives might possibly be. I am ashamed, in short, of my former passivity and of the astigmatic selfishness which allowed me to rest at ease in my ignorance of matters that did not concern me directly.

We must all watch out and speak out. Otherwise, in twenty years people will be asking, How did Jim Garrison ever get this *far?*

And the answer will be: We let him.

A short postscript that so perfectly fits the entire affair: After the District Attorney won the primary, assuring his reelection, a letter arrived addressed to Clay Shaw with the bold return address, JIM GARRISON, New Orleans, on the envelope. Another bold JIM GARRISON is centered at the top of the enclosed sheet. The letter reads:

DEAR FRIEND,
  I am grateful to you for your recent support in the primary election. I believe that together we confounded many self-appointed experts who thought that expensive advertising techniques would win no matter what the real issues were. They were wrong because you refused to be fooled. . . .

Sincerely,
JIM GARRISON

This document is tacked to a prominent place above Clay Shaw's desk.

P.P.S. Will they ever stop?
  As this book goes to the printers, yet another principal in the case has tangled with the law, this time none other than the state's main witness, Perry Raymond Russo. On August 22, 1970, Russo was arrested and booked on three counts of burglary and theft. The New York *Times* reported that Russo and a 20-year-old companion had been arrested at Russo's home. The two men were accused of the $8,400 burglary of a New Orleans residence, possession of a stolen safety deposit box and the theft of a motorcycle valued at $3,000.
  It will be more than interesting to see what action Jim Garrison takes in this matter. If he does choose to prosecute, it will be doubly interesting to see what Perry Russo might do. Or say.
  No, it seems they will *not* stop.

Editor's Note—1993

—Clay Shaw died in New Orleans on August 14, 1974. The death certificate stated the cause of death as lung cancer.

—Judge Edward Haggerty died December 2, 1990.

—Jim Garrison was District Attorney of New Orleans from 1962 to 1974. He is currently a Judge of the Court of Appeals in New Orleans. His books include *A Heritage of Stone, The Star-Spangled Contract,* and *On the Trail of the Assassins.*

—James Kirkwood won the Pulitzer Prize for *A Chorus Line.* His books include *P.S. Your Cat Is Dead, Some Kind of Hero, There Must Be a Pony!,* and *Good Times/Bad Times.* He died in 1989.

Acknowledgments and Sources

There are many to whom I am deeply indebted for their confidence and assistance over the past year and a half leading to the completion of this book.

Without the trust of Clay Shaw to begin with, this would have been a much more difficult task. Without his friendship, it certainly would have been a less rewarding one.

His lawyers, F. Irvin Dymond and Edward Wegmann, have been most cooperative; I have also come to value their friendships. A special word of thanks to Frances Tipping of Edward Wegmann's office for her aid in obtaining source material. To Bruce Eggler, also, my appreciation for his assistance.

For their time and cooperation in speaking with me either informally or during formal interviews and for providing me with fascinating glimpses into the minds and behavior of the principals in this affair, I would like to thank District Attorney Jim Garrison, James C. Alcock, Andrew Sciambra, Judge Edward A. Haggerty, Jr., Miguel Torres, Perry Raymond Russo, William Wegmann, Sal Panzeca, Tom Bethell, Dean Andrews, Jr., Aaron Kohn, David Chandler, Burton Klein, Police Sergeant Matt Perkins, Police Lieutenant Edward M. O'Donnell, Sam "Monk" Zelden, Mayor Victor Schiro, Ed Planer, Leonard Gurvich, Louis Gurvich, June and Dick Rolfe, and jurors Sidney Hebert, Oliver Schultz, Larry Morgan, David Powe, Robert John Burlet and Charles Ordes.

Warm phrases of camaraderie and gratitude go to Nina Sulzer, James Phelan, Hugh Aynesworth and William Gurvich for their invaluable assistance.

There are many others who aided in various ways during my time in New Orleans. Their help and friendship made the task and life easier. This especially applies to my trial buddies—Jerry Cohen and Martin Waldron. I would also like to mention Lloyd Burlingame, Rosemary and Jud James, John Mourain, Mrs. Edgar Stern, Marilyn Tate, Mrs. Muriel Bultman Frances Bogner, Jeff Biddison, Marge O'Dare, Helen Dietrich, Jeff Sulzer, Paula

Aynesworth, Noni Lyons, Elena Lyons, Patricia Chandler, Benjy Morrison, Donald Lee Keith, Bill Block, Carl Pelleck, Carole Oppenheimer, Roger Williams, Mike Parks, Kent Biffle, Jack Mac-Kenzie, Bill Reed, Terry Flettrich, Gail Baumgartner, Mr. and Mrs. Moise Dennery, Marty Cocita, Carroll Durand, Leo Touchet and John Messina.

My gratitude to the Stern Family Fund for their aid.

For the final preparation of this manuscript I would like to express my thanks to my dear amanuensis, Lee Powell, for her excellent work and high interest, and to Edward Powell for his proofreading.

A special commendation to Evan Rhodes for his time, patience and valuable suggestions with regard to the original uncut manuscript.

Finally, I cannot express appreciation enough to my editor, Richard Kluger, who provided me with the kind of concerned and painstaking editing that I had heretofore only heard about in publishing folklore. I will not forget his hard work and devotion to this book.

To my new editor, Michael Korda, my solid appreciation for his enthusiasm and caring and for in no way making me or this book feel like stepchildren after Dick Kluger's departure.

The testimony of Perry Raymond Russo and Dean Adams Andrews, Jr., is derived from the official court transcript as taken down by the firm of Dietrich and Pickett, Inc. The detailed daily accounts of the trial by the New Orleans *States-Item* and *Times-Picayune* together with my notes and those of fellow reporters are the sources of other testimony. I am indebted to Edward Wegmann for the transcript of Perry Raymond Russo's hypnotic session, to James Phelan for a copy of the Sciambra memorandum, to Tom Bethell for the Secret Service report on David W. Ferrie, to the District Attorney's office for the copy of Jim Garrison's opening statement and to Jim Garrison himself for my copy of his closing statement.

The following books have provided particularly helpful background information: *The Official Warren Commission Report on the Assassination of President John F. Kennedy; Counterplot* by Edward J. Epstein (Viking); *Six Seconds in Dallas* by Josiah Thompson (Bernard Geis); *The Garrison Case: A Study in the Abuse of Power* by Milton E. Brener (Clarkson N. Potter, Inc.); *Plot or Politics?* by Rosemary James and Jack Wardlaw (Pelican Publishing House); *The Kennedy Conspiracy* by Paris Flammonde (Meredith Press).

Several magazine articles also provided interesting background data, among them: "A Plot to Kill Kennedy?—Rush to Judgment in New Orleans" by James Phelan in the May 6, 1967, issue of the *Saturday Evening Post;* "Is Garrison Faking?" by Fred Powledge in the June 17, 1967, issue of *The New Republic;* "Playboy Interview: Jim Garrison," *Playboy,* October 1967; and "The Persecution of Clay Shaw" by Warren Rogers, *Look* magazine, August 26.

Index